BALLET 1·0·1

A Complete Guide to Learning and Loving the Ballet

ROBERT GRESKOVIC

New York

To the memory of my Ukrainian grandmother, Antonia

 For information address: Hyperion, 114 Fifth Avenue, New York, New York 10011.

Designed by Helene Wald Berinsky

Library of Congress Cataloging-In-Publication Data
Greskovic, Robert.
Ballet 101 : a complete guide to learning and loving the ballet / Robert Greskovic.
p. cm.
Includes bibliographical references (p. 591) and index.
ISBN 0-7868-8155-0
1. Ballet. 2. Ballet—History. I. Title.
GV1787.G74 1998
792.8—dc21 97-36516
CIP

FIRST EDITION

10 9 8 7 6 5 4 3

Contents

II • THE DANCERS

III • LOOKING AT A BALLET

IV • THE FAMOUS BALLETS

Foreword

MIKHAIL BARYSHNIKOV

When I first started going to the ballet, the thing that drew me back to it was not just the beauty of the performances, but the fact that that beauty seemed personal to me. It is like people who collect stamps. In those little pictures they see details—how many lines are laid down to make an ear or a moustache, and the inking, and the feel of the paper—that they think only they can cherish. Only to them are these things so precise and so moving. So it was for me with ballet. I was sure that I was the only one who saw how the fairy, when she raised her wand, lowered it again in a special kind of arc, first fast, then slower. That was mine, and full of mystery.

When I entered the ballet school in Riga, I began to see all this from the inside, to see the mechanics, how that arc of the wand was taught. But ballet didn't become less mysterious to me. It became more so. Here was a community of people, very secluded, who dedicated themselves to this art form. They were servants of something—messengers. They had a duty, and not to everyday life. I thought, what a beautiful way this was to live. They all had their own places in the company, each place very important and needed, whether it was a *corps de ballet* dancer or a *coryphée* or a character dancer or a ballerina. They spent pretty much all day in the theater, and then at night they gave the performance. Hundreds of people, if you include the orchestra and the stagehands, and they all worked and worked, and then for three hours at night they came together and did this thing that was not about them, but about an idea. And the audience came to see it, and then it was gone. It was a memory. The whole thing seemed to me like a ritual, haunting.

That wasn't the only mystery. The ballets, too, in their stories, were about serious and personal matters. *Giselle* and *The Sleeping Beauty*—these had to do with the great blessings and disasters that are the center of our lives, the things one is usually too embarrassed or too frightened to talk about. There they were, in crystallized form.

And again, it seemed very personal, because it was contained in the bodies of the dancers, and the body is so revealing. When a dancer comes onstage, he is not just a blank slate that the choreographer has written on. Behind him he has all the decisions he has made in life. He has already met a million forks in the road. Each time, he has chosen, and in what he is onstage you see the result of those choices. You are looking at the person he is, the person who, at this point, he cannot help but be. All the experiences he has had as a child and as a teenager, all the images that his body has accumulated, these come up as colors in the dancing, giving it sparkle and complexity. They come out through the eyes, through the pores. Exceptional dancers, in my experience, are also exceptional people, people with an *attitude* toward life, a kind of quest, and an internal quality. They know who they are, and they show this to you, willingly. But all dancers are self-revealing, and this is true no matter what the style of dancing. Whether it is ballet or Cunningham technique or Indian or Balinese dancing, the character of the dancer pours through. Within a minute, you are receiving a personal message.

For the audience, knowledge of the art can only make this experience more pointed and moving. In the pages that follow, the dance critic Robert Greskovic lays out the basics of ballet—its history, its technique—and takes us through performances of its most honored works: *Giselle, Swan Lake, The Sleeping Beauty*. He explains what first and second position are, and how the pointe shoe developed, and what makes a soloist different from a principal dancer. He quotes wonderful sources, the Hollywood choreographer Hermes Pan comparing dance and music, the Russian balletomane Konstantin Skalkovsky complaining about the St. Petersburg ballet audience. ("They look at the most brilliant adagio as a cow looks at a passing train.") He gives us interesting information, of the kind one doesn't normally get from books—for example, that the stage of the Royal Theater in Copenhagen has a "hand hole" so that when an Italian girl who has been transformed into a water nymph has to be transformed back into an Italian girl before our very eyes, someone can reach up from under the stage to whisk away the nymph costume before the smoke clears.

More than information, Greskovic gives us nuance, shading. He tells us, for instance, what people mean when they speak of a dancer's "line," and how we can see the line. This is the kind of explanation that only an expert can give you, and most experts don't. All the things that ballet fans talk about at intermission, while newcomers stand there wondering what they mean: those things are here. Finally, Greskovic salts his book with his opinions. Like a good dancer, he shows us who he is. He has been thinking about ballet—watching it, reading, writing, and talking about it—day after day for more than thirty years. He knows it through and through. Now he shares his knowledge.

Introduction

Ballet, the world seems to say, has two faces. One is the frighteningly unfamiliar, leading people to insist, "I don't understand it." The other appears quite ordinary and perfectly understandable, inspiring news reporters to describe, for example, the successful docking of one space vehicle with another as a "space ballet," confident that the reader will find the usage perfectly clear. If pressed, the person capable of having both the above reactions will say that in the first instance they're talking about the formal activity and behavior of dancers on a stage. Meanwhile, in the latter example, the word stands for any sophisticated activity smoothly accomplished that looks effortless. So, it's not ballet that people fail to understand, it's *Ballet*, with a capital *B*.

But why should this be so? If you can understand the ballets of space modules in orbit, or dolphins curvetting underwater, or air force jets in precision formation, you *do* understand the essence of ballet, even with its big *B* and its individuals on stage doing things with their limbs and especially their feet that look quite unlike what you do with your own appendages. The common denominator of this double-edged vision is perfection of participant and of execution.

Longtime dance watcher and critic Clive Barnes once suggested that the notion of amateur ballet came a little too close for comfort to the idea of amateur brain surgery. You don't have to be a brain surgeon to get his point about ballet. Nor do you already have to be what is sometimes called a balletomane. This term, which more or less means eagerly committed balletgoer and enthusiast, will take its place in the tapestry of ballet history as it unfolds subsequently on these pages. For now, to begin touching upon the fine and complex nature of ballet, let's hear from a nineteenth-century Russian ballet historian who published his impassioned views on ballet and balletgoing in St. Petersburg under the byline "Balletomane." His real name was Konstantin Skalkovsky and his actual job was that of government mining engineer.

This high-toned Russian critic expressed the highest regard for the art of ballet as it was presented on the stages in imperial St. Petersburg. He insisted that to appreciate fully the particulars of his favored performing art, the ballet audience needed to look long and hard at what took place in the theater of ballet. He suggested that prolonged and careful scrutiny of the ballet dancer's art would yield suitably substantial rewards. His phrase for the insight you'd gain was "*le pourquoi de pourquoi*"—the why of why things are done their particular way in ballet, also known as classical dancing. His view of those who didn't look carefully or caringly at the art and artists he so revered was quite dim. In one 1882 essay decrying the lack of sophistication on the part of his fellow St. Petersburg audience members, the lordly balletomane compared the attention of the public as it looked at a most brilliantly arranged dance highlight to that of a cow looking at a passing train.

Along these lines, I regularly recall something balletomane and critic Arlene Croce succinctly stated about balletgoing when I met her in my early ballet-watching days: "Ballet is a cultured art; you must pay attention." By this logic, without calling a casual viewer a cow and without suggesting inordinate amounts of cramming or research, ballet stands removed from the so-called popular arts. A given ballet can be, as indeed many are, quite popular, but the art itself cannot be said to be a popular one. Nor, for all its athletic dimensions and evident physical prowess, can we ever confuse the art of ballet with the act of *any* sport.

Athletic activity aims for quantity; the winning score becomes the bottom line. Aesthetic activity aims for quality; a beguiling, fine-grained experience motivates the goings-on. Writers and thinkers regularly try to equate dance with sport. A deft football player's ability to jump up and snag a pass might well be called a ballet move. The same with a notable rebounder in basketball. Because of their particular trappings, gymnastics and figure skating come ready-made for comparisons with ballet. Still, comparing sports, especially the most balletic ones, to ballet itself remains a classic example of "so near, yet so far. . . ."

In sports the form the athlete shows is sometimes taken into consideration, but it's never *the* consideration. In ballet, the form of the move or the position is always uppermost in the body and mind of the dancer and in the eye and mind of the viewer. Certainly ballet and specific sports share notions of efficiency, as defined in the physical sciences. Making the body aerodynamically sleek for moves where sleekness leads to maximal result occurs in both. The athlete, however, will say to hell with form in order to achieve a quantitative result. The dancer will not, at least not if he hopes to win admiration from his public and his artistic director.

One irony, in the comparison of athletics to ballet, is that writing about sports tends to be much more specific and "up close and personal" than does reportage about dancing. One dancer-choreographer commented on the blandly generalized approach to dance writing in her local newspaper: "The guy who writes about stamps writes with many more particulars than the guy who covers dance." In a similar circumstance, the talking heads who introduce ballet on television hardly get at what and how the dancers are doing, especially when you compare their chat with the takes rendered by the commentators of sports events.

This is not to say that we should welcome blow-by-blow nattering over ballet as it occurs on a television screen, but something beyond the "sweetly pretty" commentaries that now accompany most videotaped dance must be possible. Someday, with the growing interest in cable television, ballet may actually come to our home screens with the same serious and informed dimensions already accompanying telecasts devoted to movies, sports, and world history. Toward such an end this book looks at select works that stand out from the history of ballet as of lasting value and/or popularity.

Before dwelling on the key works presented in this volume, something needs to be said about them in general as theatrical entities.

Contrary to popular opinion, ballet is *not* opera without words. Probably because opera is arguably older as a form of musical, lyrical theater, and because ballets are often presented in theaters specifically designated as opera houses, many opera lovers cross over to ballet when it plays their theaters. In the process they bring with them all the factors that make them interested in opera. We certainly welcome all comers, but we don't suffer gladly notions lifted directly from opera lovers' expectations. Ballets can and do concern themselves with librettos or scenarios, and do follow narrative lines of development. But along the way ballet gained an independence from opera, and it's important to keep the two forms separated in your mind.

Even while music supermen such as Igor Stravinsky have flatly stated that "music can express nothing but itself," operagoing music lovers love the plotlines and narratives that give opera its basis to create dramatic and/or melodramatic characters. Ballet certainly has its share of similar "librettos" or "scenarios." Still, as we shall see, the most precious and rewarding veins in the strata making up story ballets are not those calling for character development or narrative nuance. They're the opportunities, sometimes connected to the story itself by the slenderest of threads, to let the dancers strut their most brilliant dance stuff. Eventually, ballet became ballet when the trappings of opera, the episodic narratives, the specific characters, the specific place and time settings all gave way to the open, endless space on the edge of eternity. There ballet dancers are free to be themselves and dance their dances unduly fettered by time, place, and personality constraints imparted to them by plot writers versus dance makers.

Ballet's coming of age will follow a "road to independence" logic when it's spelled out on these pages. The select ballets discussed in detail will further fortify this story. Still, ballet's flowering stems from more than gaining independence from its once all-important narrative or literary basis. However inspiring to ballet's life the element of music consistently tends to be, it need not be considered as playing a precisely equal role in ballet theater. Eventually, unless we're confronted by the sight of an academic music visualization (a pedantic, early modern dance way of working in which movement slavishly illustrated musical structures) any great ballet's music remains, however slightly, a less than equal partner with the dancing. My strong belief in the preeminence of what dancers actually perform over what the accompanying musicians in fact provide, may strike true believers in twentieth-century choreography as arguable, especially those committed to the masterly ballets of George Balanchine, who liked to say, "The music comes first." But I stand by this contention and my belief that ballet's power emanates from its being a visual art. Take away the music from a ballet or turn down the sound on your monitor playing a ballet video and you still have something of a ballet experience. Bring down the curtain, or turn off the monitor's picture, and you have a music concert, period.

Partly for this reason, I've chosen not to offer a discography here. Many individuals, sometimes even including me, find fortifying rewards in listening to a ballet's musical score on an audio system. I certainly do not mean to discourage such enrichment to anyone so inclined, but by the same token I do not find such preparatory or follow-up activity crucial to a full-scale ballet experience. Another reason I hesitate to single out separate musical sources of ballets has to do with tempos. Ballet dancers qualify as supermen and superwomen with regard to physical prowess and finesse, but next to none could perform the choreography created for musical scores as performed on most concert recordings. There are many recordings of music used for ballet, but while the names are the same, the tempos all too often have been changed to preclude any accommodation of an innocent dancer's ability to make visual sense of the aural element. My advice is therefore to listen to any ballet's music however much you like, but be aware that the musicians' preference for tempo, either fast or slow, may have no bearing whatsoever on dancers' movement possibilities.

For these purposes, a videography in this book makes much more sense. If the musicians involved in a videotaped ballet are at odds with the dancers, you'll know it in an instant and your sympathies will very likely remain with the ill-served dancer. When and where possible, I have selected a particular videotape example for the ballets chosen here as landmarks. My choices were made with equal parts personal preference and practicality. To be sure, videotaped ballet is not the thing, only a reduction from three dimensions to two of a single performance of the thing. I doubt anyone becomes a ballet enthusiast by way of video exposure to the art form, but I doubt anyone who has become smitten by this performing art in the flesh will fail to see the useful and beneficial nature of these audiovisual records.

Given the limits of the video market, no single tape can even nearly qualify as ideal. Indeed, along the way of watching ballets performed and re-performed, no single performance can likely be called ideal, either. Laurels to the ideal rendering of this or that ballet are most likely conferred on those ballets in the pie-in-the-sky of one's memory and imaginings. But this book, like the art of ballet itself, is about the reality of the perfection ballet's art aims for. And any reality check usually involves a ticking off of the imperfections, however minor, within the sampling of perfection in question.

In choosing the tapes to accompany the ballets named here, I often had to make judgment calls and compromises based on tapes in the public domain. (Invariably, there exists somewhere in a world like ballet's a private domain. Borrowing a term used for "unofficial" opera recordings, these are known as "pirates" and will be touched on along the way.) In many instances of the ballet examples included, one small consideration slightly outweighed some other. Whenever suitable, I'll indicate any notable wrinkles that present themselves.

In view of the large store of ballets defining its history, my inclusion of one over its alternatives will no doubt strike anyone already familiar with the field as subjective at best, preposterous at worst. Favoritism in ballet is no different from partisanism in any field. It is in this way, incidentally, that sports seems most like ballet. Preferring one team of players over others, or one kind of move over another exists in ballet as much as in baseball. When considering what some balletgoers call "the classics," I'm presented with fewer and more limited choices than I have for more recent, more contemporary choices. In the reality of the life of ballets on the stage, my choices are limited to the ballets that have survived in the flesh and blood of performance, rather than in the ink and pulp of history books. Still, some lover of Spanish-flavored ballet and its cursory connections to Cervantes's classic about the knight of the woeful countenance, might raise an eyebrow over the omission of *Don Quixote*, while some balletgoer with a fondness for the days of knighthood in Hungary might look askance at the absence of *Raymonda*.

With regard to my choices of works from the more recent past, I can't say with any certainty that I'd make all the same decisions, if I thought this through ten years from now or ten years earlier. Ten years ago, for example, *La Bayadère* would not become the contender it is nowadays. This four-act, seven-scene ballet, about which the ballet-going public outside Russia knew little more than one scene in 1980, is now done with some regularity, and there are three and a half good chances of owning the full spectacle on video. Time flies extra fleetly in the world of ballet. On the other hand, *Swan Lake*, virtually synonymous with ballet in many minds, exists in numerous versions, both on stage and on video, but none nowadays has quite the air of authenticity to its original, trend-setting beginnings as *La Bayadère*.

When it comes to the choices I've made of ballets from our century, and particularly, from our own age, the number of arguments and raised eyebrows will no doubt increase. What about *Jewels*, Balanchine's groundbreaking, full-evening, "abstract" ballet? What of Frederick Ashton's *Scènes de Ballet* or his limpid *Symphonic Variations*? All I can say at this juncture is that all these candidates, in addition to others, have been considered. Some were rejected partly because no accompanying video is now available, others, more or less due to chance. My final cut is hardly the final answer to ballet's Greatest Hits, but let's just say it's the answer this time. As for potential challenges from the Eurocentric ballet lover who might ask after examples from European intellectual choreographers, such as *Le Sacre du Printemps* by Maurice Béjart, or *The St. Matthew Passion* by John Neumeier, or *Grosse Fugue* by Hans van Manen, I can only answer that works such as these are not really alternatives to the final choices offered here. In my considered opinion, however at odds it may remain with many a balletomane, especially a European one, I can only suggest that works such as these are right where they belong, on the nebulous fringes of the big and basic picture of classical ballet.

If I can easily imagine arguments concerning my choices of work for this sampler, I can even more loudly hear the quibbles with the dancers featured in the selected video. All too often, ballet's lifeblood is described in terms of choreography and choreogapher, while the focus of the experience centers on its dancers. A century's worth of *Swan*

Lakes can come and go only because along the way the public finds Swan Queen ballerinas and Prince Siegfried princely dancers to admire and as often as not prefer over others. I may explain, and seemingly defend the dancers who lead the video performances I suggest here, but not nearly to the degree I'd have to in the face of a fellow balletgoer's personal preference. "But she's so unmusical," the non-fan of my choice might protest. Or, "But his jump leaves much to be desired." I'm not about to open here the quality-versus-quantity cans of worms suggested by such statements, but merely acknowledge the existence and operation of factors of taste. I know the why of why I prefer this dancer over that.

I doubt anyone could revere virtuosity more than I do, even as many fellow admirers of expert dancing choose to overlook details of form in the name of quantitative achievements. On the matter of quantity, the late great and greatly revered ballerina and ballet teacher Alexandra Danilova once made an apt remark. In the midst of expressing admiration for the ballerina's remarkable dancing, a fan asked her to help sort out a discrepancy: "You do such virtuoso dancing, you do impressive fouetté [whipping] turns, but you don't do extreme, multiple pirouettes—why?" "Vell, I am too beesee dahnsing," the sultry-voiced ballerina replied. Balanchine, a mentor of Danilova's, sometimes spoke directly to the point of multiple turns. Counseling his ballerinas on the subject of multiple pirouettes in rehearsal, the ballet master was heard to say, "Two, maybe three . . . after that audience starts to count."

Before looking at some ballets in our present—the only time any performance realistically knows—we need to go over the past that got us where we are. That story is long and involved. In many ways it's also changing every day as successive historians delve constantly into the often elusive past of this famously ephemeral art.

· I ·

The History of Ballet

Chapter 1

LET THE HISTORY BEGIN . . .

Before surveying the age and history of ballet, a look at dance activity in general helps prepare the way. Dance partisans like to challenge military men on the historical seniority frequently conceded to another line of work as our "world's oldest profession." (The stigma of this disreputable and sometimes unmentionable profession actually stayed with dancers of certain periods. Likewise, the selling of the body's beauty can still be read by cynical onlookers as the selling of the body itself.) The logic from the champions of dance goes something like, "Before the war, comes the war dance," or a related argument, "We move in the womb, before we do anything else." Another take suggests that humankind communicated by gesture, a language of signs, before it spoke a language of sounds and words. Historians of dance in all its manifestations, as opposed to ballet specialists in particular, look to happenings in early peoples and their rituals for our deepest dance roots.

India's Hindu god Shiva has come to us depicted as a multi-armed divinity deftly balanced on one leg and known as Nataraja, Lord of the Dance. Actual Indian dance forms appear to have been in place around 6000 B.C. From First Dynasty Egypt, circa 3000 B.C., come reliefs showing a kind of dance/body language. Acrobatic figures on later Egyptian wall paintings and reliefs help illustrate dance methods to further degrees. Greek dances reveal links with civilizations on Crete, possibly transferred from Egypt, dating between 3000 and 1400 B.C. Greek theater, with its dramas rendered by way of instrumental and vocal sound with preplanned movement, even further fill in our background.

The Dithyramb, a theatrical entity made up of song and dance that grew out of celebrations of the Greek god Dionysus, gave rise to fully formed classic Greek theater. Some key dance terms trace their roots to words the Greeks chose for participants in their dance dramas. *Korugos* and *Koruphaios*, variously transliterated from the Greek, identify those concerned with training or leading the participants of the Greek chorus (*koros*). Similarly, the construction and design of theaters that today house our ballet originate in this same world of Greek theater. Notable are the *orkestra*, the round dancing floor of the chorus, and the *skene*, the covered area behind the "orchestra" performing space. The raised platform place between these two sections was called the *proskenion*. This points to the later plan of the proscenium theater, which provided the evolving art of ballet with its ideal frame.

A renewed interest in things Greek, by way of Roman reworkings, surfaced at the end of the Middle Ages, with its chivalric codes and its Holy Roman Empire. A focus on a "classic" past led to the era today known as the Renaissance and its philosophical bent called Humanism. Men and women themselves, rather than Mother Church and its Holy Father head, gained prominence for ways of thinking about the world. Appropriately enough, male and female dancers would become ideals of the individuals making up the new philosophy. The main thrust of such activity centered in the city-states that then constituted what is nowadays Italy. These small worlds periodically featured pageants or fêtes to aggrandize local despots as they celebrated such occasions as empire-building marriages or the birth of an heir. Their affairs included music, movement, and decoration, planned for indoor and outdoor venues. In the latter instance, the events approximated our parades, specifically those that include floats and numerous marching units.

There were many precedents for grandiose Italianate court spectacles, and one in 1393 became particularly memorable—infamous, in fact. To celebrate the marriage of one of his knights to a gentlewoman of his queen, King Charles VI of France participated in a masked entertainment called, ironically enough, *Bal des Ardents*

(Burners' Ball). Organized occasions for getting up in costume and mask occurred with some regularity in this era. The theme of this *masque* or *morisco,* as such events were called, was that of Wildmen of the Forest, after the folkloric figures also known as green men, foresters, or leafy devils. The king got actively involved in the affair, dressing as one of six shaggy creatures sewn into costumes made of close-fitting linen covered by clumps of hair made from flax and pitch. For some serendipitous reason, the king momentarily separated himself from his fellow beasts to speak to a duchess just before a torch borne by a curious onlooker set the remaining quintet ablaze. When the king's flammable covering caught the fast-moving flames, the duchess smothered them with the train of her dress. Except for one other lucky soul, who threw himself in a water vessel kept by for butter making, all the other mummers died from their burns.

The entry of this sextet of wildmen at the *Bal des Ardents* was meant to be significant and dramatic, though not literally so as things turned out. But due to its notoriety, this ball gave dance history one of its earliest examples of the *entrée,* the entrance into a theatrical production of a self-contained, particular group of performers, usually dressed identically or at least thematically. These group dances and dancers would become characteristic of the opera ballets that gave rise to our ballet.

During the 1400s we find a few individuals who qualify as early ballet masters. (The term "ballet master" predates today's use of the term "choreographer," but is sometimes used synonymously. Some individuals in the history of ballet and choreography preferred the one over the other, and even now, when the Ballet Master title might appear on a ballet company's roster, most people more readily understand the Choreographer title.) Our knowledge of early ballet masters comes mostly from a paper trail. Those dance practitioners who left us written word of their art have secured themselves prominent places on the genealogy of ballet history makers. In this premature phase, the "dancing master," as such men were then called, didn't act precisely the way we expect our choreographers to act today. Those maestros did it all; today's choreographers have support from other specialists—teachers, coaches, and rehearsal assistants.

The efforts of men such as Domenico da Piacenza (or Ferrara) or Guglielmo Ebreo (known also as William the Jew of Pesaro) went toward training courtiers in the prescribed graces of court dancing. Whatever we know of these particular dancing masters, as well as another of Domenico's followers, Antonio Cornazano, comes largely from the pages of dance manuals that survive to describe and diagram the ways of their dancing art. Maestro Domenico rises to the top of ballet's genealogical charts because he cared enough or was famous enough to have his working ways written down. Literally so, in the case of his treatise, since he lived in Europe's pre-moveable type printing era.

Domenico's *De Arte Saltandi et Choreas Ducendi* (On the Art of Dancing and Conducting Dances) bothered to choose *ballo* over *danza*, both of which mean "dance" in Italian. Domenico used the former because it referred to dancing of varied rhythm, as opposed to *danza*, which identified dancing to music of unvarying rhythm. The craft and creations of Domenico and those following him led to results known as *balletti*, or *balli*, plurals for *balletto*. These Italian words, diminutive forms of *ballo*, conveniently connote to the English-speaking reader that our "ballet" has roots in court balls held in palatial ballrooms of Renaissance Italy.

At this juncture it needs to be stressed that the participants—the dancers performing their *balli*—were amateurs, members of court society. Their master teachers not only provided precise instruction in the details of such dancing—carriage of the torso, positions and moves of the feet and legs, deferential courtesies of the man to his lady—but on particular occasions they also invented new patterning, sometimes called "figures," for the dance and dancers to follow. (The literal basis of today's more familiar figure skating, the tracing of prescribed figures onto clean ice, directly relates to the dance aims of this period. Diagrams defining correct *balletto* plans look like the patterns cut by ice skaters executing their prescribed figures.)

The costuming for these court dances, when not concerned with special masquerade events, remained that of contemporary court wear. These included fairly heavy long-skirted gowns for the women, and, for the men, elaborately constructed jackets or doublets and bloomerlike shorts, sometimes called trunk-hose, over fitted tights. Both wore leather shoes with soles and heels befitting the fashion of contemporary footwear. If ever an illustration from these centuries puzzles your eye about whether the dancer pictured is male or female, period fashion offers a fairly consistent rule: If you can see the legs, it's a male dancer; if not, it's probably a woman.

When France's Charles VIII, descendent of the nearly immolated Charles VI, invaded the Kingdom of Naples in 1495 to claim its throne, he had his cultural superiority singed by the remarkable sophistication and splendor of Italian court dancing. Italian principalities of this time lavished large expenditures of money and artistic talents on their entertainments. One fête could boast direction of its cast of hundreds by the father of the Renaissance's great painter Raphael (Sanzio); another, decor, costumes, and stage machinery by Leonardo da Vinci. One of today's more informed interpretations of Sandro Botticelli's beauteous fresco, *La Primavera*, reads its parade of characters as a mythological ballet as performed in Florence during the 1470s.

In 1489, a fête reminiscent of contemporary dinner theater or floor shows made a mark qualifying as something of a first "ballet." To celebrate the marriage of the Duke of Milan, an Italian maestro of entertainments, Bergonzio di Botta, coordinated an affair combining his culinary and choreographic talents. Music, recitation, and self-contained dances—called entrées, as courses in meals are still called—wove through the event with appropriate dishes arriving in due course. A dance scene representing Jason and his Argonauts, for example, preceded the roasted, gilded lamb in the guise of the Golden Fleece.

As often as they took place in palazzo ballrooms and dining rooms, Italian spectacles were held outdoors, under the often clear skies. The cast of players and complement of events could include scenes of combat, parades of festooned chariots or wagons, and geometrically arranged equestrian contingents, sometimes referred to individually as "horse ballets."

By the mid-1500s, grandiosely scaled variety shows, known as *spectaculi*, had become a prominent part of the cultural activity in northern Italy. The variety of these mixed-bag affairs, for outdoor as well as indoor spaces, found form in presentations that might include equestrian formations, tournaments or mock combats, sometimes in aquatic settings, and even tennis games. (To this day, the term "spectacle" remains in use in France and French-speaking Canada to identify evenings at the ballet.) By this era France had adopted the Italian theatrical methods for courtly entertainments, and it is at this point in ballet's history that the French begin making their own indelible mark in the art of ballet that we have come to know.

The figurative marriage of Italian dance practices with French cultural life came from a literal wedding between a well-known Florentine heiress, Catherine de Medici, to a French royal, Henri duc d'Orléans. Circumstance, mixed with sundry amounts of palace intrigue, put Florence's Catherine in a position to run France alongside the three heirs to the throne she had mothered. The royal occasions that Catherine supervised to display the splendors of her court—marriages, mostly—owed much to the *spectaculi* native to her homeland.

Catherine's era give rise to the use of the term "ballet," which leads directly to our usage and understanding of the same term. In 1573, the French Queen Mother put on a fête to celebrate the arrival of ambassadors from Poland to offer their country's throne to her son Henri. Named *Le Ballet des Polonais* (The Polish Ballet), this indoor production helped establish the theatrical form known as *ballet de cour*, literally "court ballet." This Polish affair took a semitheatrical form. The audience viewed the central proceedings from three sides around a little stage atop a set of stairs. Once the prepared dancing was done, the admiring audience got its chance to join in the dancing, all based on what we'd call ballroom dancing.

The individual responsible for preparing the dance elements of this court festivity was an Italian in the service of Catherine. Born Baldassarino da Belgioso, and called Balthasar de Beaujoyeulx in Catherine's court, the Italian violinist and dancer turned French dance master gets credit for establishing the unified dance spectacle we would today call a ballet. The Beaujoyeulx work at the root of the family tree of ballets was another extravaganza of Catherine's. This one occurred in 1581 under the name *Balet Comique de la Royne*, which sometimes gets modernized into *Ballet-Comique de la Reine [Louise]* and is freely translated as Queen Louise's Ballet Spectacle. Ten thousand guests are said to have witnessed the spectacle, which lasted from 10 P.M. until 3 A.M.

What makes this not entirely unprecedented affair loom large in ballet's history is essentially its eye toward dramatic cohesion. Its danced, musical, and spoken segments, which were intended by its creator to appeal to "the eye, the ear, and the intellect," focused on classical mythology's Circe. Each individual scene of the six-hour spectacle related to this theme. Each qualified as a self-contained "entrance" or entrée, such as entries for Mercury, the Satyrs, the Dryad Wood, and of course that of Queen Louise herself, who appeared in a fountain-of-gold vehicle spouting water and accompanied by mythological sea inhabitants. The through-line or unifying character of the enchantress Circe and her powers to overwhelm the likes of Apollo climaxed with a bow to the French monarchs responsible for the entertainment.

With the naming of the ballet-comique, it is important to understand the use of the word *comique*. It comes from the French *comedie* and refers to dramatic theater, not necessarily comedy as we use it today to note a specific branch of theater based on humor or farce. Hence the ballet-comique referred to danced spectacles with unifying dramatic themes, rather than variety spectacles, where the elements followed one another with no particular concern for dramatic continuity. The entrée form, which was already in place before Beaujoyeulx, gained a notable sense of focus after his now famous *Ballet-Comique*. Related spectacles and, some would argue, superior and more innovative presentations occurred alongside Beaujoyeulx's, but he had the foresight to promote his work by means of printed illustration and description.

At the same time of Queen Louise's 1581 ballet in France came the publication in Italy of Fabritio Caroso's *Il Ballarino*. This manual of technical information delineated the latest dance steps and focused on the male courtier, whose province was moves of virtuosity. So as France was taking and maintaining its lead in the presentation and production of ballet spectacle, Italy held its place by continuing its development of dance steps themselves.

During this time, the execution of Italian dance "figures" extended to four-legged high-stepping steeds. The horse-ballet was another of the multiple strings for Italy's *spectaculi* bow. Masterly French draughtsman Jacques Callot documented a 1616 Florentine festival that involved symmetrical, curling lines of caparisoned horses and richly outfitted riders elaborating a procession of floats and mummers in an arenalike space specially arranged for spectators.

Simultaneously, Italy, England, and France all continued to produce spectacles carrying forward the elements in favor during the 1500s. Italy followed the form known as Intermezzi; England, that of Court Masque, a spectacle often dominated by the visions of the country's poets. Under Louis XIII, France's *ballet de cour* took a slight shift away from the extravagance favored by its late Queen Mother Catherine.

The ballet-comique, with its aim of thematic coherence, gave way in Louis's reign to the *ballet-mascarade*. These events, with no particular interest in a dramatically related theme, included segment after segment of numbers performed by artfully costumed and masked performers. Sometimes the grand event involved specific dance moments, sometimes not, including instead pantomime scenes or acrobatic gymnastic displays. Eventually, *ballet à entrée* came into being. These were spectacles of discrete yet interdependent parts. Similar in format to the *ballet-mascarade*, this form called for a series of entrances of independent groups all interconnected, however slightly, by some overarching, often mythological theme or dramatic situation.

The character of the individual entrées varied, ranging from the grotesque and burlesque to the noble and godly. Low-life characters were performed by hired "professionals," though on occasion, aristocrats, including Louis XIII himself, chose to dabble in the less than genteel roles. At the conclusion of these and other *ballet de cour* genres came the *grand ballet*, a general dance climax. In these "ballets" all the assembled courtiers, those taking part in the prearranged ballet segments, and those who just watched, joined in the ballroom dancing. All, that is, except the hired commoner dancers, who were not included in the climactic courtly throng. Sometime during the early 1600s the declamation or recitation that accompanied the appearance of the various danced entrées changed to song. For a while the term *ballet mélodramatique* named these events; eventually they became what we call opera. By the 1630s such courtly spectacles were being offered to paying customers whether noble or common.

Chapter 2

LE BALLET: A MAN'S WORLD

France's *ballet à entrée* was in full flower when the four-year-old Louis XIV succeeded his father Louis XIII to the throne. Like his father he developed a keen interest in dancing in his court spectacles. Louis's skill and prominence as a dancer were eagerly supported and encouraged by the Italian-born Cardinal Mazarin (Frenchified from Mazarini) who helped rule the Louis XIV regency. After making his ballet de cour debut as a boy, Louis made his most memorable mark as a dancer in 1653 when the teenage monarch performed a series of grand entrances in a spectacle called *Le Ballet de la Nuit*. For his final appearance, at the fête's climax during the wee hours of the morning, Louis appeared as Apollo, god of the sun, in a fancy Roman-cut corselet and kilt decorated with spiny and wavy golden rays. Dressed in the glowing golds of *Le Roi Soleil*, Louis came to be known as France's Sun King.

Among the Italian influences Cardinal Mazarin promoted in his adopted France were those of Italianate opera spectacle as well as those of the proscenium theater. This framed space established for the theater spectator the single-point-perspective design theory at work in Italian painting. To elaborate and "paint" the stage spaces, Mazarin imported another expert Italian influence, Giacomo Torelli, known as the "great sorcerer" of stage design and machinery. Another Italian, Giovanni Baptista Lulli, helped continue the momentum of Italian influence on France's ballet theater and at the same time pointed the way to making and keeping it genuinely French.

Jean Baptiste Lully, as the Florentine violinist and dancer was rechristened at Louis's court, was brought from Florence as a partner in Italian conversation for a French princess. He soon became a fellow dancer of Louis and eventually one of the king's great favorites. As the king became more and more determined to produce court ballet spectacle on a scale unparalleled anywhere else in Europe, his beloved Lully became one of its biggest leaders.

Ballet as court entertainment and courtier spectacle flourished to its heights during the dancing days of Louis XIV. During the year 1661, a number of occurrences led to the eventual establishment of ballet as an independent theater art practiced by professionals who specialized in its practices. The most important of these rests in Louis's establishment of an academy of dance in a room of the Louvre palace. Called the Académie Royale de Danse, the society began as little more than a gathering of dancing masters, thirteen originally, for the purpose of "reestablishing the art in its perfection," according to Louis's decree. Also in 1661, the king's finance minister, Nicholas Fouquet, presented a grand fête to honor Louis and to show off the new chateau and gardens of his country estate at Vaux. The housewarming's entertainment was Molière's *Les Fâcheaux*, which qualifies as the first of the genre known as *comédie-ballet*.

Previously audiences had seen their *comédies* and their *ballets*. Now they would see the danced *entrées* that came between the play's various acts as dramatically related to the playwright's scheme, rather than as decorative diversions to cover the time the actors needed to change costumes. As it turned out, both the chateau's refinements and the theatrical format pleased the king to no end, even if he considered the finance minister a treasonous servant of the state. Fouquet was arrested and incarcerated, while his chateau's architect, gardener, and decorator were taken as a team by the king to make Versailles a showplace of unparalleled monarchical splendor.

Likewise, Molière found employment with the king, developing the comédie-ballet further. Lully, favorite court composer, became Molière's collaborator, and Pierre Beauchamps arranged the dances for the dramatically related interludes. Today Beauchamps, who was appointed "superintendent of the king's ballets" in the 1661 dance academy, sits atop most genealogies of ballet's master teachers. By the beginning of the eighteenth century he would be given credit for codifying the now standard five positions of the feet, universally accepted as ballet's basic starter alphabet.

In 1669 Louis XIV established the Académie Royale de Musique for his favorite, Lully, to run. Past his physical prime, the king himself quit dancing in 1670. His absence from the stage allowed those more adept than he to take the lead without seeming to show up their king, accelerating the advancement of finely schooled dance skills. The academy's first production, an opera called *Pomone*, with dance interludes by Beauchamps, took place in a converted tennis court. In 1672, Lully established his own academy of dance within the confines of his musical organization. Despite coming after the founding of the first royal dance academy, this *école de danse* lives into our day, where, as the ballet of the Paris Opera, it maintains its distinction as the world's oldest continuous ballet academy.

The new seriousness Lully gave to the study and production of musical and dance theater led the way for those performing these arts to be highly trained professionals rather than incidentally prepared courtiers. With the increased popularity of music and dance spectacles, non-aristocratic, trained performers could appear in earthy "character" roles, but godly heroic types needed to be played by members of the ruling class. Now, non-nobles began to perform roles heretofore reserved for those with actual noble bloodlines. With class lines now blurring, gender lines came next. For a while, French theatrical spectacles were performed by all male participants; the use of masks and travesty costuming aided the transformation of young male dancers into the variously required female characters.

By 1681 the all-male situation had changed. Prominent in the cast of characters for Lully's opera *Le Triomphe de l'Amour*, which included Beauchamps as Mars, was one Mademoiselle de Lafontaine (1665–1738), a born mademoiselle, as opposed to a man dressed up as one. This female dancer, otherwise known as a ballerina, was one of four such mademoiselles in this production. While history has yet to offer the identities of the three other ballerinas, its records provide little more about Lafontaine than her name. Still, Lafontaine's likeness graces a gallery of portraits honoring France's line of prima ballerinas, the "first" or lead female dancers whose skill and personality, and sometimes influential patronage, give them precedence over their sister dancers. In contemporary reportage, Lafontaine was hailed the "Queen of Dance." But at least one prototypical ballet-watching wag wondered, "Who else, since she was the first?"

BALLERINAS AND THE *DANSE D'ÉCOLE*

By the late seventeenth century women dancers joined, though did not supersede, male dancers on the ballet stage. When maestro Lully died in 1687 (from a freak injury incurred by stabbing his foot with the point of his time-marking stick), the theatrical form known as *opéra-ballet* was in vogue. While similar to the *ballet à entrée*, these productions aimed for even more thematic and dramatic coherence. They included what we today recognize as opera—sung narrative texts, which here served to introduce individual ballets, dances that elaborated some overall theme. A contemporary writer who composed scenarios for opéra-ballet likened the danced portions to the pictures painted by Antoine Watteau, the great painter of that age. Calling the dances "beautiful Watteaus," the librettist identified them as "spicy miniatures demanding graphic precision, gracefulness of the brush and superior brilliant coloring."

The music academy and opera house in Paris overseen by Lully set the pace and standard for this form of musical entertainment. One early opéra-ballet, *L'Europe Galante* (1697), was the creation of André Campra (1660–1744), who followed in Lully's footsteps. Its success prompted the composer to remark on the number of people who attended the Paris Opera as much, or more, for the dancing as for the music. To build upon this trend and increase the popularity of such works the composer suggested a way: Lengthen the dances and shorten the skirts of the female dancers.

In 1700 a description of the art of French/European dancing, for the theater as well as for the ballroom, got written down. Published as *Choréographie, ou l'art de décrire la danse* by Raoul Auger Feuillet, the manual's "characters, figures, and illustrative signs" were an early attempt to create a dance notation comparable to that established for music. A universal system never evolved, but this early attempt came close. *Choréographie* spread throughout the Europe of its time and subsequently gave rise to other, individual systems inspired by its model. Feuillet's predecessors and/or contemporaries, Pierre Beauchamps (1636–c. 1705) and Louis Pécour (c. 1653–1729), who became dance master to the king when Beauchamps retired after Lully's death, are today generally acknowledged as co-authors with Feuillet of the information included in this volume.

The word "*choreographie*," which gives English the word "choreography," came into the French language from combining "*khorea*," Greek for "dance," with "*graphein*," German for "write." By extension, "choreographer," now all but exclusively used for dance maker, or creator, originally, literally meant "dance writer," as in one who writes down dances on paper. That designation later became known as "notator," but not for more than a century. Thus while the "choreographer" was the one who put dance sequences on paper, the dance or ballet master was the one who created them for the stage space.

By early 1700, the foundation of ballet schooling was to a great extent already in place. Some of Feuillet's terms are slightly different today, and some choreographers use the same name to identify somewhat different moves. Specifically, today's *jeté* (a jumped move instigated by a "thrown" foot), *sissone* (a jump off two feet landing on one, named after Monsieur Sissone), *chassé* (a step with one foot "chased" by the other), *entrechat* (a jumped move to "weave" the feet in the air), *pirouette* (a "whirl" or spin in place), and *cabriole* (a jumped "caper" with the legs briefly closing and opening again in the air) all remain much as they were in Feuillet's day. (Of this group, the last three moves were excluded from the vocabulary of ballroom dancing and restricted specifically to the methods of theatrical dance.)

In 1713, two years before the death of Louis XIV, the Paris Opera established its very own school of dance. The body language practiced there and indicated by Feuillet's writings eventually gave rise to the term *danse d'école*, which has come to serve as a synonym for ballet dancing. Though Feuillet's writing included working from five positions for the feet, the absolute designations of these stances, usually credited to Beauchamps and his work in the late 1600s, was first formally documented in 1725 for *The Dancing Master*, a social dance manual by Pierre Rameau (c. 1674–1748), a former dance master to the queen of Spain.

The French school of dance stressed well-mannered elegance and grace of movement over eye-catching physical feats of acrobatics and virtuosity. Pronounced acrobatic emphasis remained part of Italianate dance methods. However much the danced sequences of the opéra-ballet could appear incidental to a production's title or theme, acting perhaps to slow the thrust of the action, they didn't blithely separate from it. Italy's contemporaneous *intermedii* or entr'actes did.

Another Rameau, a musician named Jean Phillipe (1683–1764) and no relation to dancing master Pierre, made his mark within the opéra-ballet theater. His compositions ultimately gained him a fame related to that of Lully. Likewise Rameau's prominence gained him antagonism from the diehard Lully faction.

Les Indes Galantes, Rameau's opéra-ballet from 1735, gave his own partisans good cause for celebration. A lavish spectacle of singing and dancing, loosely shaped as a story of four loves in four corners of the world, the individual entries took the audience to exotic, foreign climes: Turkey, Peru, Persia, and North America. We can assume the male and female dancers performing in Jean Phillipe Rameau's premiere obeyed the particulars defined in Pierre Rameau's manual from ten years earlier. By this time, the ballroom and the ballet forms were recognized as separate.

Even while the two forms of dancing shared many aspects, the methods of the ballet stage, with its professional dancers, were seen as more demanding. In particular, the turnout of the legs and feet so that they appear more in profile to the viewer, though proscribed for the ballroom dancer, became even more pronounced for the stage dancer. Pierre Rameau's dictates for the ballroom included turned-out positioning of the legs and feet, sometimes referred to as *en dehors*, but the dance master remained aware of the stricter use of the position for specialized steps specific to theatrical dancing. His observations make clear that turnout initiates in the hip socket, explaining that "neither knees nor feet can turn out if the hips do not" do so first. Elaborating that neither *battements* (kicks, "throwing" the legs in the air), nor entrechats nor cabrioles are workable without firm turnout, the dance master notes that such moves belong exclusively onstage and are not part of the ballroom dancer's vocabulary.

Still, the look and notion of turned-out legs and feet became a strong concern of ballroom dancing amateurs. Various devices came into use for shaping, encouraging, and building turnout. Sometimes these were no more than little wooden boxes that were shaped to accommodate a standing man's or woman's feet with the heels touching and the toes pointing in opposite directions. Or they were crude machines that twisted the feet to extreme sideward-pointing positions. Other times, the contraptions were taller and more elaborate, aiming to press the full leg into profile position above the sideward-pointing feet. Few of these allowed for gradual, workable change; most forced the issue, stressed the limbs, and caused permanent damage.

Italy's infamous Casanova left us with a memoir regarding notable French stage dancing from a visit to an opéra-ballet (Campra's *Les Fêtes Venétiennes*) in the mid-1740s. Louis Dupré (1697–1774), adored by his public as "The God of the Dance," came before the Venetian as "a tall, well-made dancer, wearing a mask and an enormous black wig, the hair of which went halfway down his back, and dressed in a robe open in front and reaching to his heels." Dupré's fine figure, his measured steps, his rounded arms, his light and precise footwork, battements, and pirouettes all mildly struck the foreign observer, who couldn't believe it was all over when the dancer disappeared like a breeze to the enthusiastic cries of an adoring audience.

Other male dancers also ranked high with the French public: Michel Blondy (1677–1747), probably Beauchamps's nephew, and Claude Balon (1676–1739), sometimes spelled Ballon and dubiously said to have inspired the term *ballon* for lightness in jumps. Each acquired notable fame, though Dupré was the only one called a "god." Women remained in the shadow of their male counterparts not only because they entered the profession later than men but also because their costuming was more concealing and constricting of movement than men's. While women's feet were about all of the leg shown to the public, men in their knee breeches, or *culottes*, and hose displayed more leg and thus their dancing's legwork.

Maestro Campra's call to shorten the ladies' skirts on the ballet stage came about gradually. Like royal family succession, dance lineage comes about as a result of related generations. In the case of a *première danseuse*, as the leading female dancer or ballerina was called, the link was not necessarily through actual bloodlines but through teacher-to-pupil/protégé lines. Mademoiselles Marie-Thérèse de Subligny (1666–c. 1735) and Françoise Prévost (c. 1680–1741), respectively succeeded Mlle Lafontaine as France's "Queen of the Dance." Mlle de Subligny made her mark in part dancing alongside both M. Blondy and M. Balon, while the younger Prévost found herself paired with the aging but still active Balon. In all cases, their properly long skirts remained properly long, which did not prevent some from noting that neither ballerina was strongly turned out in the knees and feet.

Among the works in which Prévost established her fame was one she devised herself, without regard to a counterpart male dancer. Called *Les caractères de la Danse*, the solo (or *pas seul*) took the form of a series of dances illustrating different varieties of lovers, both male and female, and all performed by Prévost herself. Eventually the première danseuse became a respected teacher at the Paris Opera. She produced two famous pupils and gave the often partisan-happy ballet public one of its first artistic rivalries. Both Marie Sallé (1707–1756) and Marie-Anne de Cupis de Camargo (1710–1770) would perform their teacher's showcase of "characters." In so doing, each defined not only her artistic profile but also delineated for the public differing aesthetic schools of taste.

Sallé, known for strength in expressive pantomime as well as dance-step skill, elaborated the showcase into a duet. Thus she could accentuate expressive interaction with a partner as she performed different characters. Camargo, or La Camargo as the wildly popular ballerina was known, exemplified the more pure-dance side of her art. In performing the characters choreographed by Prévost, the star pupil focused on the physical intricacies of dance steps. Her speciality became little jumping steps, *temps d'élevation*, and steps in which the feet and lower legs delicately closed to cross each other or to beat together, *batterie*.

Earlier in the world of French ballet, Jean Baptiste Lully's loyal fans supported his work as expressive and, once in competition with that of Jean Philippe Rameau, superior to work that came to be admired for its technical, virtuoso bent. And so it was under way, the dichotomy in the ballet world between dancing that is predominantly expressive and dancing that is technically impressive. Both Camargo and Sallé initiated changes in costuming that led to making the female dancer's legwork and footwork more visible to the public.

Once Camargo became adept at well turned-out, fancy work for her lower legs and feet, she consistently chose to perform with a skirt shorter than that of proper everyday dress. Even though the shortening preferred by Camargo went little beyond baring the ankle, her "innovation" came coupled with the inclusion of *calçons de précaution* ("precautionary panties" or "modesty drawers"). This muslin, drawstring undergarment worn over hose was deemed necessary by authorities fearful that briefer skirts might produce brief glimpses of the bare flesh and anatomy above the tops of a ballerina's stockings.

To remain in keeping with the expressive dimension of a Grecian beauty sculpted by Pygmalion, Sallé appeared in thin muslin draperies. None of a dancer's normal code of dress appeared on Sallé as Pygmalion's Statue come to life: no stiff bodice, no large skirt, no hooped petticoat, no ornamented, "put-up" hairstyle. All of which caused something of a scandal in 1734, helping to sell many many tickets. Unlike Camargo's costume preference, which helped evolve the ballerina's "uniform," Sallé's undressed look was devised for the particular purpose of dressing a particular ballet.

In 1739, an Italian dancer named Barbara Campanini (1721–1799) came to Paris as both Camargo and Sallé were on the wane. Quickly known in French ballet circles as La Barbarina, the energetic Italian teenager represented the latest exponent of her homeland's dance schooling. Possessing virtuoso strength and personal brio, the popular danseuse won special praise from the likes of Prussia's Frederick the Great, who made admiring comments on her "boyish legs."

The hallmark of her dancing was speed and brilliance, especially in turns and jumps. In temperamental terms she fell in line with dancing à la Camargo, except more so. Where Camargo could confidently flutter through *entrechat-quatre*, a double crossing of the feet in the air of a little jumped step, La Barbarina could zip through *entrechat-huit*, a quadruple accent.

Chapter 4

GENTLE WOMEN AND GENTLE MEN OF THE BALLET

Meanwhile, in the courts of Russian tsars and tsarinas and English monarchs, a taste for ballet spectacle evolved on its own. In 1738, a year before La Barbarina made her debut in Paris, the Russian crown established the world's second oldest academy of ballet dancing, more or less since known as the "St. Petersburg school." Even earlier, during the second decade of the century, an English dance master named John Weaver (1673–1760) began the development of what would come to be known as the *ballet d'action*. In this brand of ballet theater, unlike the *ballet à entrée*, the dancing served to carry the chosen subject by means of movement alone, either pantomime or dance steps, without recourse to spoken, sung, or recited verse. Weaver's most ambitious and prominent creation was *The Loves of Mars and Venus*. With France's "*dieu de la danse*" Louis Dupré as Mars and England's so-called first ballerina, Hester Santlow (c. 1690–1773), as Venus, the choreographer himself performed as the antagonistic Vulcan.

The vicissitudes of contemporary taste and fashion being what they were in early-eighteenth-century England, Weaver's coordinated blend of pantomime, gesture, and formal dance steps more or less came and went with him at home. When Mlle Sallé brought her greatly admired *Pygmalion* to London in 1734 few enthusiasts for the French ballerina bothered to credit Weaver's earlier creation as the model and inspiration of her showpiece. Whatever else motivated English audiences to acclaim Sallé's work while forgetting that of Weaver, the phenomenon of a public's keen taste for a foreign star dancer would continue throughout ballet's history.

Physical theatrics, often downright acrobatic, were the mainstay of the branch of Italian popular theater known as *commedia dell'arte*, which means "comedy of the profession," as distinguished from *commedia erudita*, meaning "comedy of the gentlemen amateurs." Though interwoven with spoken Italian at home, on tour, especially in France where commedia dell'arte players gained popularity, the artists concentrated, often exclusively, on physical, gestural, and pantomimic means of performing. By the mid-1700s, a theatrical mix called ballet-pantomimes, which owed something to the commedia dell'arte workings and themes, made up the offerings at the Théâtre Italien in Paris.

The full flowering of the ballet d'action came through the efforts of two disparate individuals: Gaspero Angiolini (1731–1803), an Italian, and Jean Georges Noverre (1727–1810), French-Swiss by birth. The former had previously worked under the wing of Franz Hilverding (1710–1768), a Viennese dance master who pioneered the form of the ballet d'action much as Weaver had done. Noverre, whose accomplishments give him more historical prominence than Angiolini, had studied dancing with the "great" Dupré. The two proponents of unified dance theater, in which the means of dancing carried the particulars of theme and narrative, came near to swords drawn over their similarly geared artistic philosophies.

After Noverre published his famous *Lettres sur la danse et les ballets* (dated 1760 and often referred to in English simply as *Letters on Dancing*), Angiolini cried plagiarism, claiming the Frenchman's theorizing merely rehashed that of his mentor, Hilverding. More than a friendly feud and less than a full-scale battle, the bone of contention between these contemporary choreographers prefigured countless others throughout ballet history. In the end, the history of ballet owes a debt of gratitude to Noverre for putting formally on paper the innovative goals of himself and others, ballet d'action.

These ideas worked to establish the supremacy of the dance master over that of the composer in creating ballets. Besides stressing a need for dramatic coherence, the ballet d'action proponent insisted that the particulars of the ballet's dramatic line be rendered as expressive movement, either pantomime or suitable dance gestures. Harmony and naturalness took precedence over virtuosity for its own sake. Along with this development came a reevaluation of what dancers wore.

Up till this time dancers were costumed in a kind of uniform that varied in detailing while remaining consistent in overall cut. Both men and women essentially dressed in fanciful versions of contemporary fashion. From head to toe, the male dancer's costume began with a ringletted wig and some sort of hat, often ornately plumed. His torso sported a coat or tunic basically modeled on the skirted kind found on ancient Roman generals.

By Noverre's day these tunic extensions had grown extravagant. Often standing away from the dancer's waist like a flyaway hoop skirt, the kiltlike accessories had their own name, *tonnelet*. The male dancer's legs were covered in breeches gartered at the knee and hose; his feet in heeled, buckled, or bowed leather pumps. Capping the whole costume was a molded leather face mask, fastened with a ribbon.

Similar masks were regular features of the female dancer's uniform. Completing her costume were a wig and a full-skirted long dress with hooped petticoat and hip-exaggerating panniers. Beyond the optional wearing of "precautionary drawers," women dancers also wore hose and fashionable heeled leather pumps.

In order to dance ballet d'action reasonably, Noverre stressed costume reform to "break hideous masks, to burn ridiculous perukes, to suppress clumsy panniers, to do away with still more inconvenient hip pads." He demanded "more action and expression in dancing." By shedding the face masks, his dancers could perfect the art of pantomime by working with expressions on their own faces. Noverre's 1763 pantomime-ballet *Jason and Medea* exemplified his principles thoroughly. With its inclusion of the personifications of Vengeance, Jealousy, and Fire, the vividly expressive show sometimes shocked contemporary audiences with its violence.

One of Europe's most admired dancers, and successor to Dupré's *dieu de la danse* title, Gaëtan Vestris (1728–1808, born in Italy as Gaetano) created the role of Noverre's Jason. Vestris became renowned for his elegance and his standard-setting presentation of roles in the *danse noble* genre. This genre, also known as "*haute*" or "*sé-*

rieux," called for measured, stately, elegant dancing predicated on the articulation of the tall, long-of-limb physique. Vestris encountered Noverre's innovations about mid-career, and they affected his performing for the rest of his long career. Known variously to his public as "*le beau Vestris*" and "*l'homme à la belle jambe*," the handsome dancer with comely legs fathered a son at thirty-three with a young aspiring ballerina of seventeen, Marie Allard (1742–1802).

Smaller of build than his "god" of a father, Vestris *fils*, born Marie-Jean-Augustin and known to history as Auguste (1760–1842), made a name for himself in the genre of dancing below that of the *danse noble*. Sometimes called *demi-caractère*, to make reference to physiques better suited to colorful athletic characters rather than aristocratic ones, this one category did not prove large enough for the virtuoso talents of Auguste. Noverre's assessment of the stellar dancer's prodigious gifts suggested that with his large jumps, his quick footwork, and multiple turns, Vestris *fils* combined three types of dancers: the *sérieux*, the *comique*, and the *demi-caractère*. Looking with bemusement on the achievements and acclaim of his son, Vestris *père* noted how Auguste had one benefit denied him, that of having himself as father.

Besides Marie Allard, some of the prominent women dancers who shared stage time, and in some cases offstage time, with the father-and-son gods of the dance and the groundbreaking ballet masters included Anne Heinel (1753–1808), Marie-Madeleine Guimard (1743–1816), and one Marie-Madeleine de Crespé (1760–1796), known as Mlle Théodore. As eighteenth-century ballerinas, these women cut figures more like traditional wedding cake figurines than the leggy, short-skirted fixtures that later regularly twirled on music boxes. But to their age, the hoop-skirted, crinolined ladies were all revered ballerinas. The time when their sex would dominate the art form, leaving their male counterparts in the shadows or completely offstage, was still to come.

Mlle Heinel, a German later nicknamed "*la belle statue*," made her name in Paris partly because of her skill in executing turns, the pirouettes of the *danse d'école*. She excelled in the multiple turn as well as in the *pirouette à la seconde*, wherein the dancer took and maintained a position during the turn in which the leg held away from the stage extended straight to the side. She retired while still in her prime and married Gaëtan Vestris.

The French-born Guimard had a long and influential career in Paris. Though her extremely thin physique was frequently remarked upon, Guimard's weighty influence at the Opera was profound. Although Noverre greatly admired the ballerina, noting how her charm resulted from a blend of tenderness and voluptuousness, the feelings were not mutual. When the master of the ballet d'action (or *ballets en action*, as they were sometimes called) landed the job of directing the Paris Opera, Guimard, its leading ballerina, led a campaign against his administration, which finally led to his resigning after four years in the post. Parisian balletgoers were not always so complimentary as Noverre. Mocking the taste of the *première danseuse* to decorate her house with images of Terpsichore, mythology's muse of the dance, they referred to the delicately boned and thinly framed ballerina as the "Skeleton of the Muses."

Having gained something of a reputation as a well-read intellectual and follower of Jean-Jacques Rousseau, Mlle (or Madame, as she was later called) Théodore, left the Paris Opera before being made *première danseuse*. The "free thinker in skirts" soon made a good and prominent name for herself, however, in Brussels and London. She eventually settled with her dancer-husband-choreographer Jean Dauberval (1742–1806) in Bordeaux, where she achieved her most lasting place in ballet history. In 1789, close to the eve of France's history-changing Revolution, Dauberval featured his wife as Lison in *Le Ballet de la Paille*. "The Ballet of the Straw" was a rustic affair, set in a farmland where a landowning mother tries in vain to arrange a profitable marriage for her headstrong daughter, who has eyes for a more comely if less landed fellow. Today the work is known as *La Fille Mal Gardée*, and the heroine is called Lise. At that time it was radical for a ballet to take for its subject the middle class and present a setting that was contemporary rather than portraying a mythological past and its lofty characters.

Dauberval (born Jean Bercher) learned his craft from Noverre. The champion of ballet d'action praised his pupil's abilities as a dancer, noting how amid the rococco conventions of the day, Dauberval could create characters "full of dramatic action and interest." In *La*

Fille Mal Gardée, Dauberval's *ballet villageois* (a category of comic, rustic ballet), the choreographer helped establish a move away from the realm of gods and goddesses toward that of down-to-earth everyday life. At this early juncture, the everyday life of the ballet's hay-harvest more closely resembled the conceit of France's Queen Marie Antoinette and her quaint dairy farm on the grounds of the royal chateau at Versailles than it did the nitty-gritty milieu of France's land-working classes.

The vicissitudes of the French revolution around Paris allowed Dauberval to maintain a strong company in Bordeaux. Among his dancers and "pupils" were the Italian-born-and-trained Salvatore Viganò (1769–1821) and his wife, Spanish dancer Maria Medina (1765–1821). Acclaimed as poet, musician, and actor, Viganò followed in the aesthetic footsteps of Dauberval. The Italian made his name in dance by creating light, comic ballets but eventually climaxed his career as creator of *choreodrammi* (mimed dramas). France's revered novelist Stendahl equated Viganò's theater genius with that of Shakespeare while Germany's genius composer Beethoven wrote his only ballet score, *The Creatures of Prometheus*, for Viganò.

Viganò's skills and tastes continued to carry forward and develop Italian theatrical traditions for grand pantomimic gesture, telescoping expression with both the face and the body. Alongside his wife and partner, who was much admired for her physical beauty, Viganò also explored what he called the *pas de deux* pantomime. Drawings of these duets from the 1790s record a remarkable gestural language; they also document how far costume reform had come, especially with the fashion "revolution" in the wake of the French Revolution. Viganò's own costumes appear of much lighter fabric and are more casually constructed, while Medina's look was lighter still, cut along French Empire lines, in softer materials and uncorsetted waists. Both dancers wear softer, more flexible footwear, reminiscent of "barefoot" sandals.

Chapter 5

THE PRE-ROMANTIC AND ROMANTIC ERAS

Charles-Louis Didelot (1767–1837), half French, half Swedish, studied and worked under a variety of the eighteenth century's ballet innovators, including Noverre, Dauberval, and both Gaëtan and Auguste Vestris. Just before the end of the century, the well-schooled student created a work that looked forward to ballet as it would blossom in the nineteenth century and continue to flower into our own time. Initially called *La Métamorphose* in 1795, for an early version in Lyons, Didelot's formative *ballet-divertissement* was revamped in 1796 and retitled *Flore et Zéphire*.

With his Flora and Zephyr characters, Didelot rekindled a taste for the Anacreontic world. Anacreon, a Greek lyric poet who lived around 500 B.C., hymned the joys of wine and love. His poems inspired a school of poetry, which lasted through the mid-1400s, longing for similar pastoral pleasures. Sometimes termed Baroque or Rococo (as was the period's visual art and music), ballet entered the nineteenth century, as well as a different mode, needing a new label. The transitional phase is usually called Pre-Romantic.

For decades, the gods and goddesses of the dance had routinely portrayed the gods and goddesses of classical mythology. While their carriage indicated heads held high in the clouds, their elegant footwork told of feet firmly planted on the ground, or "on the boards" as theater argot might have it. Didelot's Flora and Zephyr were spirits, one a nymph goddess of flowers and spring, the other a personification of the mild west wind. Their feet were meant to tread the air, and with the help of wires worked by special stage machinery, these dance characters could so do.

Flore et Zéphire became Didelot's most popular and lasting work. The fame the French dancer and choreographer gained from it led to an invitation in 1799 from the Francophile Russian monarchy to direct the ballet connected with the tsar's circuit of imperial theaters established in 1783. For Russia's St. Petersburg in 1808, Didelot reversed the title names to *Zéphire et Flore* to give prominence to the male dancer starring in this version. This was Louis Duport, a French dancer who had recently made his name by way of contesting the waning powers of still famous Auguste Vestris.

Male dancing prowess peaked during this era. Vestris *fils* left the stage largely if not quite permanently and became a well-known and respected teacher. His classes, as well as those of Carlo Blasis (1797–1878), a pupil of Viganò's, helped the next generation of dancers advance significantly beyond that of their elders. Blasis actually formalized his teachings by publishing, first in Italy and then in England, manuals describing the methods and fine points of dancing in the early 1800s. Addressing, for example, the advancing expertise with ballet's particular turning move, the pirouette, Blasis gave the lexicon the term *attitude*. The "design" or posture of the turning dancer's body was characterized by a way of holding the extended leg, which in this case was determined by a definite bending of the knee. Blasis referred to the graceful position for a pirouette as being modeled on the attitude of the famous sixteenth-century statue of Mercury by Giambologna.

To his dedicated pupils in the next generation of accomplished ballet dancers, Auguste Vestris was affectionately known as "Grand-papa Zephyr." In the newer age, however, it was Didelot's Floras who pointed the way, somewhat literally as it would turn out. With the extra lightening of their costumes and footwear (gauzy, airy dresses and supple, heelless slippers), the nymphs flying about the stage could be seen to skim and alight on the earth on the very tips of their toes. Two ballerinas who led revised stagings of *Zéphire et Flore* remain in the history books as innovators of the soon-to-be pervasive new dimension, and drama, of ballet: dancing *sur les pointes*. Russia's Maria Danilova (1793–1810) and France's Geneviève Gosselin

(1791–1818) and Fanny Bias (1789–1825) each performed Flora and belong to the early sisterhood of ballerinas recorded as dancing on the tips of their toes.

The foremost, if not the very first, ballerina to enter the ballet public's consciousness on pointe was Italy's Marie Taglioni (1804–1884), particularly in a Paris production of a ballet fashioned especially for her by her teacher–ballet master father, Filippo Taglioni (1777–1871). Marie's background—born in Stockholm—included the rigorous lessons in dancing that Blasis promoted in his writings. To show off his daughter's prowess and finesse, Filippo devised various ballets for her.

Influential among these in the dawning of ballet's new Romantic era, was an 1831 *ballet-divertissement*, in the "Ballet of the Nuns," created for the opera *Robert le Diable* by Giacomo Meyerbeer. In the opera's third act, Taglioni performed the role of the ghost of an abbess rising from her tomb in a cloister bathed in moonlight. She acted to stir her phantom sisters into a dance of enticement. The scene presented vaporous figures urging the narrative's hero, Robert, to steal a talisman from a saint's statue. Special gaslight effects and those of light-catching garments conjured ectoplasmic shapes in a kind of metaphysical scene that would become familiar and popular over the ensuing decades.

In 1832, Papa Taglioni presented his Marie in a full-scale ballet that definitively launched her career as symbol of an entire era of ballet art. *La Sylphide*, with a scenario by Adolphe Nourrit, the leading tenor of *Robert le Diable*, told the story of a woodland nymph whose beguiling presence convinces a young Scotsman to abandon his plans for domestic security and follow her to her natural habitat in the surrounding forest. With its theme of instinct and impulse over intellect and societal duty, its setting within untamed nature, and its distinct costuming for the ballerina sylph and her corps de ballet, sister sylphs, *La Sylphide* established a pervasive formula for future ballet. The white, tiered, bell-shaped skirt falling from the boned bodice of Eugène Lami's costume for Taglioni at once became synonymous with La Taglioni, and eventually with any and all notions of Romantic ballet.

Once the ballet costume term tutu, coined from *cucu*, French babytalk for bottom (from *cul-cul*) or perhaps as a corruption of *tulle*, its fabric, entered the dance vocabulary some fifty years after *La Sylphide*, Taglioni's *Sylphide* skirt became the prototype for the so-called Romantic tutu. (Well into the twentieth century, fashion lingo would call "ballerina length" any skirt that fell, tutulike, to a calf-height hemline.) The light, gossamer dancing of Taglioni as the winged sprite who lived in the air and foliage of the forest, featured maneuvers and postures expertly poised on the tips of her toes. Such workings on pointe took Taglioni's audiences to the edge of their seats and to raptures of acclaim. They also helped take something that existed as a blatantly acrobatic stunt and shape it into a lyrical, theatrical trait. By way of La Taglioni, the ballet public marveled at *équilibres sur la pointe*, by which the female dancer could create diaphanous pictures fortified by armatures of steel. (Her teacher father threatened to curse his ballerina daughter if he ever *heard* her dance.)

In 1834, another foreign ballerina made her debut in Paris. Already esteemed in Vienna, her place of birth, as well as in London and Berlin, Fanny Elssler (1810–1884) came before the Parisian public most dramatically in *Le Diable Boîteux* (1836), a ballet created by the Opera's resident *maître de ballet*, Jean Coralli (1779–1854). Translated as "The Devil on Two Sticks," meaning a demon on crutches, Coralli's ballet capitalized on a fascination with local color and exotic subjects beloved of the era's Romantics, such as Alexandre Dumas and Victor Hugo. The setting was Spain, and Elssler performed the part of a Spanish dancer. Her *cachucha*, a ballet rendering of a standard Spanish dance complete with castanets, tiered-lace skirt, and hair comb, caused a sensation. It also suggested comparisons between Elssler's fiery, fancy figures on the ground and Taglioni's ethereal movements in the air.

The rivalry between Elssler and Taglioni recalled that of Sallé and Camargo. In the hearts and minds of their respective partisans, the two "goddesses" gave rise to poeticized preferences. Designations of Taglioni as "Christian" in temperament and of Elssler as "pagan" remain the day's most famous. In dancing's physical, technical terms, Taglioni's lightness and aerial prowess concentrated on ballet's *balloné* effects; Elssler's steely, stabbing toework and grounded figures dwelt more on *tacqueté*.

Giselle, ou Les Wilis, a Paris Opera creation of 1841, ten years after the triumph of *La Sylphide*, gave the burgeoning Romantic age its hallmark work. Specifically designated a *ballet-fantastique*, as opposed to a *ballet-Anacreontique*, an opera ballet, or a ballet pantomime, this two-acter was the carefully wrought collaboration of composer, scenario writers, set and costume designers, and individual choreographers. All capitalized on the concerns of the Romantic movement dominating the arts. The story concerned an earthy, peasant world visited by a philandering aristocrat and haunted by potent spirits from beyond the early graves of certain local inhabitants. The ballet's score, by Adolphe Adam, struck many ears as genuinely coherent music drama, and was produced in careful concert with the ballet's masterminds rather than out of existing musical clichés.

While *Giselle*'s title character could be seen as Elssler-like in Act 1 and Taglioni-like in Act 2, neither the Viennese nor the Italian ballerina was available to take on the new Romantic role. After making their names in Paris, both took their acts and most famous roles on the road. (In 1840, Elssler made a grand tour of America, where on the afternoon of her appearance in Washington, Congress recessed so members could see her perform. In 1841, Taglioni performed for the first time in Milan's famed La Scala opera house.) Thus the most lasting of Romantic ballet's heroines was first performed by a "new" ballerina, Carlotta Grisi (1819–1899), yet another Italian import.

Choreographic credit for *Giselle, ou Les Wilis* goes to Coralli, creator of Elssler's "Spanish" ballet showcase. Additional credit, however, particularly for the dances of Grisi, goes to Jules Perrot (1810–1892), who was by this time a famous dancer and choreographer, as well as Grisi's lover. Though *Giselle* told a story of vampires (the translation of the Slavic *wilis*), for all its Romanticism, it was no cheap-thrills spook show or grand guignol melodrama. In the words of its creators, the tragic ballet's heroine should die "a pretty death."

• • •

By the mid-1800s Western Europe had a number of internationally prominent ballerinas. (Fifteen-year-old Augusta Maywood, 1824–1876, one of America's earliest exponents of ballet dancing, made successful guest appearances in Paris during 1839.) In 1845, a savvy English theater promoter named Benjamin Lumley put together ballet's first blockbuster superstar event, commissioning Jules Perrot to choreograph a special ballet for four of the day's leading *danseuses.* In addition to La Taglioni, the event involved Grisi, Lucille Grahn (1819–1907), and Fanny Cerrito (1817–1909). (The former was a Danish-born-and-schooled ballerina who gained international acclaim; the latter, a Neopolitan ballerina, who had not made her debut in Paris but who was already popular in Italian cities, Vienna and London.)

Perrot's ballet, designated a *divertissement,* meaning a diverting, storyless display of dancing, was simply titled *Pas de Quatre* and featured its four stars in pink tutus à la Taglioni. All that has lived into the ages that succeeded the era of Romanticism are reconstructions of the rosy, gauzy dresses and the tuneful score by Cesar Pugni. With the double-edged task of devising individual dances and of giving proper due to each of his superstars, Perrot had his work and problems cut out for him. The dances seemingly proved the easier part. The ordering of them brought up the question of who would dance second to the last, before the great Taglioni, generally agreed to be the foursome's most super, as in senior, superstar. Only after a suggestion that age would be the deciding factor did the one-upwomanship subside.

With the ballerina's growing expertise in working on pointe, the female dancer held firm sway over ballet's Romantic Age. A few male dancers, such as Perrot and Arthur Saint-Léon (1821–1870), made some impact, but even the most prominent of these remained in the shadow of their female counterparts. Saint-Léon, who was a virtuoso violinist as well as an accomplished dancer of the *noble sérieux* genre, like Gaëtan Vestris, reached his dancing peak as partner to Cerrito, to whom he was married for six years. Perrot had direct links to his teacher Auguste Vestris, who taught his physically articulate but not especially comely pupil some of his personal trade secrets: "Turn, spin, fly, but never give the public time to examine your person closely."

Another Frenchman, Lucien Petipa (1815–1898), also made a name for himself in Romantic ballet's world of women. Besides creating the role of the duplicitous count in *Giselle*, Petipa won fame and acclaim in *La Peri*, a ballet-fantastique in which his skills as a virtuoso partner came into play. Choreographed by Coralli, the ballet included a scene in which Grisi, as a vision of an impassioned pasha's dream, had to drop from a six-foot-high platform into the waiting arms of her admirer. Such sophisticated supporting skill from the male dancer would become more refined and sophisticated as the century advanced, notably with work done in Russia by Marius Petipa (1818–1910), Lucien's brother.

Hoping to create another ballet blockbuster in the wake of *Pas de Quatre*, Perrot created *Le Jugement de Pâris*. This divertissement had a little more of a story, as well as a small ensemble of subsidiary characters leading to the climactic *Pas des Déesses*. The scene-setting segment included a corps de ballet of seven women and Perrot himself as Mercury. The centerpiece featured Saint-Léon as Pâris and Taglioni, Grahn, and Cerrito as the goddesses Juno, Pallas, and Venus. Though each goddess wore Romantic ballet's seemingly regulation ballet skirt, the divertissement's subject harkened a bit back to the era of French court ballet with its emphasis on the myths and personages of classical Greece and Rome.

Increasingly, the taste and influence of male balletgoers and financially supportive subscribers in Paris dictated the form ballet dancing took. (After 1830, the Paris Opera, which had retained a royal license since its inception under the Bourbon monarchy, received only partial state subsidy and became something of a private enterprise.) The great popularity of female dancers and dancing eventually evolved to a policy for presenting women in certain male roles. Calling on a longstanding theatrical tradition of "travesty," known in French as roles *en travestie* and referred to in opera as "trouser" or "pants" parts, female dancers during the mid-1800s frequently took the part of the leading men or heroes in ballet productions. At the beginning of her career in Paris, Fanny Elssler's older, and bigger, sister Therese (1808–1878) regularly performed as Fanny's "male" partner. Though the playing of older characters (usually pantomime roles) was still done by men, the male dancer was becoming a contradiction in terms in the big picture of ballet in Paris.

Chapter 6

FRENCH ART IN DANISH AND RUSSIAN QUARTERS

Fortunately for the male species of dancer, different tastes from those in France reigned in Denmark and Russia. The ruling monarchies supported the ballet as a diversion for its court and as a showcase for its country's culture, and male dancers advanced alongside their female counterparts.

The story of ballet in Denmark goes back before the era of Auguste Bournonville (1805–1879), the dancer and choreographer who would become synonymous with Danish ballet. Danish taste for *ballet de cour* dates to the 1600s, with 1634 marking the first full-scale version of such spectacle. Denmark's versions were based on both the French-style events and the related style popular in the English court. After a lull during the 1730s and 1740s, when King Christian VI showed no tolerance for theater or ballet, a resurgence began and more or less has remained continual to this day.

King Frederik V and his English-born queen, Louise, saw the opening of Denmark's first self-contained Royal Theater in 1748, which eventually featured drama, opera, ballet, and concert music. Soon thereafter, French and Italian ballet masters were imported to develop their art on Danish soil. Antonio Sacco, a follower of the *ballet d'action* of Noverre and Angiolini, set Denmark's ballet on a path similar to other European centers like Paris, London, Vienna, Milan, and Stuttgart.

In 1771, French dancing master Pierre Lurent helped establish a dancing school in the palace's own little private theater. In 1775, when another Italian, Vincenzo Galeotti (1733–1816), arrived to oversee Denmark's growing ballet tradition, the Danish ballet achieved its first flowering. Already renowned in Europe as a dancer and ballet master, Galeotti, another Noverre follower, guided the Royal Danish Ballet for the next forty years. By way of historical happenstance and Danish taste, a one-act *ballet-comique* Galeotti produced in 1786 entitled *The Whims of Cupid and the Ballet Master* exists to this day in Copenhagen, where it remains the oldest surviving ballet.

Galeotti's suite of dances by individuals from diverse cultures and climes unspools as the characters get tangled up when a mischievous Cupid plays a game of mismatching wedding couples. The approximately hour-long ballet has probably survived because of its whimsical nature, its pantomime-dominant material and its quaint look through eighteenth-century eyes at foreign peoples and behavior. Although each succeeding generation likely streamlines some details, gingerly upgrading costuming and automatically working toward contemporary physical skills, the ballet's overall shape and texture has been maintained. One reason the work is not toured much concerns the potential offense given by the cultural clichés evident in the rendering of the foreigners' behavior—for example, the presentation of Africans as wide-eyed and oversexed.

As the successor of Galeotti, French-born Antoine Bournonville (1760–1843) really accomplished only one invaluable thing with regard to the Royal Danish Ballet's growth. He fathered Auguste Bournonville, the dancer and ballet master who would revitalize and lead Denmark's ballet into a Romantic golden age all its own. Auguste trained with his father and was fine-tuned by the famous French dancers with whom Antoine had worked in Paris, Pierre Gardel and, especially, Auguste Vestris. His French finishing-school lessons gained the young Bournonville a contract to dance with the ballet troupe of the Paris Opera. While there, in addition to other achievements, he proved himself a gracious and expert partner to La Taglioni, who was happy to dance with the deft Dane.

Six years into his career as ballet master to the Danish king's company and four years after seeing the success of Filippo Taglioni's *La Sylphide*, Bournonville produced his own version. Bournonville's reworking included new choreography as well as new music. (The Paris version had music by Jean Schneitzhöeffer; the Copenhagen version, by Herman Løvenskjold.) His *Sylphide* also heralded a native, Danish sylph: sixteen-year-old Lucille Grahn. Bournonville claimed his find gave the Danes "their first idea of female virtuosity." Meanwhile, the ballet world ultimately decided that the Dane's version of *La Sylphide* gave this Romantic tale its most enduring ballet form. Nowadays, when *La Sylphide* is billed, with rarest exceptions, it's Bournonville's second version that you'll get. Taglioni's original staging has virtually disappeared from the world's theaters.

When Auguste Bournonville lost Grahn to the international circuit, he developed other female dancers in Copenhagen to take her place. Being himself a strong and accomplished dancer, the choreographer consistently created ballets that accentuated male dance prowess as much as, or even more than, female. Like the enduring quality of the Danish version of *La Sylphide*, the remarkable finesse and strength of Danish male dancers and dancing extends into the present day. Bournonville's Danish school of ballet, which he personally oversaw from 1830 through 1877, fostered and refined the ways of his adopted French school as the French strayed from those foundations, particularly with regard to male dance prowess.

While the French ballet world slipped into its tarnished Silver Age (or its age of decadence), Russia, an autocratic monarchy ever eager to emulate French court life, relived and perpetuated France's once royal ballet. Like the sixteenth-and seventeenth-century French sovereigns who imported their ballet art from Italy, the Russian tsars and tsarinas imported the most sophisticated ballet to their imperial theaters. At that point in history, however, the source was as notably French as it was Italian.

Through his work in St. Petersburg, Didelot guided the ballet of Russia's new capital to its first flowering. The way had been prepared in part by the efforts of Hilverding and Angiolini, both of whom directed the imperial theater's ballet in the late 1700s. A sibling tradition, born in the 1770s some thirty-five years after Petersburg's, was also growing in the country's former capital, Moscow. By the time of Europe's Romantic Age, Russian ballet was strong enough and sufficiently motivated to participate in the movement.

At first, European Romantic ballet lived in Russia through imports. Lucrative tsarist fees enticed such names as Taglioni, Elssler, Grisi, Grahn, and Cerrito to star in Russia's ballet before Russian audiences. Intermittently, products of Russia's own schools, in particular that in St. Petersburg, dominated its stages. Maria Danilova, through whom Didelot was early on able to introduce the expertise for dancing on pointe, came to be remembered as "Russia's Taglioni" after her untimely death at seventeen in 1810. Avdotia Istomina (1799–1848) became the object of paeans to beauty from the pen of Russia's great Romantic poet Alexander Pushkin in the 1820s.

Elena Andreyanova (1819–1857) was Russia's first Giselle, in a Petersburg production staged one year after its Paris premiere. The Petersburg-schooled ballerina was also the ballerina who danced opposite the debut performances of two of Russia's—and ballet's—most important architects. They were the Swedish-born Christian Johansson (1817–1903) and the French-born Marius Petipa. Each would play a crucial role in leading Russian ballet to preeminence in the late nineteenth century—the former as influential pedagogue, especially of male dancing, and the latter, even more importantly, as the ballet master who would help formulate what all the world would come to call classical ballet.

Meanwhile, as Johansson and Petipa established themselves as dancers in Russia, the imperial ballet troupe was being shaped by two imported Frenchman. Perrot headed the Petersburg troupe from 1851 to 1859. The once prominent partner to Grisi and popular choreographer initially came to Russia as partner to Elssler in 1848. One of the first ballets Perrot staged in Petersburg was his *Esmeralda*, with a narrative based on Hugo's *Notre-dame de Paris*. Originally called *La Esmeralda* at its 1844 premiere, the ballet that then featured Grisi was presented during 1849 in St. Petersburg with Elssler as the eponymous heroine. Perrot was succeeded as the tsar's ballet master by Arthur Saint-Léon.

The renowned violinist and dancer had early on performed for Perrot, notably in his post-*Pas de Quatre*, *Le Jugement de Pâris*. Now he would lead the Russian ballet through its final phase of post-European Romanticism. One of his most notable creations was his most Russian. *The Little Humpbacked Horse*, *or The Tsar Maiden* used familiar-sounding ballet music, by resident imperial theater composer Cesar Pugni, but took inspiration from a popular Russian folktale about a pure and simple young man and a magical, mischievous little horse. The five-act 1864 production proved an immediate and lasting success with the Petersburg public for its colorful presentation of Russian folklore as ballet subject matter.

GRAND PA PETIPA AND HIS EMPIRE

In 1862, while he was still officially a leading dancer and assistant ballet master in St. Petersburg, Marius Petipa created his first multi-act ballet for the tsar's imperial theater: *The Pharaoh's Daughter*, a Grand Ballet in three acts and nine scenes, with prologue and epilogue. Its story involved exotic Egyptian locales, in and about the Nile and its pyramids, English archaeologists, opium-induced dream states, awakening mummies, poisonous snakes, and the like. In the end, Petipa had produced a ballet spectacle that would lead to other such extravaganzas, and, most important, to what all the world would learn to call classical ballet. The transition proceeded gradually rather than abruptly once Petipa took over the position of Ballet Master in Chief to the Imperial Tsar in 1869.

In his position of leadership, Petipa produced both multi-act and single-act ballets for the imperial theaters. Mostly these sites were in St. Petersburg, and included the stages of the private palaces of the tsar and his family. Additionally Petipa's imperial duties took him to work outside Petersburg. In 1859, he worked in Moscow, where he created *Don Quixote* for the imperial theater circuit's primary Moscow theater, the Bolshoi. The public in Russia's older and less westernized capital expressed a taste different from that of audiences in the more European westward metropolis. Moscow showed preferences for broad, colorful, and comedic theatrics; Petersburg for more formal, dance-based effects. A kind of cultural rivalry sprang up. Muscovites saw the ballet art practiced by Petersburg as cold; Petersburg looked at those in Moscow as circusy and coarse.

The old capital had its own ballet history. Adam Glushkovsky (1793–c. 1870), a pupil of Didelot's, helped stabilize the ballet troupe connected to Moscow's Bolshoi Theater when he acted as its ballet master from 1812 to 1839. (The Bolshoi label exists to our day for Moscow's principal ballet troupe. Back then, however, Petersburg and Moscow each had its Bolshoi Theater—the name simply means "grand" or "big"—offering ballet and opera. Eventually, the name Bolshoi became exclusively attached to Moscow's ballet and opera, primarily because Petersburg's Bolshoi Theater was displaced by the city's now more famous Maryinsky Theater.)

In 1871, two years after the Moscow premiere of his *Don Quixote*, Petipa staged the Spanish-flavored ballet for the St. Petersburg troupe. To accommodate that public's preference for "pure" ballet dancing, the ballet master altered the ballet's overall tone, lessening its stress on pantomimic comedy and character and enlarging its opportunities for displaying virtuoso ballet dancing. By this time, aristocratic connoisseurs of ballet in Russia were established as a distinct breed. Their keen interest in the ballet art of dancing and all its fine points gave rise to a still-used name for devotees of ballet: balletomane. The word derives from "balletomania," meaning an intense, nearly mad, enthusiasm for ballet. (Similarly, nineteenth century Russian opera buffs with unbounded devotion to melodic Italian opera, were known as melomanes.) Invariably male, these individuals in nineteenth-century Russia set themselves apart from the rest of the balletgoing public.

In 1877, Petipa created *La Bayadère* for St. Petersburg's Bolshoi Theater, with a libretto concerning "exotic" India by Sergei Khudekov, a prominent balletomane and historian. More than an enduring work, this four-act ballet with apotheosis provided the history of its art with a quintessential all-dancing dream or vision scene. Previously, in 1850, acting as assistant to Perrot, Petipa rechoreographed the dances of the Wilis from Act 2 of *Giselle*. The scene of women in white ballet dresses recycled a similar one from *La Sylphide*, all of which led to a taste for a genre known eventually as *ballet-blanc*.

The ballet-blanc stood apart from the body of the narrative ballet as a pièce de résistance dominated by the ballerina and her female corps de ballet. Petipa's concept of such a scene for his *La Bayadère* upped the ante of the genre's dancing, traveling a route from what's now called Romantic dancing to what came to be called classical ballet dancing. Petipa's white-clad dancing women represented Shades or Shadows, spirits in an underworld where the narrative's hypnotized hero descends to seek forgiveness from the story's heroine, whose death he indirectly caused. Called "The Kingdom of the Shades," this climactic scene in Act 3 came to be equated with all of *La Bayadère* for the pure-dance tastes of the ensuing century, and even with classical ballet itself. Writing about this scene in 1963, British balletomane and critic Clive Barnes suggested: "If you don't enjoy *La Bayadère*, you don't really enjoy ballet."

Meanwhile, back in Moscow, another 1877 ballet premiere came and went only to return by the century's end as a work so popular it became emblematic of all ballet. *Swan Lake*, to Pyotr Tchaikovsky's first ballet score, initiated a Big Three of Russian classical ballet. Until now, with the exception of isolated composers such as France's Léo Delibes, music played a more serviceable than inspirational part in the mix of nineteenth-century ballet theater. In fact, it was Tchaikovsky's green yet ultimately golden theatrical music that delayed the full-force effect of *Swan Lake* on ballet history.

Ballet music needed to be danceable, *dansant* in musicological dance language. Tchaikovsky's fresh attempt at ballet music struck those listening for the predictable old-school sound as symphonic, and thus not *dansant*. To subtle and fine-tuned ears the score proved to be both, but a suitable, sensitive reading of the innovative *Swan Lake* score would come only when ballet mastering caught up with this Russian master of ballet music. The original setting of *Swan Lake* came from Wenzel Reisinger (1827–1892), a dutiful Austrian ballet master working in Moscow, and was based on a German folkloric tale of a princess bewitched by a genie in the guise of an owl into being a swan during daylight. Though it remained a good number of years on Moscow's ballet stages, *Swan Lake* evolved erratically over its lifetime. From the start, the form of the ballet became flexible. Musical numbers were rearranged, and eventually new performers sought and gained new dances, in one case to completely new music, to suit their personal tastes. Before it went out of repertory in Moscow, *Swan Lake* got further adjusting and reshaping by Reisinger's Belgium-born successor, Joseph Hansen (1842–1907).

In the mid-1880s, Petersburg's prolific Petipa restaged two ballets made popular over the past few decades in Paris. One was Coralli's and Perrot's *Giselle*; the other Saint-Léon's 1870 final work, *Coppelia*. The former had the distinction of having initiated Romantic ballet's golden age; the latter, made upon its choreographer's return from Russia to his homeland, represented the pinnacle of Parisian ballet's pandering to its predominantly male audience's taste for virtually all-female ballet troupes.

Petipa rethought both ballets. For the *Giselle*, he refortified its forty-year-old, Romantic dance dimension, especially the dances for the *wilis* sisterhood. In *Coppelia*, he bypassed its travesty tradition and presented its leading male character with a first-class male dancer. In the process, Petipa further evolved the *danse d'école* to a new classical plateau. By the time these 1841 and 1870 works would gain the status of "classics" in the twentieth century, they would each do so out of Petipa's particular restagings.

The decade of the 1880s finished out with St. Petersburg's fixation on visiting Italian ballerinas, who complemented the public's fascination with Italian operatic stars. Ever since ballerina Virginia Zucchi (1849–1930) had made her Petersburg debut in 1885, Petipa regularly featured the avidly admired Italian in his ballets. (An 1885 staging broadly based in part by Petipa on Dauberval's *La Fille Mal Gardée*, known in Russia as "Vain Precautions," showcased Zucchi, and led directly to versions of the ballet that would live into the twentieth century.) Russia had been preferential toward Italian ballerinas earlier in the century, but at the start of Petipa's tenure as chief ballet master, Russian-born-and-schooled ballerinas gained new prominence, sometimes in the persons of Petipa's dancer wives Maria Sorovshchikova (1836–1882) and Lyubov Savitskaya (1854–1919) and his daughter, Maria (1857–1930). The "Divine Virginia," as Zucchi was hailed in print and conversation, altered all that.

The 1890s in Russia mark a golden decade for the classical ballet that Petipa spearheaded, partly with the virtuoso strengths of Italian ballerinas. Continuing a tradition of imposing physical strength and acrobatic skill that began almost as soon as ballet was born in Italy, nineteenth-century Italian-schooled ballerinas were regularly extolled for their "steely" pointes. Or for their "leg-breaking feats," in the none-too-complimentary words of disgruntled Russian ballerina Ekaterina Vazem (1848–1937), who saw herself and her Russian sisters passed over in favor of the guest artists from Italy.

Milan-trained Carlotta Brianza (1867–1930) followed Zucchi to St. Petersburg. A year after she was engaged by the imperial theater management, Petipa chose her to dance the title role of the new production he planned for 1890. The *ballet-féerie* in three acts, with prologue that showcased Brianza, was a turning point for Petipa and for the history of ballet. Called *Spyashchaya Krasavitsa* in Russian, *La belle au Bois Dormant* by the Francophile Russian court, and *The Sleeping Beauty* in English-language ballet history, Petipa's retelling of a Charles Perrault fairy tale in ballet theater terms went into the ages as the quintessential classical ballet. The now equally famous music came from the hand of Tchaikovsky, who composed this, his second ballet score, to specifications spelled out in advance by Petipa. Rather than crimp the composer's imagination, these instructions led to a masterpiece, equally symphonic and *dansant*.

From there, Petipa concentrated on the ballet-féerie, a ballet theater form based on a genre of French drama theater called a *féerie*. This theatrical form concentrated on the realm of enchantment and supernatural beings, and called for spectacular stage effects and transformations. Hoping to capitalize on the popular success of *The Sleeping Beauty*, Petipa and his artistic collaborators—composer Tchaikovsky, designer and librettist Ivan Vsevolozhsky, and assistant ballet master Lev Ivanov (1834–1901)—created *The Nutcracker* in 1892.

Having something less of an initial success than *The Sleeping Beauty*, this two-act ballet based on a sweetened French retelling of a dark, Germanic tale by E. T. A. Hoffman, *The Nutcracker* went on to achieve an overwhelming popularity, going beyond ballet. Italian ballerina Antoinetta Dell'Era starred as the Sugar Plum Fairy in the production's second act set in the magical land of sweets. Petersburg's ever-popular child performers from the imperial theater's ballet school played the leading characters of the domestic scene in the first act.

In 1895, Petipa completed the triumvirate of Tchaikovsky ballets by overseeing a new production of *Swan Lake* for St. Petersburg. Arranged in part as a memorial concert for Tchaikovsky, who had died the previous year, Petipa's staging of the 1877 score became the one that launched the ballet toward lasting fame. Assisted by Ivanov, the Russian-born ballet master who ended up completing work on *The Nutcracker* for the indisposed ballet master, Petipa clarified the story of *Swan Lake*. He also emended and added music (by Tchaikovsky, orchestrated by resident imperial ballet composer Riccardo Drigo), and fashioned a formidable leading role for the ballerina, who danced both the role of Odette, the Swan Queen, and of Odile, the daughter of the evil genie impersonating Odette and duping the story's imperfect hero, Prince Siegfried. The double role was first performed by Pierina Legnani (1863–1923), Petersburg's latest Italian virtuosa. One particular tour de force of Legnani's immediately impressed itself on the choreographic history of the part of Odile: thirty-two successive *fouetté* (or "whipped") turns in the coda of the seductive pas de deux from the ballroom scene. The part of Prince Siegfried was created for Pavel Gerdt (1844–1917), the Russian *danseur noble* who had created the leading prince roles in both *The Sleeping Beauty* and *The Nutcracker*.

With her formidable dance strengths and her popularity with both the Petersburg public and with Petipa, Legnani dominated the imperial ballet's stage in the 1890s. To dramatize the esteem in which she was held, the tsar's troupe coined and conferred on the prodigious Italian technican and artist a new, superlative title: *prima ballerina assoluta*. Soon thereafter, Russia's own Mathilde Kchessinska (1872–1971), the first native ballerina to master Legnani's feat of thirty-two successive fouettés executed in one place, joined the visiting Italian in holding the "assoluta" title. No other prima ballerina was granted this accolade before the imperial Russian era came to an end, some twenty years later.

While the French-born Petipa masterminded Russia's ballet through the end of the century, his Russian-born assistant acquired a reputation for shading the art of ballet with music-inspired nuance.

The new depth of Ivanov's dance making suggested "soulfulness," a label thereafter applied in general to much Russian ballet. The actual amount and particular kind of choreographic contribution Ivanov made to Petipa's staging of *Swan Lake* will probably never be precisely known. The self-effacing Russian's name is traditionally associated with the ballet's two "lakeside" scenes, especially with regard to the use of the corps de ballet. These scenes (Act 1, scene 2, and Act 3) take place near the eponymous lake and involve the dancing of the corps de ballet as swan maidens. Because of the symphonic nature of Tchaikovsky's music, particularly for the segments of the ballet now identified with Ivanov, the notion of "dance symphonism" came into being.

Chapter 8

RUSSIA SURPASSES FRANCE

A full-fledged exploration of dance symphonism would have to wait for the experimentalist modernism of the twentieth century. Both Ivanov and Petipa rode out the nineteenth century in their respective fashions. Ivanov continued to live and work as an assistant ballet master, overshadowed by Petipa even as his career began its long wane following *Swan Lake*. Only *Raymonda*, Petipa's 1898 ballet in three acts, four scenes, and apotheosis of the Tchaikovsky-like colorful music of Alexander Glazunov, revealed much staying power. Despite a dramatically weak libretto, the chivalric-theme spectacle set in medieval Hungary gave the seventy-eight-year-old Petipa cause to create a panoply of dances. Petipa closed the ballet with one of his choreographic specialties, a grand divertissement of dances with no particular plotline. The libretto inspiration for these dances came from the celebrational mood of wedding festivities. All the event had to do was celebrate Petipa's leading dancers according to Glazunov's climactic music.

On the surface, the divertissement dancing so emblematic of Petipa's ballets appeared to those looking for dramatic narrative logic as extraneous exercises of ballet's art. Contemporary sensibilities concerned with overtly expressive aims or interested in total work of art (*Gesamtkunstwerk*) cohesiveness found such moments mostly decorative. Still, as they exist today, Petipa's divertissements can be seen as dance ahead of its time. By forthrightly attending to its music and to the virtuoso skills of its performers, such dancing bypassed the literary libretto dictates and entered the poetic realm of pure-dance activity.

As Petipa aged, the familiarity of his ballet tastes and principles wearied individuals both inside and outside the theater. The dawning of the new century inspired newer ideas and other preferences. The Russian school of ballet now surpassed that of France, just as that school had previously done over the Italian ballet. Following in the footsteps of Kchessinska, a string of Russian-born ballerinas gained stellar fame: Olga Preobrajenska (1871–1962), Vera Trefilova (1875–1943), Ekaterina Geltzer (1876–1962), Agrippina Vaganova (1879–1951), Sophie Fedorova (1879–1953), Lyubov Egorova (1880–1972), and, especially, Anna Pavlova (1881–1931).

Male dancers also distinguished Russia's ballet, in good measure through the pedagogy of Christian Johansson, the Swedish-born Bournonville pupil who taught prominently at the imperial school after his retirement from the imperial stage in 1869. (Petipa concentrated the better part of his mentoring on the art of the ballerina.) Besides the tireless Pavel Gerdt, the imperial ballet's male ranks were fortified by the likes of the brothers Nicolai (1869–1937) and Sergei (1875–1905) Legat, Alexander Gorsky (1871–1924), Vasily Tikhomirov (1876–1956), Mikhail Mordkin (1880–1944), and Mikhail Fokine (1880–1942).

Fokine, first as dancer and then as innovative ballet master, was among the more prominent questioners of Petipa's methods and legacy. Sensing a complacency and lack of genuine seriousness around him in the ballet at the turn of the century, Fokine composed and circulated a questionnaire addressing a potential need for reforming Russia's ballet. One of the answers he got back, from leading dancer Georgi Kiaksht (1873–1936), owing to his view of prurient balletomanes' looking for opportunities to admire young women in short skirts and revealing garments, defined ballet as "pornography, plain and simple."

Finding the current formulas of ballet to be tired, the budding ballet master in Fokine wondered about costuming, specifically, the tutu. Since Virginia Zucchi's day, the length of the ballerina's skirt had become shorter, after the adamant Italian went against the regulation-length skirt and insisted on one more suited to her physique. Fokine's costume questioning went beyond skirt length to silhouette. He asked why, no matter what a ballet's period or locale, the *danseuses* all appeared to be outfitted by what looked essentially like an open parasol.

After seeing American dance innovator—and self-proclaimed enemy of ballet—Isadora Duncan (1878–1927) on tour in Russia in 1904, Fokine gained further fuel and inspiration for his argument toward reform. While the inheritor of the imperial ballet's rich traditions saw no need to discard his academic dance schooling, he saw much reason to alter or bend its rules for the sake of dramatic unity. To impart a suitable Greek look to his 1907 *Eunice* without breaking the imperial theater regulations against bare feet and bare legs on stage, Fokine had toes with pink nails painted on the dancers' tights (Kchessinska and Pavlova led the cast). Fokine also chose, like Duncan, to extend the dance maker's choice of music into the realms of "serious" or "concert hall" music, thus going beyond the confines of that composed expressly for the purposes of dance theater.

Isadora Duncan's first Russian appearances included dances to the music of Frédéric Chopin. Inspired by a 1906 Chopin composition of hers called *The Flight of the Butterflies*, Fokine created *Chopiniana* in 1907. This suite of dances to orchestrated piano pieces evolved over the years and initially, seminarrative details of Chopin's life and work were part of its theatrics. Eventually, such specifics were jettisoned and in its final form *Chopiniana* became a hallmark as well as landmark creation. Distancing itself delicately from the aims of narrative, the self-contained ballet blanc asked that a new category be coined to qualify it. One term decided upon was "ballet of mood."

Fokine's was not a lone voice seeking change in the scope of ballet and its music. At the same time a group of artists and art connoisseurs had launched a journal called *World of Art* (1899–1904) that focused on progressive ideas in the literary, plastic, and performing arts. The editor of the journal and leader of the group was one Sergei (later Serge) Diaghilev (1872–1929), an aesthete who became Russian ballet's most prominent impresario and unofficial ambassador. The *World of Art* circle around Diaghilev included the painters Alexander Benois and Léon Bakst. Together, these artists, plus Fokine, would become part of a Diaghilev-run ballet enterprise that would give the art form a new prominence and seriousness in the twentieth century.

The seriousness of ballet in Paris during the final decades of the nineteenth century and those opening the twentieth appeared to be greatly in question. When Saint-Léon returned to Paris from St. Petersburg, he created his final ballet, *Coppelia,* in 1870. Though he had shown himself to be a brilliant dancer and came from the theatrical world of Russia where male dancers continued to share prominence with the ballerina, the repatriated Frenchman had to provide the Paris ballet public with what it expected. In the case of male dancers, these balletgoers expected as few men on stage as possible.

By this period, male dancers were largely relegated to the pantomime roles or to those of character dancers. Thus, in casting the part of Frantz, the callow hero alongside the ballerina heroine Swanilda, the ballet master chose beloved Parisian ballerina Eugénie Fiorce (1845–1908). In her boots, pantaloons, Slavic blouse and cap, Mlle Fiorce performed *en travestie* opposite Italian debutante Guiseppina Bozzachi (1853–1880), in pointe shoes, peasant-aproned tutu, and colorful jewelry.

To many observers this period of ballet at the Paris Opera is aptly named "La Décadence." Captured in numerous paintings showing the goings-on inside the theater, not the least of which are by Edgar Degas, are the regular, well-to-do male ticket holders, known as *abonnés* (subscribers), who held prepaid season tickets. Sporting mustaches, leaning on walking sticks, and dressed from top hat to toe in all black, they loom like shadows in the wing spaces or lounge in the specially outfitted *foyer de la danse*, an anteroom studio behind the stage. There these connoisseurs of *le ballet* could chat with their favorite dancers on their way on- or offstage.

Chapter 9

DIAGHILEV DOES PARIS

Two years after mounting an exhibition of Russian painting for the Paris Salon d'Automne of 1906 (fifteenth-century icons to the most contemporary of Russian pictures), Diaghilev produced a season of Russian opera. Looking to build on the momentum of these ventures, he then presented a season mixing opera and ballet in 1909. While Russia's most contemporary examples of two-dimensional art couldn't look like much more than also-rans compared to the history-changing paintings being created in and around Paris at this time, Diaghilev's Russian ballet (or Ballets Russes, as the troupe was headlined) proved to be quite another matter next to the inbred limitations of their Parisian counterparts.

The first Ballets Russes season emphasized works of strong Russian or at least Slavic character. Each had choreography, all or in part, by Michel Fokine who Frenchified his first name. For good measure, a Francophile creation called *Le Pavillon d'Armide* was unveiled first. While the composer Nicholas Tcherepnine and the designer Alexander Benois were contemporary Russians, Fokine's ballet had a libretto based on a literary work by Théophile Gautier, one of France's prominent Romantic poets and balletomanes. (In his prime, he helped author the story of *Giselle*.) This eighteenth-century-flavored, one-act ballet about a tapestry that came alive had begun life in Russia as a self-contained smaller work called "The Animated Gobelin." Since then it was a showcase for a variety of Russia's finest dancers.

Consistent to the cast of *Le Pavillon d'Armide* in both St. Petersburg and Paris was Vaslav Nijinsky (1889–1950). Playing the part of a slave costumed like a dancer in eighteenth-century court ballet, complete with wire-reinforced *tonnelet,* Nijinsky enchanted Parisian audiences with his serpentine moves and his exotic mein. While Paris's own Opera dancers included men capable of performing the ballet's pantomime characters in *Le Pavillon,* the home company had nothing like Nijinsky. However beguiling Eugénie Fiorce and her sister dancers could be in men's clothing, the twenty-year-old Russian-trained dancer of Polish descent proved all the more intriguing. Paris's travesty dancers could pose and trip on a light fantastic toe, but Russia's male dancers, of whom Nijinsky was but the most prominent, could pounce, spin, and jump with unprecedented power and grace.

Another stellar male dancer in his prime, Adolph Bolm (1884–1951), led the second of the Ballets Russes' offerings: scenes and dances from Alexander Borodin's opera *Prince Igor.* Commonly known as the "Polovtsian Dances," because of being set around the campfires of the Polovtsi, a nomadic people from the Russian Steppes, Fokine's choreographic arrangements brought primal Russia potently before French audiences. Here, without deferring to conventional ballet costume or its conventional footwear, Petersburg's choreographic innovator exercised his theories of dramatic unity and theatrical logic. Instead of ballet skirts there were harem trousers; instead of pointe shoes, sandal-like ballet slippers. Instead of symmetrical arrangements of ensemble dancers, there were individualistic groupings indicative of tribal units.

Besides a potpourri of often virtuoso, smaller dances strung together under the title *Le Festin,* which means "The Feast," Fokine's productions for this first Paris season included one almost old fashioned ballet. Set (by Benois) in a moonlit clearing near a ruined abbey, awash in luminous ice blue, the ballet formerly known as *Chopiniana* was presented to the Parisian public as *Les Sylphides*. Thus rechristened by Diaghilev especially for a public with *La Sylphide* in its reverent past, *Les Sylphides* helped crown the Ballets Russes season with a snow-white reverie.

Though Nijinsky, the ballet's lone male dancer, wore a white silk blouse and black velvet jerkin, as well as a wig of long hair done à la Chopin, his dancing neither detailed nor illuminated any particular narrative. His presence remained that of inspired poet surrounded by inspiring muses. Each of the three ballerinas who led the ensemble of eighteen corps de ballet women had her own solo—to a waltz, a mazurka, and a prelude, respectively. Only one, however, danced a duet with the poetic male dancer. In the case of this Ballets Russes season the most prominent of the prominent ballerinas was Anna Pavlova.

La Pavlova, as she would already have been known in her native St. Petersburg where she had developed a devoted following, captured the attention of Paris almost as much as Nijinsky did. (Early in her career, Pavlova needed to be identified as Pavlova II, since the tsar's ballet school had already graduated a Pavlova, one Varvara, in its past.) Tamara Karsavina (1885–1978), another of the leading *sylphides*, also made a name for herself dancing, among other roles, the waltz in Fokine's Chopin suite.

Thus launched, with its dances and dancers alike winning acclaim, Diaghilev's Ballets Russes grew and evolved over the next twenty years. In France, *le ballet*, essentially reared in Paris, had become variously predictable and frivolously diverting. Its monied, socially prominent audiences went to it largely out of habit, often to find personal or prurient pleasures. Next to Diaghilev's concentration of the imperial Russian ballet, the full-scale republican French variety looked fairly inconsequential, decadent, or both.

During the ensuing Diaghilev seasons, heretofore dubbed *les saisons Russes*, European ballet got a firm jolt of resuscitation. Russian creations and performers pointed to an art that was part of the present, not a relic of the nostalgic past. In these beginning years Diaghilev focused on presenting very Russian works: Russian music, Russian subject matter, Russian visual design, Russian dancing dominated. The slant not only represented the Russophile tendencies within Diaghilev's *World of Art* circle, it also satisfied the ever-present taste for the exotic that a local public often craves to break the monotony of its everyday existence.

During the 1910 season, Diaghilev brought back to Paris one of its own landmark creations, *Giselle*. The Ballets Russes version of the groundbreaking French ballet included intermediate reworkings by Petipa as well as fresh touches by Fokine. Even, however, with the highly acclaimed Karsavina and Nijinsky in the leads, Paris preferred the brand-new novelties Fokine created for Diaghilev. Among the most popular of these were *Scheherazade*, *Firebird*, *Le Spectre de la Rose*, and *Petrouchka*. All had decor and costumes by Russian artists. All but *Firebird* had starring roles for Nijinsky; all but *Le Spectre de la Rose* had music by Russian composers.

Scheherazade (1910), based on a tale from *The Thousand and One Nights*, probably had the biggest impact. In vibrant bursts of stage color from the scenery and costumes of Léon Bakst and surging Orientalist music by Nikolai Rimsky-Korsakov, Fokine's orgiastic episode told of harem licentiousness and royal bloodbath retribution. Its serpentine modes of movement and curvilinear groupings recalled the pictorial innovations of Eugène Delacroix, specifically his 1827 painting, *The Death of Sardanapolus*. Nijinsky danced the role of Golden Slave, the most desirable and sensuous of the Shah's male slaves.

Both *Firebird* (1910) and *Petrouchka* (1911) were based on Russian folklore. Each had a specially commissioned score by Igor Stravinsky, then a little-known composer. *Firebird* marked Stravinsky's first-ever composition for ballet. Its fantastic tale of a legendary, magical creature was actually the conflation of two different folktales. Pavlova was meant to dance the title figure, but the ballerina steeped in nineteenth-century traditions found Stravinsky's twentieth-century sonorities not at all to her liking. Diaghilev replaced her with Karsavina. Paris adored the result. *Firebird's* colorful, swirling sights and sounds framed a darting, beplumed, birdlike ballerina who comes to the aid of Russian prince and his princess bride.

Petrouchka recycled the collective childhood memories of all three of its collaborators, composer Stravinsky, choreographer Fokine, and designer Benois. The narrative about a mysterious magician and his three lifelike puppets had a metaphysical dimension; the time and place represented nineteenth-century St. Petersburg. Re-creating a pre-Lenten fair, Fokine's action delineates a commedia dell'arte-like situation. A brazen, militaristic blackamoor in concert with a cold-hearted ballerina doll eventually destroy a forlorn poetic soul who comes back to "life" after seemingly being done in by the Moor's cutlass. Accentuating open and flat body language, Alexander Orlov danced the Moor. Karsavina, picking her way stiffly on pointe, embodied the ballerina. Slouching and pigeon-toeing, Nijinsky portrayed the introspective Petrouchka.

As the sinister magician who presents all three puppets in his fair-booth of a theater, Enrico Cecchetti (1850–1928), an Italian-schooled, former imperial ballet virtuoso dancer performed the pantomime role of the Charlatan. Among the imperial ballet roles in which he gained his fame was a dual one in Petipa's *Sleeping Beauty*. For the 1890 production Cecchetti rendered both the pantomime role of the wicked fairy Carabosse and the aerial, fluttery-footwork part of the Blue Bird, a fairy tale character who dances at the wedding of the awakened princess. (Though *Beauty* was indisputably Petipa's production, the choreography for Cecchetti's Blue Bird was likely devised by the dancer-teacher himself. Petipa had a reputation for focusing his inventive powers on the dancing of women. His male dancers often depended on their teachers—Johansson, for example—to devise the dancing for their solos.) Now past his dancing prime in Diaghilev's troupe, the once impressive technician became Maestro Cecchetti, the company's master teacher.

For his 1912 season, Diaghilev encouraged Nijinsky, by now his live-in lover, to create *L'Après-midi d'un Faune*. The dreamlike ballet, set in an imagined ancient Greece, took its name and inspiration from its music, a prelude composed by Claude Debussy to a poem by Stéphane Mallarmé. Taking to heart Fokine's principles of dramatic unity, especially as they had inspired a previous Fokine ballet called *Narcisse*, Nijinsky created an archaic Attic episode of simple, spare means.

In tone, texture, and mood Nijinsky's first ballet took the form of a hypnotically animated antique frieze or Greek vase painting. Its methodically limited and constricted actions delineated an encounter between a sensually agressive animal-man and a group of unsuspecting, innocent nymphs. The dancer turned choreographer played the part of a lustful semihuman creature. Standing like a man and spotted like a beast (set and costumes by Bakst), Nijinsky's faun slipped, slinked, and padded about his landscape on a slyly playful prowl for pleasure.

The flattened, angular postures and moves of Nijinsky's choreography passed through the music's lush atmosphere like ships through a fog. Instead of directly acknowledging Debussy's score, Nijinksky worked artfully against it. Beyond the blunt body pictures and consistently grounded moves, what really caused eyebrows and tempers to go up in 1912 Paris was the sexually suggestive moments climaxing the short ballet. For the ballet's closing gesture, Nijinsky's faun went into artful, erotic spasm on a scarf left behind by a fleeing, frightened nymph.

Amid the flurry of controversy that followed the premiere, Fokine left Diaghilev's troupe. The move came partly from his own outrage and support for those who found Nijinsky's ballet disgusting, and partly from being irate over Diaghilev's favoritism toward Nijinsky's choreography. (To capitalize on the newsworthy scandal of *Faune*, Diaghilev scheduled extra performances, thus postponing the premiere of Fokine's *Daphnis* and reducing its performances to only two.) When Fokine left the Ballets Russes he began taking his notions of reform to ballet elsewhere in Europe, all of which left Nijinsky to provide Diaghilev's dancers with new ballets in the modernist mode he borrowed from Fokine.

In Fokine's view, ballet needed reforming that would yield a new ballet different from the old. Nijinksy's post-Fokine ideas and experiments led beyond what was then thought of as the "new" ballet. Nijinsky's third ballet, in particular, stands as a harbinger of so-called modern ballet or, in some quarters, as a formative work in the antiballet form generally known as modern dance. That work, performed for the first time on May 28, 1913, was called *Le Sacre du Printemps* (often referred to in translation as *The Rite of Spring*). The title comes from its original Stravinsky score, which has a reputation for innovation and influence even beyond that of the similarly sensational ballet.

If Nijinsky's *Faune* elicited a murmuring restive response from the audience during its premiere performance, *Sacre* caused a near riotous one. As Stravinsky's orchestra throbbed, thundered, and growled in the pit, Nijinksy's ballet dancers stamped, hunched, and lurched about on the stage. The aim of both composer and choreographer was to evoke scenes of pagan Russia, particularly primal rites regarding the worship of the arrival of spring, all culminating in the sacrificial dance of a chosen female virgin. The result struck many in the tradition-bound public as an affront to the eye and the ear.

As a dancer, Nijinsky had burst upon the ballet scene in Paris as if bounding through a dramatic leap. As choreographer, the sensual and powerful young man chose to offer his public dancing that was earthbound and constricted. His movement preferences reconfigured ballet's aerial creatures into sluggish, spasmatic larvalike creatures. Unlike his earlier ballets, *Sacre* featured no role for the choreographer himself. Nijinsky's tribal ballet featured the ensemble, as so many modern dance works would in the ensuing years.

In order to help Nijinsky and his dancers follow the complex structures of Stravinsky's music, Diaghilev employed a dancer familiar with a modish semiscientific system of moving the body with strict regard to music. The system, called Dalcroze Eurythmics, was named after its creator, a theoretician in Switzerland named Émile Jaques-Dalcroze. In the words of the Dalcrozean disciple assisting Nijinsky's dancers with the unusual counts of *Sacre*: "They hated it heartily." Extenuating circumstances—personal ones, created by Diaghilev's anger over Nijinsky's sudden marriage—sent *Sacre* into oblivion. (The emotionally wounded impresario preferred to have both Nijinsky and his ballet out of sight.)

The ensuing years of Diaghilev's enterprise saw further attempts at innovational or ultramodernist choreography. Some of these choreographers and their dances made lasting marks in the history of ballet, but *Sacre* loomed large by virtue of its disappearance, and its scandal-filled legend. It would be seventy-five years before a full-scale attempt was made to bring Nijinsky's choreography back to the stage. (The veracity of the results of the 1988 "reconstruction" of *Sacre* at the Joffrey Ballet inspires as much expert discussion of authenticity as the original did of aesthetic argument.)

Léonide Massine (1895–1979), another young dancer favorite of Diaghilev's, was the next principal choreographer of the Ballets Russes. More dance actor, or what's often called a "character dancer," Massine made works that showcased his ability to create characters and/or caricatures by way of gestural dance language. His most historically memorable ballet was *Parade* (1917). The title refers to a display of circuslike acts that take place in a traveling fair's theater.

Unlike the fairground setting of Fokine's *Petrouchka,* however, *Parade* came without a gloss of nostalgic folklorism. The self-proclaimed "realist ballet" had an abrasive "everydayness" all through it from the hands of Paris's most wily avant-garde. There was collagelike, urban-sound music by Erik Satie, Cubistic sets and costumes by Pablo Picasso, and variety act–style dances by Massine. The concept and libretto came from Jean Cocteau, a prominent art dabbler and poet. A master of chic and stunt who admired the Ballets Russes, Cocteau hoped to astonish the not easily impressed Diaghilev. "Étonne moi," the impresario fired in near exasperation at the poet for his none-too-thrilling concept for *Le Dieu Bleu,* a 1912 premiere that failed to rise high in anyone's estimation.

In 1920, Massine created a post-Nijinsky staging of *Sacre*. Similar in surface look, different in matters of substance, Massine's ballet proved uncontroversial and popular. By the next year, however, Massine needed replacing himself. Following something of a pattern, Diaghilev dismissed his chief choreographer because of his liaison with a female dancer in the company. The implacable impresario tested his next choreographer on a small scale in his most ambitious plan to date. Bronislava Nijinska, Nijinsky's younger sister, just arrived from Soviet Russia to join the Ballets Russes as a dancer and having the glimmer of a reputation as choreographer, was asked by Diaghilev to create individual dances for some scenes in his current grand plan. It would be his most spectacular: a recreation of Petipa's 1890 masterwork, *The Sleeping Beauty*.

Diaghilev planned his extravagance for the Christmas holiday season in London, where the Ballets Russes had gained a loyal following. (The holiday-timed run of *ballet-féerie* spectacle prefigured the extended runs of *The Nutcracker* that would become so familiar later in the century.) Translating *La Belle au Bois-Dormant* as *The Sleeping Princess,* the multi-act ballet put a fresh gloss on an imperial heirloom. The lavish production with rich decor and ornate costumes by Bakst ended up costing much more than it made.

Like the first *Swan Lake*, this first Western Europe production of Petipa's *Sleeping Beauty* has been summarily, if inaccurately, dubbed a failure. Its November-through-February run, however insufficient for recouping the great expenditures, still remains no small achievement. Even if audiences were hesitant to come in droves to a single, evening-long ballet, England would eventually reveal a deep devotion to such presentations, and *The Sleeping Beauty* in particular.

A roster of influential stellar dancers led Diaghilev's *Sleeping Princess*. Not the least of these was Carlotta Brianza, Petipa's original Aurora, who, twenty-three years later, performed the pantomime role of the wicked fairy Carabosse. Four ballerinas in their prime alternated as Aurora in 1921 and 1922. Lyubov Egorova (1880–1972), Lydia Lopokhova (1891–1981), and Vera Trefilova (1875–1943) each performed the title role when Olga Spessivtseva (1895–1991), Diaghilev's first cast and favorite "princess," did not. Spessivtseva and Pavlova once shared the pinnacle of the ballerina genealogy for Diaghilev. Probably because she left Diaghilev to pursue and direct her own career, Pavlova became the lesser of these equals to the director of the Ballets Russes. When the impresario likened his two stellar ballerinas to halves of the same perfect apple, he noted Spessivtseva as the half turned toward the sun.

Chapter 10

BALLET'S ROVING AMBASSADRESS

In 1908, a year before Diaghilev's splashy Paris seasons began, Anna Pavlova made a little tour outside Russia with mini-companies of Russian dancers. After taking part in Diaghilev's early Ballets Russes seasons, she chose to become her own impresario. As an already beloved exponent of Petersburg's ballet schooling, Pavlova had participated in a 1905 strike supporting reform of ossified theater traditions. At heart, however, the frail-looking ballerina remained conservative in her tastes.

Physically, the lean, long-limbed, and svelte Pavlova departed from norms then set by leading ballerinas such as Italy's Pierina Legnani and Russia's own Mathilde Kshessinska. (These two late nineteenth-century favorites with Russian audiences remained the only ballerinas on whom the imperial ballet conferred the title "prima ballerina assoluta.") Where Legnani and Kchessinska were full of figure and sturdy of limb, with stylishly small feet, Pavlova was more willowy, longer of foot and sharper of pointe. In 1903 an aging and about-to-be-dismissed Marius Petipa cast the fast-rising Pavlova, who had not yet attained the status of top-rank ballerina, in the title role of *Giselle*. To show off her special qualities of lightness and fragility, the master ballet master adjusted the choreography for the role of Giselle.

Pavlova also inspired the young, reform-minded Fokine. She created the role of the leading "sylph" in his 1907 *Chopiniana*, which would become known as *Les Sylphides*. Sometime earlier, for an almost impromptu solo to "The Swan" music Camille Saint-Saëns wrote for his *Le Carnaval des Animaux*, Pavlova inspired Fokine to create what would become her signature role. Originally called *The Swan* and later widely known as *The Dying Swan*, Fokine's vignette for a skimming ballerina in a white feathery tutu became an icon for ballet and its ballerinas.

Locales without longstanding, or in fact any, history of ballet, became the destination and/or mission of Pavlova's touring ventures. Having established herself as a consummate artist in St. Petersburg, Paris and London, she took her dancing and her dancers on travels that led her to North America, South America, Japan, India, Southeast Asia, Australia, New Zealand, and South Africa. Everywhere, Pavlova presented herself sylishly on as well as off the stage. Her repertory revealed her variously as an exotic woman, a fairy tale princess, a woodland or nature spirit, a Slavic icon, a dragonfly, a butterfly, a rose, or a poppy.

Fortunately for posterity, Pavlova consented, however reluctantly, to dance for the moving picture camera but unfortunately the results are cramped in space, erratic in speed, and wanting in sound. Though not the earliest film records of historically significant ballet dancers, those of Pavlova remain some of the most valuable for the era and the artistry they record. Her world-famous *Swan* was probably the most frequently filmed. No existing footage, however, includes the solo's ending—neither film length nor camera speed allowed for a complete filming of the dance—but the results do record how animated and fluid her upper body worked in this ballet. The influence of Isadora Duncan (of whom there are no official films) on Fokine's choreography becomes twice as pronounced in Pavlova's Duncan-like upper-body freedom.

Countless people got their first taste of ballet from Pavlova on her wide-ranging tours. Among those who would become famous themselves in the art the ballerina first showed them was an Englishman named Frederick Ashton. As he pursued a career in ballet himself and began reminiscing how it all began, he liked to note how he was first "bitten" by seeing Pavlova. "She injected me with her poison," was the way he put it, and from then on he was driven to make ballet his life's work.

Always considered especially delicate, Pavlova succumbed to pneumonia before her fiftieth birthday. Legend has it that in her dying delirium, she asked her attendant to prepare her swan costume. In tribute to her career, the *Swan* music she made world famous was played as a spotlight moved across an empty stage in her memory.

Chapter 11

NIJINSKA AND NEOCLASSICISM

Nowhere near the beauty nor exemplar of her art that both Pavlova and Spessivtseva were, Bronislava Nijinska (1891–1972) instead began to make her mark as a choreographer. Having successfully created some of the new dances sought for *The Sleeping Princess*, she was commissioned to reduce the expensive spectacle in "three acts, plus prologue" to a one-acter. After instilling a taste for short works in his European audiences, Diaghilev decided to pare his lengthy *Princess* down to such an entity. Nijinska was put in charge of the reduction, which she entitled *Aurora's Wedding*. The resulting twenty-minute sampler of highlights from the over-three-hour production, proved immediately and consistently popular with Ballets Russes audiences.

Next, Diaghilev put an original ballet project in Nijinska's hands. This was a new Stravinsky work called *Les Noces*. Shaped as a cantata (for pianos and chorus), the composition took inspiration from Russian peasant wedding rituals. Unlike her brother's choreographic imaginings of pagan ritual ceremonies for *Le Sacre du Printemps*, Nijinska's theatrical rendering of peasant wedding rites was based on ethnographic reality. After considering more or less direct representation of Russian-family marriage rites, Nijinska and her designer, Natalia Gontcharova, reduced the ballet to essentials. Essences of folkloric dress, limited to plain uniforms, and spare architecture, amounting to little more than bare walls with small windows, constituted Gontcharova's final designs. These plain elements framed Nijinska's nakedly classical ballet moves enacting the essence of nuptial folk rituals.

What Nijinsky had turned into a modern dance–like anti-ballet mode of movement, Nijinska made into austere but undeniable ballet dancing. Nijinska's bride, her female relatives and acquaintances, all danced on clean, sharp pointes. Her groom's male elders and friends worked in ballet slippers laced up like folk-style footwear. Both brother and sister ballet dancers answered Fokine's call for the "new" versus the "old" ballet. The older Nijinsky moved in a direction far afield from ballet's academic exercises, and willfully abandoned them. The younger sibling learned from her brother's experiments and took their interests back inside the technique of ballet. Strong on distillation and free of illustrative representation, Nijinska's 1923 *Les Noces* gave rise to what would be called neoclassical choreography. (Consciously or not, Nijinsky's ballets show the way to the world of modern dance.)

Nijinska's *Les Biches* and *Le Train Bleu*, both from 1924, carried forward her choreographic vision for ballet as a highly stylized but contemporary art. The former, which translates as "The Does" (as in female deer) and is 1920s terminology for young women, celebrates ballet women as chic young ladies. (The jazz rag–influenced music is by Francis Poulenc; the fashionable clothes by Marie Laurencin.) "The Blue Train," to translate Nijinska's other 1924 ballet, takes its name from an express train that connected urban Paris with the Côte d'Azur seaside. (Darius Milhaud composed the score, and couturier Gabrielle "Coco" Chanel designed the beachwear costumes along her signature, easy-moving, soft-cut lines.) A female character called the "Tennis Champion" (performed by Nijinska herself) wields a tennis racket in certain moments reminiscent of the way the Queen of the Wilis in *Giselle* works her talismanic branch of a wand.

Once she left Diaghilev's high-profile fold, Nijinska found work free-lancing with little troupes of her own. Due either to the impermanence of the companies in which she created her later ballets or to a lack of interest in performing them beyond initial runs, none found their way to posterity. A good number of Nijinska's eye-catching, neoclassical works live today only in tantalizing photodocumentation and in memoirs and enthusiastic reportage of eyewitnesses. With the growth of dance scholarship, especially that with a feminist bent after the choreographer's death in 1972, Nijinska and her works have become renewed subjects of eager interest. Some of this enthusiasm has the ring of hype, but some will no doubt lead to reasonably educated guessing and eventually to performances of reconstructed Nijinska works not seen since their creation in the 1920s, 1930s, and 1940s.

Chapter 12

GEORGE BALANCHINE IN EUROPE

Back in Russia, one Georgi Melitonovitch Balanchivadze (1904–1983), a young dancer with burning interests in choreography, grew restive. Russia's newly formed and less than stable Socialist state struck a dubious note in the budding ballet master, just as it had in Diaghilev and his circle. Few of the Ballets Russes Russians cared to return to their homeland after the Revolution. In Petrograd, as St. Petersburg had been renamed, former imperial school graduate Balanchivadze devised dances for himself and some of his favorite fellow dancers. (During his initially unenthusiastic student days, Balanchivadze became utterly fascinated by the possibilities of ballet dancing after fixating on Petrograd ballerinas working on pointe in their classrooms.) By 1924, he was fired with inspiration and more than ready to leave a country in disarray. So, on a would-be limited excursion outside Russia, Balanchivadze and some dancer friends made their way westward, permanently.

Diaghilev, always on the lookout for fresh talent, hired the little troupe. In addition to Balanchivadze, whom Diaghilev soon Frenchified as George Balanchine, the new Ballets Russes dancers included Tamara Geva (1908–) and Alexandra Danilova (1904–1997). When Diaghilev spoke of needing numerous opera ballets now that his dancers served as the resident troupe of the Monte Carlo opera company, Balanchine boasted that he'd quickly be able to whip up such choreography. Though his answer was impromptu and more hopeful than certain, new ballets came readily from the confident Russian.

Having proved himself a fertile creator of incidental opera dances, Balanchine gained commissions to choreograph original new ballets for the season proper of the Ballets Russes. In 1925 came *Barabau*, a semicomic work. Between 1926 and 1927 he created *La Pastorale*, *Jack-in-the-Box*, *The Triumph of Neptune*, and *La Chatte*, as well as an interlude for Nijinska's modernistic rendering of *Romeo and Juliet*. All of these works involved the latest music and newest art world trappings dear to Diaghilev's tastes. *Barabau* had decor by the Postimpressionist painter Maurice Utrillo. *La Pastorale* had a Hollywood movie theme. Balanchine's choreography had a male lead, in the role of telegraph boy, ride his bicycle on stage and allowed a good deal of sexy legwork for the very leggy Felia Doubrovska (1896–1981), an earlier emigré from Petrograd. *Jack-in-the-Box* had Danilova as "The Black Ballerina," clad in blackface and white toe shoes.

In *La Chatte*, starring the cool but kittenish Spessivtseva, Balanchine took an Aesop fable and arranged it as post-Cubist theater, complete with geometric architecture and chic costumes done by sculptors Naum Gaubo and Antoine Pevsner in newfangled plastics. The *Romeo* segment was performed in silence and showed the dancers behind an elevated curtain from the knee down.

With *Apollon Musagète* in 1928, Balanchine produced a ballet that would remain a classic of the neoclassical mode he was then spearheading. Using a score previously commissioned in America from Stravinsky, Balanchine gave the history of ballet a landmark. He later claimed that this choreographic reverie on the resplendent sun god and the particular muses who inspired his art focused and fortified his entire career as ballet master. (Balanchine always preferred the Old World designation of "ballet master" over the New World "choreographer." Petipa had been First Ballet Master to His Majesty the Emperor. His tombstone simply says "Ballet Master," and so does Balanchine's.)

Eventually called *Apollo*, the one-act ballet took shape as Balanchine went through a process of elimination. His ballet showcases a leading male dancer and three ballerinas, one of whom, in the role of Terpsichore, proves "more equal" than the others. The scenes proceed through individual solos and a centerpiece pas de deux. Graphically pictorial groupings of all four dancers, sometimes with limbs suggesting the rays of Apollo's sunny brilliance, come and go, as do pictograms shaped by configurations of two or three dancers.

Originally designed with costuming in the lightly Grecian mode, *Apollo* soon went through a process of costume and scenic simplification. (Grecian-pleated tutus became chemiselike chitons, cinched, by Chanel's design, with neckties from the fashionable Parisian haberdasher Charvet.) Balanchine's sometimes gestural, sometimes acrobatic ballet language for *Apollo* took its motivation directly from the music's almost austere character by way of eliminating a number of possibilities at hand. Stravinsky's carefully honed score, in which the tradition of nine muses got reduced to three for theatrical clarity, inspired the young ballet master to "dare not to use all my ideas."

In the following year, the last as it turned out for Diaghilev's Ballets Russes, Balanchine created two new works. *Le Bal* was a semi-surrealist work in which a mysterious woman is unmasked to reveal a hideous, aged face, which eventually comes off as well to show her as a beautiful and youthful woman. Balanchine himself danced one of the roles, and Danilova danced as the mysterious woman. Though the ballet had bold, clear designs by surrealist painter Giorgio de Chirico and a suitably atmospheric score by Vittorio Rietti (a regular Ballets Russes composer), it failed to have a life much beyond 1929, Diaghilev's last year.

Le Fils Prodigue became Balanchine's final Ballets Russes creation as well as the last production Diaghilev presented. (The impresario died during the troupe's holiday break.) Based on a Russian reduction of a parable from the Old Testament, *The Prodigal Son*, as Balanchine's ballet came to be known in English, survived, as did *Apollo*, well beyond its initial Ballets Russes performances. Balanchine created the title role of his *Prodigal* for Serge Lifar (1905–1986). The young Kiev-born pupil of Nijinska whom Diaghilev had recently hired also created leading roles in Balanchine's *La Chatte*, *La Pastorale*, and *Apollo*. The book, or libretto for the dramatic action of *Prodigal* came from Boris Kochno, who had previously authored the schemes of *Pastorale* and *Chatte*, and who served as Diaghilev's secretary and companion. To turn the biblical parable into ballet theater, Balanchine made the role of the eponymous son athletic and emotive. He made "The Siren," the ballerina role of a woman who corrupts the protagonist, icy cool, acrobatic, and academically formal; she alone dances on pointe. Along with the dark-toned score of Sergei Prokofiev and the bold paint-stroke designs of Georges Rouault, Balanchine's dramatic ballet included an ensemble of twelve men, whose physical presence the choreographer once described as "protoplasm."

With Diaghilev's death, the Ballets Russes became a rudderless vessel. Balanchine left the scrambling to keep the Diaghilevless Ballets Russes afloat to those who hoped to relive the impresario's legacy to the letter. Instead, Balanchine chose the time of change to seek his independence. (At the very time of Diaghilev's death in Venice, Balanchine was in England working on *Dark Red Roses*, a film project in which he danced and created a little ballet that served as a kind of nightclub act. The footage of Balanchine performing as a jealous Tartar lover exists to this day as a rare glimpse of his early dancing career.) In London, Balanchine devised dance numbers for variety shows. In Copenhagen, he became a guest ballet master at the Royal Danish Ballet, for which he re-created a number of ballets by Fokine and Massine. After unsuccessfully participating in the first season of the Ballets Russes de Monte Carlo, a reconstitution of the former Diaghilev organization, Balanchine found a company of his own to direct, with Boris Kochno as his artistic partner.

Named for its year, *Les Ballets 1933*, the little troupe got backing from a rich patron promoting one of the group's performers, Austrian dancer and actress Tilly Losch (1904–1975). In the company's six-month existence, Balanchine created six ballets. Three of these, *Les Songes*, later called *Dreams; L'Errante*, eventually called *The Wanderer*; and *Les Sept Péchés Capitaux*, also known as *Anna Anna, or the Seven Deadly Sins*, went on to become part of future companies run by the choreographer. Another 1933 creation, *Mozartiana* (Balanchine's first creation to the music of Tchaikovsky) would continue intermittently, in revised versions, to play a part in the ballet master's life up to his last years.

If the backer's commitment to *Ballets 1933* was not overly serious, Balanchine's was. Just as the company folded, giving Balanchine pause regarding the nature of opportunity for new ballet in Europe, a young, wealthy American entered the picture. Lincoln Kirstein (1907–1995), heir to a New England fortune, had become smitten by the exotic, foreign art of ballet. He enthusiastically made a bereft Balanchine a proposal: Why not come to America and establish ballet in a country where no such tradition existed?

Balanchine's elementary knowledge of America matched that of Kirstein about ballet. What each lacked in particulars, however, they made up for in optimistic anticipation. Balanchine knew of Hollywood's Ginger Rogers and looked forward to working in a country that produced such women. Kirstein began his wish list of new ballets for his American organization with *Pocahontas*, an Americana subject he imagined being danced to seventeenth-century English dance suites. By January of 1934, with inestimable help from Kirstein and some of his monied friends, Balanchine opened the School of American Ballet.

During the school's first year, the performing wing of the academy, named the American Ballet, gave its first performance. For its dancers, Balanchine had created *Serenade* to Tchaikovsky's Serenade in C for String Orchestra. The non-narrative work for female soloists, female ensemble, and, originally, lone male soloist, became a signature piece for Balanchine's American ballet organization. Taking its poetic, dramatic color from its music, *Serenade* became, for the mid-twentieth century, the quintessential "ballet of mood," reliving the status and impact that Fokine's *Les Sylphides* had had at the turn of the century.

Though it would become another of Balanchine's "classics" and one of ballet history's hallmark examples of plotless or abstract ballet, *Serenade* came into being innocent of such dimensions. "I didn't have it in mind to make anything," Balanchine said in an interview. "I made *Serenade* to show dancers how to *be* on a stage." The eventual or inevitable structure of his showcase included moments such as a ballerina's arriving late in a scene, incorporating a male dancer into the ballet's progress, and a ballerina falling amid the stage action.

All the "dramatic" moments of *Serenade*, Balanchine insisted, came about spontaneously, by happenstance, as his work evolved. The late-arriving ballerina did indeed come late to the ballet's 1934 rehearsals. The unexpected appearance of the lone male dancer, well into the ballet's progress, came about because Balanchine acquired a man he hadn't counted on at the start. The ballerina who falls to the floor and remains lying there became part of the ballet's "text" after an overwhelmed dancer crumpled to the floor in tears during a rehearsal.

Chapter 13

BALLET TAKES ROOT IN BRITAIN

Between the early eighteenth century—and the innovative work with ballet d'action by John Weaver—and the first decade of the twentieth, ballet theater found an interested audience in England, but not another home. With the ballet of continental Europe conveniently across the channel, for England it was just as easy to import the art as it was to develop and evolve its own school and support systems. Many of the prominent names in nineteenth-century ballet, from Marie Taglioni to Carlotta Brianza, performed in England, where it should be remembered Charles Didelot was working before being summoned to help improve ballet in Russia.

In 1897, a Danish-born ballerina called Adeline Genée (1878–1970) came to London to dance the role of "A Diamond" as part of Queen Victoria's Diamond Jubilee celebrations. The immediately popular dancer stayed, and for the next ten years served as prima ballerina in London's grand music hall, The Empire. In 1910, Pavlova performed a London season of her own, and the next year, Diaghilev's Ballets Russes, with Pavlova among its dancers, gave its first London season.

During the second decade of the twentieth century, English interest in ballet became coupled with increasing English expertise in the art. In 1912, despite a busy touring schedule, Pavlova settled in London. In 1914, England's own Phyllis Bedells (1893–1985) became prima ballerina at The Empire, as the adored Genée toured here and there, all the while working to establish ballet in Britain. In 1916, Seraphina Astafieva (1876–1934), a Russian retired from dancing with Diaghilev, opened a school of ballet in London. By the 1920s, both Diaghilev and Pavlova were able to restaff their respective troupes with English-schooled dancers.

The teaching of ballet in England was firmly formalized in 1920. Édouard Espinosa (1871–1950), a ballet pedagogue with an international background, and Philip Richardson, editor of an English magazine about dancing, founded the Association of Operatic Dancing. (Since 1936, the organization has been known as the Royal Academy of Dancing.) Genée became its first president. In 1922, another dance teaching association appeared in England. Known as the Cecchetti Society, it aimed to perpetuate the teaching methods of Diaghilev's and Pavlova's revered Enrico Cecchetti. The maestro had opened his own London school in 1918, and the society set out to promulgate his teachings farther and wider.

With the deaths of Diaghilev in 1929 and Pavlova in 1931, England was primed to produce ballet with an English accent. In particular, two hardworking women played primary roles in the birth of English ballet proper: Cyvia Rambam, a Pole, known professionally as Marie Rambert (1888–1982), and Erdis Stannis, from Ireland, known professionally as Ninette de Valois (1898–). Both had danced for Diaghilev and both worked to carry forth Diaghilevian principles on English soil. Rambert founded the Rambert Ballet School in 1920 and a performing group known as the Marie Rambert Dancers in 1926. De Valois opened the Academy of Choregraphic Art [*sic*] in 1926.

By 1931, both Rambert's and de Valois's organizations were shifting into higher gear. Rambert's performing group became a producing organization known as the Ballet Club. De Valois, already involved as choreographer and dancer with a new ballet organization known as the Camargo Society, teamed up with a theater visionary named Lilian Baylis. In exchange for creating dances for Baylis's dramatic productions, de Valois got a promise of theater time for evenings of her ballet productions. By 1935, de Valois's little British ballet company, the Vic-Wells Ballet, was on a straight path toward becoming Britain's Royal Ballet. By 1936, Rambert's troupe had become Ballet

Rambert, a name that would make its own mark in British ballet history.

Both Ninette de Valois and, even more scrupulously, Marie Rambert sought native British talents for their respective English ballets. Both were instrumental, though Rambert was first, in encouraging Frederick Ashton to create ballets. The late-starting Englishman owed a great debt of inspiration for his passionate career in ballet to Bronislava Nijinska and Anna Pavlova. Another Englishman Rambert "discovered" was Antony Tudor (1908–1987). He also expressed a profound debt to Pavlova. (Ashton loved to reminisce about how marvelously Pavlova could run, and Tudor about how she entered one ballet by walking down the stairs of her little house on pointe.)

Tudor would later make his career in the United States. Ashton, sometimes called the most English of English choreographers, made his in England, launched as he was by the encouragement of both Rambert and de Valois. His first ballet, *Tragedy of Fashion, or The Scarlet Scissors* (1926) enacted a witty, lyrical episode in a dressmaker's salon. There, mannequins paraded fashions, coldhearted clients remained hard to please, and a couturier stabbed his wounded heart with his own shears. It marked the first of many collaborations between Ashton and, until her somewhat untimely death in 1953, his favorite costume and set designer, Sophie Fedorovich. Rambert herself danced the leading mannequin.

After other ballets for Rambert and the Camargo Society, Ashton created *Les Rendezvous*, a "Ballet-Divertissement" for de Valois's dancers in 1933. His classically precise yet frothy excursion showcased big-skirted "ballet girls" and dashing swain partners. The leading pair of "lovers" was performed by former Diaghilev dancers Alicia Markova (1910–) and Stanislas Idzikowski (1894–1977). Markova began her career with the Ballets Russes as the first of its handful of so-called baby ballerinas. In her particular case, the dark-featured Markova was christened a "baby Pavlova."

Markova had been trained by Astafieva in London. Born Lilian Alicia Marks, she had her name changed by Diaghilev when she joined his company in 1925. Subsequent baby ballerinas would join Markova in Diaghilev's troupe, but the English teenager set the precedent. (Three notable other babies soon followed—Tatiana Riabouchinska [1917–], Irina Baranova [1919–], and Tamara Toumanova [1919–1996] all came from the classrooms opened by emigré Russians in Paris, and each made her name as a teenage ballerina with the Ballets Russes. The first came from the tutelage of Kchessinska; the other two from that of Olga Preobrajenska.)

While the Paris-trained baby ballerinas stayed on with the various Ballets Russes organizations that followed Diaghilev's death, Markova made her way back to England. There, Ashton expressed keen interest in forming his new ballets around her gifts. Soon the English ballerina with a Russian name became an instrumental player in the shaping of a distinctly English ballet.

Rambert and de Valois kept leading the way. Rambert's troupe, called the Ballet Club, gave its productions in the confines of a little theater named the Mercury. Markova referred to its 18-by-18-foot stage as a "postage stamp" and its evenings of ballet as "magical." Rambert used the term "blessed poverty," to indicate how the restrictions of borrowed time, cramped space, and tight money inspired choreographers and dancers to do their most inspired work. *Foyer de Danse* (1932), Ashton's homage to Degas and the French school of ballet, remains a perfect example. It starred Ashton and Markova, and featured as part of its setting the full Mercury stage, including the industrial back-wall staircase that was meant to be hidden and function as a backstage entryway.

A silent film exists in the Rambert archives showing Ashton coursing through his *Foyer de Danse*. It documents the fleet feet and richly detailed and changeable body language of the dancer-choreographer. Ashton's aerial, mercurial performance makes you wonder if the motivation to put his dancing frequently in the air and shift it about so marvelously came from knowing that there wasn't much actual ground to cover on the Mercury's stage.

A more accessible film recalling what ballet was like at the Mercury comes in the 1948 movie *The Red Shoes*. One scene, actually shot at the Mercury, hypothetically re-creates a performance of the second act of *Swan Lake*. You see and hear a crude gramophone, a swan queen ballerina about as big as the lake in the background, and a corps de ballet of swans you can count on the fingers of one hand.

You also catch a grace-note glimpse of Rambert nervously watching from "out front" in the audience for things that can, and do, go awry.

At the renovated Sadler's Wells Theater, de Valois's company had a bigger stage than the Mercury, though it was hardly expansive. Still, this did not crimp de Valois's vision for British ballet. Certain of the stellar talent of Markova, as well as that of another English dancer with a non-English stage name, Anton Dolin (born Patrick Healey Kay, 1904–1983), de Valois presented England's first full-scale stagings of three famous nineteenth-century ballets. To the English, then and now, such works have the reverential designation of classics, often "The Classics."

De Valois's most ambitious productions of full-length classics were staged in 1934. *Giselle* came first, quickly followed by *Casse-Noisette*, as *The Nutcracker* was then called. *Swan Lake*, or *Le Lac des Cygnes*, as the Diaghilev-admiring English chose to call it, came near the year's end. Each acted as a bold show of strength. As we have seen, when Diaghilev's full-scale production of *The Sleeping Princess* failed to find sufficient audiences, the impresario reduced the multi-act work to a one-acter called *Le Mariage de la Belle au Bois Dormant* (or *Aurora's Wedding*). Likewise without a large-scale complement of dancers, Diaghilev's Ballets Russes had put on reduced stagings of *Swan Lake*. Rambert's troupe presented the love duet, excerpted from the ballet's second act, and de Valois staged the whole of this act as a self-contained ballet. Now Madame, as English ballet had nick-named de Valois, reversed Diaghilevian downsizing for upgrading.

Given the grand ambitions of de Valois's projects and the realistic limits of her fledging troupe, none of her "full-lengthers," as such multi-act ballets are often called in England, amounted to definitive productions. To achieve something resembling that, quantities and qualities of personnel would have to increase, as would supporting budgets. Still, the scrupulous outline and breadth of each classic put them soundly in the consciousness of the English public.

To set the actual "text"—the shape of stage action and particular choreographic details—de Valois offered Nicholas Sergeyev a ten-year contract. In particular, she insisted that the stagings of imperial Russia's best-known multi-act ballets include the original storytelling pantomime passages that Diaghilev had largely edited out. Sergeyev, the Russian-born-and-trained former Ballets Russes ballet master, had relocated in England after Diaghilev's death. When he fled Russia after the Revolution, he had taken his dance notation notebooks. These contained records of the work he supervised for the imperial theaters of St. Petersburg. Sergeyev's documents contained various systematic "scores" of ballet choreography. The shorthand "system" in which two dozen nineteenth-century favorites were written was known as Stepanov notation, named after Vladimir Stepanov (1866–1896), the Russian pedagogue who had devised the method, which Sergeyev had studied.

In 1935, de Valois hired Ashton as her company's resident choreographer. (Conductor and composer Constant Lambert was already in place as company musical director.) Thus, by the mid-1930s, English ballet was firmly launched on a course pursuing two constants: the creation of contemporary English ballets and the presentation of touchstone proven works from the nineteenth-century repertory.

As it turned out, the evolution of de Valois's English ballet had to proceed without the participation of the popular and familiar Markova and her frequent partner, Dolin. Both star dancers severed their ties to the Vic-Wells Ballet in order to head a company of their own, the Markova-Dolin Ballet. (The star-driven showcase eventually evolved into separate English ballet institutions—Festival Ballet in turn became London Festival Ballet, and then English National Ballet.)

Markova's departure from the de Valois company left Ashton without the prima ballerina of his choice. Undaunted, de Valois proposed an unknown young dancer to star in Ashton's ballets. Born Peggy Hookham, de Valois's new protégée went on to win over a skeptical Ashton and to become one of ballet's most popular ballerinas. Her name was initially changed to Margot Fontes and finally to Margot Fonteyn (1919–1991), a name that brightened to shine like a Broadway marquee in ballet's firmament.

Chapter 14

FRED AND MARGOT

In many ways the story of English ballet's maturity is dominated by the choreography of Frederick Ashton and the dancing of Margot Fonteyn. Initially, the young choreographer found the nascent ballerina's feet and pointe work to be on the soft side—"like pats of butter," in his words. Similarly, Fonteyn found her taskmaster unbendingly difficult and impossible to please. Eventually, both "came round" and the two interacted like poet and muse.

Starting with *Le Baiser de la Fée* (1935), an "Allegorical Ballet" based on Hans Christian Andersen's eerie tale, "The Ice Maiden," Ashton regularly showcased Fonteyn in his choreography. In 1937, he created another delectable ballet-divertissement. Like the earlier *Les Rendezvous*, his new *Les Patineurs* took a rich variety of steps practiced in ballet classrooms and presented them (to some music of Giacomo Meyerbeer, arranged by Lambert) as if they were the movements of ice-skaters. Here, and elsewhere, Ashton reinforced his lasting commitment to the *danse d'école*, the strict, academic ways practiced in ballet classrooms since the days of Louis XIV.

Meanwhile the next, and most significant, of English ballet's classics came in 1939 through de Valois's continued visionary efforts. Called, à la Diaghilev, *The Sleeping Princess*, the three-act, plus prologue, Vic-Wells production relived Petipa's Maryinsky masterwork in necessarily reduced measure. (The poster-paint style of the sets and lightweight, grayish costumes were by Nadia Benois, daughter of Aleksandr, the *World of Art* designer responsible for the visual impact of many Ballets Russes productions.) Sergeyev, by way of his trusty Stepanov notation notebooks, recreated the original dances. Fonteyn danced Aurora, the title role that would be identified with her for the rest of her long career; Ashton danced a couple of subsidiary parts, but had nothing directly to do with the choreography.

The destructiveness of World War II, which England entered in 1939, prevented British ballet activity from proceeding on its ambitious way. Still, during the war years, Ballet Rambert and the Sadler's Wells Ballet each carried on. Irregular seasons and determined touring drew willing audiences wherever they performed. No grand or extravagant works got performed, but new ones, making do under crisis conditions, did.

Ashton created three new works for de Valois, starting with *Dante Sonata*, a lyrical evocation of Dante's *Divine Comedy*. To achieve his poetic effects, the choreographer called on his fond memories of modern dance innovator Isadora Duncan. Ashton presented his ballerinas, Fonteyn prominent among them, barefoot, in flowing shifts, with their hair unbound and loose.

By 1946, with the war ended, de Valois's company gained the honor of celebrating England's victory. In light of its tireless efforts to stay afloat artistically, frequently playing before beleaguered troops and war workers, the Sadler's Wells Ballet company gained the national distinction of being named resident dance troupe of London's Royal Opera House at Covent Garden. England's recognition of de Valois's company turned into a vote of confidence for ballet in general. The victorious reopening of one of Europe's best-known opera houses took the form of a ballet, not an opera, production.

De Valois chose a refurbished production of *The Sleeping Princess*, now called, more accurately, *The Sleeping Beauty*. The refreshed version of her 1939 production included new, more fanciful and colorful sets and costumes by Oliver Messel. These were loosely based on the lavish scheme devised by Bakst for Diaghilev's 1921 revival. An increasingly popular Fonteyn led the cast as Aurora. Her partner was

Robert Helpmann (1909–1986) as Prince Florimund. This time Ashton helped out choreographically, giving the Russian fairy-tale classic two new Petipa-like dances: a villagers' waltz and a divertissement trio.

Though not specifically credited, the personal embellishments and ballerina details for Aurora also bore the mark of Ashton. Whether directly or indirectly, Ashton's careful eye and taste led Fonteyn to her exemplary, individual ways with all classical choreography, even that without Ashton's byline.

Only two months after the triumphant presentation of *The Sleeping Beauty* in the Royal Opera House, Ashton had a triumph of his own. During the war he'd been affected by a contemplative composition for piano and orchestra by César Franck called *Symphonic Variations*. Now, in the aftermath of horrific wartime, Ashton offered a plotless, so-called abstract, a reverie for three male and three female dancers dressed in the manner of classic deities. The six performed their elegiac dance, together and as soloists, in a place awash with spring greens and traversed by thin, undulating black lines. Both decor and costume designs came from the deft hand and eye of Ashton's beloved Sophie Fedorovitch.

Ashton's *Symphonic Variations* was an immediate hit with its public and an eventual entrant into ballet's pantheon of hallowed classics. No dancer especially stood out in *Symphonic Variations*, but Fonteyn danced to personal prominence at its center. Her sister ballerinas, Moira Shearer (1926–) and Pamela May (1917–), served Ashton's purposes with their own individuality. So did their partners and fellow dancers, Michael Somes (1917–1994), Brian Shaw (1928–1992) and Henry Danton (1919–).

In 1948, with Fonteyn's perfectly proportioned physique stylishly dressed in a geometrically decorated tutu, Ashton showed his *Scènes de Ballet*. The choreography took its inspiration from Stravinsky's music of the same name and cues from treatises on Euclidean geometry. Continuing in his "abstract" mode, Ashton chose not to follow a scenario concerning metaphysical conceptions proposed by ballet critic Richard Buckle. Instead he heeded Stravinsky's own reflections that his music was free of literary or dramatic intentions.

Before 1948 was over, Ashton returned to ballet with literary sources and narrative aims. He choreographed a three-act version of *Cinderella*, his first multi-act ballet. The music came from Soviet Russia, where in the name of Social Realism, story ballets were a matter of course. The composer was Sergei Prokofiev and his score had already been choreographed, twice, in its homeland. But, the Iron Curtain made sampling the results less than simple. The best Ashton managed to do was to speak with a ballet writer who had seen the ballet in Moscow.

Ashton's *Cinderella* for his Sadler's Wells company honored English music hall traditions amid its reliving of nineteenth-century story-ballet formulas. The wickedly witty showman cast Cinderella's ugly stepsisters as travesty roles in England's "pantomime dame" tradition of vivid women played by men. (An even more particular precedent for such performing regularly occurred in English popular theater pantomimes, typically presented around Christmas.) Ashton performed one of the two roles himself. He played the shyer, put-upon sister to Robert Helpmann's bossy, supercilious character. The ballet's prince, heretofore a role Helpmann might automatically have danced, was played by newcomer Michael Somes.

Ashton's was the first staging of this *Cinderella* outside the Soviet Union. With its breadth of three-act development, his ballet hoped to showcase the increasing artistic powers of Fonteyn on a grander-than-ever scale. However, an untimely injury to Ashton's favorite ballerina changed the plan. Shearer, who rose to new fame the same year for her portrayal of the ballerina in the widely popular movie *The Red Shoes*, danced the title role at the Christmas season premiere.

The next year, with Fonteyn recovered, the Sadler's Wells Ballet hit new stride. In a U.S. tour under the aegis of New York's cultural impresario Sol Hurok, de Valois's national company became an international hit. America, which had budding ballet all its own, remained inherently prone to admire European artistic taste. Showcased on the unusually grand scale presented by the multi-act ballet—de Valois shrewdly insisted on presenting her full-length *Sleeping Beauty* on opening night—British ballet beguiled American audiences.

Ashton's interests in ballets with narrative or at least literary subjects led him, during the 1950s, to create successive new works. A couple of these were made especially for New York City Ballet, Balanchine's finally stable company reorganized in 1948. The first, *Illuminations* (1950), used the music of Benjamin Britten to inspire an evocation of the life and poetry of Arthur Rimbaud. The other, *Picnic at Tintagel* (1952), used 1916 music by Arnold Bax to present a little group of tourists transformed into medieval personages while visiting an enchanted castle. At City Ballet, readily establishing itself as the showplace for Balanchine's variously plotless displays of musically inspired dancing, Ashton's literary-theme ballets added some happy contrast.

Back home, where Fonteyn was still his exemplary ballerina, Ashton created another three-acter, *Sylvia,* to Leo Delibes' 1886 score of the same name. With Fonteyn and her sister huntresses in chic little helmets and prettily draped Roman military kilts, *Sylvia* replayed and made contempary the now centuries-old ballet taste for mythological worlds where ballerinas artfully brandished weapons, in this case little bows and arrows.

Moonlighting again, this time in Denmark, Ashton tried his hand at another Prokofiev story ballet. Just as his *Cinderella* was the first staging of its score outside the Soviet Union, Ashton's 1955 *Romeo and Juliet* came before what would be numerous ballet versions of Shakespeare's play according to Prokofiev. With the gently and innocently isolated dancers of the Royal Danish Ballet, England's foremost choreographer created a delicate danse d'école rendering of the somewhat bombastic and floridly emotional score.

A year after serving as guest choreographer of Denmark's Royal Ballet, Ashton found himself working for England's own royal troupe. The year 1956 marked the twenty-fifth anniversary of de Valois's Sadler's Wells Ballet. The jubilee was duly marked by a *pièce d'occasion* ballet of Ashton's called *Birthday Offering*. The showcase (to selections of Alexander Glazunov's music) featured solo "variations" by six of the company's ballerinas, framing a solo and pas de deux for Fonteyn. (Somes was her cavalier. Each of the solo ballerinas had escorts, who all danced in a rousing mazurka. The Brits nicknamed the whole affair "Seven Brides for Seven

Brothers.") It became Ashton's last work for his Sadler's Wells Ballet. In a charter dated October 31, 1956, the title of Royal Ballet was conferred by H.R.H. Elizabeth II on de Valois's ballet school and companies. (With the 1946 move to the Royal Opera House, a second company was started to serve the dance needs at the Sadler's Wells Theater).

In 1958, Ashton choreographed another multi-act showcase for Fonteyn, *Ondine*, a story ballet about a water sprite of the same name. This time the water nymph subject matter, popular in the nineteenth century, was matched up with a new, specially composed score. Like Hans Werner Henze's original music, the ballet had an original libretto written by Ashton. The only detail specifically retained from Romantic ballet's treatments of this theme was a historically famous *pas de l'ombre*, or dance with a shadow, which became legendary in Perrot's version of the ballet for Fanny Cerrito. In Ashton's newest vision of her, Fonteyn became liquid, playful, imperious, and tragic.

By 1960, Fonteyn seemed to be ending her career and Ashton was ready to fashion another multi-act story ballet for another of his company's ballerinas. Around the bold, pliant, and strong dancing of Nadia Nerina, he made *La Fille Mal Gardée*. This was a contemporary English reworking of Dauberval's 1789 landmark *ballet d'action* of the same name. Ashton's version took into consideration a great deal of the ballet's intervening history. With help from company musical director John Lanchbery, he pieced together a workable, danceable score from old sources. From Karsavina, he got memories of the Petipa/Ivanov version done in Russia, including an entire little "mimologue" for his heroine to deliver, soliloquylike, to her audience as she imagines herself marrying and raising a family with her beloved. Unlike his ballets *Romeo*, *Ondine*, and to some extent, his *Cinderella*, *Fille* proved quite durable and remained regularly on stage beyond its original run and cast.

Chapter 15

PARIS, OPERA, AND BALLET

When Diaghilev brought his Russian-style ballet to the city where some two hundred years earlier the art form had got on its feet, so to speak, Paris's own ballet had entered a period dubbed, in hindsight, as "*La Décadence*." Since 1830, when its long-standing academy of music and dance lost royal patronage and turned to private enterprise, the offerings of the Paris Opera became increasingly dependent on the tastes of its monied subscribers. After a while opera dominated, with the resident ballet company providing the necessary, secondary, dance diversions.

By 1861, when Richard Wagner's *Tannhäuser* had its first Paris performances, the obstreperous and lordly Jockey Club, an all-male society with a pervasive interest in ballet "girls," regularly arrived late. Their object was to miss the unprepossessing singers and catch their favored, comely danseuses in the then traditional second-act ballet. The problem was Wagner's antitraditional bent. Pressured to include a second-act ballet in his balletless 1845 opera, he grudgingly agreed. But, so the dramatic unity of his composition wouldn't be interrupted, he composed it for the beginning of his opera. Catcalls and jeers volleyed forth from what was known as the "Infernal Loge" when *Le Jockey* realized the ballet had come and gone. Eventually, a disgruntled Wagner withdrew his German opera from the house of Parisian furies.

After 1860, the overseeing of Paris's ballet school came under the immediate direction of the general administrator of the Opera.

The academic post of underdirector for the school then went to an illustrious alumna of the ballet company. This individual oversaw the company's super-professional class for the top dancers of the troupe, *la classe de perfectionnement*. The first to hold this professorial position for the class of perfection was fifty-six-year-old Marie Taglioni, who then served from 1860 to 1870.

The young pupils of the school have been known since early in the nineteenth century by the French endearment, "*petit rat de l'Opéra*." The image of "little rats" struck observers, Balzac included, as apt when they caught sight of tiny, bony figures scurrying about the dark, looming confines of the cavernous backstage of the opera house. During the late nineteenth century, as the mostly female *petits rats* matured to womanhood, they became eagerly sought after by the "fat cat" society of annual subscribers.

Pretty ballet women dressed lightly in gossamer skirts with corsetted bodices bloom like hothouse flowers in both pulp magazine illustrations and fine art renderings of those days. Indubitably, such behind-the-scenes scenes included the somewhat sinister presence, either implied or inadvertent, of privileged gentleman admirers. These outsiders in street wear hovered over the Opera artistes in costume as would wasps over blossoms.

Significantly, few of the surviving glimpses we have of these Parisian days capture what actually happened onstage, during the performance of a ballet. It is safe to say that the goings-on backstage in this era largely took precedence over the actions onstage.

After the wake-up call from Diaghilev's ballet, things started to change at the Paris Opera. Jacques Rouché, the theater's reform-minded director, was a proponent of the ballet as much as the opera. Eventually he programmed all-ballet evenings, something that hadn't happened since the last century. While the Ballets Russes was still active in and around Paris, Rouché began inviting choreographers and dancers connected with Diaghilev to work with the Opera company.

Spessivtseva, the "apple" of Diaghilev's eye, danced prominently at the Opera. Her appearances as *étoile*, the Opera's official designation for "star" dancers since the mid-nineteenth century, coincided with the subsequent retirement of Carlotta Zambelli (1875–1968). (La

Zambelli, the latest in the troupe's line of Italian virtuosas, would become the Opera's *professeur de la classe de perfectionnement.*)

In 1929, just following Diaghilev's death, Rouché commissioned the now out-of-work Balanchine to create a new ballet for the Opera. Specifically, the Paris troupe wanted a new staging of *The Creatures of Prometheus* (the Beethoven ballet originally commissioned by Viganò for himself in 1801). The history of ballet in general, and the Paris Opera in particular, now looks back upon this moment as pivotal. As it turned out, the visionary and brilliant Balanchine came down with tuberculosis and had to abandon his work. He left what he had done in the hands of Serge Lifar, who danced the title role and finished the choreography on his own. The rest became ballet history. Balanchine sought his fortunes elsewhere and Lifar made his in the maze of the Paris Opera.

After creating and starring in *The Creatures of Prometheus*, Serge Lifar was appointed *Directeur de la Danse* under Rouché. For the bulk of his tenure, he acted as both star and creative force for the revitalized Paris Opera. Over the next four decades, the expatriate Russian and former Diaghilev favorite put his stamp all over the French troupe. The commanding dancer onstage began demanding a new seriousness off it. One of his first stipulations was that the auditorium's chandeliers be extinguished during performances. He insisted that female dancers stop wearing their personal jewelry onstage and that male dancers shave off their mustaches. Likewise, the backstage area, especially the studio anteroom known as the *foyer de la danse*, became off-limits for subscribers seeking to rendezvous with their favorites.

After decades of decline, the stature of the male dancer at the Opera began to rise perceptibly under Lifar. His portrayal of Albrecht in his 1932 staging of *Giselle* offered an amplified version of the standard role. Even opposite the public's beloved Spessivtseva in the title role, Lifar made his distinctive mark. He achieved co-equal status for the male dancer in a showcase of Romanticism that originally spurred the supremacy of the ballerina. With Lifar officially named *étoile*, the designation no longer applied only to female dancers.

Lifar's Diaghilevian bent toward twentieth-century modernism led him to play reformer. To the centuries-old tradition for five basic positions for the feet in ballet, Lifar borrowed experiments from early Soviet ballet masters and blithely added two new ones. Called *sixième* and *septième* positions, the Lifaresque stances were little more than rethought versions of ballet's longstanding first (or *première*) and fourth or (*quatrième*) positions, respectively. Lifar's "theory" essentially deprived the standard academic positions of purposeful turnout by accentuating parallel positioning. The determined accent gave the feet and legs a look that struck modernists as chicly archaic and traditionalists as lazily turned-in.

For better or worse, Lifar's technical innovations left their firm mark on Paris Opera dancing. Through today, Paris-schooled dancing can betray details of "flat" legwork, ignoring ballet's theories of turned-out accentuation. This is especially evident in the look of the leg that's kicked in the air to lead the trajectory of ballet's most direct big jump, the grand jeté. (Lifar himself was a late starter in studying ballet, and full, pronounced turnout could not have come easily.)

Unlike those ballet traditions growing or soon to be growing in other parts of the world, the longstanding one in Paris evinced no strong single-choreographer system. As we have seen, Russian ballet matured to a golden age under the guidance of ballet master Petipa. Denmark reached impressive heights under Bournonville. Budding English ballet grew rapidly under Ashton's guidance. America, youngest of all these nations, would acquire major impetus from Balanchine and find secondary force from Antony Tudor. Though all these choreographers began their careers as dancers, each retired sooner than later to concentrate on the making of dances and building of a repertory.

Lifar's concentration on choreography mainly supported his desire to continue his own dance career. His example and energetic presence at the Opera gave rise to the development of several ballerinas from within the company. Often these dancers captured their public's attention in Lifar's own ballets. Solange Schwarz, whose signature became the extravagantly high position of her leg lifted *à la seconde*, made her mark in *Entre Deux Ronde* (1940). Yvette Chauviré (1917–) gained *étoile* status after starring in Lifar's *Istar* (1941). The eighteen-minute essay in pseudo-archaic exotica was virtually a solo showcase for the increasingly popular French ballerina. Eventually, opposite Lifar's Albrecht, La Chauviré performed the title role in *Giselle* and became La Giselle for generations of France's balletgoers.

Lifar, accused of being a collaborator with the German occupation forces in France during World War II, was ousted from the Opera for two years. He continued his career under a cloud by forming his own company in Monte Carlo, the principality where Diaghilev's Ballets Russes ended its days. In 1947, he was allowed to return to the Opera, where he worked, initially only as choreographer, until 1958. During his first season back he oversaw the premiere of his heavily symbolic *Les Mirages* and gave final form to Paris Opera Ballet tradition.

Originally known as *Le Défilé* when it was devised by Opera ballet master Léo Staats's (1877–1952) in 1926, this parade of dancers from the Opera's company and school came to be known as a *Grand Défilé* under Lifar. Rank upon rank—first of pupils of the school, then of artists of the troupe—advance toward the public from deep upstage. In the ornate nineteenth-century theater of the Paris Opera known as the Palais Garnier, this presentation emanates from the cozy, gilded, chandeliered ante-studio, the once infamous *foyer de la danse*, set just behind the rearmost reaches of the stage proper.

In Staats's version, the dancers marched to Wagner, ironically, the march from his *Tannhäuser*, the opera nearly booed off the Opera's stage by the disgruntled ballet "connoisseurs" of the Jockey Club. Lifar changed the music to "March of the Trojans" from Hector Berlioz's *Les Troyens*. The spectacle, once exclusively given only in Paris but lately, on rare occasions, presented on tour, remains one of the ballet world's most handsome and vivifying sights. Pristinely dressed girls, boys, women, and men in all white (the exception being some young men in black velvet jerkins à la *Les Sylphides*) do little more than walk toward the audience, bow a traditional *révérence*, and take places in symmetrically arrayed groupings. The accumulated effect (270 individuals strong during the mid-1990s) proves grand and gracious indeed. In its final tableau the *défilé* amasses a garden of ballet beauty, paying homage to the art form's continuity and freshness.

Just before Lifar's return to the Opera, Balanchine had been invited to serve six months as guest ballet master. Besides restaging three of his earlier ballets (*Serenade*, *Apollo*, and *Le Baiser de la Fée*), the choreographer, now a U.S. citizen, created a brand-new work for the French troupe. Called *Le Palais de Cristal*, the large-cast, four-movement ballet took inspiration for its shape from its music, a recently discovered early symphony by Georges Bizet. (The title was inspired by Leonor Fini's slightly surreal design scheme, which included painted representations of bouquets of crystals in urns. Her costume designs were color coded to precious stones—emeralds, rubies, black diamonds, and pearls—the first but not last time Balanchine would identify movements of an abstract ballet with various jewels.)

Soon, Lifar was again dancing as well as creating new ballets at the Opera, and anywhere else he could find commissions and/or roles. Following his long-running influence at the Opera, a succession of candidates tried out for the job of director of dance. Each survived, some longer than others, but few did better than cope with the numerous strictures put in place over the years regarding dancers' rights and overall working conditions.

In 1983, Rudolf Nureyev took over the job when his unprecedented career onstage, or *sur la scène*, as the French put it, was ready to focus with more concentration offstage.

Chapter 16

SOVIET RUSSIA, NUREYEV, ENGLAND, AND THE WORLD

As the Paris Opera Ballet was leaving its Lifar era, Britain's Royal Ballet was primed to leave its Margot Fonteyn period. By 1961 Fonteyn had been on the ballet stage nearly thirty years. She had gone through one-and-a-half partners—Michael Somes, who took over when Robert Helpmann retired from partnering/prince roles, was now ready to move on to less physically demanding character and pantomime roles as well. The Royal Ballet had schooled and brought along other women since Fonteyn. Consecutively, Moira Shearer, Nadia Nerina, and Svetlana Beriosova each gained prominence during Fonteyn's prime. Now that she was passing that prime, further English talent shone. Merle Park, Lynne Seymour, and Antoinette Sibley each made notable debuts in the increasingly large Royal Ballet repertory.

Even as Fonteyn was pondering her predictable departure from the English stage, however, the ballet world's spotlight was fixed on a riveting newcomer. He was Rudolf Nureyev (1938–1993), or, Noureev as the French transliteration of his Russianized Tartar name would have it. After a late start at the ballet academy in Leningrad that was heir to the school of St. Petersburg's imperial ballet, the prodigiously gifted young dancer gained great prominence. The twenty-three-year-old, whose shaggy long hair predated that of the Beatles, made cultural news in the Soviet Union for his impassioned and powerful dancing. He also made security police news by ignoring local Socialist politics and by paying far too much attention to people and activities in the "decadent" West.

After the 1917 October Revolution, in which Bolshevik forces took charge of overthrowing the imperial government, ballet in Russia went through hard times. Part of the difficulty stemmed from economic austerity measures surrounding the chaos of violent change and civil war. Another part was philosophical: What place should the aristocratic art of a privileged few have in a Communist system leery of all things from the old order? "None," bellowed many gruff voices for the new order. Fortunately for ballet, however, a high-ranking Bolshevik, Anatoli Lunacharsky, the First Peoples Commissar for Enlightment, proclaimed otherwise. "Art," he orated, "creates human types and situations, which we live on from century to century and which are real to millions of people, like a part of real life, for example, *Don Quixote* and *Hamlet*." The people, the ballet-loving Bolshevik noted, love and need their ballet.

During the first years after the upheaval, ballet joined all the Soviet arts in a spirit of experimentation. Two compatriots of the young Georgi Balanchivadze, Fyodor Lopukhov (1886–1973) and Kazian Goliezovsky (1892–1970) helped lead the way. Acrobatic maneuvers amplified the art of partnering. Contortionist posturing took body line and shape to new extremes. A pose called "the ring" appeared: a ballerina, balanced on pointe with one leg extending high behind her, reached up and over her head to take hold of the foot of her raised leg. The ring shape took form as the eye traced a continuous line flowing through the arch of the torso into the back-reaching arm grasping the foot of the crooking raised leg.

Balanchine had left Russia with his experimental ideas in 1924 as post-revolution living conditions continued to deteriorate, and soon the artistic climate that allowed ballet its modern adventures deteriorated as well. Ballet, like all Soviet art, must appeal readily to "all the people." Commissars after Lunacharsky said yes to ballet only as long as it blatantly communicated uplifting themes. Narrative ballets in which innocent and good common people came out on top of oppressive imperialists were in favor. Non-narrative "exercises" in gymnastic moves inspired by "pure" music were not. Socialist Realism, *Da*; Formalism and Abstraction, *Nyet.*

During the 1930s, socialist realist doctrines came down from on high, where a ruthless Joseph Stalin oversaw all facets of Soviet life. Soviet ballet had to turn back from the kind of experimental dance making Lopukhov did a decade earlier. One of his grandest, and most short-lived, ballets was a "dance symphony" called *The Magnificence of the Universe*. Taking inspiration from its music, Beethoven's Symphony no. 4, Lopukhov's ballet dealt with the theme of creation, but without a particular story. Balanchivadze and Alexandra Danilova were among the cast of eighteen that danced the work's sole performance in 1923.

The full flowering and development of the pure-dance ballet would have to take place on ground more fertile and friendly than that of the Soviet Union. The dancers and choreographers who could not or would not leave Russia had to knuckle under or work around State-determined restrictions.

Lopukhov led his fellows in Leningrad (as imperial St. Petersburg, then Petrograd, was now called) in working around the system. As the director of the former imperial ballet, eventually called the Kirov Ballet, the Soviet ballet master became a protector of the Petipa heritage left to his theater. For the most part he rethought and/or restaged nineteenth-century masterworks. Variously he would carefully scalpel out their "imperialist" impurities or put a New Order spin on Old Order business. Along the way, Lopukhov had his old ballets dressed and designed in ways more streamlined or appropriate to the visual tastes of the day.

Meanwhile, back in Moscow just after the turn of the century, another inherently Russian approach to ballet in the twentieth century was begun by Aleksandr Gorsky (1871–1924). The Petersburg-schooled dancer and choreographer actively worked to revitalize the neglected ballet in Moscow's Bolshoi Theater. Much of Gorsky's innovation concerned naturalism and an emphasis on characterization. He strongly supported the dramatic theater theories of Konstantin Stanislavsky and Vasili Nemirovich-Danchenko, who had opened the Moscow Art Theater in 1898. In restaging many of Petipa's nineteenth-century spectacles, Gorsky worked specifically to accentuate "local color" wherever and whenever appropriate. He softened or broke the plainly geometric and symmetrical shape of static ensemble groupings. He discouraged formalized pantomime and called for more naturally expressive acting. Like Stanislavsky, he often concentrated on ensemble elements, sometimes encouraging individualized portrayals within "crowd" scenes. Many of Gorsky's "after-Petipa" productions came, much to the disgruntled aging ballet master's dismay, while Petipa was still alive. Gorsky's 1920 production of *Swan Lake* and his 1922 staging of *Giselle* have had a lasting influence on Bolshoi Ballet productions throughout the twentieth century.

During the 1930s in Leningrad, a former ballerina and pedagogue became artistic director of the ever superior-seeming troupe in the former imperial city. Agrippina Vaganova (1879–1951) had a distinguished but not legendary name as a strong dancer. To indicate her strength without exaggerating her magic—or as some ballet connoisseurs call it, "perfume"—Vaganova was known as the "Queen of Variations." (This unofficial title spoke volumes in ballet lingo. The term "good soloist," or to be more fair to Vaganova's nickname, "great soloist," really says "not-quite-a-ballerina.")

Vaganova retired from the stage in 1916 and the next year began what would become her life's great work, that of teacher to student and professional dancers alike. From the mid-1920s through 1951 she taught at the former imperial school, taking over instruction of the top graduating classes of women. Her connection to the company affiliated with the school also remained close. First and foremost, as the teacher of its "class of perfection"; secondarily and partially, from 1931 to 1937, as its choreographer and artistic head.

It was during Vaganova's artistic directorship—1935, to be precise—that the Leningrad troupe acquired the name Kirov Ballet. The identification, more or less current to our day, came alongside renaming the former Maryinsky Theater as the Kirov Theater, where the ballet had danced since the late-1800s. Henceforth, Russia's two flagship companies became known, for short, as the Kirov and the Bolshoi.

While the matriarch of Leningrad's ballet worked assiduously to perfect the expressive methods of its dancers, several Soviet ballet patriarchs worked to satisfy the watchful authorities with ballets in which expert Soviet performers could shine along acceptable party lines. Sometimes this meant things like changing the tragic ending of *Swan Lake*. Tchaikovsky wrote music and Petipa shaped choreography showing how the lovers die only to be united in the afterlife. Soviet reformists preferred a "happy ending," so the prince overcame the evil genie and could live happily ever after with his swan-returned-to-princess-form. Other times it meant brand-new, socially significant Soviet creations with Soviet librettos, Soviet music, Soviet choreography, and Soviet dancers.

In 1932, Vasily Vainonen (1901–1964) choreographed *The Flames of Paris*, in which heroic French revolutionaries win against decadent monarchists. In 1934, Rostislav Zakharov (1907–1984) created *The Fountains of Bakhchisarai*, a tale loosely based on Pushkin, in which an innocent Slavic princess triumphs spiritually over the oppressive forces of barbaric infidels. In 1940, just before the worst of World War II hit Leningrad, Leonid Lavrovsky (1905–1967) finished the first Soviet, and arguably the most influential of all subsequent stagings, of Prokofiev's *Romeo and Juliet*. In this danced version of a literary classic, 1930s socialist realism insinuated itself on Renaissance Italy, where mercantile members of Verona prove to be vile characters.

Vaganova's pedagogy left its indelible stamp, not only on her Leningrad company, but also to a notable extent on the "rival" Moscow troupe and other groups around the world interested in emulating the ways of twentieth-century Russian dancers. Her star pupils make up a Who's Who of twentieth-century star ballerinas: Olga Mugalova (1905–1942), Marina Semyonova (1908–), Galina Ulanova (1910–), Tatiana Vecheslova (1910–), Natalia Dudinskaya (1912–), Olga Lepeshinskaya (1916–), Alla Osipenko (1932–), and Irina Kolpakova (1933–). Some of these women made their fame performing in Leningrad, others, in Moscow, where they were transferred after graduating.

As ballet mistress and choreographer, Vaganova shaped countless dances and details of dances that later audiences would come to see as classics of Russian ballet. Since all of this work took place behind the Iron Curtain, the actual particulars are still barely known in the West. By the time the Kirov, which Vaganova did so much to influence, began to tour in the West, the pedagogue had died. Much of the Kirov's "after-Petipa" ballet was performed in versions touched up by Vaganova and others even though it simply bore Petipa's name as choreographer.

In 1934, Vaganova set down her thoughts on teaching in book form. Though less than a syllabus, her *Fundamentals of the Classic Dance* became a bible for revealing the nuts and bolts of Soviet ballet technique. Her theorizing included analysis of the French and Italian methods of ballet and made a case for how her preferences sprang from taking the best of both. Of course, the Vaganova blend included a strong dose of elements that were inherently Russian. Probably the most pronounced area of Russian accent came in the use of the dancer's back. The pedagogue's emphasis on the arching of the lower back and waist into a stretched and strongly curved spine, became a signature of her dancers' silhouette, or *plastique*. Whether she would have said so or not, the physically pronounced detail came to be called the "Russian" or "Vaganova" back. In 1937 Latvian-American writer Anatole Chujoy translated Vaganova's treatise into English as *Basic Principles of Classical Ballet* and a larger number of readers could learn the legendary teacher's "secrets" of ballet. Five years after Vaganova's death in 1951, the Soviet establishment named the Leningrad Choreographic Institute after its by then world-famous teacher and theorist.

In 1939, Vakhtang Chabukiani (1910–1992), a dancer from Soviet Georgia with something of Lifar's passion for dance, and probably more taste, choreographed *Laurencia* for the Kirov Ballet. The ballet, based on a story of a peasant uprising in Spain, starred Natalia Dudinskaya and Chabukiani as the heroine and hero who overwhelm and slay the evil ruling forces. Along the way, Chabukiani's ballet gave the ballerina a theatrical time of jumping and turning in flounced lace skirts. With his own part, Chabukiani allowed for opportunities to kick up his heels, click some castanets, and smolder sexily along the way.

Chabukiani's passion and power fired the Russian ballet world in a way no other male dancer had quite done since Nijinsky. Moscow's Bolshoi Ballet had developed something of a reputation for particular strength in male dancers, but part of that distinction sprang from the fact that the troupe had no special constellation of ballerinas to take precedence. In fact, contemporaneous with Chabukiani came Aleksei Yermolayev (1910–1975), a standard-setting virtuoso with Moscow's Bolshoi. Still, in the more eagerly watched arena of Leningrad, Chabukiani captured the greater attention. It even followed him when the Georgian firebrand returned to his home base troupe in Tiblisi, as artistic director and chief pedagogue.

Chabukiani's star still hung in the Leningrad firmament when the green but burningly eager Nureyev entered the Kirov school at seventeen, an age when many are ready to leave. The upstart from Ufa—in a republic much farther away than Georgia—made his way, not without controversy, through several years at the school. He irked the administrators but impressed Leningrad's most revered men's teacher and "king" dancer maker, Aleksandr Pushkin (1907–1970). At his graduation performance Nureyev danced in the pas de deux from Petipa's *Le Corsair*. The choreography was lately, indelibly associated with Chabukiani, who had choreographically amplified some of its choreography while giving some of its most definitive performances.

Soon Nureyev was dancing with the Kirov in other leading roles strongly associated with the flamboyant legendary Chabukiani: Blue Bird in *Sleeping Beauty*, Acteon in the "Diana and Acteon Pas de Deux" from *Esmeralda*, Basilio in *Don Quixote*, and Frondoso in *Laurencia*. During this period of emulating Chabukiani, Nureyev even sprouted a slivered mustache like his idol's.

Nureyev's heart-stoppingly intense and big-scale dancing became the excited talk of Leningrad, where such talk didn't come easily. Part of his impact stemmed from his unbridled individuality, offstage as well as on. It was one thing to play the rebel peasant, overthrowing oppressive landowners; it was something else to live a life, overturning roles of conformity and political decorum. As the Kirov began negotiations for a newsworthy Paris and London tour, Nureyev's bright talent seemed outweighed by his brash disregard for Communist isolation and aloofness.

If it hadn't been for pressure from the French producer of the Kirov Ballet, Nureyev would have been kept off the Paris tour. But word in the passionately interconnected ballet world travels fast, even through the Iron Curtain, especially when it communicates in terms of a "next Nijinsky" or a "pantherlike" performer.

Parisian audiences were hardly disappointed in the new firebrand on stage. Soviet authorities could hardly have been more displeased by his "westernized" behavior off. The fearless virtuoso had won rave reviews for performances as Solor in "The Kingdom of the Shades" from *La Bayadère* and as the prince in *Sleeping Beauty*. For other reasons the authorities decided to call him back to the Soviet Union just as he was to depart for the London leg of the tour. The ballet panther smelled a political rat, and bolted. He sought political—read: artistic—asylum in France.

Chapter 17

RUDI IN ENGLAND AND AROUND THE WORLD

During his isolation in Soviet Russia, the artistically hungry and ambitious Nureyev harbored hopes of enriching his budding career by working with all the best in the West. Most particularly, he wanted to study alongside the great Danish *danseur noble* Erik Bruhn (1928–1986) and to work with master ballet master George Balanchine. With Balanchine across the Atlantic Ocean in New York City, and Bruhn just north in Copenhagen, Nureyev more easily found his way to Denmark.

This is where Margot Fonteyn reenters the picture. In her capacity as popular, well-known ballerina, she had been asked to organize a benefit gala performance. Shrewdly, she tracked down the media's darling defector and put him on her program. So far, Nureyev's free world performing had come only with the International Ballet of the Marquis de Cuevas, a vanity ballet troupe out of Monte Carlo established by a weathly Chilean.

London's well-knit group of balletgoers had been fixated on Nureyev ever since his Paris appearances with the Kirov. Some had slipped over to get a preview of the new star before his expected performances in London. All were crushed, as it turned out, at his absence from the season, and few could afford now to miss his English debut. For the occasion of Fonteyn's gala, Nureyev—or Rudi as he'd soon be known in familiar English—danced a specially choreographed piece by Ashton. This was *Poème Tragique*, an impassioned solo, complete with billowing silk cape to a piano composition by Aleksandr Scriabin, a composer chosen by Nureyev.

Among the excited audience members at this gala was Ninette de Valois, the Royal Ballet's eagle-eyed Madame. Her enthusiastic analysis of the newcomer immediately included plans for her company. Fonteyn, in de Valois's opinion, shouldn't think of leaving the stage, she should think of recharging her career opposite Nureyev. Initially the self-aware Fonteyn foresaw such a pairing as "mutton to lamb." But Madame prevailed, and Fonteyn went into high-gear preparation for the new partnership. The "experiment" began with *Giselle*. The rest, as late twentieth-century ballet history now knows, became legendary.

Fonteyn and Nureyev became "Rudi and Margot" to their adoring fans. These hippie-era balletomanes were characterized as "groupies" by a media that was hungry to put a contemporary spin on a traditional art. The pairing of the mature English ballerina with the blossoming Tartar danseur gave the more thoughtful ballet watchers much to ponder regarding the partnership. Even skeptical or negative voices on the Fonteyn-Nureyev phenomenon contributed invaluably to the unprecedented discourse. Notable and consistent couplings had come along before, but this one, in part an untried experiment and in part a promotable commodity, piqued interest in the physical/emotional chemistry at work.

Nureyev spurred not only his partner's profile but also the dancing of the Royal Ballet in general and its male dancing in particular. In 1963, this brazen male dancer who worked tirelessly, and sometimes shamelessly, to demand equal time in ballerina-dominant works from the nineteenth century, made a big effort on behalf of the female corps de ballet. He staged "The Kingdom of the Shades" scene from Petipa's *La Bayadère* with a lone, bravura male part, which he naturally assumed himself, and a luminous ballerina role (for Fonteyn), and showcased the precise academic schooling of the Royal Ballet's female ensemble.

The Kirov season from which the stellar danseur defected had included this heretofore unfamiliar "Shades" excerpt to great acclaim. Now the ex-Kirovite showed his commitment to passing along such traditions and treasures as ballet master, as well as dancer. Soon he cast the Royal's own David Wall (1946–) in the lead role of Solor, to show how his tutelage could affect some of the West's brightest young talent.

English ballet, meanwhile, carried on past Ashton's generation, even while the architect and master himself continued to create works. John Cranko (1927–1973) and Kenneth MacMillan (1929–1992), both products of the Sadler's Wells Ballet, showed interests and gifts for creating ballet choreography. Cranko's career was short-lived—he died soon after assuming the directorship of Germany's Stuttgart Ballet. MacMillan's took off after he choreographed what came to be the most popular ballet version of Prokofiev's *Romeo and Juliet.*. Though the aspiring heir to Ashton created his three-act ballet for two young and fresh Royal dancers, Lynne Seymour and Christopher Gable, the "hot" team of Fonteyn and Nureyev put the ballet on the map internationally.

When Fonteyn eventually had to curtail her career, Nureyev had already acquired a number of new partners at the Royal, notably Merle Park. By this time, with his aspirations to dancing far and wide in as varied a repertory as he found suitable, he had grown increasingly interested in staging ballets himself. Sometimes these were revisions of nineteenth-century landmarks, *Raymonda* (1964), *Swan Lake* (1964), *Don Quixote* (1966), *The Nutcracker* (1967), and *The Sleeping Beauty* (1972), for example; other times, he made new ballets from scratch, such as *Tancredi* (1966), *Manfred* (1979), and *The Tempest* (1982).

Soon the dancer without a country was joking, only half-seriously, that he was also a dancer without a company. His influence on his adopted Royal Ballet had been great, but not without a price. The pairing of Anthony Dowell (1943–) with Antoinette Sibley gave the Royal a stellar partnership of its own, but their rise proceeded with some restraint due to the dominance of Fonteyn and Nureyev. During the directorship of Norman Morrice, who followed MacMillan, who followed Ashton, the Royal put a ban on outside guest artists. The company was making a concerted effort to build up and promote dancers from its own school and ranks.

Nureyev's touring itinerary around this period became a jet-age version of Pavlova's ocean-liner style during the 1920s. His trips to the States were largely limited to appearances with touring companies. Following the Royal years, he performed with ballet companies from Canada (Toronto's National Ballet of Canada) and Australia (Melbourne's Australian Ballet). Sadly, though, his longed-for association with Balanchine never materialized.

Chapter 18

AMERICA, BALLET, AND BALANCHINE

After 1934, Balanchine made America his home and in the process made America a home for ballet. Until that time, the fairly young and prosperous country only knew ballet as yet another European art form. In this case, it seemed an almost exclusively Russian form.

In Europe, the multiple heirs to Diaghilev's legacy settled into two rival troupes, one called the Original Ballet Russe, the other Ballets Russes de Monte Carlo. In effect, each Russianized company based itself on Diaghilev's formula: a moderately sized ensemble overshadowed by leading dancers, often billed as "stars," offered one-act or excerpted multi-act ballets on mixed programs. Both companies enjoyed popularity on their American tours.

During the 1930s, working for one or another Ballet Russe organization, Massine created a series of so-called symphonic ballets. These plotless works, set to serious concert-hall music, came with strong dramatic and thematic subjects. For the 1933 *Les Présages* (to Tchaikovsky's Fifth Symphony), it was the destiny of man; for the 1938 *Seventh Symphony* (to Beethoven), the creation and destruction of the world.

With Balanchine's 1934/35 *Serenade*, the Russian who came after Massine as ballet master for Diaghilev had his own style with plotless ballet. The difference between the so-called abstract ballets of Balanchine and of Massine came, figuratively and literally, in their programs. (In the older, more literate world of musicology, "program music" existed in contrast to "absolute" or "pure" music. Program music addressed itself to specific literary ideas, aiming to create pictures in the ear's mind of a particular time, place, and/or event.)

The printed program for Massine's plotless, symphonic *Les Présages* listed the dancers of its various sections by such names as Action, Temptation, Movement, Passion, Fate, and Destinies. The ballet's individual sections, corresponding to the music's movements, came with identifications beyond their musicological ones; for example, "First Movement: *Andante, Allegro con anima*. Man's life with its diversions, desires, and temptations." The dancers in Balanchine's plotless *Serenade* were identified only by their names in the printed program. The music came with no elaborated descriptions other than the composer's markings regarding tempo.

For Balanchine, music acted as poetic inspiration, not as unbending slave driver. Massine's use of "serious" music remained seriously committed to its structure and shape. His transfer of music into dance terms strictly (some said slavishly) obeyed the musical methods. In this impetus, his large-scale ballets resembled the smaller-scale works called "music visualizations." These displays were promoted earlier in the century by pre-modern dance American practitioners such as Ruth St. Denis and Ted Shawn.

In their way, Massine's ballets were self-consciously abstract. They aimed to distill and reduce musically dramatic sentiments to specifically expressive forms of movement and posture. Balanchine, who increasingly eschewed narrative, overt characterization, and plot, disliked the word *abstract* when applied to ballet. He wondered how this label borrowed from painting could be a sensible term for ballet, which of necessity takes place only with human beings—male and female dancers—onstage. He suggested the term "storyless." But even then he questioned the too narrow thinking regarding the definition of story. In his view, and in light of ballets like *Serenade*, where one man at the start and another at the end encounter the ballet's prominent women, simply putting a man and woman together onstage enunciates a story of some kind.

By 1938, Balanchine's right-hand man Lincoln Kirstein published a polemic entitled "Blast at Ballet." In his essay the Yankee arts patron, determined to establish a truly American ballet, belittled a current assumption in the States that ballet automatically meant Russian ballet. His prose coined the term "Russianballet." Given the appearances and successes of Ballets Russes this and Ballets Russe that, the Russian connection had credibility, but not, if Balanchine and Kirstein had their way, absolute certainty.

Their way took time. Makeshift companies out of their School of American Ballet came and went. None became permanent, not even the one that came with hopes of stability when New York City's Metropolitan Opera took on Balanchine and Kirstein's ballet as resident troupe (1935–1938). Upon leaving the European-styled opera organization after a series of artistic disagreements, Balanchine was reminded all over again of how ballet-unfriendly "traditional" opera houses could be.

For a few years Kirstein spearheaded a troupe without Balanchine's direct participation. Named Ballet Caravan, the American troupe's repertory stressed overt Americana, with works such as *Filling Station* by Lew Christiansen (1902–1984) and *Billy the Kid* by Eugene Loring (1914–1982). For some of this time Balanchine was applying his inherent international sophistication to the American institutions of musical theater and Hollywood movies.

In between the conservative bent toward old Europe at the Metropolitan and the limited slant for localized American subject matter in Kirstein's Ballet Caravan, Balanchine kept his sights fixed on the lively powers of ballet dancing. His aim was to keep the honored traditions of classical dancing fresh and contemporary. Ballet would become American by integrating itself into American life while being danced by American dancers.

Meanwhile, Richard Pleasant (1906–1961), an American architect turned ballet company manager, teamed up with Lucia Chase (1897–1986), an American heiress turned ballet dancer, to form their own American ballet venture. Originally called Ballet Theatre (eventually, American Ballet Theatre), Pleasant's and Chase's organization took a middle road. It core unit sprang from the Mordkin Ballet, a Russified group directed by an ex-Bolshoi dancer for his American students. Likening its aims to those of a museum or art gallery, Ballet Theatre proposed a wide-ranging character for itself.

Tried, true, and famous works from ballet's past would exist alongside new creations from the present.

Fokine's *Les Sylphides* (1909) opened the troupe's first program, and the Russian, now living in New York City, became something of a mentor to the company. Soon, however, Antony Tudor, Marie Rambert's "discovery," found his way to Ballet Theatre. Never a prolific dance maker, the British dancer and choreographer became closely identified with Chase's company. (Pleasant left soon after founding Ballet Theatre, and Chase was joined as co-director by theatrical designer Oliver Smith (1918–1994).

Tudor arrived in the States with the high recommendation of Agnes de Mille (1905–1993). De Mille, who would have her own notable career as a choreographer with Ballet Theatre and elsewhere, knew inspiration when she saw it. Tudor's work, simultaneously European, contemporary, and classical, gave rise to a new ballet label: psychological ballet. Starting with his 1938 *Jardin aux Lilas* (sometimes performed as *Lilac Garden*), Tudor worked ballet's rarefied ways of moving to identify specific, dramatic, human emotion.

In *Jardin*, a foursome of lovers mismatched by societal forces, socialize in a garden of lilacs. There, they can at best steal desired moments; otherwise, they must live uncomplainingly with their unhappiness. None of this was indicated through traditional pantomime. The turn of a head or the gesture of an arm or hand elaborated plain ballet dancing into the emotions Tudor was after. Everything sprang organically from the music. (In the case of *Jardin*, this meant a "Poème" for violin and orchestra by Ernest Chausson.)

Pillar of Fire (1942), Tudor's first original creation for Ballet Theatre, made ballet theater out of a small-town situation involving spinsterhood, self-righteousness, and pure love. The psychology of Tudor's heroine, named Hagar after a biblical character, telescoped confidently from Tudor's delicately shaded, classical choreography.

In 1944, Jerome Robbins (1918–), a New York City born and variously trained dancer with Ballet Theatre, created his first ballet for the company. In the process, he created an enduring American classic. Much of the Ballet Theatre repertory that Robbins had been dancing came in the form of standard Russian, or Russianized, fare.

His ballet *Fancy Free* moved wholeheartedly in a contemporary direction. Its characters were American sailors; its locale, New York City. The music was by New Yorker Leonard Bernstein; the design by Ballet Theatre director Smith. The result was a smash hit.

During this time Balanchine staged some of his older ballets for Ballet Theatre, and created a couple of new ones including, notably, *Theme and Variations* (1947). Named straightforwardly after its Tchaikovsky music, Balanchine's ballet made a showpiece of classical dancing and radiant, regal personages of its leading dancers—Cuban-born ballerina Alicia Alonso (1921–) and Russian-born *danseur noble* Igor Youskevitch (1912–1994).

Chapter 19

AMERICA, NEW YORK CITY, AND BALLET

As it proceeded to establish itself, Ballet Theatre kept aiming for a wide variety of ballets, including staples with Russian pedigree. Meanwhile, the ubiquitous Ballet Russe de Monte Carlo continued to sport its Old World aura. At the same time Kirstein and Balanchine had launched another separate scheme. This one, called Ballet Society, begun in 1946, was a subscription series that solicited interest and payment for ballet in advance of specially created programs of new works. Everyone wanting to see Ballet Society's offerings needed to subscribe, including journalists who normally expected complimentary press tickets.

For Ballet Society's first outing, Balanchine took some of his recent earnings and commissioned a score from Dutch composer Paul Hindemith. Called *The Four Temperaments* by its composer, the chamber work was structured as three musical themes and four variations. The names of the four medieval humors, or personality types—Melancholic, Sanguinic, Phlegmatic, and Choleric—identified the musical variations. Balanchine's innovative choreography heeded all the drama he heard in Hindemith's music and steered clear of any literal, subject-matter references suggested by the words.

Kirstein's art world connections and tastes led him to commission costume designs for *The Four Temperaments* from Kurt Seligmann, a visual artist with a taste for the occult. His wildly fanciful clothes constricted the dancers, obscured the choreography, and dismayed Balanchine and were eventually discarded in favor of what could be described as practice costumes. (The simple basic leotard and tights for women and the tights and T-shirts for men, sometimes in black and white, sometimes all white or all black, became the trademark style of dressing Balanchine's ballets. In such "uniforms" the dancing could be seen most cleanly and directly. The look also made minimal stress on the production budget.)

During 1948, for what would be its last season, Ballet Society presented two differently "undressed" Balanchine ballets. *Symphony in C*, a retitled rendering of *Le Palais de Cristal* of the Paris Opera Ballet, was given in basic black and white costuming. The attendant men wore tights and plain tops in black; the predominant women wore no-frills "classical" all-white tutus. (The shorter, leg-baring classical tutu essentially differed from the leg-clouding Romantic one in length.) *Orpheus*, the society's final premiere, had a specially composed score by Stravinsky and artfully rendered, austere costumes and scenery by Japanese-American modernist sculptor Isamu Noguchi. (At the time he was closely associated with designing the stages for many of Martha Graham's modern dance works.)

The beauty of Balanchine's bare-bones classical ballet profoundly struck one influential Ballet Society attendee. He was Morton Baum, head of New York City's City Center Theater, a venue with a low scale ticket price policy. His enthusiastic reaction to Balanchine's distinct vision of American ballet led him to invite Ballet Society to work along with New York City Opera as a city institution and in 1948, New York City Ballet was born.

With a starpower ballerina in the person of Maria Tallchief (1925–) and an eager disciple in Jerome Robbins, who came from Ballet Theatre (BT) to work alongside Balanchine, the New York City Ballet (NYCB) got forcefully under way. With a trimmed *Firebird* (1949) and an encapsulated *Swan Lake* (1951), Balanchine offered Ballet Russe staples in stagings with his own stamp. In 1951, with BT's organization faltering, Tudor signed on at NYCB. So did BT-Tudor dancers Hugh Laing (1911–1988), Nora Kaye (1920–1987), and Diana Adams (1926–1993).

After BT got back on firmer footing, Tudor and the dancers associated with him reestablished their connections with Lucia

Chase's organization. Adams, however, stayed at NYCB to inspire an inspired Balanchine. From here on, the growth of the two dominant American ballets went fairly separate ways. Chase's and Smith's BT, known since 1956 as ABT, for American Ballet Theatre, continued to balance tried and true "classic" repertory works with brand-new ones. Balanchine's and Kirstein's NYCB stressed the ongoing creation of brand-new or newly furbished ballets.

ABT made a point of following the star system. By this formula, leading dancers, sometimes imported from foreign companies where they had originally made names for themselves, became as much a commodity of a season as the ballets in repertory. The casting of ABT's ballets became as much, or more, a selling point as the individual works themselves. During the 1950s and 1960s the names of Jean Babilée (1923–), Erik Bruhn (1928–1986), Carla Fracci (1936–), Violette Verdy (1933–), Rudolf Nureyev, and Toni Lander (1931–1985) variously became associated with ABT. Some stayed with the company longer than others. Bruhn and especially Lander remained long enough to make ABT synoymous with their mature careers.

In contrast, Balanchine's NYCB advanced differently. Leery of depending on a particular dancer, especially particular "outsider" dancers arriving with growing reputations, swelling heads, and fine-print contract stipulations, Balanchine programmed his seasons for his evolving ensemble troupe. Would-be ballet sophisticates dubbed these ways a "no-star" system. The description was meant pejoratively—it implied a bent toward choreography over dancing, an overall lack of glamour, and a cult of chill artists devoid of overt personality.

New Worlders—people who came to ballet fresh, without excessive preconceptions—found the results of Balanchine's system beguiling. One of their number liked to answer complaints about Balanchine's so-called non-star system by suggesting that the choreographer was in fact only about stars; indeed, his was an all-star organization. Starting with Tanaquil LeClercq (1929–), an early scholarship student to the School of American Ballet, Balanchine's company developed numerous stellar dancers. None of these men and women, however, got billed above the title of the company or were promoted as starring in this or that ballet. Their numbers included Patricia Wilde (1928–), Jacques d'Amboise (1934–), Melissa Hayden (1923–), Edward Villella (1936–), Patricia McBride (1942–), Allegra Kent (1938–), Suzanne Farrell (1945–), and Gelsey Kirkland (1952–).

In the late 1960s and 1970s, the United States lived through a period variously described as a "dance boom" or a "ballet boom." Fonteyn and Nureyev, heading various tours of Britain's Royal Ballet under the aegis of savvy impresario Sol Hurok, had a lot to do with igniting the fires of interest. Partisans for them, or for other foreign stars, and boosters of local, homegrown dancers fanned the flames of ballet interest and debate. Chase consistently tried to counterbalance her own American dancers with the foreign performers she also promoted.

With the public largely disposed toward assuming the superiority of the foreign ballet artist in an art as "foreign" as ballet, the Russian, Danish, English, and French dancers at ABT often overshadowed the local talents. American-born dancers such as Sallie Wilson (1932–), Bruce Marks (1937–), Ted Kivitt (1942–), Martine van Hamel (1945–), Cynthia Gregory (1946–), Mariana Tcherkassky (1955–), and Fernando Bujones (1955–) could often be counted on to bemoan the unfair advantage accorded at ABT to such foreign-born individuals as Ivan Nagy (1943–), Natalia Makarova (1940–), Mikhail Baryshnikov (1948–), Michel Denard (1944–), Yoko Morishita (1948–), Seymour, and Nureyev.

Balanchine remade his Russian ballet for American tastes and worked almost exclusively with dancers from his school. In the individual cases, he hired dancers with foreign schooling. But this was only on the assumption that these select men and, on rarer occasions, women commit themselves to remaining with him long enough to immerse themselves in his company's particular aesthetic.

Three separate events from 1967 help define American ballet at the time. In February, ABT presented its first full-evening production of *Swan Lake*. This was staged by England's David Blair (1932–1976) in the tradition of Petipa's 1895 landmark St. Petersburg production. In March, Toronto's National Ballet of Canada (founded in 1951) presented the premiere of a two-act production of *Swan Lake* with all new choreography by Erik Bruhn. This tightened the original four-act scheme and, among other rethinkings, insinuated a mother complex into the character of the prince. In April, NYCB gave the premiere performance of Balanchine's *Jewels*, a three-act production that would go down in the history books as the first full-evening nonstory/plotless ballet.

However adventuresome both ABT's and National Ballet of Canada's 1967 productions were with regard to company history or budget, each remained safely under the wing of *Swan Lake*'s unquestioned popularity. (Balanchine once quipped that all ballets should be called "Swan Lake," thus guaranteeing large and interested audiences.) ABT wasn't the first American company to put on a complete *Swan Lake*. That distinction went to the ballet troupe associated with the San Francisco Opera. (In 1940, San Francisco Ballet, then known as San Francisco Opera Ballet, produced a four-act version under the guidance of one of its early founding ballet masters, Willam Christensen.) Still, ABT's production was the first to claim direct links through English ballet's Russian connection to the production that put the ballet in lasting shape. The newness of Chase's production stemmed from its conscious re-creation of an Old World pedigree. Bruhn's semi-Freudian, Canadian *Swan Lake* chose to move in an opposite direction, reworking a nineteenth-century folktale according to twentieth-century sensibilities.

Balanchine's non-narrative, contemporary *Jewels* steered clear of remaking or rethinking a historical masterwork. Its three "acts," linked by visual design, made dancing the subject. The particular music of Gabriel Fauré (for "Emeralds"), Stravinsky (for "Rubies"), and Tchaikovsky (for "Diamonds") provided inspiration perfectly free of additional literary constraints. The separate color schemes—aqueous greens, vibrant reds, and sparkling whites—might well be found in a *Swan Lake* evoking seasonal hues, ballroom interiors, and moonlit clearings. In fact, with Tchaikovsky's Symphony no. 3 floating and surging through the all-white "Diamonds," which includes a large female corps de ballet, visions of *Swan Lake* swans arise even without *Swan lake* particulars. Fantastic stories often acted as glue holding together moments of fantastic dancing. In Balanchine's ballet picture, the filler was cleared away to make room for more dancing.

Chapter 20

BEYOND THE PARIS OPERA AND BEYOND PARIS

To paraphrase Tsar Nicholas I, who once reminded a Frenchman that St. Petersburg was Russian but not Russia, it needs to be stated that Paris Opera Ballet was French, but not all that France had to offer, ballet-wise. In spite of the reforms instituted at the Paris Opera by Serge Lifar, working conditions could still prove daunting. Roland Petit (1924–), a Paris Opera alumnus with visions of choreography dancing in his head, chose to take his fight elsewhere. With a group of young and eager dancers and help from former Diaghilev collaborator/librettist Boris Kochno, the young modernist became the main choreographer for a new troupe called Ballets des Champs-Élysées. Prominent among the then little-known dancers sympathetic to Petit were Jean Babilée, Nina Vyroubova (1921–), and Renée (later Zizi, and Petit's wife) Jeanmaire (1926–).

Petit's ballets could at once show the influence of intellectual thought associated with French existentialist philosophy and an unapologetic, showy sexiness reminiscent of the popular theater, or music hall. His *Le Jeune Homme et la Mort* (1946) starred Babilée in paint-smeared dungarees and Nathalie Philippart (1926–) in a Cocteau-designed evening gown, draped in the style of Madame Grès. His *Carmen* (1949), in which the thoughtful choreographer danced opposite the leggy Jeanmaire, could have been called "The Philosopher and the Showgirl." Petit went on, often with Jeanmaire, to work for musical theater and for the movies.

Marseilles-born and trained Maurice Béjart (1927–), another popular French dancer and choreographer, also declined the "privilege" of heading the ballet bastion of the Paris Opera Ballet. He made his name as a choreographer during the 1950s in experimentalist works exemplified by *Symphonie pour un Homme Seul* (1955). This work used a nontraditional "sound" score (by Pierre Henry and Pierre Shaeffer), or what the French call *musique concrète*. Early on he directed his own companies, the first of which was called Les Ballets de l'Étoile. He showed a preference for dressing dancers in the simplest, barest essentials, offering what the French might call *la danse nu*. Soon, with his troupe known (in translation) as the Ballet of the Twentieth Century, Béjart's repertory was sports arenas and other "in-the-round" spaces. Many of his dancers came out of his own modernist ballet school called Mudra. This East- and West-influenced academy trained dancers in a body language somewhere between clear classicism and idiosyncratic modernism.

With a pronounced and promoted interest in the male dancer, and with his female dancers as often off pointe as on, this ballet looked like a definite hybrid. Béjart's *Le Sacre du Printemps* (1959) presented Stravinsky's 1913 music as a 1950s calisthenic ritual for bestial men and wan women. Dressed in the all-over tights now known as unitards, the whole faintly orgiastic affair had the look of a decorative athletic event. Its ranks of sweating bodies, dominated by male dancers dressed in what resembled wrestler's singlets, sporting fashionably long haircuts and wearing heavy eye makeup, led to the choreographer's and company's signature style.

A blend of ballet's methods with those of the century's self-proclaimed modern dance came upon the scene out of Germany between the two world wars. Kurt Jooss (1901–1979), a late starter, had come to dance through the teachings of movement theorist Rudolf Laban (1879–1958). Laban's personal theories shied away from tenets of ballet, and his teachings helped establish the German roots of modern dance. (Eventually, Laban's work led to establishing a method of notating the mechanics of dancing. To our day this internationally recognized and used diagrammatic method is known as Labanotation.)

Once on his own in a country where ballet already had a local history (some of Noverre's innovative work took place in Stuttgart),

Jooss blended Laban's theorizing with the ballet's precepts. *The Green Table*, subtitled a "Danse Macabre in Eight Scenes" (1932), became Jooss's best-known work. Made for a choreography competition held in Paris, where it won first prize, the expressionist ballet made a name for its genre and its creator. Its dramatically inflected dance language produced dance-acted vignettes about war and wartime. Jooss himself created the dominating figure of Death. As a cross between the mythological Mars and a skeleton out of German woodcuts, the omnipresent character marched and skulked around, claiming victims along his implacable way.

Seeing *The Green Table* in Stockholm soon after its premiere inspired Swedish dancer and choreographer Birgit Cullberg (1908–) to study under Jooss. Thereafter, from the 1940s onward, she formulated her own blend of modernist movement and ballet. Cullberg's efforts, which kept a Jooss-like accent on theater while strengthening her mentor's borrowings from ballet, betrayed a strong taste for dark psychological drama. Her most lasting work, *Miss Julie* (1950), is based on August Strindberg's play dealing with class strata and sexual appetites. Around this time, Maurice Béjart worked with Cullberg. In addition to performing the leading role of Jason in her *Medea*, he also choreographed, at her suggestion, an original version of Stravinsky's *Firebird* for Swedish television.

Outside the self-contained traditions of the Danish Royal, British Royal, and Paris Opera, Western European ballet took the shape of a mosaic in the second part of the twentieth century. If any throughline could be sensed, it followed the path of Jooss, Petit, Cullberg, and Béjart.

The exceptions to this influence included the Stuttgart Ballet of John Cranko (1927–1973), whose debt was to British ballet, in which he apprenticed. Though based in Germany, Cranko's troupe, which he directed as his creative workshop until his untimely death, maintained a strong English dimension. This character mostly revealed itself in the multi-act story ballets he created. These include *Romeo and Juliet* (1958, revised 1962), *Onegin* (1965, revised 1967), and *The Taming of the Shrew* (1969). Each found an immediate longevity with the Stuttgart company as well as, eventually, in companies around the world. With the exception of Kenneth MacMillan

(1929–1992), his close contemporary in England, Cranko explored the full-program story ballet more regularly than anyone else in Western Europe.

MacMillan came to prominence at the Royal Ballet after Ashton retired from full-time work with the company. Like Cranko, he created both one-act and multi-act narrative ballets, as well as abstract works. Unlike Cranko, he did not meet an untimely end and did become heir to Ashton's domain within the Royal Ballet. MacMillan's original multi-act ballets were all made for the Royal Ballet: *Romeo and Juliet* (1965), *Anastasia* (1971), *Manon* (1974), *Mayerling* (1978), *Isadora* (1981), and *The Prince of the Pagodas* (1989). All of these ballets outlived their initial seasons, and most have been revived by the Royal Ballet with a couple becoming part of the international repertory.

Chapter 21

STARRY NIGHTS

Ballet history has regularly shown how individual dancers fire a public's interest and imagination as much as, and often more than, particular ballets do. The French call such exemplary performers *étoiles*, or stars, and the fuel for increased interest in ballet during the 1970s in America came in good measure from these popular, charismatic, and virtuoso dancers.

Lucia Chase's American Ballet Theatre made a point of hiring popular dancers, especially for high-profile seasons like those in New York City. Prominent among these in the early 1970s were the Danish-schooled Bruhn, Italian-schooled Fracci, and the Soviet-schooled Makarova. The term and notion of "superstar" readily applied to the charismatic appearances of Nureyev, often with Fonteyn. And in 1974, the dance world gained a new star: Baryshnikov. The prodigy from the same Leningrad academy as Nureyev had defected in Canada, and Chase signed him right up.

Mikhail Baryshnikov was the third of Leningrad's exemplary talents to bolt from their home company and seek artistic freedom in the West. As the latest, and youngest, he embodied the progressive nature of ballet dancing. The eighteenth century's Gaëtan Vestris grudgingly recognized this pattern of next generation superiority and when confronted with the advanced gifts of his own dancing son, Vestris *père* reminded everyone of the young man's unique advantage—having Gaëtan for a father. Baryshnikov was only ten years younger than Nureyev, but he was in a way his predecessor's heir. Each had been formed, approximately a decade apart, by Leningrad's master men's teacher Aleksandr Pushkin.

Baryshnikov not only had the advantage of being further down the line of the pedagogue's teaching career, he also had the benefit of Pushkin's teaching at a more leisurely pace. (Nureyev arrived at the Leningrad academy at seventeen without a solid foundation; Baryshnikov came at fifteen with sounder basic schooling.) Each found early acclaim, from both teacher and ballet watchers. Baryshnikov appealed by way of his precise power, deft control, and unprecedented strength. The only problems he presented to his Soviet artistic directors were those related to physical type. Baryshnikov danced like Apollo but was built more like a Pan. According to their ballet scales, he resembled a big godly boy rather than a godly young man.

In the West, especially America, where Baryshnikov landed and made his home, the ballet powers viewed his talent as limitless, and, given his appeal at their box office, happily had him dancing any roles he'd like. This meant that the ex-Soviet dancer, steeped in that system's tradition of casting by body-type, had to exercise restraint and/or selectivity himself. This, he did, sometimes to the chagrin of directors wanting him to perform roles he thought unsuited to him physically, if not technically. (For example, the prince in *Swan Lake*. Here was a role that many a company was happy to offer the superstar, only to come up against, in most instances, a self-imposed veto regarding it as "unsuitable.")

Partisans for Camargo versus Sallé, Taglioni versus Elssler, Pavlova versus Spessivtseva continue to speak out whenever high-profile virtuosos dance in the same era. Nureyev, the Rudi people would insist, was Baryshnikov's superior; he was more passionate, a better actor. Baryshnikov, the "Misha" people would counter, was a more powerful and awesome classicist; he had more inherent artistic taste on stage. And on, and on, it would go.

Meanwhile over in NYCB's closed shop and/or safe haven, Balanchine's non-star stars inspired their own champions. Earlier in the troupe's history, a prominent dance writer and champion of Maria Tallchief tried to tout his favorite over Melissa Hayden, a potential rival for similar roles. "There is only *one* Tallchief," the would-be connoisseur stated flatly in highest admiration. "There are, of course, *two*," a far more clever writer retorted, reminding the hyperbolist and the world that Maria's sister, Marjorie, was also a ballerina.

During the Fonteyn/Nureyev/Makarova/Baryshnikov 1970s, Balanchine's firmament included McBride, Villella, Verdy, Kent, Martins, Kirkland, and, after a hiatus, Farrell. Each proved a star in the true, if of necessity, lower-case use of the term. The closest of these to a S star in the publicity-machine sense was Villella. His appearances on television and in glossy journals showed him off as an American-born challenger to Nureyev in terms physical prowess, artistry, and virtuosity. Farrell, on the other hand, gained prominence mostly in the "bell-jar" of Balanchine's company. She came along as an early recipient of a scholarship program that resulted from a huge grant given to Balanchine (much to chagrin of numerous other struggling ballet directors) by the Ford Foundation. The svelte, fair-haired, leggy young woman made other beloved ballerinas look thicker, dumpier, heavier than they actually were. Farrell broke the ballerina mold of her time much the way Pavlova and then Spessivtseva did in theirs. She was strong without being tough, daring without being scary, and virtuoso without being self-congratulatory.

For better or worse, depending upon which partisan you heard from, Balanchine's obsession with Farrell affected his entire company and a good deal of its public. The ballet master's landmark *Jewels* said a lot about his way with dancing and his dancers. For example, a mercurial Verdy and a mysterious Mimi Paul (1942–) led the cool "Emeralds" segment. A sassy yet sweet McBride alongside a cocky Villella galvanzied the boisterous energy of "Rubies." Finally, capping all the splendor, squired around with deft and gracious support by d'Amboise, came the magisterial Farrell, kittenish, slightly icy, and brilliantly faceted as the centerpiece of "Diamonds." Outsiders peering in on Balanchine's inner sanctum concocted all sorts of stories, some of them fixed with raised eyebrows toward the ballet master's "relationships" with his ballerinas. "Mr. B.," as the boss was usually called by his company, liked to answer outside pryings into his "real" life by noting that it was "all in the programs." The program for *Jewels* names Balanchine's chosen composers and dancers; Farrell's name, leading "Diamonds" with that of d'Amboise, culminates and punctuates the entire affair. There are no character names, no synopsis of the ballet's action, no indication of narrative, and yet *Jewels* says a great deal about Balanchine, ballet, and the NYCB.

In 1978, Baryshnikov's name was printed in Balanchine's programs. The young Russian dancer got a dream contract, artistically if not financially, to be part of the revered Russian's NYCB. Nureyev's longstanding hope for a similar berth remained unfulfilled. Baryshnikov's connection to NYCB, which ended in 1980 when he assumed directorship of ABT, fell short of giving him his fondest wish. Though he danced numerous parts in many Balanchine ballets, many of them originated by Villella, the eager disciple failed to acquire the most sought-after plum: an original role created expressly for his talents by the master ballet master. Jerome Robbins, however, did create two original ballets with Baryshnikov in them, *The Four Seasons* (to Verdi), and *Opus 19* (to Prokofiev), both in 1979.

Chapter 22

A TOP THREE AND MORE

American ballet grew largest in New York City with both Chase's and Balanchine's organizations basing themselves there. Of the two, only NYCB acquired a permanent home theater where it could regularly perform before culture-conscious New Yorkers. ABT became the company that toured, taking its ballets and dancers regularly around the United States with New York remaining an option, not a given. American cities outside New York, with isolated, odd exceptions, came to know Chase's ballet fare more than Balanchine's.

NYCB and ABT were not, however, the only ballet acts to be experienced in the States. Between 1929 and 1938, enterprising individuals in Atlanta (Dorothy Alexander), San Francisco (Willam Christensen), Dayton (Josephine and Hermene Schwarz), Chicago (Ruth Page and Bentley Stone), and Philadelphia (Catherine Littlefield), founded ballet companies and schools, albeit on a smaller scale, throughout the country. Eventually these organizations gave rise to what became known, not always happily, as America's regional ballet movement. In the initial locales and further regions American ballet took root and variously took off. Among the notable flowerings into the late twentieth century are the Pennsylvania Ballet, the Boston Ballet, the Houston Ballet, Pacific Northwest Ballet, the State Ballet of Missouri, and the Pittsburgh Ballet.

By the mid-1950s, an unlikely ballet-trained young man named Robert Joffrey (1928–1988) went on his way to establish a regional-scale ballet troupe with New York City–style aspirations. Eventually called the Joffrey Ballet, the smaller sibling of NYCB and ABT gained prominence as the United States's third-tier ballet contender. The younger generation Joffrey set his troupe's sights somewhere between those of NYCB and ABT. The former presented itself largely, though not exclusively as one man's—Balanchine's—creative workshop. The latter showcased multiple and successive contemporary choreographic voices alongside stagings of so-called classics and/or popular favorites from the past.

Joffrey, a self-made ballet enthusiast, counterbalanced his own study of ballet technique (with a far from ideal physique) with an avid interest in ballet history. His company, built more on the scale of the average "regional" troupe, would partly become a workshop for the often-fulsome choreography of his co-artistic partner Gerald Arpino and for the latest-trend evocations by the scene's younger generation. Additionally, Joffrey's ensemble troupe pursued a sidelight of retrieving "disappeared" landmarks of ballet history. Ballet pundits reduced the three leading American ballet institutions during the 1970s boom years to: Neoclassical for Balanchine's company, Classical for Chase's, and Pop for Joffrey's. None proved entirely accurate, but all stuck, at least on the surface.

By the mid-1970s each of the Big Three in U.S. ballet went into a high gear all its own. Balanchine directed and dominated two festivals of all new ballets. One in 1972 celebrated the music of Igor Stravinsky; another, in 1975, the music of Maurice Ravel. At that time ABT's star dancer ranks increased. Notable name dancers such as Makarova and Baryshnikov upped the ante to superstar status. Few of the old or, especially, new ballets in which ABT presented its stellar dancers, proved especially memorable, but the star-loving public came regardless. At the Joffrey, rare restagings of historically important ballets made news. A series of these were by Massine, including the 1917 Diaghilev-commissioned *Parade* (1973), with designs by Picasso.

Robert Joffrey went at the task of restaging long-unseen works from the past with a "bring 'em back alive" verve. As an intensely avid, self-made ballet historian, he left no stone unturned in his effort to put onstage a work that included all the documented details that were part of the original staging. "Reconstruction" was the name given to restaging works that didn't have a continuous performance history.

Some of the hiatuses between a work's most recent performances and Joffrey's revivals proved longer than others. But if Joffrey put his mind to restaging a work, he didn't let the fallow years, no matter how long running, stop him. Between 1967 and 1976, Joffrey oversaw the restaging of four seldom seen ballets by Jooss (*The Green Table*, *The Big City*, *A Ball in Old Vienna*, all from 1932, and *Pavanne on the Death of an Infanta* from 1929) and three by Massine (*Le Tricorne*, 1919, *Le Beau Danube*, 1933, and *Pulcinella*, 1920, in addition to *Parade*).

For brand-new ballets, Joffrey looked outside his company as well as in. Sometimes he strayed quite far afield. Eventually, his commissions for works from outside the confines of ballet proper gave impetus and prominence to a new wing of the ballet repertory. The name most frequently suggested was that of the "cross over" ballet.

Chapter 23

AT WAR AND PEACE WITH MODERN DANCE

To understand crossover ballet, it's necessary to look back over the preceding decades. At the start of the twentieth century, when Europe's ballet was gaining a foothold in America, an original dance form, variously named as barefoot, aesthetic, interpretive, or modern dance sprang up. In the beginning the two—ballet and modern—coexisted as sworn enemies. Russian ballet reformer Michel Fokine found little to admire in the theatrical dance alternative. He once characterized modern dance as "ugly mother standing in wings watching ugly daughter perform ugly movements on stage as ugly son make ugly sounds on drum, is modern dance." The likewise ugly disagreements back and forth counteraccused ballet of being European, elitist, artificial, and effete. Modern dance, the argument went, was American, democratic, natural, and expressive.

The battle, however, didn't last. By the 1940s even staunch modernists like Martha Graham suggested that her dancers, at least her male dancers, bone up with the aid of ballet technique classes. In 1947, ABT commissioned modernist Valerie Bettis to choreograph a new work, called *Virginia Reel*. Tudor, with his use of ballet moves to reveal the psychology of his ballet's characters, helped break the ice that supposedly prevented ballet methods from being expressive, and therefore serious. Dancer-turned-choreographer Glen Tetley (1926–), trained in both modern and ballet, began creating works for ballet companies during the 1960s. His *Ricercare* (1966) came from an ABT commission. His signature became a modern-dance-inspired love of floorwork and a love of lifts, usually for sleekly clad male and female dancers in unisex leotards.

In 1973, Joffrey commissioned a postmodern experimentalist named Twyla Tharp (1941–) to make a ballet for his company. To assure the presence of her own brand of quirky dancing in a work made for a differently geared group, Tharp included her company of modernists alongside Joffrey's ballet dancers. She named her ballet choreographed with two companies *Deuce Coupe*, after a Beach Boys' song she used as a score. With its ballet-skilled young men and women performing gracefully alongside boogaloo-happy modernists, Tharp gave the Joffrey a zany mix of a ballet that became a hit, and put the idea of such experimentation before the public in a new way.

Tharp's interest in ballet and its dancers reached new heights when ABT commissioned a work from her. The 1976 *Push Comes to Shove* starred classical ballet's then supreme exemplar Baryshnikov, framed by other ABT principal and ensemble dancers. With such a high-profile success to its credit, crossover ballet became part of ballet's formerly "closed shop."

Ballet, it turned out, was where the dancers were, and where the big-time attention tended to be. During this period of growing "outside" interest, modernists with reputations for success in their own worlds were willingly coaxed to moonlight in ballet. Joffrey continued to explore the crossover experimentation he had a hand in selling to the public and ABT kept toying with the idea, including further Tharp commissions.

Balanchine, though consistently open to including diverse choreographic voices at NYCB, never saw fit to look outside ballet's own confines. Isolated examples of Graham for a 1959 collaborative ballet (*Episodes*) and Merce Cunningham, a former Graham dancer who had studied at SAB for *The Seasons* (1947, Ballet Society) and *Summerspace* (1966), all stood as exceptions. The expatriate Russian once succinctly explained their presence in his company matter-of-factly as "friends of Lincoln's."

Kirstein, ever interested in presenting ballet as a living, contemporary art, kept seeking ways to interconnect ballet with the aesthetics of the day. Balanchine, a grateful recipient of Kirstein's promotion, found no reason to thwart his benefactor's ideas. He also saw no reason to adopt the "modern dance" aspects of such thinking himself. The classical ballet master once described the difference between his approach to dancing and that of a contemporary modernist: "She wants every one of her dancers to dance like her; I want my dancers to dance like themselves."

After overseeing a festival of Tchaikovsky and another Stravinsky celebration, Balanchine fell ill and died in 1983. NYCB's organization, which included its affiliated School of American Ballet, was initially run by Peter Martins, Jerome Robbins, and Kirstein, but eventually Martins held the job solo. The Royal Danish Ballet dancer, who retired from the stage to concentrate on his director's duties, had begun to choreograph while still a dancer for Balanchine. His consciously classical dance making betrayed a self-consciously neoclassical bent. For an American Music Festival (1988), the first of NYCB's post-Balanchine new ballet festivals, Martins commissioned several non-ballet choreographers to create new ballets for his company.

Once Baryshnikov found himself at the helm of administrating ABT, he called a halt to the stream of casting guest dancers to lead the repertory which by this period had reached overflow proportions. Baryshnikov's aim was to build a stronger ensemble company and to reward the best of those dancers with the best leading parts. For repertory he produced a mix of works. Two main sources fed his purposes: nineteenth-century classics he knew from Kirov stagings and twentieth-century Balanchine works he'd come to know from acquaintance with NYCB.

The new works Baryshnikov acquired also had two strains. One came from honoring ABT's tradition of full-length classics, which in some measure Baryshnikov took a direct hand in re-creating and rethinking. Previously, Lucia Chase had given him commissions to stage fresh versions of *The Nutcracker* (1976) and *Don Quixote* (1978). For his own company he rethought *Cinderella* (co-created with Peter Anastos in 1983) and *Swan Lake* (1988). His commissioning of brand-new contemporary ballets went to a mixed array of choreographers, a good many of whom were not associated with classical ballet. These included Lynn Taylor-Corbett (1946–), David Gordon (1936–), Karole Armitage (1954–), David Parsons (1959–), and Mark Morris (1956–). Beyond marking profound changeovers in almost all the world's major ballet institutions, the 1980s also witnessed the bottoming out of the much touted ballet boom.

Joffrey continued to commission attention-getting crossover ballets as well as historical revivals. The most newsworthy of the latter came in 1987. It took the form of an educated-guess reconstruction of Nijinsky's long-lost 1913 *Le Sacre du Printemps*. The grand plan was put together by dance historian/researcher Millicent Hodson and her art historian husband, Kenneth Archer. In addition to "new" old ballets and brand-new works by newcomers, Arpino continued to provide confections of his own. In 1988, when Joffrey succumbed to AIDS, the founder's focus ended and the troupe went into a period of uncertainty.

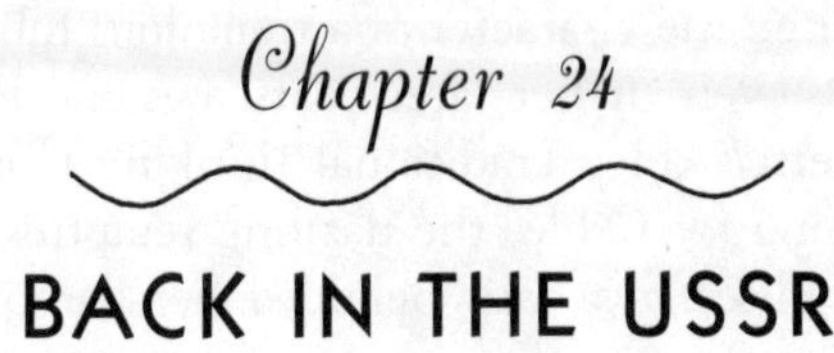

Chapter 24

BACK IN THE USSR

Between the Bolshevik Revolution and the mid-1950s, the Russian ballet continued in virtual isolation from the rest of the world. The companies of Leningrad's Kirov Theater and of Moscow's Bolshoi dominated all of Soviet ballet. No full-scale sampling toured outside the Communist Iron Curtain to Free World countries and reports from visiting correspondents, random films, and the odd small-scale tour gave the West its only tastes of the once unparalleled imperial ballet. (Marking the first tour of Soviet ballet dancers, Leningrad's Vahktang Chabukiani and stellar ballerina Tatiana Vecheslova [1910–1991] appeared in the States in 1934.)

During the mid-1950s, fuller forces came, full force. Paris got a conglomerate troupe in 1954; London, an all-Bolshoi company in 1956. New York got a similar Bolshoi in 1959. Most of the attention from these appearances focused on the dancers. Galina Ulanova (1910–), who was then in her late forties and who danced in the 1940 premiere of Lavrovksy's *Romeo and Juliet*, was still performing her role. Honored as "prima ballerina assoluta" by a Soviet system continuing a title established by the tsar's ballet, Ulanova gained much attention and acclaim in the West.

Maya Plisetskaya (1925–), Ulanova's temperamental opposite, became the superstar for the next Bolshoi generation. Niece to the Bolshoi's groundbreaking leading male dancer, Asaf Messerer (1903–1992), Plisetskaya became her uncle's most renowned pupil. Bold of accent, lean of limb, and long of neck, the Bolshoi ballerina prided herself on taking class with the men and emulating their prowess. If Ulanova epitomized the character of a tremulous Juliet, Plisetskaya's emblematic role, even in her later years, became the dual one of *Swan Lake*'s Odette/Odile. Traditional thinking found her athletic powers more fitting for Odile, the dazzling temptress and imposter, while plenty of Plisetskaya fans heralded her baroquely serpentine Odette, the White Swan queen.

Messerer, a pupil of Gorsky's, had made his mark as a dancer by showing forceful athletic skill. His technical feats, such as landing a double air-turn in an arabesque pose, specifically enriched the vocabulary of the male dancer, first in Russia and then, by example, around the ballet world. Eventually his class of perfection was schooling dancers beyond his own virtuoso skills.

Aleksei Yermolayev (1910–1975), a product of the Leningrad school who later joined the Bolshoi, also advanced the art of Soviet male dancing. Something of a kindred spirit to Chabukiani's fiery personality, Yermolayev demonstrated impressive athletic strength, especially in the elevation of jumps, and a vivid burning personality in his histrionic acting. Yuri Zhdanov (1925–1986) and Nicolai Fadeyechev (1933–), both frequent partners of Ulanova (and in Fadeyechev's case, Plisetskaya), represented a cooler temperament for athletic Bolshoi dancing.

While other individual male dancers caught attention here and there, it was the emphatic, forthright dancing of the male contingent overall that gained notice on its Western tours. Soviet ballet's taste for acrobatics pervaded its choreography, and the deft yet unshakable strength of the men with big lifts and sometimes big catches of its ballerinas presented a picture of unusual physical strength. (It should be stressed that in Eastern Europe the circus is considered an art form of its own, not simply a quantitative spectacle.)

But the influence worked both ways: Outside its inner sanctum, Soviet ballet learned how hopelessly naive and old-fashioned its narratives and characterizations could strike others. By the early 1960s, a choreographic voice who had experienced Paris sought to refresh Soviet ballet. Yuri Grigorovich (1927–), a dancer turned choreographer, captured the attention of both the Soviet and Western ballet worlds. While under the thumb of official censors, he didn't dare stray into the forbidden world of formalist abstract ballet, but he did try to choose his narrative subjects with an eye for shaping them into ballet theater that didn't rely on the silent movie–style acting with which he grew up. Modernizing Soviet ballet to Grigorovich meant working with an all-dancing, no-pantomime formula.

After gaining a name in Leningrad's Kirov Ballet with *The Stone Flower* (to Prokofiev, 1957) and *The Legend of Love* (to Arif Melikov, 1961), Grigorovich landed squarely on the ballet map in 1968 with his staging of *Spartacus* for the Bolshoi Ballet, where he had become artistic director and ballet master four years earlier. *Spartak*, as the ballet and its Shostakovich score were already known in Soviet Russia, takes the life of a heroic, rebellious Roman slave for its subject.

Before Grigorovich's version, the ballet had been produced twice with little success. With the new staging, audiences in both the Soviet Union and, eventually, the West took to its sweeping, broad-stroke action and vivid characterizations, as did many critics from the respective locales where the Bolshoi traveled. Even those who didn't take wholeheartedly to Grigorovich's all-dance, no-pantomime scheme tended to praise the ballet's all-heart-and-soul dancers. Bolshoi Ballet artists such as Maris Liepa (1936–1990), Vladimir Vasiliev (1940–), Natalia Bessmertnova (1941–), Ekaterina Maximova (1939–), and Nina Timofeyeva (1935–) all led early performances of Grigorovich's *Spartacus*, as each then entered the pantheon of great Russian dancers.

In Leningrad, where the older, cooler, more refined Petersburg schooling still held sway, leading male dancer Konstantin Sergeyev (1910–1992) was in charge. Less a choreographer of original ballets and more a restager of older ballets, Sergeyev gave the world his Petipa productions of *Raymonda* in 1948, *Swan Lake* in 1950, and *Sleeping Beauty* in 1952. Because of the Maryinsky Theater pedigree as the revered "House of Petipa," many equated these stagings with the hallowed originals of ballet history. In fact, Sergeyev himself, and Vaganova and Lopukhov before him, took a strong hand in giving these sacrosanct ballets their classic shape.

Sergeyev's dancers, like those under Grigorovich, included some of ballet's most notable artists. Once they began to tour outside the Soviet Union—which they got to do when the Kirov followed the

Bolshoi's lead—these men and women set standards as high as, and yet different from, those of the Grigorovich's dancers. The top-rank roster of Sergeyev's Kirov included Yuri Soloviev (1940–1977), Irina Kolpakova (1933–), Alla Sizova (1939–), and Alla Osipenko (1932–). This list reads even more impressively when considering the exclusion of the Kirov's biggest late-twentieth-century names: Nureyev, Makarova, and Baryshnikov. So big were the holes left by these defections from the Kirov that by the second defection—Makarova's in 1970—Sergeyev lost his job as company director.

Oleg Vinogradov (1937–), who eventually assumed directorship of the Kirov, had little or nothing to say as a choreographer. Some of his stagings of Petersburg classics—after-Petipa, after-Sergeyev, after-Vaganova, after-Lopukhov—proved, with odd exceptions, to be worthy heirs to their august histories. But once more it was the dancers he developed that distinguished his regime. These included Tatiana Terekhova (1952–), Konstantin Zaklinsky (1955–), Altinai Asylmuratova (1961–), Zhanna Ayupova (1966–), Faruk Ruzimatov (1963–), and Yulia Makhalina.

Chapter 25

FAR FROM DENMARK

By the mid-twentieth century, Copenhagen's Royal Danish Ballet was more than two hundred years old. With the 1879 passing of Bournonville, its most influential and prominent ballet master, the troupe proceeded to live comfortably on its past. Hans Beck (1861–1952), once a dancer under Bournonville, kept his predecessor's specifically Danish romantic era ballets on the stage, in good order. In the early decades of the twentieth century, with a sense that ballet history was passing Copenhagen by, the Royal Danish Ballet invited first Fokine and then Balanchine to work with its dancers. Neither innovator made Copenhagen his home, but one of Beck's pupils, the Danish-born-and-schooled Harald Lander (1905–1971), took over where the guests left off.

In his efforts as Royal Ballet Master from 1932 to 1951, Lander consciously stressed a twentieth-century profile for an alma mater steeped in Old World nineteenth-century traditions. Lander's directorship encouraged both revivals of classic works (by Bournonville and others) and premieres of ballets made especially for the dancers under him. Under his regime, classical dancers such as Margot Lander (1910–1961), Toni Lander (1931–1985), Børge Ralov (1908–1981), as well as Erik Bruhn came to national and, in the cases of Toni Lander and Bruhn, international prominence.

Études, originally made for the Royal Danes in 1948 as *Étude*, starring Margot Lander, became Harald Lander's best-known ballet after he revamped it for the Paris Opera Ballet in 1952. For a score,

Lander chose well-known piano-fingering exercises by Karl Czerny (specially arranged for orchestra by Knudåge Riisager). The classical, classroom ballet's aim was to make dance theater out of the barest bones of ballet practice itself. Once outside the confines of Royal Danish decorum and its nineteenth-century-nuanced dancing, Lander's ballet turned into a showy, almost circuslike display of one-upmanship technique. Beyond its new life in Paris, *Études* found particular favor in the repertories of English National Ballet (formerly London Festival Ballet) and ABT.

Under Lander's directorship, the Royal Danish Ballet began to tour and show its strengths, subtle and otherwise, outside its homeland. As a result, the greater ballet world developed an eager taste for Bournonville's local color masterworks, and for the way the Danes enlivened their humane characterizations. Rich, vivid pantomime stood out among the company's impressive strengths as much as, or in some cases even more than, keen dancing prowess.

Once the Danes gained an interested and impressed foreign audience, the expertise of its male dancers was widely heralded. Henning Kronstam (1934–1995), Fleming Flindt (1936–), and Niels Kehlet (1938–) gained top laurels after Bruhn, who was variously hailed as the age's most nearly perfect exponent of classical ballet. (These expert opinions included that of Aleksandr Pushkin, Nureyev's and the Kirov Ballet's revered male pedagogue.) One reason for the extra-strong showing of traditionally strong Danish ballet men came from the tutelage of Vera Volkova (1904–1975), a Russian émigré who became the company's artistic advisor and pedagogue after Lander left.

Under Volkova's pedagogy and the successive directorships of Flindt and Kronstam, both former pupils, the Danes refortified their Bournonville past with touches of the present. As a result, certain technical details were upgraded; for example, pirouettes gained virtuoso dimensions and the women's pointe work gained new prominence and technical strength.

Soon after the troupe began to tour widely, individual Danes departed to pursue their careers outside Denmark. Stanley Williams (1925–1997) left the Royal company and became an influential teacher at SAB. Besides Bruhn, Toni Lander, Peter Martins (1946–),

Adam Lüders (1950–), and Ib Andersen (1954–), all made their fame as much or more outside Copenhagen as in. In the case of these men, each was hired by Balanchine and featured with due prominence in his shaping of the repertory at NYCB. In the case of Martins, his stellar performing career at NYCB evolved into an even more prominent position as director.

Chapter 26

LEADING MALE DANCERS LEAD

When just about every leading ballet company needed to find a new director in the 1980s, something of a trend developed for filling the post: leading male dancers with little or no experience in choreography invariably got the jobs. Baryshnikov took on artistic direction of ABT in 1980 and Martins began directing NYCB in 1983. Nureyev became director of the Paris Opera Ballet, also in 1983, and stayed on until 1989. He was succeeded by Paris's own star dancer, Patrick Dupond (1959–), who held the position until 1995.

Anthony Dowell (1943–), England's exemplar of male classical ballet dancing, became artistic director of his Royal Ballet in 1986. Peter Schaufuss (1949–), a stellar and restless alumnus of the Royal Danish Ballet, served as artistic director of London Festival Ballet (now English National Ballet) from 1984 through 1990; he directed his Royal Danish alma mater troupe from '94 to '95.

NYCB stellar dancers Edward Villella and Helgi Tomasson (1942–) each became artistic directors upon leaving the company Balanchine established. After a series of short-lived ventures, Villella established Miami City Ballet in 1986, and has continued as its artistic director. Tomasson, trained in Iceland, Denmark, and America, took over the pop-inclined San Francisco Ballet in 1985 and made it into a more classically based company.

So far the biggest contributions of these men's directorships have been less in the realm of adding to historically important pieces of choreography and more in the area of developing important dancers. Kyra Nichols (1958–), inherited from Balanchine's era, tops a list of illustrious NYCB ballerinas. Beyond her, it was the men of Martins's company who took the laurels: Damian Woetzel, Peter Boal, Ethan Steifel, and Kirov import Igor Zelenski. At ABT, legacies from Baryshnikov's efforts include Julie Kent and Wes Chapman. In the case of Tomasson's upgraded SFB the presence of the company and the school's Elizabeth Loscavio helped gain the troupe high praise. The eventual presence of Yuri Posokhov, a Bolshoi-trained dancer, added further luster to SFB.

One of the biggest effects Nureyev had on the bastion of the Paris Opera came in the area of promoting young dancers. Danseur étoile Manuel Legris tops the list of Nureyev's male ranks, with danseuse étoile Sylvie Guillem more than topping the ballerina roster. Guillem's appearance on the international ballet scene had an effect similar to that of Pavlova and Suzanne Farrell before her. Her extreme flexibility, leanness, and sky-reaching extensions prompted artistic directors from Moscow to Melbourne to seek female dancers with similar traits. London's Royal Ballet already had a dancer of related and, some would say, superior gifts in Darcey Bussell, a protégée of MacMillan's. As luck would have it, just as Guillem was making a name for herself and Nureyev's Paris Opera regime, the gymnast turned dancer left to become permanent guest artist with Dowell's Royal Ballet.

In Russia, with the Soviet Union dissolved, the ballet circuit became much less tightly controlled and much less lavishly financed. Dissatisfaction with Grigorovich, who represented something of Soviet dictatorship style, led to the appointment of Vasiliev as artistic director of Moscow's Bolshoi Theater in '95.

The final judgment of history's harsh reality still awaits a good many of these artistic directors from similar backgrounds. Baryshnikov has left the ballet directing and dancing phase of his career to pursue a modern dance–based alternative as guiding light and leading performer for the White Oak Dance Project, a non-ballet troupe of variously schooled dancers.

Meanwhile, in Germany, two American men who hardly made names for themselves as leading male dancers comparable to the men listed above became leading forces of European ballet. Wisconsin-born John Neumeier (1942–), artistic director of the Hamburg Ballet since 1973, headed the ballet troupe and later the ballet school of the state-subsidized opera house. His lengthy canon of works includes a bent toward dramatic effect through imposed intellectual theorizing.

To the tastes of Europe, where Neumeier's works are popular well beyond Hamburg, his streamlined and bare-bones dance pictures look Balanchinean. To American tastes, where his work has not found a strong audience, his intellectualization of music and deconstructionist rethinking of standard librettos appears more Béjartian. Neumeier's choreography for standard concert symphonic music, especially that of Gustav Mahler, more closely connects his aesthetic to Massine than to Balanchine.

William Forsythe (1949–), a former member of the Joffrey and Stuttgart ballets, became artistic director of Germany's Frankfurt Ballet in 1984. In his position as chief choreographer, the Europeanized American created a body of works that captured the interest of just about every other artistic director of his generation. His often grand scale, austere extravagant spectacles, with throbbing and boisterous electronic scores, dramatic lighting, and body-revealing costuming represented for many the latest word in contemporary ballet. The nature of his theatrical effects and the occasional inclusion of absurdist spoken monologues connect his ballet theater to the dramatic theater of another American-born European guru, theater and opera director Robert Wilson.

James Kudelka (1955–), a Canadian-born and trained dancer, has gained a similar reputation as a leading choreographer in Canada. Of the three companies that play leading roles in Canadian ballet—Les Grands Ballets Canadiens in Montreal (established 1956/57), the Royal Winnipeg Ballet in Winnipeg (established 1938/39), and National Ballet of Canada in Toronto (established 1951)—Kudelka has had strong connections to both the Montreal and Toronto institutions. His choreography has also been prominent at American companies such as ABT, SFB, and the Joffrey. In 1996 Kudelka assumed the artistic directorship at NBC where his often modern-dance-like ballet interests have a place to evolve and expand.

Chapter 27

HARLEM, CUBA, CHINA, JAPAN, SOUTH AMERICA

About ten years before the aforementioned succession of male dancers took the reins of companies wanting new directors, a leading male dancer with NYCB made a different move. Arthur Mitchell (1934–), the first black man to reach principal dancer status at NYCB, left Balanchine's company. With his mentor's support and encouragement, he started a troupe of his own dedicated to offering opportunities in ballet to disadvantaged youth. First, like Balanchine, Mitchell opened a school. With the full-time assistance of Karel Shook (1920–1985), a teacher dedicated to offering ballet training to people of color, the Dance Theatre of Harlem (DTH) was founded in 1968. Its school opened in 1969. Its company's first professional performances began in 1971.

Various ballets by Balanchine and original works commissioned by Mitchell, who only occasionally created choreography himself, helped shape the DTH repertory. Frequently the offerings stressed the "theater" element Mitchell intentionally put into his organization's name. A mini-repertory of ballets by designer-and-choreographer Geoffrey Holder (1930–) focused on the Afro-Caribbean-related music and dance forms. Holder's *Dougla* (1974) became an early signature work. Set to a score of drumming and dressed like a grandly orchestrated carnival, Holder's ritualistic parade promoted the company's classical virtues even though it utilized none of classical ballet's signature details, such as pointe work or pirouettes.

As Balanchine did before him, Mitchell specifically rethought the ballet classics he acquired for his company. *Firebird* (1982) and *Giselle* (1984) became two of DTH's most popular efforts. In the case of the former, Stravinsky's Russian fairy tale acquired new tropical-forest details according to fantastical scenic and costume designs by Holder. John Taras (1919–), a ballet master with strong connections to Balanchine, created new choreography befitting the relocated tale. The company's *Giselle*, sometimes called *Creole Giselle*, remade a Slavic folk-tale set in the Rhineland as an American tale located in the bayous of Louisiana. Former Ballets Russes de Monte Carlo leading dancer Frederic Franklin (1914–) restaged the ballet largely according to the familiar Coralli-Perrot-Petipa version, all the while adding appropriate shadings to accommodate the new libretto.

By the late twentieth century, the world's various ballet schools and companies existed without direct links to the spheres of Western European aristocratic courts that gave birth to the art form. Early in the century world tours of the indefatigable Pavlova took her to places like Cuba, Chile, and Japan. Cuba had already seen the likes of Fanny and Therese Elssler on their tours in the mid-nineteenth century. By the mid-twentieth century, local ballet classes helped inspire dance careers for brothers Fernando (1914–) and Alberto (1917–) Alonso. A similar inspiration augmented by foreign study gave rise to the international fame of Cuban-born Alicia Alonso, Fernando's wife. (The virtuoso ballerina led Balanchine to create a classical showpiece called *Theme and Variations* in 1947 for Ballet Theatre.) In 1948, the brothers Fernando and Alberto Alonso, as director and choreographer respectively, teamed up with ballerina Alonso to create Ballet Alicia Alonso. Soon this troupe and an affiliate school became the Ballet de Cuba, and finally, after the Revolution, Ballet Nacional de Cuba. As would happen in China later, Communist allied countries regularly received support from the closely knit system of ballet in the Soviet Union.

Ballet came slowly to isolated Japan. During the second decade of the twentieth century, European teachers opened schools there. Russian dancers toured during the twenties, notably Pavlova in 1921. American interpretive dance and the "music visualizations" of Denishawn also left favorable impressions in Japan on tour, as did the budding Chicago-based ballet of Ruth Page, in 1926. A number of semiprofessional troupes sprang up in the wake of these appearances. Ballerina Mikiko Matsuyama founded the Matsuyama Ballet in Tokyo in 1948. With Matsuyama's ardent Communist husband, Masao Shimizu, as director, the Japanese company made a strong impression on tours to China. One of the most welcome offerings on a 1958 tour was *The White-Haired Girl*, a ballet staging of a popular piece of Chinese opera. Since then the company and its school have continued and grown under second-generation leadership from Mikiko and Masao's son, Tetsutaro Shimizu, working alongside his ballerina wife, Yoko Morishita.

In 1960, under the influential tutelage of Soviet teachers, another Tokyo-based ballet organization began. With its beginnings as a performance wing of the school, the first to teach ballet according to the Russian method, the Tokyo Ballet matured into a company strongly influenced by foreign ballet masters. A Bolshoi-pedigree *Giselle* was staged in 1966, French choreographies came in 1969, and Alberto Alonso's *Carmen* in 1972. The troupe made an extensive tour of Europe in 1975, and in 1976 held a ballet festival that featured such guest artists as Margot Fonteyn, Alicia Alonso, and Maya Plisetskaya. The festival has continued every three years, ever since.

Ballet came in earnest to China only after the establishment of the People's Republic of China, with its links to Soviet Russia. Russian teachers from both the Bolshoi and Kirov companies helped establish the country's two main ballet schools. One was in Beijing, another in Shanghai. Dai Ai-lian (1916–), an English-schooled dancer and pedagogue, took charge of running the Beijing school (established 1959), and its affiliate company, Central Ballet of China, so designated in 1980. The other school, Shanghai School of Dance, opened in 1960. Both ballet centers in China included in their training ingredients of the country's centuries-old practice of virtuoso acrobatics, as well as some indication of its equally old martial arts.

With its first flowering during the years known as the Cultural Revolution, Chinese ballet gravitated to bluntly propagandist works. Two such creations dominated the repertory. Beijing produced *The Red Detachment of Women* and Shanghai created *The White-Haired Girl*. Each realistically set, multi-act narrative ballet, with specially commissioned scores from Chinese composers, included the presence of rifle-wielding women on pointe. One couldn't, however, confuse these 1964 ballets with their nineteenth-century Romantic ballet antecedents. In the 1846 ballet *Catarina, ou la Fille du Bandits*, Lucille Grahn wore a standard ballet skirt and brandished her firearm as a pretty prop. In the twentieth-century Chinese ballets, no such frivolity was allowed. In fact, tutu-style skirts were forbidden; any showing off of legs was unthinkable. As a matter of course, uniform female ballet dress consisted of pajamalike trousers, cut for a thigh-concealing modesty. This changed with the end of the Cultural Revolution, and a more pervasive Russian ballet influence prevailed, complete with standard ballet skirts, tights, and toe shoes.

Chapter 28

POST-SCRIPT: DANCERS, DANCERS, DANCERS

Unlike the history of opera (ballet's one-time symbiotic sibling), the history of ballet does not conveniently trail off during the twentieth century. There is significantly more to ballet's present than living on the glories of its past. Ballet lives on actively, and regularly finds new works produced almost as readily as new dancers. For convenience's sake, this narrative ends in the 1990s. An awareness of the three hundred years prior to this era helps the interested ballet-goer fit his or her own ballet watching into the continuing story of ballet history.

Each time we witness ballet in our era, we can't help but fortify our view with precedents that indicate how the current example weighs against former ones. With the apt presence of the Sun King so prominent in ballet's beginnings, we might smile and say how there is nothing new under the sun, even as we attend some ballet's world premiere. There are, however, constantly and gratifyingly, plenty of new dancers under the sun.

Ballet's history, like most histories of the performing arts, often dwells on the creator of "the work"—in our particular case, the choreographer. In related film history and film theory language, we view ballet's history in "auteur" terms. Many a ballet enthusiast will likely argue, however, that first and foremost the public goes to the ballet for its dancers. As we have briefly seen, some promoters have played directly to such motivation and headlined star dancers "above the title" (as Hollywood would say) of the company or of the repertory being offered. At the end of the proverbial day, in the equation balancing the ballet being performed and the dancers performing it, the scales tip toward the importance of the dancers themselves.

Certainly, the choreographed ballets and, as a result, the creators of them play an incontrovertible role in the history and process of ballet. But it remains in the bodies of the dancers to flesh out the aims of the choreographer. The boys and girls (in the case of child dancers) and men and women of the ballet stage are ultimately what we see at the ballet.

Dancers, however, are more humanly fragile and susceptible to injury, so ballet advertising usually emphasizes the ballets being offered. George Balanchine voiced the trouble with ballet marketing on the strength of its most popular dancers by noting that if an advertised dancer was unable to appear, he'd have to give the people their money back. Invariably, however, as ballet advertisements sell numerous ballets by name, they're still dominated by overwhelmingly strong pictures of the company's most eye-catching dancers or dancer.

· II ·

The Dancers

Chapter 1

LADIES AND GENTLEMEN OF THE BALLET

Texts accompanied by illustrative plates in historical books of ballet tell us a little about where our dancers come from. The carefully practiced art of dancing held a key place among the "arts of the gentleman" (fencing, musicianship, and riding were others). Acrobatic skills and feats also became part of the dancer's art; so did mummery, the pantomimic art of playacting in unusual costumes and masks.

With the establishment of full-time dancing academies, as opposed to isolated lessons in the rites of passage for well-bred young adults, professional dance training entailed an incremental process that began in childhood. In his 1737 letter to the empress of Russia, French ballet master Jean Baptiste Landé requested a dozen Russian children (six boys and six girls) to start a school. The St. Petersburg institution grew to be one of the most renowned in the world, and its select pupils became known as the "children of Theater Street." (The appellation, from the street where the school was located, also served as the title of a 1977 documentary film about the institution, narrated by Princess Grace of Monaco and now available on video.)

As women began playing a greater part in ballets, the art of dancing grew in details specifically suited to the female physique. Acrobatic stunts for standing on the toe tips led to the art of pointe work, which women perfected as their own. In Paris, the children of the ballet academy became known as "les petits rats"; in the States, an even slangier nickname for young, female ballet students was coined: "bun heads." The French argot refers to the girls' lithe, all-limbs physique; the American phrase focuses on the tightly and neatly pulled back and knotted hairstyles almost universal to the look of the girl ballet student.

You can decide for yourself if your interest in ballet and its dancers coincides more with notions stressing that "ballet is woman," as George Balanchine prominently voiced, or that "ballet is man," as Maurice Béjart liked to proclaim. Or, that the presence of both men and women dancers means that ballet is equally male and female, as voices for equality like to maintain.

Of the prevalent attitudes toward gender in ballet, the one toward female supremacy now has a longer and more popular history. In the scheme of standard English grammar, the reflexive pronoun "he," automatically preferred for following nouns with no specified gender, was regularly changed in the case of "dancer." Until the watchful practices of our current age, dance literature would repeatedly presume to bypass standard usage and write "the dancer . . . she." (The sometimes oppressively anti-ballet thinking of feminist writing in the so-called dance studies of higher education is likely to pass over this lapse, or construe it as yet another example of anti-woman sentiment. Such watchdog thinking probably assumes that the word *she* is chosen because the word *dancer*, after years of connection to women, has largely negative connotations.) In some quarters "the dancer . . . she" was automatically associated with the woman, beautiful and mysterious. In the words of a very Old World, very non-feminist Russian balletomane, recognizing a dancer was simple: "Show me her face, and I'll tell you if she can dance."

Technically, dancers are made, not born. Realistically, however, natural gifts make the process more agreeable and the dancer more special. One of the reasons Balanchine gave to defend his view that women were ballet's dominating force stemmed from his view of the inherent flexibility and pliability of the female physique. The athletic practice known as gymnastics would seem to corroborate this. Men and women gymnasts compete in near-equal measure, except in the realm of "rhythmic" gymnastics, which includes only women. (From the extremely attenuated and extraordinarily flexible look of world champion rhythmic gymnasts, it would appear that few if any male physiques could approximate the characteristics of these women. We have only to look briefly at the men's floor exercises to see how much less inherently flexible even highly skilled male gymnasts are. For a point of fact, pay close attention to the different look of the men and the women as they extend and hold their lifted legs to the side.)

Before separating the men from the women for our purposes of looking at dancers, we can look at male and female students together. Though the biggest and most specialized schools hold separate classes for boys and girls from the very beginning of their training programs, they don't really have to. Ballet basics are basic to the dancing of both men and women. Most experts agree that the ages of nine or ten mark a good starting point for ballet training. Some systems, such as the school of the Paris Opera, include eight-year-olds. Many smaller schools and individual teachers take students even younger, but these individuals must work with extreme care not to stress the child's delicately developing muscles and bones. (Unfortunately, some still do not, to disastrous results to legs and feet.)

All classes begin at the barre. The horizontally fixed pole, traditionally of wood and fixed slightly away from the wall, serves to support the dance student as he works with one side of his body at a time. (The functional use of the barre is said to come from an earlier use of a hanging cord, like a bellpull, on which a courtier could anchor himself while practicing various ways for swinging or kicking his leg.) The youngest ballet pupils often begin their training in a ballet classroom with work that asks them to hold on to the barre with two hands, while facing it. In special cases the pupils actually stand behind the barre, delicately pinned where their backs can feel firm straight support against the wall.

Barre-work is primarily stationary. The student works one side of the body at a time more or less remaining standing in one place. Beginning exercises stress elongated, vertical posture centered by an erect, lifted spine. The *battement tendu*, an energetically stretched action of the foot leading the leg, is often simply called *tendu*. The movement trains the dancer's limbs to stretch out and away from a specific position of the feet, and then to return to that same precise position.

Historically there are five set positions for the feet. These began life in court dancing, and have continued into the classrooms and stages of contemporary ballet. In First Position, the feet support turned-out legs by pointing to the extreme side, with the heels touching. In this way, the feet in first position form a continuous, straight line cutting across the viewer's path, left-to-right/right-to-left. Second Position, or *Seconde* in Franglais balletspeak, opens the heel touching First Position so that a space about equal to the length of one of the dancer's feet separates the stance. Third Position, a nowadays rarely used stance best suited to seventeenth- and eighteenth-century ball-room manners, closes the First Position in so that the heel of one foot overlaps the heel of the other. Fourth Position, is another opened stance. Instead of keeping both feet in a side-to-side alignment, this stance has one foot directly aligned in front of the other. Thus, the heel of the one foot aligns with the toes of the other and vice versa at a figurative one-foot space interval. Fifth position closes fourth so that the alignment of heel-to-toes and toes-to-heel has one foot and leg touching the other. This is the tightest or most closed of the stances; it's considered the strongest. Fifth position gives the dancer his most compact base, readying him to move or extend either leg or foot in any direction with a minimal readjustment of balance.

In addition to working for strong stretch in the legs and for automatic return of the foot from an outstretching position to a precise, stable one, *tendu* practice aims to reinforce ballet's prescribed "line" and silhouette. (In his role as pedagogue, Balanchine stressed over and over the crucial importance of tendus for the professional as well as for the student dancer.) The repeated practice of the foot's leaving and returning to a given position by sliding away and then closing back in again, instills the dancer with "muscle memory." This means that the action becomes second nature, that it can eventually be accomplished without consciously and methodically thinking it through.

A strong but not stiff torso anchors the activities of the limbs in an elegantly calm center. The student also works his arms and hands, likewise positioning his neck and head in direct relation to the activity of the lower body. A conscious interplay of oppositions, of details such as the tipping the head and/or angling the shoulder in a direction opposite that taken by the leg, is based on the art term and theory *contrapposto*. The notion comes from the Renaissance, where it identified Italian sculpture's reclaiming of Greek notions for making the static, symmetrical, frontal figure more dynamic, asymmetrical, and expressive.

Chapter 2

MEN AND WOMEN AT WORK

Ballet's noble tone and French vocabulary apply to all its dancers. Still, in its evolutionary history, its essential aims and manners have become specifically accented by the locales where such dancing took root. In the individual nations where it became a serious endeavor—France, Russia, Denmark, England, and America—ballet lives closely related to its siblings but not identical to any of them—kissing cousins all, but not separated-at-birth quintuplets. The characteristic ways in which ballet is taught and performed in each of its major centers have come to seem like so many dialects of the same root language. In ballet parlance, they have become distinct "schools" or "techniques."

Some observers, many writers among them, would also suggest the word *style* here. I wouldn't. I find it too nebulous a notion and glib a handle, too often settling for a cosmetic surface that overlooks nuts-and-bolts workings. But, I do recognize, and so will you if you look at ballet with concentration and admiration, distinguishing features to the French School, the Russian (formerly Soviet) School, the Danish School, the English School, and the American School. It is important to bear in mind, that each of these schools lives and changes with its times. You can't so much pin-down this or that school (or technique) as you can find in its current phase links or breaks to its past.

For a good part of their schooling and for most of any ballet class, male and female students practice the same exercises and hone the same physical skills. We've already stressed ballet's emphasis on vertical balance and lengthened-through-the-spine demeanor. Ballet dancers all tend to look as if they keep their heads in the clouds. Up there, there's no cause to frown or otherwise contort their faces as they breathe in a rarefied atmosphere. The artful moves their legs and feet make can be variously busy, powerful, and long-reaching, but they must never appear hectic, overanxious, or harried.

All ballet classes include a central portion known as "center" because it takes place in the center of the classroom, where, away from the helpful support of the barre, the dancer needs to practice his moves self-sufficiently. Center largely concentrates on what are called *adagio* exercises and movements. Meaning "at ease," these delicately unfolding, lengthening, and controlled moves and postures show the dancer at his most serene. The pronounced accentuations that are worked and displayed here emphasize the dancer's line. Line is something you come to recognize, even when you can't quite define it. Many observers, professional journalists among them, erroneously or glibly think dancers with long, lean, willowy limbs produce "long line." They don't, automatically. Such physical details simply mean that such a dancer's body can more readily or easily display longer lines of limb in space. But incidental lines are not the same thing as ballet's essential line.

At heart, line is central to all front-rank ballet dancing. It's an internal dimension, a sublime inner connection of all the physical aspects that make up the dancer's physique. Line emanates from an artful alignment of parts and expresses itself as something far greater than a mathematical whole. True ballet line has little to do with the shape of the dancer's limbs and everything to do with harmonious coordination of each part seen as a totality. If dancers were sculptures, line would be the defining armature around which the clay of their form gets centered and directed. Dancers with bulky-muscled limbs can, with scrupulous control and unerring coordination, achieve perfection of line, while those with agreeably lean and linear musculature can fail to do so if they lazily trade on their "good looks" and neglect to shape and hold themselves with unbroken, careless energy. Line is able to ground external surfaces with an inner understanding. Great dancers with impeccable line behave as if they're able to see themselves from our vantage point, all the while showing themselves to us in a supremely internalized, unending harmony.

"Broken line" comes from lapses in concentrated coordination of interconnecting the torso to the limbs as well as connecting individual limb segments to the whole of the extremity. Line makes flesh realize geometry's premise that a straight line is the shortest distance between two points. It also reinforces the grander geometric premise that there are no such things as straight lines but really only arcs of circles with infinite radii. "Line for days," says the voice of enthusiasm for a dancer with unerring, unmistakable line.

Probably the best place to discern and admire line, or lack thereof, is to watch a dancer perform from some distance. Indeed, a dancer's line doesn't stop at the ends of his extremities, it continues theoretically into the space around him. The cheapest seats in the theater often afford a perfect vantage point for observing the dancer and his dancing whole. If he has impeccable line, you'll see it; no position he takes will fail to emanate from a strong center, where it will endlessly open out and reach well beyond itself. If his line is imperfect, you'll see that, too. It will look snagged or smudged or stunted. It will stop, or at least disturb, your eye. It will draw your viewing pleasure up short.

Both male and female dancers work for perfection of line. In fact, line beams throughout a dancer's body. Depending upon the focal point of a particular movement or posture, its imaginary-line force can stretch from from head to toe as well as from the fingertip of an arm outstretched forward to the opposite fingertip of the arm reaching in a backward direction. Sometimes the toe tip, capping the stretch of a leg away from the lean of a torso, can have the effect of an aureole at the tip of a magic wand. This is especially true, when the toe tip in question is dressed in the shiny satin of a pointe shoe.

To the novice ballet-watching eye, line may appear more evident in the female dancer as she displays herself balanced on the tip of her toe, her pointe. When a foot position other than that of flat contact with the floor is called for, men traditionally work in a position less sharp than the woman's pointe. The "not pointe" and "not flat" position is called *demi-pointe*. It means working on the ball of the foot, with the heel lifted sometimes quite high in the process. Some schools distinguish among a slight lifting of the heel, a medium lift, and a very high lift as quarter, half, and three-quarter pointe, respectively. Sometimes the demi-pointe refers to all varieties equally; occasionally, a distinction will be made for "high half toe." For learning purposes and for specific effects, women also work on demi-pointe, but, especially since the late twentieth century, full pointe positions have become a most pervasive rule for female dancers.

Women since the early nineteenth century have been working confidently on full pointe, which is to say balancing their full body weight on the very tips of their toes. Eventually, the specially made shoe, reinforced with stiffening that's called "blocking," helped make this a way of working for any woman properly trained rather than only for those with especially strong toes. Nowadays, pointe work more or less determines the generic use of the word *ballet*. Because of its tiny base and resulting near-frictionless contact with the floor, as well as its tapered, sleek look, the pointe-shod foot helps refine and further finish a dancer's line.

Getting herself onto pointe, just as it does for getting the male dancer onto demi-pointe, means raising the heel from the floor. The French term for this action is *relevé*. Activating the relevé gracefully and smoothly, and integrating it into the overall texture of dancing, has become another of ballet's fine details. Sometimes the action is treated with a slight brusqueness, as it becomes a little spring of a jump. Other times, it's done more pliantly, in steadier, tinier increments. In this latter case the process is called "rolling up." Balanchine preferred and fine-tuned this second way, and sometimes made analogies to an elephant's trunk as the image of strength and softness he felt it conveyed.

The look of the female dancer's foot on pointe as she balances her full weight on it can appear differently from school to school. Some schools work for a direct, straighter line from the top of the arch of the dancer's foot into the line of her straight toes. Other schools work for accentuation of the full arch of the foot so the toes seem to curve the foot's shape back under the beveled arch of the entire pointe. In the former, the blocked toe shoe seems to define and support the shape of foot on pointe; in the latter, the foot seems to bend the shoe into a shape that indicates something of a croissantlike curve.

The set ballet poses involving "extensions," which is to say positions that involve lifting, reaching, and extending the leg away from the hip and/or waist, accentuate the dancer's line. Two big categories of poses involving extensions are classed as arabesques and attitudes. Arabesque poses and positions take their basic name from the fanciful tracery lines inherent in Islamic art. Attitude came into the ballet vocabulary because of a specific adoption by Italy's Carlo Blasis. Blasis took the bent-knee "attitude" of the famous sculpture of Mercury by Giambologna as a position for turning, and *voila,* all such bent-knee positions became attitudes.

The basic difference between arabesque and attitude designs concerns the character of the extended leg. In arabesques the knee is straightened; it acts to lengthen the leg fully. In attitudes, the knee is specifically bent and flexed, so the lower part of the leg defines a direction in space different from that indicated by the upper leg. Both arabesques and attitudes become complete body positions and designs by harmonizing the work of the legs with that of the arms in coordination with the torso, head, arms, and hands. Even the eyes and their sightlines play a part and make finishing touches that accentuate line's ability to extend beyond a dancer's physical limits.

Depending on pedagogy and aesthetic tradition—the school or technique in question—arabesques come in a variety of set designs. Usually, these are identified by numbers. First, second, third, fourth, and in some cases, fifth arabesque designs exist for a dancer to perfect and a ballet master to draw upon. Poses with attitude extensions are usually categorized according to the way in which they meet the eye of the audience. The French terms *croisé,* meaning "crossed," *ouverte,* meaning "open," and *effacé,* meaning "shaded" all variously apply to distinctions from one attitude design to another. (The term "standing leg" consistently defines the leg on which the dancer balances as he diversely works and/or lifts his other leg, which appropriately enough is called the "working leg.") Croisé, effacé, and ouverte descriptions exist in ballet to distinguish poses where the working leg and/or arm is the one closest to the viewer (known in theater lingo as downstage) from those where this leg and/or arm is farther away upstage).

While much of ballet's physical power is concentrated in work of the legs and feet, a good deal of its "perfume" comes from the use of the arms and hands as they complement or contrast with the legs, torso, neck, and head. Ballet classes all include exercises called *port de bras* that stress the use and positioning of the arms. Literally meaning "carriage of the arms," these arm movements and positions have set designs and numbered designations. Every national school of ballet has its specific arm arrangements for each set arabesque and attitude, as well as for each of its "directions of the body," which display the dancer in croisé, effacé, or ouverte angles to the audience. Like the positions for the feet, positions for the arms have a set number of alternatives, designated by numbers that, unlike the positions of the feet, vary somewhat from school to school. In some cases positions have names. Arms raised and slightly rounded to frame the dancer's head are called *en couronne* because they act like a "crown" or crowning design to the dancer's overall posture. When both arms are held at different angles in front of the dancer as he stands in profile or at an angle to the audience, the positioning can be called *à deux bras*.

Unlike leg positions where the knee either stretches the leg taut and straight or bends it at a decided angle, arm positions tend to use the arm's central joint, the elbow, less extremely. Depending upon the taste of the ballet master or mistress, as well as on the traditions of the school represented, the bending of the arm at the elbow and at the wrist tend to be more matters of individual taste and choice. As a rule the shoulders are held down firmly but not tensely, the elbows are gently flexed to give the line of the intended curve, and the wrist directs the hand with its individually positioned fingers into some kind of harmony with the arm's arc. Proportional length of arm, individual size of hand and fingers, and the relation of all this to the dancer's neck and head all come into play regarding the precise character of the carriage of a dancer's arms. The great Marie Taglioni, for example, is pictured in lithograph after lithograph wearing a choker and bracelets of pearls in a variety of roles. The reason for this consistent style of costuming had much less to do with theatrical appropriateness and much to do with the fact that she had inordinately long arms and neck, and the pearls helped stop the eye from dwelling on their attenuated length.

It's appropriate at this juncture to reiterate that as art of the human body, ballet gets its finesse from defining many distinctions among few elements. The ever-trenchant Balanchine frequently noted how limited the human body was regarding its elements: Two legs, feet, arms, and hands; one torso, neck, and head. So, distinguishing between extensions bent or straight, as they are shown to audiences from points of view either open or crossed, acts as a process of delicately lightening and darkening a set of primary colors.

• • •

Various turning moves occur during "center." Ballet's most familiar turn is the pirouette. When the ballet dancer pirouettes, he lifts one leg, which he places in one of a variety of specified positions, and by means of prescribed momentum-gathering initiations, spins around on the balancing leg. Normally the dancer keeps his lifted leg bent at the knee as the toes point to the knee of the standing leg. This toe-pointing-to-knee position of the working leg with respect to the standing leg is variously known in ballet parlance as *passé*, as it indicates a moment when the foot passes the knee, or *retiré*, indicating a foot retired to the knee.

Pirouettes can involve single, double, triple, and more revolutions. They can be done on demi-pointe, as they usually are by men, or on full pointe, as they usually are by women. Multiple pirouettes are beguiling to the eye, and the more multiple the revolutions, the more virtuoso the feat. Still, Balanchine sometimes reminded his dancers of too much trickiness with pirouettes. As far as number of revolutions, he was known to say: "Two, maybe three . . . after that the audience starts to count." A specific pirouette, called a grand pirouette, has become traditionally but not exclusively the province of male dancers. In a grand pirouette, the dancer begins by initiating the turning momentum with his standing leg while his working leg is extended straight to the side, at about hip height. As he pumps his way through such rotations, the dancer's extended leg acts something like a compass point. The specific position for the leg extended straight to the side away from the standing leg is called *à la seconde*, so pirouettes in this position are sometimes called *pirouettes à la seconde*. Once the momentum has been instigated, the dancer can climactically bend his working leg in so the foot points at the standing knee as his turn spins continuously through as many revolutions as the impetus has allowed.

When a female dancer initiates her pirouette in the supporting arms of an attending partner, she's doing a "supported pirouette." With her partner's hands to guide, steady, and keep her centered over her pointe, the pirouetting dancer can spin longer than she could unsupported. When she stands in front of her male counterpart and takes support for centering her turn from a finger the man usefully drops from the hand he holds raised over the woman's head, the resulting turns are known as "finger turns."

Sometimes the term *tour* is used to describe the dancer's turning moves. An airborne tour, in which a dancer springs from the floor and turns around while in the air, is called a *tour en l'air*. Traditionally, this is a step practiced mostly by male dancers. The usual number of revolutions in the air is two, though individual dancers become comfortable with three. Often, these tours are referred to as *double tours*. When any grounded tour is initiated by lightly but decidedly striking the floor with his toe tip, the term *tour piqué* is used. *Piqué* means "struck" in French and often English-speaking balletgoers call these moves "piqué turns." Like pirouettes, piqué turns can be multiple in revolution. Both men and women do them, but because women usually execute them on the smaller, friction-minimized pointe, they tend to be more multiple, mercurial, and more striking when performed by women. When half turns are strung in quick succession one after another into looping full turns, the results are called *châiné* turns, or sometimes *tours déboulés*.

Turns can be distinguished as much by the direction of their momentum as by the shapes taken by the working and standing legs. The two varieties with regard to direction of momentum are *en dehors* and *en dedans*. The former, anglicized as "outside" turns, refer to revolutions where the turning momentum points away from the standing leg; the latter, anglicized as "inside" turns, refers to turning momentum directed toward the standing leg. In the former, the dimension seems to open out, rather like the easy unspooling of a length of thread. The latter is perhaps a little more like tightening a screw in its place. (Don't try to think of clockwise and counterclockwise at all; they're not consistent or apt analogies for *en dedans* and *en dehors* turns.) Outside turns give the effect of opening up and radiating outward; inside ones have a look of wrapping up and pulling inward.

One of ballet's most emblematic or clichéd turns is the so-called *fouetté*, which is short for *fouetté rond de jambe en tournant*. This special kind of turn will be discussed later in reference to *Swan Lake*, but for now it is sufficient to note that the key distinction for these turns comes from the *fouetté* part of its name. Meaning "whipped," the word describes the way in which the dancer's working leg whips around the standing leg in the course of the turn's successive revolutions. Depending upon their execution and their prominence in a ballet, fouetté turns can whip audiences into a frenzy of enthusiasm.

Small jumps also are part of center work. The overall term *jeté* has come into use to describe most of ballet's jumping moves. Little shifts from one foot to the other are ballet's most elemental jetés. When these shifts get bigger and more forceful they are called *grands jetés*. When big jumps involve turning moves the shorthand term *tours jetés* is often used. The most frequently seen tour jeté is technically a *grand jeté en tournant*. By the time big or ballet grand jumps come into play during a ballet class, center work has given way to moves "across the floor," usually on a corner-to-corner diagonal path of the classroom.

Ballet's various jumps are often generically called jetés. The French *jeter* means "to throw," and in the course of executing a ballet jump a dancer throws his impetus-making leg into the air he's jumping through. Unlike competitive athletes who strain to make maximum distance or height with their jumps, ballet dancers subsume any such effort and aim to project a sense of riding through the air with the greatest of ease. In actuality there are two distinctions of forward-traveling, space-eating grand jetés. The first, the true and plain grand jeté, lifts off and into the air by way of a gracefully, if forcefully, thrown and stretched front leg, drawing in its wake an equally effective and efficient, stretched-back leg. At full scale such a grand jeté streaks into and through the air like a hurled javelin. The second grand jeté is known in the Russian school as *grand jeté pas de chat* (meaning "big catlike jump") and the English school as "flick" jeté. This jump is led and climaxed in the air by a leg that folds in before it snaps open, a little like a booster rocket, to extra-accentuate and sustain the jump at its peak. This type of grand jeté has the snappier accent of sharp salute than a streak of lightning.

Small, fast, and fine ballet moves qualify overall as *batterie* because they tend to involve "beating" moves of one leg and/or foot against the other. Ballet lingo calls all variety of *batterie* or "beats." The most common of these moves are *entrechats*, which involve quick crossings of the lower legs on the way into and out of the air (or, in dance parlance, "elevation") of jumps. In effect, entrechats look like flutters of the lower leg and feet, almost as if they propelled the jumping dancer into the air. Depending upon the virtuosity of the dancer doing the entrechat, the step is named according to the number of crossings possible while in the air. *Entrechat-quatre* and *entrechat-six* are the two most frequently called upon forms of the step. On occasion, highly expert dancers, usually male, execute *entrechat-huit*.

The twentieth century's legendary Nijinksy gained acclaim for performing *entrechat-douze*, a feat also credited to eighteenth-century dancing Salvatore Viganò's dancer and the choreographer's Papa Onorato. It hasn't been recorded with any regularity in our own time. Since technical skills tend to advance and increase quantitatively with the generations, Nijinsky's twelve overcrossings of his feet in the air make us wonder why the feat hasn't been repeated. My hunch is that soon after Nijinksy's time—he stopped dancing in 1919—dancers stopped doing entrechats with hiked-up bent knees and consistently worked with stretched knees and straight knees. The act of bending the knees as the dancer went into his jump allowed for more time and height above the floor, when one could throw in a few more crossings of the feet. Nijinksy's bent-knee method of executing entrechats was the preferred way of Italian pedagogue Enrico Cecchetti. Though the influential maestro's principles still continue to be felt in the dancing of Italian ballet troupes, and to some degree in that of some English and English-influenced companies in

Canada and Australia, his bent-knee entrechats have all but disappeared, as has *entrechat-douze*.

A grand jeté that involves the making of full-length contact and rebound of one leg against the other is called a *cabriole*. Its name drives from a word meaning "to caper" and is related to "capriole," a kicked-out jump performed by horses. Like almost any of ballet's set moves and steps it can be done to the front, side, or back. (When dancers practice all three of these alternative directions during their barre work, the exercise is said to be *en croix*, because its front-side-back-side-front accent describes the shape of a cross.) Cabrioles are usually given to male dancers and when executed to the front present an image of the dancer sitting in the air.

BOYS TO MEN

Because men were ballet's first dancers and because we don't often think of men first in ballet, let's start with them. From their beginnings as gentlemen schooled in the necessary arts, male dancers struck figures of elegance and decorum. Italian traditions identified the necessary, courtly quality as *sprezzatura*, which has been defined as "a studied elegance and seemingly effortless grace." The term is found in a 1528 courtier's handbook called *Il Cortegiano* by Baldassare Castiglione. In more contemporary terms, the trait could be defined as "cool."

Sometimes ballet's lordly, cool air overrides all else in the man's dancing personality. The times when it doesn't often amount to the exceptions that prove the rule. Such exceptions even account for some of ballet's more newsworthy men. If and when the men in question reveal an unexpected "edge" as intention rather than ignorance, their contrary, going against the grain of ballet's manners can lend them a notable complexity. So-called bad boys of ballet gain immediate attention because of their unbridled depature from ballet's cooler side.

Dance literature traditionally borrows names from classic mythology to identify male dancer personalities. Apollo, god of light and the arts, appears reincarnated in towers of ballet elegance; Dionysus, deity of fertility and wine, in the bodies of more fiery individuals. Apollonian and Dionysian sides can, however, come and go in the same dancer, depending on the role being performed. Still, one of these two personality traits tends to override the other throughout a career, and ballet lovers frequently have a decided preference for the one over the other. My experience, if not my personal taste, has detected a preference for the hot-blooded over the cool types, but ballet wouldn't be ballet without its dignified princes. And ballet's bad boys wouldn't command special attention if the good guys weren't in control in the first place.

Labels and catchphrase designations change with cultural eras, but those we continue to use for men in ballet stem from historical categorizations that distinguished male dancers accordingly as noble, demi-character, or grotesque. These literal translations come from early ballet's distinguishing among the *noble* or *sérieux*, the *demi-caractère*, and the *grotesque*.

The primary determining factor comes from body type. Tall and long-limbed physiques traditionally indicate the grave and ultimately noble dance character. This manifests itself in classic story ballets with princely roles, and in non-narrative, classical showpiece works for cavalier roles—escort/partner to the ballerina. Middle-range stature and proportion of limbs suggest brighter "color" of movement activity and personality or character. The prince's friends, for example, or solo roles less consistently coupled with a female dancer counterpart. If the grand or "serious" genre calls forth the personification of Apollo, the *demi-caractère* suggests the figure, stature, and fleetness of Mercury, the gods' favorite messenger. Shortest of all in stature and/or appearance, due to a thickness of limb, would be the grotesque, rustic, or comic dancer. In story ballet traditions these are the acrobatic jesters or buffoons; in non-story ballets, the eye-catching, athletic solo roles. (It remains a matter of physical science that the lower the center of gravity the individual has—that is, the shorter the dancer—the easier and quicker he'll be able to get off the ground and stay in the air of a jumped or turned move.) By the book of tradition, such male dancer designations remain in ballet to lesser and greater degrees depending on artistic directors' tastes in general and dictates in particular.

"Deh-pohrrrt-mahnt" is how Russian-born-and-trained ballerina and teacher Alexandra Danilova enunciated deportment as the imperative demeanor young men need to acquire with their ballet schooling. It is related to the behavior we expect of military men in dress uniform when they're on official duty. The School of American Ballet's founding patron, Lincoln Kirstein, likened the rigors of ballet academies to those of top, elite military academies (West Point was his favorite model). The Russian tradition, from which almost all ballet schools today descend, grew to its full scale in a world of spiffy military officers regularly "at attention" to their autocratic emperor or tsar.

The manner and the manners of men in ballet also reflect the behaviorial tone set by the chivalric code of romance. The knight in shining armor dedicated to the service and protection of his lady love still shines forth, however delicately or peripherally. In imperial Russia, the formal decorum held almost as much offstage as on. Before performances began and during intermissions of ballet at the imperial theaters, all the men in attendance stood in front of their places, facing the audience, not taking their own seats until the lights went down.

Nowadays, of the world's major ballet institutions, only Britain's and Denmark's royal ballets survive in proximity to still-working royal palaces. But the men in all ballet companies embody an air of noblesse oblige in the ways they present and carry themselves onstage before their public. Unless he is "in character" for some particular role, the male dancer won't be caught lazing about onstage, leaning on something for support, or sinking into his hip with arms folded in between dances. Depending upon his personal stamina and the degree of difficulty and complexity contained in his choreography, the danseur, as the male dancer is sometimes tagged, will only let down his guard to his fellow dancers and company personnel after he's exited into the wings. There he's as likely to breathe hard, fold forward, or collapse on the floor as he's unlikely to do on stage. (Ballet lingo even has a nickname for its most physically demanding choreography. A strenuous dancing role is known as a "puff," which means the dancer expects to be winded after getting through it. But even with "puffy" roles, the dancer needs to wait until the choreography gives him an official exit, before he can do the huffing and puffing to regather his strength.)

Chapter 4

CORPSMEN AND MIDDLEMEN

Similar to the stratified French court that formulated it, ballet has its own stages of hierarchy. Nowhere are the strata of a ballet company more specifically spelled out than in Paris itself. At the Paris Opera Ballet, the world's oldest continuous ballet troupe, the levels, or *cadres du ballet* as they are called in military manner, remain many and various. Linking the multitiered troupe to its similarly graded school, Paris Opera Ballet ranking starts with a transitional level for finishing students called *stagiaires et surnuméraires* (apprentices and "supers," or extras). Then there are levels largely equated with what other troupes call the corps de ballet. Paris Opera Ballet calls them, in ascending order, quadrille (formerly separated into *deuxième quadrille* and *premier quadrille*) and coryphée. The term *coryphée* comes to ballet from the *koriphaius* of Greek theater—the leader of the chorus. In more class-conscious ballet companies (often those connected to class-conscious societies), coryphée remains in common use to designate the strongest, usually most senior, members of the ensemble.

After coryphée comes a uniquely French rank for soloist dancer known as sujet (once designated as *petits sujets* and *grands sujets*).

Next in ascending order, come the higher ranked premiers danseurs, from which the rest of the world gets the term "first dancers." Interestingly, even in the land where the female dancer overwhelmed all, the term maintains, to this day, its masculine form. Highest and most "French" of the Paris Opera Ballet rankings comes the category known as *grade suprème*: the *étoiles*, the most stellar of the first dancers.

Corps de ballet literally means the "body of the ballet," and at the Paris Opera, the whole of its ballet troupe falls under this designation. Outside France, the term corps de ballet tends to refer to the body of dancers who dance as an ensemble. As such these dancers are not featured individually as soloists. The men and women of the ensemble give a ballet company its base. They constitute the broadest, widest segment of the company's pyramidal structure. (Some smaller-scale ballet companies, numbering, for instance, under thirty or so dancers, maintain a chamber-style structure that groups all its dancers together and moves the individual members around according to need.) Often simply called "the corps," the ballet ensemble comes out of a tradition where such dancers were employed to frame the more central dancer (or dancers) with both posed and animated groupings.

Nowadays in England, Royal Ballet ensemble-rank dancers are classed as Artists. The ladder to the top of their rankings goes through First Artist, Soloist, First Soloist, Principal Character Dancer, and, finally, Principal. Denmark's Royal Ballet includes its very youngest dancers under the headings ballet children and ballet aspirants, then lists its largest rank simply as ballet dancers and its select top rank as solo dancers. Imperial Russian traditions that predate the Soviet era included corps de ballet, coryphée, soloist (demi- and first-) and first dancer rankings. In the case of the latter, premiere danseuse was used interchangeably with "prima ballerina." (The special and rare rank was the addition of "assoluta" to that title.) The Soviet period, with its abhorrence of all class-system labels, tended to list all dancers of a given company as artists of the ballet. When pressed, usually by Western presenters, the roster would list leading dancers in larger print ahead of a longer listing of ensemble dancers in smaller print. If further pressed for rankings, the company would identify "corps de ballet" beneath a list of leading dancers called "principals" or "soloists." In general terms, most ballet hierarchy follows a three-tier system: corps de ballet, soloists, and principals.

Overwhelmingly, as ballet evolved in the nineteenth century, the corps de ballet consisted mostly of female dancers. In England, such performers were simply called Ballet Girls. Sometimes, in the practice made popular in France, the "girls" of the ballet might portray men. In nineteenth-century imperial Russia, however, with its cadres of male cadets handsomely uniformed around all its cities, especially in the country's cradle of classical ballet, St. Petersburg, men played men onstage. On occasion, the tsar's Finnish regiment, a military unit stationed in Petersburg to guard Russia's Baltic coast, even appeared onstage as extras to amplify ballet stagings.

In the larger companies of our day, men number nearly as many as women in the corps. In line with the tradition of calling corps de ballet women ballet girls, corps de ballet men are often referred to as ballet boys. However unpopular this linguistically inaccurate designation has become through consciousness-raising trends, it can still be found in use today. Part of the reason "boys and girls" came in use for male and female ensemble dancers stems from the youthful air ballet dancers present. The typically lean dancer's physique tells more of pre-maturity than of post-maturity.

Western, democratically inclined troupes tend to see corps de ballet rank in entry-level terms: corps today, at the top tomorrow. Old World European traditions, notably those clinging to Russian ballet's family tree, designate rank earlier. Leading dancer talent regularly gets identified out of school and corps de ballet dancers tend to be developed as such, and more or less remain so employed throughout their careers.

Uniformity is regularly the name of the game in the corps de ballet. Unofficial jargon separates "tall boys" from "short boys" in the workings of the male corps so the ensemble can be grouped into uniformly harmonious units. Both tall and shorter men need to be well rounded. (Leading dancers have the luxury, in tailor-made roles, of displaying their better steps while steering clear of moves that don't come so readily to them; not so for corps dancers.) Besides being able to move through a wide range of ballet's specific steps, the corpsman needs to jump and turn with equal skill. Furthermore, he must be able to lift and otherwise support his female counterparts in a variety of required, partnered moves. When heeding the particulars of execution for any or all the above, the "ballet boy" must also pay heed to staying in harmony and/or literally in line with his fellow dancers.

In concept, "individuality in the corps" is something of an oxymoron. Or so it has been until more recent times, notably in the era of George Balanchine. The founder and guiding light of New York City Ballet altered the concept of regimented uniformity in the corps de ballet. Balanchine's vision of the corps de ballet definitely included the dimension of individuality. It allowed for personal distinction within its ranks. Answering criticism for his company's lack of strict regularity in the dancing of his corps de ballet, Balanchine likened his preferred, individualized effects to those of an unclipped garden. His response further concluded that more precisely controlled corps effects resembled the less lifelike sterility of the carefully trimmed formal garden. In other quarters, the witticism "corpse de ballet" was coined when a lack of liveliness overwhelmed the work of the corps men and women.

However stiff or bland the corps de ballet might appear at its least lively, it still stands out positively in extra-large productions from literal extras, the "walkers on" or "supernumeraries" who are sometimes hired to fill out a cast of characters. Even lower-rank ballet dancers walk and carry themselves with an air that non-ballet personnel cannot readily approximate. A ballet teacher once suggested that ballet dancers tend to bang their shins and/or stub their toes more readily than "civilians" because they're not practiced in cautiously looking down. Rather, they're constantly looking slightly upward and proudly away from themselves. (Wry and witty former prima ballerina Alexandra Danilova liked to suggest a slight upward cant of the head to her pupils, describing its character as "little bit snooty.")

Though a dancer's walk can look self-conscious to the eye used to seeing pedestrians on foot, it's anything but. It's nothing more than second nature, finely practiced behavior based on the pliant and de rigueur pointing of the feet as they stretch into each step. The seeming oddness of such walking looks especially pronounced for male dancers. Ballet's regulation slipper (heelless, soft, and short-soled of thin kidskin leather) has something to do with it; its second-skin support gives the foot the look of a specially streamlined but essentially bare foot. (In their specially constructed and stiffened pointe shoes, women seem forced to walk their artful way by virtue of the dictates of their particular footgear.) The fact that a seemingly barefoot man would walk any way but casually flat-footed, beachcomberlike, strikes the eye bred on everyday sights as most unusual. Contemporary fashion regularly offers the woman footwear that variously redistributes the carrying of her weight. From high, high heels to flat or low, almost nonexistent heels, the average eye is used to seeing women walk with concern for carriage and poise. In America, in particular, ours is hardly a world where we expect our men to "trip it, as you go, on a light fantastic toe," as a John Milton couplet suggested.

The ballet man's walk may be second nature to him, but it's anything but casual. The automatic pointing and stretching of the foot, through to toes, appears natural and unnatural at once. Corps de ballet men, like platoons of military troops, conduct themselves with practiced formality. In their ballet classrooms, ballet men stand neatly spaced at their barre, variously stretching, kicking, and extending their legs in a synchronicity that has the effect of a centipede's single-minded movements. All ballet dancing obeys strict rules, and the obedience of the corps de ballet to those strictures stands multiplied by the numbers involved. According to Balanchine, one of ballet's most influential masters and one who put women well before men in his hierarchy, the man's part in ballet was to escort or attend the woman. The archetypical role of the corps de ballet man, in this view, keeps him ever ready to offer his arm and put his attentiveness to the ballet woman's service. The tuxedoed escorts accompanying formally gowned women at debutante cotillons or at many traditional wedding ceremonies perform civilian roles related to ballet's artistic ones.

As we've seen, the middle ground between ensemble dancer and top-ranking dancer varies somewhat in name and kind from one national tradition to another. Still, the general term soloist suffices overall to designate a dancer who gets to shine in, but not dominate, a given ballet. Traditionally the rank is earned by proving oneself in the corps de ballet. (In the tradition of *egalité* in the Paris Opera

Ballet system, all the ranks must be gone through, and only those who've reached the sujet or soloist plateau can legitimately dance semiprominent roles.) In some cases, the soloist is an expert dancer whose physique or stature prevents him from assuming a wide range of principal roles, but whose prowess or athleticism may well surpass, in quantities at least, the dancing of the leading man.

In the words of Danilova, "goot solovist" is another way of describing an accomplished dancer whose talents ultimately fall short of leading dancer caliber. Sometimes soloist level dancing is the final step in the proving ground toward first dancer stature. The term "demi-soloist" and the related "demi-solo" denote the lower end of this plateau. In ballet's traditions toward symmetry, double and quadruple numbering provides stage pictures and actions with convenient framing devices. Sometimes the male parts of such arrangements are referred to as "side boys," to indicate the place these semiprominent dancers occupy in a ballet. Side boys act as lesser soloists, who still stand away from the amassed corps de ballet. Side boys often become soloists.

Many solo roles were choreographed by their ballet masters to test or build the strengths of the potential leading dancer. Modern publicity and established reputations being what they are, many audience members may know beforehand who'll be dancing the leading roles, but only those in the know will recognize the solo dancer. In the end, this becomes part of the ballet world's scheme. Eye-catching displays in isolated moments of a ballet make the audience ask, "Who was the side boy on the right?" or "What's the name of the young man who did the solo in the first act?" Many a star begins his sparkle in little showcase solos while he's still fairly unknown. There have been several times in my experience when either or both of the soloists dancing the "Peasant Pas de Deux" in *Giselle* left a bigger impact on their audiences than the so-called stars in the leading roles. Frequently, because of the more-acting-than-dancing nature of the choreography for the leading male dancer, the forthright dancing of the pas de deux man can better capture an audience's attention. It's not unusual to hear an interested, beginning ballet watcher come away from Act 1 *Giselle* saying things like, "Well the lead's okay, but that 'peasant' in the pas de deux can really dance."

Chapter 5

PRIMO BALLERINOS

Impressive dancing and impressive dancers aren't that difficult to recognize. Anyone with an interest and two good eyes can do so with no formal ballet-watching education. To recognize, however, the full depth and breadth of the real dancer in low-key, nonflashy moments takes more careful looking. First dancer status is conferred by ballet directors, usually after the individual has proven himself. The proof must come in more than physical aptitude and strength, though these elements are not negligible.

Besides being finely schooled and agreeably built, the first dancer needs to be able to make his special qualities count onstage. Any soloist who makes his audience ask about him, even to the point of taking attention away from the guy in the leading role, is well on the way to achieving first dancer rank. For lack of a more scientific name, the word *hunger* comes to mind to identify the special eagerness first dancers bring to their work.

In yet another example of male ballet dancers being less well served than female, you will find no consistently used labels for leading male dancers. Dance chat and journalism regularly use "ballerina," even throwing around with reckless abandon "prima ballerina" (of which more ahead) when referring to female first dancers, but no such consistent terminology springs to mind in the case of men. Though first dancer is perfectly well understood and comes with a decent sense of history, it is not widely used as such. If anything in English, the French form, premier danseur, is more prevalent. Americans coined the term "principal dancer" to name all the top-ranked dancers of a given ballet company. Only rarely will anyone complement the use of prima ballerina with its Italianate counterpart: *primo ballerino*. Though this is a legitimate Italian term, English usually calls on it only for comic effect.

The one categorization for male first dancers that has some prevalence in English-language ballet discussion is the *premier danseur noble*, sometimes shortened simply to *noble* with the English speaker often swallowing the delicate French *l* as well as the silent *e*. This comes down to us from the *noble* or *sérieux* genre established in ballet's beginnings. These "ideal" guys need to be tall, dark or fair, and handsome, though according to eighteenth-century traditions, dark hair was *de rigeur*. Sometimes their kind is so sought after and scarce, they needn't necessarily meet dancing's most virtuoso demands. In some instances, dancers who don't physically fit the bill still get a chance at a *noble* role, until a legitimate candidate turns up. Equal opportunity Americans often stop themselves from dwelling on the compromise aspect of such not-quite-appropriate examples. Concern arises in these instances about a nebulous unfairness that deprived the dancer in question of ideal physicalities. Sometimes benighted members of an audience even root more enthusiastically for the underdogs—the shorties, the guys with bunchy muscles or caricature proportions—who get to play the prince, than they would for the storybook types who physically fit the bill to a T. But, resist it though many earnest Earnies and Earnestines will, happenstance standards such as a dancer's physique made their place in ballet's history for apt and longstanding reasons. Once somewhat aggressively queried about his then unusual taste for tall dancers, Balanchine simply stated: "I like tall, with tall you can see more; with short, you can see less."

In the case of the tall and comely male dancer, we all see more, whether we admit it or not—more physical scale than we see on less large individuals, as well as more legibility and visual distinction than we see on averagely featured men. When these dancers get to strut their stuff and move as ballet demands, we see further riches. Even if the *noble* fails to jump quite as high as his shorter, mercurial fellow dancer, he can extra-impress by virtue of the fact that he gets so grand-scaled a physique into the air. We may be delighted to see a streamlined gazelle leap, but we're awestruck by the sight of a Lipizzaner stallion capering its full girth and weight up and off the ground.

It's important, when understanding and analyzing the *danseur noble*, that his alternate name was originally *sérieux*. In this vein his manner tends to be stalwart; his mood more grave than mischievous; his emotional temperature more slow burn than red-hot fire. Overall, the *danseur noble* is a pillar of godliness, the epitome of *sprezzatura*. No matter how European and archaic this Italian word, its connections to imperturbable manner and towering carriage finds universal precedent from Asia to Africa, from Japanese emperors to Ashanti chieftains.

Just as dancers' personalities lean either toward the Apollonian or Dionysian, so do tastes in the audience. Unfortunately, sometimes we don't admit our biases to ourselves, and we blame the object of our scrutiny for lacking qualities we might have no business expecting. One narrow-minded viewer's cardboard prince is another enlighted onlooker's knight in shining armor, oftentimes with his visor down. Unlike more mercurial energetic types, Apollonian cool dancers behave as if they don't have to draw attention to themselves, feeling confident that attention will automatically be paid to their magnetic manner. He remains like the mountain convinced that Muhammad will come to him.

Not all principal male dancers qualify as *danseurs nobles*, just as not all male dancers with *danseur noble* temperaments gain principal dancer level. If the noble Apollonian dancer tends to bring to mind the cool of polished marble, the more fiery Dionysian dancer calls forth something more like the earthen densities of hand-molded terra-cotta clay. One bespeaks a high sheen, the other a high-heat firing. As I've indicated, the more actively animated dancers—the slightly obstreperous Dionysian or the fleet, soaring Mercury-like fellow—tend to make more immediate contact with their respective audiences. Sometime those manning the top of a company's roster aren't solidly connected to any of the above strains. Every company has these fellows: not quite fish and not quite fowl. On odd occasions, these types can become a kind of kingly bee, but not often. These performers who don't quite hold our attention on their own, even while they're billed at the top of the cast list, can often be the mainstay of a company while it seeks or breeds its own undeniable stars.

In quarters peopled by dance watchers who either live in the idealized past or who want mega-media attention to confirm a dancer's stellar status, you might hear how there are no stars anymore. (I suspect there's never been an age where the maturing generation doesn't decry the absence of stars comparable to those that initially inspired them.) What's often meant is that the thoroughly known and revered dancers the complainer misses are no longer around to comfort him with their familiarity. Don't listen to these naysayers. Look for yourself. However rare, starpower is born in every generation of dancers. And true stars are those dancers who bring their abilities to stage where savvy artistic directors showcase them and a public "gets" them. They all have a certain hunger to come before us and an equally certain generosity for satisfying that hunger in front of a public looking on with unending curiosity, appreciation, and pleasure.

Every generation of balletgoers discovers its own stars. In so doing, the contemporary crop puts into perspective all those who have come before. The branch of the family tree on which the stars of a current day flower takes its strength from the succession of related stars who previously grew to their fame. You can often deepen your appreciation for a favored star by tracing his artistic bloodlines. A quick scaling of ballet's male tree could start at the junction where Apollonians diverge from the Dionysians.

For simplicity's sake let's see history's "dieu de la danse," Gaëtan Vestris, give rise to the Apollonian branch; and, to keep it all in the family, let's view Auguste Vestris as pointing toward the Dionysian. We've already seen how Papa V. only acknowledged his son as a viable heir because Auguste had the unique essence of his father's genes and influence. With regard to the little one's potential, wags likely suggested that the less than classically handsome Auguste would be well advised to keep in constant, mercurial motion before his public, because if he paused overlong in stasis one might notice how homely he really was.

I'm using Vestris *père* and *fils* as handy primogenitors of their progeny that make up the individual branches of ballet supermen bred along national as well as temperamental lines. Most of the names in the list below that predate my personal era and moving picture records find their way to my hall of fame via written reports on their talents and the kind of instinctive reaction that grows with other instincts one lives by as a balletgoer. In the following list the names are organized by nationality, usually of the dancer himself, but sometimes of the adopted country where the dancer grew to fame. Those names marked with an asterisk indicate dancers whose special gifts are reliably recorded on videotape.

• *French Apollonians:* Maximilien and Pierre Gardel, Lucien Petipa, Arthur Saint-Léon, Cyril Atanasoff, Michel Denard, Jean Yves Lormeau, Laurent Hilaire*, Manuel Legris*. *French Dionysians:* Louis Duport, Jules Perrot, Serge Lifar, Jean Babilée, Jorge Donn*, Patrick Dupond*, Nicholas LeRiche*.

• *Russian Apollonians:* Pavel Gerdt, Lev Ivanov, Sergei Legat, Mikhail Mordkin, Nikita Dolgushin*, Konstantin Sergeyev*, Yuri Soloviev*, Nikolai Fadayechev*, Vladilen Semyonov*, Mikhail Baryshnikov*, Aleksi Fadeyechev*, Yuri Posokhov, Vladimir Malakhov*. *Russian Dionysians:* Vasily Tikhomirov, Leonide Massine*, Vaslav Nijinsky, Vahktang Chabukiani*, Maris Liepa*, Vladimir Vasiliev*, Rudolf Nureyev*, Valery Panov*, Irek Mukhamedov*, Farouk Ruzimatov*, Igor Zelensky

• *British Apollonians:* Anton Dolin, Hugh Laing, Michael Somes*, John Gilpin*, David Blair*, Anthony Dowell*, Mark Silver, Bruce Sansom, William Trevitt. *British Dionysians:* Walter Gore, Harold Turner, Alexander Grant*, Christopher Gable, David Wall*, Wayne Eagling*, Ashley Page, Michael Clark*.

• *Danish Apollonians:* August Bournonville, Valdemar Price, Børge Ralov, Erik Bruhn*, Henning Kronstam*, Peter Martins*, Arne Villumsen*. *Danish Dionysians:* Hans Beck, Hans Brenna, Fredbjorn Bjørnsson, Nils Kehlet, Ib Andersen, Nikolaj Hübbe*.

• *North/South American Apollonians:* Lew Christiansen, Frederick Franklin, Igor Youskevitch, Fernando Bujones*, Jacques d'Amboise*, Arthur Mitchell*, Royes Fernandez, Ivan Nagy*, Helgi Tomasson*, Ronald Perry, Patrick Bissell*, Kevin McKenzie*, Rex Harrington, Peter Boal*, Ethan Stiefel. *North/South American Dionysians:* William Dollar, Jorge Esquivel, Edward Villella*, Paul Russell, Damian Woetzel*, Julio Bocca*, Carlos Acosta.

Chapter 6

CORPS DE BALLET FÉMININ

No matter how masculine the gender of the names given to the cadres of a ballet troupe, women have tended to overwhelm the ranks and dominate the presentations. Completely or predominantly female ensembles abound in the history of ballet, especially in those works that have survived over the years. So-called big ballets are thus named because they include large numbers of dancers—usually large numbers of female dancers. Once the expert talents and strengths of individual women established ballet's Romantic era, echo-, or sibling-, or mirror-images of these heroines regularly accompanied and attended showcased ballerinas in the course of a given ballet.

The ballet blanc is generally understood to be an otherworldly episode or interlude expressed by the dancing of the female corps de ballet. Another traditional scheme made popular as a result of Romantic ballet's fixation on the female dancer was called *le jardin animée*, or the "living garden." There, the luxuriant blossoms were invariably equated with the female ballet ensemble. Balanchine, who authoritatively moved ballet well beyond such nineteenth-century plot devices by doing away with narrative in general, nevertheless clung happily to such essences. For his taste, the ballet blanc and the jardin animée weren't interludes in a bigger picture, they were the entire picture. He once noted that a choreographer could "put sixteen girls and a stage and fill it—it's everybody, the world. But," he felt compelled to continue, "put sixteen boys, and it's always nobody." While this remark stands forthrightly for Balanchine and a good many other ballet-watchers, it does not have to speak for you.

Like their male counterparts, female dancers usually enter a company's ranks at the lowest ensemble level, which we are calling the corps de ballet, remembering that in French tradition this same identification refers to a company as a totality. (I say usually because there are exceptions to this pattern. Prized pupils of influential teachers and ballet masters can begin their careers at higher levels. Nijinksy and Pavlova both entered the imperial Russian ballet at coryphée level. Other times the corps de ballet becomes a short-lived formality and the dancer gets promoted higher, even directly to the top ranks, in swift succession.) On the average, young women enter corps de ballet positions at the ages of sixteen, seventeen, or eighteen, frequently just after she finishes her graded years of schooling.

During our century, especially in America, where Balanchine's influence was strong and pervasive, the average corps de ballet dancer became known for her ability to dance with a skill once thought of as the province of the higher-ranked dancer. What began as ranks of so-called ballet girls, lining up and variously surrounding and framing the central and expert ballerina, became a carefully schooled unit of skilled female ballet dancers. Each individual in these ensembles worked with a desire, at least at the start of her career, to make it to the rank of ballerina herself. Somewhere along the way, however, when promotion out of the corps fails to take place, the once hopeful dancer takes a turn and remains a senior, professional corps dancer. Some of these remain content to serve time as such; others become disgruntled and leave the field.

In the glory days of Russia's imperial ballet troupe, when benefit performances were regularly held so that the box office proceeds could go directly to the pockets of the dancer being honored, there remained specifically scheduled benefit performances for the dancers in the corps de ballet. In this way, the imperial theaters acknowledged the importance of the corps and its individual artists. Every now and then today we hear of a dancer who seemingly has the potential for a career as a more featured dancer admit that he or she prefers to stay in the corps where the pressures are less pronounced than in the upper ranks.

Within the ever-waggish world of Paris Opera Ballet, there is even a special designation for a senior member of the female corps de ballet. She is *le ballerine près de l'eau,* which means "the female ballet dancer closest to the water." The water image refers to the standard big ballet backdrops of fountains; the oldest corps members would be positioned at the back of the ensemble, right next to the background. (For a brief but accurate taste of such a scene, see the ballet sequences included in the classic 1925 silent film, *The Phantom of the Opera:* hordes of ballet girls rowed in long lines stretching from the footlights to the deep positions upstage.) If the Parisian wags are to be trusted, we can assume that unlike the logistics of today's corps de ballet, where places are determined by height—"tall girls" toward the back, "small girls" toward the front—in Paris, the positioning was decided by age—"young girls" up front, closest to the public; "old ones" in the back, at maximum distance.

As the nature and accomplishment of the corps de ballet dancer evolved in history, so did the function of the corps itself. Balanchine's taste for a kind of individual accent within a corps de ballet's group mentality has been discussed. In the ballet master's twentieth-century view, and in his original choreography, the female ensemble became more organic than decorative to the stage pictures. His ballet "girls" (and when called upon, "boys") worked more in flux than in stasis to fill out his stage pictures.

Traditional nineteenth-century corps de ballet formations stood or moved like so many paper dolls, the groupings repeated and interconnected with strict regularity. At any given moment the corps de ballet tended to be posed for a harmoniously arranged and regimented still picture. Even in ballets where Balanchine made specific reference to nineteenth-century models, he kept the energy and state of flux at higher levels. What formerly came modeled on still images, then became more reminiscent of the techniques of motion pictures. In numerous nineteenth-century ballets, for example, rows and ranks of women would settle into lines and hold them, as if a freeze frame in film, whereas Balanchine's corps de ballet moved into its lines and groupings only to start moving off into further arrangements, rather more like a filmmaker's dissolve.

Nowadays, the nineteenth-century tradition more or less holds sway as a way of working for the corps de ballet in companies such as the Royal Danish and British ballet troupes. A similar sense of delicate regularity holds true for Russian companies, while an almost uncanny cohesion of ensemble work marks the efforts of the Paris Opera Ballet. New York City Ballet, and certain satellite troupes run by directors once connected to Balanchine, go for the energy of the individual over the rote behavior of the whole.

Depending on the particular organization, the ranks above the corps de ballet level offer the female dancer graded chances to stand out decidedly from the unison work of the ensemble. On her way to performing solos of her own, the corps de ballet woman may find herself in the realm of the coryphée, dancing "demi" roles. These little solos, or moments of prominence, often come in pairs or perhaps quartets. They offer the public a chance to begin focusing on individual personnel. Some members of the regular balletgoing public will already be aware of a certain dancer by the time she's given her position of semiprominence. As often as not, the dancer picked out from the corps to assume greater artistic responsibilities will be somewhat familiar to the dance watcher. As well as inspiring the questions such as "Who was that?" when they take on solo roles, some dancers make us notice them even in the corps de ballet. So the "girl" you picked out from the crowd by virtue of her standout way of moving, or at first merely a way of looking, will often come before you in a demi-solo role. Temperament, as well as sheer physicality, lead us to fix on one dancer or another, all by way of looking for ourselves.

For some reason, compartmentalized classification according to body and personality type is less pronounced and traditionally defined than that for the male dancer. Only within the ironclad formulations of the fiercely unionized Paris Opera Ballet are there such minute gradations of dancer rank from lowest to highest level. The same ones already indicated for the men apply as well to the women—the first and second quadrilles, the mimes, and the grand- and petit-sujets.

Ballet solos, called "variations," abound in works that have direct or implied connections to nineteenth-century prototypes. One of the hallmarks of the great Marius Petipa was his interest in and development of the female dancer by way of solo dances. Only one ballerina ultimately figured prominently in Petipa's individual creations, but he had at his disposal more than one accomplished dancer at the height of his reign as ballet master in chief of the tsar's troupe. Thus his multi-act ballets, and the formula they created, came to include solos, sometimes in series or at least in matched sets, where talented dancers other than the leading ballerina could be featured. As we shall see in extant Petipa ballets, these solos could, and did on occasion evoke individual aspects of the lead ballerina's character.

Often created especially for up-and-coming dancers, as both ways of developing their talents and testing their strengths, individual solos or variations continued to serve similar functions after Petipa. Sometimes the aim of these solos was to give plain opportunities for a certain dancer to show off her particular brand of virtuosity. Balletomanes in our day will distinguish favorite solos in conversation by calling them names such as the "jumpy" one, or the "swoopy" one, or the "turny" one. In each case the original dancer on whom the choreography was devised probably had special gifts, say for soaring through jumps or for melting through languid poses or for turning brilliant pirouettes.

Chapter 7

QUEEN BEES

Ballet's true queen bees, since the seventeenth-century's Mlle de Lafontaine (no relation to our age's Margot Fonteyn), have captured their titles through the acclaim of their public and the promotion of their artistic mentors. In French she's a *première danseuse, une ballerine*, but to all the world she's a ballerina. Even the Francophile Russian court took the Italianate form of the word to label its most stellar leading female dancers. Ballet moves and steps in Russia were called by their French names—plee-aye, pah dah boor-eh—and they were counted in Russian—eyas, dvah, tehree—but their foremost female dancer executants were identified in the Italian—bah-lah-reenah.

The English chose to borrow the term "soubrette" from female opera singer classification (a light soprano voice) to identify a dancer who's not fully suited to ballet's most fluorescent and luminous roles. Soubrette roles and soubrette dancers tend to be energetic or spunky in mood and unmysterious in temperament. In Russia, there came to be a distinguishing of ballerina roles by a kind of choreographic-cum-temperamental coloration: classical or lyrical. The former type, and the repertory she would best illuminate, was associated with dancing that had a sharp, strong, brilliant edge to it. The latter had associations with more languid, fragile, and "singing" qualities.

None of these categorizations proves wholly useful and clear-cut. True ballerinas, which is to say exemplars of their art and their era and not just literally female ballet dancers, come in nearly as many varieties and shades as there are women who fit the bill. Like her premier danseur counterpart, the première danseuse is a rare bird of her species. She is both physically and athletically superior to her sister dancers. Like her fellow male dancers, she tends to display that ineffable hunger to do what she does so well. Ideally she should do this work effortlessly, de-emphasizing its difficulty all the while revealing how physically difficult it must indeed be.

In essence, the ideal ballerina should seem *Woman* rather than just another woman. The Russian balletomane who said of female ballet dancers, "Show me her face, and I'll tell you if she can dance," was of course being arrogant, high-handed, and chauvinist, but he was also saying something of a truism. The era in which this statement was recorded, around the 1920s, marked a time when acting her part was as prevalent as dancing it for the ballerina. In such cases the balletomane's statement in part reflected the ballerina's need to "speak" with her face as much as with her dancing body. But even into our evolving age, where acting by the ballerina, in the sense of dramatic, theatrical "interpretation," might not be called for, the legible, theatrically vivid face still plays its part. If you are to play the part of superwoman, it never hurts to look the part. And only the most overly earnest dance watchers will say that average, nondescript facial features won't be a hindrance.

On the other hand, ballet is not a traditional beauty contest. Many a physically beautiful woman has entered the world of ballet only to make a hasty or not-so-hasty retreat, when it became clear that her physical and/or mental strengths were not up to the rigors of ballet dancing. (The same cold facts pertain to the men's side as well.) Similarly, the agreeably or ideally theatrical face cannot take precedence over the ballerina's other, equally important physical aspects. One ballerina, recognizing and seeing through would-be ballerinas who use their faces to "work" a performance and compensate for their lack of physical strength and acumen, calls such performing "eyebrow dancing." Or, as a balletgoing wag once observed: "Lots of things with the eyes and face, not much with the legs and feet!"

As Woman, the ballerina is a woman with highly skilled legs, feet, torso, arms, hands, neck, and head. Traditionally and variously she is also a figure or character of some mystery. She leads the company she dances for as its finest exponent of ballet's art. She is a model for her company's lower rank—usually but not always younger dancers—and she sets standards for the public before which she appears. In Balanchine's words she is the "queen," while her male counterparts are her consorts. Those who are put off by the queenly image usually feel that way because they're galled by the scent of aristocracy and elite privilege. If they'd go one step more they'd realize that ballet's ideals need ultimately to be met by the workings of a meritocracy, not an aristocracy. You don't have to be born into the right family, you have to be born with suitable physical, mental, and artistic attributes into any family. Ballet and ballerina careers are definitely not for everybody (what career is?), but those they exclude tend to be those whose suitability is lacking, not those whose family tree is lacking.

A simple list of ballerinas who made history with their artistry could handily begin with Marie Taglioni and Fanny Elssler, whose careers just postdate those of our convenient male primogenitors, father and son Vestris. We recall how nineteenth-century French ballet critic and Théophile Gautier coined a connoisseur's view of La Taglioni as a Christian-type goddess and Elssler as a pagan-type divinity. Another way of seeing this would be to characterize our two broad ballerina strains according to the stress on aerial moves (or *temps d'élevation*) versus grounded (or *terre à terre*) qualities. In both cases, Taglioni represents the former and Elssler the latter.

Like the male hall of fame, this one also has national concentrations, but unlike the men's roster the women's is more complicated. Italy's Taglioni and Vienna's Elssler had careers that crossed so many borders, they cannot be associated either with their country of origin or with the particular country in which they made their names. Similar patterns hold true for a good number of the ballerinas on this select list. With that in mind, this hall of fame will bypass country designations and move in two general tracks. (Asterisks indicate ballerinas suitably documented on videotape.)

• First the Taglioni branch, with its strain of aerial and/or lyrical qualities: Fanny Cerrito, Lucille Grahn, Emma Livry, Marfa Muravieva, Virginia Zucchi, Ellen Price, Valborg Brochsenius,

Anna Pavlova, Olga Spessivtseva, Felia Doubrovska, Adeline Genée, Galina Ulanova, Alicia Markova, Marina Semyonova, Irina Baranova, Alla Shelest, Yvette Chauviré, Nina Vyroubova, Margrethe Schanne, Margot Lander, Irina Kolpakova*, Natalia Bessmertnova*, Tanaquil LeClercq, Sallie Wilson, Allegra Kent, Carla Fracci*, Svetlana Beriosova, Lynne Seymour*, Suzanne Farrell*, Natalia Makarova*, Noella Pointois, Lis Jeppesen*, Gelsey Kirkland, Alessandra Ferri*, Altinai Asylmuratova*, Patricia Barker, Darcey Bussell*, Julie Kent, Svetlana Zakharova, Alicia Graf.

• The Elsser branch, with its *terre à terre* accents and/or its clear classical bent, evolved into a line of great variety: Carlotta Grisi, Adele Grantzow, Ekaterina Vazem, Pierina Legnani, Carlotta Brianza, Mathilde Kchessinska, Elizabeta Gerdt, Tamara Karsavina, Alexandra Danilova, Carlotta Zambelli, Tamara Toumanova, Tatiana Vecheslova, Rosella Hightower, Margot Fonteyn*, Natalia Dudinskaya*, Nora Kaye, Alicia Alonso*, Nadia Nerina, Maya Plisetskaya*, Maria Tallchief, Diana Adams, Toni Lander, Ekaterina Maksimova*, Alla Sizova*, Nina Timofeyeva*, Antoinette Sibley, Karin Kain*, Merrill Ashley*, Elizabeth Platel*, Kyra Nichols, Sylvie Guillem*, Elizabeth Loscavio, Yulia Makhalina*, Dianah Vishneva, Paloma Herrera.

· III ·

Looking at a Ballet

Chapter 1

LOOKING AT BALLETS

In *A Chorus Line*, one of Broadway's longest-running hit shows, three dancers sing "At the Ballet," a song that recalls their earliest impressions of ballet. A total experience—the dancers, the dances, the dancing—makes up the ballet for lyricist Edward Kleban. But what about *a* ballet? We've seen what contributed to ballet's history and what it means to be a ballet dancer, so how do we define a ballet? A spectacle with dancers to music? Not necessarily, at least so far as the music ingredient is concerned. Or, even indeed, in so far as dancers are concerned: remember Renaissance horse ballets, and don't forget the "space ballet" journalists write of when one space module docks with another. Spectacle? Well, that depends on how narrowily or broadly you define a spectacular event. If the masterminds of Louis XIV's *ballets de cour* looked in on *Moves*, a 1959 Jerome Robbins ballet performed in silence, they'd probably assume they were something far removed from their art form. Likewise if we looked in on one of Louis's spectacles we'd probably think we were seeing a stately pageant, but hardly a ballet. Balanchine once defined dance as movement organized in space and in time, which is usually but not always defined by music.

European expatriate, American poet, and dance critic Edwin Denby put the process of making a ballet into poetically plain terms by writing:

Making a ballet takes an unbounded patience from everybody concerned. An outsider is fascinated to be let in on the minuteness of the worksmanship. But then he finds no way out of that minuteness. Listening to the same few bars pounded again and again, watching the same movements started at top speed and broken off, again and again, the fascinated outsider after two hours and a half of theater finds himself going stir crazy. Seeing a ballet in the theater the momentum of action and music carries the audience into a world of zest and grandeur. In performance the dancers look ravishing. In rehearsal they look like exhausted champions attempting Mt. Everest, knowing how limited the time is, step by step, hold by hold, roped together by the music, with the peak nowhere in sight.

Nowadays we understand, however broadly or vaguely, that ballets are choreographed, even if in England this process can be referred to as writing. "To write a ballet" in the English of England, doesn't mean to write out its particulars longhand, or even to record its workings in some form of notation. It means to devise, create, and arrange the ballet's movements. The turn of phrase comes out of an era, most prominent in the nineteenth century, when ballets were formally written out as running narratives before anything else was undertaken. In those days, the musical composition would come next as the composer in question closely followed the particulars given in the written libretto or scenario. The scenic and costume designs would also proceed to follow the dictates of the ballet's "book," which is another synonym for its scenario. Finally would come the composition of the dances by the ballet master.

The Story Ballet

We have seen that ballets have for a long time come onto their stages as gestural and motional renderings of specially devised stories or plots. *The Loves of Mars and Venus,* from 1717, is one early example for which we have thorough documentation. During the nineteenth century every ballet creation beyond a diverting solo, duo, or group number aimed to tell or illuminate a literary work. Sometimes the story named in the title was already familiar to its audience from current or historical literature (*Don Quixote*, for example), other times it was an original tale written especially for the stage (*La Bayadère*). In the case of the already familiar work, its transition from literature to libretto had to take into account the difference between the privately contemplative experience of reading and the publicly visual one of ballet spectacle.

Whenever a story is written as the basis for a ballet, it needs to be created with an eye to its translation into theatrical spectacle, pictorial tableau, and opportunities for dancing. I say "is written" to emphasize that the story ballet did not end in exhaustion of its genre when the twentieth century found cause to explore the story-less ballet. Story ballets were a given in the nineteenth century, but they are not simply fossils in the twentieth. Balanchine once reduced the suitability of one kind of narrative over another for ballet potential by posing the problem of the "mother-in-law." Mother figures, it seemed to him, could be established with some ease on a ballet stage, but mothers-in-law could not. Historically, then, successful ballet scenarios came from the pens of ballet-aware writers or from the ballet masters themselves, acting as their own librettists.

"Ballet-aware" means being cognizant of ballet's limits and its reaches. Hermes Pan, choreographer of Hollywood musicals, compared the special expressive powers of dance with those of music when he made note of things "unheard of in words, but hinted at in music." Dance in general, and ballet in particular will be able, in its fashion, to evoke and suggest things—states of existence, moods of emotion, images of transport—that words cannot.

For starters, it helps for a ballet's plot to concern itself with dancing in one way or another. Ballet is not a realistic art form; it's a lyrical, poetic one. If a ballet aims to relate a story, it must do so according to the special means of classical dancing. Narrative ballets aim to tell the story as written down in a scenario. The story can take place in the so-called real or everyday world, or in a romanticized hallowed past, or in a fantastic realm past, present, future, or in a mixture of all three. Whatever its line of development, the plot or theme must be spelled out with the means of dance in mind. Those means, of course, include pantomime. They can even include spoken words, but not so much so that you're back in the milieu of dramatic rather than dance theater.

Music, as we shall see, can become a full-out substitute for a scenario as a ballet's inspiration. But when music serves to support a scenario, it must also support the scenario-inspired dancing. In nineteenth-century terminology this meant being *musique dansante*, which is to say music suitable for dancing. During the 1800s the suitability came in the form of music for processionals, waltzes, polkas, and the like. Specially called-for ballet solos (variations) and pas de deux also needed to be supported by music that would inspire and impel the expressive physical vocabulary of *danse d'école* dancing.

During their nineteenth-century heydays, narrative ballets came in a variety of forms. Beyond the simple, one-act "ballet," which told the awaiting audience it would see a danced rather than spoken or sung narrative, there came the "grand ballet." Sometimes referred to nowadays as the "big ballet," this meant a danced narrative on a huge scale, involving an especially large cast of performers, numerous acts and scenes, often with prologue and apotheosis, and lavish settings and costuming. "Pantomime ballet" meant a work largely driven by pantomime or so-called character performing; these qualified almost more as "opera without words" than as occasions for ballet dancing. "Fantastic ballet" referred to a danced story that had supernatural aspects and otherworldly forces. (If either the *ballet-pantomime* and the *ballet-fantastique* took on extra-large scale they would accordingly also qualify as *grand.*) The "fairy ballet" or *ballet-féerie* meant a work whose story involved the prominent presence of fairy characters and sometimes were ballet theater renderings of the literary genre known as fairy tales. The "ballet divertissement" or *divertissement* eschewed the complexities of plot and narrative and offered plain displays of prettily dressed ballet dancing. But this form wasn't a kind of narrative, it was an alternative to narrative ballet, and as we shall see next, became the precursor of a pervasive ballet genre in the twentieth century.

So given appropriate, dance-friendly material the story ballet proceeds to expound its particulars in gesture, pantomime, and movement that make for legible theater. By turns its musical accompaniment should establish apt atmosphere, fortify the intended emotions, and give the dancing per se something to sink its feet into. Ballet's history is stocked with individual innovators who worked tirelessly to interrelate particular storylines with welcome opportunities for dances, to make the dancing that dancers are trained to do, and that a dance-going public wants very much to see, part and parcel of this or that storyline.

The story ballet's design, both in terms of scenic elements and costuming, works for a similar rapport with the narrative material as well as with the needs of dancers. However realistic or fantastic the story's time and locale, for example, the stage needs to be freed up enough to accommodate the required number of dancers and to allow for their potentially space-eating movements. Given the tastes of our post-cinematic age, even story ballets born in a previous century now seem beholden to fluid, motion picture methods. Fades, dissolves, and the like become the aim of scene transitions and transformations.

Ironically enough, some of the Old World methods can still not be beat, or in some extra-ironic instances, not even recaptured more than a hundred years after their heyday. An intriguing case in point is that of Sweden's Drottningholm Court Theater. A marvelously equipped little jewelbox that flourished in the eighteenth century, it was closed in 1792 and shut down after its king was assassinated. Idly rediscovered and reopened in 1921, it gives our technologically advanced age a thing or two to think about regarding scenic effects. Simple but effective sound effect devices, such as a thunder box and a storm sheet, and the turn of a capstone wheel for deftly efficient scene changes to take out one world of, say, foliage and bring in another of Baroque architecture, still impress the eye and elate the spirit. Smooth-running trapdoors permitting quick, vertical entrances and exists by means of well-oiled elevators also helped produce charming special effects. (For a thumbnail demonstration of this eighteenth-century theater, sweetly and clearly narrated by Margot Fonteyn, be on the lookout for Part 5, sometimes called "Magnificent Beginning," of her 1979 six-part television series called *The Magic of the Dance*.)

In a similar vein, Copenhagen's Royal Theater included a simple device called a "hand-hole." This little opening and its fitted plug in the stage boards allowed a hand to come up from beneath the stage to help with a quick-change costume transformation. Many high-tech modern stages have no such simple devices, just as they do not allow for once-standard trapdoor appearances and disappearances. When the Royal Danish Ballet tours its nineteenth-century productions to would-be latest-word-cutting-edge twentieth-century theaters, it will invariably have to create special scenic devices to hide the costume-transformation assistant, who really needs only a hand-hole to do his job efficiently.

The stages for story ballets need to be "decorated" appropriately for the time and place of their narratives. The aptness, however, can take many forms, and doesn't necessarily mean the photographic realism of a museum diorama. Ballets, even those that take place in real-world places—Italy's Verona and environs, for example, in the case of *Romeo and Juliet*—are still ballets, not travelogues to foreign climes where people dance. Like all lyric theater, such as opera, ballet is a formal rendering of often informal material. It's an art of poetic evocation, not realistic reproduction. Its momentary characters, locales, plots, themes, and emotions provide the dancer and his choreographer with opportunities to color, shade, and rework anew ballet's own artful ways of movement and stasis. A village square rendered as bright and candy-colored as a children's book illustration seems a far more appropriate surrounding for the harmoniously elegant "villagers" that many a ballet company's dancers present than would an earth-toned facsimile of some outpost caught in a snapshot.

A license similar to that for story ballet scenery works for costuming as well. Dancers need to be dressed for the particulars of the story their ballet entails, but they also need to be allowed to dance unencumbered. Secondarily, their dancing needs to be seen without distraction from costume parts that, while not restricting movement, might still act to confuse the eye of the viewer.

Ballerina costuming got inalterably changed with the advent of the "sylphide" dress of Marie Taglioni. The cloudlike tulle skirt beneath the neatly fitted and tailored bodice became a prototype for the "ballet dress." The ballet blanc became popular, as did the ballet blanc tutu. The generic doublet-and-hose look for the noble hero became almost as standard soon after that. Along with discarding the man's extravagant *tonnelet*, the change from women's long skirts, puffy panniers, and space-eating hoops led to ballet costuming so practical and popular that it remains in place to our day.

The ballet dress with its frothy, layered skirt and sleek, snug bodice may seem an incongruous way of dressing for a forest villager named Giselle or a town villager named Swanilda, but these women are ballerinas first and foremost. And her male and female friends are ballet dancers as well. We are "at the ballet" when we meet them as villagers, foresters, or vampires; we are not at an anthropological enactment of natural history and indigenous customs. However beguiling or moving or transporting a ballet's story might be, it's still only the peg on which to hang the ballet dancing.

The "Romantic-length" tutu gave way to the shorter, stiffer, more leg revealing and freeing skirt that constitutes the classical tutu. This more crisp silhouette dresses the ballerina for various manifestations of the fairies who dominate the *ballet-féerie*. The male silhouette changed less radically, especially with regard to the look and freedom of his legs. The *culotte* or knee breeches of the eighteenth-century dancer gave way to fitted hose with tunic, briefs, and sometimes gaiters over them.

As milling and knitting techniques advanced through the Industrial Age, garments more and more form fitting came into use. Tighter and tighter tailoring led to the "tights" look for legs in snug-fit hose. Bare legs and bare feet, as premodern dance innovator Isadora Duncan learned over and over again in her groundbreaking career, were considered a scandal on the legitimate stages of nineteenth-century dance theater, so tights were cut and colored to suggest a nude look when appropriate.

To cover the skin and yet bare the form of the dancer's body to neutralize the dancer away from specific costume defining specific character became desirable as the story ballet gave way to ballets without stories. It bears noting here that the body-fitting suit devised by a French acrobat and trapeze artist name Jules Léotard became one of ballet's basic costumes. By the mid-twentieth century, the variants of the leotard devised in the late nineteenth century were worn by both male and female dancers for working both on- and offstage. In women's fashion the leotard resembles a one-piece bathing suit; in men's, a kind of wrestler's singlet.

Whatever the dramatic thrust or theme of the story ballet, or for that matter of the non-story ballet, it's the presence of the dancers, especially the leading dancers, that draw audiences to the theater. As the form and formula of the story ballet evolved, it consistently worked to showcase in due course and in proper measure its leading dancers. By the age of Petipa, which is now equated with a golden age of classical ballet, the inspiring stories not only needed to be dance-friendly, but friendly enough to allow for the inclusion of various pièces de resistance that had proven popular with the public for showing off the latest beauties and strengths that ballet had to offer. Balletgoers didn't expect, or indeed want, every ballet to be set in Spain, or in India, or in ancien régime France, but they did come to expect and crave the presence of the large group dances, character numbers, and central pas de deux and the variations for the prima and primo dancers.

Pageantry and colorful presentation would frame or set the scene for the work of the individual leading dancers. Without special regard to the time, place, and mood of the narrative, the story ballet came to include the *grand pas d'action*, which was a formal display of ballet dancing that had delicately worked into its choreography some attention to the narrative's particular points. The formula, perfected in the heyday of Petipa and used with subtle or not so subtle variation ever since, went as follows: entrée for the leading pair of dancers, pas de deux for them, individual solos for each, and coda or recapitulation dancing, bringing the two back together again. The centerpiece of this discrete island of dancing in a sea of scenic expanses, expositional pantomime, and large-scale pageantry remained the pas de deux. Nowadays, the pas de deux from such pas d'action tends to be called somewhat artificially the *grand pas de deux*. The *grand* part is really the full panoply of elements, and the pas de deux is technically and simply the pas de deux, even when its manner and effect make for the grandest of theatrical occasions.

In the case of the multi-act story ballet, the pas de deux, which freely translates as "dance for two," puts the ballerina and her partner (sometimes literally, sometimes figuratively called her cavalier) on pointed display. Often times called an adagio or "supported adagio" due to the support the one dancer receives from another, this physical and musical showpiece brings the audience in close to the ballet's and the story's leading figures as they get intimate with one another. In the non-story-ballet pas de deux, the form has been consistently if not exclusively seen as a love story even if a specific narrative plays no part. But in the classical ballet mood of Petipa, it's important not to overemphasize or overproject the amorous nature of such duets in their nineteenth-century mode.

The pas de deux of Odette and Prince Siegfried in *Swan Lake* is marked "Love Duet" in Tchaikovsky's 1877 score, but it's not a smooch session. Pas de deux such as this one in a work with specific links to the medieval code of chivalric love between a knight and his lady should not be thrown into another world's sense of lovemaking. Story ballets such as *Swan Lake* were created for the highly formal world of the tsar's ballet. The ballerina's skirt might have revealed her legs a bit more than those of the proper women in the audience, but it also stood out from her waist, where it kept her partner at something of a proper distance. Even the would-be natural and appropriate detail of eye contact in pas de deux like this one should not be overplayed. The ballerina embodying the high standards and values of the leading character in many a story ballet performs her pas de deux *with* her prince/cavalier/partner, but she's performing it *for* her audience. Just as he does. Therefore too pronounced a relationship between the two dancers leaves the audience out of it. Both the hero and heroine of a story ballet should allow the audience in, so it can stay in touch with what makes them special and admirable to us.

With regard to dramatic/narrative coherence, somewhere between the story-advancing *grand pas d'action* and the storytelling expositional pantomime and pageantry, nineteenth-century narrative ballet traditions included another tier of dancing: the divertissement. These diversions, often for little more than entertaining decorative effects, often came in strings. One after another, somewhat like the entrées of a *ballet de cour* spectacle, they'd come on in various configurations—pas de trois, pas de quatre, pas de cinq, etc.—and display some aspect of the theme by which they were loosely organized. They might be a string of fairy tale characters (as in *Sleeping Beauty*), or a set of national dances (as in *Swan Lake*), or a spread of sweetmeats (as in *The Nutcracker*). These diverting fillers help fill out the story ballet with perhaps more actual and varied dancing than the narrative plot particulars necessarily allow.

Chapter 2

BALLETS WITHOUT STORIES

Savvy ballet masters made sure there were no undefinable mothers-in-law in the scenarios for their story ballets. Meanwhile a reform-minded Michael Fokine decided there needn't necessarily be any characters in a ballet. The Romantic music of Frédéric Chopin, beloved of concertgoers and favored by the rebellious Isadora Duncan as dance inspiration, inspired Russia's Fokine to create a dance reverie with no narrative handle. *Chopiniana* as it was first called and conceived in 1907, aspired, even as it eschewed all interest in narrative, to be significantly more than a divertissement based on musical themes of Chopin. After a couple of reworkings, the ballet jelled in 1909 under its new title, *Les Sylphides*. Except for its Old World title, suggested specifically to Fokine by Diaghilev because it established the new ballet's links to the old, *Sylphides* became a first. Its music-inspired dancing made it a ballet without a story and its self-contained cohesion made it something more than a string of divertissements. For lack of anything better to call the storyless creation, ballet historians chose the term "ballet of mood." All during this time Fokine was promoting his ideas and his dances as the "new" ballet, which he contrasted, unfavorably, with the "old" ballet of Petipa and ballet masters of the previous generation.

What *Les Sylphides* did was re-create the *ballet blanc* as a self-sufficient creation. In the "old" ballet, we'd have to watch and wait through a narrative framework to get to a dramatic reason to pause on such a luminous, moonlit reverie. In his new ballet, Fokine didn't lead into and then come away from the dream state or vision scene his dancers conjured up. He just put it all out there, and then brought it to its own ending, all by way of listening carefully to orchestrated renderings of Chopin piano pieces. In *La Sylphide*, the man among his sylphs was a mortal, with a name, James. In *Les Sylphides*, a similarly central young man was simply called Youth. His inspiring muse/sylphs weren't even called that much. They were simply listed in the program by their dancer names alongside the name of the music they danced, Waltz, Prelude, and Mazurka, in the case of the solo numbers.

Initially, Fokine's reform-minded work didn't give rise to further storyless ballets, but rather to similar scaled narrative ballets. The old, multi-act *grand ballet*, with its scenario determining its music, gave way to the newer one-act ballet where the music and libretto had more even say in determining what followed; the visual and choreographic elements still played some lesser role.

Following some post-Fokine experiments in the burgeoning Soviet state after the Bolshevik revolution—Lopukhov's *Magnificence of the Universe*, for one prime example—Balanchine took the occasion of his arrival in America to create a *Sylphides*-style reverie. Naming his one-act, storyless ballet *Serenade* after its inspiring Tchaikovsky score for strings, Balanchine helped establish ballet itself as well as so-called abstract ballets themselves in the United States. The contemporaneous, music-inspired "symphonic" ballets of Massine lived somewhere between the old story ballets and the new storyless ones.

Ballet music, which had steadily gained a rigor and seriousness that had been lacking in the previous age, soon replaced the "book" as the motivating force behind choreographic works. Diaghilev along with Fokine had something to do with this new emphasis. Balanchine, who paid a debt of recognition to both these men after his own career began to grow, played an even bigger part. Music, in the hands and minds of choreographers like Balanchine, moved up on the totem of ballet priorities. The composer and his musical composition now come more or less ahead of all other creators concerned with a ballet's authorship. What previously was called the ballet's book by a writer considered the ballet's author slipped into lesser prominence.

If a written element was wanted, it came in the form of a program note, which invariably followed all the ballet's other credits, including its dancers, while its author was merely named in the signing of the program note. In our own day the composer will often have top billing, the choreographer second, the designers will figure next (in scenery, costume, and lighting sequence), and the dancers after that. If the music is played live, its conductor will be prominently billed. Then, often in tinier print, *might* come a program note. This usually succinct and brief commentary is placed in footnote position.

For a while, even Balanchine's music-inspired ballets that were unconcerned with all narrative took on somewhat literary, poetic titles: *Ballet Imperial*, *Concerto Barocco*, *Concierto de Mozart*, *Le Palais de Cristal*, *Caracole*. Then, Balanchine decided to let it be more plainly known that music could inspire ballet theater and show no need to fancy-up itself. He created works such as *Theme and Variations*, *Symphonie Concertante*, *Symphony in* C (a renaming of *Le Palais de Cristal*), and *Divertimento No. 15* (a reworked and rechristened *Caracole*). In England around the same time, Ashton created *Symphonic Variations* and *Scènes de Ballet*, both abstract works and both named precisely for their non-narrative musical compositions.

All this might recall that in our modern dance a species known as "musical visualization" came into being during the 1920s. This form of dancing took its reason for being from the structure and texture of the chosen musical accompaniment. The results, often slavishly mirroring the music's methods, frequently made for dull theater, and sometimes the dullness of these non-story, non-ballets led pundits to claim there wasn't much going on in the newfangled storyless, music-motivated ballets of Balanchine and his kind. Such works were christened abstract to link their aesthetics, not always favorably, with those of the currently fashionable and controversial visual art movement of non-figurative painting. But Balanchine, among others, who saw abstraction as largely geometric and non-objective, found abstract ballet a misnomer. "Storyless" sat better with Balanchine, but even that didn't exactly fit the bill. "How much story do you want," he wondered. "You put a man and woman on a stage together, and already it's a story." Very likely, a love story.

So by the mid-twentieth century the world had ballet as narrative and ballet as mood or evocatively poetic theater. Costume-wise and scenically, you can usually spot these two species quite readily. Your normal, average narrative ballet tells the eye of a place, however fanciful, peopled by characters, however fantastic, of some sort. The typical non-narrative ballet tends to take place in a neutral or nonspecific space that contains dancers as dancers. "Athletes of god," to translate *athletae dei* from the classic Latin, or "acrobats of god" in the phrase turned by Martha Graham, pass serenely, wildly, and everywhere in between through storyless ballets as themselves.

M. Léotard's form-fitting garment became one kind of uniform for the dancers in such works. In a variant on the word *leotard*, dance-wear manufacturers came up with a related garment, a "unitard," a full-body form-fitting suit that has become another kind of uniform for storyless ballets. (Unitard is an Americanism, as is bodytights; in England, the term "all-over tights" finds favor.) Ballet watchers even use the terms "leotard ballet" and "unitard ballet" to define entities they feel fellow dance watchers will readily understand. In case you're still a little fuzzy on the difference between a leotard and a unitard, think of the former as looking like a woman's one-piece bathing suit and the latter as a pair of long johns or Dr. Denton's. When the costume of choice for a storyless ballet includes the wearing of a leotard, the full "costume" includes tights, as well as dance slippers and/or toe shoes. Standard operating procedure, largely established by Balanchine's use of basic dance wear as basic costuming, has the female dancer wear her leotard on top of her tights, meaning she puts on her leotard after she pulls on her tights. For the men, the opposite holds true; they pull their tights on after getting in a leotard.

The combination of leotard and tights produces a simple black and white effect: Women in black leotards with "regulation" pink tights and toe shoes and men in black tights over white leotards, which then look like T-shirts, and white socks and ballet slippers. As a result the "black-and-white ballet" became a twentieth-century counterpart to nineteenth-century ballet blanc tradition. The British, who maintained a strong reverence for the Diaghilevian concept of the "total work of art," where strong-concept visual design played its pronounced part in creating a ballet, often referred to these nondesigned schemes as "practice clothes ballets." It should be stressed, however, that while the black-and-white, leotard-and-tights look recalled that of the clothes dancers wear for practice sessions, Balanchine saw each of his individual black-and-white ballets as "costumed" by way of intentional simplicity, not from casual neglect.

In their way, leotard or black-and-white ballets ask ballet lovers to focus on the ballet itself. If you assume all black-and-white ballets look alike, you are judging a ballet by its covering. Initially it may well be the stories and their related costumes that help you distinguish one ballet from another in the mind's eye, but your memory of the dancing—the eye-catching steps, the couplings of two or more dancers, the configuration of groupings—will remain extra vivid if those moves, postures, and positions are revealed as plainly and unimpeded as possible.

If we've learned to equate a black-and-white leotard look and a sleek unitard look with the storyless ballet, should we assume that any time we find a stage full of more prettily dressed male and female dancers, say with the former in spiffy tunics and matching, sleek tights and the latter in frothy ballet skirts and pretty bodices, that we must be seeing a story ballet? Certainly not. Just as Fokine took the ballet blanc and treated it as a self-sufficient entity, so other choreographers, Balanchine prominent among them, remade ballet history's *jardin animée* as a world of dancing unto itself. Sometimes the ballets that qualify as storyless, are called "pure dance" ballets or "all-dance" ballets. This may sound oxymoronic to listeners who assume that dancing is what makes a ballet qualify as a ballet in the first place. But, when this distinction was first being coined, the standard "pantomime ballet" wasn't something from ballet's ancient history.

Chapter 3

GETTING BALLET ON THE STAGE

We've already discussed the turn of phrase "to write a ballet." We know not to take its meaning literally. Choreographers, who once wrote out the scenario for their ballets, nowadays mostly "write" the thing in the space of a studio with the bodies of dancers who will perform it in the end. Ballets are "writ on the air," to quote wordsmith-and-choreographer Agnes de Mille, when they're being created. But what about writing ballets on paper? Can it ever be done? Well yes, it can be, and it has been. Nowhere near as universally as music can be written down, but still, choreography can be put on paper for others to read. This kind of writing is called notation, and the ballet in question is said to be notated rather than written down.

Notation systems have been around since the fifteenth century; by the eighteenth century, with Raoul Feuillet's system, the attempts got more and more serious. Though no system gained pervasive acceptance, today two stand out as strong. Labanotation, formulated by Rudolf Laban in the 1920s, and Benesh notation, copyrighted by Joan and Rudolf Benesh in 1955, have gained some popularity. Labanotation is strong in the United States; Benesh in Britain. Both work alongside staffs of the music that accompanies the dance sequence being diagrammed. The former is read vertically, with the musical notation running in the left vertical margins of the page; the latter is read horizontally, with the musical staff just above and parallel to the notation symbols for the dance movements. Unlike music notation, which just about any composer, vocalist, intrumentalist, and many a musicologist can read, these two dance notations can be read only by skilled notators, who in some instances have the title choreologist. Few dancers so qualify, and even fewer dance historians and critics.

So, what's a troupe to do if it has no choreologist on hand, or, even if it does, where does it turn if no one has ever notated the ballet it wants to stage? It does what ballet has done throughout its history. Following what all the world calls an oral tradition, the system for putting a ballet back onstage after a hiatus of any sort involves the tutoring of the new dancers by the old. And so it goes, the dancer familiar with the part demonstrating for the dancer learning the choreography for the first time. The process of demonstration will undoubtedly then also involve moments of correction.

Artistic administrations of ballet companies traditionally have a two-tier system of individuals who are responsible for seeing that the wishes and repertory of the artistic director are carried out satisfactorily. (Artistic Director nowadays more or less replaces the title Chief Ballet Master, or Ballet Master to His Majesty the Tsar, in the case of Petipa.) The higher of the two subsidiary positions is one originally known as *régisseur-générale*. This "first lieutenant" oversees much of what needs doing to get the required ballets onstage and in shape. He may or may not actually oversee, hands-on, individual rehearsals, but he knows the ballets intimately and has an authoritative, near-last word on any conflicts or questions that might arise.

With such an imprecise way of handing down steps and physical details, small or even not so small variables can creep in. Alternatives can enter the mix with the successive individuals involved in passing along a ballet's particulars to subsequent casts. This is particularly true in the case of ensemble or soloist level choreography; gray areas can appear where a dancer will want final clarification. Dancers crave consistency as they prepare to rehearse. They invariably want to establish what they call "the version," meaning the precise counts and/or physical accents wanted in this particular case. This is where the *régisseur* may well be brought to make a decision and set the choreographic "text" that the company will call its own.

This process of teaching the steps and outline of a ballet previously unknown to its dancers is called "setting the ballet." If the particular work has been notated and if the company wants to work from this kind of source (not all, in fact, have faith in such scores), the notator/choreologist will be setting what might be called the ballet's bare outline. Invariably, such a setting might also be amplified by a dancer or dancers who were part of a previously staged version of the work. This filling in of the outline by way of amplifying the blocked-in steps is often referred to as "coaching."

Coaching can be a very delicate matter. Few dancers worth their salt want to repeat another's precise, personal effects; each wants to find how to impart his own. Invaluable coaches are those who give the current dancer reasonable leeway to individualize the choreography without distorting its outline. Details such as how precisely to use the head, in terms perhaps of, say, the angle to the focus of the eyes, or the arms, say in terms of exact ease or tension at elbow, shoulder, wrist, or fingers can be worked out so that the current dancer makes the most of his individual temperament and physique.

After fine-tuning acts to oil the machinery of the choreography while getting it up and running, the company's second-tier rehearsal personnel come into the picture. Once called *répétiteurs* (an offshoot of *répétition*, French for "rehearsal"), more often than not today, they're called ballet masters and mistresses, sometimes assistant ballet masters or mistresses. These men and women take the dancers through the set version of a particular piece of choreography and help put the physical material in the bones and muscle memories of all the dancers involved. This is the polishing and honing that makes the choreography true to both the choreographer's intentions and the particular dancer's individuality. In most large-scale troupes there are individual ballet masters and mistresses for the leading dancers, as well as those to work with for the corps de ballet. In taking the corps de ballet through rehearsals the person in charge will likely call as often for attention to "lines"—the rowed formations that generally aim to remain straight and evenly spaced—as well as "line"— the individual harmonious alignment of each dancer's personal body language.

The *régisseur*, in concert with the artistic director, oversees the ultimate bringing together of all the elements for the specially called "stage rehearsals," and ultimately the final "dress rehearsal." With regard to the ballet in question, it is of course always the choreographer, if he is alive and available and who may or may not have a permanent place in the company, who gets the last word. If this individual doesn't have a permanent place in the troupe, the artistic director, *régisseur*, and the individual ballet master or mistress in charge of polishing the ballet through rehearsals keep their eyes and ears open so they can be the choreographer's surrogate eyes and ears when the ballet is put fully in their caretakership.

Chapter 4

REVIVALS AND RESURRECTIONS

We've just detailed how a ballet company keeps the works in good order that come and go in the general circulation of ballet repertory. A company's repertory—that is, the bill of fare out of which its individual programs are made—usually strives for variety and novelty. Even extra-popular works will be taken out of circulation at some point to make room for others and to prevent the public from growing tired of its favorite pieces. Regulars following a ballet company season by season tend to note what's in and what's out with each current season. No one company can offer all satisfaction to all tastes. Some will show a dominance of narrative works, others of non-narrative ones. All will probably have their share of new works intermingling with old works.

Most companies with solid longevity have established profiles with regard to the kinds of works they favor. Of course, this can change, but overall some preferences emerge to fix the company's character in the view of history and the mind of their public. Russia's post-imperial, one-time Soviet ballet kept a stress on narrative works involving displays of vivid emotion. Denmark's Royal Ballet tradition, which reached a golden age in the Romantic ballets of Bournonville, has tended to show a preference for such works over the years, even when it chose to accentuate a contemporary slant. Britain's Royal Ballet also came of age and matured along lines that emphasized narrative and dramatic characterization. Balanchine's NYCB took the other route, stressing non-narrative, non-dramatic works in favor of what are sometimes called neoclassical works. American Ballet Theatre, seeking a different profile from NYCB, accentuated, as soon as it could afford them, multi-act story ballets. Canada's National Ballet, taking Britain's Royal Ballet as its model, opted for a similar stress on drama and acting in its profile.

Sometimes, regardless of story or storyless preferences, a company will make a special point of bringing back to its stage a work not seen in some time. Here, you'll likely hear the word "revival," by which the company tells you that a once popular work from the past is being done afresh, with new dancers and old virtues. Revivals can have a buzz of excitement about them for both novice and veteran dancegoers. The former will have its own opportunity to see why a much-talked-of work from the past has the strong reputation it does. The latter will have a chance to rekindle its fondness for a once-familiar ballet. Sometimes revivals come back not only with new dancers but also with new visual designs framing the old choreography. Other times, they'll come back by way of attempts to re-create all the former aspects, except those of previous generation dancers. The Joffrey Ballet, formerly of New York and now of Chicago, built its first-generation reputation on a scrupulous restaging of revivals that sought to re-create all aspects of the original version. Sets, costumes, and choreographic text all aimed for original intentions so far as they could be decided upon. When, for example, the company staged Agnes de Mille's popular *Rodeo,* which was by then a perennial staple at ABT, the Joffrey version went back to the original designs, which ABT had over the years rethought and altered.

And then there are those ballets that came and went and remained gone for so long that they leave a gaping hole in ballet history—ballets that had reached a point of proverbial no return. This happens when there are no comprehensive records left, no reliable moving pictures or notation scores, and no sufficiently reliable individuals to tell a new generation in depth what the original was like. When a ballet goes out of repertory for an extended period of time, it becomes known in the lore of the field as "lost."

Once-famous ballets that get lost feed the mysterious myths of legend. Invariably, these legend-laden artifacts come up in discussions that arise whenever wish lists are drawn up to identify the most sought-after of the special ballets that are no longer around. When concerted efforts are made to go against the odds and reclaim such ephemeral works from oblivion, the process goes well beyond setting the ballet and beyond rehearsing its fine points. Now we are in the area known as "reconstruction."

The intrepid individuals involved in reconstructing a ballet find themselves working with various bits of information. These may include still photographs, drawings, diagrams, extant written and musical literature—reminiscences, reviews, essays, working notes, film fragments—and any eyewitnesses, either professional or amateur, who might still be around to be queried about the lost work. If and when the work gets finished, the result still stands as a kind of educated guess about the ballet reconstructed. The individuals in charge of bringing ballets back from oblivion need to be well versed in the methods and means of the original work's time, place, and other particulars so they can fill in details wherever necessary. In many cases these specialists don't qualify as a company's ballet masters or mistresses, and sometimes they're not even ballet masters or mistresses at all, but rather historically minded dance lovers who like such detective work.

A good case in point comes from the 1987 reconstruction of Nijinsky's legendary and controversial *Le Sacre du Printemps*. The only full staging that exists today was done for the Joffrey Ballet by dance historian and researcher Millicent Hodson and art historian and researcher Kenneth Archer. The result of their seven-year research is performed by both the Joffrey company and the Paris Opera Ballet. The credits for this staging attribute the choreography to Nijinksy, with specific note that it was "staged and reconstructed" by Hodson. (For a thorough documentation of the process by which a ballet not seen in nearly seventy-five years came back to the stage, see *Nijinsky's Crime Against Grace: Reconstruction Score of the Original Choreography for "Le Sacre du Printemps"* by Millicent Hodson [Pendragon Press].)

In the jargon of academic literary discourse on ballet and its possibilities, there is an awkward term for a species of ballet staging that falls somewhere between a reconstruction and a simple restaging. In opera and theater similar entities are said to be products of "updating." For instance, playing Shakespeare's *Richard III* in Nazi Germany, or setting Mozart's eighteenth-century, Italianate *Le Nozze di Figaro* in New York City's Trump Tower. In dance, especially when the change of scene involves an adjustment of other factors, say an amplification or a distortion of the traditional musical element or of the standard choreographic material, the process is called "versioning." Sometimes both the aim and end result appear to be mere grabs at widespread publicity. Other times, the outcome strives for and achieves fresh illumination of longstanding, and perhaps stale, traditions.

All that viewers need concern themselves with when watching any and all ballets, reconstructions and versioned creations included, is how effective the result is for them as dance theater. Once and if you find yourself taken with a given ballet, you might well be motivated to explore its background more fully. In that process you might learn of details big or small that do not jibe with what you saw onstage. Or, with regard to more personal experiences, you might not find a present-day version of a familiar ballet corresponding precisely with your past acquaintance with it. All this spells out the element of change that can seem so discomforting to your expectations.

As our history has told us, ballet grew and evolved to our day through a useful process of change. It would be as foolish for us to reject all change out of hand as it would be to accept it without question. Ballet is an art of standards and traditions that need room to grow but not license to alter arbitrarily. The "letter" of ballet can and should change realistically; the "spirit" cannot, if it means to keep its integrity intact. As the shapes of bodies change with fashion, diet, and other contemporary circumstances, so will the shapes bodies can make in time and space. But as classicism's principles of balance, harmony, *contrapposto*, and central focus maintain themselves, the changes of details will not yield a change of theory.

"Old school" diagrams of arabesque postures, for example, can seem at odds with contemporary displays of the same pose. Time was when the extended leg was kept firmly in the hip socket and the angle of lift from the floor was a conscious ninety degrees. Nowadays, ninety-degree angles for extended legs can look timid at best, tight

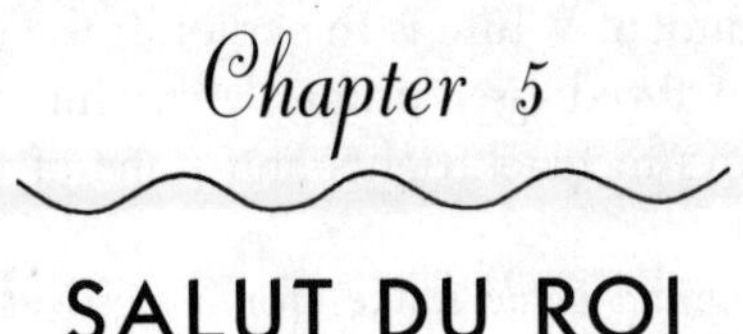

Chapter 5

SALUT DU ROI

Even in the extremes that ballet keeps finding as the outer limits to its ways of moving and positioning the body, the *danse d'école* honors the deportment that comes from its beginnings in the world of practiced manners and deferential behavior. The last look you have of the dancers who perform for you on a given night comes during their curtain call—what's known, and practiced, in ballet classes as the *révérence*. This is a bow, initially to the teacher giving the class, and eventually to the public giving the dancer its unswerving attention. In the traditions for women the mode of bowing is known as the curtsy. For the men it's simply the bow. Both come from courtly behavior patterns.

At the Paris Opera Ballet, as we have learned, there is even a self-contained bowing ceremony, which has the effect of a mini-ballet. Called a *grand défilé du ballet de l'Opéra,* this presentational affair began during the 1920s and took its present shape just after World War II in 1946, under Serge Lifar's direction. In neat stage-wide rows, smaller lines, and then individually, all the Opera's dancers, ranging from youngest pupils through senior étoiles to the dance director of the company, advance downstage with a measured tread and graciously bow before the public. They approach the public and they bow. No more, no less. When the ceremony takes place in the older of the company's theaters, it emanates from the once infamous *foyer de la danse*, which is set as deep upstage as the theater goes. As the series of bows is completed, the dance pupils and dancers take up places framing the stage, with their groupings recalling a perfectly arranged French garden. White is the color of the girls' and women's tutus. The men are also dressed primarily in white tights and bloused shirts, with the boys in black tights and some of the young men in black tunics.

Paris Opera's *grand défilé* makes for a sight at once simple and sumptuous. But the end of every ballet performance encapsulates the grand affair on its terms. Bows, also called curtain calls, can get raucous in a theater, but the wildness traditionally stays on the audience's side of the footlights. However dramatic and emotional the performance might have been, the *révérence* tradition returns things to the ballet's light-filled realm of grace and decorum. (The major and only occasional exception to this scheme comes in what are known as curtain calls "in character." This means that if the character played by a dancer is particularly evil or comic or in any way eccentric, the dancer will hold that quality as he bows before his public.) The activity of the curtain call is little more than a bowing of the head, a sweeping or raising of the arm, and a sinking to the knee in the case of the ballerina. But, as our witty Madame Danilova said once to American premier danseur Jacques d'Amboise: "Jacques, you dance like prince, but you bow like peasant." She then proceeded to show him how to salute gently to the public on the right, left, center, and rafters of the house. Each one being a simple opening reach of his arm directed by the energy of his hand.

Dancers, and particularly seasoned dancer couples, end up finding their own ways of bowing like princes and princesses. When those ways reach the level of a routine, their adoring fans can be felt waiting for their favorite part of the individual ceremony. Curtain calls come first, onstage with the curtain up full height. In this case the entire cast takes part, as does the conductor (and, when apt, any solo musicians). Often the curtain call involves the presentation of bouquets to the leading dancers. American tradition limits the floral tributes to female dancers; sometimes the male dancer will be presented with a wreath. Why this fear of flowers should be so regarding men I have no reasonable explanation. No one seems to blanch when all Olympic champions, male and female alike, are given bouquets of flowers along with their medals. And no one thinks twice in Russia when bouquets go the danseur as well as to the ballerina. Sometimes bouquets are thrown, informally and spontaneously, during the individual curtain calls that take place in front of the curtain. Here, with the houselights up and the dancer as close to his public as he can get onstage, the audience gets its most close-range look at its adored dancers, those athletes of God.

· IV ·

The Famous Ballets

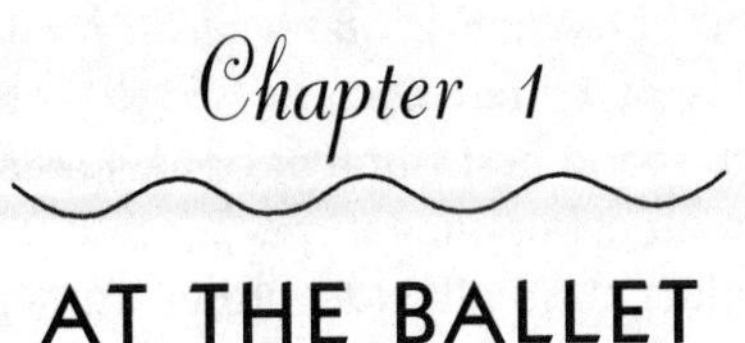

Chapter 1

AT THE BALLET

In "Notes on Choreography," a 1945 esssay of helpful hints for America's early audiences about the "new" art of ballet, Balanchine wrote the following:

> A ballet may contain a story, but the visual spectacle, not the story, is the essential element. The choreographer and the dancer must remember that they reach the audience through the *eye*—an the audience, in its turn, must train itself actually to *see* what is performed upon the stage. It is the illusion created which convinces the audience, much as it is with the work of a magician. If the illusion fails the ballet fails, no matter how well a program note tells the audience that it has succeeded.

We're now going to look carefully at individual ballets. Obviously, the way to do this is to watch them performed in a theater. The essential appeal and beauty of ballet come from "being in the moment," to paraphrase a notion of modern dance matriarch Martha Graham's; that is, the moment of performance when standards of perfection stand ready to be met as we look on. Balanchine consistently referred to the "now" of ballet as its lifeblood. Before copywriters for athletic shoes coined "Just do it," Balanchine suggested, "Do it, now."

But we can't always enter these desirable moments. "Now" continually fades to "then" on the pages of history in our mind's eye.

Or, before you've ever seen a ballet live for yourself, "then" can remain recorded on videotape (or laser disc). I will consistently refer to video recordings of ballet, because video's method is the most convenient one for the largest number of us. Laser discs undoubtedly are superior in quality, but videotapes represent the more popular and available product. (As all videophiles know, within videotape technology the qualitatively superior Beta format similarly lost out to the quantitatively superior VHS.) Meanwhile DVD (digital video disc) technology enters the mix.

As we look at some of ballet's most popular and classic works, I'll bring in video examples. In some cases, these will not have much more weight than an F.Y.I. memo. Even in the best of instances, I'm not at all convinced that full-scale, physically alive ballet presented on the small, flat picture tube can do enough approximate justice to itself to win you over in advance. Unlike the audio recording of music, which allows its art form to be isolated and amplified for the private contemplation of the listener enthusiast, the video recording collapses the space and shrinks the scale of the artistry it captures.

On the other hand, after acknowledging the limits of videos, I find it self-defeating to ignore them and not take advantage of the potential they *do* possess. Even without resorting to the freeze-frame and slow-motion technical features of video pictures, you will find a kind of under-the-microscope clarity to dance effects that fly by so quickly on stage. You will find your own rewards in seeing ballet on video. Tapes can rekindle familiar, pleasurable sights, inform you of unexpected ones, or give you more than a hearsay hint of bygone dance and dancers that history has deemed significant.

Also unlike audio recordings of popular musical works, video recordings of popular ballets are not nearly so plentiful. In some cases, the videos are those of televised events which, once you are aware of them, could be taped off the air. Commercially available examples (see Videography) often represent at best a compromised example of an incomparable ballet. So, although no videotape is a legitimate substitute for an in-theater ballet experience, and not all of these imperfect substitutes are equally imperfect, very few ballet videos are thoroughly worthless. As I focus on the select repertory of deservedly well-known ballets, I'll call on videos that pertain to the subject.

To supplement your fuller understanding about famous ballets, you might find support in listening to the music as it has been recorded. As I said in the Introduction to this text, I have chosen not to dwell specifically on the area of recorded music for ballet. This is not to say that such a study would be without value. My attention focuses on videotapes, which of course include recordings of the pertinent music and recordings of the all-important dance moves to that music. As I have indicated, recorded ballet music too often neglects tempos that would suit dancers and moves headlong with tempos that suit the conductor. Still, ballet music CDs usually include accompanying literature that spells out the music's structure more fully than videotapes do the choreography's structuring. So do not hesitate in your own pursuit of learning what makes a ballet tick to explore this musical area as you see fit. Not all ballet music is available at all times. Most music stores have regularly updated catalogues of the current releases. If more than one selection exists for your purposes, you might gravitate to the one performed by an orchestra connected to an opera house that also has a ballet company—say the orchestra of London's Covent Garden, which serves both the Royal Opera and the Royal Ballet companies, or the orchestras of either St. Petersburg's Maryinsky Theater or Moscow's Bolshoi Theater. Sometimes the salesperson may be able to advise you. If you want to make sure the recording will give you what you are looking and listening for, ask if it can be exchanged if it proves unsatisfactory when you play it at home.

Too few videotapes include packaged notes. Most settle for the space available on the outside of the packaging box. Even this can vary—some labels give a full list of the dancers performing all the featured roles, some list only the most featured dancers. In many instances when the latter is the case, the tape itself will identify the cast more fully. In such cases, you might like to jot the names down on an index card and slip it inside the box before you store it. In the beginning, balletgoing with the help of videotape may simply entail getting to know the ballets themselves. Eventually, you'll likely become as interested, or perhaps even *more* interested in individual dancers. As we have learned, dancers in subsidiary parts today may find themselves in prominent roles tomorrow. Someday as a retrospective exercise you might like to go through your videotapes and focus on the career of a favorite dancer, following him or her from early subsidiary parts to bigger, more varied leading ones.

Before each ballet I discuss here, I'll note pertinent videos or the fact that no reliable video now exists. In the case of those ballets with a useful video example, I'll place the example in the context of ballet's variable world and history. Since most of the designated classics get performed widely beyond the locale of their origins, I'll point out how our example relates to the ballet's original intentions.

As for acquiring these videos to build a ballet video library, use ingenuity and follow your hunches and instincts. In some cases, a commercial video will change labels; in other instances, it may be dropped from circulation. Ask for the most recent video catalogue at your video source; most ballet videos will be in a Performing Arts section. If you cannot find it listed in the current market, check the establishment's Performing Arts rental section, if it has one. Sometimes titles taken off the market remain on rental shelves.

In order to get what you're looking for you might have to be doggedly persistent and politely insistent. Some videos are filed oddly. For example, if you are looking for the tape of *Sleeping Beauty* recommended here, it just might be catalogued under *The Bolshoi at the Bolshoi: The Sleeping Beauty* as its packaging says. So if you know a title exists, don't take no for an answer. Come prepared with as much information as possible—the title of the ballet, the names of the featured artists, the ballet involved, even the theater in which the performance was filmed. Stick to your convictions, and make the salesperson stick to the search. Comb mail-order catalogues as well. (See mail-order sources in the Appendix.)

Before you purchase a video you might like to rent a copy and see if you want to own it. You may find that a video suggested here less suits your tastes than an alternate you find. Go with the one that speaks to you, but remember, if you use it to follow the focus given here, your version will have variables not necessarily taken into consideration. Also, as you meet fellow ballet watchers who are videophiles, ask what they have acquired. In some cases, the tapes on the commercial shelves began as televised dance on public television. In these cases the original telecast version might have included commentary by hosts and interviews with dancers that are not included in the commercial product. You may well find these additional elements informative. Seek them out; investigate their information.

If you are ever in New York City, you should visit the Dance Collection of the New York Public Library for the Performing Arts at Lincoln Center. The Jerome Robbins Archive of the Recorded Moving Image has vast video holdings. With the exception of tapes held for professional use only, the tapes may be viewed on the premises by the public. You may access the collection's catalogue database on-line by using the Internet by way of telnet to nyplgate.nypl.org. The login and password is nypl. There, you can find out ahead of your visit or just for your own information, what has been videotaped and with whom and when. That knowledge can lead you to other sources of such tapes. Many individuals have large private collections; seek these people out, express your interest.

This beginner's survey will proceed with an eye toward established popularity, not historical chronology. The time-line and through-line can be found in the historical survey of part 1 of this text. I wouldn't go so far as to say you need to start where this repertory of favorites does, or that you should proceed in the same order laid out here. You may well find yourself starting at a point that falls midway, or indeed with some ballet that does not appear. There are no rules to making your way through the world of ballet. My guess is that as you proceed to act upon your own growing interest, you will pass through the works on view here if not in total, then in good measure.

So now, quick, name a ballet that automatically says "ballet" to most people . . .

Chapter 2

ROMANTIC CLASSICAL BALLET: *Swan Lake*

• • •

Original Choreography by Marius Petipa and Lev Ivanov
Music by Pyotr Tchaikovsky

Did your guess jibe with the first ballet of this concentration? If you guessed *The Nutcracker* you were close—see the next chapter in this section. Swans and Sugar Plums regularly surface in the minds of average citizens when they're prompted to conjure up images of ballet.

Even if you've never said as much to yourself before, chances are the notion of a sleek, linear, graceful creature gliding on calm waters and that of a rarefied ballet dancer already makes sense to you. As you'll see, for a work that's so pervasively popular and so synonymous in many people's minds with ballet itself, *Swan Lake* isn't exactly a universally consistent, tangible entity. In effect, the ballet born in 1877 has become almost as much an idea as a recognizable quantity in the ballet world.

For *our Swan Lake* I've chosen a video performance recorded in 1980, with Britain's Royal Ballet led by the Royal's own Anthony Dowell (who eventually became its artistic director) and ex-Soviet ballerina Natalia Makarova. Because of its popularity, there are numerous *Swan Lakes* on video, including versions from Russia (Leningrad/St. Petersburg, Moscow, and Perm), Vienna, and the United States; a Paris version is on the horizon. The selection here comes by way of British traditions that did invaluable work bringing Russian-born classics to Western audiences. It appropriately illustrates some of the various shadings that have gone into clarifying the essence of this perennial classic.

About this video:

Swan Lake, Music by Pyotr Ilyich Tchaikovsky with the Royal Ballet, starring Natalia Makarova and Anthony Dowell, 1980 (released 1982), 173 min., Color.

This video exemplifies the English way with the principles of Russian ballet. By featuring a ballerina from outside the confines of the English school, it also gives examples of the Royal Ballet's consistent interest, especially since the 1960s, in employing high-profile guest artists from outside its fold. The filming was done before a live audience in what the British call "one off" circumstances, which in video means once through, no stopping for retakes and no filling in other, more smooth footage. (The delicate but distracting occasional clicking and crackling in the background comes, inexcusably, from the still cameras of photographers shooting the performance.) Even as a novice, you'll see a few "wrinkles" or "bobbles" in the dancing. But these understandable imperfections should serve here, early in our look, to remind us of one of ballet's most thrilling elements. All signs within the workings of ballet point toward achieving perfection—of strength, of finesse, of line, of stamina, of harmoniousness. Carefully shot and edited film or videotape ballet can find ways to smooth over happenstance imperfections and re-perfect them. Live performance cannot. And there's the thrill. Recorded imperfection, like recorded perfection, freezes the thing as an artifact or reminder of itself. Live imperfections only make more palpable, more human, live perfection. Take the little imperfections you come across on this video as examples of the proverbial exceptions that will prove the power and beauty of ballet's rules in the moment of performance, in a theater.

We'll go through the first of our ballets and its video with a double focus. Primarily, of course, we'll be looking at the particulars of *Swan Lake* as the ballet before us; secondarily, I'll be spelling out the particular way in which I intend to view all subsequent ballets.

Always read all the information provided with the video, even though all too often it tends to err on the side of thinness. This is often the case for the notes provided in the copy of theater programs as well. In ballet, even more than with opera, frequently there are variations between the recorded version of the "classic" and the currently performed version. Studying and noting the particulars of a recorded rendering of a ballet before seeing it can, and should, only prime you for seeing the actual performance. You shouldn't go to the theater with the video recording playing in your mind.

This video production of *Swan Lake*, alas, is one of those maddening ones with scant credits on the packaging, no separate notes, and onscreen credits only at the end. I'm going to spell those credits out here so you won't have to start at the end to satisfy your curiosity about the identity of a certain dancer. On the other hand, being left on your own with unidentified performers can become an extra-rewarding experience. Some "name" dancers gain that status from hyperbole manufactured by overeager journalists. Other non-name performers may simply have been passed over or be ahead of the reporters. So names as labels of fame, or non-fame, can lead you astray. Every now and then it's good to just watch X, Y, or Z unidentified by name or stellar reputation, or lack thereof.

CAST

Odette-Odile	Natalia Makarova
Prince Siegfried	Anthony Dowell
Baron von Rothbart	Derek Rencher
Queen Mother	Gerd Larson
Wolfgang, the Tutor	Garry Grant
Pas de Trois	Sandra Conley Roslyn Whitten Michael Coleman

Cygnets	Angela Cox
	Julie Lincoln
	Jennifer Jackson
	Anita Young
Two Swans	Judith Howe
	Pippa Wylde
Master of Ceremonies	Wendy Ellis
	Karen Paisy
	Derek Deane
	Mark Silver
Spanish Dance	Rosaline Eyre
	Jacqui Tallis
	Christopher Carr
	Ashley Page
Leading Czardas	Julie Lincoln
	Graham Fletcher
Neapolitan	Rosemary Taylor
	Wayne Sleep

and

Artists of the Royal Ballet Company

The Orchestra of the Sadler's Wells Royal Ballet
Conducted by Ashley Lawrence

Leader
Paul Wood

Original Choreography by Marius Petipa and Lev Ivanov
Additional Choreography by Frederick Ashton, Rudolf Nureyev
Production Supervised by Norman Morrice, Michael Somes, Jill Gregory

Scenery and costumes designed by Leslie Hurry
Supervised by Audrey Price

(I cannot here, nor elsewhere in this introductory volume, pause to consider the individual personnel involved in bringing the stage action to the video or motion picture medium. These crucial directors, camera operators, etc., all worthy of attention, get duly credited on the screen. You'll probably form your own opinions quickly regarding those who've gracefully aided your look at a ballet and those who have confounded it, but they are subjects for another time and another study.)

Conspicuously missing from the credits to our *Swan Lake* is identification of the authorship of the story ballet's actual story. In fact, history remains uncertain of who authored the original libretto (published in 1876) for the 1877 *Swan Lake*. Some Russian sources credit a theater head named Vladimir Begichev and a dancer colleague named Vasily Geltzer. The narrator of this videotape confidently accepts these identifications and serves them to us without reservation. More serious investigators admit there is no certainty. Some presume that the composer himself gave a hand in the libretto's reshaping of the Germanic tale about a princess bewitched into the form of a swan.

With regard to the revised libretto or scenario, which gave rise to the staging that led directly to the stature *Swan Lake* possesses today, we know that Tchaikovsky's brother Modest had a hand in it. That was for the 1895 production, which followed closely on the heels of an 1894 concert staging of the ballet's second act to memorialize Tchaikovsky, who had recently died. When people say "original" choreography for *Swan Lake* in our day they invaribly refer to this rethought 1895 staging. The original staging by Julius Reisinger, with subsequent changes along the way, has not survived in any way, and no one to date has even thought to attempt reconstructing it. Almost no staging of *Swan Lake* today, even those where great pains have been taken to honor the 1895 version, fails to rework the libretto in some way to suit the production's own purposes.

For the purposes of this Royal Ballet production, largely if not precisely based on the historic 1895 staging, Ashton reordered and reworked the libretto's and score's various parts to suit his dancers and their schooling. Our tape's narrator tells us of the central female character, whom he calls the Swan Princess. Other versions, most other versions, will refer to the female protagonist as the Swan Queen. The program simply gives us her names: Odette and Odile.

Tchaikovsky's overture, or "Introduction," sets a hauntingly sad and plaintive mood. In actuality, its melody prefigures but does not yet state what will become the ballet's recurring "swan theme," the score's great and only leitmotif. (Leitmotif, generally associated with the romantic music theater of Richard Wagner, is a consistently recognizable musical statement that becomes associated with a particular element—tangible or intangible—in a musical composition. Another Wagner connection comes from the similarity between Tchaikovsky's "swan" motif and one Wagner composed in relation to the heroine of his *Lohengrin*, a romantic opera in which a swan also figures prominently.)

From its very start, Tchaikovsky's mood-making, subtly colored music reveals its originality. This distinction was recognized from the start, but not necessarily admired. The Russians used the word *simfonizm* to identify the "symphonic" quality found in what was Tchaikovsky's first ballet score. Detractors of the result found its symphonic character unsuited to dancing, which they felt needed more recognizable oom-pah-pah qualities inherent to familar formula waltzes and polkas. The music and its related action were described in 1877 by one waggish Petersburger:

> A magnificent green park. In one of its glades Mr. Gilbert II (also the noble Prince Siegfried) celebrates his coming of age, and on account of this orders the villagers to dance. Nothing can be done; grudgingly, but putting on a happy appearance, they begin to jump clumsily.
>
> "But why do you dance so badly?" Mr. Vanner (the Prince's tutor) asks them sternly.
>
> "Ah, forgive us! To do otherwise to Mr. Tchaikovsky's music is impossible; it is worse than marching in ¾."

The swan-related theme in the ballet's introduction stirs in volume, then quiets and cues the rising of the curtain. Quickening and brightening activity provides general entrance music for the scene's peasants and youthful courtiers. More pronounced fanfare moments herald the individual entrances of more important personages: first, that of the prince's aged tutor, and finally, with somewhat more brassiness, the arrival of Prince Siegfried himself. These two performers, Grant and Dowell, portray their respective characters in apt measure to their type. The tutor is a character role: Grant is heavily made up and in his more "clotheslike" costume, he comes across more as an actor than dancer. Dowell, a premier danseur, is the ballet's hero. He's dressed more like a dancer than Grant. His normal danseur decorum serves as the basis for his character. He will "shade" his classical dancer's quality to fill out his princely personality, but he won't overemphasize actor business. Someone looking for more fulsome naturalism might find this mode of performing and Dowell's particularly elegant way with it stiff, but I find it in perfect harmony with the nonrealistic tone of inherently classical ballet theater.

We sense festivity in the general air and spirit of the gathering. (The libretto tells of the Prince's birthday.) The artful milling and bustle of the participants come from a combination of small-scale pantomime, naturalistic gesture, and "blocking," wherein the stage director (probably Ashton) has carefully plotted the traffic patterns of the seemingly spontaneous gathering. What we don't find here but may encounter onstage, is busy acting business aimed at making the scene more realistic. (The term "dire mummery," to indicate desperately naturalistic pantomimic carrying-on, has been used in England to decry such misguided dramatics in the formal theater of ballet.) Note how the stage delicately clears for the Prince's appearance, and then for slightly more formal dance presentations, as ballet-skirted female courtiers present their prince with festive garlands of flowers, and youthful male courtiers in smart tunics and tights pay obeisance to their princely friend. Unlike the other participants in the scene, these men and women wear ballet shoes (pointe shoes for the women; ballet slippers for the men). The others more rustically clad wear firmer "character" shoes or boots.

The whole of this opening "scene" is literally named thus by the composer. Tchaikovsky originally composed some eleven *scènes* for his score, which numbers twenty-eight sections. These musical *scènes*, which frame various others designated "Pas" or "Danse" or "Valse," etc., indicated sections where the story or drama would be carried forward by way of emotive gesture or pantomime. The selections with specific dance names were meant to provide the dancers with opportunities to express themselves in moments of "pure dance" and to give their audience concentrations of what it had come to the ballet to enjoy and admire.

The first of *Swan Lake*'s dances comes in the form of a waltz. Marius Petipa's original production included a big group number for twenty-four couples. Their dance involved the use of little stools, baskets of flowers, and a maypole. Ashton's choreography is for six men and six women in more formal ballet dress. Hewing to the waltz as a social dance for couples, Ashton works the twelve-dancer ensemble predominantly as six couples. After taking their places on distinct musical cues and in the direction of the Prince, the six twosomes work hand in hand, at first doing little more than shifting places and bending and leaning their torsos away from one another on the waltz's lilt. Ashton has a penchant for emphasizing the dropping back of the head of the dancer to enrich the pliancy of the spine and the torso. Throughout the dance, Ashton keeps shifting the upper body against the direction of the lower body, variously honoring ballet's love of contrapposto. See how often he has the dancer lead the shoulder in the direction opposite that of the stepping leg. This becomes especially rich when the men step backward through long, soft fourth position.

Arranging and rearranging the ranks of six couples as two threesomes, the choreography works toward more ballet-step individuality, calling on gently emphatic lifts, long-reaching steps that pause in pliant postures, and little, softly beaten jumps (cabrioles). A lined-up foursome stands across the center of the stage as four couples frame the line dance. The arrangement expands and contracts. The men turn pirouettes in attitude (or bent-leg extension) and guide the women in promenade turns. When the music changes texture to an almost pantomimic degree, the choreography has the women, by way of dance movements, coax the Prince to join in. This he does, alternately with all six—three women on each arm—and individually, as he pays each one some momentary attention as a dance partner.

Once the waltz's own internal motor revs back up to its full momentum, the six men return and, after politely bowing to reclaim the women from the Prince's attention, reform a group of twelve and close out the waltz with individual flourishes: bigger jumps, brisker turns, bigger lifts, and elegantly rocketing entrechats. A climactic circle, like a playfully excited carousel, brings the dance to conclusion as each couple settles into a prettily posed unit, one after another, seriatim, like decorously falling dominoes. The finishing pose is held on the music's final cadence. Like various musical punctuations—thumping chords, tonics, and the like—dance numbers have a way of wrapping up, and coming to a definite end. In Broadway lingo, a number that finishes clearly and emphatically, so the audience knows for certain that it's over, is said to have a "button." Finely wrought ballet numbers also have buttons. If the audience doesn't know a segment is ended and applauds in the wrong place, it's usually the fault of the choreographer.

Another *scène* follows, and as it moves into its purpose, the Tutor helps pass about some drink as we catch brief sight of an unknown trio of dancers. But before they can be brought into the action, another entrance is made. The Queen or Princess Mother comes on preceded by her retinue. The women courtiers present her with flowers, as do the women briefly introduced at the scene's start. Then the Queen summons her page, who carries on a pillow a present for our birthday Prince: a crossbow. But the Prince's excitement over his gift is tempered by the Queen's commanding reminder that his coming of age means he must choose a bride from princesses like those who accompany her. A distinct pointing to the ring finger signifies the Queen's pointed message, and the hardly enthusiastic Prince acquiesces for the moment.

After his insistent mother's ceremonious departure, Prince Siegfried finds the two women and a man who greeted him just before the Queen's arrival ready to dance for him. This is the first of the formally set and composed dances that bear some relationship to the original 1895 production. In outline and concept, the pas de trois follows the popular pas de deux formula of the era: introduction, pas de deux, variations, coda. One of the characters in the original concept of *Swan Lake* was Benno, confidant and close friend to Siegfried. In most productions where this character is included (our video not being one of them), it is he who dances in this trio.

The Pas de Trois

After dramatically appropriate nods of courtesy to the Prince, the trio retreats to the upstage right corner. There they position themselves facing the audience with their arms raised *en couronne* and the feet and legs braced to launch into a self-contained ballet dance. Connoisseurs might even connect the dancers' positioning and readiness with that of a ballet class, when dancers form twosomes or threesomes and cross the classroom floor from far corner to near. Novices probably react with related thinking: This is different from the scene-setting activity of group work with pantomime and gesturing and from the more formal but still social dance–related waltz offered earlier. This is a little ballet within our ballet. *This* is what really makes ballet *Ballet*. Ballet aestheticians will argue, with good reason, for classifying *Swan Lake* as a great Romantic work. But, here, when the story gets confidently suspended, we get a thumbnail example of why *Swan Lake* should be considered a Classical ballet. Don't let one label or the other confuse your watching and admiration of this island of classical dancing.

In this staging, which came to the Royal Ballet by way of stagings put on by former imperial ballet master Nicholas Sergeyev, the "intrada," or introduction, introduces all three dancers, before taking the shape of a duet once the woman who will perform the first of the variations (solos) makes an early exit from the opening section. It's full of jumps—bigger ones for the man, lesser ones for the women. Most of the man's jumps are cabrioles; most of the women's are similarly geared sautés in arabesque making for a climactic shape related to that of the man and his cabrioles. (*Sauté*, broadly meaning "hop," refers to jumps from one foot to the same foot.) For the man, whose legs are revealed full length in tights, the arabesque-line jumps look crisp and clean; for the women, in tulle skirts slightly shorter than those of the courtier women from the waltz, the related jumps look more delicate and fine.

Before the trio reduces momentarily to a duo, the man plays partner to each woman. Once, he'll help center the pirouettes of the woman on his right; then, in loving obedience to classicism's faith in simple, strict symmetry, he'll repeat himself with the solo woman on his left. These moments of virtuosity are the most exposed of their kind up to this point, and each tells further of the depths and beauties of physical power and finesse that lie at the heart of classical ballet. After a moment that looks like a three-dancer grouping, one of the women slips out and leaves us watching a duet. The cabriole jumps that were the man's feature now become the woman's as the man supports her in a gentle lift that permits her to float through her own cabrioles. After more separate and partnered moves, the Prince's female "friend" unspools a length of successive (*chaîné*) turns that gets punctuated by a presentational supported, multiple pirouette. All the turns in this dance have been outside, or *en dedans* in direction.

The names of individual steps, by the way, are only important if you want them to be. Their "look and feel" are ever important if you want to gain the most pleasure from the efforts of both dancer and choreographer alike. Sensitively wrought steps give dancing texture, character, and mood. You can only appreciate those dimensions by thoroughly taking in all the particulars at play. Of course, the more you watch the better you get at seeing, but with interested eyes even first looks reveal riches. Balanchine has written about the process of watching ballet by stressing the paying of close attention and the participation of our memory in that activity: "The spectator must be willing to assimilate what is shown on the stage and possibly to be disturbed by it (for the ballet has spiritual and metaphysical elements, not merely physical ones) and to retain in his memory the preceding ones that are being performed and the ones that follow."

Now we're ready to see the ballet's first solos and soloists. Formal solo dancing means more than a dancer dancing by himself. It means when all the eyes of the audience as well as those of the dancers/characters framing the stage are on the solo being performed. *Swan Lake*'s "Pas de Trois" is a perfect example of a showcase for dancers ranked as soloist. It's here in any given performance that a young dancer coming up through the ranks might be getting his first big chance to shine before a public that might previously have only caught sight of him in the ensemble. Coming as these soloists do in threes, helps us move gradually toward meeting the principal dancers, and, of course, the all-important ballerina. Actually, the first solo dance Tchaikovsky composed for this pas de trois is cut here, momentarily. (In this staging, it will return, as we shall see; in many others following the 1895 *Swan Lake* original, it remains cut from the score altogether.)

The female "friend" who left the stage during the intrada dances the first of these three solos. Tchaikovsky composed an "Allegro semplice—presto" number, which the first woman soloist confidently paces through largely on pointe, shifting emphases from leg to leg and fluttering into some entrechat-six fillips, eventually getting far enough upstage to zip through a diagonal path series of chaîné turns amplified by intermediate *piqué* turns. Next comes our solitary male soloist, whose "Moderato" variation allows significant time for him to take to the air. (The man's solo will be as *en l'air* as the woman's was *à terre*. As you see from the start, he even throws a jump into his run onstage to take his place for the beginning of his solo.)

His jumps alternately expand in the air of their elevation (more cabrioles and leg-position-changing *grand jeté en tournant*), they also beat and shoot upward with geyserlike trajectory—double tours en l'air and entrechat-quatre jumps alternating with entrechat-six. (If you want a quick way to tell a quatre from a six remember the former closes with the same foot front that began the jump; the latter finishes with the foot that began the move in the front, closing to the back. Of course, it's also more crossings of the feet as well, with the quatre beating back then front again and the six beating back, front, back. Each foot participates in the beat, thus each beat has a "two-count." If you see too many beats to make a quatre and the front foot closes front again, you probably saw entrechat-huit.) Our male Royal soloist turns a quintuple pirouette, which finishes extra fancily in arabesque, before launching into a *manège* (or arcing circuit) of turning jumps known as *tour de rein*, because as a "turn of back" each revolution takes the dancer in the air while leaning his torso backward as if aiming toward the middle of the circle his jumping describes. He finishes with a (slightly insecure) triple pirouette. (Records of the 1895 staging indicate that a quintuple came at this point.)

The second of the women dances her solo last, an "Allegro" number. It's even more pointe happy than the first female solo, remaining ever more *terre à terre* throughout. Her final diagonal, successive turns start with alternating a piqué attitude turn with a double (standard) piqué turn, and eventually more chaîné turns. (In case you wondered, the attitude turn is en dedans and the standard passé turn is en dehors.) One at a time each dancer returns to perform the pas de trois's "Allegro vivace" coda. Female soloist no. 1 has jumps in place and in a manège, the man has more athletically "beaten" jumps (teasing "entrechats" to the front and expansive "cabrioles" to the back). The second female soloist spins through repeated, supported, triple pirouettes. All three point and counterpoint each other for a delicately shifting symmetry and an equal share of focus before ending in a sculpturally pretty three-dancer grouping.

Next comes what Tchaikovsky called a *sujet*. The "subject" in this case becomes a little dance by a "peasant" gal, chosen by the Prince's tipsy tutor, who dances on her own once the old fellow who chose her drops out after trying to participate in a dance himself. This leads directly to a festivity concluding "Polacca" or "Polonaise" for the merrymakers. The subject the *sujet* pantomimes is a request to the Prince that he permit everyone left to dance. Both the request of the female peasant and the noblesse-oblige response from the none-too-animated or interested Prince include one of ballet's most frequently used pantomime signs: two hands lifted overhead and curled around each other signify "dancing." In this case our female character executes the sign amid a request for permission to allow dancing; in response, the Prince signs consent to let the dancing commence, to which he then shows mild attention to the proceedings, but little more. The "Polacca" comes named in the score as a "Danse des Coupes," which means "Dance with Goblets." Our production eschews involving this prop and lets the peasantry (twelve couples strong) dance its delicately rousing hearts out amid animated ranks that weave neat wheeling rings. (The choreographic credit for this non-goblet "Goblet Dance" should be Ninette de Valois, one of British ballet's primogenitors, but for some reason it's not spelled out on these credits.)

The polacca's conclusion clears the stage and leaves Prince Siegfried and his tutor alone in a twilight. Without much dramatic or gestural introduction, a new scene and mood ensue. A new musical number starts; it's the previously cut variation ("Andante sostenuto") from the pas de trois. Its voice is that of the plaintive oboe and, upon removing his cloak and passing it to his attentive tutor, the Prince steps directly into his first solo. Sustained, *allongée* poses, mostly languid arabesques, shimmeringly smooth pirouettes, featherlight and snow-silent jumps, and torso wreathing ports de bras keep all the athleticism in a pervasive mood of melancholy. After a soft "button" of an ending, the air fills with the first sounds of Tchaikovsky's pearlescent swan theme.

In the full score this comes with Act 1's "Andante" finale, which is cut here. In this version, following the 1895 Petersburg tradition to make the original Act 2 into Act 1, scene 2, we hear the "swan theme" as it's introduced in the (Moderato) *scène* written to open Act 2. Intimates of the Prince enter on the swan theme and present him with his crossbow. One of them mimes the gesture of shooting with the crossbow, which the Prince accepts and leads them away on their hunt. Sometimes this scene includes the miming of a sighting of a flight of swans, but not this one. Unfortunately our video's narrator tells us of the ballet's upcoming events *over* the playing of the swan theme scene. He tells us of Siegfried's desire to hunt at the edge of Swan Lake and of the sight he comes upon of the swan's transformation into a beautiful "girl" (narrator's word). He further tells us that this woman is a princess, bewitched into swan form by an evil genie, who watches in the form of an owl over her and her sister swans/maidens when they shed their swan form between midnight and dawn. We learn that this evil spell can only be broken by an unswerving vow of first love from a man pure of heart.

Act 2 (or Act 1, scene 2), The Lakeside

A great winged creature has made a phantomlike appearance as the mists lift along the lake that stands in view. One detail not part of this Royal Ballet production is standard elsewhere. During the playing of the swan theme music, with its plaintive oboe voice and its "still waters run deep" mood, many productions include the sight of swans gliding serenely across the lake. The detail has been in place since the ballet's beginnings. Some of the reports on the 1877 production make fun of the misbegotten wooden swans that appeared in the first staging. (For a good rendering of this effect see *Swan Lake*, The Kirov Ballet, starring Galina Mezentseva and Konstantin Zaklinsky, c. 1986, 144 min., Color.)

During the playing of the next scene, one more worldly and bright of tone than the otherworldly and shadowy previous scene, Siegfried stays alone at the lakeside as his hunter friends go elsewhere. After regarding the skies and gesturing about the presence of creatures to hunt, the Prince is halted mid-aim by a surprising sight. As the music of his scene closes, a female dancer enters urgently by means of striding steps and a big jump. She wears swan feathers in her hair, and a swan's down trimmed tutu. In short, a ballerina has made her entrance. This is the moment that most seasoned balletomanes wait for, and that neophytes automatically recognize because it has been so pointedly set up. Invariably, even with more staid British audiences (almost all audiences are more staid than U.S. ones), there'll be applause recognizing that *the* entrance has taken place and that *the* ballerina has appeared.

Next comes another *scène*. It starts with Odette, the Swan Princess (or Queen), in a brief moment of privacy. She seems to yawn and bathe in the moonlight, stepping first into elemental yet individual first arabesque and then slipping into a lunging, croisé pose that first arches backward and then folds, downcast, forward. Trained in traditions emanating from the ballet world that originally produced *Swan Lake*, as our Odette, Natalia Makarova reveals her beautifully proportioned physique, most beautifully revealed in her "classical-length" tutu. Hers will be a Russian rendering of this English production's view of classical ballet's universal language. Her arabesques will be Russian in detail and personal in part. Instead of a taut, smooth extended leg, firmly directed with a fully straightened knee, Makarova's "swan" arabesques will "float" behind her in a direction slightly softened by a gently crooked knee.

No sooner is the radiant, regal woman gradually released from her swan state, when Siegfried approaches her. The meeting is a mixture of wonder and apprehension on both their parts, with wonder overwhelming his and apprehension hers. In the ensuing give and take of his decorous curiosity and her guarded fear, all duly supported by the sometimes racing heart beneath the scene's music, these two particular dancers make an intriguing aesthetic mix. In the reaction of Dowell's Siegfried we can see more than flickers of questing pantomime. In the presence of Makarova's Odette, we see predominantly classical posturing and poses. Dowell betrays a belief in mime; Makarova, a fear of it.

The scene's climax is meant to be mimetic dialogue between Odette, telling of her plight and explaining how it might be remedied, and Siegfried, swearing all necessary compliance. (Though some productions nowadays retain this fully articulated pantomime, none is currently on videotape.) At the appropriately boisterous moment, Baron von Rothbart, the evil genie in his owl guise, appears to reinforce the power of his bewitching spell. Once more Dowell reveals pantomimic reactions to the drama and Makarova continues to strike gestural but not mimetic dance poses. Odette prevents Siegfried from attempting to destroy the genie with his arrow, pausing in arabesque balance before his crossbow.

In the agitated heat of confusion that Rothbart's appearance caused, Siegfried goes off after Odette, who has stolen away. Immediately, the action segues into the next scene, which appropriately enough is known as the "Entrance of the Swans." Filing on in this production like a slightly nervous chain of birdlike women, are twenty-four female corps de ballet dancers. Snaking back and forth by way of prancing *pas emboîté* (meaning "boxed") steps alternating with sautés in arabesque, these two dozen women in feathery white tutus fill up the stage as ranks of tremulous swan maidens. Configuring and reconfiguring as lines, wedges, and rings they finally come to rest off to the side in an angled grouping as their sorcerer disappears and Siegfried's fellow hunters come upon them. Confused and with crossbows drawn, the hunters are directed to desist in their hunting efforts by the gestural commands of a returned Siegfried. All of which gets punctuational pleading from an imploring Odette, who rushes on to shield her sister swan maidens from all harm.

What follows is a suite Tchaikovsky wrote as "Danses de Cygnes." Here, and throughout this lakeside act, our production honors what most traditional *Swan Lake* stagings call the choreography of Petipa's assistant, Lev Ivanov. We may never know just how much of what came down to us from the 1895 production is actually the work of Ivanov or Petipa. This version of the *Cygnes* suite begins with the swan maiden's waltz. At the start three lines of eight women stand like rows of poplar trees. From there the ranks expand and contract, sweeping some dancers to the side to pose as others shine in the center. Besides the signature use of first arabesque positions and winglike reaching and expanding ports de bras, the swan corps de ballet makes frequent use of a lightly galloping step known as *pas de chat* (or "step of the cat"). English-school swan maidens use both their backs and arms more demurely than currently schooled Russians do. But the back and the arms help create much of the effects for swan corps de ballet dances.

Petipa's reordering of numbers placed Tchaikovsky's pas d'action next, even though the composer had placed it later on in the suite. The "White Swan Pas de Deux" is sometimes referred to musically as "Love Duet." This is because Tchaikovsky composed his pas de deux by way of recycling music he had written as a love duet for *Undine*, an opera (on the subject of a water spirit, by the way) that he had abandoned. *Swan Lake*'s "Love Duet" ensues after Siegfried has entered to search for Odette among her sister swan maidens. Odette reenters at last, cued, as was traditional in the nineteenth century, by a harp arpeggio. She sinks to her knee and folds forward.

Pas d'Action

In the world of ballets like *Swan Lake*, the pas de deux, often if not always a pas d'action (or a dance carrying forward the story's action), was the pièce de résistance. In form and mechanics, the supported adagio, as it was sometimes called, presented the leading dancers in a harmoniously coordinated showcase, especially the ballerina. However expert she was physically, in the pas de deux her expertise became magnified. Her ability to sustain and expand herself in space gained further fullness by being able to count on the coordinated strength offered by her partner's support and assistance.

The "lakeside" pas de deux, or adagio, begins when Siegfried reaches over Odette and tenderly guides her rising to stand full height, on pointe. Her first move, a finger turn (or a turn supported by a partner's finger), takes her to the first of the duet's many and various softly unfolded arabesque poses. The main voice of Tchaikovsky's music here comes from a violin. The corps de ballet gets intermittently "orchestrated" into the action, acting as a frame to the drama of its queen. Sometimes to respond to the music's flowing line, the Swan Queen's extending leg softly unfolds by calculated degrees to fully stretched extension; other times, her leg sweeps straight and softly into its extending positions.

As a pas d'action the duet does not merely give opportunities for the ballet's hero and heroine to dance together or separately, in the manner of the earlier pas de trois. Without resorting to overt pantomime, the dance dynamics tell of the Swan Queen's desire for comforting and of her sometime urge to go away. In downward plunging moments, known as *penchée* (leaning, inclining) moves, Odette seems to plummet sorrowingly toward the center of the earth; in a variety of back-leaning postures known as *cambré*, she seems at once imploring heavenwardly and drawn beyond herself by forces unknown. A series of leg-opening lifts (based on the dynamics of *sissone*, a jump from two feet to one) have the effect of making Odette try to fly off and away from her earthly misery. In most cases her port de bras adds winglike assistance to all her desires to escape captivity. None of Odette's supported pirouettes spin front and center as ready displays of virtuoso ability, as they do in the pas de trois. Each element of this pas de deux weaves emotively into what follows. When Siegfried takes position in the upstage left corner before bringing Odette downstage in a series of supported moves and big overhead lifts, he does so with the seeming intent of preventing the Swan Queen from leaving the clearing. (We may assume, incidentally, that the big lifts in which Odette arches back, legs, and arms open as if in a silent wail, at full arm's length over Siegfried's head, are post-nineteenth-century innovations. Dance strength, costume cut, and general decorum would have made the lifts executed by Dowell and Makarova unlikely in 1895.)

A series of sorrowfully unspooled supported pirouettes, luminous leg extensions, and moments for Odette to sway gently cradled in

Siegfried's arms (echoing and elaborating on the duet's opening moment) all precede a final series of finger turns for Odette with Siegfried at the point of an open V-formation of swan maidens. The music accompanying the duet's final moments comes not from Tchaikovsky's hand but from the Russian imperial ballet's resident composer and conductor Riccardo Drigo. Petipa wanted something different from Tchaikovsky's own, almost wild allegro coda and commissioned the house composer to fashion something more in keeping with the mood established along the way by the duet. Drigo's work has since become the standard ending to the pas de deux. Meanwhile, a few choreographers still use Tchaikovsky's ending: Balanchine, for instance, in his one-act rendering of *Swan Lake*, which is presently unavailable on video.

In succession, as the music trails to a conclusion, Siegfried walks Odette around in a small circle and guides her through a gentle finger turn, first a single, then a double, then a quadruple. Amid this sequence, Odette does what are known as *petit battement sur le cou de pied*, which means little beatings of the (working) foot at the ankle of the (supporting) foot. The fluttering shimmer of the action has the effect of visualizing a heartbeat. As closure to the entire "Love Duet" Odette swooningly falls out of her final finger turn and then returns to her upright position only to plummet one last time into a deep reaching arabesque *penché*. In a minimum of business and a maximum of focus, Dowell completes the picture of heart-stopping introspection by breathing with perfect sympathy into the calm stillness Makarova's Odette achieves. For me this simple, inanimate moment says "at peace."

(For a version of the "Love Duet" as a duet à trois, honoring the fact that in 1895, Petipa let Siegfried's friend Benno share in the "labor" of partnering, due to the advancing of age of Pavel Gerdt, the original Prince, see *The Royal Ballet* with *Swan Lake*, Act 2, featuring Margot Fonteyn as Odette, Michael Somes as Siegfried, and Bryan Ashbridge as Benno, 1959, 132 min., Color. For another look at Makarova's Odette, four years earlier in another production, see *American Ballet Theatre: Swan Lake* with Makarova and Ivan Nagy, 1976, released 1988, 122 min., Color.)

The gears change radically in the "Dance of the Little Swans," the next part of the suite. Sometimes called the "Pas de Petits Cygnes" or simply the "Cygnets," this is probably the most familiar number in *Swan Lake*. If ever you've seen four jokesters interlink crossed arms in a side-by-side lineup and and pump through a chirpy little dance, you've seen the essence of this number. The effect this dance "without arms" makes, is one of a colorful embroidery. It has the texture of legs and feet doing fine-thread cross-stitching as the upper bodies do slightly more heavy bigger cross-stitches. If you follow the four-way unison footwork you'll see steps classified as *échappé*, *entrechat*, *relevé-passé*, *pas de chat*, and *emboîté*. This is followed by another waltz, sometimes referred to as a "General Dance." Its nickname is usually "Big Swans" since it comes directly after the little swans. (Most companies regularly cast their shortest dancers in the roles of cygnets and their tallest as big swans. In our video, the latter is performed by two coryphée level women, but other productions use four, presumably to balance symmetrically with the quartet of cygnets.) Because of the yeastier and more booming nature of its music, this waltz usually tends to be based on big jumps and big poses in arabesque. And so it is here, even if these English grands jetés look less grand than many a Russian rendering of the same steps. (For an example of what I mean, see the Kirov *Swan Lake* mentioned earlier.)

Now Odette returns, alone. The stage, by the way, remains "set" with the swan corps that did not dance in either the little or big swan dances. This is Odette's solo, the only one of the lakeside act. She brings with her the melancholy with which she left. She starts croisé, which is to say not directly facing the audience, but at a slight angle, with her downstage leg crossing the upstage one. She unfolds her upstage leg and via a move known as rond de jambe en l'air she softly kicks it upward, having gone onto the pointe of her supporting leg. At the top of each of three successive *développé* moves (developed or unfolded), she has faces directly front, directing her movements' entreating qualities directly at the audience. As the music continues its rising melancholic mood, Odette makes more entreating moves. Twice on a diagonal path, she jumps through two graded, varied sissones that end in a tremulous balance in an arabesque made particularly swanlike in the arch of her torso and the cast-back nature of her arms and hands. Makarova, a ballerina famous (or infamous, depending upon taste) for preferring extremely slow adagio tempos, takes special care throughout her solo to hold and sustain the choreography's frequent moments of balance. These details stand in stronger than usual contrast once she enters the solo's final phase: After returning twice to the upstage left corner to start, restart, and start yet again a diagonal stretch of piqué turns, she sets off into them with the almost feverish energy heard in the music. For punctuation, she aims to hit one more grand and still swan arabesque, before exiting.

A most insistent and driven coda follows, involving all the swan maidens, repeatedly in balloné steps (accenting the lower part of a raised working leg in toward the supporting leg). Emotional heat stirs up further as four swan maidens at a time hop, on a flat foot, in arabesque, lowered heads and stretched arms on a consistent line. Technically these moves qualify as *arabesque voyagé*, but generically they might be called flat-foot hops and they have both a gravitas and primal charm that make them so beguiling to behold. Finally, Odette joins her sisters, making her way on her familiar diagonal path by starting a move facing her downstage corner and finishing it after flipping (*fouetté*, in strict terms) position to end facing upstage.

Before striking one more flushed-with-energy-and-anxiety swan arabesque, Odette backs up, center stage, facing the audience with a furious series of rélevé/passé and entrechat moves that make you think she'd like to jump out of her own skin. Siegfried's return at the climax acts to lift Odette heavenward as the familiar swan theme fills the air. Rothbart returns on his crag, the light of dawn suffuses the scene, and after her swan sisters snake out in a long curling line, Odette arches potently back toward Rothbart and away from Siegfried. Then, on the music's rippling diminuendo, she skims out in a trail of pas de bourée suivi steps as, facing flat upstage, her back and arms ripple sensations telling of a return to her bewitched swan form.

Act 3 (or Act 2), The Ballroom in a Great Hall

Our narrator tells us now of betrothal celebrations in Siegfried's castle the evening after events at what he calls Swan Lake. (the ballet's libretto, by the way, does not similarly refer to the lake where Siegfried meets Odette as Swan Lake.) We learn that our Odette-smitten Prince will find none of the six princesses a suitable bride, and that he'll be duped by a mysterious nobleman's daughter, whom he takes to be Odette. Once he learns of his deception, the Prince realizes that Odette must be forever condemned to being a swan.

At curtain up, the castle's great hall readies for further festivites. A master of ceremonies greets and announces the arrival of dancers from individual nations: Hungary, Spain, Naples, and Poland. Next the six prospective fiancées and finally the Queen Mother and Prince Siegfried. A fanfare announces the arrival of a quartet of dancers, two couples dressed in traditional classical ballet costume—tutus and tiaras on the women, and tunics and tights on the men. Their dance, almost as straightforwardly separate from the action as that of the pas de trois, has the air of high entertainment at this celebrational gathering. In fact, the music, from a "Pas de Six" Tchaikovsky wrote for this act, but which Petipa cut from his 1895 staging, is rarely used nowadays in *Swan Lake*. But Asthon found it inspiring, and in 1963 made his pas de quatre. (Originally it replaced the first act's pas de trois, but eventually it was placed in the ballroom act.)

The music is bright and brassy and the two men and two women start out, linked hand in hand, side by side in a faint echo of the configuration taken by the little swans. The pas's opening, to the music's intrada is full of grace note and big-stroke physicalities. With the women in very short tutus and the men using their legs and heads most freely, the tone here is brighter and more baroque than anywhere else in the ballet. The first solo is for one of the women (Paisy). Originally made for up-and-coming Royal ballerina Merle Park, the almost sassy and kicky dance is said to be based by Ashton on the teasing social dance known as the cha-cha. A double solo for the men follows to an almost boisterous portion of the dance suite. Harkening to the predominance of horns, the dance covers the stage with simultaneous, alternating, and counterpointing big jumps, big kicking steps, and rapid turns. The next female solo (Ellis) was made for soon-to-be Royal ballerina Antoinette Sibley. Dominated by a lively oboe, its intricacies are said to be based on the then hot disco dance known as the Twist. A dashing and thrilling coda brings back all four dances and eventually sets them rollicking and bolting through to a breathlessly excited finish.

Another waltz ensues, at the behest of the Queen. Its purpose is to introduce the Prince to the princess candidates for his fiancée. He chooses none, even as his mother insists, and only the arrival, and dancing, of two couples of Spanish dancers momentarily deflects her royal displeasure. This is the first in the suite of "National Dances" that Tchaikovsky wrote to satisfy a popular form of divertissement dancing. Divertissements or diversions often occurred within the context of narrative ballets to lard the event with the local color favored by a public eager to see dances from far-off places.

Swan Lake's Spanish dance is traditionally a two-couple number and so it is here, with men in smart boleros and heeled boots and women in heeled pumps, flounced skirts, and mantillas. The choreography is usually ballet/flamenco with swooping back bends and hands held as if brandishing castanets. (Tchaikovsky composed his bolero-style music with hopes the dancers might actually play castanets themselves.)

The Hungarian dance takes the form of a couple dance called the czardas, in this instance for four subsidiary couples and one central duo. Instead of Spanish *tanceno* or heel-to-floor work, the accents here involve the clicking together of heels and elbow-jutting port de bras with one-hand-on-hip and one-behind-the-head angularity.

Unlike the two previous national dances, which show reasonable links to the dances that graced Petipa's 1895 ballroom scene, the "Neapolitan Dance" is pure fantasy and pure twentieth-century invention. Ashton created it in 1963, the same time as the "Pas de Quatre." For the start, both the male and female dancers have tambourines. Unlike the character shoes involved in the costuming of the other national dancers, these "Neapolitan" dancers wear ballet shoes—soft slippers for him, pointe shoes for her. They work their feet and their lower legs with mercurial, virtuoso finesse. Dizzying beats, intricate jumps, and quick-stabbing pointes create a heated cushion of air for this dance to ride upon. Soon the aerial gets more expansive as the two dancers cover space more hungrily. Fanciful coronet playing only spurs the dancers on more confidently, all of which segues musically into a "Tarantella," a one-time folkloric dance of exorcism. After the beribboned revelers toss their tambourines to some helpful Hungarians, they link hands and swing each other around and around, wrapping and unwrapping themselves over and over to steal kisses. Once unhooked from their prancing, kissing circuit, they flourish their hands as if to say, "It wasn't anything!"

It's back to character shoes—boots on both men and women—for the final national dance, a mazurka. A Polish court dance quite popular in Russia, this rendering was put together for the Royal Ballet by Nureyev. Set for four equally prominent couples, the dancing displays traditional foot-brushing steps and gentle solicitations between the mustachioed men and the toque-wearing women. Meanwhile, you may well notice that Dowell's Siegfried reenters the ballroom during this final "divert." Odd and almost distracting as it looks, it has only one reason for being: if the dancer playing the Prince had to sit still through all the national dances his muscles would go cold and perhaps stiff. So making the most of the melancholy mood that makes him wander in and out, Dowell is likely better warmed up for having spent some useful time offstage preparing his muscles.

A "surprising" fanfare announces unexpected guests, an unfamiliar nobleman and his daughter, Odile, who looks to Siegfried remarkably like Odette. The casting of the same ballerina as both Odette and Odile goes back to the first staging. As one parody of the convention made clear, when noting that Pelagia Karpakova played both roles: " 'How like Mlle Karpakova she is!' exclaims Siegfried. 'Why are you so surprised?' wonders [Benno]. 'You see that it is she, only in another role!' " Since then Odile has regularly, if not exclusively, been performed by the same ballerina, in a tour de force challenge of opposing characterizations.

Much less longstanding is the identification, almost everywhere accepted nowadays as tradition, of Odile as the Black Swan. Until the 1940s, Odile was simply Rothbart's deceitful daughter. The color of her costume could be anything from graded aurora borealis hues (as in the 1895 costume sketch) to reds, golds, or greens. In 1941, Alexandra Fedorova-Fokine staged the "ballroom act" of *Swan Lake* for the first time in the United States, and called her excerpt "The

Magic Swan." Probably because she wanted it to be distinct from the usually excerpted "lakeside" scene with its then popular "White Swan Pas de Deux," the swan ballerina at its center, dressed in jet black, would be known as the Black Swan. Makarova wears the now-traditional black tutu, though she eschews a traditional costume from her native Russia which would feature the two-pronged panache of black feathers that figure on most Soviet-Russian Odiles. Though these look blatantly like devil horns to non-Russian eyes, to Russians they probably tell of their intended source: the feathery peaks that demark the horned-owl, emblematic bird from that part of the world.

Odile and her character's color and costuming aren't the only traditions that have been adjusted since *Swan Lake* came into the world. Another detail that Tchaikovsky might not recognize is the particular music for Odile's seductive duet with Siegfried. The music almost universally hailed nowadays for the "Black Swan Pas de Deux" was originally written by the composer for a duet in Act 1. Petipa is the one who transposed it to the ballroom scene after Tchaikovsky's death. It's this music that Dowell and Makarova dance to. Ears that are sensitive to key signatures will hear the awkward change made from the introductory passage to the opening bars of the pas de deux.

Eyes that are sensitive to the workings of one pas de deux over another will see that while Siegfried's duet with Odile is brighter and flashier than his encounter with Odette, this ballroom duet still qualifies as a pas d'action. Even as it displays the ballerina's dance prowess in a bolder fashion, it still carries along in its formal elements the particulars of the impostor duping the dazzled Prince. In his deftly skilled hands as a partner, Dowell's Siegfried manages to support Makarova's Odile and yet let her appear to maintain her independence, a sense of her being always one step ahead of him, confidently leading him on. Her teasingly dizzying turns and her arms masking her face all tell us what she's up to even as her prince remains too dazzled to see it clearly himself. (The presence of her "nobleman" father indicates how much more effective this *duet à trois* might be if the Odette pas d'action still involved Benno.) When Odile plunges into penché postures, they're as fluid and deep as Odette's, but much more calculated and much less inevitable. Odile's winglike arms betray more edge, less comforting warmth. Her sustained balance in arabesque is more brazen, her cast-back head and arms tell more of wild laughter than of imploring resignation.

The ballroom solo of Siegfried moves in marked contrast to his coming-of-age contemplative one. Dowell's clean, clear jump and shiningly spun turns get showcased here and reveal his state of elation and pleasure. Odiles's solo is full of confident turns—outside pirouettes, and inside piqué attitude turns. A series of teasingly "overturned" tours, known as *renversé* turns, that she leaps into with both feet first, have a now-you-see-me-now-you-don't sly and almost discombobulating air. Finally she circuits the stage with repeated turns (the piqué and chaîné variety), zipping into a climactic length of them before planting herself confidently in a stock-still finish. (To be sure, the camera's magnifying lens catches the little insecurities that are part of Makarova's way with dancing—she was not born one of nature's innate turners—but it also documents her fearless nature to "go for it" with pleasure.)

A thumping coda lets Dowell display more of his elation through elevation and turns, and brings Odile to a virtuoso moment that has been part of the ballet since its 1895 staging. This, if you've ever had an even slightly knowledgeable conversation about the Black Swan, means Odile's famous fouettés. *Fouetté* simply means "whipped"; in the instance of *Swan Lake*'s ballroom scene the term stands for *fouetté rond de jambe en tournant*, which is a long way of saying "whipped circling of the leg while turning." The nickname fouetté is easier to say and think about, but technically it applies to a variety of moves, and you should know when you use it to apply here you're speaking in shorthand.

Ballet history has it that Pierina Legnani, the steely-toed Italian virtuosa who performed Odette/Odile in Petipa's landmark staging of *Swan Lake*, was a technical whiz at turns on pointe. Previously, in *Aladdin* and in *Cinderella*, she wowed her public by executing *sur place*—"in one spot," thirty-two successive fouettés . . . en tournant. Finding fresh opportunity in the racing music of Tchaikovsky's pas de deux, she and Petipa decided to insert her specialty. The rest is history. And, while this or that brave ballerina substitutes some other, more personally agreeable steps in this place, most end up taking flack for it in both official and unofficial commentary after the fact.

(For a successful and effective alternative to the Legnani legacy, see: *Swan Lake*, Bolshoi Ballet, with Maya Plisetskaya and Nikolai Fadeyechev, 1957, released 1984, 81 min., Color. For an eager acceptance of Legnani's Black Swan bravura, see Alicia Alonso pull out all the stops on the famous fouettés and add a few steely-toed challenges of her own in hops on pointe in sustained arabesque pose: *Alicia*, including the Black Swan from *Swan Lake*, 1973, 75 min., B&W and Color.)

Makarova's final pas de deux pose suggests Odile in a pleased moment of triumph. In shape, her posture looks very like one that her Odette might take, except for the tone. There is a beaming, self-satisfied cant to her braced stance with head and arms thrown back. In a similar pose Odette would be sighing; the Odile version has a good laugh. Agitation and resolution ensue with the act's final *scène*, in the swiftness of which we hear bits of the fiancée's waltz. Siegfried pleases his mother by choosing Odile for his bride, and Rothbart insists on a sworn declaration. When Siegfried swears his troth, two fingers proudly raised to heaven, confusion and hurly-burly rain down. Odile unleashes her most wicked look of laughter, and, as an apparition of Odette appears outside a window, Siegfried realizes his error. The court clears out as Siegfried rushes into the night, through the vaporous smoke left in the wake of Odile's exit, and the Queen is left disconsolate.

Act 4 (or Act 3), The Lakeside

The last act of *Swan Lake*, as our narrator notes, takes us back to the "enchanted lake." There Odette, grieving over Siegfried's betrayal, is kept from drowning herself by her swan-maiden sisters. When Siegfried arrives to tell of his having been tricked, the two vow to end their lives together in the lake. Rothbart tries to prevent them from doing so, knowing that Odette's death will destroy him. But the lovers seal their pact, and disappear into the lake's waters as Rothbart is vanquished. In a final apotheosis, Siegfried and Odette remain united in death as they could not be in life.

Of all the ballet's acts, the fourth is the least standard. While renderings of Petipa's and Ivanov's 1895 scheme for this final act can be found nowadays (see the previously mentioned Kirov and ABT videos), stagings that frequently hew to the original often take liberties here, which is certainly what Ashton has done. The choreography for Act 4 of this Royal Ballet production is exclusively his. So is the ordering and choice of music. In more academic circumstances, I might lean away from this production as it caps a staging that mostly honors and re-creates a classic's successful and traditional workings with a scheme all its own. Petipa and Ivanov worked most on their last act, ordering new music (orchestrations of related Tchaikovsky compositions for piano) and reworking several details of the original libretto.

Ashton has kept to the outline of the revised libretto, but he has gone back to much of the 1877 music, using none of the 1895 additions. In the process, he has limpid and fluid choreography that raises to fresh heights the effective powers of the female corps de ballet. We shall see further "choreographic writing" for the female corps that matches the beauty Ashton has wrought, but we will not, in my view, see these efforts bettered.

The act opens on Tchaikovsky's entr'acte music, as Rothbart, first from his crag of a perch and then at the center of the stage, sweeps through, mesmerizing and controlling the twenty-eight swan maidens in their linear formations. Once they've gathered and their sorcerer has departed, they dance with a melancholy tread to the score's "Danses des Petits Cygnes." (These almost weeping numbers should not be confused with the brisker "Dance of the Little Swans" from the first lakeside scene.) The result is a sublime corps de ballet display. The steps are little more than walkings on and off pointe, but there's strength in numbers and the follow-the-leader lines snake, curl, and ring about the stage like moonlight on ripples of water. The picture is made extra shimmering by the constant embellishment of upper-body carriage, especially in the use of the arms, head, and neck. Ashton brings his corps de ballet segment to a close with a kind of majestic whisper. His linear, clustered, and circling formations finally configure as in a stage-wide lineup that has the spread and breadth of a swan in flight. Softly, the gigantic winged display, with the individual dancers' arms acting like tendrils of down, floats forward with the ease of a mist. With apt motivation from Tchaikovsky, it finally comes to rest like a great winged bird on a nest. A gift for choreographic grouping is as rewarding as a talent for inventive movement. Some choreographers have one or the other; some, like Ashton, have both.

The supple geometry and soft mood of the moment is immediately broken, musically as well as physically, by the start of Tchaikovsky's "Allegro agitato" *scène*. Odette's shifting moves reveal her not knowing where to turn. Her sorrowing gestures weigh her down; her distress discomforts her swan sisters. They prevent her from attempting to hurl herself into the lake.

Boisterous sounds, full of percussion, bring back Rothbart who claims possession of Odette with big lifts, his owl wings often menacingly outspread to exert his authority over all the swan maidens. Climactically, Siegfried returns, amid the storm Rothbart has conjured. He finds Odette and, on bended knees, begs forgiveness.

An interlude of Ashton's special devising follows. Using an especially lachrymose variation from the long-ago discarded "Pas de Six" of the ballroom scene, Ashton hears the lamenting woodwinds calling to Odette as she leads out row upon row of swan maidens. Between leading out each group she returns to comfort the distraught, prostrate Prince. As they exit, by means of nibbling *bourrée* steps on pointe in fifth position, the swan maidens show the elemental, expressive nature of elemental ballet steps. When Siegfried's all alone, and the music builds in volume and texture, Odette stirs him to his feet and into a duet of almost distracted and abandoned poses and movements. They end with a repeat of the pose that began the first lakeside scene's "Love Duet."

Another mood change comes from Tchaikovsky's "Scène, Finale." A vengeful Rothbart comes between the lovers, almost literally tearing apart their embrace. A resigned embrace signifying determination to end her life in the lake takes Odette away from Siegfried, and into the lake, by way of a *grand jeté pas de chat*, into the upstage wing. Siegfried follows suit, and Rothbart is left to writhe in the knowledge that his spell has been broken. The "released" swan maidens reenter in a flush of energy, spurred on by the music Tchaikovsky wrote to accompany the original libretto's call for a flooding of the lake. As the evil genie passes weakly through their ranks to expire on his rock, the swan maidens ripple like sea anemones and finally line up to bow before the sight of Siegfried and Odette, sailing off in a swan-drawn boat to the afterlife.

(For a look at a rendering of the originally intended flood, see *Rudolf Nureyev/Margot Fonteyn in Tchaikovsky's "Swan Lake"*, 1966, approx. 106 min., Color. For a more dramatic staging of the suicide, see the ABT video mentioned earlier, and for a dramatic conquering of Rothbart by Siegfried and a Social realist Soviet happy ending, see the Bolshoi Ballet video also mentioned above.)

Swan Postscript

So now, you've seen the Swan Queen die in *Swan Lake*. But technically you haven't seen ballet's almost equally famous solo called "The Dying Swan." This is a separate ballet, a vignette, really, that has nothing to do with *Swan Lake* whatsoever.

"The Dying Swan" began life in 1905 as "The Swan." Choreographed by Michael Fokine for Anna Pavlova as a *pièce d'occasion*, the solo is set to the "swan" portion of Camille Saint-Saëns' *Carnival of the Animals* suite. In this case, it's an evocative cello solo. It acquired the name "Dying Swan" as the tremulous Pavlova interpreted its dramatic arc as one going toward the expiration of life.

Made up of little more than supple upper body and arm movements and *pas de bourrée suivi*—teeny, nibbling steps that are often as even and smooth as a string of pearls—the choreography has doubtless had a resonating effect on the look of Odette and her "body language" ever since. Most Odettes borrow something from "The Dying Swan" lineage in their leave-taking at the end of the first lakeside scene. Certainly, Makarova does. There is a silent, almost complete 1925 film of Pavlova doing her solo, to which sound is often post-applied. No complete extant version is now on commercial cassette, but it is part of a television series called *The Magic of the Dance*, hosted by Margot Fonteyn, which may be rerun occasionally or eventually made available commercially.

Probably the ballerina most identified with the role since Pavlova is Moscow's Maya Plisetskaya. Almost any film or video about the legendary Soviet ballerina includes at least excerpts from "The Dying Swan." You can see her do the complete five-minute, twenty-seven-second solo, while in her seventies, on a video: *Essential Ballet: Stars of the Russian Ballet*, 1993, 117 min., Color.

POPULAR BEYOND BALLET

The Nutcracker

• • •

A ballet in two acts, four scenes, and prologue
Choreography by George Balanchine
Music by Pyotr Tchaikovsky

If *The Nutcracker* was your candidate for the first and foremost ballet in the world, maybe that's because you've already seen some version of it. Or, perhaps it's because you associate ballet with *The Nutcracker Suite*, a popular selection of musical excerpts heard in many a background at Christmastime. If you've never seen any production of *The Nutcracker* anywhere—on the stage, screen, television, or on ice—and are now pursuing your interest in ballet, you're probably not doing so in America.

If, by the way, you want to show how far beyond square one you've gotten in your ballet interests, be sure to remind anyone who says *Nutcracker Suite* when he means *The Nutcracker* that the former is a musical suite sometimes rendered as a mini-dance version of the latter, which is what actually qualifies as the real thing. (Unlike *Swan Lake* and its variously amended score, however varied the choreographic stagings, *Nutcracker* tends to use Tchaikovsky's score as the composer wrote it.) The original staging of *Nutcracker* came in 1892. Because of the collaborative authorship between ballet master in chief Marius Petipa and his assistant Lev Ivanov, the ballet prefigured the creation of the "memorial" *Swan Lake* three years later.

Because of the ballet's broad popularity, *Nutcracker* has come to us in a wide variety of versions. Because no chain connects recent Russian productions with the 1892 original, there is no particular reason to give them special consideration. Neither of the two prominent English versions proves particularly notable, including the one that aims to restage Ivanov's choreography as approximately as possible.

The video I have chosen here records the American production that was probably more responsible than any other for giving rise to the nationwide popularity the ballet possesses in the United States in the twentieth century. This is the production devised by Balanchine in 1954, recalling the staging he was brought up with when he was a young student and dancer in St. Petersburg (1915–1924).

About the video:

> *George Balanchine's The Nutcracker* (Darci Kistler, Damian Woetzel, Kyra Nichols, Bart Robinson Cook, Macaulay Culkin, Jessica Lynn Cohen), 1993 (released on video, 1994), 93 min., Color.
>
> This filming records the granddaddy of all American *Nutcrackers* in a quasi-stage, quasi-sound studio setting. It documents American dancers of New York City Ballet, the company that Balanchine founded and with whose dancers he first choreographed his twentieth-century rendering of the nineteenth-century *ballet-féerie*. The cast also includes a movie personality, as is often the case when ballet moves from its local culture center to the popular big screen. He is Macaulay Culkin playing the little nutcracker/little prince. The rest of the children's roles are performed by pupils of the School of American Ballet, the academy Balanchine founded upon landing in America.

As is sometimes the case with "major motion picture" affairs, *Nutcracker* was released with related CD recordings; in this case, two differently conceived ones. One offers the score almost exactly as it's played in the ballet (see below); the other, the same score with overdubbed narration telling the story of the ballet and its happenings. Since the film also includes some narration, less wordy than the CD's, it makes more sense to listen to the music "plain," the way it would be heard in the theater. This could be the ideal way to study ballet music that has a direct relationship to the ballet theater. Because the music you're hearing actually accompanied the kind of dancing it was composed for, you can assume the tempos and textures are not merely fancyings of the conductor or musicians involved. Additionally, the CD's accompanying booklet notes for the recording without narration give more careful and accurate scene-by-scene account of Tchaikovsky's musical structure. (*Music from the Original Soundtrack/George Balanchine's "The Nutcracker"*, New York City Ballet Orchestra, David Zinman, Conductor), 1993, 73:33 min.)

Like the *Swan Lake* video, *The Nutcracker* video has very sketchy labeling, the full cast credits appear only onscreen, at the end of the video. They're given here, in the manner of a printed program you'd be given in the theater.

CAST

The Sugar Plum Fairy	Darci Kistler
Her Cavalier	Damian Woetzel
Dewdrop	Kyra Nichols
Coffee	Wendy Whelan
Marzipan	Margaret Tracey
Tea	Gen Horiuchi
Candy Cane	Tom Gold
Hot Chocolate	Lourdes Lopez and Nilas Martins
Mother Ginger	William Otto
Fritz	Peter Reznik
Grandparents	Edward Bigelow and Karin von Aroldingen
Frau Stahlbaum	Heather Watts
Dr. Stahlbaum	Robert LaFosse
Herr Drosselmeier	Bart Robinson Cook
Marie	Jessica Lynn Cohen
The Nutcracker	Macaulay Culkin

Unlike *Swan Lake*, where the ballet's libretto was authored out of various sources into a somewhat original narrative, *Nutcracker*'s story comes mostly from an already familiar source, E. T. A. Hoffmann's "The Nutcracker and the Mouse King." Specifically, it is based on a slightly less dark and grotesque retelling of the same tale by Alexandre Dumas *père*, which he called "The Nutcracker of Nuremberg." Almost all currently performed or videotaped versions return to the Hoffmann/Dumas sources. Often, effort goes to "darkening" the tale with Hoffmann's penchant for the weird and metaphysical.

Balanchine's production, recorded here with all the costumes Barbara Karinska created and only slight adjustments to the stage settings designed by Rouben Ter-Arutunian, closely follows the 1892 libretto. This was originally put together out of Dumas's narrative by Petipa and the general director of the imperial theaters, Ivan Vsevolozhsky. Beyond the basic narrative, which various choreographers have followed, Balanchine has honored a premise of the original concept that is frequently abandoned, namely the use of children themselves in the roles conceived as child characters. Probably the most consistent adjustment made in the rewriting of *Nutcracker*'s libretto concerns the characters of the children. Striving to make more "adult" versions, choreographers often cast the children's roles of Act 1 with adults acting as children. This frequently allows for the transformation of the "children" into the adult heroes and heroines who appear in Act 2.

In broad outline, the original narrative, frequently maligned as being thin and untheatrical, thus motivating the frequent reworkings, goes as follows: Marie, the small daughter of the Stahlbaums, spends Christmas Eve among her friends and family. Accompanied by his young, well-mannered nephew, Herr Drosselmeier, Marie's clockmaker-magician godfather, arrives at the gathering. His entertaining behavior betrays both mischief and mystery. Among his presents is a grotesque-faced nutcracker for Marie. Her fiesty little brother jealously breaks the toy and Drosselmeier repairs it in a makeshift manner. After the party's conclusion and night falls, Marie goes to find the nutcracker to comfort her as strange events occur. Drosselmeier madly appears atop the room's clock and mice overrun the parlor and engage in battle with the household's toy soldiers. At a crucial point in the battle, now led by the rodents' Mouse King, Marie throws her shoe and fells the belligerent king. At his demise, the Nutcracker is changed into a little prince, who had been bewitched into his grotesque state by the Mouse King's evil mother. In reward for her valor and innocent devotion to the Nutcracker, Marie is taken to the land of snow and then to the Land of Sweets. There, at the court of the Sugar Plum Fairy, there is rejoicing for their prince released from his spell and the Sugar Plum Fairy commands a celebration and entertainment of dancing. Capping the divertissements of sweet confections, comes the dancing of the regal fairy herself. All the kingdom salutes and blesses the marriage of their golden prince and the good Marie.

Tchaikovsky's overture, which reveals no leitmotifs (*Nutcracker* is his only ballet without them), sparkles as if full of air and light. There are no potentially brooding cellos or double basses to be heard. Just as the curtain would rise at its end, so the pop-up proscenium stage with its drawn curtain takes us into the theater of *The Nutcracker*. As he did for the structure of *Swan Lake*, Tchaikovsky composed sections he called *scènes* for episodes meant to carry the narrative by means of pantomime or acting gestures. He also composed dance portions, each duly named to support the kind of dancing appropriate for evolving the narrative in pure dance methods.

Act 1, The Home of The Stahlbaum Family, Christmas Eve

The "Prologue" (to Tchaikovsky's *scène*) shows Marie and her little brother Fritz outside the parlor where they learn, by peeking through a keyhole, that the Christmas tree is nearly finished being trimmed. Familiar tussles, telling how siblings will be siblings, occur. Guests arrive, both adult and child. Their miming refects the warmth, grace, and eagerness sounded in the music. (In an unintentional and negative example, a child here and a parent there oversteps the comfortable bounds of pantomime and resorts to behaving like a gulping goldfish. Mime is *not* speaking without sound, nor mouthing the statement so the "listener" can follow the familiar lip movements of being spoken to. It's a gestural, separate language that can be shaded by facial expression, but should not be accompanied by open-mouthed articulations. Rule of thumb: When the dancer is mouthing to shape pantomime, he is probably floundering and improvising, because he hasn't been instructed well in distinct ways of formal mime expression.)

On a building musical cue, we enter Scene 1, where, in the momentarily darkened parlor, wide-eyed children approach the prettily lighted tree and all its presents. Tchaikovsky's next musical section, "Marche," finds the Stahlbaums leading the children in a little dance, eventually for six couples, with the mischievous Fritz having to partner with his mother.

Another social dance follows quickly on the heels of the "Marche." This is called "Petit Galop des Enfants et Entrée des Parents" and takes the form of the fathers escorting their little daughters, followed by the little sons assuming their roles as dancers without any assistance from their parents. This square dance–style activity, with the dancing children and parents moving to the center of the floor and back again to wait another turn, is a delicately figured performance without the showiness of ballet's athleticism or acrobatics. The "Entrée des Parents" segment comes almost as an interruption of the figured dance. More adults, additional children, and a set of grandparents arrive. Holiday drinks lead to a toast and presents get distributed.

A darkening of mood comes with the next section, a *scène dansante*. The owl-topped grandfather clock strikes eight, and an unusual latecomer arrives. Covered in black, he carries large boxes and has with him a young boy. After hiding under his big top hat, the mystery man, in the swirl of his large cape, pops up to reveal that he's Godfather Drosselmeier. Marie is relieved and pleased at his identity, but she's a little shy and taken aback when her godfather presents her to his nephew. The two children take each other's hands, but the younger Marie finally pulls hers away, not knowing precisely what to make of the unknown acquaintance. He shrugs off her behavior (a little too broadly for Balanchine's intention of mysteriousness, in my opinion).

Old man Drosselmeier, with unkempt hair, dangling watch fob, and a patch on one eye, makes the rounds of greeting the adults but clearly he seems more comfortable with the children. First he complies with the kids' call for magic tricks. Then he produces life-size dolls from the packages he brought: a pair of commedia dell'arte dolls (Harlequin and Columbine) and a military automaton (a fearsome soldier). Each respective "doll" performs a miniature dance: Harlequin and Columbine, a pas de deux and the soldier, a *pas diabolique;* that is, a driven, possessed dance. (Originally, both dances were intended for pairs of automatons, in a reversal of the characters presented. The first dolls were a militaristic pair, and each popped out of off-putting "packages"—the military canteen maid from a head of cabbage and a soldier from a meat pie. The second pair came out of large snuffboxes. (For an approximation of these original intentions, see *The Nutcracker*, with The Royal Ballet, starring Leslie Collier and Anthony Dowell, 1985, 102 min., Color.)

Once again, the party becomes more intimate with the start of "Scène et Danse du Grossvater." Drosselmeier has more presents up his sleeve including a stick horse, which proves to be a momentary attraction, once he produces his most special gift. From under his coat, he pulls out a toothy, white-haired doll-like fellow, who can crack nuts in his jaws. Pantomime and music tell of cracking nuts, and eventually Drosselmeier presents the funny-looking little man to Marie. (Some of the movie's added sound effects overwhelm those deftly fitted by Tchaikovsky into the musical mix.) Marie is enchanted. Fritz is jealous. He snatches the nutcracker from his sister's loving arms, and in a fit of pique drops the wooden doll to the floor, breaking him. The godfather is dismayed, but not daunted, and uses his handkerchief as a kind of bandage while a sympathetic nephew Drosselmeier gives Marie a small white bed for her nutcracker to rest on. The two innocents take each other's hands for the second time, expressing their mutual admiration. This time Marie finds no cause to pull abruptly away. Interludes of lullaby peacefulness between the girls and their dolls are broken by the rat-a-tat-tat noises of the boys with their military hats and drums.

Introductory music and a calling for the "Grandfather's Dance" (an Old World tradition for the last dance of a social gathering) find Drosselmeier encouraging his nephew to escort Marie through the dance. The group activity, in which both young and old participate in couples, includes a stately section and a brisker one. After closing on the Grandfather Dance's more frantic note, the lullaby that marks the soothing to bed of Marie's nutcracker returns and the party breaks up in an almost yawning tone. The scene's final soft stroke has Drosselmeier and Frau Stahlbaum respectively leading away young Drosselmeier and Marie, who have taken each other's hands one more time and betray no interest in parting.

Here is where Balanchine adds an interpolation of music Tchaikovsky wrote for another of his ballets. It's an "Entr'acte" for a violin solo, originally intended for and then cut from *The Sleeping Beauty*. Unfortunately, the video includes a bit too much narrative chatter over the lyrical reverie, but unencumbered in the theater it serves to take little Marie in her nightgown back down to the parlor to be with her dear, lonely nutcracker. As the violin's "song" intensifies, it brings back Frau Stahlbaum to make sure Marie is safe and sound and brings on Drosselmeier to repair the nutcracker's jaw.

At the end of the violin's solo, Act 1, scene 1's final musical *scène* resumes. The parlor takes on a wilder atmosphere and the music (overrun by a few too many dramatic storm sound effects on the tape) indicates a change in the air. Marie thinks to put her nutcracker in his own bed, and discovers an almost diabolical Drosselmeier atop the owl-crested grandfather's clock flapping like a night bird himself while large and bothersome mice overrun the room seemingly at her godfather's instigation. The music indicates a mounting tension and the proportions of the room start to change. The toy cabinet and soldiers dwarf Marie and finally the Christmas tree to the score's most majestic elaborations grows to a towering height climaxing at the score's grandest peak as the now-outside french windows detail how enormous the parlor has become.

Act 1, Scene 2, The Battle

Almost everything in Marie's world has grown huge except her and the Nutcracker, and soon he too transforms on his little bed and grows to match the scale of everything else around Marie. The Nutcracker takes charge of leading the soldiers and directs a valiant but losing battle against the belligerent mice. The arrival of the mice's seven-headed Mouse King threatens to turn the tide decisively against Marie's nutcracker when the brave girl hurls her slipper at the king and distracts him enough for the Nutcracker to slay him. After seeing the Mouse King expire, the Nutcracker cuts off his crown and displays it as the victor.

Act 1, Scene 3, A Fir Forest in Winter

Tchaikovsky's next, and final scene of Act 1, rolls in like a vaporous mist, for a dreamy "Andante" *scène.* It's a floating journey to a far-off world, where the Nutcracker waits with his trophy crown still in his hand. The scene swells to a climax, and crashing cymbals at once show the Nutcracker transformed magically into a little prince as Marie awakens amid the falling snows of a forest of fir trees. The little prince crowns her with the hard-won coronet, and leads her away.

Tchaikovsky's "Valse des Flacons de Neige" (Waltz of the Snowflakes) begins with music that curvets and cascades along with the snowflakes, cuing the individual corps de ballet dancers dressed as wintertime Taglionis for a wintry ballet blanc. After six musical *scènes* and five low-keyed dances—a march, a gallop, two doll dances, and grandfather's dance—we come to a full-scale ballet dance. Balanchine's choreographic circles and swirls by way of lineups, formations, leaps, and spins follow Tchaikovsky's momentum. After starting lightly, the scene's falling snow gets thick and heavy, bathing the dance in near-blizzard effects. In the theater, as on the screen, the actual falling snow (paper confetti, of course), builds up along with the dancing. A wordless choir adds to the music's texture, and downy pom-pom wands become extensions of the snowflake women's hands. (These props resemble those used in 1892, when similar sprays of downy balls came from the tips of hand-held wands.) A final double ring for all sixteen women in a radial cluster, climaxes the waltz, after which the snowflake women drift into the night as our little prince and little Marie return to continue their journey.

Act 2, *Confiturembourg,*
The Kingdom of the Sugar Plum Fairy

At this point, another *scène* is sometimes begun during the usual curtain-down overture. Golden-winged and haloed little girl angels skim about a brightly glowing new world landscaped by sweet treats as if displayed in a fancy confectioner's shop. The floor-length, standout skirts of the angels' dresses hide the locomoting activity of their feet. The look of gliding, almost as if on ice comes from a Russian dance tradition performed to a folk round called Beryozka, which means "birch tree." As do the women who dance in the Beryozka, the little angels carry green branches in one hand. The effect is achieved by taking unseen, fast, tiny steps and maintaining the kind of serene demeanor as if being buoyed along by helpful powers.

The *scène*'s cue for "curtain up" acts to signal the entrance of the beneficent Sugar Plum Fairy, who glides on accompanied by music shimmering with dainty sounds from the harp and the celesta. This last instrument is a kind of sophisticated toy piano, which when Tchaikovsky first learned of its existence while composing *Nutcracker*, found it "divinely beautiful." Balanchine wastes no time letting us hear more of the celesta's divinely beautiful music. As soon as the Sugar Plum Fairy deftly rounds up the little angels, she dances for them to the variation (or solo) Tchaikovsky composed for the later pas de deux. Its delicate tintinnabulations twinkle like light passing through cut crystal. Sugar Plum picks through it on pointe as precise and intricate as a laser. There are few jumps involved in her dance, and these take the shape of quick or soft dartings more than grand arcs. Her dancing is mostly made of piqué steppings onto pointe and a variety of turns, all of which variously fill her skirt of pink mist with air and light showing how expressive her legs are. Some of her high stepping and leg-lifting accents allow her skirt to clear a way for her "singing" legs. Complementing the grace of legs and feet is the graciousness of her upper body, with wand-flourishing port de bras blessing her surroundings with glistening, rococo flourishes. Momentarily, her feet skim, in pas de bourrée suivi complemented by rippling arms, showing sweetness where a dramatic Swan Queen might show sadness. In one highlight she comes directly forward, stepping into three successive en dedans pirouettes, before pausing in a double en dehors pirouette capped by a third spiraling spin called a *soutenu* turn. In another subsequent line she recedes from us in high-stepping half turns before following the music's accelerating force through a diagonal of relevé turns and more piqué turns.

If you'd like a "study" example of Balanchine's notion of ballet as an art of many distinctions among few elements, study this solo for its subtle shifts and changes of weight, direction, and posture. If you'd like to see how Balanchine's Sugar Plum solo borrows and reconstitutes elements from what we currently believe to be Ivanov's choreography, look at videos documenting Ivanov. (For example, Leslie Collier in the Royal Ballet *Nutcracker* video cited earlier in this chapter, and Violette Verdy in *A Trip to Christmas/The Bell Telephone Hour*, 1961, 47 min., Color.)

The next *scène*, the score's last so designated section, heralds the entrance of all the divertissement dancers representing various confections, exotic treats, and beauteous things. All of which leads to the arrival of the little prince and Marie in a walnut-shell boat. Upon being welcomed to his kingdom, the prince prepares to tell the tale of his adventures as a nutcracker. His "mimologue" is the first of two segments Balanchine credits directly back to the Ivanov production of his own youth. All gesture, with no mistaken "mouthing" of the particulars, articulates how when he was asleep in a far-off place with Marie lovingly watching over him, what should appear but whiskered, toothy rodents on the attack. At once he bravely took up arms against the pack's king, with whom he fought ferociously until Marie threw one of her shoes at the king, allowing the prince to take the advantage and slay the evil mouse. (Unfortunately for the full nuance and expression of the pantomime, Culkin proves adequate, but not inspired by the musical and movement subtleties of his "danced monologue." Neither his gesturing nor his moving about "sings" the way it could have if he had been living the life and work of a serious student of ballet like his predecessors. The fact that he once did go to the School of American Ballet helps, but ultimately not enough.)

The music and the staging tell of rejoicing at the victory, and the Sugar Plum Fairy enthrones Marie and her prince in the place of honor for a celebration of dancing. And, after the fairy passes artfully back and forth before her guests, accentuating her brief exit dance with grand jeté pas de chat twice over, she whisks herself away as the divertissements begin.

First comes "Hot Chocolate," "*Le Chocolat*" in Tchaikovsky's titling. Dominated by an exuberant trumpet and decorated with chattering castanets, the music scores a dance for a leading couple and four subsidiary couples. The choreography features skirt-swirling kicks and jumps for the women, and staglike leaps for the men with flamenco-styled arms and hands all around. Balanchine's vignette relives the *escuela* bolero dancing bred in eighteenth-and nineteenth-century Spain as a cross between ethnic Spanish dancing and ballet.

"*Le Café*" or "Coffee from Arabia," as our narrator says, is often called "Arabian" in ballet companies. Here it's a female dancer's solo, belly-dancer-like, with finger cymbals on each hand. Tchaikovsky's music is based on a folk tune from the Caucasus region of Georgia, where Balanchine's ancestors came from. Though Balanchine's choreography works on pointe, it does so selectively, letting the sinuous, serpentine airs of the music keep in a hootchy-kootchy world. (Originally, Balanchine made the solo for a male dancer as a hookah-smoking nobleman and four adolescent girls as parrots. The female soloist remake dates from 1964.)

"*Le Thé*" or "Tea" features a male soloist popping out of a tea chest rolled about by two fan-wielding female assistants. Rather like a jack-out-of-his-box, the man in silk pajamas spins like a top and jumps like a rabbit. His climactic jumps are big and climax in spread leg positions known as "the splits." They are variants on *soubresauts*, a class of jumps from two feet to two feet, the variety being the achievement of "the splits" at the peak.

Tchaikovsky's "*Trepak*," referring to a Russian folk dance and originally called a dance of *buffons* (or "jesters") in these divertissements, becomes Balanchine's second direct link to the 1892 choreography. Though he calls his number "Candy Canes," Balanchine retains the use of the hoop as a prop and the detail of jingle bells decorating the costumes. He also keeps to the original number's "scale" of performers by providing his leading Jester with a complement of smaller jester companions. The original lead was an athletic dancer named Aleksandr Shirayev, and he is often credited as the probable creator of his dance's acrobatic choreography. Whether it was the creation of Petipa, Ivanov, or Shirayev, the dance with the hoop now part of Balanchine's *Nutcracker* is sometimes called "Hoops" for short. It demands that the leading dancer, a man, be equally adept at turns and at jumps—in other words be what company members classify as "a turner and a jumper," and in this case one who can aim his dancing body through a hoop, all on Tchaikovsky's vigorous music. Ringing the tricky, central "hoopster" are more of the ballet's energetic student dancers. These eight, usually performed by girls but intended to be boys, are the eldest of *Nutcracker*'s student dancers. They don't have to jump through their hoops, only to raise them high or wheel them wide arcs in the air.

Called "*Les Mirlitons*" (meaning "reed pipes") in the score, the succeeding divertissement ended up in the suite without a sweet to go with it. Early on Petipa considered identifying the number with "cream pastries," but it didn't last. Balanchine calls his divertissement for a lead female dancer and ensemble "Marzipan Shepherdesses." These shepherdesses make lace in space by constant openings and closings of the feet and leg positions. The almighty fifth position keeps coming back to center the dancer before having her move away, often to second position and back again. Unlike Sugar Plum's soloing through pliant pointes, the lead Marzipan Shepherdess reveals more steely toes. All five women spend some of the piping dance jumping gingerly onto both pointes at once. Usually they demurely hold their pan pipes as if playing sweet pastoral airs while their feet and legs move like benign switchblades. In addition to much else, this is also a little showcase of batterie. Entrechat, rond de jambe en l'air, and the step Balanchine once let a square dance caller identify as "whickety-whack," the *gargouiallade*, actually a pas de chat–like jump with a rond de jambe en l'air for each foot. Also see the successive single en dedans pirouettes into a climactic triple, all as prelude to the final, multiple pirouette en dehors, finishing in a kneeling pose otherwise known as "pirouette to the knee."

With "Mother Ginger and the Polichinelles" or "*La Mère Gignon et les Polichinelles*" we get more student dancers, who play the well-behaved children of a "relative" of the "Old Woman Who Lived in a Shoe." Polichinelles are simply Frenchified versions of the family of Pulchinello from Italy's commedia dell'arte. We recognize them anglicized as Punch and Judy characters. Tchaikovsky's music borrows from a French folk song but few Americans in the late twentieth century will likely recognize it. Girl students make up this entire cast, though the children in the pink humpbacked outfits represent boy characters. La Mère herself is played in travesty by a man for Balanchine, just as she was for Ivanov. The movie camera dwells a bit overmuch on the improvised antics of "Mother Ginger," but you see enough of the little quadrille (four-couple dance) to see its innocent yet solid geometry. One repeated piqué-first arabesque shows an elemental move at its most elementary. Over and over these steps get stuck on demi-pointe, on the music, with care by diligent student dancers working and counting their little hearts out. Ditto for their elementary combination of *échappé, changement, rélevé-passé.* In the end they return to conceal themselves under their mother's enormous skirt, before she exits like a hen with her brood.

The "Valse des Fleurs," planned as a *grand ballabile*, closes the divertissement segment. In nineteenth-century tradition, the *ballabile* form meant a large group number with no solos. Tchaikovsky composed a lush, expansive waltz for what Petipa planned as a re-creation of the similarly grand number he staged for the "Valse Villageoise" in *Sleeping Beauty* two years earlier. Balanchine breaks the solo-less tradition of the *ballabile* by creating another ballerina role to lead his "Waltz of the Flowers." He calls her Dewdrop and she sweeps and soars among her sister waltzers with the ease and power of Zephyr. (Petipa's plan and Ivanov's execution included men as well as women in the mix—not so Balanchine's.) Besides twelve corps de ballet women in rosy pinks, he includes two "demi" women in faint lavenders to head the ensemble. All these women in tiered Romantic-length ballet dresses configure about the Dewdrop ballerina like a garden of lushly petaled blossoms.

The waltz begins in earnest to what sounds like hunting horns decoratively reverberating through the verdure of a woodland. Dewdrop holds central attention as queen of her landscape, often framed as if by a formally planted forest of trees lilting in the breeze. Frequently in the luminously strong and regal demeanor of Kyra Nichols, who is dressed in a kilted fantasy of a military uniform, complete with a helmet of crystal beads, we imagine we're seeing Diana, mythology's huntress goddess. In her expansive poses of sustained balance, Dewdrop looks at once like a huntress *and* her primed bow and arrow. (Karinska's costume seems to be made of rosewater and whalebone.) The waltz's yeastier, more robust airs cue Dewdrop's solo appearances as she leaps like a hurled javelin and turns with the naturalness of a jet of gyroscope. The more airy and lightly textured musical moments spur the ensemble into lineups and clusters that simultaneously expand and lighten the stage picture, as the layered skirts of the "flowers" float like a rising perfume. Three little quartets of "flower girls," led by the demi-pair, skim and prance, linked by crossed arms, in what may be Balanchine's homage to Ivanov's famous cygnets' dance. Eventually a stage-wide linked line of all fourteen flowers breaks into two gatelike wings that sweep open as Dewdrop streaks off into another of her exits. Her final, climactic reentry brings her directly toward the audience down center stage as two facing rows of inward bending flowers bend backward like the parting of a pink sea. Bold jumps and boldly struck arabesques all delicately weave into the waltz's lilting and surging climactic close, with Dewdrop finally alighted at the center of what looks like a gigantic floral spray.

(For a solo-less rendering of this *grand ballabile*, see what the Russians call "The Rose Waltz" in Vasily Vainonen's 1934 *Nutcracker*. The Kirov Ballet's production of the work includes twelve corps de ballet couples and four demi-couples. *The Nutcracker*, Larissa Lezhnina and Victor Baranov, Kirov Ballet, 1994, 100 min., Color.)

With the divertissements thus completed, the narrator says, "Into the great room the Sugar Plum Fairy herself came with her cavalier to dance for Marie and her prince." No mention of "pas de deux," though that in fact is what Tchaikovsky composed at Petipa's instructions, requesting an adagio with colossal effects. By the end of the next chapter on *Sleeping Beauty*, you'll have been introduced to all of the various pas de deux composed by Tchaikovsky. Once you've seen and heard all of them you can pick your own favorite, but I think Petipa's challenge toward "colossal effects" gave special inspiration to his composer and that this pas de deux has a grandeur unmatched by any other such pas. Frequently, this Tchaikovsky pas de deux, like that called "The Black Swan" and the one we'll learn about in *Sleeping Beauty*, often gets performed as an isolated showpiece. (It's also popular on the ballet competition circuit.) Often such duets get fancied up with the title of "Grand Pas de Deux," though however grand they are in effects, they still remain pas de deux. The "Grand" designation properly belongs only to the "Grand Pas d'Action" or "Grand Pas," sometimes specifically designated as, for instance, "Grand Pas Classique" or "Grand Pas Hongroise (or Hungarian-styled grand dance)."

Balanchine's choreography for the pas de deux of the Sugar Plum Fairy and her Cavalier is his own. But, just as he did with the Sugar Plum's solo, Balanchine pays passing homage to Ivanov's original choreography by working with similar steps and effects in different ways and to different parts of the music. Tchaikovsky labeled the supported adagio portion of his composition section "Andante maestoso," literally "flowing majestically." And so it does. Pose upon pose occurs majestically from a give-and-take rapport of support and independent dancing on the part of the ballerina. A dramatically grand-scaled croisé arabesque twice appears as the capstone of a double pirouette caught and supported by hand from the attentive cavalier. Note how continually the cavalier fixes his own artful posturing after he's secured his ballerina's balance and position at the climax of a phrase. See how effectively Sugar Plum's deep-reaching, supported arabesque penchée finds contrasting echo in a lushly yielding, supported *cambré* ("back bent") swoon.

See how smilingly she repeatedly unfolds, on tickling harp *glissandi*, out of easy en dedans pirouettes into a large-scale, croisé arabesque penchée, all making effects that appear flowing, majestic, and seemingly spontaneous. Immediately following are a sequence of "caught" first arabesque poses that Sugar Plum strikes on pointe, and, with the assistance of her cavalier, meltingly transforms into radiant second arabesque postures onto a flat foot. (This is a specific effect Balanchine borrows from Ivanov.) A buildup in the music leads to a rushing separation of both dancers and a coming together again with Sugar Plum caught sitting on her cavalier's shoulder. (Sometimes called a shoulder–sit lift, this is an example of an effect Balanchine borrowed, in altered form, from Ivanov, who worked with a related parting-before-coming-together lift, which we'll find he borrowed from Petipa's *La Bayadère*.) As the majestic tone and momentum of the duet flows toward its conclusion, Sugar Plum gets to spiral through successively multiple pirouettes that drop dramatically into sudden cambré poses, also recycled from Ivanov's choreography. Note how the turning over of the palms by both the ballerina and her partner further expand and enrich the flow of the visual, majestic momentum.

On its way to its impending conclusion, the duet passes through a little "special effect" moment of Balanchine's that recalls one of Ivanov's. After Sugar Plum hits another excited First Arabesque poised on pointe, she appears to travel, gently pulled along by her cavalier, in that pose as if on ice. In Ivanov's pas de deux, the cavalier, Prince Coqueluche, spread out a gossamer veil like Sir Walter Raleigh and whisked his Sugar Plum on a brief, smooth ride as she stood on two pointes. (For an approximation of this effect, see the Royal Ballet *Nutcracker* mentioned above earlier in this chapter.) In Balanchine's case, the effect comes from a small piece of sheet metal, which, as the ballerina stands on it, gets pulled along as she maintains her balance. A spiraling path into a miniversion of what we'll learn to call the "Rose Adagio" in *The Sleeping Beauty* follows before a crescendo-matching entrechat-embellished lift, supported pirouette, a tossed-in-the-air pose and a final "catch" in ballet's "fish-dive" pose. In our next chapter, we'll see that this catch pose comes from the punctuation of Petipa's *Sleeping Beauty* pas de deux, created two years earlier.

(If you're curious about the precedents for Balanchine's pas de deux in Ivanov's choreography, as I suggested for noting the comparisons in the Sugar Plum Fairy's solo, you can compare this pas de deux with Ivanov-structured renderings in the two videos mentioned earlier in this chapter—the Royal Ballet's and *A Trip to Christmas*.)

At this point in all formal and formula nineteenth-century pas de deux should come the variations, the solo dances for both the danseur and the ballerina. We've already seen how Balanchine transposed the ballerina's solo to the beginning of the act. Therefore, so as not to overfocus on the danseur who has neither a specific name nor a particular dramatic role in the narrative, Balanchine cuts out the variation composed for the Cavalier and moves directly into the coda, which is the finale of every standard pas de deux. This one begins with a boomingly athletic, aerial circuit for the Cavalier (Woetzel): Two cocky double cabrioles define his entrance, a huge *tour-jeté* follows, closing with a *manège* (repeated steps done in a circular path) of brazenly sharp-shooting coupé-jeté moves, all done, in spite of their gracefulness, with almost attack-dog force. Kistler has her own energetic manège, mostly piqué turns, with some turning *pas de chat* moves for good measure.

When he comes back, Cavalier/Woetzel stays put and spins through a virtuoso set of grands pirouettes, turning so many and so quickly he goes beyond the trap of seeming to make the audience count—he does so many, so variously, there are almost too many to count. Kistler/Sugar Plum's turns mostly take the form of supported pirouettes in front of the finally still Woetzel. After a spiraling length of chaîné turns, the ballerina falls into a climactic swoon in her cavalier's arms. The final pose of the pas de deux turns out to be a more voluptuous and curvaceous version of the ending to Ivanov's version. What was for Ivanov a ballerina in strict fifth position leaning atilt in her cavalier's arms becomes for Balanchine a swooning ballerina caught serenely in her partner's spontaneous grasp.

With its cinematic fluidity and without de rigueur curtain calls for our leading dancers, *Nutcracker* rushes toward its inevitable conclusion. Tchaikovsky's "Valse Finale et Apothéose" and Balanchine's re-capitulation choreography pour forth as one after another all the divertissements reappear and breeze through brief reminders of their distinct dances: Hot Chocolate, Polichinelles, Candy Canes, Marzipan Shepherdesses, Coffee, Tea, and Dewdrop with her Flowers. Notable for their reappearances are Coffee, with her double piqué turns on demi-plié pointe ending through extension to arabesque, and Dewdrop's successive, deliberately slow relevé turns extending into arabesque balance, with the climactic fifth one held longest as a sustained balance. Most pronounced of all the reentries is that of the Sugar Plum Fairy lifted over and over by Cavalier in a posture that unfolds and opens into a développé, front. A final lift catches Sugar Plum high up in the air and brings her down with ease and control, enough for her to beat her lower legs and feet on their way back to the stage. (If you want a sense of how adept a Cavalier is with the fine art of partnering, watch the way he sets down the ballerina, almost more than how he lifts her up. Expert partners, without a show of fuss or muss, set their ballerinas down with delicate control, keeping watch on the process and working their strength to assure that she's securely on her own balance before pulling away.)

In Woetzel's arms Kistler is secure enough to wave back on all the other leading participants during the descent from her final lift. All of which happens in a flash of finale force that Balanchine is so skilled at. Piqué-arabesques straight to the audience and tour-jetés momentarily away from it fill the stage with wave upon wave of energy, as the entire cast returns finally spinning almost madly to take places that frame a climactic pose for the Sugar Plum Fairy in a happily open croisé, arabesque-penchée. More mellow music follows as Sugar Plum, wand once more in her gracious hand, salutes Marie and her Little Prince on their return journey.

The movie's final credits manage to give a semblance of the experience of curtain calls, although the Act 1 characters have to be shown in outtakes that are not the same as proper curtain calls. These latter approximations of curtain calls give a sense of so-called character calls, which mean taking bows in the personality of the character being portrayed rather than as the performer himself. Many audience members find this conceit entertaining. I do not. Dance artists work hard at a range and depth of parts, and I feel it's a special pleasure to see them at the end of any given show as themselves. To my way of seeing, the "real" dancer behind the character makes the characterization all that much more remarkable. Otherwise, the naive onlooker could assume the dancer was merely playing himself, and where's the art in that? (All of the Act 2 dancers manage to show themselves simply in simulated "proper" curtain calls; those of

Act 1 have no choice, as they're shown in actual moments from their performances.)

As a postscript, it should be noted that *Nutcracker* is a frequent subject for "versioning." Some of this comes from a kind of cynicism about the work's popularity, especially in America. Therefore, the urge to poke fun at the sacred cow becomes hard to resist. Some of these rethinkings of the original material and intentions are slight, such as a Joffrey Ballet production by Robert Joffrey, which sets the whole Germanic Christmas scene in Currier and Ives' early America. Or medium slight, such as in Graham Murphy's version for the Australian Ballet, which takes the narrative into a reflective memory lane experience for an old ballet teacher, whose reverie starts by having her come across the familiar music on her kitchen radio. (This is on video, but as of this writing only in PAL VHS format.) *The Hard Nut*, Mark Morris's non-ballet version for his modern dance company, rereads the entire score in terms of 1960s and 1970s suburban United States as seen in comic book terms. This is also on video: *The Hard Nut*, 1992, 87 min., Color.

Chapter 4

CLASSICAL CLASSICAL BALLET

The Sleeping Beauty

• • •

Ballet-féerie in three acts with Prologue
Original choreography by Marius Petipa
Music by Pyotr Tchaikovsky

And *The Sleeping Beauty* makes three. This is the final component of our look at ballet's Big Three Tchaikovsky story ballets. As we've learned from ballet history, its 1890 premiere makes it chronologically the composer's second ballet composition (*Swan Lake* being first). Furthermore, with regard to now standard Petipa stagings that have come down to us, it's actually first in the sequence. (Petipa didn't choreograph *Swan Lake* originally.) With all three of these works firmly fixed in the standard ballet repertory, *Beauty* remains the best example of narrative ballet theater in which the art and act of classical ballet directly carry the spectacle.

Unlike the underlying narratives to *Swan Lake* and *The Nutcracker*, the basic story of *The Sleeping Beauty* is already known to most people coming to the ballet of the same name. Fairy tale connoisseurs know that the full telling of the story includes a good many twists and turns not common to the average retelling of its plot, which goes something like this: A lovely princess is cursed to die an early death by an offended wicked fairy, but her spell is softened by a good fairy who turns the would-be demise into a deep sleep. After a hundred years of slumber, a valiant prince comes upon the princess, kisses her awake and pledges his troth. The original story, which comes from the version told by France's Charles Perrault in his seventeenth-century collection of such tales, is not nearly so simple and has its goodly share of additional grotesque details, such as an evil plan by the princess's mother-in-law to eat her daughter-in-law and her children in fancily cooked dishes. (Perhaps the elimination of this figure and her story tell us that, like Balanchine, Petipa believed there could be no mother-in-laws in ballet.)

This is a ballet-friendly retelling of Perrault with no one getting cooked in a sauce. We see the princess meet her fate, even though her protective parents hope to prevent it. Eventually, however, the good fairy's prediction comes to pass and we watch an extravagant celebration honoring the marriage of the good prince and princess, and their being united in lasting bliss. I do not mean to characterize the amending of Perrault's narrative as an act of frivolousness toward a frivolous goal. When ballet theater remains true to its means and methods it yields profoundly poetic theater. Ballet cannot redo what literature does with the written word, but it can do something different, something only a language of the human body in mute gesture and expert prowess can achieve.

This Moscow Bolshoi Ballet video of *Sleeping Beauty* was less an obvious choice than a useful one. I felt, all things considered, that a Russian company performance was a must. The most obvious Russian possibilities in the St. Petersburg traditions that brought *Beauty* into being in the first place struck me as variously compromised. None was precisely more illustrative of the ballet's original intentions than this Moscow company version. And, in some pertinent details, the Bolshoi Ballet version, staged by a graduate of the Petersburg tradition, proves much more appropriate.

About this video:

The Bolshoi at the Bolshoi: The Sleeping Beauty, Nina Semizorova, Alexsei Fadeyechev, 1989, 145 min, Color. (The packaging may show an incorrect running time of 94 min. and an incorrect identification of the conductor; he should be Aleksandr Kopilov, not Algis Zhuraitis.)

Taped on the gigantic Bolshoi Theater stage, this recording

documents the Moscow company usually known for its more flamboyant and emotive spectacles in a cooler, atypical mode. Staged by Yuri Grigorovich, according to various Petersburg source materials and individuals in 1963 and revised in 1973, the Bolshoi Ballet *Beauty* bypassed some of the "improvements" that had become part of the Leningrad Kirov (formerly known as Petersburg Imperial) Ballet staging. Nina Semizorova, the ballerina in the pivotal role of Aurora, was a pupil of Galina Ulanova, the legendary Petersburg-trained ballerina long associated with the Bolshoi Ballet. Aleksei Fadeyechev, as Prince Désiré, represented a princely danseur noble unlike any Petersburger on video. With Yuri Vetrov in the crucial role of the wicked fairy Carabosse, the Bolshoi staging stuck more closely to Petipa's original concept than the versions promulgated by the subsequent balletmasters from Petipa's home theater, the Maryinsky.

Both the cassette's packaging and the opening credits give little more than minimal cast listing. I'll save the mention of the less prominent dancers, who do not get identified until the final credits, for appropriate mention along the way or at the end.

Tchaikovsky's "Introduction" opens with the first of the ballet's two leitmotifs, the boisterous and almost violent theme of the wicked fairy Carabosse in "Allegro vivo" mode. Then, like a balm of antidote and serenity, comes the "Andantino" of the Lilac Fairy's soothing theme. (In Russian, "lilac fairy" sounds as if it comes from serenity: "fea seereny.")

The ballet's opening curtain comes with a "March," which has a down-to-earth tone of everyday—albeit everyday *palace*—behavior. The first personage we see is Catalabutte, the king's master of ceremonies, overlooking his guest list for the Prologue's first scene: "The Christening (or Baptism) of Princess Aurora." (Catalabutte's name is a reworking of the name of a rival king in Perrault's tale.) The invited courtiers arrive in couples and, as is sometimes Grigorovich's shtick, embellish their reasonable walking steps with slightly outlandish dancing steps. (For a far more reasonable and Petipa-like rendering of this activity, see, *The Sleeping Beauty*, The Royal Ballet,

1994, 132 min., Color.) Catalabutte, unidentified in any of the credits, oversees the whole affair with aptly officious prancing and scurrying about. The bringing in of the baby princess in her cradle followed by the anticipated entrance of king and queen (also unnamed in the credits) with a suite of royal pages, once further gates have been parted, completes the setting.

After one more nervous check and approval of the guest list, the scene changes to the ballet's next segment, a "Dance Scene." In Grigorovich's staging, this episode brings on the invited fairies to gracious strains of a waltz related to the Lilac Fairy's theme. First we see the retinue of the Lilac Fairy, twelve fairy women and six men holding lilac-topped staves, then Lilac herself, followed by five other fairies, all in different color tutus. A gestural interjection from Catalabutte cues what should be the more dance-dominated portion of the scene, which as I've pointed out, Grigorovich makes more or less "dancey" throughout. By now you should understand that Calatabutte's gesture means "to dance," as he circles his raised hands one over the other in gracious command. In this case it cues another little waltz meant to prepare for the presentation of the fairy's gifts. (Originally attending pages, with cushions holding emblems of the fairies' individual gifts, would be part of the action.) A brief interjection of dancing from the Lilac Fairy's male attendants occurs in the waltz's most robust passage. Entrechat jumps dominate their brief appearance. Ballet's waltz step, known as *balancé en tournant*, dominates the dancing of the fairy women.

On gracious command from the king, the celebration continues. Now the ballet's action moves to the "Pas de Six," the choreographic heart of the Prologue, in which the good fairies will bestow their gifts on the infant princess. The pas opens with a series of dance segments for all the fairies, and their attendants. One step, which will become prominent in the Lilac Fairy's solo—a leg kicked high to the side as the dancer rises on pointe and then brought down in an arc to rest in front of her in phase with a crossing of her wrists (technically a *rélevé-grand battement rond de jambe*)—becomes a kind of choreographic leitmotif. Sometimes, diagonal lineups of fairies face the cradle of the princess and direct their port de bras toward her, in gestures of blessing.

Next come the individual fairy solos, or variations. Each was calculated by its choreographer and composer to symbolize some individual character trait bestowed upon the newborn princess. As the Fairy of Tenderness, in white, Elvira Drozdova personifies Beauty and Candor. (Petipa called her Candide.) A leggy languor dominates her solo, with her arms lilting like tree branches in a breeze or as caressing gestures tracing the loveliness of shapely arms. The Fairy of Carefreeness (Olga Suvorova in a golden tutu) dances in a more spritely manner. (Petipa called her Coulante and specifically associated her with "Wheat Flour.") Grace and the gift of dancing are the attributes she brings as she picks sharply through her "Allegro" music with various piqué steps. In palest pink to delicate pizzicato plucking of strings, comes the Fairy of Generosity (Inna Petrova). She peppers the stage with the daintiest piqué steps as she skims nimbly. Feathery hops on one pointe climax by flicking into a kicking up of the heels known as *temps de flèche* (meaning "arrow step"). Named "Miettes Qui Tombents" by Petipa, referring to the Russian custom of sprinkling bread crumbs in a baby's cradle to assure the girl's fertility and a life free from hunger, she is sometimes nicknamed the "Crumb Fairy." In lemon yellow, with her fingers aflutter as if singing a tinkling song, comes a Fairy of Mischievousness (Olesya Shulzhitskaya). Her gift is that of eloquence, of singing, and of laughter. The penultimate variation is that of the bold Fairy of Bravery, here in strong orange (Natalia Malandina). Hers is the gift of energy and commanding temperament. The physical detail of a pointed finger lends extra authority to the port de bras accompanying the energetic and almost brusque footwork. (Petipa called her Violente; nowadays this solo is often called the "Finger Variation.")

The climatic dance is for the Lilac Fairy. Her attribute is wisdom, which according to Russian custom gets bestowed on a child placed beneath a lilac bush. Framed by her retinue of twelve female attendants, Nina Speranskaya dances to a waltz Petipa planned as a *variation volupteuse*. The high and smooth rélevé-grand battement rond de jambe mentioned earlier figure quite prominently here. The choreography for the Lilac Fairy solo, now part of most productions credited to Petipa's hand, is known to be by one of the ballet master's heirs, Fyodor Lopukhov. Petipa's original production had two separate versions of the solo, both now seemingly "lost." One of these Petipa versions was made specifically for his daughter, Maria, who was not known for her virtuoso technical skills; the other was for an alternate dancer, who was more adept.

A brisk "Allegro giusto" coda (meaning strict or suitably timed allegro) wraps things up. Agitation starts to hang in the air as the music and dancing pulse at a nearly nervous pace. All participants in this fairy world come back to dance, with the Lilac Fairy once more in a strong central position. Turns en dedans dominate her culminating appearance, leading some *Beauty* watchers to remark that while the other fairies consistently and exclusively turn en dehors, Lilac turns both en dedans and en dehors, thus showing her superior prowess of expertise.

The Prologue concludes with Tchaikovsky's "Finale," which begins in a lulling mood. (The libretto calls for the fairies to present tokens of their gifts to the baby princess, but this staging glosses over these details. For a more particular rendering of the moment, see the Royal Ballet video mentioned earlier in this chapter.) A stirring uneasiness ensues. The cause soon appears in the form of a little chariot pulled by three gnomes and three rats. The bent and aged fairy Carabosse emerges from the vehicle, accompanied by duly menacing and sour music. She's hunchbacked and walks with a cane. Here, the part is played (by Yuri Vetrov) *en travesti*, as it was in 1890 (by Enrico Cecchetti). A sarcastic air colors the fairy's behavior, mocking the king and queen and savaging the master of ceremonies by tearing at his hair.

A momentary appeal of sweet music and pleadings from the good fairies only inspires more mockery and a diabolical little dance that leads to her offering a christening gift. In turn she admits the princess will grow to be a lovely young woman, but then will prick herself on a needle and die. Carabosse and her suite relish the consternation created and bask in the wicked laughter blaring through the music. (The video fails to record one particularly pathetic and shocking moment for the court as the queen falls to the ground pleading with Carabosse. The king, attempting to bring her to her senses, quickly returns the queen to her feet, reminding her of who she is.)

A harp arpeggio announces a mood change. The Lilac Fairy

reenters. She has yet to formally present her gift. In only the most general of terms within this staging, she predicts that the princess will not die from her mishap but will merely fall into a deep sleep, from which she will be awakened by a kiss from a handsome prince. (To see these particulars in clear pantomime, see the same Royal Ballet tape.) What the Bolshoi staging reveals is another sampling of the Russian "fear of mime" exemplified in Makarova's no-pantomime performance as Odette. In place of what twentieth-century Russian ballet tended to see with embarrassment as the sign language of the deaf and dumb, we see as Soviet ballet's penchant for generalized heroic gesture. Without a scenario to tell us what's transpiring here, we can only assume that Lilac is telling Carabosse: "No, you don't; you'll be vanquished by my sister fairies."

Carabosse's furious exit, with its "You haven't seen the last of me" gestures, fades into the distance as the Lilac's beneficent presence and lulling musical theme bathe the whole scene in a serenity that says good has triumphed, and will continue to win out over evil.

By the end of the Prologue, we have seen various and substantial examples of classical ballet dancing; in this instance, mostly from female ballet dancers. Yet we have still not seen *the* ballerina. I emphasize "the" because the role of the Lilac Fairy is considered a ballerina part. Sometimes lone female roles such as this get nicknamed "big ballerina" roles, which means roles for tall ballerinas. The "tall girl" ranks that exist within ballet troupes often provide the company with its "tall girl" ballerina. These are frequently, though not exclusively, women whose repertory consists of roles for women exclusive of male partner counterparts.

However, my observation referred to the fact that after this prologue richly stocked with solo female dancing, we still have yet to see the ballerina of *The Sleeping Beauty*. Before we meet her, in the next act, a word about her "type." Ballerinas don't fall into consistently ordered families of kind. The noble, the demi-character, and the grotesque don't readily apply to women as they do to male dancers. Identifications like "Romantic ballerina," as opposed to "Classical ballerina," come and go, and sometimes prove useful. The former are said to excel in works associated with the Romantic era and with roles that reclaim aesthetics of that time. These ballerinas are sometimes said to be creatures of the air, meaning that steps of elevation and postures of weightlessness come naturally to them. Classical-type ballerinas represent to the eye more of a brilliant prowess, of clean terre-à-terre foot- and legwork and more angular geometry of choreographic shape.

In Russia, where of course *The Sleeping Beauty* was born, Aurora is a "classical" ballerina's role. The originator of the part was Carlotta Brianza, an imported virtuosa of the Italian school "virtuosa" known for their extra-strong technical abilities. In particular, Brianza was praised for her impressive "steel pointes."

By contrast, Odette/Odile is considered "lyrical" in nature, a word related to other people's use of "Romantic." Though in her Odile character the Swan Queen ballerina needs to be less meltingly nuanced and more "brilliantly" defined, the sense remains of a link to the Romantic world of *Swan Lake*'s libretto.

Lilac Fairy candidates might be called "independents" in that tall girl ballerina roles tend to be free of consistent character mates, if not free of partnered moments per se. So let's now see how Petipa's grand plan shows us, after an already agreeable act of female ballet dancing, what's so special about our title-role ballerina.

Act 1, The Spell

We have arrived at Princess Aurora's twentieth-birthday celebration. (And don't let anyone nostalgic for "sweet sixteen" parties tell you Aurora's turning sixteen, if the staging claims to be faithful to Petipa. Petipa's libretto states clearly that Aurora has reached the age of twenty.)

Tchaikovsky's first *scène* ("Allegro vivo") begins as a busy affair with some women trying to practice the forbidden art of working knitting needles. They're caught, sentenced to execution by the implacable king, and finally pardoned by intervention of the merciful queen. (Originally, it was the four princes we shall soon meet who obtained the clemency of the king.) Emotions appear to rise at the relenting of the king as Tchaikovsky and the libretto take us directly into a lush waltz. Here the garden gates open, revealing a grand terrace at the foot of the palace stairs, down which spill sixteen couples of adult villagers. They begin to animate to the lilt of Tchaikovsky's "Valse Villageoise." (This is the success that Petipa hoped to recapture in the "Waltz of the Flowers" for *The Nutcracker*.) Eventually, the ranks swell to include twelve couples of child waltzers, and the props include baskets of flowers, threaded lengths of blossoms, and garlands. Over the years the number has become known as the "Garland Dance." However, as much as I wish the choreographic rendering here had less of an "attack and thrust" accent, I believe this Russian-heritage number is truer to the dance's original concept than the recorded British version, with its smaller scale forces. (If ever New York City Ballet puts on video the Peter Martins staging of Petipa's *Beauty*, we will have a record of the most beguiling "Garland Dance" around, the one Balanchine re-created in 1981 for a Tchaikovsky festival.)

But what of our ballerina? A short *scène* gives the action a potent cue of anticipation. Four dashing princes stride onstage, bowing graciously to the monarch, eight violin-playing pages (adolescent girls dressed as boys) spill down the stairs, followed by eight tutu-wearing friends, as a nervously gesturing Catalabutte signals an eagerly awaited arrival. All eyes go center, upstage, where at the top of the stairs and descending down their length comes Princess Aurora. Without any pause for mimetic pleasantries, she's dancing, mostly through jumps—heel-kicking pas de chat and bigger, leg-splitting grand jeté pas de chat, turns that open out into high kicks, spiraling chaîné turns, and a little length of coupé-jeté dartings.

After a show of affection and obeisance to her royal parents and gracious acknowledgment of her four princely suitors, Aurora is ready to reenter her music, and commence the act's protracted, four-part pas d'action. The first, and most dramatic of its segments is the adagio that has come to be known almost everywhere it is danced as the "Rose Adagio." The nickname comes from the fact that during the course of her dance with four suitors, Aurora is twice presented with roses, one at a time, from each of the princes.

An elaborately extended harp arpeggio precedes the start of the adagio. High développé extensions à la seconde, supported individually by each prince or cavalier, launch Aurora into it. Almost immediately she takes a balanced position on pointe in attitude pose; each of her cavaliers momentarily takes her hand as she momentarily takes it away to sustain her balance independently. A tradition for sustaining these unsupported balances to make a show of serene independence came into *Sleeping Beauty* history with Margot Fonteyn, once she made the role her own during the 1940s. Since that time, Aurora's held attitude "balances" have become part of the ballet's tradition, even though the detail comes from outside Russia. Sometimes Aurora's balances are known as *equilibres*, French for "balance."

In our tape, Semizorova seems to be straining to achieve an effect not native to its Russian history. In the Royal Ballet tape already mentioned, Viviana Durante honors the nouveau tradition of drop-dead balances with unfailing aplomb. Incidentally, the Italian-born ballerina holds her attitude leg in the "tighter," more true 90-degree bend at the knee than does Semizorova, who works, understandably, with the more open angle of flexion preferred by Russian teaching.

The adagio continues with other moments for Aurora to dance individually with each of the prospective suitors. Prominent in this ceremony is the presentation of a rose from each cavalier and the turning of supported pirouettes in each case. The number of revolutions increases during the sequence: A single en dedans turn with her first cavalier, a double with the second, triple with the third, and a quadruple with the last. All the while, as the adagio builds and increases momentum and volume, the attendant pages, maids of honor, and garland-bearing villagers group and regroup, frame and reframe Aurora's dancing.

A climactic presentation of more single roses and different turns upon acceptance leads to the adagio's most spine-tingling sequence: further balancing in attitude, this time with each cavalier taking Aurora's hand and walking in a full circle around her as she maintains her attitude-balanced pose. Such moves fall into the category of *promenade* (literally, walk) and are a standard part of the pas de deux vocabulary. Primarily, as is true in this instance, the aim is to let the ballerina display the beauties of her line, posture, and strength from all angles; in effect, "in the round," as is said of freestanding sculptures. Semizorova's theatrical way of releasing the theatrical breath of her keenly held pose is to slip from attitude to arabesque extension and plummet softly into a penchée position, before spinning through one final multiple pirouette. (As you can see in the Royal Ballet video, an alternative to climaxing the promenaded balances is a dramatic opening of the attitude position to one of arabesque, and an extra little balance in that position before coming back down to earth.)

In a hall as vast as the Bolshoi's, and with a public less clap-happy than American audiences, the video allows for a full hearing of the adagio's closing music. Most often in American theaters the applause for the elegant conclusion to a most artful "coming of age, endurance test" is so overwhelming that Tchaikovsky's final chords are drowned out.

The end of the wonderful and highly popular "Rose Adagio" does not mean the end of the pas d'action. However as much as Petipa's scheme pleases the pleasure and thrill-seeking balletgoer, it manages to do so with the "action" of its narrative comfortably in sight. Aurora has presented herself to her court (and to us, her public) as a radiant and strong young woman. With regard to our videotape, it's wise to try to discount the slightly old-fashioned wig and makeup on Semizorova. Only a viewer accustomed to Soviet-styled details such as this marcelled wig and doll-face makeup can fail to wince at it on first sight. Still, after getting over the initial discomfort, our eyes can see that Semizorova herself feels perfectly at home and natural in this guise, and her unself-consciousness can then melt away the odd surface and reveal the simple heart beneath it all.

Continuing the pas d'action, a "Dance of the Maids of Honor and Pages" follows. Often referred to as Aurora's Friends, these dancers trip through their "Allegro moderato" dance in sets of four. First, two quartets of violinist-pages appear; then two separate quartets of "maids of honor." One set in all white initially act as a unit à la Ivanov's cgynets; another, as slightly "bigger girl" friends in pale gold, dance more openly and independently, recalling some of Aurora's steps themselves. All this precedes "Aurora's Variation," a solo also composed as "Allegro moderato." The new "drama" here centers on Aurora performing for all assembled—court, visiting princes, and public alike—completely free of any and all other dancer support.

(Her culminating manège of single piqué turns into chaîné turns, finishes early, as is the custom in Russian productions, omitting the longer ending that Tchaikovsky originally wrote, and that our Royal Ballet tape includes.)

Like the coda to the Prologue's "Pas de Six," the one for Act 1's pas d'action coda is "Allegro giusto." In the usual recapitulation manner, the maids of honor begin the emphatic culmination in two separate foursomes (the second of which momentarily pair up with the four suitors). Most dramatically, Aurora returns and the tension mounts as she bounds first downstage on a diagonal, and then with new energy, moving upstage in a series of teasingly strung together little cabrioles, pas de chat, and *renversé* turns. These seem to turn over at the last minute as the torso leans out of the turn and then gets pulled dramatically into its strong momentum. A bleating interruption of the dance's swaying pulse makes for a nervous change of mood. A woman wrapped in black appears and presents a thread-wrapped needle, something of a cross between a knitting needle and a spindle.

There are efforts to prevent Aurora from toying with the object as she blithely circuits the stage with leg-opening turns and turning jumps reminiscent of unspooling fibers from a spindle. Soon it pricks her finger. Nervous, more foreboding music follows. A woozy-looking Aurora falls into a temporary faint and then arises with the music's accelerations into a dance of giddiness. Known as Aurora's "Danse Vertige" (vertiginous dance), there is a frenzy and the-world-is-turning-all-around-me air to her movements, which end as she falls back in a swoon. With all assembled frozen in a tableau, the shrouded figure reveals herself to be Carabosse; all the onlookers come to just before the vengeful fairy disappears into the ground (through a use of a trapdoor).

The brash thematic music of Carabosse gives way to the soothing strains of the Lilac Fairy, who appears, with her retinue. After Aurora is carried to her bed chamber by six chivalrous pages, Lilac rises above the scene. Hoisted by flying machinery, she floats on high and oversees putting the entire palace to sleep. Though both Petipa and Perrault call for a palace engulfed in protective briars, creepers, and brambles, this production makes little show of such atmosphere. As the music rises and spreads like overgrowing, tendrilled vegetation, all that really closes in here are the palace gates, eased in place by the fairy's retinue.

Only one crucial character has yet to appear. He is the heroic prince, whom the Lilac Fairy predicted would break the spell. In Petipa tradition, the Russians call him Prince Désiré. For some reason, otherwise reliable English stagings of Petipa's work have been known to call him Prince Florimund. Each of our Tchaikovsky-Petipa ballets has showcased a danseur prince as well as ballerina princess. But each has been different, especially in the case of the prince. Siegfried revealed himself to be a man of good heart but weak character. Sugar Plum's Cavalier and/or Prince Cocqueluche, remains little more than a gracious walk-on royal, who performs nicely but doesn't tell us much. *Beauty*'s soon-to-appear Prince Désiré will be as good of heart as Siegfried but less flawed of character.

The character of *Sleeping Beauty*'s prince has remained constant in all stagings using the original 1890 libretto, but the concept has varied. Pavel Gerdt, the original interpreter of the Prince Désiré role, wore heeled pumps more in the manner of a Louis XIV courtier than a nineteenth-century ballet dancer. This had less to do with the fact that he was forty-five years old at the time, than it had to do with authenticity of period. Another pertinent factor was the de-emphasis Petipa put on the dancing of the men in his ballets. Petipa remained steadfastly interested in the roles and dancing of the ballerina. When his ballets required a male solo, he often sent the dancer in question to the teacher of the men's ballet classes—notably a Bournonville disciple, Christian Johansson—where from their classroom steps and combinations they might acquire the material for their solo dancing.

With subsequent productions changes in the role of Désiré came almost immediately. When Nikolai Legat, a successor of Gerdt's in the role, danced the prince he performed more athletic choreography in less "authentic" footwear. Prince roles have more cause for amplification and rethinking in nineteenth-century "big ballets" than the already substantial roles of ballerinas. We'll see evidence of this kind of "upgrading" in the tape discussed here. (For a kind of ultimate example of expanded-upon Prince Désiré role, see Rudolf Nureyev in his own staging of it: *The Sleeping Beauty*, starring Rudolf Nureyev, 1972, 90 min., Color.)

Act 2, The Hunt, the Vision, the Awakening

An airily supercilious Galifron, Prince Désiré's tutor, greets a hunting party of courtiers during Tchaikovsky's bucolic and mellow entr'acte and *scène.* Fokine once suggested that besides dance itself, ballet worked with "mime, pantomime, and static groupings." As a shortened form of pantomime, mime and miming can stand for more casual, individualized silent acting on the part of the dancer. All of which is separate from formally set, often declamatory gesturing that spells out a particular narrative point: Recall the little prince's pantomime upon arriving in the court of the Sugar Plum Fairy. As I've indicated, given their fear of pantomime syndrome, Soviet-Russian ballet artists may mime but they shy strongly away from its more explicit counterpart, and do not open their mouths to help articulate their miming.

With due mimetic flourish from Galifron, Désiré arrives with a burst of athletic energy during Tchaikovsky's "Colin-Maillard" ("Blind Man's Buff") music. (Tchaikovsky's title comes from the French name for the game.) Dressed in autumnal gold with a scarlet cape, Aleksei Fadeyechev soars onto the scene with vaulting, air-filled grands jetés, softly spun turning jumps, and splitting coupé-jeté leaps, all telling more of elation than athletic bravado. In scale and ease of execution, all of Fadeyechev's dancing would probably astound the likes of Gerdt and Legat. But then, they also appear astounding next to the accomplishments of many of Fadeyechev's peers. Like so many Russian dancers, Aleksei is a second-generation dancer; his father, Nikolai, had a great career as Bolshoi Ballet *danseur noble extraordinaire*.

Tchaikovsky wrote the music that our prince "rides" so expertly to accompany a playful game of "touch" for the members of the hunting party. (The key word in the game, by the way, is "buff" meaning buffet, or touch, not "bluff" as so many people like to say, probably because the individual who is "it" must be blindfolded.)

What follows is another *scène* and dances. Tchaikovsky wrote four separate ones for the members of the prince's party. The miniature court dances were planned by Tchaikovsky and Petipa to allow for a minuet of duchesses, a gavotte of baronesses, a 6/8 dance for countesses, and lively 2/4 dance for marchionesses. Taking the central countess by the hand, our prince dances the minuet and then sits beside her as the rest of the party performs the "Dance of the Marchionesses." This production eliminates the other two dances of the suite—frequently all four, or at least three, are cut. In some stagings, the earthy music written for the "Dance of the Countesses" accompanies a solo for the prince. (For an example of this dance transposed to the prince see *The Kirov Ballet: "The Sleeping Beauty,"* 1996, 160 min., Color.)

The dramatic point of the suite and the following "Farandole," a dance for the peasants who are part of the entourage, is to establish the monotony of riches in the prince's life. Still, there is subtle variety within the set of courtier and peasant dances. The royals maintain their decorum and strict vertical carriage throughout their dancing, which qualifies as classical court dance. The peasants, in their more rustic costuming—no wigs, baggier garments, heavier shoes—are freer of movement, making for "character" dancing.

The sound and miming of hunting horns signal the departure of all but the prince to hunt. Left on his own, in another musical *scène*, the prince leaves the world of daily tedium and enters a haunting realm of sadness. In our video, he dances to music meant for miming and establishing of mood. Grigorovich's original choreography includes many of the steps the prince danced upon entrance. Only here their accent and tempo have changed. What was sunny and warmly eager has turned mellow and contemplative. Poses and moves achieve a scale as grand as that of the opening dance; now they're breathing more like a sigh than a flush of happy energy. High-reaching *effacé*—arabesques in various *fondu* (literally, "melted") postures breathe with yearning, like overwhelming melancholy thoughts. The prince's hands and arms embellish his moves with accents of lush gentleness.

After the Lilac Fairy materializes, the prince dances alongside her as if under her spell. They frequently dance in unison, as if he were her shadow. Out of the darkened depths of the landscape the vision of Aurora appears, surrounded by sister "shades" (or phantom visions). Petipa's plan indicates that the Lilac Fairy's conjuring of Aurora comes by a wave of her magic wand. Although Grigorovich's Lilac had a wand in her hand during the putting-to-sleep of the kingdom, here she's empty-handed. I think the wand is as apt a prop for Lilac as the cane is for Carabosse. The latter prop, too often left out of many *Sleeping Beauty* stagings, is happily an effective part of this production.

I suppose the mimophobic Soviet ballet found that a wand would deprive Lilac of the freedom to dance and force her towards too much miming. Petipa not only welcomed pantomime and miming, he even had Lilac's costume altered after the Prologue so she could mime more comfortably. For her part in the subsequent acts, Petipa had his fairy change. After initially appearing in her classical tutu, or *tarlatans*, as the costume was sometimes called (because of its fabric), the fairy godmother subsequently wore a longer, more dress-like garment, sometimes called a chemise (because of its looser, less formal look). (See the Kirov Ballet tape mentioned above for an example of the Lilac Fairy in a more informal costume for her presence in the "Vision" scene.)

In this minimally mimetic staging, however, Lilac's missing wand is only part of the story. Absent too are some points that can only be spelled out in pantomime. One missing detail is especially unfortunate. One *Sleeping Beauty* watcher used to translate the pantomime in which Lilac formerly questioned the prince's melancholy before producing the vision of Aurora, with a wave of her wand, as: "Boy, have I got a girl for you!" No such moment is identifiable in our tape. (A fair indication of this fairy-to-prince exchange in pantomime can be found on the Royal Ballet tape I've previously referenced.)

After a sprightly solo entrance for the vision of Aurora, in a diagonal of huge coupé-jeté leaps that manage to be light in tone in spite of their boldness of energy, the stage fills with the princess's sister visions. (Petipa indicated the retinue of Aurora as protective nymphs, creatures of the waters in this terrain, but over the years they've been made less specific. In this production, Aurora's "sisters" have tiny leaves hanging from their costumes and in their hair and appear as woodland spirits of the autumnal forest surrounding the scene.)

We have come to the act's pas d'action. A ballerina-announcing harp arpeggio signals its start. In spite of all its warm coloring—roseate autumn hues, blush pinks of morning, and lilac flora—here is a ballet blanc. Here comes the all-dancing episode with our hero, heroine, and good fairy at the center. Grigorovich's version includes select, un-Petipa moments for the prince to take up the choreography of the princess and the fairy and mirror their movements, but these are not oppressively outlandish. (For that dimension, see the "Vision" scene in the Nureyev *Sleeping Beauty* mentioned above, where Nureyev's prince shamelessly appropriates Aurora's dancing for himself.) The rich-bodied sound and mood of the cello dominating Tchaikovsky's music make the whole scene shimmer with passion. The fluidly arranged and rearranged corps de ballet repeat effects we'll see in Petipa's earlier *La Bayadère* and prefigure effects we've seen in the lakeside scenes of Petipa's production of *Swan Lake*. When the shifting lines of visions (twenty-four strong) cross and crisscross with their artfully extended arms and legs meshing and layering, they make for a "living" set. Mostly, the corps de ballet represents the bramble overgrowth guarding the sleeping princess and her palace.

Now the vision of Aurora has a solo. The almost celebrational waltz that Semizorova dances includes repeated, high-reaching battements that fork into passé position. Sometimes this move is described, somewhat erroneously, as an enveloppé move, because it appears to be the opposite of a *developpé* move. (Strictly speaking, *enveloppé* is a French school of ballet term for the pulling-in impetus of the working leg for a specific en dedans turn.) Actually, Aurora's "Vision" solo music was not written for this pas d'action. Petipa replaced a more sedate number that was intended here, for the one that remains part of Russian stagings. It was borrowed from a suite for the precious meals and stones from Act 3, originally meant to accompany a dance for the "Gold Fairy," whom Petipa originally described as "burnished gold." (To hear the original music and see a solo with steps related to the Petipa-lineaged, Russian solo, see the

Royal Ballet *Sleeping Beauty* mentioned above. The choreography is by Frederick Ashton, who makes use of *enveloppé* moves. The Kirov tape also includes the originally composed "Vision" solo and choreography of its own.)

The "Presto" coda to the pas d'action, brings the "Vision" scene to a close. After spritely dancing from corps de ballet and now-you-see-her-now-you-don't appearances by Aurora, the prince watches her vanish instantly, as if by the wave of a magician's wand. The retinue's dancing includes an insistently repeated use of ballet's *ballоné* step, which by its clean, flapping in-and-out accents stirs up the atmosphere like a rising mist.

The prince's enthusiasm to find his disappeared vision is clear from a jumping circuit he makes of the stage, prominently and elegantly exploding through some tours jetés. Tchaikovsky's *scène* is labeled "Allegro agitato." With the appearance of Lilac in her barque, alas wandless, the journey to find the princess begins. Tchaikovsky's "Panorama" accompanies the trip, like a sonorous haze hovering over a quietly flowing water current. Mobile scenery is used to help dramatize the prince and fairy's travels toward the shrouded palace.

Today the unrolling panoramic scenery tends to be misty landscape scenes but originally it showed hunting parties, complete with hunting dogs, all frozen in their tracks by the sleeping spell. In fact, the original unrolling scenery lasted longer than the score Tchaikovsky had provided, so the composer had to provide more music to fit the remaining yards of scenery. As a result, the world got the pejorative term "yard music," meaning music composed by-the-yard to fit some theatrical need. (The mouthed "conversation" caught on this video between Fadeyechev and Speranskaya during their panoramic ride, by the way, is not bush league, lip-synching mime, it's actual talking. It's something Russian dancers invariably do onstage when they're off to the side, and something most other dancers wouldn't ever dream of doing.)

What should follow, but was cut before *Sleeping Beauty*'s premiere performance, is the violin solo Balanchine uses in his *Nutcracker*. Instead, the ballet moves directly into its "symphonic entr'acte and *scène*." Here, and in many productions, we watch Carabosse and her gnomes and rats lurk about the landscape in vain hopes of preventing the Lilac Fairy's foretold kiss of awakening from occurring. (Here's where the crone's cane would make a great foil opposite Lilac's wand, and in productions where it's prominent, the prince's sword.)

The actual battle of wits begins with an acceleration of the musical pulse. Carabosse knows she will be vanquished once Désiré and Lilac approach the slumbering palace. Unfortunately, we don't see the slight snag that Petipa intended when he indicated the prince's bewilderment and lack of knowledge of how to awaken his beloved. The set pantomime should go something like:

> Prince: What can I do?
> Lilac: Come on, boy, use your head!

Then he should run to her bedside and kiss the sleeping princess on her brow. Today, however, almost all productions make it a smacker on the lips, Hollywood-style. No production I know of, not even the often detail-perfect Russians', and certainly no video, maintains the Old World decorum of a kiss on the forehead.

The act's finale, to Tchaikovsky's "Finale" (Allegro agitato) is a brief, bursting affair of fanfares, after a great gong sounding the breaking of the spell. Petipa calls for an immediate and dramatic lifting of all cobwebs and gloom and a reviving of an entire kingdom. Our tape makes little of the removal of a hundred years' darkness for the return to the shining light of day, but the Royal Ballet video includes a good show of the sudden transformation. Tchaikovsky's rousing wrap-up makes for an excited flourish of a conclusion.

The creators of *The Sleeping Beauty* planned a curtain at this point and then a break before Act 3. Our Bolshoi *Sleeping Beauty* bypasses both and moves the awakened court directly into its next and final episode. It's too bad, given this potentially thrilling changeover, that the staging doesn't make more of the dramatic transformation. A mere parting of some gauze gates and the turning on of more lights doesn't quite dramatize the ballet's narrative climax.

In fact, the scene that opens the last act of *The Sleeping Beauty* illuminates the ballet's original inspiration and features a parade of Perrault's fairy-tale characters. Ostensibly they arrive to help celebrate the wedding of the awakened princess; practically they become a fresh excuse for the divertissement dancing that is a popular part of ballet theater's formula. Petipa planned a full complement of these characters, most of whom do little more than take part in an opening procession. Grigorovich's production includes only those individual characters who have dances to perform in the celebrational suite. (For a sense of the full cast of Perrault's characters, see the Kirov Ballet tape, which starts out with Blue Beard and his seven wives and includes most of the characters Petipa specified, including Donkey Skin and Prince Charmant, Tom Thumb and His Brothers, and the Ogre and the Ogress.

Act 3, The Wedding

The "March" Tchaikovsky wrote to open the act and bring on the royal court before the king, queen, and Aurora and her affianced prince is cut here. (See the Kirov tape for an understanding of Petipa's plan to bring on the newly awakened princess and her heroic prince in formal courtly attire, which after exiting they'll change for tutu-and-tights dance clothes before returning to dance their final pas de deux.) Grigorovich's celebrational act begins with Tchaikovsky's "Polacca" (or Polonaise, a processional dance of parading couples in a ballroom setting). In Grigorovich's reduced cast of characters we see: Little Red Riding Hood and the Wolf, Cinderella and Prince Fortuné, Blue Bird and Princess Florine, and Puss in Boots and the White Cat.

The divertissements begin with three-quarters of the pas de quatre Petipa planned for his fairies of precious jewels and metals. During the musical "Intrada" (Introduction) we are presented with the fairies of Silver, Gold, and Sapphires (Drozdova, Malandina, and Petrova, respectively). Their feet flutter like facets through entrechats; their legs and arms, in gently struck and held arabesque poses, tell of refracted rays of light. In due course, they give the stage over to their most prominent sister, the Fairy of Diamonds (Maria Nudga). She climaxes the "Intrada" with bolder dancing that includes a variety of grands jetés. We have already seen how the Fairy of Gold's music found its way into the "Vision" scene as a solo for Aurora. The music for the Fairy of Silver (a polka, "Allegro giusto") brings back our trio. Petipa suggested the "sound of coins" be heard and the dancers' little hops on two pointes almost make little hammering sounds themselves. (The "Sapphire" solo was originally cut as it is here, but can be heard and seen in all its mildly eccentric, irregular glory—unusual 5/4 musical time—in the Royal Ballet *Sleeping Beauty* in a glorious dance by Ashton.) The "Diamond" solo (Vivace) came from the start with suggestions of "sparks" and "electricity," and fluttering hands and feet help materialize those offered by the tinkling music. A throbbing and insistent coda finally brings all four fairies into the dance at once, where they perform a climactic series of relevé pirouettes from sharp fifth position.

"White Cat and Puss in Boots" (Maria Zubkova and Mikhail Sharkov) is the suite's first *pas de caractère*. To an artful approximation of meowing and clawing, two storybook cats playfully cavort and tease each other. Puss tends to leap about by way of grand jeté pas de chat while White Cat does so through plain, Russian-styled pas de chat.

The suite's most famous number is the "Pas de Deux" composed for the Blue Bird and Princess Florine (Alexander Vetrov and Maria Bylova). The stellar role is the man's: the Blue Bird. (Show your knowledge readily, by the way, if any balletgoer asks about the blue birds. Only the male is a blue bird; his female partner is a princess, according to Perrault's tale and Petipa's libretto.) Originally this was performed by Enrico Cecchetti, the influential Italian dancer and pedagogue who probably had a good deal to do with devising the virtuoso choreography still identified with the role today. In essence, the duet is a self-contained pas d'action, telling, in classical dance terms, the story of the Blue Bird who taught a princess to fly. We see our princess hear a birdlike song in the air, and our bird hover, flutter, and soar about like a creature of the air. We see "lead and follow" dancing as Blue Bird shows Princess Florine the way for taking to the air. A lengthy diagonal and sweeping arc of aerial steps end for Blue Bird with successive entrechats, finishing up with an energetic double tours en l'air. (Unfortunately these standard Blue Bird steps do not sing their sweetest and most beguiling song with the Bolshoi's Vetrov. Nor do they in any of the currently available alternate videotapes. The best compromise is Kyril Melnikov's supple and airborne if not clean performance on the Kirov tape. Blue Bird is one of the most difficult roles in the classical male repertory, and as you watch *Beauty* for yourself you'll see the challenge and recognize the champions whenever they appear.)

Florine's solo is also a classical challenge, but a less demanding one. It's set to the flute air the princess harkened to when we first saw her. This rendering is slow of tempo and cautious of approach. (Much more reliable and impressive is Leanne Benjamin's performance in the Royal Ballet's video, and much more imaginative, if slightly eccentric, is Elena Pankova's on the Kirov tape.) Blue Bird's next appearance begins the coda, in perhaps the pas de deux's single most famous sequence: a diagonal of a specific variant on ballet's *brisé volé* step. The name means "broken flying" and Blue Bird seesaws in the air, alternately jackknifing legs and feet forward from his torso as they cross and recross each other and sweeping them backward in a body-line posture sometimes called *temps de poisson*, meaning "moment of the fish." (Blue Bird's first diagonal in his solo also features temps de poisson positions.) More terre-à-terre moves, largely turns, dominate Florine's coda appearances. A climactic diagonal with the princess on her "teacher's" arm shows, at an almost breathlessly brisk tempo, how much the pupil has learned about becoming airborne, as the flying instructor shadows his fledgling pupil.

Two more *pas de caractère* follow. First, a Red Riding Hood, full of wonder and some bewilderment, meets up with Wolf, full of confidence and bluster (Olesya Shulzhitskaya and Andrei Melanyn). Their encounter has her skittering about and miming her eagerness to get to Grandmother's, while the wolf jumps about the innocent girl trying to make things go his way. After seeming to elude him, Red Riding Hood is outsmarted and carried off, in a proper shoulder lift, of course. (To see the dance done with the set pantomime that Grigorovich has discarded in favor of more generalized miming, see the Royal Ballet's rendering.)

Next comes a duet between Cinderella and Prince Fortuné (Suvorova and Sergei Gromov) that's often cut in contemporary stagings. (You won't find it on the Royal Ballet version.) Except for the trying-on of a slipper that's in the possession of the prince, there is little in Grigorovich's choreography to characterize this duet as the "story" of a virtuous scullery maid and the prince seeking her hand. Six candelabrum-bearing lackeys stir into the mix, which turns into more pas de deux than pas de caractère. An additional character number, called "Pas Berrichon" for Tom Thumb and His Brothers, featuring the "Ogre" is not given in this production, nor in many others, partly because it needs a well-matched septet of little boys to play Tom and his six brothers. (For a charming rendering of the pas, see the Kirov video with its confident contingent of boy ballet students.)

An elaborate musical introduction sets the stage for the pas de deux that brings together in final, formal dance terms the story's heroine and hero. Grigorovich sets up the duet by giving the stage over to fairly athletic dancing, full of various *grands jetés*, for the Lilac Fairy framed by her retinue. (For a more courtly ceremony as an "intro," see the Kirov video with its participation of adolescent and child pages attending the fairies of precious stones and metals.)

Now, costumed in wedding whites, Aurora in tutu and tiara and Désiré in tunic and tights even sport powdered hair. Their duet begins with the traditional adagio, this one "Andante non troppo" (flowing, but not too much so). It's a culmination dance like no other in these Tchaikovsky-Petipa ballets. It's a happy-ending capstone for two characters we've gotten to know. It doesn't need to be a pas d'action, and except for a sense of shared wedding vows, which the original staging seems to have incorporated into the choreography in some mimetic way, nothing really needs to be advanced. The wedded couple can simply perform the sublime choreographic coordination and couplings that are the core of classical ballet's "double work." And in so doing their dance illustrates the essence of their achievement. Theirs is a shared world of refined gallantry, impeccable balance, easy grandeur, and clear, interrelated open body language. However beauteous and fanciful Aurora's posturing becomes, or that of Désiré, the pas de deux reinforces the greater, grander effect produced by the configuration of the two taken together. At moments, such as for Aurora in attitude balance and promenade, we are reminded of other, earlier Aurora "moments." A building of momentum leads to a three-times-over climax for the princess to spin through en dedans pirouettes that end falling into her prince's arms.

A nouveau tradition, similar to that of Aurora's "balances," has come to *Beauty* history in the form of the so-called fish dive. Instead of falling back into a kind of swoon (such as that of Russian-company Auroras and Balanchine's Sugar Plum Fairy), most Auroras today spin into their *en dedans* pirouettes at this point, only to be swept up in their prince's arms to pose in a "fish dive." This tradition came with Diaghilev's noteworthy production called *The Sleeping Princess*. The partnered move was put in this place by Bronislava Nijinksa. Popular and eye-catching though these moves tend to be, they do pose a theatrical question: Would Petipa have put fish dives here *and* chosen to end this adagio with a similar pose? You'll find some connoisseurs bemoaning a lack of fish dives, almost as much as they will a lack of fouetté turns for Odile. But decide for yourself if such a lack is all that detrimental to this experience.

The adagio's climax is laced with beautifully simple and spare elements of the classical vocabulary—shining first arabesques most prominent among them. A final promenade in effacé attitude balance into *penchée*, then unsupported first arabesque leads finally to a little toss of Aurora in the air and a gentle catch in a smiling fish dive. As if to underscore the wondrous ease and simplicity of the entire adagio, for a coup de grâce Désiré punctuates the very last pose with a release of both hands from the work of partnering.

Variation one goes, as tradition has it, to Désiré. Its musical mode is "Vivace" and Fadeyechev's dancing is vibrant and virtuoso. Double, direction-changing cabrioles float on high with powerful ease, and double tours en l'air that end in quiet, easy arabesque, occur repeatedly, each time in an opposite direction. A *manège* of shooting *coupé-jetés* lead into turning jumps that fan-kick open like billowing, sun-billed clouds. The whole circuit drops to a kneeling pose to stop in cool glory.

Variation two, "Andantino," shows Aurora as both playful and coquettish. To the music's sweetly bowed and delicately plucked strings, she keeps shifting weight, and intricately changing positions from those fine and close to the ground to others more open and hovering over it. Three-times-repeated sissone jumps climax with smilingly satisfied and varied pauses in simple fifth position on pointe. After retreating to her upstage left corner she comes downstage walking on pointe in *pas de cheval* (step of the horse), all the while circling her hands at the wrist in a characteristic detail of Russian folk dance. As the music heats up, so does Aurora's boldness, and the princess spins through both piqué and chaîné turns before hitting one more grand first arabesque.

The coda of Aurora and Désiré brings both back into action and provokes more of their power and finesse. Fadeyechev hurls himself, calmly, coolly through double assemblé air turns and Semizorova does some playful jumps of her own. Both then slide back on a diagonal through hops (nicknamed chugs in American ballet lingo) in arabesque position. Together again, Désiré and Aurora configure one more pose as she hits a final attitude balance, this one to the front.

A strangely somber "Sarabande," which was written to come next, is usually cut, as it is here. Grigorovich's *Beauty* moves directly into Tchaikovsky's "Finale," a concluding "Mazurka" for *all* the assembled. It starts with the courtiers, and then includes entrées by all the fairy-tale characters to recapitulations of their individual musical motifs. As the momentum rebuilds the entire cast rearranges into another group dance. Fanfares, and an "Apotheosis," herald a salute to the wedding couple. Tchaikovsky tucked "Vive Henri Quatre," a French song about the Bourbon king whose dynasty the ballet particularly celebrates, into the Louis XIV milieu of this last act.

The final tableau finds Aurora and Désiré front and center, and all the assembled, fairy-tale characters and royal court alike, pay them homage. The Lilac Fairy once more rises above the scene with her wand, this time blessing the participants rather than putting them under a frozen spell.

Chapter 5

MATURE ROMANTIC BALLET

Giselle

• • •

Original Choreography by Jean Coralli and Jules Perrot
Music by Adolphe Adam

Giselle is not our oldest icon from ballet's Romantic era, but it is the most famous and most frequently performed. On Romantic ballet's time line, the 1841 two-acter followed the 1832 *La Sylphide*, the seminal work that prepared the way for *Giselle*. And, as in so many such cases, the prototype was superseded and improved upon as the trend it initiated evolved. So we'll look at *Giselle* before we look at the earlier *La Sylphide*.

The video I've chosen documents a performance of American Ballet Theatre that includes the presence of "superstars" with Russian-Soviet pedigrees. Natalia Makarova and Mikhail Baryshnikov both came from Leningrad (as Petersburg was then called) and through their stellar reputations they connect this ballet born in France to its rejuvenation in Russia. The whole production, with its well-researched British staging and its American dancers filling out the picture, stands as a solid sampling of the kind of presentations ABT was putting on during the late 1970s.

About the video:

Giselle, American Ballet Theatre, with Natalia Makarova, Mikhail Baryshnikov, Martine van Hamel, 1977 (released 1988), 95 min., Color.

Unfortunately the packaging notes are minimal and no synopsis text appears on screen. The production was directed by David Blair, after Coralli and Perrot. For the record, beyond the characters of Makarova's Giselle, Baryshnikov's Count Albrecht/Loys, and van Hamel's Myrtha, Queen of the Wilis, the cast includes: Frank Smith as Hilarion, Kirk Peterson and Marianna Tcherkassky in the Peasant Pas de Deux, Berthica Prieto as Bathilde, Ruth Mayer as Berthe, Alexander Minz as the Prince of Courland, George de la Pena as Wilfred, Richard Shafer as the Squire, Nanette Glushak as Moyna, and Jolinda Menendez as Zulma.

Filmed on the stage of the Metropolitan Opera House, where ABT's production had its premiere performance, the recording includes a live audience, who pay due homage responding to the performance and to their favorite dancers. There is added history here since Makarova made her debut with American Ballet Theatre in this very production seven years earlier, and Baryshnikov did the same for his U.S. career three years before this taping. (As an alternate, I'll be referring with some regularity to a staging arranged by Britain's Peter Wright, and led on video by the internationally renowned Rudolf Nureyev and Royal Ballet–linked Lynne Seymour: *Giselle*, 1979, 78 min., Color. Other leading roles are taken by Royal Ballet personnel, the ensemble comes from Munich's Bavarian State Opera ballet company.)

To call *Giselle* a "fantastic ballet" may sound like gushy balletomane enthusiasm, but the label is literally apt in this case. *Giselle, ou Les Wilis*, to give the work its original full title, qualified in early nineteenth-century terms as a *ballet-fantastique*. The categorization informed the public of a ballet that involved fantastical, supernatural elements. (Similarly, a ballet version of *Faust*, a famous dramatic poem by Goethe, also qualified during this era as "fantastique" since it too involved dark, metaphysical dimensions and a powerful spirit world.) As we have seen, *Sleeping Beauty*, with mostly benign fairies, qualified as a *ballet-féerie*.

The concept and particulars of *Giselle* came from Théophile Gautier, a ballet-loving poet and theater critic of his time, who wrote the scenario with help from Jules-Henri Vernoy de Saint-Georges, an opera-loving dramatist and librettist. Unlike *The Nutcracker* and *Sleeping Beauty*, with their basis in already familiar fairy tales, *Giselle* was an original story. Like *Swan Lake*, it took a narrative shape all its own by borrowing from a variety of previous sources. Prominent among these were Slavonic tales of Wilis (vampirelike maidens) who died before their wedding days and practiced passions for dancing beyond the grave. Also affecting Gautier's story of Giselle, a Germanic maid fated to become a Wili, was *Fantômes*, a creation by Victor Hugo, France's leading Romantic man of letters. In Hugo's creation, a beautiful Spanish woman dies at daybreak after a night of frenzied dancing.

Giselle tells of an innocent German peasant maiden who falls in love with an unfamiliar villager named Loys. Hilarion, a local gamekeeper who seeks Giselle's hand for himself, mistrusts the stranger. Giselle's love for dancing troubles her mother, who worries about the exertion on her frail daughter and fears an untimely death could lead to her daughter's joining the band of vengeful Wili spirits. Everyone's worst fears come to pass when Hilarion discovers that Loys is really Albrecht, a philandering count. When Giselle learns that he is already betrothed to Princess Bathilde, a gracious woman whose acquaintance she has just made as her hunting party passed through Giselle's village, the shock of betrayal deranges the peasant maid and leads to her death. Haunted by his part in causing Giselle's madness and demise, Albrecht seeks solace at her grave in the forest. There he finds her "shade" or "spirit," as well as those of the Wilis, on the night the Wili queen has chosen to initiate Giselle into her ghostly sisterhood. The encounter leads to the downfall of Hilarion, who becomes ensnared by the Wilis. Eventually Albrecht is saved through the loving efforts of Giselle. In the end—the most changed element of the scenario over the years—Albrecht is either left alone with memories of his lost Giselle or, as was originally devised, is rescued by Princess Bathilde, in whose arms he swoons.

As ballet scenarios go this one has a familiar ring, even if you limit comparisons to the ballets detailed here so far. Odette was bewitched and betrayed; Aurora fell into deathlike sleep. Siegfried rushed full of remorse to seek his beloved's forgiveness; Prince Désiré found himself chasing a phantom vision of a beautiful woman he'd come to idolize. Still, while elements of the narrative are related to each other, the basic ballet theater of *Giselle* differs from that of *Swan Lake* and especially *Sleeping Beauty*.

Let's consider what we might call "silhouette." Ballets called "classical" bare the dancing body more than those from the Romantic era. The tutu that a disgruntled Michael Fokine would complain looks too often like an "open parasol," remains the dance uniform of ballets such as *Swan Lake, The Nutcracker,* and *Sleeping Beauty*. Not so in *Giselle*, which comes from an earlier era when ballet dancing was more a matter of footwork than leg work. Especially so in the case of female dancers, whose footwork was then evolving and developing in the area now known as pointe work. Certainly the ballet skirts associated with the mid-nineteenth-century *Giselle* were short in comparison to those of the preceding era, but they would become shorter still in the ensuing eras. The look of Romantic era ballets, with their frequent fixations on the realms of air and night spirits, had become formulaic by the time of *Giselle*. Gauzy, layered fabrics helped highlight the artful ways in which a ballerina's feet and footwork could allow her to tread delicately on the ground and to move deftly into and through the air.

Some observers choose to apply the word *soft* to ballet from the Romantic era. It's not an inappropriate distinction, but it can be a trap, leading in the extreme (of both expectation and execution) to a limpness and/or droopiness that borders on the absurd. (Balanchine scoffed at a certain lugubriousness around the Old World ballet, and even created the term Gisellitis to describe the "disease.") But in its clear and poetic plan, the ballet displayed dramatic weight and narrative substance. In its contrasting halves, the two-act *Giselle* presents earth versus air, day versus night, and the physical world versus the metaphysical. Its authors and choreographers were even ballet savvy enough to formulate a ballerina part that combined the essences of the day's two leading and divergent female exemplars.

The Romantic literary movement, which gives the ballet of this time its name, focused on the ideal which restless, poetic individuals often sought. The setting of the search, sometimes heedless and hell-bent to the brink of self-destruction, was usually the everyday world from which the aspiring, wistful poet hoped to escape. In ballet renderings of the yearning drama, the male "seeker" pursued the ideal and/or unattainable female in the form of a spirit, ghost, shade, or sprite. Frequently the latter were creatures of nature, sometimes with a touch of the demonic and/or lethal.

As we have seen in our brief history, Marie Taglioni gained significant prominence for the entity known as the ethereal Romantic ballerina. Her strong dancing produced effects of ineffable lightness. Likewise, we saw how Fanny Elssler, Taglioni's "rival," made a somewhat different effect. Her dance prowess created deftly grounded effects that idealized terre-à-terre dancing to new earth-bound grace. Gautier, the originator of the idea and co-author of the libretto for *Giselle*, found the essence of Taglioni's aerial dancing "Christian" and that of Elssler's earthy artistry "pagan." Carlotta Grisi, a younger ballerina with neither ballet's aerial nor *tacqueté* ("pegged," to indicate intricated pointework) labels dominating her reputation, created the title role. Admired by Gautier for her artless, effortless acting as well as for her accomplished dancing skills, she proved an ideal interpreter of the ballet's heroine and no doubt a good reason for its immediate success.

Grisi's dances were shaped not so much by the ballet's first choreographer, Jean Coralli, then chief ballet master of the Paris Opera, but by Jules Perrot, the ballerina's common-law husband. Her Albrecht was Lucien Petipa, brother of ballet's soon-to-be-renowned Marius. It eventually turned out that it was Marius Petipa who would reshape and secure *Giselle* for all ballet history. Petipa danced Albrecht opposite Elssler in Russia in Perrot's St. Petersburg production, and soon, in his capacity as ballet master, was making changes that today mark almost all versions of the traditional choreography.

Many people fairly deplore Adolphe Adam's music for *Giselle*. (Its naïveté was the main reason for Balanchine's derision.) The ballet's admirers remind us, however, how alive and substantive the music becomes when heard, as it was intended, alongside the dancing. No one can deny that Adam's composition includes an early and well-wrought use of leitmotifs. Unlike the more select use of leitmotif found in Tchaikovsky's *Swan Lake* (one significant motive) and *The Sleeping Beauty* (two), Adam covers all the protagonists and antagonists. We hear identifiable musical themes for Hilarion, for Giselle's love for Loys, for the Wilis, and for the huntsmen. Some of the motifs find their way into the mix as "musical reminiscences" that prefigure or echo in scenes they don't necessarily dominate.

The orchestral "Introduction" heats things up quickly, with a slightly foreboding tone that quiets into pastoral air. American Ballet Theatre brings the curtain up during it, presenting Hilarion prematurely to us. He's back from his early morning hunt, and leaves one of his rabbits on the door of a cottage. His exit comes as he mimes tender affection toward the abode where he left some game. What follows should actually cue the ballet's opening curtain, "Les Vendangeurs" (the grape-gatherers). These prettily dressed villagers do little more than pass through, crossing from downstage left to upstage right. One lovey-dovey couple stays a little longer, sitting on a bench, but not for long. They're soon teased out of their momentary tryst by fellow peasants.

Slightly more nervous and darker-toned music brings back Hilarion, presenting him with his musical motif. He shows deference to an older woman, Berthe, who has emerged from the cottage he presented with the rabbit. He graciously gestures his pleasure in making the gift and the woman shows affectionate gratitude. A burst of suddenly boisterous music and a dashing entrance for a young man wrapped in a cape, changes the scene again. "Entrée de Loys" frames on the danseur's entrance. He's tailed by a similarly attired attendant and moves excitedly, if somewhat furtively.

He immediately slips into a hut opposite the cottage and emerges capeless and swordless. (In some productions, in order to dramatize the ruse of the noble Count Albrecht playacting as the rustic Loys, Albrecht comes out of his cottage with his sword still in his belt and has to have Wilfred, his squire, remind him of his carelessness. (You can see this enacted in the video with Nureyev mentioned above.) General disapproval and/or worry from Wilfred to Albrecht is about all we get here from this miming. Note, however, the clarity, gravity, and dignity of Baryshnikov's telling gestures. (Likewise, try to look past the excessive mouth-opening display put on by Nureyev in the alternate tape.)

A sense of excited anticipation in both the music and in the behavior of Albrecht brings us to "Entrée de Giselle," Adam's and Perrot's rendering of the ever important "entrance for the ballerina." Just as I stressed how prettily dressed these Rhineland peasants were, I stress the "ballerina-ness" of Giselle. You may on occasion hear "thoughtful" and in-the-know balletgoers ridicule costuming for our villagers and heroine as absurdly pretty and not "believable" enough. Such pedantic and pedestrian thinking tends to forget that *Giselle* is a *ballet*-pantomime, a *ballet*-fantastique. To expect ethnographic detailing in this context is to forget one is watching a ballet.

Like Romantic literature and painting, Romantic ballets were interested in local color, but only so far as such colorations of bygone times and faraway places helped illuminate the poetics of the work at hand. The balletgoing public was interested in these fanciful spins only so far as they gave fresh impetus to ballet dancing. So don't expect Giselle to come onto the scene in homespun and mud-caked sabots. And, don't let otherwise seasoned ballet enthusiasts tell you the pretty costumes are not plain enough. (For an extreme example of a pretty ballet skirt on the peasant called Giselle see Natalia Bessmertnova's in *Giselle*, Bolshoi Ballet, 85 min., Color, 1974. For an in-between example, see the slightly finer version worn by Seymour in the Royal Ballet production.)

After an impetuous Albrecht "raps" with musical accuracy on Giselle's cottage door and then steals out of sight, the door opens and our ballerina has made her entrance, this time as a carefree and smitten Giselle. An ebullient circuit of *sauté*-balloné moves, a pause to mime the fact that she heard someone knock, and climactic series of energetic and lighthearted *ballotté* steps. (Meaning "tossed," these moves give the impression of rocking back and forth like a boat on a wavy sea; the French school of ballet term is *jeté bateau*, or boatlike step.)

Giselle is halted in her elated, artful romp by sounds of Albrecht, sometimes mimed as teasingly "blown" kisses. A change of musical and emotional mood occurs when Albrecht comes out of hiding and hovers affectionately about Giselle. After the overwhelmed and shy young woman tries unsuccessfully to go back to her cottage, the two begin to interact through miming and dancing. Albrecht's miming, in this case, asks Giselle to dance for him. (In an uncharacteristic commitment to the methods of sign-language pantomime, Makarova forgoes her usual fear of mime and goes through the artful motions of one sign after another, signifying her love of dance and of Loys, etc.)

Their rapport brings us to the act's "*Scène d'Amour*." Arm in arm they skim sideways in ballet's *glissade* (gliding) steps. When Giselle sits briefly on a bench she absentmindedly allows her skirt to take up the whole seat. Smiling protestation from a make-room-for-me Albrecht causes her to attempt another return to her cottage. Albrecht's showing of his sworn love for Giselle, two fingers raised to heaven—just as Siegfried signed that fateful moment in the ballroom—causes the bewildered woman to seek counsel from nature. After retrieving a marguerite (or daisy) from her mother's garden, she calls Albrecht back to their bench, beckoning with her hand and gliding through glissade.

Once seated, she plays "he loves me; he loves me not" with the flower's petals. As she proceeds, a negative outcome seems evident, so she quits playing in distress. Albrecht picks up the offending flower and shows that it does predict a positive answer. (Some Albrechts make a show of forcing the issue by removing the odd petal before playing the game for Giselle. The camera on Baryshnikov doesn't show conclusively if he does this or not; Nureyev is clearly shown "editing" the flower.) The concluding part of their "love scene" has Albrecht following behind Giselle in a joyous course of bounding grands jetés.

The ebullient mood is cut short by a scene with Hilarion. The gamekeeper, who hopes to win Giselle's hand for himself, confronts her with his dismay over her falling for Albrecht/Loys. Their miming, Hilarion's insisting on his devotion and Giselle's gentle but firm insistence that she cannot return his interest, leads to a confrontation between Albrecht and Hilarion. When things get to the possibility of drawing weapons, Hilarion, with his hunting knife in hand, notices how automatically Albrecht goes to draw a sword, which of course he's not wearing in his guise as Loys.

Calm and sunny spirits return with the reappearance of the vineyard workers who earlier passed through the village. The scene is entitled "*Retour de la vendange et valse*," which cues the "return of the grape-gatherers and a waltz" led by Giselle dancing happily for both her beloved Loys and her fellow villagers. The waltz that Giselle begins to lead by herself, with her female friends framing her in the background, restates the musical motif heard during her first entrance. So too, does the *balloné* step motif. Eventually she coaxes Albrecht to join her, which he does somewhat shyly. After Albrecht joins Giselle, the village men join their counterparts in framing the action. At the height of the lovers' (and the music's) excitement, Giselle and Albrecht travel downstage, arm in arm, leaping through jumps known generally as grand jeté-passé because the legs pass one another in the air in the arc of jumping.

A momentary uneasiness in the music cues a vignette for a faint-feeling Giselle. She reveals her "little spell" off to the side, where an evidently worried Albrecht indicates his concern. The general dancing of the peasant ensemble, formed in a centrally fixed rotating lineup that has become stock-in-trade for ice-show numbers, continues to dominate the episode. Climactically, a determined recovery takes Giselle back into the dance.

Here, production director Blair, as many other stagers of *Giselle* have likewise done, has added the music Adam wrote to climax his "*Pas des Vendanges*" which originally was placed at the end of this act. (The Nureyev-Seymour video has all of the music for this pas in its proper place in a version of the duet created by Mary Skeaping.) The rearrangement provides Albrecht with a mini-solo. In his traditionally consistent solo, Baryshnikov travels upstage. His passage is dominated by entrechat-cinq moves (the odd numbered entrechat always lands on one foot with the other positioned just off the floor to shoot out in a new direction) as well as by floatingly free sissone-ouverte. (The extra-virtuoso Baryshnikov throws in some quietly huge coupé-jeté moves that aim upstage and land downstage, like rolling over in bed.)

When the dancing Albrecht links up once more with Giselle their sometimes excited, other times intimate dancing à deux leads to a game with kisses. As Albrecht offers his hand to Giselle, by means of the musical sweep of his arm in contrasting thrust of his arabesque leg, the noble count finds the innocent peasant eager to pass kisses from her hand to his. (According to Anton Dolin, England's legendary mid-twentieth-century Albrecht, the game should be one of the aristocrat's offering to take Giselle's hand for the purpose of a decorous kiss. But the woman untrained in the ways of courtly love doesn't quite know what to make of the "ceremony" and decides to offer her hand back, kissing it first. For an explication of this and other salient details of *Giselle*, see *A Portrait of Giselle*, with Anton Dolin, 1982, 90 min., Color.)

Once more, ballet's conventions need to be remembered and accepted. Sticklers for a logic based on a literal reading of the ballet's subject will scoff at waltz music being danced by Germanic peasants in a Rhineland of long ago. But just as ballet skirts and ballet slippers belong here, so does music befitting ballet's particular kind of dancing. Writing to Heinrich Heine, the poet whose folkloric *De l'Allemagne* helped inspire *Giselle* in the first place, librettist Gautier noted that the ballet was set "on the other side of the Rhine, in some mysterious corner of Germany." Then he added, "Do not ask more of the geography of a ballet, which is unable to indicate the name of a town or a country in gesture, its sole means of expression."

When Petipa restaged Perrot's ballet for imperial Russian audiences, he inserted the newest conventions of his era alongside those of Perrot's. At this point in Act 1, he commissioned music from Ludwig Minkus for a standard, formula pas de deux for the leading ballerina and her partner. Though this dance is not now part of any Perrot-linked staging, its music can be heard. The Joffrey Ballet's Gerald Arpino used it to accompany a Romantic pastiche pas de deux he choreographed under the title *L'Air d'Esprit* in 1978.

A mimetic scene follows the delicately festive waltz. Giselle's mother dominates the action. She mimes her concern for her daughter and her passion for dancing. Though the scene is shortened here (as in most productions), to exclude Berthe's mimologue telling of the ghostly fate that awaits young women who die before their wedding day, hints of this message remain. The older woman emphatically crosses the wrists of her arms stiffened in front of her and subsequently folds her crossed arms over her breast in the manner of a corpse. Besides being revealed in Berthe's worried expressions and in her vestigial pantomime, the warning about becoming a Wili can be heard fleetingly in Adam's eerie leitmotif for the Wilis. (And yes, all shivers and shudders known as the "getting the Willies" would seem to come from the same source.)

Hunting horns tell of an approaching party. Their sounds disturb Albrecht in his charade and cause him to quit the scene. As they get closer Hilarion takes advantage of Albrecht's departure and steals into his cottage. We have come to "La Chasse" (The Hunt). Blair's production includes the presence of one real dog handled by a squire. (Originally, the prince and princess heading the party arrived on horseback. In a subsequent Paris staging the party numbered forty, and besides the Prince of Courland and his daughter Bathilde, other courtiers in the group also entered as equestrians.) The presence of royal visitors brings out most of the villagers, and finally Berthe, who upon being asked in a succinctly pantomimed request, gives the visitors refreshment.

A late-appearing Giselle ultimately plays hostess, and after being discovered almost boldly admiring Bathilde's rich garments, the innocent villager has a "conversation" with the gracious aristocrat. Giselle indicates matter-of-factly that she has made her own dress and more happily that her real love is for dancing. The two women then share thoughts of love; their pantomime signs matters of the heart and points to the place of the wedding ring on the ring finger. The enchanted princess then presents the beguiling young woman with a present, a chain of gold.

In a show of gratitude, Giselle presents two villagers—remember the couple who rested briefly on the bench on their way the vineyards?—to perform a dance for the royal visitors. This "Pas de deux des Jeunes Paysans" (often called the "Peasant Pas de Deux") was part of the first production but not part of the ballet's original plan. It was an interpolation, specifically arranged to existing music by one Frederick Bergmüller to satisfy the tastes of the day for diverting displays of virtuoso dancing. Waggish tongues even had a name—a *fromage* (cheese)—for such blatant and extraneous goodies of dancing.

Typical Paris Opera machinations also stood behind the addition, which entered *Giselle*'s scheme at the insistence of an influential and wealthy "patron" or "protector" of the pas' intended *danseuse*, Natalie Fitzjames. In all *Giselle* productions that include the "Peasant Pas" (and not all do include it—you won't find it on the Nureyev video, for example), the emphatically punctuated dance sticks out rather brightly from its more mellow, smoothly blended surroundings. The only vestigially appropriate dramatic logic of the duet is to put the male and female dancer performing it squarely in the eyes and minds of the audience eager for displays of fancy dancing. As mentioned earlier in regard to up-and-coming solo dancers, many times these unnamed characters have stolen the show from the leads and started to make a name for themselves. The part of the male peasant, for example, served to showcase the debut of Baryshnikov, here our exemplary Albrecht, in the company in which he was trained, the Leningrad Kirov Ballet.

Our video has Mariana Tcherkassky and Kirk Peterson as the leading "peasants." Both, incidentally, went on to higher-level careers after this: hers culminating in principal dancer status with American Ballet Theatre; his as leading dancer and eventually artistic director of Connecticut's Hartford Ballet. Blair's version of their pas appears to have grown out of some standard version that has come down to us through the ballet's history. Russian troupes regularly perform their rendering of the number, which includes free-association links to the changeable history the duet underwent in Petipa's various productions. This version shows itself to be somewhere between a pas d'action and divertissement pas de deux. The Petipa showpiece pas de deux came after Coralli's and Perrot's days, and this Bergmüller number looks and sounds betwixt and between.

The bright "Polacca" start brings both dancers before us in a sunny and energetic mood. More intimate partnering follows for the mellower "Andante." Three solos ensue, each to less than a minute's worth of music. First the man dances to music marked "Pesante" (for "weighty," as in "heavy"). His choreography has a stress on aerial moves and batterie including *brisé-volé*, the "broken/flying" step we saw worked into the solo for the "Blue Bird" in *The Sleeping Beauty*. The "heavy" character of the music gets acknowledged in the smart landings the dancer must make out of one aerial move before taking off for the next. The woman's solo is "Allegretto," or "pretty lively" rather than "very lively," and it too includes sunny *temps d'élevation* (aerial steps) with brisé-volé details, though all have less force and emphatic landings. Incidentally, it displays pronounced pointe work not likely possible in the 1840s, thus counterbalancing aerial emphasis with a terre-à-terre dimension. Next comes a second male solo, this time an "Allegretto pesante," combining both the preceding musical qualities. In visual and physical texture, the "peasant" man displays steps and accents related to his first solo and covers more space with them. A waltz brings both together in something less formulaic than a coda, but its acceleration serves a similar flourish-making purpose.

A restatement of the "Hunt" music cues the little celebration to break up, after which, we see Hilarion and hear his music as he emerges from Albrecht's hut with a suspiciously fine sword and hunting horn. (In some productions only the sword is retrieved; the hunting horn has been hung nearby, at the Prince of Courland's behest, to reassemble the party when necessary. The Royal Ballet production includes this detail.) But just as Hilarion prepares to produce what he's found to Giselle and Berthe, the mood changes abruptly to one of cheery, emphatic spirits.

We have come to the "*March des Vignerons*" (March of the Wine Growers). An upbeat, high-stepping entrance brings on a full complement of Giselle's fellow villagers. Climactically, they call her out of her cottage (by way of musical, rhythmic clappings) and crown her Queen of the Vintage. Their numbers are neatly amplified by six young women all in a row, signifying, as such attendant women often do in the world of nineteenth-century ballet, special friends. In a company that has such designations, these roles might well be cast from the coryphée ranks of the troupe. (The original libretto calls for a vine-bedecked wagon to be brought out to act like a "coronation coach," but Blair's production doesn't include one. Again, Peter Wright's staging for the Royal Ballet does honor this tradition.)

After accepting the honor enshrined on a bench in this case, and being presented with a homemade scepter minus a matching crown, Giselle is ready to show her gratitude, her pleasure, and her love of dancing by performing a solo. The *pas seul*, now part of just about every *Giselle* with claims to Coralli and Perrot's staging, is actually another interpolation, this one dating from Petipa's stagings from the 1880s. The music is probably that of Ludwig Minkus, then composer to the Russian imperial theaters; the choreography that of Petipa. Blair places it as part of the crowning festivities. (Wright tags it on to the hunting party scene, where it acts as an entertainment offering for the royal visitors, rather like the "Peasant Pas" does for Blair.)

After quickly winning permission from her mother to dance yet another dance, and stealing loving looks in the direction of Loys, Giselle takes her place upstage left and commences her pas. Makarova treats the dance as the delicate showpiece it was meant to be. Hoping to almost toy with each of her solo's individual highlights, Makarova takes the variation at an exquisitely slow tempo. As a lyrical ballerina type (according to Soviet Russian categorization), she draws out and fills out the choreography's nuances. She works to sustain her balance, to catch and hold dance high points and to make as buoyant and pliant as possible the respective leg extensions and footwork. She has her conductor trained to follow her passage through space as much as he follows the music's carefully composed sounds through time.

The first arrived-at effect, a simple first arabesque piqué, takes as much if not more time descending off its point of balance as it does striking it. The musical term *cantilena* (smooth, melodious, not rapid), which applied to operas of Donizetti and Bellini, has also been used to describe Adam's ballet score. Makarova has used the term, dancewise, to describe a desirable quality, when appropriate, that she sought in her own dancing, and eventually in the dancing of those she was coaching. She works to float through the various turns of her solo, as if the music's floating quality were some ether she could actually swim in.

To a delicately insistent violin passage, Makarova executes a string of so-called hops on pointe while counterpointing her working leg with ronds de jambe en l'air augmented by pausing and placing the circling leg to attitude-front position. The gestural import thus goes from shyly beckoning in the direction of beloved Loys to sweetly pointing in the direction of her loving mother. A final manège of piqué turns, with her skirt held proudly away from her turning legs, takes her happily to a climactic set of chaîné turns, out of which she demurely drops in head-lowered reverence.

A *galop général* (general, lively round-dance) follows for the villagers, in neat and regular rows of steps (for the females) and somewhat less tidy arrangements (for the men). Giselle and Loys join them at a high point, only to have Hilarion enter on a wrenching musical change and lead into what the score calls the "Finale du ler Acte et Scène de Folie" (Finale of the First Act and Mad Scene). Pantomime based on displaying the "evidence" of Albrecht's sword and hunting horn involves an accusatory Hilarion, a bewildered Giselle, and a trying-to-remain-calm Loys. Hilarion's sounding of the hunting horn brings back the Courland party. Bathilde's familiar and loving greeting to Albrecht brings a distressed Giselle to the knowledge that it's the princess and not herself who's engaged to Albrecht. As Giselle tears the princess's gift from around her neck, she collapses into the start of the "Mad Scene."

Espisodes of female heroines unhinged by the reckless and thoughtless nature of would-be heroic men were a familiar part of the dramatic arts of *Giselle*'s day. They were, for example, something of a plot motivation for glorious flights of vocal artistry in the *bel canto* operas of Donizetti and Bellini. (It's also of incidental interest to note that Carlotta Grisi, the original Giselle, was as accomplished a singer as she was a dancer.) Gautier's libretto sought to end the life of his deranged protagonist in a "pretty death." Today, ever since Elssler performed Giselle in Russia during the late 1840s, the ballet's "Mad Scene" stresses a more acted aspect, as enunciated by Elssler, than the danced one preferred by Grisi. (Petipa, who played Albrecht to Elsser's Giselle in Russia, is largely responsible for this choice, as he included it in his influential stagings of the ballet.)

As do all traditional Giselles, Makarova begins her descent into madness by tearing off the necklace presented by Bathilde and by letting her hair come down. (Traditionally a sign of grave stress and anguish, sometimes associated with mourning, unbound hair was a sight seldom seen on the ballet stage. Usually it was seen only in the case of travesty performance, where a woman playing a male role could then properly present herself with her hair undone and flowing loose.) Gone is her *cantilena* quality. She stares blankly, walks awkwardly, more or less dropping her weight onto her heels, and gestures as if in a trance. Adam's music reprises the "love scene" that accompanied Giselle and Albrecht's earlier amorous moments together. Since Petipa's day the music has been amended. Originally, church music played a part as Giselle imagined the wedding she would never have. The reprise of the scene with the marguerite has been retained.

Bone-chilling, blood-curdling music surfaces when Giselle steps on the telltale sword that Albrecht threw to the ground after being confronted with it by Hilarion. After toying with it, almost as if it were a serpent she was teasing, Giselle presents its blade as if to stab herself. In all productions the weapon gets taken away from her by Hilarion. But just *when* it's taken varies. Most times it's taken away before Giselle can do herself any harm. Sometimes, however, it's pulled from her grasp just *after* she manages to graze herself. The detail is dramatically crucial, since Giselle's grave in unconsecrated terrain is justified, according to Christian tenets, if she has died from a self-inflicted wound. If she dies of a weakened, broken heart, as most often she seems to do, the non-cemetery plot burial becomes unwarranted.

In any case, Makarova does not wound herself. (Seymour does.) She does, however, become oblivious to most of her surroundings. To the musical reminiscence of her dancing alongside Albrecht, her legs and feet appear to repeat their dance absentmindedly. More mysterious music recurs, and Giselle works herself into a frenzy as the uncomprehending onlookers watch in helpless fright. After a penultimate rush into her mother's arms and then to Albrecht's, she collapses in death. The music heats and stirs up in density and volume. Immediately, Albrecht accuses Hilarion of being responsible for the tragedy, and the gamekeeper counters by accusing the count himself. The villagers try to keep Albrecht away from the dead Giselle and her grieving mother, but he persists and ends on his knees near her corpse. Most stagings have Albrecht try to plead for his own good name and finally quit the scene in dramatic flight. (See Nureyev in his video, fleeing with his cape billowing in his wake.)

Act 2

The scene changes from day to night; the mood, from workaday to mysterious. Oliver Smith, this production's designer, has given the forest an open airiness that goes against the initial plan for the wood to be dense and dark. The music's introduction sounds ominous, detailed with tolling church bells and chilling frissons along the way. We see Hilarion fashioning a wooden cross to mark Giselle's resting place. His work is initially mildly distracted by the haunting atmosphere and he is eventually spooked by the apparition of veiled figures who appear among the trees and along the marshes. The ballet's creators planned a scene of high-spirited peasants playing a game of chance near this would-be sacred spot, but after initially including it in his production, Blair cut it, just as Petipa had in his reworking of Perrot's staging.

Now, like a mist rolling in—oftentimes a dry-ice fog pours over the stage—Myrtha, Queen of the Wilis, appears on music called "*Apparition de Myrthe et Évocation Magique*." With her veiled body held rigor-mortis stiff, she skims on tiny, successive moves on pointe in fifth position. You'll often hear these steps called *bourrées*, when in fact they are a specific kind of *pas de bourrée*, which is three-part changing of weight from one foot or pointe to the other and vice-versa. Sometimes, Myrtha's traveling variation of this step is more officially called *pas de bourrée couru* (running pas de bourrée) or *pas de bourrée chaîné* (chained pas de bourrée), the Russians call them *pas de bourrée suivi* (meaning connected pas de bourrée, because the one increment successively and eagerly follows the other).

After removing her veil she begins a solo dance that includes authoritative arabesque positions: on the flat, as opposed to the pointe of her foot, she steps and rotates (en promenade) in first arabesque, capping the revolution with a mesmerizing arabesque-penchée. Further bourrées act to define and consecrate her "territory." More arabesque moves, first alternating with second, take

Myrtha further into her evocational dance. (These sliding hops, or "chugs," establish a *voyagé* accent that will recur in this ballet and that we saw in the coda of *Swan Lake*'s first lakeside scene.) Repeatedly, she balances still, poised (on piqué pointe) in attitude position with her arms up and away from her torso, as if giving a chilling command.

After folding into a bow low to the ground, she arises to more energetic music and dancing. Grands jetés and sautés that switch positions midair dominate her variation. (Petipa substituted the now familiar variation, likely composed by Minkus, for the one that Adam included. No doubt he needed music more suited to the more athletically classical dancing he arranged for the solo dance.) Martine van Hamel's queenly character maintains an implaccable and impassive demeanor that in no way breaks character to acknowledge applause.

The high-pitched voice of the flute signals another change of mood, bringing us to the "Pas des Premières Wilis." Myrtha now wields some flowered branches. According to Gautier's specifications these should come from the shrub of rosemary, the herb of remembrance. As divining rods the twigs call forth the Wili sisters over whom Myrtha is queen. After being commanded to remove their bridal-veil coverings, twenty sisters encircle their leader; two more prominent ones then enter one at a time. All are dressed in the ballet blanc "uniform," full, long-skirted tutus. Moyna and Zulma, the two "lieutenant" Wilis, nowadays mirror each other as well as their other Wili sisters, but originally each was a distinct and separate character. The former was an odalisque, or member of some shah's harem; the latter, a *bayadère* from an Indian temple. (No such distinctions remain, and in some U.S. ballet companies nicknames arise: Laverne and Shirley gained some prominence during the era of the TV sitcom.)

After surrounding Myrtha in regular, regimented dancing where the arms sometimes seem to salute their mistress, the Wilis separate into two flanks, and first Moyna and then Zulma dance solos. Nanette Glushak, the first of these, has an ease and suppleness that gives her relevé-arabesque penchée moments a special reach and depth. As Zulma, Jolinda Menendez hasn't got enough strength in her waist and lower back to extra-dramatize the sweeping renversé turns that highlight her solo. All twenty-two Wilis fill and then clear the stage for another solo dance of Myrtha's. Big jumps, big poses, and commandingly held balances distinguish her foray.

With heads lowered, the corps de ballet as Wili horde, starts to move in accumulating rows with steady insistence. Hopping—chugging—in allongée (elongated) first arabesque, they obey the growing insistence of the accelerating and seesawing tone of the strings dominating the music as if swarming insects. A climactic and emboldened entrance for Myrtha has her rocketing back into the Wilis' midst where she recommands their dancing leading it front and center.

The high-energy temperature and mood drops for the start of the next scene. The new music, "Apparition de Giselle," signals the reappearance of Giselle as a Wili spirit. After incantations and surrounding the spot fixed with the cross, the Wilis pull away. On a commanding gesture from Myrtha, without the rosemary-branch scepter Gautier indicated here, the white-clad Giselle appears on top of her grave. With a regal swipe of the Wili queen's hand, the spectrally pale Giselle spins into a vertiginous spiral, hopping en dehors in low arabesque. Subsequently she unspools into *assemblé* moves (jumps in which the feet come together—assembled—in the air), casting about in the air like the clapper of a bell. After an almost demonic diagonal of fanning coupé jetés, she strikes one more softly floating arabesque pose, sometimes called *arabesque à deux bras*, after the positioning of both the dancer's arms toward the front of the torso, and exits near her grave.

After harkening gestures from Myrtha and her subjects indicate someone is approaching, the alerted Wilis clear the scene. On a new and plaintive air—"Entrée de Prince et Apparition de Giselle"—Albrecht appears. The dominant instrumental "voice" on our tape is a violin, but the arguably more melancholy and haunting oboe was Adam's choice and is more or less traditional. Pacing as if in a trance of deep thought, Albrecht proceeds wrapped in large cloak, carrying an armful of lilies. These flowers associated with death that will become the talisman of Giselle's ghost have become the signature bouquet for Albrecht to carry. Given their strong association with Giselle herself, my hunch is that they misguidedly became Albrecht's flowers somewhere along the way. I suspect the Paris Opera's florid Serge Lifar, one of the twentieth century's first important Albrechts outside Russian productions, may have been responsible for the hero's co-opting the heroine's flowers as his own.

In any case, bouquet in hand and cape filling with air, the remorseful count wanders, as if in a fog as lachrymose as the music, until he finds Giselle's grave, where he places his floral offering. Higher, trilling sounds signal another presence. The white-clad Giselle appears and disappears and appears again, slipping by Albrecht as she passes momentarily through his grasp in a gentle lift. In its original staging, both Giselle and her sister Wilis made various appearances by means of wires worked in conjunction with stage machinery.

After she flits through the background deeper upstage, Albrecht explodes in the air of her appearances by way of a pristine and expansive grand jeté en tournant. (The Russians call this move *grand jeté entrelacé*—interlaced grand jeté—and you'll not likely see a more perfected textbook demonstration of the turning jump than Baryshnikov's singular example.)

As Albrecht kneels, enraptured by his encounter with Giselle's spectral appearances, the one-time joyous peasant maid encircles him in sustained floating moves. In essence she executes what ballet-class terminology would call "unsupported adagio," practiced during the "center" portion of the ballet lesson. Makarova works with consistent care if not complete success to make each extension, each pointe-balanced pose, each reaching and unfolding action "sing" with the *cantilena* quality of unbroken momentum. Soon, Albrecht is on his feet and dancing in mirror-image phase with Giselle, eventually, momentarily, coupling with her to lift her at arm's length above his head as if she were hovering over him in midair. (These signature Giselle-Albrecht lifts, with him supporting her horizontally at the hipbone, are sometimes called a "bird" lift.)

Separated, the two arc side-to-side past each other in grander, less quick-timed versions of the assemblé moves Giselle swung through in the sudden animation of her "Wili Initiation" dance. The music's agitation and Giselle's brief disappearance make Albrecht agitated. When Giselle returns, she carries a lily in each hand and, as if engaged in a kind of chase, both the enticing Wili and the remorseful count soar through grands jetés en tournant. At the peak of their encounter, Giselle crests twice through *grand jeté pas de chat*, releasing a lily behind her at the top of each jump. In her wake Albrecht twice bolts through grands jetés in his attempt to catch the "offered" lilies. (In the case of the National Ballet of Cuba's famous but sight-impaired Alicia Alonso, the execution of this catch-as-catch-can trick became a different lily game. The technically prideful ballerina would strike an arabesque balance on pointe in lieu of grand jeté and hold the lily over head, where her Albrecht could jump to retrieve it. The feat is documented on a videotape: *Giselle*, starring Alicia Alonso, Azari Plisetski, 1964, 99 min., Black and White.)

Left with only his lily reminders of Giselle, Albrecht finds her returned yet again with more lilies. (Part of the concept of the original staging included the use of mechanically moving tree branches and leafy shrubs from which Giselle could "appear" to offer more lilies to her beloved before "disappearing" from sight. Random productions in our era make attempts to re-create these devices for having the Wili spirit materialize among the foliage of the forest.)

Just as Albrecht spills the presented lilies on Giselle's grave, a new sense of urgency stirs in the music. We have come to the "Entrée d'Hilarion, Scène et Fugue des Wilis." As Albrecht flees downstage, Hilarion is chased and trapped upstage by ranks of Wilis, arms pointing menacingly in his direction. Their lines and circles surround him to prevent his leaving their territory. With Myrtha stationed implacably downstage left the Wili sisters engulf their victim like a whirlpool of immovable force. The method to their madness is to compel their captive to dance to death. When he's not surrounded, Hilarion is casting about in jumps and turns meant to exhaust him.

Hilarion's gestured plea for mercy and relief, on bended knee before the Wili queen, is met by gestures that pantomime the fact that the gamekeeper (her hand gestures in his direction) must remain (finger points to the place) and dance (hands roll over one another overhead). The ultimate Wili configuration is a corner-to-corner diagonal line; the huntsman's final, desperate plea to Myrtha for relief is met with a pantomimed gesture signifying death: hands raised calmly overhead cross the arms at the wrists as they forcefully bring the gesture directly down to conclude as fists crossed below the waist.

After Hilarion whirls headlong out of sight and, the libretto tells us, to his end, the Wilis go off two-by-two, to a kind of insistent "traveling" music. If you want to note the difference between ballet's common jeté and its standard grand jeté, follow this sequence. The first two jumps, one to left the other the right are jetés, the next two are more forceful grand jetés. (As I've said before, ballet is essentially an art of many distinctions among few elements; technically, then, this sequence involves twice executing *jeté dessus* [jeté over] and then twice doing *grand jeté en avant en attitude* [large jeté to the front in attitude position]. But don't worry about the finer points until you get your bearings on the basic ones.)

Noting that as a pack, the Wilis move in pairs, the dance critic Arlene Croce likened their emblematic exit to the way the Hells Angels motorcycle gang tends to travel. On the first appearances and disappearances of Giselle, Croce had another witticism: If in any way ill timed or too coyly presented, these peekaboo comings and goings come close to the classic cartoon situation of Tweety Pie the canary wondering aloud about catching sight of Sylvester the cat: "Thought I thaw a puttee tat!"

When the Wilis return, almost as soon as they've left, they're led by Myrtha, once more brandishing her rosemary-branch wand. They reposition themselves on their tightly packed diagonal line. Trailing in, as if drawn from the forest by the Wilis' powers, is Albrecht, up against their frigid wall. However, just as the merciless queen is about to answer the count's gestured plea for mercy with her familiar "death sentence," so to speak, Giselle breezes in, spreads her arms, a cruciform, and leads Albrecht to the protection of the cross on her grave. In this staging Giselle positions herself like a cross more than letting the hewn cross work its godly powers over the godless queen. Here, Myrtha should specifically make an attempt to wield her powers by means of her scepter, only to have the branch wither in the face of Christian powers. But instead of seeing it shrink before the power of the cross, in this production we watch van Hamel hurl it to the ground in dismay.

As a deeply melancholy violin is heard, Myrtha's gestures command that Giselle obey her and begin an enticing dance. The libretto says that while the cross overpowers Myrtha's magic and thus protects the moral Albrecht, Giselle is still bound as a Wili to do her queen's bidding. That bidding asks that the ghostly young woman dance so beguilingly she will make herself impossible to resist and lead Albrecht to leave the refuge of sanctuary and bring himself out in the open once more.

Adam's "Grand Pas de Deux" now begins. The "grand" designation is a musical and theatrical one. The reference tells us that this is the ballet's pièce de résistance. The Romantic era term predates the "grand pas de deux" of Petipa's classical ballet era, where it refers to climatic pas de deux of a strict formula: entrance, adagio, male variation, female variation, coda. (The pas de deux that Petipa interpolated into Act 1, discussed above, that is no longer included in stagings of *Giselle*, followed this formula.) This duet begins with a solo adagio for Giselle; its opening dramatic move is a calculated développé of the right leg after it's slowly drawn up to the passé position. In character and tone, this unsupported adagio moment represents an even more concentrated rendering of the ballet-class centerwork exercise. After sweeping her extended à la seconde leg to arabesque, Makarova inches around through en dehors promenade in arabesque-allongée. A similar but not identical sequence to the other side, climaxing in a first arabesque penchée pose, proves to be the enticement Myrtha intended. Albrecht joins Giselle, and the two commence a supported adagio.

With Albrecht's "support" Giselle's dance grows more languorous, artfully attenuated and dreamlike. A good many overhead lifts from her beloved make the Wili spirit seem to float and hover in reverie. Romantic ballet's arabesque à deux bras repeatedly occurs throughout the adagio. On the duet's closing, singing sigh, the sorrowing Albrecht kneels while the forgiving Giselle stands behind, and each raise one arm ahead of them, as if rising from the same breastbone.

A sign from Myrtha impels Giselle to continue her dance with a mind toward exhausting her beloved. This begins with Giselle's more sprightly moves (delicately shimmering sauté-rond de jambe en l'air moves), which lead to light *soubresauts* (jumps from two feet to two feet) that pause in the air in arched-body positions sometimes characterized as *temps depoisson* (or "timed like a fish"). Along the same diagonal and to a repeat of the same music, Albrecht does his first solo dancing in this pas de deux. First come softly struck, potent cabrioles to the back, then on a musical "reminiscence" from the "Pas de vendanges," Albrecht does precisely the same step sequence he executed for Giselle's pleasure in the village gathering. Metaphorically, this direct quote goes toward revealing how essentially unchanged Albrecht is in his present state from his recent past.

After wrapping up his solo with a fine-spun pirouette en dedans en attitude, he rejoins Giselle, essentially helping her "float" her jumps to hang hauntingly in the air. The whole of the adagio finishes with Giselle solo, responding to the "sawing" strings with entrechats and successively repeated rélevé-passé steps. The sequence of back-traveling entrechats has been known to begin with a series of entrechat-quatre and finish with one of entrechat-six, but Makarova does all quatres, executing the second set more briskly than the first.

Following a sequence of repeated pauses and held poses in arabesque, she whisks herself on another diagonal of turning steps, initially based in balloné moves then in chaîné turns on pointe and finally in impetuously held first arabesque balance.

Albrecht enters for his solo to Adam's "Andantino." In Baryshnikov's case this takes the form of powerfully athletic yet clean-as-a-whistle double cabrioles-front alternated with abandoned *sissone-fermé* (a leap from two feet landing on one before bringing the other in to meet it). Typically, Baryshnikov adds an extra back-leaning tilt to his torso, lending the look of almost reclining in the air. After tossing off a *grand jeté en tournant battu* (large, turning jump, beaten), he hurls himself smoothly into a *double assemblé*, the nickname for a jump shaped like an assemblé that turns over twice in the air before landing. More ecstatically abandoned tour jetés and a series of smoothly rocketing and revolving double tour en l'air ultimately leads to a dreamily vertiginous sextuple pirouette that opens à la seconde on the seventh revolution to spin through one tour à la seconde, and finish precisely "to the knee," meaning in a kneeling final pose.

Adam's brief "Andante" brings Giselle on with another offering of lilies, this time for her queen. Myrtha, however, waves off the flowers, gesturing that the dance to the death proceed, which sends Giselle into an almost reckless dance. Her music is another of Petipa's interpolations, a waltz, composed by Minkus on one of Giselle's musical themes. She travels upstage, sweeping into jumps that change directions midair. More entrechats and ronds de jambe en l'air act to fill the air with further palpitations. After enticing Albrecht back into the dance, Giselle travels on an exiting diagonal by means of grand jeté pas de chat followed by Albrecht, who tears after her with one whomping grand jeté.

The "Finale" of the grand pas de deux begins with a musical passage sometimes called "Ensemble des Wilis." Now the Wili sisters reenter the action as a group, restating, in more agitated terms, their formations and steps from earlier rituals. Flying into their midst with a dance force that appears to capture in one individual the full frenzy displayed by the nearly two-dozen strong Wili group, Baryshnikov's Albrecht shoots through a diagonal of *brisé* (broken) steps that cut the air like gleaming shears. He immediately travels upstage, making his turning jumps look artfully looser, signifying a loss of will and control, and then beelines back downstage with an even more intense and cutting sequence of brisé moves. (In the video with Nureyev, you'll see him dance almost continually in an innovation of his own. He chooses to dance from the very start, where traditionally the Wili ensemble reenters the dance on its own. In addition to the pulsating dance of the Wilis, Nureyev rebounds repeatedly through entrechat-six, as if his feet were possessed by the will of the ghostly sisters.)

Taking himself through yet another set of leg-splitting jumps, Baryshnikov's Albrecht finds Giselle. She immediately begins to travel in successive hops in arabesque. In dance terms, the danseur partners his ballerina through a repeated set of actions called *temps levé* in arabesque. In terms of the building dramatic narrative, Albrecht appears to take rest and solace in the shadow of Giselle's dancing. The choreography presents an image of Giselle's "subbing" for Albrecht, of her distracting or fulfilling Myrtha's demands as the exhausted count gets some respite.

After Giselle and Albrecht separate once more, presumably due to Myrtha's power of insistence, the entire floor of the forest is filled with dancing. Front and center, the bonded lovers lead the entire Wili contingent (minus the immovable Myrtha) in hypnotically regular moves. Repeatedly, all jump through sauté-fouetté-arabesque moves that have the effect of artfully pulling them in opposite directions over and over again. Near the end, the spirits remain willing to continue with the mad dance, but the body of Albrecht is weakened to the point of total exhaustion. On command of Myrtha and in light of no answer to pleading gestures from Giselle and Albrecht, the count must continue to dance. As he does, elaborating on the preceding sauté-fouetté moves with cabrioles, he collapses once more, with seemingly no further reserves of energy.

Just then, as the merciless Wili queen readies to make Albrecht complete his dance to the death, the sound of chimes delicately peal through the darkened music of the night forest, telling of the breaking dawn. Myrtha and her sisters can no longer hold sway as the sun's light filters onto the landscape. Adam's final musical number is called "Lever du Soleil et Arrivée de la Cour." While the "rising of the sun" remains part of the action of the ending of *Giselle*, the "arrival of the court" has mostly been dispensed wth since Petipa's revision of the ballet.

We see two dramas play out. Upstage, with their backs to us, the Wili queen and her subjects pay homage to the fading night and slip out of sight. Downstage, the independent Wili bids loving farewell to the lover, who, though lost to her, has been saved from the Wilis' torment. Caressing him one last time, Giselle hovers over and about Albrecht as if she were vaporizing into the day's light. The dazed lover takes his ghostly beloved into his arms as she seems to fall back to rest on the air. Once she slips from his grasp, Giselle backs away in skimming pas de bourrée suivi steps on pointe. Drawn to her grave, she can no longer see, sense, or feel her lover. He watches her exit hopelessly. He seeks to remain in contact by gathering up the lilies covering her grave. In a daze, he backs off, absentmindedly strewing the flowers as he goes. Their trail is all that remains of his journey seeking Giselle's forgiveness, and he collapses in one last swoon.

Today you'll see a variety of endings to *Giselle*, with none that

I know of choosing to enact the "return of the court"—Bathilde, Albrecht's squire, and various courtiers arriving to rescue the count from the wilds of wood. Some stagings use the brassy, robust "return" music to accompany Albrecht's bewilderment awakening from his dream/nightmare. In addition to the arriving courtiers, the original staging also intended Giselle to slip back into the earth where flowers spring forth. Her last gesture to Albrecht in this rendering should be a lone flower—a rose, to be precise—presented by her disembodied hand as she slips away forever. Sometimes Albrechts remain standing in grief with one of Giselle's lilies still in their hands, a kind of reminder of the intended ending.

If you'd like to fast-forward ten years to a "next generation" Giselle and Albrecht, see the movie *Dancers*, 1987 (released on video, 1988). There you'll find Baryshnikov not only still dancing Albrecht with mellowed, full powers, but you'll also see his personal ideas about producing the ballet. You'll see Giselle as Wili spirit appear among leafy shrubs and on bowing tree branches, as well as Myrtha's magic scepter as a rosemary sprig. You'll also find in the ingenue role, Julie Kent, a then corps de ballet dancer who went on after this movie to become a ballerina and dance the lead role of Giselle to deserved acclaim.

As with all well-known and famous ballets, *Giselle* has its share of updated and rethought productions. One of the most imaginative and appropriate was created especially for Dance Theatre of Harlem by Frederic Franklin. While the choreography is based primarily in the traditional Coralli-Perrot-Petipa version, this *Giselle*, sometimes called *Creole Giselle*, has a rewritten libretto by Arthur Mitchell, the company's artistic director, and Carl Michel, the production's designer. The familiar outline of *Giselle* remains intact, but the details have been shifted. The setting is a sugar plantation in a free-black colony around the Louisiana bayous. The second act takes place on the edge of a swamp; Albrecht enters not on foot but in a flat-bottomed skiff poled by his squire, and the Wilis are called "Miseries." (See *Creole Giselle*, with Dance Theatre of Harlem, starring Virginia Johnson, Eddie Shellman, and Lorraine Graves, 1988, 87 min., Color.)

Chapter 6

BALLET EMBODYING THE IDEAL

La Sylphide

• • •

Choreography by August Bournonville
Music by Herman Løvenskjold

Moving backward in time, we come to the oldest of the ballets among our selections. With the exception of Galeotti's *Whims of Cupid and the Ballet Master*, which the Royal Danish Ballet has more or less kept in active repertory since its 1786 premiere, *La Sylphide* is the oldest extant ballet in all of international ballet. Although the landmark *Sylphide* was created by an Italian in 1832 for Paris, it is the remake, choreographed in 1836 for Copenhagen by August Bournonville, that has survived to become popular in ballet history and into our own day. As of this writing the only video recording of Bournonville's complete *La Sylphide* is not on videocassette but on laser disc. This excellent recording and performance on the Royal Danish Ballet's own stage, with Lis Jeppesen and Nikolaj Hübbe, has been shown on cable television. So has a less remarkable staging led by what was then called London Festival Ballet and featuring Peter Schaufuss and Eva Evdokimova, but it is not available commercially on either disc or tape. If you have no access to laser disc facilities, watch your cable TV listings for reruns of either of these recordings or ask some longtime balletgoers if they taped them.

Because Bournonville's *Sylphide* is the one you'll likely see in a theater, it will be the one I concentrate on. For passing reference, I've incidentally named the only "complete" *Sylphide* now commercially available on videotape. This is an extravagantly filmed performance of Pierre Lacotte's free-hand reconstruction of the original *La Sylphide* by Filippo Taglioni, Marie's father. I'll call it a "supplementary video" and refer to it at appropriate moments as we work through Bournonville's version.

About the supplementary video:

> The Paris Opera Ballet Company in *La Sylphide*, starring Ghislaine Thesmar and Michel Denard, with Laurence Nerval, Mathe Souverbie, Yvette Bouland, 1971, 81 min., Color. This video may be catalogued under P for Paris Opera.
>
> The French-made film with French-language introductory narration documents a large stage, large-cast approximation of an early nineteenth-century ballet pantomime complete with the flying machines that created the special effects of the age. It includes details that Bournonville re-created for his version, and a completely different musical score by Jean Schneitzhöffer. (Schneitzhöffer's music has become as rare a fixture in the ballet world, as has Taglioni's choreography. One of his melodies, however, has been recycled into a fairly popular score for "classroom ballet" called *Etudes*. When you come across this work, which is based on piano-scale studies of Karl Czerny by Knudåge Riisager as well, you'll hear echoes of the original *La Sylphide* in the segment where the leading ballerina of *Etudes*, dressed like a sylphide, dances with a gallant partner.)

Unlike the titles for our preceding ballets, the one for *La Sylphide* tends to remain in the French-language wording of its first manifestation by Papa Taglioni for daughter Marie. Actually, Bournonville's now internationally known ballet that took its inspiration from Taglioni's work was, and indeed still is, called *Sylphiden* at home in Copenhagen's Royal Theater. For a time during the late 1960s and 1970s, American Ballet Theatre tried to anglicize the ballet's possibly forbidding and esoteric title by calling it *The Sylph of the Highlands*, but eventually *La Sylphide* continued to prevail.

As we shall see, the motivation to rechristen *La Sylphide* in a way that steered clear of using the word *sylphide* partly stemmed from a potential confusion with *Les Sylphides*. But this is another story that will be told in the wake of this one.

Bournonville's *La Sylphide* owes much to Taglioni's, but not everything. What struck the impressionable twenty-five-year-old Dane studying in Paris from his one look at Taglioni's ballet was the wondrous presence and performance of La Taglioni and the marvelous stage machinery in the Paris Opera house. Realizing that back home in Copenhagen, he would have neither of these ingredients to fortify his *La Sylphide*, Bournonville remade the work to his purposes. Not all of these were compromises from supposed higher standards. The Danish sylph would be the ballet master's prize pupil, Lucile Grahn, whom the ballet master had schooled in standards set by Taglioni. The leading male role of James, the young Scot whose dreams the sylph preoccupies, would be more than a "pedestal for the prima donna," as Bournonville himself noted while creating the part for himself.

All Bournonville really took wholesale from Taglioni's Paris ballet then was its outline—the libretto, and its trappings. The author of the narrative scheme was Adolphe Nourrit, an operatic tenor who had performed the title role in Meyerbeer's opera *Robert le Diable* (1831), miming opposite Marie Taglioni's dancing in the seminal Romantic opera ballet known as the "Pas de Nonnes" (or "Ballet of the Nuns"). We no longer have this ballet around in its Taglioni rendering except in sundry pictorial records, including some famous ones by the great Edgar Degas. But we do have history's verdict on the ballet's inspirational impact on the ensuing age of ballet Romanticism. As André Levinson, the conservative but dedicated ballet historian-critic, put it when scrutinizing the pre-Romantic ballet from the vantage point of fully fledged Romantic ballet: "Ballet was a divertissement. It became a mystery."

Nourrit's *La Sylphide* retells, with requisite poetic license, a tale set in Scotland about a brownie (or male sprite) of the hearth who tempts away half of a wedded couple, destroying domestic tranquillity. The source was *Trilby, ou le Lutin d'Argaïl.* Nourrit's libretto concerns the enticing powers and eventual destruction of beauteous female sylph. (The term sylph to identify a woodland nymph, comes from a derivation of the Latin *silva* for forest.) Our sylph visits James Reuben, our young Scottish groom-to-be, on his wedding day. While trying to resist the beguiling sylph's enticements to have him abandon his domestic surroundings, including his innocent bride-to-be Effy, James bewilders his fiancée, gets testy with his rival for Effy's hand, and is brashly dismissive with Madge, an old hag who steals in to take warmth from his hearth.

After he can resist no longer, James leaves everything behind and follows the sylph to her forest home. Once there among her sister sylphs she continues to elude his grasp. Finally, he meets up once more with the hag he threw out of his house. She pretends to get past any hard feelings and offers him a means of capturing the sylph—a specially desirable scarf. When the gossamer shawl proves irresistable to the sylph, James teases her with it and eventually wraps her in it. But instead of capturing her and winning her for his own, the scarf, which was hexed by Madge and her witches' coven, first deprives the sylph of her wings and then of her life's breath. Realizing he's been revenged by the witch, James is forced to see his one-time betrothed on her way to marry his rival and to watch his beloved sylph float away from him forever. He's left to swoon in darkest despair.

We have seen that the dramatic duality of *Giselle*'s two acts rested in a rustic everyday world in daytime versus a wilder landscape at nighttime. *La Sylphide*'s two halves contrast interior farmhouse life with an exterior realm of the natural wilds of a forest. James is not so much a calculating philanderer as an impetuous dreamer. The sylph who visits him as a vision and in his dreams has been viewed as epitomizing the "beautiful danger" inherent in the world of Romantic art. Sometimes the enchantress/sylph and the ogress/witch are viewed as a Romantic duality, as sister or kindred spirits.

James meets a tragic end in his efforts to pursue his dreams, but in the words of Romantic era critic Jules Janin, our reaction to his fate is meant to remain complex: "Poor James! and yet who dares to pity thee? He must also pity the poet, the lover, the dreamer, all souls who are wrapt in visions of the ideal." Into our day a related caveat surmounts the so-called old stage of Copenhagen's Royal Theater where Bournonville first presented his *Sylphiden*: EI BLOT TIL LYST goes the Danish for "Not only for pleasure," a word to the wise about the deeper powers of art.

Løvenskjold's overture breathes into life before bellowing with indications of unsettled dark forces in lowing strings and woodland horns. Then it switches gears and tempo, animated by higher strings (the violin will come to be identified as the "voice" of the sylph). At the curtain's rise and the start of the score's "Introduction," we find the sylph, in a cloud of white gauze, poised at the feet of a Scotsman asleep in his easy chair. A solo violin cues the flower-crowned woman with transparent wings on her back to rise up. With gestures that suggest the sleeping Scot's sweet dreams and her own teasing presence in his reverie, the sylph rings the young man's chair and the room of his household with dancing passages that suggest a creature of the air. She skims through rippling moves on toe tip and delicately strikes (*piqué*) or pliantly springs (*relevé*) into arabesque poses that suggest hovering and floating moments.

Soon she's to-and-froing in a little dance of elation, sometimes circling one foot as if stirring the air (ronds de jambe en l'air), sometimes slipping into low little jumps or lightly sweeping into higher, leg-beating ones (cabrioles back), sometimes changing directions by stepping into one position facing this way (in arabesque) only to pull the extended leg in and reextend in a new and different direction, and effortless bounds about the room in a contrasting direction. Gestures signaling a sudden, bright idea precede the sylph's "flight" back toward James, on whose brow she plants a whisper of kiss.

The awakened young man shows happy if bewildered interest in the visitor. She poses demurely during his expressions of curiosity and darts about the room energetically to elude his desire to take her in his arms. Eager arabesque poses and spritely grands jetés artfully "float" the sylph away from James and his impetuous attempts to embrace his vision. Her final coursing comes from pointing to the chimney over the fireplace and her disappearance up its flue.

The sylphide's mercurial departure marks the end of Løvenskjold's "Introduction." Schneitzhöffer's first episode ends similarly in Lacotte's pastiche of Taglioni's ballet. Beyond this point, the Paris Opera staging bears less and less relationship to that of the Royal Danes. But before or after you see Bournonville's devising of this scene you might like to note the especially lovely dancing, particularly with regard to footwork, of Ghislaine Thesmar as a sylphide à la Taglioni.

While neither Bournonville's nor Lacotte's stagings overstresses the use of pointes—it is imperative to recall that *La Sylphide* inspired a taste for more and more pointe work on ballet stages—Thesmar's sylph works much more off pointe than on, compared with Danish-tradition sylphs, specifically with Jeppesen as caught on this video record. What's intriguing and impressive is how much variety of texture, scale, and finesse of footwork Thesmar reveals without more than minimal recourse to working on her pointes. As it turns out in the scheme of both Taglioni's and Bournonville's *La Sylphide*, pointe shoes only appear on the feet of the sylphide and her sister sylphs. Later in the era, in *Giselle* for instance, not only the Wilis but Giselle and her female friends dance in pointe shoes.

Also of note contrasting extant Bournonville and guessed-at Taglioni, is the amount of mimetic encounter between the awakened young man and his dreamlike vision. Bournonville's sylph finds herself engaged in a brief "conversation" of gestures with James, where the otherworldly creature faces and "answers" the young man. Lacotte's "Taglioni sylph" largely eludes being sighted by her James. Once awakened he senses the apparition from his dream more than her appearance. In a striking dramatic moment, Lacotte's James sights the sylphide only long enough to see her slip away, up the chimney.

Løvenskjold's second scene, called "Effy's Entrée" and marked "Andantino," is mostly expositional. It introduces Gurn, a rival for Effy's hand, and Effy herself, happily welcoming her wedding day. With Anna, Effy's aunt, also on hand, the scene unfolds in pantomime. Sensing the distracted nature of James, Gurn hopes to show Effy his constancy. Anna looks a little apprehensive at the lack of solicitation on the part of James. Effy feels his distance when her kiss to awaken him elicits an expression of disappointment that she is not the source of his earlier kiss. James summarily dismisses Gurn's

dience, while the highest level was upstage, farthest away from the audience.

Bournonville's stress on dance as an expression of joy—an outpouring of energetic emotion—regularly took the shape of space-eating moves, often with arms opening out from the breastbone, as they so often do in these two male solos, as if to signal an embrace at the height of a jump aiming straight downstage, in the direction of the audience. As consistent as the wide opening out of the arms comes Bournonville's preference for the position of the extended leg in attitude (rather than arabesque position) for big jumps and big poses. The video record of Hübbe's James nicely documents the climactic en dedans pirouette with which Bournonville wrapped up the whole number.

At this point in the ballet, No. 6 in the score and called "Reel," the Scottish folkore material surfaces with strong local color. Løvenskjold's music is based on a legitimate Scottish number known as "Strathspey Reel." The choosing of partners for the couple dance indicates how distracted James is when Effy's mother has to remind him that he's expected to perform this traditional dance with his fiancée. Once the couples are all paired up, including the slightly absurd one of Gurn and a girlchild "Villager," the balleticized folk dance spreads out with its terre à terre accents and almost percussive footwork. In other words, we're treated to music and movement that qualify as a character dance. Since this is a communal dance, its participants include villagers of all ages, and most stagings of Bournonville's choreography include children, usually three couples besides the girl dancing with Gurn, in the complement of villagers.

As the couplings and lineups work through their paces, James keeps being pulled away by sightings of the sylph, whom no one else appears to see. First he sees her atop the stairs, then flitting across the length of the room. His dropping out of the group dance to chase the "phantom" obviously bewilders Effy.

The act's finale (the score's No. 7) begins in a briefly mellow mood. As Effy gets accoutered off to the side for the wedding ceremony, James looks proudly at the wedding ring he'll soon confer on his bride. But the sylph reappears (the libretto says from the fireplace, the Royal Danish video has her come in the front door) and teasingly appropriates the ring for herself. Next, she gestures to the outdoors where she indicates James should follow. In some productions, such as the Danish one mentioned here, the sylph places James's tam-o'-shanter at his feet to encourage his departure. In all of them, the sylph's enticements work their wonders and James dashes outdoors in pursuit of his vision.

From there the music builds, as the assembled prepare to toast the bride and groom and see them wed. After lifting their glasses to a nonexistent James, eager anticipation turns to heated agitation. Anna, showing concern for her absent son, sends out men to look for James. Effy freezes remembering the old woman's prophecy. Gurn comes in from his look outside and mimes his sighting of James chasing a winged, floating creature. After his previously unfounded claim to such a sight in the armchair, the guests dismiss Gurn as daft again. Effy pulls off her wedding ornaments and seeks comfort for her confusion in the arms of her friend Nancy (a semiprominent character) and her would-be mother-in-law. Darkness and heaviness in the concluding music weigh down the scene as the curtain falls.

Act 2

The time is the dark of night, and the place is a wild landscape, menacingly overgrown with vegetation, and according to Bournonville's specifications outside the mouth of a cave. No. 1 in the score is "The Witch Scene." Over a roaring fire, a charred caldron emits sulphurous vapors, as Madge, our familiar witch, stirs some brew. Her sister witches contribute grotesque ingredients to the concoction, a little like the Weird Sisters do in Shakespeare's *Macbeth*. The musical atmosphere has its shrieks, bellowings, and churnings, all of which give way to a rollicking mood of drinking-songs. Part of the cause for celebration by Madge and her companion witches is the gossamer scarf that is retrieved from the pot. Bournonville notes that it's spun and woven by these sisters as a "rose-colored drapery." (Don't think too ill of sparkling versions that might emerge from the kettle; a report of Taglioni's staging notes a "spangled scarf."

Whatever the distinctions of its material—bilious green, rosy pink, or sequin spangled—the freshly brewed scarf gets tucked about Madge's person as she exits and the scene evaporates. In some productions the witches fly (on wires) out of sight, and with others, as in the Danish one being observed here, the caldron is made to disappear (through a stage trapdoor). In all, the scene ends with the departure of Madge and her coven and the arrival of dawn upon the forest realm of the sylphides.

The violin voice of the sylphides comes up afterward, with the sunrise Bournonville calls for. Instead of menacing landscape, a pastoral one materializes for No. 2, "James and the Sylphide, the Forest Scene." A new sylph is introduced, and she skims into view by way of tremulous pas de bourrée couru on the violin's trill. Initially executing a développé to first *arabesque*, she pivots (en promenade) in place, in pose. A gentle penchée move caps the moment, and a pliant rising onto pointe leads the lone sylph to call on two companion spirits. They frame their central sister and, after lightly moving from one side and then another, all three harken to approaching sounds and slip out of sight.

James enters, entranced by the sights he finds. Then, as if floating from on high, his sylphide enchantress glides to the ground. (Simple rather than elaborate stage machinery characterizes Bournonville's rendering of *La Sylphide*, inspired by Taglioni's. Whatever else Lacotte's filmed production re-creates from Taglioni's 1832 staging, it utilizes much of the *grande machinerie* typical of the elaborately equipped Paris Opera house. Thesmar and her sister sylphs appear to soar, float, and fly over, around, and through their lushly wooded landscape, aided by a complex series of wires, stage levels, and individual hydraulic lifts.)

After alighting, the sylph notices the wonder with which James surveys his bucolic surroundings and signs how welcome he now is to her domain. They stand facing each other and exchange pledges of love by raising their hands and pointing fingers to heaven. A more animated and lighthearted musical passage shows an inspired James taking his beloved sylph into his embracing arms, but the object of his desire demurs. Slightly puzzled and put off, James finds the sylph teasing him by removing his cap. She then darts away, first to pick him some strawberries, then to scoop some fresh spring drinking water in her cupped hands. Her breathlessly light runs on pointe prettily recall the liquescent nature of what she carries.

Each time the sylph treats James to the delights of the landscape, he tries to hold her in his arms, and every time she slips away. Next she has him follow her as she chases and catches a butterfly for him. This last little offering elicits something of a reprimand from James, who insists the sylph let the fluttering insect go free. Musically and mimetically the butterfly scene counterposes fluttering hands and fingers with trilling sounds to explain itself.

Bournonville's narrative has James become a little frustrated and melancholy at this point, all of which the sylph perceives and seeks to remedy. In the words of the libretto, "She knows a way." Her way takes the form of a brief scene in which she introduces her sister sylphs to her beloved (No. 3, "The Sylphide Calls the Sylphs") and leads directly into a seven-part divertissement (No. 4, "The Sylph Scene"). The extended segment of dancing that makes up Bournonville's divertissement took the shape we find today a good time after the ballet's first performances. Nearly thirty years later, probably around 1865, Bournonville revised his initial stretch of sylph dancing to include even more.

The reasons for this expansion likely stem from Bournonville's desire to emulate *Giselle*, a ballet popular ever since its premiere in 1841, the year the Danish ballet master saw it himself. Thus the *ballet-fantastique* that grew out of seeds planted by earlier Romantic ballets—led by *La Sylphide*—spurred Bournonville to refortify *Sylphide* with lessons learned from its own offspring. Ultimately, the heart of Bournonville's ballet blanc included two added solos for James, one for the sylphide herself and a trio of "leading" sylphs. The music came from additional Løvenskjold (the trio) as well as from Josef Mayseder (the second solos of both James and the sylphide) and probably from Holger Paulli (James's first solo, which postdates Bournonville altogether). So our looking at *La Sylphide* after *Giselle* is not merely a convenience reflecting the lesser popularity of earlier work; aesthetically, in part at least, Bournonville's *Sylphide* is an heir of *Giselle*.

The suite begins with the sylphide's développé-arabesque penchée moves calling forth her sister sylphs from both sides of the forest clearing. After a musical introduction that sounds not unlike that composed by Adam for an entrance of his Wilis, Bournonville's sylphs (eighteen in number in current Danish productions) group together in pairs that is not unlike the face-to-face configurations of Coralli's Wili dances. Løvenskjold's "Andante con molto espressione" (flowing with much expression) underscores the gracious, soothing nature that rises from the evolving formations configured by the harmoniously lilting women. Their pairings reform into single rows, a smoothly revolving ring, and a softly angled wedge saluting their queenly sylph, who appears to float and balance at the end of a tree branch.

When our singular sylph comes into the midst of her mirror-image sisters, she dominates with a solo dance. A flute accompanies her dancing, which includes delicately poised moments of balance on one pointe. These movements variously blossom from airily unfolded (by way of développé moves) extensions to the front or to the side. Weighty and meatier musical accompaniment follows for James's first solo, in the interpolation (probably of Paulli) mentioned above. As if cued by the sylph's final gesture, James bounds and rebounds, embellishing sailing assemblé jumps with beats, specifically "sixes," and confidently bolting upward into straightforward entrechat-six. For the climax he alternately bolts into varied entrechats and emphatic double air turns; in the case of Hübbe's performance, you'll see three double tours en l'air with one to the right, the next to the left, and the last to the right again. A pas de chat to pose triumphantly, with arm up in the style of the Scottish Reel, puts James in a "finished" pose to punctuate his dance and stand ready to accept his audience's applause.

Out of the prettily linked surround of standing and kneeling sylphs, three slip out to start their own little dance, faintly echoing the moves of the dominant sylph. A fourth sylph continues the violin-accompanied number with a mini-solo. (In the case of our Royal Danish video, the dancer is the eye-catching Silja Wendrup-Schandorff, who would herself reach ballerina rank and perform *the* sylphide in the future.) The Danes refer to this trio (interpolated from Løvenskjold's "The New Penelope") a "Belt Dance," though I don't know why. The number ends as a kind of quartet that splits into two halves in order to set the stage for the sylphide's second solo.

For this outing the happy woodland spirit behaves in an even more spritely fashion than she did in her first solo. Repeatedly and with variations, she takes fleetly and gently to the air, frequently filling out her moves with feathery batterie of several varieties. Her music is dominated by the finesse of wind instruments. James takes up immediately where the sylph leaves off; her relevé to arabesque, facing downstage, prefigures, in contrast, his relevé into attitude, facing in the opposite direction. (These back-to-back solo-dancing showcases make up the Mayseder interpolations cited above. And, though not jarring in their "different" nature, they break the musical voice identity established by Løvenskjold. For these moments the violin, consistently the sylph's "voice," transfers itself to James.) Just as the sylph's second solo, "Pui lento" (more slow), reveals a more heated-up physical dimension, so does the one for James, "Pui mosso" (more moved, as in "quicker"). Mayseder's violin music accelerates teasingly, and after James's grand initial poses in strong, effacé attitude balance, he zips through a series of space-eating jetés, entrechats, sauté-ronds de jambe en l'air, grands jetés, and a wrapping-up air turn.

The sylph rejoins the action as if entering a fray for the divertissement's rousing coda. Her moves take little time to build to a physical expansiveness almost equal to that of James. Her music includes the sound of hunting horns at its start. Her jetés, turning jumps, and grands jetés further fire up James, whose final foray is his biggest yet, as hardy horns help him marshal his physical force into grander grands jetés and more forcefully reversed turning jumps. After a series of *saut de basque* moves—single followed by a double—he tears out by way of excited brisé steps. (Much of the articulation and accent evident in the latter half of the divertissement for the sylph and James shows how Bournonville may have modified his ballet's second act in emulation of the effects presented by the second act of *Giselle*.)

The excitement affects the sister sylphs as well. And, as if called onto a stage burning with a heat for dancing, first our four demi-sylphs then the full complement, led by James and the sylphide, perform a group dance almost as demonically charged as that concluding the action of *Giselle*. Climaxing in a stage full of grands jetés in attitude directly aimed toward the audience, the sylph sisterhood, the sylphide, and James all wind down in unison. The final move is a grand preparation of rich port de bras before a neat wrap-up with a wrapped-in, multiple en dedans pirouette. The scene's final tableau has the sylphide posed somewhat demurely in an arabesque-penchée in front of James, backed up by a semicircular double frame of kneeling and standing (on pointe) sylphs. On our Danish video, James holds one arm up: "Look everybody, one hand!" the gesture seems to say. (Indeed, in some very old photographic records of this moment, James has both arms raised—"Look, *no* hands!"—as if reminding us that he has still not got ahold of his dream figure.)

If you find yourself especially enamored of the all-dancing aspects of *La Sylphide*, you can find this dance dominated scene isolated and featured on *I Am a Dancer*, originally released as a film and now a video showcasing Rudolf Nureyev in his heyday (also starring Margot Fonteyn, Carla Fracci, Lynne Seymour, Deanne Bergsma, 1973, 90 min., Color). Though the excerpt excludes the "Belt Dance," it does open with a session of Nureyev rehearsing the sylph corps de ballet in the closing moments of the coda. As recognizable Bournonville, the overall shape and tone are a little skewed. Nureyev's James dances with a very Russian accent; Fracci's sylphide with a very Italianate one; and the score's been very souped up. One detail of authenticity does hold, however, as the ensemble of sylphs numbers twelve, Bournonville's original number. (The sixteen seen in the Royal Danish video are not inauthentic, as the ballet master upped the size later on.) Sixteen appears to be the number in the Paris production as well, as that's how many figure in the video of Lacotte's staging. The number seems unusually modest for a Paris production.

Along its characteristically extravagant lines, the Paris video documents flashy and probably inauthentic dancing for Denard's James, even as Thesmar's Sylphide remains a model of feathery and showy (but not show-offish) footwork lovingly detailed, but not overridden by precise pointe work. The Paris Opera scenery, said to be based on the original by Pierre Luc Ciceri, also qualifies as grand and elaborate. But this is historically justified. Ciceri's settings for the earlier *Robert le Diable*, which showcased Taglioni's "Pas de Nonnes," were famous (or infamous) in the extravagance with which they filled the eye and taxed the Opera's production budget.

Even as the stage full of dancers moves out of the picture-perfect grouping, James, the gallant danseur, does not break character to partner his sylphide/ballerina and assist her exit from the tableau. He acts more as something for her to lean against than as a partner practiced in steadying her by holding her at her waist. (On our Danish video, Hübbe stretches out his arms so Jeppesen's sylph will have more support to call on should she need to find it as she comes off pointe and slips away.)

How near yet so far these visions are from the grasp of James becomes clear in the intervening scene, No. 5, "James Chasing the Sylphide"—"Allegro ben agitato" (lively, much agitated). The more he chases after one group or another of clustered sylphs, the more they elude him. Finally, the sylphide reappears only to disappear again after a graded series of running grands jetés-pas de chat leaps. With impassioned energy and desire, James leaps after the departed sylphide with a more emphatic version of her flying jump.

A "Moderato" intermediate scene, No. 6, "Gurn, the Witch, and Effy," returns the action to pantomiming the narrative. Gurn sends some fellow villagers off to look elsewhere while he looks over the clearing in view. After he triumphantly discovers James's tam, he bumps into Madge, who has entered the scene. (In Taglioni's version and the Paris video, this interlude with Gurn is absent. Instead, the hag simply meets up with James. Though Bournonville says that Madge enters from her cave, there is no cave in sight on the Danish stage. (There is one, however, in the French scene.) The witch convinces Gurn, somewhat reluctantly at first, to forget about the tam (she actually tosses it away) and to think about his prospects for marrying the fair Effy. (By now you should recognize all the miming that notes these particulars.)

Effy and her aunt Anna come upon the scene. Effy's first concern is to discover any sign of James. On Madge's sinister insistence, Gurn feigns ignorance and relates finding none. Pushing the young man almost as a goat would, the witch sends Gurn to his knees to ask

Effy's hand for himself. The hag then works on Effy, reminding her of the palm-reading prediction. The apprehensive Anna takes her opinion out of the mix, and Effy finally extends her hand in acceptance to Gurn. Effy's melancholy and circumspect manner tell that she may not be completely convinced in her new decision. The party goes off, with only the guileless Gurn seemingly comfortable with the turn of events.

An aside or two about the strength of Royal Danish Ballet miming and acting seems more than appropriate here. You'll not likely ever see better dance acting and miming. All the nuances of the sixth scene of Act 2 in the Danish video come across with formidable ease and clarity. No one overdoes anything, but nothing looks unsure or halfhearted. No open-mouth wordless speechifying mars the playing and articulation of this fairly complex scene, which intermixes misgiving, bewilderment, innocent eagerness, calculated deceit, and resigned distance. However reliable and deep the traditions for dance acting go in the schooling of Royal Danes, extra credit should be given the individual gifts of Morten Munksdorf to play a simple, sunny spirit; of Ann-Kristin Hauge, playing a reflective, heartbroken fiancée; of Englund's slyly pushy and sinister seeker of revenge; and Kirsten Simone's torn mother and aunt, keeping a lid on her own confusion and dread.

Løvenskjold's scene No. 7, "James and the Witch, the Scarf" says "Allegro con fuoco assai" (lively, with rather fiery force). It brings on James still in pursuit of his beloved sylph. Though now not anywhere in sight, he still hopes to capture her. Instead of his woodland spirit, however, he meets up with Madge, who enters coyly stroking the "magic" scarf she possesses. Feigning indifference to the man who recently cast her from his hearth and home, Madge plays hard to get and finally expresses in angry mime her hard feelings for the way James treated her. The quick thinking and impassioned Scot hopes to obtain the irate witch's forgiveness by giving her his money. This she casts away in wild disdain. In his confusion regarding her behavior, James is made to kneel at Madge's feet, where he watches her proudly tout her powers, before producing a long, gossamer, rose-colored scarf. (The Danish production's scarf is pink with discrete sparkling flecks. The shiny bits may be honoring the "spangle" mentioned for Taglioni's scarf, or they may represent drops of dew, since Bournonville's libretto compares his rosy scarf to a "blossom.")

After having James kneel once more at her feet, the hag wraps her scarf about the swain as he should do to the sylph in order for the talisman to work its magic and capture the creature forever. You'll note in Madge's mime a streak of fingertips tickling a vertical strip of air. When you relate this "sign" to that of Giselle's mime answering Bathilde about the origins of her garment, you see their common thread, so to speak. Such gesturing tells of handwoven pieces of clothing. The scene's emphatic, cymbal-crashing climax finds Madge with her arms triumphantly raised in the air and James in loving possession of the garment he feels will help him capture his sylph.

The ballet's finale begins with No. 8, "Entrée of the Sylph"—"Andante tranquillo" (flowing tranquilly). Madge hears the "approaching" music before the sylph appears and cagily gestures to James to hide the scarf so he can produce it at an opportune moment. The violin sets the sylph's tone and the scene's melancholy mood. A flute passage breaks the mood and we see the sylph listening to its birdcall air. Her relevé-arabesque poses on pointe with fluttering fingertips tell us that she hears something and what that something is.

The scene now segues into a new musical mode, "Allegro non troppo" for "James and the Sylphide." James hopes to distract her himself. She keeps a little distance, strikes an arabesque-penchée pose in front of him, and then, just as he goes to reveal the enticing scarf, the innocently distracted sprite floats up a tree to retrieve a bird's nest. (The "flight" is managed by more of the Danish stage's simple machinery, a little, levered, seesawlike elevator.) James gently reprimands the sylph to return the nest to its natural place and then produces the scarf.

Now in a dance with emphasis opposite those of the encounter between James and the sylph at the window, the sylph claps her hands in sheer delight at what she sees and dances in pursuit of James, who flourishes the desirable scarf in his wake. They both perform cabrioles-back facing each other, almost as if teasing with "let me have it,"–"no, not yet" banter. Bournonville's narrative says the sylph reaches for the scarf "greedily" and then has James wrap her in it, just as Madge had demonstrated.

As the young man happily entwines the sylph in the gossamer length of material, the wound-up creature begins to show distress. When he is able to pull her into his embrace wrapped in the scarf, the sylphide becomes enervated and limp. The music's mood changes to somber. "The Death of the Sylphide" follows, as a funereal adagio. Heavyhearted horns accompany the sylph's separation from James. She turns away from him and we see her wings fall from her back one by one. As she's about to swoon, her sister sylphs come to attend her. In a pose reminiscent of those that would be associated with the sorrowing Odette of *Swan Lake* or the final moments of *The Dying Swan*, the sylphide breathes heavily, delicately folded over, collapsed to the ground.

After two attendant sylphs help the sylphide up (as Myrtha's Moyna and Zulma helped Giselle), she approaches James. Her gestures to a dirgelike passage for violin tell of fading energy and fading light. Her hands flutter the length of each of her arms, as if tracing the dissipation of energy. As James looks on horrified, she removes the wedding ring she slipped from his finger in the farmhouse and gives it back. As he buries his face in his hands, the sylph maidens form a cortege and carry away the sylphide's lifeless body. Though her removal of the wedding ring seems a mere return of a token, the gesture figures in Bournonville's libretto as a sign from the sylph for James to confer the ring on the woman for whom it was originally intended.

We see no definite sign of the sylph's wishes for James and Effy to wed, but we do see the impossibility of such an act as the wedding party of Gurn and Effy passes. James watches their procession, knowing all is lost to him. Madge now reappears, waving ironically to the newlyweds and their suite. Next, to suitably bellowing and sinister music, the hag bangs her cane on the ground to get James's attention. When he lunges at her angrily she rears taller and reminds him again of how he once mocked her. Her answer to his aggression is to rise to her full height and hex him into a swoon. Musical "reminiscence" or "memory motifs" of the sylphide tell Madge that the sylphide's spirit is being sent to the trees. Diabolically she wakens James to see his lost beloved "carried" into the air by child-sylphs as her sister spirits float on their pointes in a hypnotic cortege on the ground. Questioning both the sight of the ascending sylphide and the implacable Madge, James, as if railing at a bad dream, sees the witch once again "tell" of his offense to her, and finally drops back into a lifeless faint.

Whether James is physically or just emotionally dead is left uncertain by Bournonville. His libretto says: "Overwhelmed with grief, the unfortunate James casts yet another look at his airy mistress, and falls to the ground in a swoon." The playing of the swoon tells something individual about each James. His ultimate state is the accumulated result of his acted and danced portrayal. Romanticism wants the ending tragic, which in either case it is. You can decide, at the performances of *La Sylphide* that you attend, precisely what constitutes the tragedy you've seen.

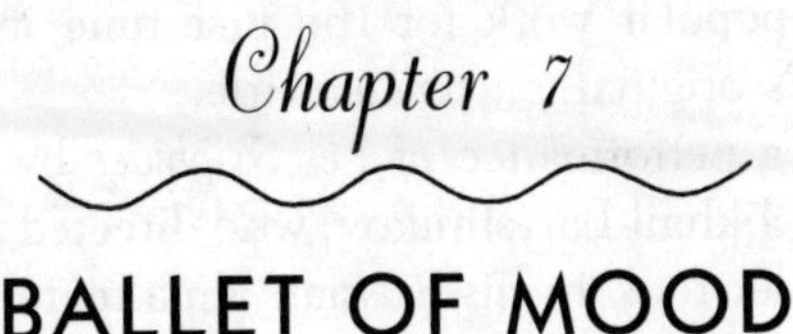

BALLET OF MOOD

Les Sylphides

• • •

Choreography by Michael Fokine
Music by Frédéric Chopin

If you've seen *La Sylphide* more than once are you ready to claim you've seen *Les Sylphides*? All joking aside, it's not surprising how much confusion arises among balletgoers confronted with *Les* and *La* and sylphides.

We couldn't move away from ballet's sylphs without consideration, and I hope clarification, of the difference between Fokine's early twentieth-century *Les Sylphides* and Taglioni's or Bournonville's mid-nineteenth-century *La Sylphide*. As we've touched on in our historical overview, Fokine's 1907 *Chopiniana* was rechristened by Diaghilev in hopes of connecting the newer, self-contained *ballet blanc* and "ballet of mood" to French ballet's hallowed past. In the years following its arrival on the European ballet scene, *Les Sylphides* became one of the art form's most popular works. Something about Fokine's choreography and Diaghilev's title obviously worked wonders on the public.

But that Western European and American public was not then especially familiar with *La Sylphide*, which had faded from view in Taglioni's version and remained isolated off the beaten track (in Copenhagen) in Bournonville's version. The Danes must have understood the potential for confusion, because when their Royal Ballet staged Fokine's popular work for the first time in 1925, it did so under the ballet's original *Chopiniana* title.

I've chosen a performance of *Les Sylphides* by American Ballet Theatre, led by Mikhail Baryshnikov, who directed this staging along the lines the ballet took in his Russian alma mater, which nurtured Fokine in the first place. This videotape captures Baryshnikov's incomparable performance as the ballet's lone male dancer. The Russians characterize this male role as a "youth"; Western Europeans and Americans sometimes refer to him as a "poet." The originator of the role was the legendary Vaslav Nijinsky. In addition to documenting Baryshnikov's Russian-heritage dancing, the video documents the dancer's work as ballet master during his tenure as ABT's artistic director, during which time he encouraged links between his American dancers and his own lineage at Leningrad's Kirov Ballet. The stage picture for his *Sylphides* includes the presence of the backdrop (by Alexander Benois) that the ballet used for its first Paris performances.

About this video:

> *American Ballet Theatre at the Met: Les Sylphides*, *Sylvia Pas de Deux*, *Triad*, and *Paquita*, 1984, 100 min., Color. Also available on laser disc.
>
> For our purposes, we're only paying attention to the *Sylphides* portion, but the other ballets should prove interesting as well, though none have Baryshnikov performing in them. With Baryshnikov onstage among his own company's women, we get a sense of the Russian heritage behind his dancing and directing and how those traditions and tastes affected the dancers whom he guided, coached, and partnered. *Sylphides* (as the ballet is sometimes called, with a sibilant stress on the pluralizing *s*) is available in other videos (see Videography); each has its idiosyncrasies, but none ultimately distorts Fokine's grand plan.

Mikhail Fokine's *Chopiniana* was born in St. Petersburg in 1907. It was reworked there in 1908, when, entitled *Réverie Romantique—Ballet sur la Musique de Chopin*, sometimes known as *Chopiniana—Second Version*, it took something of the shape it showed to Paris in

1909 under its new title: *Les Sylphides*. The first cast to present *Sylphides* to the world was stellar indeed: Alexandra Baldina, Tamara Karsavina, Anna Pavlova, and Nijinsky.

Indeed, the Leningrad Kirov staging that guided Baryshnikov toward shaping his production used the pre-Paris *Chopiniana* title when performing the work. (You can find the Kirov's *Chopiniana* leading off a seven-ballet videocassette called *The Maryinsky Ballet*, 1991, 147 min., Color.) Baryshnikov's 1980 rendering of the work for ABT kept one eye on the ballet's Russian pedigree and another on its local history. Fokine staged the work for ABT's inaugural season in 1940, and thereafter tinkered with a work he said remained virtually unchanged.

Faced with the grouped tableau of women in white tulle ballet dresses surrounding a lone young man in white tights and bloused shirt under a black velvet tunic, you might find the sight more than familiar and Old World, especially after admiring the sights of *La Sylphide*'s second-act divertissement. But it's important to remember that the sylph or Wili scenes of previous Romantic era ballets come framed by a narrative. What comes before, and after, these earlier ballets blancs is a dramatic situation in which the airy and/or ghostly women establish a kind of island of repose. Either they are a mysterious part of its particulars or they are a respite from them. In *Les Sylphides* they appear without introduction or context.

The label "ballet of mood" stuck to *Les Sylphides* when dance observers sought to identify Fokine's one-act creation and found that while it was more than a divertissement, none of the current terms, such as Romantic ballet, pantomime ballet, fantastic ballet, and grand ballet, proved applicable.

No doubt the example of Isadora Duncan, the American "barefoot aesthetic" dancer on tour in Russia, where she performed to "pure" concert music of composers such as Frédéric Chopin, inspired and emboldened Fokine to use such hallowed music for the ballet. Having chosen such music, the innovative ballet choreographer took his inspiration directly from it, rather than from the normal ballet source, the literary libretto. The suffix "-iana" refers to miscellany about a particular subject. In 1911, the critic Valerian Svetlov (born Ivchenko) wrote that *Chopiniana* had "no plot, no dramatis personae," only "garlands and bouquets of melodies and dances." He dubbed it a "priceless gem of a ballet—ballet for ballet," thus echoing the art-for-art's-sake philosophies in the other arts.

When he reminisced in his own memoirs about preparing the dancers for his plotless ballet of sylphides, Fokine spoke more of the ballerina who had given the world "*la sylphide*" rather than of the sprites themselves. In his words, after putting finishing touches on his female dancers, he felt surrounded by "twenty-three Taglionis." Not twenty-three sylphs, but as many embodiments of a particular ballerina. Whatever the ballet's trappings, the moonlit, "ruined" landscape, the winged women, the melancholy Romantic man, Fokine referred to his costumed cast as dancers, not as characters. (Their numbers, by the way, can and do vary. Fokine's specific tally of twenty-three still pertains in Russian stagings—the abovementioned Maryinsky *Chopiniana* has this number—but it can vary elsewhere. ABT's staging numbers nineteen "Taglionis.")

It seems likely that Fokine's emphasis not only on costuming "*à la Taglioni*," but also coiffeurs, led to the standard look of the "serious" ballerina for a good part of the twentieth century. Often achieving this image has been taken to extremes of caricature and dowdiness. It was, I would suggest, the severe, and severely beautiful, Olga Spessivtseva and her post-Sylphide/Giselle coiffeur, parted in the center, pulled flat, tight, and over the ears in a low chignon, that set this arrangement in stone, so to speak. Ironically, if you look at prints of La Taglioni as La Sylphide you see far less severity and much more fancy, even to the effect of showing some ear. (See the less than severe hairstyle on Thesmar as Lacotte's Taglioni.)

The ballet's musical selections include mazurkas, waltzes, a prelude, and a nocturne, all composed for piano in the first half of the nineteenth century. Current practice in Russia opens *Chopiniana* with a rousing military polonaise but it's not used elsewhere. The somewhat out-of-keeping overture is a holdover from the ballet's earliest manifestation as a danced suite more directly related to the career of the composer. (Jerome Robbins uses the same polonaise to start up his brilliant comic ballet, *The Concert*.) Though Duncan went on stage with her Chopin piano music as it was written, Fokine felt compelled to make them more appropriate to an opera house.

He had his chosen pieces orchestrated by contemporary musicians for more of a ballet score accompaniment. Over the years various composers have taken Chopin's piano compositions in hand and orchestrated them. Composers as famous as Alexander Glazunov and Igor Stravinsky have been called upon to do the work. ABT's orchestrations are credited to Roy Douglas.

Critic Svetlov thought of "blue pearls" when he saw the ballet on stage in Paris in 1909. ABT's stage picture recaptures such an image: Nineteen still women in long, white ballet dresses group about an equally still young man; all are bathed in a kind of pearlescent blue moonlight. Benois's setting, a wood of bare trees landscaping a ruined Gothic structure near a mausoleum, is painted in a similar scheme of warm blue grays. For late-twentieth-century eyes, there are shades of both *Giselle* and *La Sylphide;* in Paris neither of these precursors was in current circulation.

Fokine's choreographic program reads simply as a list of musical pieces in the printed program: Nocturne, Waltz, Mazurka, Mazurka, Waltz, Waltz. The individual and/or ensemble dancers who embody these numbers are listed by name in the order of their appearance. The printed program for our video would read as follows:

Nocturne

Cynthia Harvey, Marianna Tcherkassky, Cheryl Yeager, Mikhail Baryshnikov

Waltz

Cynthia Harvey

Mazurka

Cheryl Yeager

Mazurka

Mikhail Baryshnikov

Prelude

Marianna Tcherkassky

Pas de Deux

Marianna Tcherkassky and Mikhail Baryshnikov

Waltz

Marianna Tcherkassky, Cynthia Harvey, Cheryl Yeager,
Mikhail Baryshnikov, and Ensemble: Alina Hernandez,
Anna Spelman and Melissa Allen, Julie Bickerton, Gabrielle Brown,
Elizabeth Carr, Suzanne Goldman, Careen Hobart, Elizabeth Laing,
Kristi Lowe, Valerie Madonia, Meg Potter, Nancy Raffa,
Carla Stallings, Lisa Sundstrom, Mary Wilson

After a brief musical introduction, during which the artful cluster of female dancers around the lone male begins to open out and rearrange, the "Moderato" Nocturne in A-flat, op. 32, no. 2 sets the grouping astir, with ensemble animation slowly being dominated by the presence of a soloist. She will be the ballerina who dances the suite's waltz, probably the least prominent of the ballet's solos. She (Harvey in our video) holds center stage, framed and "echoed" by two intermediate and fourteen ensemble dancers grouped in two equal halves. It's not until she breaks away and moves to exit that the male dancer and the two remaining ballerinas poised at his side enter the action. After the second of the soloist women also exits, the danseur engages in a somewhat urgent mini-duet with the leading ballerina (Tcherkassky and Baryshnikov, in our case).

You'll note how active Baryshnikov's participation becomes. In equal measure, he partners and dances alongside the ballerina. Three times in the process of guiding his partner by her hand through gentle direction-changing jumps that glide into arabesque poses on pointe, he sweeps smoothly into emphatic yet lyrical cabrioles to the back. (Rarely have these been more lyrical *and* emphatic than Baryshnikov's.) Likewise, the softly expansive tour jeté and grand jeté that follow in the design of duet. (Compare the young man's "dancing" part in the duet with that of the nondancing participation for the princes in the supported adagios from *Swan Lake* or *Sleeping Beauty*.)

After an energetic little solo of her own, the secondary ballerina (Yeager) is joined by the male dancer in another brief duet/encounter, all of which soon becomes a trio with the reentry of the leading ballerina (Tcherkassky). With a ballerina in each hand, our poetic danseur supports his "muses" and postures center stage as the nocturne subsides. The ending leaves him to spiral through a simple, but full *soutenu* (sustained) turn and pose by himself on delicate demi-pointe, center stage, with arms *en couronne* (in a crown/frame), as if suspended in his own dream. All his attendant muses remain still in a garlanded arc that frames him at a distance like a floral hedge.

A solo the Russians still refer to as the "Eleventh Waltz," the Valse in G-flat, op. 70, No. 1, comes next. The numerical designation for the female dancer's solo reinforces the work's purely musical motivation. (Probably the waltz accompanying the dancer is No. 11 in some Chopin compilation familiar to the Russians.) On our tape, Harvey does the honors, entering and taking her starting pose as if she were but one part of the shifting ensemble that rearranges itself into further "plastic" groupings. The "Molto vivo" (very lively) music inspires a dance that starts out dominated by eager grands jetés (alternately croisé and effacé).

Soon the waltz ballerina's "decorative" port de bras turns delicately gestural. At the depth of her frequent penchée poses, she takes her softly opened hands away from her lips in emanations that suggest the voicing of love messages. In related moves, she rises to arabesque on pointe and while descending to full-foot support for other arabesque-penchée moves, she gently ripples one hand in front of her along the way, as if blessing or sweetening air she enters. Even though we see transparent wings at her back, we feel the presence of wings in hovering flight from the various, soft undulations of her outspread arms. More "spoken" sweet nothings float from her lips by means of hand gestures and more grands jetés recur before she lightly spirals into a pose balanced in fifth position on pointe, with her back to the public.

A more vigorous solo begins next, Mazurka in D, op. 33, no. 2, after the ensemble women have regrouped as three more regular and even lines. One stands along each of the stage's "wing sides" and one along the back. From the upstage right corner comes the female "Mazurka" soloist. Over the years, this solo has usually gone to the most featured of the ballet company's ballerinas, who was regularly identified as the "Mazurka/Pas de Deux" dancer. The tradition began with Pavlova at *Sylphides*' 1909 premiere. It broke over the years, for ballerinas whose strong points didn't include vigorous jumping ability and tended more toward adagio qualities. (Fonteyn was in this category.) In these instances the main ballerina's role became known as "Prelude/Pas de Deux." It's the alternate tradition that our tape follows.

Thus, Yeager dances the female mazurka. Technically, this dignified and elegant dance of Poland was a couple dance, often performed by four or eight couples. European courts, especially the Russian court, developed a pronounced taste for this elegantly playful dance form. Chopin wrote more than fifty mazurkas for piano, adding greatly to its variety. Fokine's female-solo mazurka is a ballet dance in which the traditional brushing and heel-clicking steps of the pure mazurka play no part. Instead, flying grands jetés, alternating second and third arabesque dispositions to the split-leg, climactic postures, dominate the solo. Punctuational poses in *arabesque-piquée* on pointe get struck in third arabesque and, with lush grace-note flourish, finish by means of alternately sweeping arms, in long-reaching second arabesque line. If you want to see for yourself or point out to someone else the essence of épaulement and the particular character, beauty, and "drama" of épaulé postures, the pauses for *Sylphides* mazurka ballerina are as apt as any I know. And if you miss the first one at the end of her initial string of grands jetés, you have three more chances to admire it as the punctuation of three similar sets of jumps and then one last chance, when the soloist uses her épaulé move to initiate her final exit.

Yet another regrouping of the ensemble "sylphs" occurs during the musical introduction to the next section, another mazurka. Baryshnikov's ABT production follows Russian-Soviet tradition and uses what *Sylphides* tradition calls the "fast mazurka" (Mazurka in C, op. 33, no. 3), which Fokine replaced, once the ballet was being given outside Russia, with the "slow mazurka" (Mazurka in C, op. 67, no. 3). (An ABT telecast from 1978, not yet commercially available, records the company's previous staging, one with links to Fokine's later *Les Sylphides* intentions. In this performance Ivan Nagy dances the slow mazurka with which Fokine replaced his original choice. *ABT: Live from Lincoln Center*.)

After whisking from downstage left and spiraling (*soutenu*) into readiness, upstage right, the youth/poet begins. His first moves travel as actual mazurka steps, which include gentle hops and smooth brushing actions. Two times he jumps through sissone to land in softly buoyant arabesque-allongée, with one intermediate pause in attitude-croisé. Two feather-light but firmly beaten, high-flown cabrioles front (one effacé, the other croisé) bring him back downstage, where he unwinds into adagio-timed turns in arabesque and in attitude. After a repeat of the same sequence in the opposite direction, Baryshnikov readies to enter a different lilting sequence. At this point in mid-solo, he displays (thanks to a rewarding camera close-up) a kind of half-smile, a facial expression sometimes associated with Nijinksy and telling of a most private state of bliss. A diagonal path moving largely backward upstage entails more variations on mazurka steps, this time embellished with entrechats and a tour-jeté, the final execution of which leads into his finishing, kneeling pose. Throughout his solo, his full-sleeved arms sweep and arc and "dance" in various ways that harmonize with lyrical monologue. He finishes with a sweeping gesture that yearns into the center of the stage space. (The slow mazurka ends with the dancer yearning in an offstage direction.)

The suite's final solo follows, the "Andantino" Prelude in A, op. 28, no. 7. (Sometimes the opening bars act as the ballet's overall introduction, though not here.) To set the stage for the Prelude ballerina, the sister sylphs take places as three ringed groups. The softly whispering air created by Chopin finds the ballerina (Tcherkassky) initially poised in fifth position on pointe, with one hand eagerly and luminously cupped near her ear, listening for essences. The expressiveness of her breathing, seen in her back, also dominates her posturing. Softly pliant landings, downy soft and smooth pas de chat jumps, and cat's paw-like caresses of the feet to the stage make this solo seem to suspend the ballerina in the moonlit air. A diagonal path traced upstage by way of two soft *piqué* steps gets momentary reversals through half-turning *assemblé* moves. Each lands in rich plié position, almost like a bird nestled in a nest. A weightless walk through fifth position on pointe takes the ballerina to one final whisper of a pose, in which one hand configures a "one-finger" hushing gesture.

As the ensemble rearranges to settle into two-dancer units that stand cheek-to-cheek as they frame the stage, the Valse in C-sharp

Minor, op. 64, no. 2 opens. It's marked "Tempo giusto" for "strict or suitable time." This pas de deux comes from the ballet's earliest manifestation and remained consistently part of Fokine's scheme as it evolved toward his ultimate *Les Sylphides*. Although the duet has become traditionally known to start with a lift that we first catch sight of already in the air, this detail does not occur on our tape. On the vast Metropolitan Opera House stage, Baryshnikov and Tcherkassky enter walking behind the formation of paired sylphs. After a melancholy cello introduction, the young man lifts his muse into the arcing flight that begins the pas de deux proper. If we thought Tcherkassky hovered breathlessly of her own volition in her Prelude, here, she hangs even more profoundly in the air lifted by her partner. Her lift looks like a miraculously held and unfolded grand jeté pas de chat in dream time. Reversing the diagonal path the pas enters on, the couple gently retraces its steps in a kind of reverse emphasis. Now the danseur lifts the ballerina so that she appears to recline, pausing in a supine position of reverie. In phase with her lightly beaten cabrioles to the back, her partner dances through his own arabesque position. Some partnering poets actually mirror the ballerina's cabrioles; Baryshnikov instead does *temps levé* ("time raised," a light hop) in arabesque.

In quicker-timed moves reminiscent of the contemplative Prelude choreography, Tcherkassky dances on her own as Baryshnikov stands off to the side, seemingly lost in his own thoughts. On some of the waltz's most insistent music, the danseur momentarily leaves and the ballerina moves front to strike a first arabesque on pointe and then travel backward in her pose by means of pliantly sprung, successive relevés. Her "elated" travels take her to rejoin her partner. From their upstage-left corner, ballerina and danseur proceed back downstage in a series of partnered moves highlighting supported first arabesque sequences for the woman. These evolve through grand rond de jambe en l'air transitions into arabesque-penchée moments that tell of whisperings from muse to poet. Along the way, and into a supported turn that extends a first arabesque in the opposite direction, the inspired man lovingly traces the shapes made by his partner's arms. During the course of this enraptured evocation of inspiration, the ensemble women shift their positions to end up softly sunk in reclining poses.

When the music reaccelerates, poet and muse appear to chase and follow one another: the man backs into variously torsioned cabrioles while the woman scurries toward and past him in liquid pas de bourrée couru. After another series of big lifts, in which the ballerina executes développé-front postures, the two dancers couple upstage, center stage. There, linked side by side, they begin a series of ballet's waltzlike balancé (rocking) steps. Over and over they glide and alternately twirl "in and out and under the arches" shaped by their linked arms. A final acceleration repeat begins with the man seeming to draw the ballerina toward him by caressing her wings as she skims on her feathery working pointes in parallel first position. In the faint flush of the moment, the man dances energetically, all the while continuing to partner his ballerina. Keeping decorous hold of her hand as he dances gives the effect that her energy and expertise flow into him, demonstrating direct connection between inspirer and the inspired.

As the man lets go of his muse and spirals through a privately celebratory soutenu turn, the muse skims out of sight. The then bereft poet follows in enraptured pursuit. Simultaneously, the stageful of sister dancers clears as well, leaving the stage empty for the first time. We have come to and past the ballet's musical and theatrical climax.

For a denouement, the ensemble reenters to begin the "Vivo" (lively) Valse Brillante in E-flat, op. 18, no. 1. This begins when two flanking groups take their places near the wings and a fanfare launches a brightened waltz. Now the ensemble dances with a new vigor and brightness, like that in the music. Many of their moves restate those of the solo ballerinas. There is much scurrying on pointe, hopping through épaulé arabesque, floating of winglike arm movements and some "blown kisses" gesturing. Presently the Prelude ballerina skims into their midst, restating her dance moves, which in turn the ensemble sylphs mirror.

With a lull in the waltz's full force, the ensemble gently wafts forward with rocking *balancé* steps restating those of the pas de deux couple "waltzing" forward near the end of their duet. Likewise, their small jumps faintly echo the lifted jumps the danseur performed with his ballerina to punctuate their waltzing. As soon as the ensemble is regrouped in another linear formation, the danseur lyrically soars through the space of the frame. He takes off into expansive tour-jetés that are softened and suspended in the air by means of a delayed, almost "beaten" accent to his legs as they pass each other in the jump's flight. (The Russian term *grand jeté entrelacé* becomes especially fitting for *Sylphides*' rendering of ballet's big turning jump.)

Without missing a beat or pausing to catch his breath, the danseur rejoins his ballerina and repeats the balancé sequence they executed near the end of their pas de deux. Now the ensemble creates a variety of waltz steppings to complement the couple's. Their momentary exit sets the stage for the reentrance of the Waltz ballerina. She has a side-to-side running and jumping sequence before facing her standing sisters, whose arms wave like branches in the wind as if directed, like a conductor, by hers. After she breezes out, the third ballerina delicately bounds to center stage, capping her stay with relevé turns in attitude and finishing it with sweetly leaning pose in fourth position croisé. As our waltzes noticeably conclude, the ensemble forms four evenly spaced rows marking the stage's front-to-back dimensions. Down their center "alley" skims the pas de deux ballerina, while down the side lanes follow the two semiprominent ensemble dancers. An emphatic pause, and gathering of musical and motional momentum occurs as the entire ensemble formation shifts around in a block that acts to draw on, as if by magnetic force, the four leading dancers.

Then in regular step-step sauté-arabesque moves the stageful of dancers forms four more neat rows, each headed by one of the leading dancers. All is ensemble now. And, unison activity: temps levé in epaulé arabesque followed by soutenu turns into pas de bourée en tournant sur place, twice repeated, until a final telescoping of musical energy and texture that sends the principles into classroom-style port de bras exercises, which lead to the taking of places held at the ballet's start. (In more than one detail, this summational moment recalls the end of *La Sylphide*'s divertissement: the grand port de bras exercise, the ballet women framing the ballet man and his favored ballerina.)

Chapter 8

ROMANTIC TURNING CLASSICAL

La Bayadère

• • •

Choreography by Marius Petipa
Music by Ludwig Minkus

After *La Sylphide* and *Giselle*, but before *Swan Lake* and *Les Sylphides*, there was *La Bayadère*. The 1877 "Ballet in four acts and seven scenes with Apotheosis," which fancifully told a story set in Hindu India of intrigue, jealousy, and retribution from on high, included a fabulous *ballet blanc* as one of its episodes. As the multi-act ballet spectacle appeared during the ensuing century, the singular "white" scene consistently captured the imagination and tastes of the public. In more recent times audiences have come to view the ballet-within-a-ballet as vital and contemporary as almost any new work around. Called "The Kingdom of the Shades" (meaning "Underworld of the Spirits"), the segment finally came out from under its proverbial bushel locally in 1961, when Leningrad's Kirov Ballet showed it to the West on one of its then rare tours. Since then, not only has this lone scene become a repertory staple, so has the full-scale work.

In 1980, Leningrad-born-and-trained Natalia Makarova directed a staging of the complete *La Bayadère* for the first time ever outside Russia. Her work also marked the first time in sixty-odd years that the ballet's original, cataclysmic last act was produced anywhere.

While the popular ballet remained in repertory in Russia, its originally intended last act was dropped during the second decade of the twentieth century, due in good part to the fact that the machinery necessary to produce the required effects of devastation could not be operated or properly repaired. Nowadays, the once rarely seen full-length production has become more and more widely staged and performed. (In 1996, the PACT—Performing Arts Council of the Transvaal—Ballet of Pretoria, South Africa, produced the complete ballet, with its own educated guessing for staging the long-gone last act.)

I have chosen a Kirov Ballet staging from a 1977 video because it presents a production with reasonably consistent links to Petipa's own production, and because it is from this staging that all subsequent versions of the ballet have grown. Furthermore, the performance takes place on the stage of the Maryinsky Theater (called the Kirov Theater in 1977) where Petipa oversaw the last adjustments he made in his own creation. The fabled "Kingdom of the Shades" is performed in its full context, with a full complement of thirty-two corps de ballet women filling out the *ballet blanc* to impressive scale.

About this video:

La Bayadère, Live from the Kirov Theater, Gabriela Komleva, Tatiana Terekhova, Rejen Abdeyev, 1977, 126 min., Color.

This video reveals grand ballet spectacle in the nineteenth-century mode on a grand, strength-in-numbers scale. Most of the various tinkerings done to Petipa's staging over the years are presented here. Since 1920, the "Shades" scene has closed the ballet, reflecting the necessary elimination of the original last act with its outmoded and unworkable stage mechanisms. (For Makarova's approximation of the fourth act, which she put together with help from historical advisors, we can look at the only commercially available staging of her production: *La Bayadère*, The Royal Ballet with Altinai Asylmuratova, Darcey Bussell, Irek Mukhamedov, 1991, 124 min., Color.)

Though classified simply as a "Ballet"—that is, without any of the era's qualifying distinctions such as pantomime, grand, or Romantic—*La Bayadère*, or *Bayaderka* as it was known in Russian, fits all these descriptions. Actual Indian dancers known as *bayadères* in French toured Europe at the beginning of the nineteenth century, feeding Romantic era tastes for exotic local color and for sensuality entwined with chasteness. Several precedents on the ballet stages of France and Italy predated Petipa's original ballet in Russia. One was an opera ballet by Auber based on a work of Goethe's and called *Le Dieu et la Bayadère*. It featured Filippo Taglioni's choreography and Marie Taglioni's dancing—in particular, dancing that involved the manipulation of a shawl or scarf, which I'll discuss later in our *Bayadère*. Another source of reference for Petipa's ballet came from the Russian production of Verdi's Egyptological *Aïda*, for which the ballet master supervised the dances. With his librettist, the historian and critic Sergei Khudekov, Petipa included in his ballet not only a triangle of protagonists similar to that in the popular opera, but also a lavish processional scene related to that of *Aïda*'s spectacular "Triumphal March."

Critics looking for ethnographic or anthropological accuracy around the time of *Bayadère*'s premiere carped about the anomalies and, to put it kindly, "artistic liberties" found in the ballet. Those critical sentiments, however, pale in comparison to some of our own day's harsh accusations of crimes against everything from India's culture to women's rights. But however off the mark of historical accurarcy Petipa might have been, he was on the mark for creating a Romantic kind of ballet theater. All I usually say to ethnographical, anthropological, and sociopolitical carping at works like *Bayaderka*, is a modified refrain of what Balanchine said to the complainers who found his *Union Jack*, a Scottish Tattoolike ballet inauthentic as a military parade: "If you want the real thing, go [elsewhere.]" In Balanchine's case the specific answer was "Fifth Avenue" where you could see a real parade; in *Bayaderka*'s case, I suggest you go to India on a package tour.

Petipa's India, and that of the ballet's composer Ludwig Minkus, remains European in flavor, with a strong Russian tone. The story involves the love of a handsome and brave Indian warrior named Solor for a bayadère named Nikiya. The temple dancer is coveted by the temple's high priest, known as the High Brahmin. When the

Rajah insists that Solor keep his engagement with the Rajah's daughter, Gamzatti, Solor is thrown into confusion. He has promised himself to Nikiya in an oath over the temple's sacred fire. This oath has been witnessed by the rejected Brahmin, who vows revenge. This he aims to achieve by informing the powerful Rajah of Solor's commitment to Nikiya. Learning of this pact between Solor and the temple dancer, Gamzatti sends for Nikiya in hopes of persuading her to abandon her vows with Solor. Nikiya not only refuses these pressures, but in a moment of anger makes an attempt on Gamzatti's life with a dagger. Now Gamzatti seeks revenge as well. At a celebration of the betrothal of Solor to Gamzatti, Nikiya is commanded to dance. Having been presented during her dance with a basket of flowers, which she believes are a present from Solor, Nikiya dances happily, until a snake hidden among the flowers fatally bites her. Distraught over the tragedy he feels he caused, Solor seeks solace in an opium-induced stupor, where he dreams of entering the underworld and making his peace with the ghost of Nikiya. (In the eliminated last act, Solor awakens to find Gamzatti determined to marry him. During the wedding ceremony, the ghost of Nikiya appears, distracting Solor, whose behavior disconcerts Gamzatti. At the moment of taking vows, the temple collapses on all assembled; in the aftermath, Nikiya and Solor find each other in the afterlife.)

In the extensive libretto (eleven pages' worth in one book offering its English translation), there are only occasional indications of dancing: a "Djampo" dance for the bayadères, a "tortured" dance for the fakirs, a "divertissement" in the Rajah's apartments, "festival" dances for the betrothal celebrations, Nikiya's solo dance for the engaged couple, a "comic" dance to amuse a distraught Solor, and then, most prominently if succinctly, the word "Dances" to note the happenings of the underworld. Today's productions include more dancing throughout *La Bayadère* than was part of the original plan, but except for the "Dances" indicated as the ballet blanc, all remain framed by the narrative.

Our video credits this *Bayadère*'s choreography to Vakhtang Chabukiani, the celebrated Russian dancer, and to Vladimir Ponomarev "after Petipa." This credit is uncharacteristically straightforward for the Soviet Russians, as their Petipa ballets often come with direct credit to Petipa for choreography. In choreographic identification, the "after" qualifier indicates that between the ballet's original staging and the current one some revamping or filling in has been done either because the original "text" has been lost, as in forgotten, or has been deemed unsuitable for contemporary tastes.

Casting credits for our video are minimal: Nikiya—Gabriella Komleva; Solor—Rejen Abdeyev; High Brahmin—Gennady Selutsky; The Rajah—Yuri Potemkin; Gamzatti—Tatiana Terekhova. (According to a member of the troupe at the time, the soloists in the Kingdom of the Shades scene are Ludmilla Lopukhova, Ludmilla Kovalova, and Olga Iskanderova.) The handsomely rendered scenery, also uncredited on our video, is said to reproduce the designs prepared for Petipa's 1884 version of his 1877 ballet. In nineteenth-century tradition, individual stage decorators designed the individual acts: in this case, Scene 1, pagoda exterior—Alexander Kvapp; Scene 2, palace interior—Konstantin Ivanov; Scene 3, gardens, and Scene 5, underworld—Peter Lambin; and Scene 4, Solor's apartment—Oreste Allegri.

The overture gives us a taste of the mysteries we'll encounter in the underworld and its shades. Curtain up for Act 1, Scene 1, "The Festival of Fire," comes with a "Moderato" scene that's mostly mimetic. (The decorated curtain, by the way, is a handsomely painted wall-like affair called a portal curtain, which dates from 1914, when Alexander Golovine designed it for St. Petersburg's Maryinsky Theater. He painted it in reds, which were subsequently changed to blues by Simon Virsiladze in harmony with the blue of the auditorium's decor.) Magedaveya, an agitated fakir (religious ascetic) slips in and out sight before a suite of spear-carrying warriors enters in advance of their leader, Solor, who takes the stage in a flash to an appropriate musical flourish. With Toloragva, his "lieutenant" warrior companion, the princely hunter exchanges pantomime about the hunt at hand, which he intends to excuse himself from in order to participate in the lighting of the pagoda's sacred fire. In a soliloquy-styled aside, the warrior signs his interest in the temple and its residents, especially the beautiful bayadère Nikiya.

Solor calls on his fakir confidant to aid him in calling forth the temple dancer, but the religious man shows reluctance and fear. The warrior ceases cajoling and gestures commandingly. Amid all the miming you see the gesture telling of the sphinxlike Brahmin (a ceremonious placing of the hands on the shoulders and moving in alignment down the chest), and another for the pure-hearted Nikiya, the bringer of water from the sacred springs (a two-hands open sweep to the top of the shoulder to indicate the balancing of a water jug). "Maestoso" (majestic) music brings a group of monks out of the temple, preparing the way for the entrance of the High Brahmin. He appears (note the hands-to-shoulders design to his posture) and summons the chief fakir, who brings on his fellow ascetics to light the sacred fire. Their scrabbling entrance, hand-waving incantations, and slinking departure leave the scene set with a lighted fire that's a ready focal point for the bayadères' dance.

Flutes signal the start of the score's "Andante delicato" (delicately flowing) music, which brings veiled young women out of the pagoda. The ceremonious dance they perform around the fire and in the direction of their high priest includes folding their hands into "at ease" positions like those of the Brahmin and opening them out in two-raised-hands salutes. Crooked arm, hand, and leg gestures hint at the "water jug" attitude of Nikiya and the multi-arm designs of sculptures of Indian deities such as Shiva.

Another "Maestoso" number follows, as the Brahmin sends for Nikiya; in the meantime the fakirs whirl into a frenzied dance around and over the sacred fire. With a brief ballerina-announcing harp arpeggio, an "Andante sostenuto" (flowing, sustained) cues the appearance of Nikiya, covered by a veil. Except for the crouching crawl of the fakirs and the stately anticipatory moves of the Brahmin, the entire stage is frozen as the leading bayadère treads center stage, where the priest removes her veil with exquisite near-trembling attention. A solo flute (the Hindu Lord Krishna's favorite musical instrument) begins a "Moderato assai" (very moderate) solo for Nikiya. Deep postures, reaching arms low to the ground and on high, as well as hands and eyes raised to the heavens, shape the dance as an invocation to the gods. (Incidentally, you might note how Nikiya's final spinning moments in her solo redo with variations the opening moments of Giselle's Wili initiation solo—an en dedans promenade in low arabesque into chaîné turns.) The Brahmin witnesses all of this as if it were directed specifically toward him.

A change of musical mood to "Allegro molto" (very quickly), sets the scene for the enraptured Brahmin to express his passion for Nikiya. After directing the fakirs and bayadères to continue their dancing around the sacred fire, the priest fixes his attentions on Nikiya. Their back-and-forth miming works up a full head of steam, with the temple dancer reminding the holy man of his place, and the Brahmin showing he'd give it all up for her love. But Nikiya is horrified and steadfast in standing up to his advances. The scene winds to an end as the bayadères offer sacred spring waters to the thirsty fakirs and Nikiya learns from Magedaveya that Solor will announce his presence by clapping his hands to signal her. The jealous and spurned Brahmin witnesses this exchange suspiciously.

A mimetic interlude between an agitated fakir and an excited Solor follows. It's detailed with gestures telling of the proposed "clapping" signal and hush-hush signs for "mum's the word." Harp arpeggios fill the air for Nikiya's next entrance, through the temple's portal. Lost in thought and solitude she collects more spring water, distracted by thoughts of Solor's impending arrival. She ruminates through another flute-dominated passage, dancing while looking for her beloved Solor. His three claps call her to his arms. The two entwine in a delicately impassioned duet, "Allegro non troppo" (quick/not too much). Nikiya's part in the pas de deux is one full of long-reaching leanings away and reachings outward, all lovingly supported by Solor. At a climactic moment she's caught in the high lift (held at full arms' length overhead), known as the "bird" (see *Giselle*, Act 2).

With the next, and final, musical segment "Allegro appassionato" (quick, impassioned), the duet heats up to more enraptured rushing about that includes an ecstatically caught shoulder lift and Solor miming eternal allegiance to Nikiya. All of this is overseen by a furious Brahmin, whose approach terrifies the fakir into helping Nikiya slip back into the temple as Solor steals into the forest. The "curtain line" is for the Brahmin, who rushes front and center with a fist-making gesture that shows his determination to crush the intended mating of Solor and Nikiya.

Act 2, Scene 2, The Rivals

The set in the original libretto is a "magnificent hall in the palace of the Rajah Dugmanta." An "Allegro moderato" overture introduces us to a vaulted space framed by numerous ornate columns. Officers and fellow warriors of Solor await the arrival of the Rajah, whose entrance comes with a fitting musical flourish. After salutes to the Rajah, the gathering lifts toasts toward a portrait of Solor. (Such an image, the 1877 libretto's authors were quick to point out, was anachronistic to India's Hindu world, but its usefulness toward narrative clarity overrode its "impurity." No further arguments, however, were advanced for other moments of poetic license.)

What happens next in our "after Petipa" production, is what Makarova's production calls the "Djampe" dance. (Makarova places it a little later in the scene.) All the libretto tells of is a "divertissement." The "Molto moderato" number with a "Vivo" coda takes the form of an entertainment by court dancing girls. Six young women, and then two more prominent ones, dance while holding above their heads a scarf that streams from one side of their trousers. With an emphasis on balloné steps and gentle hops in attitude (extended front), scampering into little jumps where the back-extended leg flips into attitude (extended back), the dancers seem to be jumping through their own hoops. The coda includes a variation on such steps, when, at a brisker pace, the dancers' working legs whisk back and forth against the flourishing of their scarves. This emphasis is known as *en cloche* for its bell-clapper swinging motion. Though the eight women all wear pointe shoes, their dance does not involve going to full pointe position. It's a ballet version of local color dancing that purposely refrains from working on toe tip.

Narrative action resumes with the exit of the dancing girls and the warrior men. After the Rajah summons the serving woman who attends his daughter, Gamzatti, the princess enters and greets her father. Their meeting indicates the impending marriage between the royal daughter and the worthy Solor. Notice that as the ballet's second ballerina, Tatiana Terekhova, enters on the video (to traditional ballerina-homage applause from her audience), she is wearing heeled pumps, not pointe shoes. This is because her first scene is one of pantomime, not dancing. The nineteenth-century tradition that separated the worlds of mime and dance included costuming as well. As we have seen from the Lilac Fairy of *The Sleeping Beauty*, mime is best dressed in "sensible" shoes and "everyday" costume, while danced scenes require ballet shoes and "ballet" costuming. (Though Makarova's production includes a scene closely modeled on this one, her Gamzatti does wear pointe shoes.)

After Solor's "lieutenant" announces the approach of the warrior groom-to-be, the Rajah sends his daughter to veil herself for meeting her fiancée. It is here that Solor enters. The Rajah's prideful and insistent reminder of the upcoming marriage disconcerts the warrior, who nevertheless composes himself when presented with Gamzatti. At this juncture, where Makarova placed the "Djampe" dance that we've already seen, the Kirov interpolates a dance for Nikiya accompanied by a "slave" partner. (The music for this is not by Minkus but by Cesar Pugni, and comes originally from *Esmeralda*, a ballet based on Victor Hugo's *Notre Dame de Paris*, first produced in Russia in 1848.) If the framed and painted portrait of Solor hanging prominently on the room's wall is an anachronistic touch for Hindu India, this artfully acrobatic adagio in the floor-show tradition associated with Las Vegas nightclubs represents anachronism writ large. Nikiya, who's meant to have a pointed entrance later on in the scene, spends a good deal of the dance in her partner's arms like a large, caught fish. The climactic moment comes when she showers two armsful of lilies in homage to Gamzatti, who gets veiled ceremoniously by two little girl handmaidens. (The nouveau choreography dates from the 1950s and was devised by the Kirov's dancer-choreographer Konstantin Sergeyev.) You'll find this oddity in Nureyev's production for the Paris Opera Ballet as well as the Kirov's.

A foreboding musical scene ("Maestoso") follows. Solor looks apprehensive as Aya (Gamzatti's serving woman) announces the High Brahmin's arrival. The Brahmin remains suspiciously mum as he gestures for privacy with the Rajah. As the place clears of all but the two men, the music begins to stir dramatically and darkly. The Brahmin gestures toward the portrait and toward Gamzatti's apartments, and after clutching himself as if pained, mimes the oath over the fire made by Solor and Nikiya. Both Solor, who slipped out as he realized what was about to transpire, and Gamzatti, who watches the exchange from behind a pillar, learn of the Brahmin's vengeful information. Gamzatti sends Aya to summon Nikiya, and the Rajah shows clear determination to crush the duplicity, which the Brahmin realizes means destroying the bayadère.

To a "Moderato" melancholy air, Gamzatti enters in a kind of reverie. She looks toward the portrait of Solor and dreams of her wedding day by toying with her bridal veil. After she tries to lose herself in thought, Aya announces the arrival of Nikiya. After pleasantries, during which the temple dancer bows deferentially to the princess and the royal daughter admires her rival's beauty, the scene heats up. Gamzatti offers Nikiya a bracelet as a gift, which is politely declined, and then compares her wealth to the bayadère's humble situation. Climactically the princess brusquely points the dancer to Solor's portrait.

Now the music changes to "Allegro vivo" as the two communicate in an emotional, back-and-forth flush of charge and countercharge. Gamzatti gets more and more imperious; Nikiya, trying to keep her respectful demeanor toward her princess, refuses to deny the truth of her sworn vows with Solor. Gamzatti's imperial insistence gets overwhelming with further efforts to ply the dancer with jewels (a necklace this time), and Nikiya's polite refusals get more frantic. Finally the rivalry peaks as Nikiya finds and picks up a dagger, which she threatens to use on Gamzatti. Due to Aya's intervention, Nikiya's hand is stayed and she flees in horror at what she intended. Then, just as the Brahmin had done at the curtain of Scene 1 and as the Rajah had done previously in this scene, the princess points in the direction of Nikiya's exit and shows fist-clenching determination to punish the dancer for her disobedience. (The rhythmic applause during the recorded curtain calls is typical of Russian audiences. The various shots the camera momentarily makes of the baroque Maryinsky auditorium and foyer show what the public of Petipa's 1900 revival of his ballet would have seen at that time.)

Act 2, The Bayadère's Death

The setting is an exterior of the Rajah's palace, with a colonnaded porch surrounded by a garden. The action opens with a grand procession "Tempo di marcia giocosa" (march time, joyfully), in the manner of *Aïda.* All the participants in the celebration of the princess's betrothal parade on in stages. Petipa's original staging included 230 personnel (dancers and supernumeraries). The Kirov doesn't quite muster this many but comes close. (So does Nureyev's version.) Amid a variety of spear and fan carriers, as well as ranks of holy men, the Brahmin parades on, as does a cadre of warriors followed by the Rajah and Gamzatti, each carried onto the stage in palanquins, deluxe reclining chairs. A gilt statuette, and rows of men carrying garlanded pikes and women with fans prepare the way for Solor's entrance. He comes on seated atop an elephant preceded by children made up as Ethiopians. (The *Bayadère* elephant is one of the ballet's more famous, or infamous, props, depending on one's feelings for papier-mâché behemoths on trundle wheels. Most audience members, happily willing to suspend disbelief, welcome the artificiality with good humor. Makarova's staging dispenses with the dear old "fellow"; Nureyev's does not.) A loosely snaking line of almost raucous Indians tears through, followed by a contingent of veiled women holding parrots on their wrists. To wrap up the procession, Solor dismounts from his elephant, and after presenting the royals with a trophy of a tiger, takes Gamzatti's hand and leads her to the palace porch, where the rest of the royal party will observe the festivities.

A short, introductory dance (cut in Makarova's staging) for twelve women with fans, twelve men with pikes, and eight Ethopian children begins the celebrational suite. An "Allegro moderato e soave" waltz (moderately lively and smooth) follows for twelve women with parrots. (Makarova uses this musical number to accompany her dance for women with fans, attended by male dancers.) The waltz's piquant grace notes elicit both gentle piqué steps to contrast with lilting balancé waltz steps. All the while the "characters" who performed earlier stand in neat ranks framing the stage for the waltz dancers.

With the stage richly, if neatly, framed by subsidiary personnel and dancers, the classical heart of the act can reveal itself. A "Moderato" musical number cues the entrance of tutued dancers to introduce a grand pas d'action. Four women in tutu skirts and bare-midriffed Indian "choli" tops perform the first grandly formal ballet dancing of the production. Straightforward, prehensile pointe work, and clear, strict arabesque positions and the like tell the eye more of ballet dancing in India than of Indian dance performed by ballet technicians.

Three more divertissements follow, interrupting the flow of the grand pas d'action. But we mustn't blame Petipa. This entire suite came into its present shape along the way. All of the three ensuing divertissements postdate *Bayadère*'s original plan, some postdate Petipa. The first, now variously called the "Bronze" or "Golden Idol," dates from 1948, when it was called "Little God" and danced by its choreographer, Nikolai Zubkovsky. (The uncredited Kirov dancer here, I believe is Boris Blankov.) It's an acrobatically athletic solo with gestural borrowings from Southeast Asian dance, and references to the Hindu Lord of the Dance, Shiva. Most of the character touches come from the angled arm positions and lotus-blossom plastique for the hands. Otherwise, it might well seem a generic exotic ballet solo.

The next diversion, the "Danse Manu," which may or may not refer to a *manouche* (French for "gypsy"), focuses on a lone woman dancing on her pointes while balancing a water jug on her head as two adolescent girls (on pointes) try to get the teasing woman to pour them a drink. It's a tinkly, perky dance where polka steps on pointe keep recurring. So do skittering runs, pas couru, on pointe. The final chase of the water-carrying woman and the girls goes through runs on pointe that finish in a flourish of a pas de chat. There is a seemingly direct history from this number back to Petipa's 1877 staging. And, in Russian ballet history, per se, several eventually famous female dancers made early appearances as one of the girls. (The dancer is Olga Vtorushina.)

Barreling and thundering on the delicate heels of the "Manu" trio comes the "Indian Dance," which is loud, fast, and furious, with a louder, faster, and more furious still coda. Eight bare-chested men with strings of bells crisscrossing their torsos are led by a ninth with a tom-tom, all kicking and madly working their arms. Into their midst comes a more wildly limb-flinging man and woman. It's anyone's guess what kind of Indians are being portrayed by these eager overachiever dancers, perhaps the intention was to indicate the "savages" cliché associated with the Americas, or to show some imagined sect in India. Whatever, the dancers throw all caution to the winds and build into a kind of unbridled kick-line.

Next, with a "meanwhile back at the pas d'action" straightforwardness, we find two more tutu-wearing dancers launching into a continuation of the grand pas d'action opened some four dances back. Big jumps, big piqué-attitude poses, and big relevé-grand battement moves electrify the "Allegretto" (pretty lively) atmosphere and set the scene for the dance entrance of Solor and Gamzatti. Now the princess is wearing toe shoes and a tutu. She and her partner/fiancé enter in a series of various grands jetés and turning grands jetés. These get performed side by side, one after another, and crisscrossing each other's path, traveling side to side, corner to corner, and most dramtically straight ahead, toward the audience. The Soviet Russian school exemplified throughout this tape was well known for the strength and power of its jumps, especially its big jumps. Of the two dancers leading the pas d'action, the ballerina, Terekhova, has the more impressive elevation.

What immediately follows, the adagio and the solos for the leading characters, all qualify as revisions made some thirty years after Petipa's death. The central supported adagio—to somewhat moody "Andante" music, originally composed for the fourth act, and no longer played in Russian stagings—dates from 1941. It was created by Vakhtang Chabukian and Vladimir Ponomarev. (If you listen carefully, and let your imagination fast-forward to the doom-filled cataclysm of the story's vengeful conclusion, you can hear, particularly in the trilling flutes, exceptionally apt music for the shade of Nikiya to appear and disappear to as she haunts her one-time lover and disconcerts her one-time rival.) To accompany and fill out the pas's central adagio the four women who framed the couple throughout their entrance now flank it, as two trios, since a "knight" danseur has entered to work with each pair of subsidiary women. Here another detail of the Soviet-Russian school is pronounced as the danseur supports his ballerina in especially grand, big poses and in big acrobatically coordinated lifts.

At a climactic point the two knights flank Gamzatti and lift her between them. Just before the adagio's ending, they lift and hold her high between them where she poses regally like a cold-spring jet from a potent fountain. Though Petipa might be admiring of such athletic lifts and sights, he would also be surprised by them. The costuming, decorum, and technical skills of his day would have disallowed maneuvers of this sort. During the final lift, for example, the ballerina gets support from her partner's hands bracing her at the ankles and the thighs. No such points of contact would have been countenanced as proper in the imperial Russian ballet.

The succeeding "Allegretto delicato" (pretty lively, delicate) brings back the tutued quartet that opened the grand pas d'action. Their brief dance, in side-by-side rows, is graced with delicate entrechats, runs, and hops on pointe. It lasts only a little longer than its curtain calls, and helps give the leading dancers a rest period.

Abdeyev's Solor variation follows. It begins plainly, with Solor entering upstage right and taking a matter-of-factly posed preparatory position. His readiness cues the start of his "Allegro pesante" (lively, weighty) music. And he's off, sailing into a manège of easy various grands jetés—grand jeté en tournant with a staglike climax at the peak alternating with grand jeté pas de chat. Lushly torsioned balancé steps then lead to turns à terre and en l'air. A concluding manège of easy coupés jeté steps takes him through chaîné turns to a flourished position, kneeling on one knee.

True to the formula of grand pas d'action the ballerina's variation comes next. To give it due prominence and attention, the neatly seated row of women from the "Dance with Fans" rises to stand in her presence. She too takes what ballet class terms a *grand préparation* before the start of her music and solo. Big leggy, kicking jumps (cabriole devant and grand jeté pas de chat) and a plainly big kick (relevé-grand battement) dominate the beginning. Turning waltzing steps (balancé en tournant) lead her into serene, sharp en dedans turns in attitude, capped by a multiple en dedans pirouette. A diagonal of more spinning turns, now all en dehors, takes her to a concluding manège and diagonal circuit dominated by soaring grand jeté pas de chat jumps.

This wouldn't be a grand pas without a grand coda, and this one starts with the filing onstage of the "parrot" dancers and the repositioning of the "fan" dancers. The music is marked "Tempo di valse brillante," and it shines with bright energy. *Piqué*-poised steps, waltzing and scissoring moves cover the stage as the eight Ethiopian children thread around and through the dozen fan and dozen parrot dancers. Finally Gamzatti returns, flanked by the first quartet of grand pas dancers. Dead center-stage, she whips through a set of kicking turns the Russians nickname fouetté en diagonale. These are en dedans turns that sweep from high battements to the side (à la seconde) into attitude posed half-turns. This sequence segues into another of more familiar fouetté turns, the successive, en dehors variety we've seen for Odile in *Swan Lake*.

The bright, formal, all-dance character of the interpolated mid-twentieth-century grand pas d'action contrasts sharply with the nineteenth-century dramatic, pantomimic nature of the act's concluding scene, an "Allegro" one. The mood immediately becomes one of gloom and sorrow as we see Nikiya enter and almost writhe in emotional agony as she's bidden to dance for the betrothal couple. Her arm-twining and leaning poses appear to pull her in two directions at once. While seeming to desire an exit from the scene, she's drawn to reach toward her beloved as he sits uneasily next to his fiancée. The dominant plaintive violin sounds the lament we feel in Nikiya's plastique. Her dancing takes her from posing in fifth position on pointe like a column of incense smoke to a cantilevered croisé-arabesque allongée posture that vibrates like a tense heartstring.

As Nikiya tries, during a dramatic pause, to leave the place, Aya presents her with a basket of flowers, which she's led to believe is a gift from Solor. More lyrical, effacé-arabesque allongée poses for Nikiya show her enjoying the floral gift. Furtive glances between the fakir and the Brahmin, and knowing ones from the Rajah to Aya, unsettle the seeming serenity of the moment. Increasingly free moves and a pleasurable mood peak when (to a rowdy, upbeat musical interpolation) Nikiya launches into a frantically energetic little dance. A good deal of it has her almost bouncing repeatedly on her pointes. After a wildly swirling finish, the bayadère gestures lovingly with individual blossoms toward Solor until she rears back in terror, having discovered a snake hidden within the basket. In a kinetic burst of energy, Nikiya mimes her accusation that the viper was planted by the Rajah and Gamzatti. The Rajah regally refutes the pointed guilty finger and the Brahmin hopes to win Nikiya back by offering her an antidote if she'll be his. Seeing Solor committed to Gamzatti, however, Nikiya declines saving herself and expires. Abdeyev's Solor falls, Albrecht-like, at Nikiya's side, which seems related to the intentions of the origin staging; but, in Makarova's the unfaithful warrior exits uneasily escorting Gamzatti at her insistence.

Act 3, The Appearance of the Shade

This act has two scenes, the first with a restive Solor in his apartment in the Rajah's palace. The opening segment, a "Maestoso, ma non troppo lento" interlude (majestic, but not too slow), shows the distraught warrior in need of diversion, which the fakir hopes to provide in the person and art of a snake charmer. Eventually the fakir's dance speeds up and involves curling two votive candles amid his spiraling dance, which the original libretto calls "comic" and which ends when the flutist and the fakir slip out, thinking Solor is asleep. After smoking a hookah on his divan, the distressed and drugged warrior senses the presence of the shade of Nikiya, as we see a woman clad in a white tutu.

Harp arpeggios signal the start of a deeper dream and multiple white-clad shades. The libretto tells us simply: "Clouds descend." Now, we are in Scene 5, "The Kingdom of the Shades." Originally set in an "enchanted place," Petipa called for a more shadowy, moonlit realm in 1900. (In the words of Tamara Karsavina, the ballerina who saw the "Shades" scene revived more than fifty years after participating in it, the episode should possess a "blue transparency of night.") Petipa's inspiration for the choreographic design for the "Entrance of the Shades" came from a Gustave Doré illustration of angelic souls filing, like wisps of vapor, into the "Paradiso" of Dante's *Divina Commedia*. A high-pitched "Andante," dominated by searing strings, trilling flutes, and harp, fills the air as a zigzagging line of women in white tutus file forward down a direction-changing ramp from a deep upstage.

We have come to another, arguably quintessential, example of the ballet blanc. All that Petipa's otherwise detailed libretto tells its reader about this extended display of classical dancing comes in three succinct words: "Dances" and "Plastic Groupings." All the "shades," like all the sylphs and Wilis, are dressed identically in white—in this particular case, in short classical tutus with luminous veils tracing the line of their arms from the nape of the neck to the wrist. The shorter, stiffer tutu evolved for the ballet over the years, as *La Bayadère*'s Romantic nature gave way in part to ballet's classical era.

Over and over, the ballet women step into pliantly open and achingly long arabesques. Technically these oft-called *penchées* are arabesques allongées counterpoised on working legs softened by plié à quart (half of a demi-plié). A richly back-bent (*cambré*) position, with arms en couronne and working leg pointe *tendu* (stretched and pointed on the floor), dramatically closes each arabesque before stepping into the next.

The image of an eagle with a majestic wingspan plays a part in Dante's "Paradise," as well as in Petipa's sublimely unfurled arabesques. Makarova consistently uses the term *cantilena* to describe the singing line that should thread through both each individual dancer's line and through the interconnected line of the entire configuration of dancers. (The Kirov uses an ensemble of thirty-two shades, though Petipa sometimes included more—forty-eight, reportedly—for his 1900 revival.)

At about the midpoint of the approximately six-minute sequence, the bayadère-shades regroup in a block formation. There, in simple unison, they delicately angle and float their limbs in plain ballet positions that act as if materializing a mist. Finally, they break ranks and separate into pointe *tendu*-braced lineups, one facing offstage right, the other, left. Presented with the sight of these regally still, impassive women, audiences tend to get demonstrative in showing their appreciation for so simple yet stirring a ritual. Writing about the scene in 1963 as done by Britain's Royal Ballet, critic Clive Barnes suggested: "If you don't enjoy *La Bayadère*, you really don't enjoy ballet."

A less melancholy harp introduction cues the start of a waltz as three "solo" shades enter and begin to dance center stage as the ensemble shades echo and counterpoint their moves along the sides of the stage. Bold and mesmerizing jumps, along with elated, pliant hops, characterize the three women's still dreamlike but brighter dance mood. To a sighing musical punctuation, the full ensemble lines reform into two facing groups. Led by the three soloists, all strike smart, *épaulé* arabesques that trigger them to scurry offstage, the ensemble groups crisscrossing between each other as they go. (Dante's poem mentions "jubilant, interwoven souls.")

A feverish "Allegro" passage brings an agitated Solor into the empty space. He spies, then loses sight of, Nikiya's shade. After a sequence of leaps, partly ecstatic and partly pained, the questing warrior arrests himself statuesquely, gazing offstage. Nikiya enters in light, striding running steps. Like that of *La Sylphide*, Nikiya's music, an "Andantino," is dominated by a solo violin. With a climactic, light bounding step, the shade of Nikiya springs to arabesque on pointe, balanced behind her kneeling beloved by way of a hand on his shoulder. Almost hypnotically, Solor hovers about her and lovingly supports his ballerina/vision in a finely drawn out adagio of poses exquisitely unfolded and firmly held.

The whole mood is chaste and cool as Solor's introspective demeanor makes Nikiya's presence seem like his inward vision. Repeatedly, Nikiya's shade unfolds her leg (through développé action poised on pointe) to balance in expansive big seconde position and then continue through adagio fouetté continuum into further moments of *cantilena* arabesque. A diagonal of successive grand jeté pas de chat and some forceful supported pirouettes spike Nikiya's adagio through-line with almost vehement outbursts of imperious reprimand. Following the shade's path as she backs into an exit by way of pas de bourrée couru, Solor walks mesmerized, as if drawn to a brightening light.

Though the preceding scene involved Solor in supporting Nikiya's adagio moves, its purpose is essentially one of introduction. We have seen, elaborately, "The Entrance of Nikiya." Next comes the central adagio of our ballet blanc. The musical "Andante" begins with the filing onstage of the sister shades, in pairs, in two flanking diagonals. Solor reenters, searching their numbers for his singular Nikiya, rather as we've seen Siegfried do in the "Love Duet" of *Swan Lake*. Like Odette, Nikiya returns to revel at last. The adagio starts with her taking a low lunge into a grand, cambré preparation as Solor salutes her in a lunging bow of his own.

After arising out of her forward and back-bent preparatory pose to spring into an en dehors turn in attitude, Solor makes the adagio a duet and supports her turn through one more revolution. He also lifts her high in a set of sissone lifts that open to land in effacé arabesque or to extend a leg, croisé, to the front. Many of the duet's climactic poses and movements relate to the plastique of the duet in the "Festival of the Fire." Only now, with Nikiya's figure more formally attired and her limbs more free and visible, she takes on a forceful, independent mood. The effacé attitude poses supported by Solor's embrace and the arabesque-allongée moments steadied at arm's length are more independent. In these taut postures she tends less to cling to her beloved and more to assert her individuality; in the latter, she appears more to shoot away than to shy away from overwhelming intimacy.

As at the very start of the adagio, Solor continues to stand apart, while Nikiya continues to dance independently of her partner. The grieving warrior only lends support intermittently, catching Nikiya's shade mostly to help prolong the punctuational poses she hits to finish her individual dance phrases. The penultimate sequence leads to a moment for Nikiya, where she's rocked, as if swooning in Solor's arms, before being lifted to rest prone, curved upward on her partner's shoulder. The final pose has the bayadère poised in glacial attitude-croisé pose, with the warrior kneeling behind and at her side. In silhouette Nikiya's pose looks like famed Giambologna's Mercury re-sculpted in white marble with all angles sharpened and all extended limbs emboldened.

As our ballet's protagonists leave the stage, the corps de ballet, which has been striking various poses and little groupings to frame the adage, strikes another pose. It's the so-called, at least in the United States, B-plus pose, or *attitude à terre* here and there. In Russian-Soviet schooling, and in *La Bayadère* in particular, the posture has a torque all its own. Note the intriguing mix of strongly arched and held torso against the equally strong, yet somewhat languid, lightly extended leg. The consistent harmony and uniform energy and plastique from dancer to dancer tells a marvelous mix of things: haughty grandeur, strict formality, sculptural refinement, and voluptuous poise. Theirs are the riddles of the sphinx. Compare, as a point of information, the stances held by the Royal Ballet's corps de ballet in their staging. You can learn a good deal about a company's overriding aesthetic from so seemingly mundane a detail as the way a corps de ballet of women stand still.

With no further ceremony, one of the three soloist shades who led the waltz (Ludmila Lopukhova) slips through her line of sisters to dance the first of three variations. Each is about a minute long. This one is "Allegro," almost with a vengeance, as the soloist all but chases through the choreography's circuit of runs and little hops on pointe, smooth piqué-attitude turns bang into bolting *grands jetés pas de chat*, and briskly sprung relevé pirouettes from fifth position. A culminating diagonal of forceful relevé-élancé in first Arabesque leads almost demonically to the final pose, a *relevé* to croisé attitude front.

With equal lack of further ado, the second shade variation follows. During the early Soviet era, this jumpy (as in jump-filled) solo got nicknamed the "Vaganova Variation" in honor of the celebrated soloist (and eventual pedagogue) who put her stamp and perhaps even choreographic preferences on this dance. The "Allegro moderato" number begins with a downstage traveling diagonal of cabriole effacé jumps. (Olga Iskanderova does the honors on this tape.) More cabrioles follow (*grand* and *petit*) as do repeated, alternating relevé moves to attitude-front position. After seemingly throwing in one happy *saut de basque* (a jumped turn), the variation comes to a stop with the soloist risen in triumphant fifth position on pointe with arms thrown up, out, and away in a kind of effortless celebration.

A "Moderato" variation completes the trio. (Ludmila Kovaleva dances here.) It begins with studied deliberation: a sissone-ouverte jump that ends in high second position, *assemblé battu*, and a single stately en dehors relevé pirouette. Further measured relevé moves follow, one of which involves a calculated fouetté move to arabesque épaulé, until the solo goes into its own high gear. Successive sauté moves that open to first arabesque precede a final downstage diagonal of pas de bourrée couru in parallel first position. The punctuation mark here is a sweetly explosive grand jeté pas de chat to a kneeling pose.

A brief brass fanfare signals the start of what amounts to a third adagio for this ballet within a ballet. Balletomanes have been known to call what Nureyev's production refers to as "Adagio with Gauze for Solor and Nikiya" as the "Toilet-Paper Variation." As stated early in this section, there is precedent for a *pas de châle* in the dance Marie Taglioni's father created for her in our *Bayadère*'s precursor, Auber's opera ballet *Le Dieu et la Bayadère*.

The "Allegretto" number begins with the entrance of Nikiya and Solor who are linked by holding opposite ends of a long white scarf. To a lachrymose violin, Nikiya flexes through a variety of *relevé* moves that take her to various arabesque and attitude poses. All the while Solor lends discreet support by letting the scarf become an extension of his strength and control. When Nikiya passes through a series of en dedans relevé turns in arabesque that eventually pull into an en dedans pirouette (in standard passé pirouette position), Solor acts almost like a fisherman, with the gossamer scarf as his fishing line. Once she lets go and her partner whisks the veil off in his exit, Nikiya appears to take to the momentum of her last pirouette and swing into a series of solo turns and jumps: grand jeté en tournant into double en dehors pirouettes that open into arabesque. The sequence gets repeated two and a half times, traveling upstage, center stage. After scurrying back downstage with more runs on pointe and pauses in relevé-passé en tournant, she skims into a climax similar to that of the third shade, and ends posed, on pointe in attitude-croisé.

Nikiya's still, delicately planted single figure stands like a calm before a storm, once the ballet blanc's "Allegro con spirito" coda is under way, which is immediately "lively, with vigor." As the three solo shades launch into a series of brisés, pas de chat, arabesque-sauté, and entrechats, the ensemble women become eagerly animated once more. Soon the entire sisterhood has filled the stage. The three soloists act as leaders, whom the full ensemble follows. After skittering on pointe farther downstage en masse, the block of white shades, thirty-five-strong, electrifies the air with a flush of steps that do little more than continually shift weight from one foot to the other.

A "Vivace" capstone to the coda begins when the shades once more move to the sidelines and Solor and Nikiya enter the cleared stage, more or less directly on the heels of the ensemble's climactic pas de chat. Solor lifts Nikiya so that her sauté-arabesque moves seem to soar and hang in the air. A solo manège of tour jetés takes Nikiya around the stage and out of sight. Solor returns to thread a few lengths of jumping moves through and around the stage. Abdeyev does not include the double assemblé moves that have in more recent times become part of the coda's choreographic tradition. This has been so ever since Nureyev's connection to the ballet in the 1960s. The aerial turns in question show the dancer making himself as tall and long as he can; their effect is like that of a log rolling through the air at a slightly tilted angle. (Mukhamedov does them on the Royal Ballet tape, and in the thus far only European-format video of the Paris Opera Ballet production, Laurent Hilaire also does them.)

Once more the stage floods with the thirty-five shades, whose vigorous dancing takes up where they left off. A demonic diagonal of soutenu turns, and a back-traveling length of arabesques voyagés reversed into piqué turns for Nikiya help telescope things to their conclusion.

In the case of this Kirov production, that conclusion takes the form of a final grouping where Nikiya and Solor pose, united, amid rows of reclining shades arrayed around them on the floor. As discussed, since 1920 the original intended last act has been dropped from Russian productions. For a brief time the ballet ended with a tagged-on scene showing Solor returning to his room, where he took his own life in despair. Once that scene was dropped, the ballet ended with the lovers united in the underworld kingdom of shades.

If you watch Makarova's staging on video (or stage), you'll have a sense of what was originally intended. Such guessing has to include the act's music as well as its choreography. (In the case of Makarova's staging, the conductor and music arranger John Lanchbery became the composer.) As we've seen the "Little God" or "Bronze Idol" solo that comes in the Kirov's second act opens Makarova's last act. The music for Gamzatti's last act solo is a pastiche of that used for the snake charmer scene. (Makarova's choreography is a swirling general dance for one dancer, who in the happy case of the Royal video happens to be one capable of making the general almost particular, the daring and beauteous Darcey Bussell.) We've also seen and heard music used for the original pas d'action in which Nikiya's shade disrupts, as in *La Sylphide*, would-be tranquil preparations for nuptials. In the Makarova production video, a regally implacable Asylmuratova dances the intrusive presence and does her best with the new, generally unsettling music.

The destruction of the temple, complete with slow-motion camera work happens right on cue of its new music, "Vivo assai" (extremely lively). To characterize the intended Apotheosis, a vista of swirling clouds and musical themes from earlier scenes all come together in Makarova's staging. Lanchbery's finale is "Vivo agitato" and underscores Nikiya's leading the way up some celestial stairs by holding high a long scarf that Solor grasps by the other end. The original staging called for the sighting of Nikiya's shade through the rains of the Himalayas. Petipa wanted us to see her, on high (probably flying on wires), with her now similarly spiritual beloved situated at her feet.

Chapter 9

RENEWING CLASSICISM

Apollo

• • •

Choreography by George Balanchine
Music by Igor Stravinsky

The ballet blanc sylphs of Taglioni, Bournonville, and Fokine, and the shades of Petipa all inspired Igor Stravinsky in 1927 when he composed his *Apollon Musagète*, a "Ballet in two scenes, with Apotheosis." The innovative Russian composer responded to an American commission for a small-scale ballet by conceiving an episode from classical Greek mythology for the classical school of ballet. Stravinsky's music and thematic scenario aimed for a purity related to that of the pure-dance segments of narrative ballets. The essence of the ballet blanc guided him to create a score divested of "many-colored effects" and "all superfluities."

The "white" ballet that resulted from Balanchine's choreography took its inspiration from what the choreographer called the composer's "white" music, "in places as white on white," as he saw it. The younger but equally innovative Russian ballet master took what he would later describe as profound insight from Stravinsky's music. It encouraged him to eliminate various options and artistic ideas in a search for clarity.

During its first years of groundbreaking performances, the ballet's full original title, which means "Apollo, Leader of the Muses," changed variously, and today it's universally and simply called *Apollo*. Because there is no reliable version of Balanchine's complete choreography commercially on video, *Apollo* will be one of the ballets in this section that we'll look at without a primary video for assistance.

A related video now on the market is an excerpted version of the ballet, performed by an uneven cast. Before I give the particulars of this supplementary video, it should be noted that two better videos of *Apollo* have been televised and might someday show up on the commercial market, be re-telecast, or be available in a dance video archive near you. These are a 1982 performance originally shown on *Great Performances: Live from Lincoln Center* with Peter Martins, Suzanne Farrell, Kyra Nichols, and Maria Calegari and a 1989 *Great Performances: Dance In America* with Mikhail Baryshnikov, Christine Dunham, Leslie Browne, and Stephanie Saland.

About this supplementary video:

> *The Balanchine Celebration, Part One: New York City Ballet*, Selections from (among other ballets) *Apollo*, with Nilas Martins, Isabelle Guérin, Zhanna Ayupova, and Patricia Barker, 1993, 86 min., Color.
>
> This *Apollo* excerpt was performed on a gala program and includes ballerinas from three different countries, backgrounds, and national traditions. This *Apollo* takes place at the New York State Theater where Balanchine originally supervised the staging of his latest and final version of his earlier, longer ballet. In this tape, therefore, you'll see excerpts of the truncated rendering.

The Greek god Apollo remains a favorite with artists of all disciplines. He was the god of music, poetry, and dance, as well as of the plastic arts, science, and philosophy. Essentially he was the god of the intellect and the enemy of barbarism. Apollo was the bringer of light, and as such could dispel darkness of all kinds. We will recall that ballet's great early champion, Louis XIV of France, became known as "The Sun King" in good part because of his portrayal of Apollo in the *ballet de cour* spectacle called *Le Ballet de la Nuit*.

Likewise, the muses or sources of artistic inspiration have become favorite subjects of the arts that they are said to motivate. In fulfilling his commission's chamber-size specifications, Stravinsky reduced the full sisterhood of nine muses to three. Thus the dramatic situation became at once classic, resembling as it did the three-goddesses-and-one-god unit of the "Judgment of Paris" and yet beyond the already ballet-familiar unit with one man torn between two women: Siegfried with Odette and Odile, Albrecht with Giselle and Myrtha, Solor with Nikiya and Gamzatti, to name but three we've already focused on. In established ballet tradition, two represented prosaic dramatic conflict; in the new tradition, three made for opened-up poetic possibilities.

The Apollo of Balanchine and Stravinsky achieves godliness only at the end of their ballet. They show us Apollo's maturing process more than his maturity. In ballet terms, the means by which this is achieved have come to be known as neoclassicism. After playing his part in the avant-garde thrust of Diaghilev's Ballets Russes, Balanchine went back to his most classical ballet roots when choreographing *Apollon Musagète*. Diaghilev likened the result to "pure classicism, such as we have not seen since Petipa." In a program note for the ballet's first performances, Stravinsky called the ballet's scheme a "play without a plot."

The "neo-" or new aspect of Balanchine's *Apollo* came from its directness, from its confident sense of classical ballet's ability to illuminate its theme or subject without recourse to Old World pantomime or pre-published libretto. When a contemporary journalist looking for manners and attitudes reminiscent of classical Greek statuary and other familiar classical references sarcastically questioned Balanchine's choice of having Apollo appear to walk on his knees, asking when the choreographer had seen Apollo do so, the undaunted ballet master retorted by asking when the writer in question had seen Apollo.

Though I don't know of Balanchine being anywhere on record giving the example of ancient Greek kouroi as a starting point for his ballet's vision, I'll suggest so here. Sculptures of these young men, said to have been part of the cult of Apollo, are known to us through the simple, almost rough-hewn statues that date from before the golden age of Greek classicism. In their simple, formulaic shaping, their elemental geometrics, their half-smiling expressions, and their forthright, striding stance, they relate handily to Balanchine's warding off expectations of aesthetics related to more "mature" and refined sculptures, like the famed *Apollo Belvedere.*

The young Balanchine's staging underwent various changes toward maturity, much as the ballet's title figure does in the course of the ballet. The costumes, originally credited to André Beauchant, the Faux Naïf painter chosen by Diaghilev for the project, changed from artful glosses on standard tarlatan tutus to freer tunics cinched with neckties. (Since the painter was unfamiliar with ballet costuming, Apollo's chiton, red trimmed with gold, and the ballerinas' dresses were suggested by Diaghilev himself. The rethought tunics were designed by innovative couturier Coco Chanel.) Beauchant's design scheme, a floral frontcloth (or dropcurtain) and a roughly painted setting with a mountain and cut-out horse-drawn chariot, remained part of the production initially. After briefly toying with a surrealist landscape of hillocks turned into heads (by Pavel Tchelitchev), Balanchine settled for a bare stairway leading to a little platform and a small "kitchen" stool as an elemental way for setting the scene. The costumes got sparer and sparer. For Apollo, tights (black or white, depending on the comeliness of the legs in question) and a one-shoulder, handkerchieflike top; for the muses, leotardlike white tunics with brief skirts.

The muses chosen by Stravinsky and animated by Balanchine are: Calliope, personification of poetry and rhythm, Polyhymnia, representative of mime, and Terpsichore, signifying in dance the rhythm of poetry and the eloquence of gesture. The full score and the original staging included the presence of Leto, Apollo's mother, and two goddess handmaidens. These subsidiary characters dominate the ballet's first scene, a Prologue called "The Birth of Apollo." The three women with one man cast of characters mentioned above play out the ballet's second scene: "Apollo and the Muses."

Fifty years after its premiere performance, for a staging with Mikhail Baryshnikov at an international dance festival, Balanchine dropped the gesturally narrative prologue from his ballet. After further excising the first of Apollo's two variations from the remaining scene, which he then reinstated, Balanchine left his prologue-free version of

Apollo as the definitive one. Today you may find both versions being performed. In the instance where a company might offer the cut and uncut stagings in a single season, the less than graceful tagged-on "with birth" (meaning the inclusion of Apollo's birth scene) has been known to distinguish the full staging from the cut one.

I'm going to "view" the Prologue in this section, even though it's not recorded on commercial tape and many companies perform the truncated version ballet. (The complete *Apollo*, with Prologue, has been filmed more than once. One notable film—1967, BBC, London—features Jacques d'Amboise with Suzanne Farrell, Gloria Govrin, and Patricia Neary; another—1969, CBC, Montreal—documents Peter Martins with Suzanne Farrell, Karin von Aroldingen, and Marnee Morris.)

A musical introduction offers fragments of the score's central "Apollo" melody. It's just about enough music to cover a screen crawl of the ballet's credits. With the curtain's almost immediate rise, we see the nymph Leto in a back-bent position, seated atop the stairway's landing. The synopsis of Apollo's beginnings according to Stravinsky reads as follows: "Leto was with child and, feeling the moment of birth at hand, threw her arms about a palm-tree and knelt on tender turf; and the earth smiled beneath her, and the child sprang forth to the light. . . . Goddesses washed him with limpid water, gave him for swaddling clothes a white veil of fine tissue, and bound it with a golden girdle."

Barefoot and tossing her loose hair as she bends her torso and arches backward, Leto writhes to her music's eventually accelerating drive. Now reaching an arm out and away from her person, then unfolding her legs, at one moment angling them apart in a taut V-shape, the mother goddess soon appears to have delivered herself a mummy-stiff, standing young man. With his upper body bound in a winding sheet, the youth's eyes are downcast and his arms trapped at his sides. Two ebullient women enter, leaping. Their linked arms make a ring around the young man as he hops forward in small lurching jumps. They cradle him momentarily and he wails silently. Each woman finds an end of the lengthy fabric enwrapping the "newborn," and starts to circle around him as they unwind his bonds. As soon as his two arms are free, he uses them to gather his own force.

Shaping himself into a seemingly spontaneous approximation of ballet's preparation for pirouette, he works both arms and pushes off his feet into the whirl of an en dedans pirouette. Having completed any number of revolutions and freed himself completely of his winding clothes, he stands surprised by his "arrival." Showing bewilderment, on evident music, he hops haltingly on the two feet supporting his animated legs. Finally, the bare-chested young man stands with his arms free and easy at his side, and his head and gaze upward.

To strains of the Apollo theme (in shining C-major), the two handmaidens enter in a configuration that's been nicknamed "the wheelbarrow." One walks behind the other, who takes support from her vertical sister as she moves forward crouched on her pointes, kicking and fanning her legs in the air as she proceeds. She carries a lute, as her attendant mate steers her toward the standing young god. The two flank Apollo and, as the music takes on a steady strumming character, they hold the lute across his chest and work his arms in the action of playing its strings. By the end of the sequence, we see a fascinated man whose arms open out and close in on the lute as one arm of each handmaiden echoes the gesture. A ceremonious exit for Leto and the two goddesses closes out the Prologue.

Scene two, "Apollo and the Muses," begins with the man god standing firm and tall in a variation on ballet's *croisé* position. His torso is now dressed in a one-shoulder, triangular top and he holds his lute against his upstage hip. His downstage arm wheels widely and repeatedly as Stravinsky's music sounds like a breathlessly strummed lute. (The score's solo instrument is the violin, with the sounds from its strings becoming the music of Apollo and his lute.) A more methodical musical mood shows Apollo studying his instrument and then concentrating his strumming in his hand, fairly furiously. Loping from side to side, he holds the long-necked lute at both ends, lifting it over his head as he jumps, staglike, as if to test the dance moves that his music's sounds inspire. His handling and brandishing of the stringed instrument has a curiously exploratory air. At moments, he seems to treat it almost like a Chinese back-scratcher.

With further curiosity, as if treating the lute as measuring stick, he places it facedown on the ground and practices dance moves. He steps on tentative demi-pointe to try out arabesques that alternate croisé and effacé positioning. He backs away from the "silenced" musical instrument by swinging into further arabesque positions (effacé) and then reverses the impetus and alternately kicks his legs (croisé) forward to "fall" (*tombé*) along a little diagonal that ends with him almost walking on his knees. Arabesque-open stances lead him to suitable preparatory moves into pirouettes—deliberate ones, en dedans with the working leg in attitude-front.

When he picks up the lute once more, in another oddly formal way, he returns to the scene's opening position and wheels again through strumming moves. This time his music making has new power. From both upstage corners and the downstage-right one, come three ballerinas, first skimming in light pas de bourrée couru and then proceeding to stride, still on pointe, through smooth and high grand battement-front. As the object of their advance, Apollo revolves (en dedans en promenade) in low attitude position.

With the arrival of the ballerina muses we have arrived at the ballet's pas d'action. All three hail the young god with hand-held-high salutes that halo his head. He salutes them in turn and they bow in response, one leg clearly extended croisé pointe-tendu. He kneels in their midst and, as he raises his lute high over his head, like a majestic jet of clear water, each of the muses bows in rich arabesque penchée around Apollo. Their upthrust arabesque legs mirror the line of his raised lute. (Note that these and similar arabesques in this pas qualify as true *penchée* positions. Compare in your mind's eye or on your video screen the difference between these and the so-called *penchées* executed during the "Entrance of the Shades" in *La Bayadère*.)

To music that now seems to settle into the flow of a calm narrative, Apollo and the muses go through an acquaintanceship. All three in sequence rest their heads on the young god's shoulder; after which he offers his hand to the three simultaneously. In the first of several troika configurations, the danseur/partner/god guides all three of the hands he holds through a grand épaulé position that motivates three more arabesque-penchée positions. With something of a flourish, he "tags" each muse into her own relevé-élancé first arabesque, twice over. Each muse finishes her arabesque in a demure kneeling pose, one hand to her chin. Watching them, rowed side by side as they skitter about on their pointes, he cleaves their lineup and separates Terpsichore momentarily from her sister muses. After catching her gently as he falls back into his arms, Apollo picks up Calliope and Polyhymnia, one under each arm, and lowers them to kneel at his sides. Next we find Terpsichore taking one of Apollo's hands and one of her kneeling sisters' and wreathing and looping a steadily measured flourish round and round the entwined threesome.

The next segment opens as the muses bend and reach their torsos with arms en couronne in staggered timing that makes for an evolving three-leaf clover. All the while, Apollo leaps back and forth around the muses' one-behind-the-other lineup. At times it looks as if the ballerinas' port de bras means to set up hoops for the godly danseur to jump through.

Once more paying equal homage to all three, Apollo takes each muse through a variation on standard supported pirouette. One by one the ballerinas take what looks like a preparation for a finger turn; in the process of turning, all spiral down into grand plié and finish the turn with a *grand rond de jambe* sweep of the working leg. After springing through little bucking moves in parallel first position on pointe, the muses get teasing "crack the whip" gestures from Apollo before prancing, coltlike, to pose in a row on their knees. Then, in a ring of linked hands and in a configuration that appears to turn inside out the earlier penchée grouping, the foursome has the muses facing out from their circle while Apollo faces toward it. Anchored by the steady, standing Apollo, the muses send their penchée legs soaring upward like three Klieg light beams in the center of a circle of arms.

A restatement of the three-leaf clover design of arms segues into a leisurely swirl of all four characters moving in a cluster as their looped and linked arms and hands create over and under moves, in and out of the arches configurations. This delicately curvilinear and airy passage leads to a more archaic, rough-hewn segment. Lined up side by side, with their heads tilted in one direction and their hands cupped under one another's chins, the foursome, with Apollo as kind of a pivot point, inches around on its heels, with toes stiffly lifted from the floor.

Undoubtedly, Balanchine took his cue for his almost awkward locomotions from the music's vaguely scratchy texture. A more airy subsequent musical passage and a loving nudge from Apollo takes the muses to their pointes and sends them off in a little train formation with their heads thrown back. The pas winds to a close with a presentation of attributes as Apollo gives the muses symbols of their art. Each ballerina rushes forward, takes her prop and, in a kind of dancer gesture of gratitude, extends an attitude extension front: Terpsichore gets a lyre, the musical instrument associated with song and dance; Polyhymnia, a mask, the sign of the mime; and Calliope, a scroll, the material of the poet. Two softly stressed chords send the muses in two sideward hops to await their solo turns, while, for his part, Apollo takes two similar hops and plumps down to sit in judgment of their performances.

Now come the variations; Calliope's "Allegretto" first. (This is where the video mentioned at the top of this section begins.) The muse of lyric poetry—Kirov ballerina Zhanna Ayupova on our tape—begins by writing arabesques with her legs and by scrawling calligraphic gestures on her scroll and in the air with her pointed finger. After putting aside her tablet, Calliope gets more declamatory with her mime-scented dancing. Analysts of Stravinsky's music note that the rhythm of the cello solo we hear to be based on an "Alexandrine," a line of poetry in iambic hexameter. More and bolder arabesque poses, with gestures telling of open-mouthed oration, punctuated by sudden contractions of the torso, lead to a spiraling circuit of turns where a fanning extended leg appears to write on the air in tandem with a pointed finger. Sissone leaps, mirroring more open-mouthed expressions, work from big to smaller and finally a still, bent-forward pause. A more delicate picking around on pointes follows, before a recurrence of the contracting torso giving impetus to open-mouthed expressions. After seeming to write a final thought on the palm of her hand, Calliope hides her hand behind her back and approaches Apollo with some caution. When she kneels at the god's knee and opens her palm, he turns his head disapprovingly.

For her "Allegro" variation, Polyhymnia, mask in hand, comes on in a flash. After a pulsating start, with a plainly delivered pirouette, she launches into a dance that has her holding one finger to her lips as she prances, pawing one extended leg repeatedly in front of her, like a pony. She too seems to write on the air with one extended hand. Her leg extensions include clear attitude positions as well as arabesques and plainly extended, straight-leg positions front. Elated piqué poses in attitude lead to piqué turns in attitude, which lead to sissone, and grand jeté moves. A felicitous diagonal strings together a series of double piqué en dedans pirouettes that finish by extending into effacé arabesque. More fanciful writing on air and prancing on arcs and diagonals, leads to a climactic en dedans pirouette. And here, for the first time in her dance, the muse removes the finger from her lips, and on suitable musical sound, excitedly "blabs" with a wide-open mouth. Apollo makes a disapproving, cabalistic sign with his hands, as the mime who could not remain silent (Pacific Northwest Ballet's Patricia Barker) slips out of sight. (As you've read elsewhere on these pages, silently mouthing the words of a pantomime message is cheating and coarsens the formal practiced art of pure pantomime.)

When Terpsichore (Paris Opera Ballet's Isabelle Guérin) begins her "Allegretto" variation, she too has the air of a fine-bred colt, one that's more serene and less impulsive of character than Polyhymnia's. Her first moves, braced in fourth position on pointe, include actual *pas de cheval* (step of the horse) pawings and contrapposto twistings of the torso, from the waist. All this happens along the ballerina's temple-column vertical axis, heightened by the holding of her lyre in two hands, high above her head. After she puts down her prop, she dances more freely, twisting and spiraling through delicate renversé positions before taking some polka steps as lead-ins to smoothly open grands jetés with arms proudly en couronne. She alternates regal, relevé first arabesques by playfully walking on her heels, recalling the "archaic" moments of the pas d'action. To some of the music's more teasing and "Ritardando" (held back) moments, she toys with positions determined by shooting an extended leg up and back and by stepping forward in a way that gives slinking play to her pelvis. Climactically, she repeats her earlier en dedans renversé twists by reaching into each one through a wide and calculated lunge. Playful, side to side, hootchy-kootchy-tinged pas de bourrées lead to a high kicking approach toward the seated Apollo. Stationed proudly in front of him, Terpsichore flutters her hands as they draw her arms to shape her almost literally bending-over-backward pose as a kind of grand show of reverence.

Actually, the variation's final note cues not Terpsichore but Apollo. With his muse back-bent in a croisé pointe-tendu body position, the young god shows his approval of her art by saluting her, much as he did all three muses at the beginning of the pas d'action, on the music's final stroke.

Taking center stage, the young god and judge begins his second variation. To a majestic opening, the "Lento" (slow) solo lets Apollo shine as master of the dance art he just finished observing. An opening pose, in clear fifth position, with his arms raised like the frame of a lyre, immediately takes off into an entrechat that lands him kneeling with his arms cast back like an eagle's half-open wings. After a deliberate return to vertical stance, a tightly coiled soutenu move takes him to further entrechats that open out into soccerlike kicks. In a lunged pose with one arm raised and the other behind his back, he alternately opens his fists to starbursts of splayed fingers. (Balanchine has said these gestures were inspired by blinking electric lights in London's Piccadilly Circus. One Apollo he rehearsed personally claimed to have been told that the opening and closing of the hands meant: "Bar and grill, bar and grill!")

An almost introspective musical and physical passage follows the show of bright lights. After pacing around as if losing himself in thought with battement-battu steps, as if absentmindedly kicking up dust or kicking a random tin can, his kicks grow into larger ones. In place, and alternately kicking his legs from one side to the other, Apollo takes on the raw athleticism and image of a soccer player. All of which returns him (and his music) to the earlier lyre salute to the heavens. A pose sometimes known as the "crouched eagle" comes again as well, and leads Apollo upstage to begin a diagonal of parallel leg strides forward on clear three-quarter pointe. Four times over, the young god steps and prepares for double pirouettes, never descending from his demi-pointe stance.

Another length of pacings still on firm three-quarter pointe and accented as if archaic *chassé* (one foot chasing the other) moves, leads to a retaking of the "bright lights" gesturing lunge and a melancholic mood. A brief passage of introspective back-and-forth reachings heat up to more athletic kicking moves and a kneeling pose with the arms describing a lyre's frame. When he rises, it's to take a straightforward preparation for a pirouette and spin into an en dedans pirouette in attitude front that segues into an en dehors soutenu-styled pirouette that takes him to a seated position on the floor.

For this particular moment, an innovation can be seen in the taping made for *Dance in America*. Baryshnikov executes a rond de jambe par terre sweep of the working leg to connect his pirouette directly into his next pose. It's for reasons such as this, that it behooves you to seek out another video version of *Apollo* for educational purposes.

From his half-seated, half-reclining position on the ground, Apollo directs behind him an upstretched arm, one commanding finger pointed. The gesture calls Terpsichore, who reenters and, with delicate precision, touches her index finger to the one Apollo extends. Thus connected, the muse turns her standing pose in a direction opposite that of Apollo. We have come to the ballet's central pas de deux.

Over the years, *Apollo* watchers have commented on the echo in this finger-to-finger moment to the nearly touching fingertips in Michelangelo's *Creation of Adam* fresco, where God the Father is about to stir an inanimate Adam to life. I've never known Balanchine to make this claim for his motivation. In any case, what we see here is Terpsichore's purposely making contact with Apollo's fingertip. Thus, with a moment of "preparation" complete, the pas de deux music begins. To my eye, the fingertip-to-fingertip starting point dramatizes how supported adagio can begin with the tiniest point of contact between two dancers.

The pas de deux adagio music begins with the fine sound of delicate strings. Terpsichore sends various high extensions over the seated god: a high *écarté* ("separated, wide-apart") position grows from développé movement, a serene arabesque allongée follows, which after revolving en promenade plummets to deep arabesque penchée. After sitting briefly, as if on a tree stump conveniently suggested by Apollo's bent knees, the muse entwines her arm with Apollo's, which leads both characters to standing positions. Once Terpsichore takes a plain piqué arabesque on pointe, decorously supported at the waist by an attentive Apollo, the configuration evolves into heightened dramatic theatricality. A creamy penchée split arabesque motivates Apollo to take his muse into his arms and next support her split-leg position on his shoulder, as she drapes herself there, bent over backward.

More deep leaning poses follow, including an arabesque penchée that culminates after Apollo helps guide and draw Terpsichore's arm into a rich épaulé position. (We've seen similarly lush and luminous moves in Balanchine's pas de deux from *The Nutcracker*, which in fact the ballet master borrowed from an earlier Ivanov scheme.) Contrasting the "singing" and "looping" dimensions of these supported arabesques, come more of those heel-digging archaisms for walking on toes-up flexed feet. More contrast follows as the flexible Terpsichore repeatedly slides into splits on the floor before arising into further effacé-arabesque allongée poses.

Leaning placidly against Apollo's hip, the muse gets carried around by her god in a leaning, demi-arabesque position. Out of a standard finger turn, the ballerina ends up sitting angularly on her partner's thigh. (The source of this maneuver might well be the related moves found in the Argentinian tango, which had found popularity in 1920s Paris.) A teasing, back and forth exchange follows to a particularly chirpy musical segment. Repeatedly, Terpsichore flutters into brisé steps that alternate with relevé-développé arabesque. Each time Apollo tries to mirror her moves, he only succeeds in twirling, left and right, through simpler, single en dedans turns. He shows more success at mirroring his muse's stepping, over and over, from one side to the other, into arabesque *fondue* (melted) with arms than with eye-shielding or harkening hand gestures.

The brief workout winds down after facing tour jetés lead into the two kneeling face to face. Apollo offers his muse his two hands, and Terpsichore eccentrically and geometrically takes them by placing her elbows in offered palms. When she in turn angles her palms in Apollo's direction, the god momentarily rests his head in them. From here, Apollo turns away from Terpsichore, and, supporting her with his hands behind him and over his head, lifts her to rest prone and arched on the back of his head, neck, and upper back. Thus poised—he like Atlas taking a world on his shoulders; she like a bird coasting in gliding flight—the two configure what has been called the "Swimming Lesson" but could just as easily be seen as a "flying lesson." Both god and muse serenely stroke their arms in the air, the one in coordinated counterpoint to the other, until Apollo rises from his knee after letting Terpsichore slide down his back. As their adagio's music sighs to a shimmering close, the two arch dreamily in cambré poses as their swimming/flying arms draw the backbend into being. The ballerina braces her back-curving posture into the back of the danseur's arched lunge. In the end, both extend, their arms open, out, and down as they lift their gaze upward.

The musical burst of the score's coda awakens Apollo and Terpsichore from their adagio reverie and brings Calliope and Polyhymnia back into the picture. The young god and favored muse exit, as the attendant muses rock in place as if steadying their respective steeds before taking off at a gallop. Now their bouncing arms, led by pointed fingers, have the sense of working a horse's reins. Relevé-sprung arabesques with arms whisked en couronne and with half-turns directed by épaulé arms take the sister muses to a diagonal of "bookend" turns, over and over facing, mirroring one another. Things heat up further when Terpsichore takes center stage and steps through a reprise of some of the more teasing steps from her variation, slipping on and off pointe, seeming to dart this way and that.

Landing back in their midst, almost as if dropping from the skies, Apollo sails impetuously through assemblé jumps that accent half-turns in the air, as well as through back-traveling slides in arabesque and skiddings that appear to stop and change directions impulsively. He strikes a kind of "strong man" stance that appears to hook Calliope and Polyhymnia on his flexed arms and spin them, like a carnival ride. A pause, and a recharging of energy brings all four characters into a pulsing dance in unison. Soon the muse threesome gallops by way of relevé arabesque moves and pulls Apollo along so that he appears once more to be walking on his knees. A break in the accelerating mode of the coda shows Apollo tending particularly to Terpsichore, whom he lifts while flanked by her sisters. A final spin for the god in low extension, front, appears to draw the muses to him, where on a dashing musical cue they clap their hands and make a pillow of their group's palms, where Apollo rests his head.

A resoundingly tranquil call, reminiscent of the scene's opening air, comes seemingly from on high to awaken the dreaming young god. As he rises to hear its message, the muses sink back in deference to the god. Playfulness gives way to stateliness. The three muses kneel as a unit as Apollo salutes the skies. Like the struts of a fan, the legs of the muses reach up from their sitting positions to touch, magic-wandlike, Apollo's outstretched hand. Then, shaping his arms in a ring, the young god provides a place for each muse to ring her arms. Slowly, in incremental stages, the sisters arise from their seated positions and the foursome moves as a unit of circled arms, curling round and round one another like a billowing cloud.

In *Apollo* "With Birth," the curling foursome dissipates and forms the ballet's so-called sunburst or peacock image. In it, Apollo stands braced in effacé lunge position, arms extended to front, usually à deux bras, while the muses all group behind him, fanning in the process of their postures an array of arabesque legs: Terpsichore is most downstage, lunging on her standing leg and extending her working leg in demi-arabesque; Polyhymnia is next extending to high arabesque; and Calliope is most upstage, reaching her arabesque leg to strong penchée height. However, in *Apollo* "sans birth" the sunburst/peacock comes later, as the ballet's closing image.

On the way to the ending, in both versions, Apollo offers his hand to all three women and moves upstage as if he were leading his troika rather than the other way around. A steady pulse in the music suggests a journeying pace as Apollo is followed at regular intervals by the three muses in a single file. In *Apollo* "With Birth" the four move slowly up the stairs "toward" Parnassus. There, with Apollo at the stairs' pinnacle and the muses evenly spaced down the steps behind him, a final tableau is struck: The god of light arrays his arms to the heavens, the muses hold their first arabesque in a graduated diagonal, and Leto and her handmaidens have returned to swoon at the sight.

In *Apollo* (sans birth), we see no staircase and observe no ascent to Parnassus. Rather, the "sunburst" that originally occurred momentarily, just before the ballet's final journey to the realm of the gods, is posed with protracted emphasis.

Chapter 10

NEO-ROMANTICISM, NEO-PRIMITIVISM, AND NEOCLASSICISM

Diaghilev's Ballets Russes Triple Bill

Now that we've looked at a couple of individual ballets from the repertory of Diaghilev's Ballets Russes, we'll look at a program's worth of three others. With his company limited in size, Diaghilev could not offer a repertory of large-scale, multi-act spectacles. (His one attempt to do this, by amplifying his troupe and taking on large expenditures, came, as we have seen in our historical survey, with a 1921 production, *The Sleeping Princess*, which as we also saw failed seriously at the box office.) The so-called triple bill began with Diaghilevian programming. Sometimes such mixed programs will be called "mixed bills," or when they include fewer or more individual items can be referred to as double bills or quadruple bills, etc. We're going to look here at a hypothetical one: Michael Fokine's *Le Spectre de la Rose*, Vaslav Nijinsky's *L'Après-midi d'un Faune*, and Bronislava Nijinska's *Les Noces*.

Though no actual reasons existed to prevent this bill from being programmed by Diaghilev in his day, practical, personal, and artistic ones did. The works, each created by and for Diaghilev's company, cover a time span when internal vicissitudes would have made this particular grouping unworkable. *Spectre*, as it's known in ballet-world shorthand, was created in 1911, *Faune*, in 1912, and *Noces* in 1923.

Today, however, each of these works maintains a place in a kind of pantheon of modernism, and thus may well find their way onto a bill of historic highlights. Depending on a company's marketing point for "selling" Diaghilevian masterworks, our trio might be grouped on a single bill, where it could be specially advertised as an "All Diaghilev" offering, or each could appear singly, enriching the "mix" of a bill with history-making landmarks. Realistically, however, following current program-length tastes, an additional work would likely find its way onto this bill to fill it out to "standard" duration.

In dance world parlance, each of these ballets qualifies as a "revival." None dropped away from active repertory long enough to be called "lost." If it had, putting it back onstage after a protracted absence would qualify it as a "reconstruction." Revivals, as I've noted earlier, take some extra doing, but not so much major research and educated guessing as reconstructions. We'll consider the particular routes to our revivals as we move along.

For neatness sake, I've placed the "pieces," as ballets are sometimes called, in chronological order. For theatrical sake, chronological sequence is hardly a priority. Program order is something most companies work carefully at. Whether it's a triple or quadruple bill, the order is usually determined according to what qualify as "opening" ballets and "closing" ballets. The middle of a mixed program is traditionally considered in pride-of-place terms. At this point in a performance the audience is thought best primed to be attentive, and thus ready for the main course. "Closers" can be considered desserts and/or chasers to the rest of the program, and traditionally includes work to send audiences home in an energized, stirred mood.

If our bill's first two works were to be billed back to back, they might well be separated with what theater lingo dubs a "Pause" (usually less than five minutes), rather than a full intermission (approximately twenty minutes long). The video recommended for viewing alongside this entry is one on which all these works appear, with an added fourth, which is not part of my discussion, in place for good measure. The videocassette's title is *Paris Dances Diaghilev*. I choose it not only because it conveniently jibes with my three-part choice, but also because it presents the dancers and dancing of the world's oldest exponent of the danse d'école, the Paris Opera Ballet. With this example, therefore, you'll see French-schooled dancers in Russian-created ballets that once served as a wake-up call to the would-be august and superior ballet of sophisticated Paris. The "Paris" of the program's title is something of a pun, since all the included ballets once shone in Paris (and except for *Spectre* all had their world premieres there), and because more than fifty years after their heyday, these ballets make up a pointedly historic program of dancing by the world's most famous Parisian ballet troupe.

About this video:

> *Paris Dances Diaghilev/The Paris Opera Ballet: Petrouchka, Le Spectre de la Rose, L'Après-midi d'un Faune, Les Noces*, 1991, 84 min. (approx. 35, 10, 12, and 28 min. respectively, individual ballet running times), Color. Booklet of text, with essays and full cast credits included with cassette.
>
> This nicely produced program, and video, includes some of the Paris Opera Ballet's most stellar performers. Almost all the leading dancers who appear in these ballets were products of Rudolf Nureyev's artistic administration, which had just come to an end before this program was filmed. Nureyev, almost as much an avid amateur dance historian as he was a dedicated professional dancer, long revered Diaghilev's legacy. This program represents the works he felt strongly and positively about. The French dancers performing them, do honor to the pieces on this tape in good measure because of Nureyev's pervasive influence upon them.

Both *Spectre* and *Faune* remain closely linked to the name and theatrical legend of Vaslav Nijinksy. In the case of *Faune*, we find a double Nijinksy connection, since the super-stellar dancer created the ballet's choreography as well as performed the title role. Of the two, *Spectre*, with choreography by Fokine and Nijinsky's legendary performance attached to its leading role, has proven the more tricky to revive in our time. The very nature—some would say "perfume"—of the leading male role of the rose/spirit as conceived by Fokine and interpreted by Nijinksy has proved elusively beyond the steps themselves, especially if approaching the work with expectations bred by the literature accumulated in the wake of Nijinsky's fabled, fabulous performances. If it weren't for this particularly impressive performance on video, I might not be focusing on the ballet within the limits of these pages. But with this extraordinary performance by the Paris Opera Ballet's Manuel Legris preserved on video, we can get closer to *Le Spectre de la Rose* than many other hopeful attempts have gotten in recent times.

Le Spectre de la Rose

The ballet's title, which translates as "The Spirit (or Ghost) of the Rose," comes from a poem by Théophile Gautier (who also wrote the libretto for *Giselle*). *Le Spectre de la Rose* was the title of a Gautier poem that opens with the lines: "*Je suis le spectre d'une rose/Que tu portais hier au bal*" (I am the spirit of a rose/That you wore yesterday to the ball). The ballet's inspiration came from a contemporary poet, Jean-Louis Vaudoyer, who quoted Gautier's line when writing about another Ballets Russes work (Fokine's *Carnaval*) in which a discarded rose played a part. This led him to imagine a separate ballet on a rose theme, for which the music of Carl Maria von Weber (1786–1826) would seem apt, since the composer was a favorite of Gautier's. After Vaudoyer aired his idea with Diaghilev's star stage designer Léon Bakst, the proposed libretto went to Diaghilev, who welcomed it with enthusiasm, especially as the new ballet could be pinned to the centennial of Gautier's birth.

The scheme was simple. A young woman returning to her home from her first ball, sinks into an easy chair, reminiscing about the the event after breathing the scent of a rose she was given. Into her rose-scented reverie bursts a roselike spirit who, after dancing around her, dances with her before disappearing again into the night. Bakst designed the Biedermeier boudoir and the woman's girlish ball gown, cap, and evening coat. He also designed the Rose's petal-covered tights and cap.

An aside about ballet design: Two of these ballets had costume and scenic design by Bakst. With the *World of Art* journal in Diaghilev's past, the plastic arts and its leading artists played a most important role in Ballets Russes productions. Diaghilev based his ballet theater on the well-orchestrated collaboration of musical, decorative, and choreographic creators. Each of the three ballets covered in this section tends, without fail, to return to our stages today as entities that include reproducing the original design as well as original choreography and original music.

I haven't taken time to dwell especially on the design elements of our previous ballet examples because, unlike their choreographic and musical elements, the "visual art" ingredients tend to vary a lot more. A "new production" of a popular ballet today tends to mean a new visual surround—that is, costuming and scenery, while the music and choreographic features remain as close to the original as possible. A new production of Fokine's *Spectre* or Nijinsky's *Faune* or of Nijinska's *Noces* would merely mean a rebuilding and painting of the original designs and refashioning of the originally intended costumes planned for the ballets' world premieres. This is not true to the same degree for any other ballet we've covered so far.

Fokine's memoirs recount how swiftly he concocted his choreographic variations on waltzing, first for the Rose's solo soaring and bounding solo and then for the duet between the half-awake woman and her phantom rose partner. Nijinsky's sister noted that the steps themselves were nothing much and quite banal, and that her brother's inspired intuition for getting to the essence of dance and characterization made them into the much-admired theatrical moments they became. In the end, the Rose disappears into the night and the woman is left with vivid memories of her dream.

The musical introduction we hear (in Hector Berlioz's orchestration of Weber's piano piece, "L'Invitation à la Valse") sounds meditative and melancholy as the resonant voice of a cello. A sweet, smiling woman enters in belted evening coat, ribboned cap. In her almost hypnotic circuit of her room, she removes her coat and keeps staring off into space. (Our video is especially well identifed onscreen and in notes so I won't pause over names.) During the introduction's protracted conclusion, the "Young Girl," as Fokine's program would call her, slips onto her easy chair as she caresses, then drops the rose she had tucked into her bodice. In a brightened and almost boisterous musical surge, a dancer appears on the room's windowsill and, after pausing in fifth position on demi-pointe while curling his arms overhead, equal parts floral tendrils and floral perfume essences, he alights into the room. One arabesque-line sissone brings him to kneel on the floor in a port de bras–embellished lunge. A rebounding grand jeté and a sailing grand assemblé put him into the air again and again.

The waltz's sweetly galloping tone sends the Rose/Spirit circuiting in pliant sauté arabesque moves, effacé positions alternating with croisé linked by clean and soft chassé steps. When the flute surfaces like a chirping bird, the rose presses on into a series of en dedans turns—in arabesque position, then attitude and finally passé position. Chaîné turns, another grand assemblé and a wheeling around into tour-jeté brings him back for more of the same. Further repeats get accented with variations. Tour-jetés get a grace note of batterie before opening, for example. Eventually, the waltz's hesitant mode gets more pronounced and the Rose stands behind the chair hovering over its sleeping occupant (as the sylphide hovered over the sleeping James).

All through his rebounding and curling flight of the room, the rose winds his arms in port de bras best described as art nouveau in character. Now, in a stationary pose, his arms become the focus of his dancing. Undulating, twining, and pulsing, they act to tease and call the young girl with their perfume. Initially these port de bras lushly proclaim the rose's own intoxicating beauty and eventually they work with caressing attention to become the sleeping beauty's escort and partner. Arising as if in a trance, she "floats" through skimming pas de bourée suivi, mirroring in her upper body the moves the Rose shadows behind her.

Making no clear recognition of the Rose's existence, she responds dreamily to his presence. Even in some of ballet's more traditional and usual supported adagio moves—leaning in arabesque-penchée balance on his outstretched arm, for example—she remains focused as if alone in her reverie. The Rose continues to attend and elude her. When she stands, gazing upward, he kneels adoringly at her feet. Alternately and presently when she kneels lost in dreamlike thought, he towers over her, poised on demi-pointe with his arms rising in undulations like heat waves.

When she sinks back to her chair once more, the music blazes forth with new energy and the Rose takes to the air once more with renewed strength. Alert cabrioles to the back and sailing, open tour-jetés take him to fresh, ecstatic heights. Cabrioles to the front and double assemblés take the excitement of musical dance energy higher still. Another of the Rose's arm-undulating appearances behind the sleeping girl's chair acts to awaken her. As James is in *La Sylphide*, the slumbering mortal is startled awake, elated by unknown forces. She dances through her excited state with runs on pointe, soutenu turns bouyantly spiraled by demi-plié accents, and a series of floating arabesque-piqué. After seeming to reach side-to-side with gestures that appear to catch the perfumes in the air, the ballerina/girl gets supported and shadowed by the danseur/rose. He expertly guides as her gently galloping partner through a chassé-sauté-arabesque sequence that builds to her own delicate jumps (chassé-tour) and to being suspended at the top of arabesque-sauté lifts.

All this climaxes when, out of separate turns, the rose stops in an adoring, kneeling pose and the girl comes to a halt, fixed upon the presence of her partner. As she excitedly chases toward him on her pointes, he backs away, enticingly eluding her through back-traveling arabesque-sauté and tour-jeté moves. A briefly partnered encounter, where they dance together and he dances with extra excitement (sissone-battu and entrechats-six) for the girl, before she falls once more into her chair and the Rose throws himself adoringly at her feet. A final reprise of his ecstatic jump sequence leads the Rose to hover over the sleeping figure in her chair one last time. The Rose rises in arabesque-effacé while bringing his arm over as if to bless the dreaming girl with one blown kiss. After completing his capstone caress and closing in his penultimate arabesque, the Rose swerves toward a window. In a buoyant run and an all-out grand jeté (or in Legris's particular case, a grand jeté pas de chat), he flies through the open casement and out of sight.

Ever since Nijinsky's Rose first flew into the night, the *Spectre* leap has become wildly famous. Or, preposterous, as exaggeration has piled upon exaggeration over the years, dooming to certain disappointment all attempts after Nijinsky's. Sober memoirs, notably Fokine's own, have attempted to bring the human feat with superhuman expectations back to earth. Factors suitable to achieving Fokine's intended effect include a humanly scaled setting on an intimately scaled stage. On the third program of the *Magic of the Dance* series, you will find a performance of *Spectre* with Mikhail Baryshnikov and Margot Fonteyn recorded on the stage in Monte Carlo where the ballet had its premiere.

As you'll likely experience with the "Rose Adagio" of *Sleeping Beauty*, you will not have an easy time hearing the music for the denouement of *Spectre*. A repeat of the ballet's contemplative opening moments, meant to accompany the awakening of the girl from her ecstatic dream, can be difficult to hear under the prolonged applause for the exit of the rose/spirit. Usually by the time the applauding audience wakes up to pay attention to the dreaming young woman and she arises to pick up the rose she dropped, the ballet has come to its ending. Intrusive though such heedless demonstrations of appreciation can be, in this case, the applause can seem like an external echo of the internal stirrings experienced by the young woman.

Pause
L'Après-midi d'un Faune

A year after he starred in *Spectre*, Nijinsky choreographed his first ballet. It was called *L'Après-midi d'un Faune* and starred the choreographer himself in the leading role. Its inspiration came from Claude Debussy's *Prélude à l'après-midi d'un faune* (1894). Debussy's impressionistic tone poem had taken its inspiration from "L'Après-midi d'un faune," an 1876 poem by Stéphane Mallarmé, a forebear of the literary Symbolist movement. After playing a key role in several of Fokine's post-Petipa "new ballets" Nijinsky with his younger sister, Bronislava, had begun experimenting on a post-Fokine, newer "new ballet" language. The visual inspiration for *Faune* came from the flattened, hieratic images found in Greek vase painting and bas-reliefs.

Faune takes place on a shallow strip of stage, a little deeper than the area in front of the curtain known in theater lingo as "one," because it represents the amount of space demarcated by the stage's first (or front-most) wing space. In some traditions, vaudeville for example, musical or dance numbers taking place in "one" were brief occurrences meant to occupy the audience's attention while a more elaborate scene change was taking place beyond this place, in wings two through six. Nijinsky's ballet occupied the space forward of the second wings.

As the video's notes explain, the aim of Debussy's tone poem was not to illustrate the events that occur in the verse, but rather to evoke their atmosphere. Nijinsky, by the way, hadn't read the poem behind his ballet's score. Instead, he took cues for his "choreographic tableau" from the music's indication of its happenings. The event depicted in the ballet is simple: A faun (a satyrlike countryside deity, half-human, half-animal) dreamily suns himself on his rock. He espies some nymphs who have come to bathe nearby. All but one take flight when the intriguing creature approaches, and finally even that one slips away, leaving behind, in her haste, one of her veils. The bereft faun then takes the talismanic remnant and proceeds to act upon its sensual associations by caressing its fabric and falling erotically onto it. The naturalism of the climactic, erotic gesture, which was said to represent the faun's first sexual experience, has a cloudy past. Nijinsky's premiere performance provoked controversy, with cries of obscenity and scandal. Historic sources presume, especially when the police were sent to observe the season's remaining performances, that the masturbatory naturalism of the premiere was subsequently toned down.

In any case, *Faune* has come down to us as much more than a spasm on a perfumed veil. In its abandonment of standard danse d'école vocabulary, it takes ballet beyond the "new ballet" expositions of Fokine and prepares the way for much of what would become known as modern dance. Even when straying from danse d'école formula, Fokine maintained something of ballet's physical tone. His warriors and maidens in "The Polovtsian Dances" of Borodin's opera *Prince Igor*, for example, point their toes and jump with ballet-plié elasticity, even if there are no pointe shoes or turned-out positions in evidence. Nijinsky's *Faune* took Fokine's ideas on Greek frieze postures into flatter, sharper, and more pronounced reductivism.

From a musical point of view, Nijinsky's ballet goes artfully against rather than coordinated to the motor energy of its score. Debussy's musical "afternoon" sounds lazy, warm, and voluptuous from the start. The languid air of a flute, a musical instrument aptly associated with the pipes of the faun, sensually floats through the air. The sight we find is one of a rich, almost ropy tapestry in which the faun on his rock appears to be part of camouflage patterning. Bakst's rich, flat landscape of autumnal earthen hues and the faun's brown and white markings intermingle like sunlight on foliage.

Obviously the choreographic text we're following is that of the Paris staging, but you might be interested to know that however standard this choreography has become, there are still alternative versions of Nijinsky's choreography. The most prominent of the variants comes from a 1989 restaging of the ballet that worked from heretofore undeciphered notations by Nijinsky himself. A 1991 volume of *Choreography and Dance* (vol. 1, part 3, Harwood Academic Publishers) documents the process of staging *Faune* according to Nijinsky's notation. The journal comes with a companion videocassette recording of Juilliard Dance Ensemble (student dancers) performing the ballet. Credit for staging the work goes to Jill Beck, and to dance notator-decoder Ann Hutchinson Guest for direction. Many details are at variance with the Paris version, though I suspect to the naked eye, once over, the basic outline agrees from one to the other.

We see our faun lift his pipe as if creating some of the sounds we hear. Likewise, we see him stretch and gesture the savoring of two bunches of grapes. However sinuous his postural tone, the faun moves through gestures and positions that emphasize flatness and bluntness: no pointed feet, no carefully gauged croisé or effacé positioning, no gracefully curved and separated fingers. Instead, the vocabulary includes heel-first flexed feet, hingelike shifts going from one profile view to the other, and flat hands with fused fingers held at back-of-hand or palm-front angles. The faun's man side made him thoughtfully alert; his animal aspect made him all thumbs with gestures.

The next time we hear the flute theme recur, a trio of nymphs enter in frieze profile linked by arms loosely entwined. Three others (two, and then one) come into view, eventually balancing and making the three, two, one appearances into symmetrical trios. (One of the second group of nymphs was played by Nijinska. Our Paris tape has her come on sixth and strike an almost Balinese pose; the Juilliard version has this loner enter fourth.)

The presence of a seventh, more prominent nymph whom Nijinsky wanted decidedly taller than her sisters, captures the faun's keen attention. (She enters last in our version, earlier in the Juilliard staging.) Standing central in the frieze lineup, she methodically begins to undo some of her garments in preparation for bathing. To the resonant reedy sounds of a clarinet, the faun stirs and starts to a standing position as the bathing nymph removes layers of her outer garments. Her attendant nymphs shuttle back and forth, arms regularly crooked and raised, almost like a dressing-room screen between the riveted faun and their mistress in her ceremonial ablutions. The quizzical, intruding presence of the intrigued faun causes the attending nymphs to flee, one trio with one of the mistress's discarded veil layers; the other with another.

Bakst's nymph costumes are well documented in his bold, handsome sketches. Each production that attempts to re-create his setting and costumes depends to some degree on interpretation. Where the all-important veils costuming the seventh nymph are concerned, we can find further variety. Our Paris tape shows a simple, stole-like veil that remains for the faun to carry away. The "Nijinsky notation" tape has him picking up an undone, pleated garment. Photographs from the original production show something more like the Paris veil, but the Juilliard researchers undoubtedly have good reasons behind their choice. In the end, I'd say, go to your Nijinsky *Faune* with however much knowledge you've got, but regard the results with open eyes of common theatrical sense. To my way of seeing, the smaller, more decorative veil makes a more workable talisman prop than a capelike muu-muu.

Reacting with bold, goatlike antics to the frightened nymph sextet as they carry away the divested garments, the faun shows more awe and gentleness toward the seventh nymph. When she finds herself alone, with the intruder, she attempts to retrieve her final veil and escape. But he becomes mesmerized by her, and she by him. His clumsiness now looks more vulnerable than arrogant. He stands on excited, high demi-pointe and thrusts his flattened-hand arms forward in a stiff attempt at embrace. The music surges in key with its previous levels. In a little "show-off" moment, the faun struts like a satyr playing peacock and scoots into the one jump of the ballet. (Though you may read that this leap represents stepping over the stream of the waterfall in the background, it's probably best seen as a jump for joy and show of strength.)

Back and forth the two go from this point. The faun stays riveted on her every move and makes more of his awkward, futile attempts at embracing her. She remains cool, angling herself in polite downcast deference or calmly, but regally keeping him at arm's length. After dropping her veil, the nymph finds her arm crooked inside the angle of the faun's similarly bent arm. As she has consistently held herself in her encounters with her admirer, the nymph stays in a low, canted bow, while the faun remains standing above her. In a trice, however, she takes advantage of her lowered position and slips out from his arm and exits.

The faun's melancholy stillness at her departure turns to wide-eyed interest when he realizes she has left her last veil. He picks it up with his stiff-fingered, flattened hands. With his head thrown back and a chuckling oboe as his voice, he appears to laugh at this triumph. Three sister nymphs appear to try to retrieve the veil, but after mocking the faun with sharp arm gestures, they leave empty-handed. More head-up-and-back ecstatic posturing follows, as does more mockery by way of brisk, hieratic arm gestures from other sister nymphs. Alone once more, with the languid flute sound returning, now pierced by tingle of delicate cymbals, the faun fixes dreamily on his trophy of fabric. He hypnotically ascends to the top of his rock. His flat, stiff hands hold and fondle the fine fabric as best they can. He finds reverie in its touch and after sensing its softness and its scents, he spreads it out on the rock and ceremoniously lowers himself onto its length. As muted horns and spare harp sounds float over those of the flute, the faun produces a pelvic spasm in his prone position as his arms stiffen at his sides. After dropping his head back for another of his unguarded animal "cries," the creature sinks his head onto the veiled rock as if the subsiding flute chord were his personal lullaby.

Intermission
Les Noces

Les Noces (or *Svadebka*, in its original Russian title) has been variously translated as "The Wedding" and "The Peasant Wedding." Its composer, Igor Stravinsky, thought "little wedding," as in small town/village little, would be most accurate, as long as "little" didn't signify small and darling. One free-form translation of the Russian word, actually the diminutive for wedding, suggests a meaning that says, "All the women weep and all the men get drunk."

Classified by Stravinsky as "Russian choreographic scenes," the score first came to the ballet stage in the choreography of Bronislava Nijinska. It was the first piece of independent choreography she did for Diaghilev's Ballets Russes. The impresario was reportedly happily certain of his faith in Nijinska when she informed him that however ethnographic and ritualistic the musical and vocal material was meant to be, she remained convinced the ballet's women should work on pointe. Her reasoning went that this danse d'école device would help elongate them in the manner of Byzantine mosaics of saints.

Nijinska's *Noces* is by no means the only version around nowadays. The score has gained popularity not only with subsequent ballet choreographers but also with some non-ballet ones. Our tape renders the Nijinska "text" reliably, since Nijinska's daughter Irina, a dancer turned ballet mistress, supervised its staging. (Except for the use of a French-language translation of the poetic, peasant Russian text, the Paris production carefully honors the aims of the 1923 original.) As with Diaghilev's careful choice of Bakst as a suitable visual-artist collaborator for his *Spectre* and *Faune* projects, the selection of Natalia Goncharova led to designs now inseparable from the ballet's musical and movement elements.

The text of Stravinsky's songs was mined from carefully gathered wedding verses of peasant Russia. The music accompanying his choral and solo singers came from an orchestra of percussion, dominated by four pianos. It was an idea of Diaghilev's to put the pianos plainly on stage as if part of the decor. In a similar vein, Goncharova's design scheme proceeded toward a reductive outcome, when the fanciful, colorful costumes she first proposed struck Nijinska as wrong for the music and the dance images she had in mind. The final decor included bare walls with a little window or two, a plank platform and a bedroom door. The costuming consisted of simple wool dresses over muslin blouses for the women, whose hair was bound in kerchiefs, and woolen knickers, muslin blouses, and stockings for the men, with shoes laced up to the knee. The costume palette stayed with chocolate browns and warm creams. Even the pointe shoes were dyed brown. The color scheme for the set was earthen gold, blue gray, and black.

The so-called practice clothes look that Balanchine took for his *Apollo* (and that you'll find in numerous "black-and-white" Balanchine ballets now in standard repertory), can trace precedents back to *Noces*. Goncharova's final costuming came about after suggestions that the ballet be dressed similarly to the clothes dancers wore when they were rehearsing. The result was a delicately Russianized version of the chemises, blouses, and head coverings worn by female dancers and the knickers, hose, and shirts favored by male dancers.

Noces inaugurated Nijinska's modernist ballet career and helped establish a branch of ballet that would be known as neoclassical. Fokine's proposed new ballet encouraged a kind of naturalism within ballet's formal confines, using pointe dancing sparingly, often for otherworldly or fairy-tale effect (see his *Firebird*). Nijinsky's experimentations, which he worked out to a great degree with Nijinska, strayed specifically into small corners of dancing where anti-ballet plastique prevailed (see his *Le Sacre du Printemps*). Nijinska, as we shall see here, saw fit to accommodate ballet's formalistic vocabulary without the "kid gloves" extraneous rationale and yet refreshed and expanded its expressive range.

Our video opens with nicely informative credits over a shot of the setting for the ballet's final scene. Stravinsky's musical form is a cantata, a concert-style (as opposed to stage-style) vocal work with instrumental accompaniment that is meant as a kind of unacted opera, or a short oratorio, which otherwise resembles a cantata. The ballet begins as soon as the music, a wailing outburst, for part 1, Scene 1 first tableau: "The Benediction of the Bride: At the Bride's House, The Tresses—sometimes called "The Consecration of the

Bride: The Braid." The stage is set simply by a bluish wall containing a single window.

The intended musical tone is one of lament. The singing proceeds to bemoan the parents' loss of a child and a daughter's loss of her youth and virginity. We see the bride's parents, waiting off to the side, and a grouping of maidens framing the bride. Nastasia, as the songs tell us the bride is called, hunkers prostrated amid the firmly postured surround of her sisters, who shape configurations at once angular and curled. In increments related to the music's pulse, the grouping animates and the bride rises up. The tresses and braiding mentioned in the lyrics come into Nijinska's choreography highly stylized. Brown cords, the length of separated "double-dutch" ropes, stream from beneath the bride's kerchief almost to the stage wings. Four women on each side of her take up the symbolic braids as if they were sailors taking up the mooring lines of a boat. In their places, they shift and stab their pointes in response to the music's instrumental and vocal accents, rather like a piano's hammers hitting the strings. With ramrod straight posture, the women also jackknife their arms in stiff and regular counterpoint to the raw musical textures. (The French-language lyrics somewhat sweeten and soften the brusquer sound of the intended Russian text.)

Nijinska's friezelike grouping holds as the lyrics alternately voice the thoughts of the bride's friends and the bride herself. Like a central figure in an icon, she remains framed by her female companions as if she were a saint flanked by angels, or by sister saints. At one moment they rest on one another as if their folded arms were an embroidery-stitched border. Even when she's a regular part of their groupings, the bride remains apart due to the contrasting light (cream in color) of the women in brown head scarves. After shifting through variously struck dense goupings, the women haul in the braids and, like nautical rope, pile the coils on the arms of the bride. After saluting her as she holds her weighty, lengthy braids, the women break into a lighter, quicker dance that mirrors a texture in the song of the female chorus. Freed from their "braiding" theme, the women jump a little, sometimes shaping their sautés on two feet, as if they were jumping rope, and shift their weight in flat-to-the-front pas de bourrée moves that make them look like bells with two working clappers. Throughout their movements, the women often hold their hands as blunted fists or as flat spatulas, never in minuet-graceful florets.

As the bride's mother and father move toward the bride, her attendants uncoil her braids and prepare for what the lyrics say about the removal of the red ribbon from her hair (the symbol of impending loss of virginity). After a repeat of their bell-clapper pas de bourrée moves, the young women move aside as the older man and woman hold their arms stiffly toward the bride. (Nijinska includes not even a stylized rendering of the ribbon's removal; indeed, no red fiber or fabric is evident anywhere.) Finally two of the "bride's maids" take up the braids once more, and ceremoniously arrange themselves so that their heads rest one on another, "braided" into a totemlike configuration. After the last two women drape the braid over the grouping and add their heads to the arrangement, the bride leans her elbows on the totem's top and stares out from her vantage point in hypnotic concentration. Just as the elders fix their concentration and body positions toward the bride, the scene should go black, though the video takes no time at all to effect a transition to second tableau, which Stravinsky wanted to flow directly out of the first.

We are now in Scene 2: "At the Bridegroom's House," for "The Benediction [or Consecration] of the Groom." The hut's wall for this scene is a yellowed expanse cut by two windows. Cinematic bleeds tell us of the dominant presence of the groom's mother and father, as well as the groom himself (Fetis is his name). Nijinska shows us a tableau where the groom is framed in semicircular fashion by twelve of his male friends while mother and father stand like sentinels on either side of the grouping. After ceremonial bowing of the center of attention to his attendants, and vice versa, we see a pumping step in place marked first by our groom and then by his friends. The chorus sings lustily of more hair and its preparation, specifically a combing and oiling of the young man's tresses. The pulsing leg work acts graphically to indicate that act.

When the combing stops, the friends ceremoniously salute the groom's head, bowing in a kind of bower around him. Further praise comes to him, as, in a moment reminiscent of the bride's maids' arranging themselves head upon head for the bride, the men lean successively on the groom's shoulders in halolike layers on his right and left. In a methodically predetermined shift, the group literally bends over backward to form what could be taken for a pyramid by a team of circus acrobats.

A lighter choral air sends the men into smaller units. One quartet moves like a four-sectioned caterpillar, while another grouping jumps similarly but more athletically than the bride's attendants did. Two of the non-dancing men ceremoniously lead the groom toward his father, as the others begin to group in a bent-forward lineup. The groom obediently bows to his father. Further and bolder echoes of the women's jumps animate a cluster of men, all of whom brandish crooked arms capped by fists in muscle-man attitudes. An abrupt musical stop cues the men to regroup as the groom approaches his mother at the other side of the stage. Behind him, like a wall of lamenting angels pressed one onto the other, the men move as a solid unit. After getting the gesture of his mother's blessing, during which the chorus sings of the actual religious ceremony, the score pulses with wilder agitation.

As the groom rests his head between his mother's hands—reminiscent of Apollo in his muses' hands—one group of six starts to jump athletically and punch the air as a climax to their leaping. Soon their jumps stir the other six, and as the male and female choruses weave their voices back and forth in "call and response" fashion, the two sextets of men act separately and in unison to contrast the hypnotic calm of the groom and his parents with a wild outburst of energy. During one of the score's most cacophonous passages, the twelve friends mirror the groom's steady gait and posture as he walks back toward his father with his arm bluntly curved up before him.

As the groom reaches his goal, and bows once more in his father's direction, the men again launch themselves into a jumping group. Like the eye of a hurricane, the groom paces center stage as chorus and percussion rain in the air and the twelve men ring his stock-still presence with bent-forward bounding paces punctuated by jackknifing jumps that have arm embellishments half like bodybuilders' posing accents and half like wings from quaking fowl. (This ring of bucking jumps has been reworked in dance history from time to time. Modern dance innovator Martha Graham's "bison" jumps were often done by women.)

Scene 3 follows directly, taking us to "The Departure of the Bride"—sometimes translated as "Seeing Off the Bride"—at "The House of the Bride." The video notes are uncharacteristically inaccurate, adding "The Wedding" to the scene's description. One of the more modernist dimensions to this ballet is the fact that of all the events shown in "The (Little/Peasant) Wedding," none addresses the ceremony itself.

The scene commences back in the home of the bride, precisely where we left off. The bride stares intensely from the top of the totem grouping of attendants, just as she did when we last saw her. The groom's mother and father and the man and woman who serve as the village's matchmakers begin the dance off to the side. Their traveling and curvetting jumps recall jumping moves from the previous scenes, but these display more freedom, eagerness, and unleashed energy. The groom's mother and the female matchmaker coil, rather like a coiling lariat, the bride's braids once more and pile the rings on her upper body. Her mother and father form a "London Bridge" arch, toward which the resigned, and hardly elated young woman advances in low-lunging, deliberate paces, her braids weighing about her like a yoke.

All the other guests follow her path, proceeding with more lively "kick up your heels" accents and energy. Soon the singing takes on a moaning character, and all the guests except the bride's parents stand and pace in place with halting impetus. When the choral moans die away, leaving only solo female voices, the men and women drop to the ground, prostrate, facing toward the wings as the bride and mother of the bride reach toward one another. Eventually the bride falls among the prostrated guests, leaving her mother to gesture imploringly through the scene's final lament. The soprano and mezzo-soprano soloists sing lyrics about the loss of a darling child. The tradition being expressed here by the bereft woman concerns that of keeping the mothers of a peasant wedding's bride and groom from attending the actual ceremony. After ceremoniously putting her fist to her forehead and crossing her chest as if beating her breast, the bride's mother opens her arms in an entreating gesture and finally folds her torso forward on the line: "My own sweet child . . ."

Part 2 of the ballet comes, as did the ensuing scenes of Part 1, directly out of the previous scene's closing moment. Video does all this smoothly, perhaps too fancily in this case. Stravinsky's "Attaca subita" (without a break, immediately) instruction and Nijinska's simple construction calling for the raising (or lowering) of elementary backdrops, quick blackouts and lights-up all mean to keep things moving at an unbroken, steady pace. The women's wail subsides with dramatic diminution.

Scene 4, "The Wedding Feast" in "The House of the Groom," is the only tableau of this part and lasts about as long as the three previous ones put together. (Stravinsky's score subtitles the scene as "The Red Table," but the ballet does not. In Goncharova's setting there is no table at all.) It's a two-level space: an upper, spare but intimate level shows the corner of a plain room, where we see a door and some benches; a lower level, the stage proper, is not so much a place as an open space for dancing. The scene begins with a start, as the chorus thunders and percussion pours forth a rain of sound. More than in any other section, the "Feast" lyrics amount to so many snatches of conversation, such as one might experience at a loud and lively gathering. (Stravinsky likened the fragmentation to that used by James Joyce, whose modernistic novel *Ulysses* was published in 1922, the same year the score of *Noces* was.)

Nijinska contrasts a scene of placid immobility with one of throbbing activity. The bride and groom and their respective parents sit stiffly on benches in the corner of the room on the set's upper level. The bride's female friends, sixteen strong, and the groom's male friends, also sixteen in number, dance in neat rows and forceful unison on the vaster, neutral dancing ground below. The two groups remain in separate units. The women pummel the stage with their pointes and neatly slash the air with their arms in various pas de bourrée bell-clapper moves and emboldened warriorlike arabesque-piqué pauses. The men pump through their "combing" steps and swing into steps that have the effect of jogging and marching in place.

In dramatic and dynamic contrast, the bridal couple stands and dances decorously on the ledge of its space while the thirty-two men and women on the "stage" below move in intermingling, shoulder-to-shoulder lines. These folk dance–style units recall the now famous "Pas des Petits Cygnes" we find in *Swan Lake*. (Swans, incidentally, figure in the lyrics of *Noces*. A white swan is associated with the bride; a gray goose with the groom.) Soon the guests are all amassed in one block, with the men and women dancing in unison and in canonic imitation of each other's steps.

When solo voices stand out from the chorus with words of the bride's mother to her new son-in-law, Nijinska gives the stage to a couple of soloists (Francoise Legree and Jean-Yves Lormeau) here as the "First Bride's Maid" and the "Best Man." With the rest of the ensemble backing them up as a kind of rough-hewn frieze, the young man and woman mirror each other's jumping steps and moments of repose. All the while, they hold their hands in soft fists and their arms in simple curves, frequently pausing to accent their heel-first flexed feet at strong angles. They move though the music as if it held imaginary hurdles and hoops for them to clear with their bolting jumps. Two "Bride's Maids" and two "Ushers" join these leaders by leaping over a hedgelike row of reclining women. (With their arms curved over their heads as they recline on the floor, the women seem to be restating in blunter, simpler fashion, the plastique of the shades that surround Solor and Nikiya in their Pas de Deux from the "Kingdom of the Shades" scene of *La Bayadère*.)

The full ensemble comes back into the dance after the women first arise and almost hypnotically take up the men's coming step. A full ensemble shift, with chains of men and women linked one behind the other, regroups the guests into two strong triangular wedges. The First Bride's Maid, positioned at her triangle's apex, becomes the first to move out. Her dance, to a female vocalist's sweet and gentle telling about a white swan's bathing, is made up of jeté steps to the right and to the left followed by little runs on pointe. The Bride's Maids follow in her footsteps, all with arms raised and curved bluntly overhead. The "Best Man" enters the dance when the music and singing gets darker in tone. He wiggles through shifting jumps and moves straight into plain pirouettes that get triggered by a heel-first position struck on apposite percussive notes.

rises to stand erect, their series of gestures seem to pull the ringing chimes out of thin air.

Two "levels" of action now transpire. The family group enacts a ritualistic opening of doors to the couple's bedroom. (The actual opening is done by the mothers. Unlike other productions, for some reason the Paris set includes no indication of a bed, which is usually painted on the expanse behind the closed doors.) At about the stroke of the sixth chime, the doors close and the upper level of the set disappears behind drawn curtains.

With equally ritualistic movement, the single unit of guests rearranges in a hieratic tableau made up of groupings seen earlier. Before the first thirteen of the fifteen chime strokes, some or all of the guests point a flat hand straight overhead and on the chime's sound pull it down in a fist, as if causing the ring. Along the way, rows of men and women kneel at the side and a totem of women rest their heads on one another's midstage. Finally, with the thirteenth chime, kneeling groups fold forward and a cluster of five men frames the Best Man. With only the sound of chimes left—the voices and pianos have gone silent—the Best Man sits on their shoulders and completes the picture. The men's central arrangement is marked by symmetrically upcurved arms that seem to salute and/or bless the onlooker, giving the stage picture the shape of a celestial gathering rendered by a Russian icon painter.

After Diaghilev, ballet was forever changed. Some of the innovations offered by his Ballets Russes led to the revitalization of ballet's continuing traditions in our century. Some of the explorations influenced the modern dance that would evolve on its own during the twentieth century. Fokine disparaged some of the trends he saw advanced by Nijinsky in his choreography. (When further tastes related to Nijinsky's seemingly "anti-ballet" elements became pronounced in the workings of European and American modern dance, the word *ugly* was used by its detractors, and then, contrarily, coopted by its promoters as a viable aesthetic option for their art form.) Wh[illegible] Nijinska remained loyal to her brother's work and would read-[illegible]nt out what she saw as weaknesses in Fokine's work and meth-[illegible] remained closely allied to the precepts of academic classical [illegible]actice.

Chapter 11

SUNNY AND FUNNY AND FINE

La Fille Mal Gardée

• • •

A Ballet in two Acts
Choreography by Frederick Ashton
Music by Ferdinand Hérold, orchestrated by John Lanchbery

What strikes us about *La Fille Mal Gardée*, and probably struck its eighteenth-century audiences, is that its action concerns contemporary characters and their human foibles and behavior. In place of familiar mythological Castor and Polluxes or hapless Jasons and wrathful Medeas, Jean Dauberval's rustic and comic ballet d'action offered the "girl and her beau next door," namely the mind-of-her-own Lise and the hard-to-resist Colas.

We are not, however, going to look at the *Fille* that made ballet history of the eighteenth century—that is, the one Dauberval created in 1789. Instead, we'll scrutinize *the Fille* of our century, the one Frederick Ashton choreographed nearly two hundred years later in 1960. I say "the" *Fille* not because Ashton's was the only one to appear during our century; it certainly was not. (Nijinska, to name but one other twentieth-century choreographer, brought a *Fille* to our stages in 1940.) But none of the other *Filles* in our era has gained the noteworthy reputation that Ashton's has. His deservedly popular version of *Fille* is neither reconstruction nor pastiche. And yet it is not unconnected to its rich historical lineage and can be respectfully considered an homage.

The stretch from 1789 to 1960 is quite a reach, and Ashton was much more inspired by his past than interested in reproducing it. This is an English creation, not a would-be French re-creation. Its two-act scheme draws upon all of Ashton's artistic influences—Russian (especially Nijinska's) and Italian ways with ballet dancing—and upon the information that he could obtain regarding his subject's nearly two-hundred-year-history. Ultimately, everything in this *Fille* passed though the prism of Ashton's own English way with ballet theater, his interest in narrative and in literary source material.

There is only one video of this production, and while it has primarily been available on laser disc, it has also been marketed on tape and been shown on cable television. Luckily, the lone recording turns out to be a very worthy effort. With regard to casting, the recorded *Fille* does not come directly from the heart of its source. A good, if slightly truncated, record with virtually the original cast was made in 1962, but is available only in special library archives. (See *La Fille Mal Gardée*, 1962, sound, black & white, 88 min., telecast on BBC-TV, London, produced by Margaret Dale.) Even if our video doesn't possess such an "original cast recording" dimension, it does come from a time and place directly connected with Ashton and his artistic hand. The choreographer was still alive when the video was made and he had approval of its casting, which includes dancers for whom he showed a personal preference. One original cast member, Leslie Edwards, appears in our video in his original mime role.

About this video:

> *La Fille Mal Gardée*, The Royal Ballet with Leslie Collier, Michael Coleman, Brian Shaw, and Garry Grant, 1981, 98 min., Color.
>
> This solidly English performance of French-born ballet should help you get your bearings for watching the same choreography performed by other troupes, English and otherwise.

Originally called *Le Ballet de la paille, ou Il n'y a qu'un pas du mal au bien (The Ballet of the Straw: or, It's Only a Short Step from*

Bad to Good), the ballet came to be known as *La Fille Mal Gardée* (The Ill-watched Daughter) for a London production in 1791. As we've seen, ballet master Dauberval's subject matter, while not wholly original to the dance stage, was not typical. The lives and loves of the common folk were unusual in a theatrical tradition stocked with classical mythological characters replete with gods and goddesses. *Fille* had a not untypical convoluted life getting beyond its beginnings in Bordeaux to arrive in our time and our world. The original 1789 uncredited music was a potpourri of some fifty musical numbers based on folk tunes. In 1828, for a production of the now-popular ballet, Ferdinand Hérold composed a more coherent score, based in part on some of the original tunes. A further layer of *Fille* history was added in 1864, when ballet master Paul Taglioni acquired a new score by Peter Ludwig Hertel for his version of Dauberval's ballet in Berlin.

Fille found a place in the hospitable environs of Russian ballet in 1885 with a staging by the ballet master team we know from the Petersburg *Swan Lake*, Petipa and Ivanov. At first called *Lisa and Colin* in Russia, *Fille* soon became known there as *Vain Precautions*, as it's been called there ever since. Ashton found enthusiastic support and inspiration for his planned remake of *Fille* by way of a direct link to the ballet's Russian heritage. Tamara Karsavina, a former Diaghilev ballerina who had grown up with *Vain Precautions* and whom Ashton revered and referred to as a "goddess of wisdom," blessed the project with reminiscences of Russian productions past, and offered the advice that the entire ballet "should charm with innocence and should not be interrupted by any other mood."

This is largely what Ashton labored to do—to create a ballet of unhurried grace, delicate wit, and simple sweetness. His inspiration became strengthened by his abiding passion for the tranquillity of the English countryside. His preparation included listening to Beethoven's *Pastoral Symphony*, subtitled "Recollections of Country Life" by that composer. Upon reflection, Ashton viewed the ballet he created as his "poor man's *Pastoral Symphony*."

While there has been, and will likely continue to be, an eagerness to put a sociopolitical spin on *Fille* as the ballet born of turbulent political times and fraught with class-level distinctions regarding monetary worth and so on, very little of such thinking pertains to the ballet's actual subject matter. The original libretto, so far as we can tell, gives no support to reading the ballet's plot in terms of a mercenary mother's preference for a well-off but backward nincompoop over a charming but penniless swain as a suitable husband for her daughter.

In any case, Ashton had a direct hand in shaping a libretto for his ballet and for overseeing the visual concept devised by his chosen scenic and costume designer, Osbert Lancaster. Likewise, he worked closely with conductor and composer John Lanchbery as he adapted and arranged the score from extant source materials. As our video's screen credits remind us, the libretto is "after Dauberval" and Hérold's music is "freely adapted." We'll see how much of *Fille*'s musical history was reclaimed by Lanchbery as we proceed through our look at the ballet, scene by scene. Essentially Lanchbery's arrangement takes as much as it can from eighteenth-and nineteenth-century sources, strengthening its cohesion by creating transitions and by shaping the theme tunes of the older music into leitmotifs. As we have seen, this musical device was used early on by Adam for his *Giselle* score, and, coming after that, Hertel's score shows some use for identifying its musical moods with specific characters.

The video offers a brief on-screen synopsis of Act 1. This tells us of sunrise on the farm of the widow Simone, and of her daughter Lise who is in love with a young farmer, Colas. However, widow Simone wants her daughter to marry Alain, the son of Thomas, a well-off vineyard owner. Lancaster's watercolorlike front-drop, based on popular French household prints, is framed by a painted red curtain decorated with words spelling out the ballet's title. Beyond its lettered swags we see a sun-filled landscape with trees, haystack, and cows. The introductory music includes imitations of ambient sounds and "voices" heard while contemplating a farmyard countryside.

Act 1, Scene 1: The Farmyard

Half-awake farm lads enter the house's courtyard and, after yawning and stretching, depart for the fields just as cock and hens stir in their chicken coop. A cock-a-doodle-doo cry rises from the lulling music as the rooster jumps down from his roost. Waking-up movements, feather plumpings, and frissons, and strutting soon animates the four white hens and the iridescent rooster. A rousing musical surge leads to the "Dance of the Cock and Hens." A male dancer plays the rooster; four female dancers, the hens. Though they are covered in feathered outfits from head to toe, the bigger man and the more delicately boned women fit their roles and characters to a perfect degree.

Little prancings in place, fly-away side-to-side sissone jumps, and wonderfully deft renversé pulsings in place all have the delightfully odd look of being at once like chickens and related to the daily formed by Enrico Cecchetti. Ashton had an equal interest in the comic turns of the music hall and in the carefully calibrated workings of the Cecchetti school of ballet which influenced his early career. (Lancaster's head-covering bird masks help dramatize the head-emphasis so distinctly part of Cecchetti's canon and Ashton's ways with ballet dancing.) A mini-chorus line enlivened by pecking heads, échappé steps, sauté-passé moves and arm/wing flapping pulsations in place cap the chicken's wake-up dance.

A much more serene musical mood comes with "Lise and the Ribbon," all based on music Hérold borrowed from Rossini's opera *The Barber of Seville*. Firstly, it cues an entrance for Lise, a dreamy young woman yawning, stretching her arms. Her actions take her to see if anyone's in the hayloft and to shoo away the chickens. Lest we forget what sort of performance we have before us with all of its trappings of "straight" theater, we note by the pointe shoes she wears that our "rustic girl" is a ballet heroine. Like the male dancer playing the rooster chicken, the women hen dancers wear soft ballet slippers. Therefore even in her miming and playacting mode, Lise shows us the touch of a ballerina.

A slight rumbling and rattling in the score sends Lise into hiding as the farmhouse shutters open and we see Madame Simone. Here, as has been traditional since the 1789 staging, when she was called Ragotte, Simone is a travesty role. In addition to being in line with longstanding theatrical traditions known to Dauberval, the male portrayal of Simone in Ashton's *Fille* comes out of a specifically English line of so-called pantomine dames. Ashton knew this theatrical tradition well, and was himself a terrific mimic, especially of grand-dame personages including such sacred cows as Queen Victoria. (Brian Shaw appears on our tape; Stanley Holden originally created the role for Ashton.)

Madame Simone doesn't yet realize that Lise is about, and, as the day brightens, the chickens make a pecking-order exit, single-file. Out of Simone's sight, Lise takes up a bowl of cream, and in her first dance *sur les pointes* so far, she weaves about in pas de bourrée couru. She stirs a wooden spoon as she goes, letting her liquid steps echo the smooth, creaming action of her domestic tasks. Next she finds a ribbon and, laying aside her bowl, plays and dances with it. This solo, with the ribbon acting as a little jump rope, stole, and garland, begins a ribbon-motif for the ballet.

A tradition for "dances with ribbons" (*pas de ruban*) dates at least as far back as Dauberval's time; a ribbon dance was probably in place in *Fille*'s first performance. Historically, these dances where fluidly manipulated linear props act to embellish and elaborate choreographic design share a kinship with the *pas de châle* that we saw worked into *La Sylphide* and *La Bayadère*. Ashton's use of pointe work and locomotion on pointe tell of his own late-twentieth-century era. The briskly sprung relevé moves and the clean, direct piqué steps "lift" the playfulness of Lise to a reverie plain. Left with her own thoughts and her pretty ribbon, the farmer's daughter rises to a higher level of existence. By now, we recognize this music as Lise's own. She ripples and circles her ribbon in the air to frame and extend her dance by means of fluid paths and lines. (Ancient Chinese ribbon dances and the "ribbon" routine of contemporary "rhythmic" gymnastics all resonate from Lise's solo with her ribbon.)

The miming of her personal amusement and delight as she plays and dances with her ribbon, delicately weaves her solo into the story unfolding. It winds down to its conclusion in a more pronounced mimetic mode, as the daydreaming young woman ties her ribbon in a bow on a ring attached to the barn. Her kissing its streamers and then striking a hand-to-heart posture tells us of her hopes that the ribbon remain a talisman and a signal to her beloved of her presence and devotion.

A more robust musical segment follows immediately upon Lise's exit. We have come to Colas, the entrance and introduction of Lise's swain. He enters accompanied by six of the farmhands we saw at sunrise. While Colas's companions wear pants that button below the knee and buckled, leather-soled and heeled pumps, our hero wears tights cut like *culottes* (French-aristocrat breeches), knee hose, and ballet slippers. In pantomimic mode the scene shows Colas being teased about his feelings for Lise, as he tries to catch a glimpse of her in the farmhouse windows. After dropping away from the group on its way to start the day's work, Colas, pitchfork in hand, resumes his search for Lise. After a look inside the barn, and on the recurrence of Lise's musical theme, Colas sees the tied ribbon. A flourish of music cues for him to stand in fifth position relevé as he points to and then approaches the ribbon left by Lise. As her musical theme continues to play, Colas ties Lise's ribbon in a bow on his pitchfork and blows kisses in its direction. Happily, he sashays upstage in flex-footed marching steps with his beribboned stick over his shoulder, his thumb proudly locked under his armpit.

We now come to his music, for "Colas's Solo," which is markedly more weighty than that of Lise's theme and that of the Lise-theme variant that underscored his finding of her ribbon. After flexing his feet in two emphatic relevé moves, somewhat like musclemen flexing their biceps, Colas marches downstage in his elated state, punctuating his pace with peacock-proud double tours en l'air and a quadruple pirouette. From this beginning he launches into a variety of direction-changing jumps interspersed and sometimes combined with various sorts of batterie.

Some of the jumps are small, low, and fast; others grand, proud, and emphatic. All of them weave through the music's soft thumps and sweet tone. A felicitous wrap-up in music finds Colas moving directly out of three successive low air turns into a continuous, finely convoluted grand pirouette. He spins into en dehors turns à la seconde, en attitude, and back to seconde again, before winding through a turn in passé position, all of which gets punctuated by a braced stance indicating a salute to the ribbon on his pitchfork. All through the dance the farming implement has been proudly brandished and worked into the shape, line, and character of his solo.

A reverie interlude lets Colas sample cream from the bowl left by Lise. This mood is rudely changed, when, after attempting to peer behind the house's shutters, he's set upon by Simone, who opens them, knocking Colas in the nose. "Colas and Simone" is full of musical bluster, as the young man tries to show politeness to the old woman, who wants to show him the door. In a flurry of musical energy she hurls things at him—vegetables, her mobcap, a plant. When Lise arrives after Simone has seemingly disappeared, the two sweethearts have a brief moment of smiling intimacy. But Simone reappears, wedging her way between Colas and Lise and momentarily directing the young man away.

Just as the annoyed and glowering mother tries to get her lackadaisical daughter to sweep up with a broom, a sextet of blue-smocked young men enter. Their happy-stepping dancing preludes the appearance of twelve young women for the score's "Villagers" number. The straw-hatted men kick up their heels elegantly in cabrioles (to the back) and in *pas ciseaux* (or scissorslike step) (to the front). As usual with Ashton, the dancer's torso regularly and lushly contrasts the work of the arms against that of the legs. Specifically, positions generally categorized as épaulé (shouldered) tend to appear in the process of Ashtonian dancing. (Note how the "boys" wheel an arm forward for their cabrioles and how they take it behind their backs when they work their legs to the front.) The sun-bonneted women weave through the men's ranks with similar "arming" torsos flourishing atop bright leg- and footwork. Like Lise, these women wear pointe shoes, which allow their part in this general dance to display the finesse of rising and standing and stepping onto toe tip.

Soon the danced entrée becomes a block of unison activity that pauses to become a block of mime. Now their arms don't decorate or celebrate their dancing, they make their case for how much they hope to be paid for their work with sickles in the grain fields. After showing how they'll mow with their tools the villagers hold up three fingers as a wage request. "Two" is suggested by Simone, but Lise agrees with the request for "three," and so three it is. The sickles are given out, and the music sends the ensemble into a joyful, jumping prelude to their scampering exit. The last two young men try to whisk Lise along with them, but Simone notices and holds her back.

A brief mime scene, "Simone and Lise," follows. Performed to music that's characterized by a kind of bluff hectoring tone, Simone tries to put Lise in her place and instructs her to do something useful—like churning butter. Colas slips in after Lise bumps into her mother as she tries to get away. (He goes to the hayloft, where Lise went during her first entrance.) The two lovers pause in a vignette of a duet behind Simone's back. He briefly pulls her toward him in a couple relevé-élancé arabesque moves before she twirls into his arms, posed momentarily in éffacé arabesque poised on pointe. In a climactic follow-up, Colas sweeps Lise into a high lift, where she's held in a kind of split penchée arabesque. To cap the stolen moment triumphantly, Colas sustains the lift with only one arm once Lise is poised in her radiantly open pose.

Meanwhile Simone comes out of the barn with the butter churn. The scene winds to a close after Madame pinches her own toes with the butter-maker in an impatient demonstration for the lackadaisical Lise. After her mother limps away to suitable diminishing music, the rascal daughter returns to her halfhearted churning, rising on and off pointe through échappé and relevé moves.

"Lise and Colas" begins as the young man bounds into a stag leap, holding his pitchfork over his head, while the young woman stares in a reverie into space. His intrusion on her daydream startles her into mechanical repeats of her churning moves. He tries to coax her away with him, but she gently demurs. Then, with an oboe delicately stating Lise's music, she recognizes her ribbon tied onto his pitchfork and, in a short mime scene, shows how touched she is by his acceptance of her ribbon. Isolated dance moves then prelude a lyrical and melancholy rapport that's marked by Lise's show of tender affection. To test his honorable intentions, she ties his willing hands with her ribbon. He teasingly tries to kiss her and she retreats to her bench and her churning activity. When she asks him to help with the chore, he displays his bound hands, which she obligingly unties.

His desire to help with butter-making soon passes to a desire for courting.

Lise slips away, rather like Giselle and her halfhearted attempts to scoot back into her cottage. Colas almost literally reels her back in by tossing a long ribbon in her direction. Once she takes hold of her end, he winds (by way of chaîné turns) in her direction, wrapping himself in his end of the ribbon (echoes of *La Bayadère* shades and Apollo's birth scene). After he unspools back to his place, she winds in his direction (chaîné turns on pointe) and gives him a peck on the cheek. Her unwinding back to her "side" leaves both lovers to hold their ends of the ribbon and dance like two cherubs holding up a drapery swag. Soon they team up, horse-harness bells jingle within the music, and Lise plays show pony to Colas's charioteer. Each prances; she like a filly, he like a dashing coachman (pas de chat, pas de cheval, and pas flêche all intermix). Eventually they change roles, he takes the ribbon-as-bit in his mouth and gallops about. He's more cart horse than show horse in his playfulness.

As the playful, perky mood subsides the two become enmeshed in an adagio in which the ribbon entwines them together. It proceeds intimately, but chastely, as Colas's supporting work comes from holding and working the ribbon that links them more than from making direct physical contact with Lise. As their adagio shimmers quietly through a passage of looping the ribbon around one another, it blossoms, half magically and half matter-of-factly into an X symbol: Having undone the artfully ringed ribbon from their torsos into a childlike cat's cradle, they stand linked by the sign of a kiss.

More direct kisses follow. Colas kisses the ribbon and presents it to Lise as their music continues to float in a dreamy atmosphere. He stretches the ribbon in a direct line between them and ripples it for her to skim along in pas de bourrée suivi steps that bring her into an arabesque-penchée embrace of her lover. After returning to her end of the ribbon, the two twirl it playfully and she spools back to him, ready to be lifted high overhead where she can twirl, poised in à la seconde extension around and around and around again. Lise melts into a serene effacé-arabesque penchée pose. Colas then slides her along the ground as if it were smooth as ice. One more twirl, wound in by the ribbon, puts the two in further kissing position that's interrupted by the appearance of Lise's girlfriends.

"Village Girls" presents a changed mood. Lise pretends to be engrossed once more in her butter-churning duties, as Colas steals away. After a little mimetic exchange between Lise and her friends about her innocent chores, the number becomes a happy girlish dance. The eight friends form an animated lineup led by Lise in a follow-the-leader set of piqué turns. As the music builds, the farmhouse daughter starts to weave and twirl amid her friends. The merrymaking is interrupted by the arrival of Simone, now changed into her dressier frock and determined to stop the frivolity and get Lise ready for some more formal activity. Her reluctance leads Simone to pick her headstrong daughter up and put the girl over her knee. As Madame attempts to spank her naughty offspring, the music heralds a new mood.

"Thomas and Alain" begins as a potbellied gentleman farmer struts on accompanied by farmhands toting moneybags and followed by an awkward, freckled fellow with a squashed hat and an umbrella. As Simone nervously rearranges Lise's petticoats to their "pre-spanking" position, she greets Thomas with a strained grin. The marchlike music shows a pompously stiff father and a backward son who appears to have learned to strut for this would-be formal occasion. Alain, the young man, peeps out from behind his father, half-shy and half-proud. Simone sends Lise to change as Thomas warily tries to show off his son, who moves in the strangest ways. At a key point, Alain pops out of sight, hiding behind his red umbrella, which has opened suddenly like some giant, leaning mushroom. Making light of the occurrence, the young man folds his umbrella and, after pawing the earth like a donkey, launches into his music's boisterous, building energy as if riding a braying donkey. Amid his carrying-on, Thomas's lackeys put into his hands the bags of money they've been holding, so he can present them as dowry for his son to lay claim on Simone's daughter.

When Lise returns, changed and refreshed, the hapless Alain attempts to show his amorous interest in her. His lack of finesse, to say the least, shows him shoving a bouquet at her and poking a pointed finger that turns inadvertently intimate when it lands on her bosom. A hurried settling down puts Lise, Simone, and Thomas on the bench as Alain performs a little dance of his own. The dominant accompanying instrument for his fatuous solo is the tuba. From a starchy, stiff torso, Alain's dancing combines dry, angular, and brusque leg work with rigidly rounded arms and coyly extended pointed fingers. Some of his steps and port de bras dumbly echo those of the field workers. The endings of his moves are consistently heavy-footed and sometimes seem to catch him by surprise. His forced turn-out is accompanied by lapses into pigeon-toed stance. He lands some of his air turns by finding his back facing his public.

Alain's almost reckless goose-stepping for his three-member "audience" gives Lise a start. Instead of continuing to giggle at his ineptitude, she stands apart, leery of him. We soon see why. The next time he clomps through his silly steps he stumbles, somersaults, and lands on the laps of Thomas and Simone.

Hunting horns introduce bucolic music: "Off to the Harvest." Two of Colas's male companions enter with one leading a pony-drawn cart. Lise and Simone, having put on their bonnets, get into the cart and, with Thomas walking gallantly alongside, depart to oversee the work being done in the fields. For Alain's part, he pretends in his own little world that his umbrella is a hobbyhorse and tags behind the party as if being borne by his own steed. Ashton's plan is for this to be the end of Act 1, scene 1, and the segue into scene 2. Some productions call the ensuing scene, Act 2, but the ballet is prearranged to use the scene-changing time behind a painted curtain for the occasion of "crossovers (passings from stage wing to the other directly opposite)."

Act 1, Scene 2: The Cornfield

As the music merrily continues in its traveling mode, we see an intermediate drop curtain that shows a verdant landscape framing a grand chateau on a distant hill. In brief, this segment tells of Simone's corn crop and of the harvesters' celebrations. First to cross over, from our right to our left, are the four hens and their rooster companion, strutting, pecking, and flapping as they go. Next comes

Thomas's cart, escorted by the wine grower and pulled by the pony. Simone expresses awe at the sight of the impressive house on the hill, and the party moves on. Alain trails at the rear, now scampering as if his brolly as bronco were bucking a bit and giving him a rougher ride. Before proceeding he retreats whence he came and reemerges as the willing "horse" to a wagon playfully arranged out of ribbons held by Lise's friends. With ribbons streaming from Alain's mouth like reins and others twirling in circles where a coach wagon's wheels would be, the eight women and one man exit as a pictorial unit.

Close on their heels comes Colas, now sporting a short dressy jacket and brandishing a bottle of wine in each hand. He parades happily through some jeté-passé steps and momentarily puts down his bottles and dances between the pair as if it were a small obstacle course for him to negotiate. Having zipped through a few beaten steps, he performs grand soubresaut and grand ciseaux steps in a sweet show-offish mode. Some proudly prepared and executed en dedans attitude turns cap his little display before he retrieves his bottles and proceeds (by way of brisé steps and sissone-ouvert moves) to the fields. His exit cues the raising of the drop curtain to reveal the harvesting field with twenty-four workers (twelve men and twelve women in alternating lines of six) carefully arranged in rows, swiping their sickles in neatly timed unison. Each holds a sheaf of grain (which looks more like wheat than corn, but never mind). The steps are unisex in unison, the women don't opt for pointe work, and the overall mode is one of mimetic musical gesture delicately demonstrating the action of cutting grain. After dancing alongside each one's bundle of stalks, arranged rather as if on some farmland chessboard, the young men and women clear back to make way for the entrance of Colas. This segment relives the "Pas des Moissoneurs" (Reapers' Dance) that was part of Hérold's original score.

"Colas" names the next number in Lanchbery's score, as the handsome local youth greets the harvesters with his bottles of wine. With his hands happily high in the air, he bounds about, first in plain grands jetés then in joyful grand jeté en tournant. Soon he has two flanks of the assembled workers jumping by his example, to his tune. He mimes that the working should now cease. Noon-hour chimes ring through Colas's excited music. Now with their sickles put aside, the men and women rally around Colas. After passing out the bottles of wine, Colas finds the eight "friends" of Lise spiraling around him as he gives each one his hand to support her in a little tour jeté. As each hands off to the next, the friends raise their free arm in a simple flourish that echoes the line of a sickle while displaying a kind of freedom from labor. Soon all hands are grouped around Colas, following en masse in his happy, jumping footsteps.

Just after the chicken and rooster quintet struts through the scene, the landowners arrive in their rustic chariot. After all due respects are paid by the harvesters to Madame Simone and her party, the "Picnic" scene unfolds. Its dominant event is another of ballet's inadvertent pas de trois. We've discussed the one in Taglioni's *La Sylphide* where the sylph interrupts a duet between James and Effie and only the torn James can "see" her. Then there was the wedding duet for Solor and Gamzatti, expanded to a trio by the phantom appearance of Nikiya, "seen" only by a distraught and guilt-ridden Solor. Here we have a clever Colas intruding deftly into a would-be duet between a bemused Lise and a duped Alain. Lanchbery's music for the trio is borrowed from Hérold. Specifically, Ashton's arranger based his composition on a pretty adagio originally intended for a divertissement composed especially for an extraneous suite of dances named in the score as "Pas de M. Albert," after the ballet master and dancer who performed them.

Ashton's dance is hardly extraneous. Its comic timing, with continually shifting emphasis so Colas can be Lise's partner in a dance where Alain thinks he's the partner, tells a good deal about the characters involved. Lise is almost innocently complicitous in dividing her responses to Alain's and Colas's attentions. Colas is a deft thinker, taking immediate and sweet advantage of Alain's distracted moments. While Alain is blissfully unaware of the ongoing moves that allow Colas to steal intimacies with Lise behind his back.

The mini comedy of errors begins as Simone and Thomas encourage their respective offspring to conduct themselves nicely through a little dance, while the elders themselves move aside for a coy little gambol of their own. The Alain-Lise duet begins with

Alain being so pleased by his proximity to Lise and being so careful with lending her dancing gallant support that he remains oblivious to all else. When Lise nudges Alain to be fawned over by her girlfriends, she gets swept up on Colas's shoulder while the duped little fellow gets tickled by the "helpful" friends. Dancing face to face with Lise fails to let him see Colas hiding behind her. A happy, twisting set of in-and-out-of-the-arches arm moves gives Colas a chance to slip under one arch and cuddle cheek to cheek with Lise as Alain thinks he's holding his fiancée securely by her hands. A deliciously delicate sequence, where Lise moves from demi-extension front through grand rond de jambe en l'air into arabesque-penchée, leads Alain to follow the soaring line of her arabesque leg with a complementary salute in the direction of its upward angle while Colas gets to hold hands with Lisa at the bottom penchée move.

After a successful back-and-forth playfulness, the sly young woman ducks out of her expected place by calling one of Colas's companions to replace her. Now Alain is startled to find himself embracing an "unamused" young man. Some melancholy horns begin the dance's final segment. Lise appears nowhere to be seen. The harvesters turn their heads side to side in negative answers to Alain's miming of "Have you seen Lise?" But soon a Rossinian acceleration inspires everyone to move into a happy whirlpool of a dance with Alain smiling at its center. Immediately, however, clouds pass through the music once more and Alain finds himself alone among sweetly paired couples. After unsuccessfully trying to insinuate himself into some of them, Alain forgets what he's missing and, as the music once more accelerates to a lightheaded frenzy, he's lost in the swirl of it all.

The giddy frenzy of the "Picnic" dance changes to a sweeter, more floating air for "Flute Dance," which follows as a male field hand mimes the playing of a flute solo. His piping finds him swaying and stepping from one side to the other as well as fluttering through repeated entrechats-quatre. In stages his "playing" draws the other harvesters into a dance around him, like ripples breaking the surface of still water. Initially, as the music maintains its lightness and delicacy, the women draw about him, twirling and opening out in steps on pointe. When the music gets more hearty, the men step in, jumping forthrightly and gallantly pairing up with the women. Soon they make an ensemble of couples and form lines and rings. With their flutist as leader, they link into a chain dance that spirals and snakes around the stage. A final ring wheels a boy-girl-boy-girl merry-go-round of successive grand jeté pas de chat leaps about the flute player.

A brief "Quarrel" comes next. Ashton requested this incidental scene to clear the stage for his main event, an undisturbed pas de deux for his lovers. So on comes an interloping Alain, who snatches the flute from the player's hand and tries to show off his own musical talents. Discordant notes abound from his inept attempts to provide the men and women with music for dancing. Their halfhearted willingness to dance to his tune turns as sour as the music, which thwarts any attempt at graceful dance movement. The tuba of Alain's farmyard solo blurts again in our ears. A Rossinian chase sequence scores a teasing game of "Who's got the flute?" as the men and women toss the instrument around so that Alain goes this way and the flute gets tossed the other. When the confused fellow finds himself being toyed with by the guys and being tickled by the gals, Thomas comes to his rescue and takes the boy away from the foolishness.

Now we come to the "Fanny Elssler Pas de Deux." The pas is so called because its music comes from a duet originally interpolated into the ballet for the renowned Elssler nearly ten years after the composition of Hérold's score. Musicologists would be justified describing the music for the pas de deux as cobbled together from various tunes in Gaetano Donizetti's opera *L'Elisir d'Amore*; a Paris Opera librarian and copyist named Leborne did the work. Still, the pastiche serves rather like the peasant pas de deux does in *Giselle*; it stands out plainly as a showcase for two ballet dancer/characters. Accordingly, the number is structured as introduction, ballerina's solo, adagio, danseur's solo, and coda.

With the picnickers calmly seated at the sides of the stage and in the background, Colas and Lise jaunt on for an introductory dance. Back and forth they go at first, at one point seeming to work their heads one to the other in a braiding move that gently echoes the pecking moves of the chickens. Eventually they prance side by side lifting their knees alternately in unison. In a speeded-up mode, Colas moves with feet-front *emboîté* ("boxed," literally) steps as Lise matches the energy and "fizz" of his steps by slightly sharp runs on pointe. When they separate as Colas draws back, gently sailing into an assemblé-landed pose saluting his partner, a flute passage cues Lise's solo moment in this introduction.

She literally leaps at the challenge, jumping (grand jeté-croisé) into a series of sweeping-leg turns and stances on pointe that are variously fixed with dead-still pauses that hold the pose delicately but dramatically. Most of these picture-still poses appear suddenly, often just as the move leading up to it changes direction of body-part emphasis. A less piquant set of moves follows. Lise approaches Colas on a diagonal path by way of melting arabesque-penchée and kneeling poses that sweep around as her arms draw her torso in a richly torsioned rotation. Additionally an arabesque-piqué sequence follows with feathery flourishes. After some spritely twisty springs to fifth position, the dance heats up once more. Sauté-passé moves lead to little cabrioles front and then Lise jumping (grand jeté pas de chat). And, after more "dead still" pauses, Lise peppers the stage with hops on her pointes interspersed with mini-sets of fouetté turns, the last of which climaxes in a sequence of eight fouettés, with the working leg alternately changing for the final five turns. She ends in a smilingly demure fourth position lunge, with one hand on her shoulder and one reaching out, up, and away.

A gracious but not grandly formal bow from Lise makes way for the adagio of the pas. Lise's girlfriends create a semicircular grouping where eight pink ribbons radiate from its center. The effect is partly that of a fan and part that of Venus on Botticelli's half-shell. As soon as the pose is struck and the harp begins the musical segment, Colas and Lise arc sweetly toward each other while slipping in between the arrayed ribbons. Presently, both lovers have four ribbon ends in a hand. Lise takes an attitude balance on pointe with one hand in Colas's and the other, with its ribbons, above her head.

A grand promenade results, with the lovers as central points for half-wheel formations—the ribbons are spokes and the girlfriends the wheel's frame. When lovers separate, we see two smaller fan shapes. When each kneels, the fan arrangement sinks gently to the ground. The his-and-her rays rearrange twice more until Lise stands central to the grouping and all the ribbons emanate from her hand. And, as she executes développé-grand rond de jambe to attitude balance on pointe, Colas promenades and steadies her to a croisé pose—imagine Aurora's effacé attitude balances taking their calm stillness from rays beaming from the hand she holds over her head.

Once Colas leaves his lover in singular, arrested balance, the women begin to run lightly in a circle like so many pretty carousel horses. The ribbons they hold act like the carousel's canopy and help secure Lise as she rotates like the centerpiece sculpture of a carousel. Colas runs teasingly through the revolving ring twice, the second time he stays to lift Lise as she releases the ribbons with a fluttering gesture that seems to direct them into the women's hands.

As Colas sets down Lise for an adagio moment all their own, the women arrange the ribbons like a latticed backdrop, made in essence out of the X's we associate with the marks for kisses. When Lise arcs round and round her lover in moves spiraled by the work of his partnering, the women regroup as flanking quartets connected by triangular ribboned lines. A screen of diamond shapes follows and segues into separate diagonal wings of women holding out the ribbons like benign longbows strung with invisible arrows. With the adagio's diminuendo, Lise sits softly on Colas's knee, and as each arcs an arm to frame the other's beloved face, the adagio ends on the denouement of the ribbons released like so many plucked heart/harp strings. (The camera in our video sadly misses the moment, pulling away from the tableau and moving in for a close-up at the very moment the ribbons get released.)

With gracious bows toward the audience woven into courtesies to each other, Lise and Colas separate. She moves to the side; he to a position for starting his solo. All the steps worked into his elated display are based on "classroom" steps identified with the pedagogy of Cecchetti. (As you watch Coleman dance his solo, it is informative to recall that the dancer and teacher whose teachings inspired Ashton's steps for Colas was the originator, and likely co-choreographer, of the "Blue Bird" role in *The Sleeping Beauty*.) He starts off with a series of Cecchetti-styled grand jeté en tournant moves sweetly punctuated by relevé-posed, attitude-croisé balances with a hand lightly placed on each shoulder. The double tours en l'air that cap this sequence has a similarly sweet punctuation. After seemingly finishing "to the knee," the move's momentum continues and Colas pops back to a standing position, with another variation on a hand-to-shoulder port de bras. Somehow the whole of this climactic pause has the "feel" of a sprung arrow and its emptied bow. More grand jeté and cabriole moves, as well as jumped turns à la seconde keep Colas confidently in the air. A multiple pirouette spools into the start of another jumping sequence, this one a manège of coupé jeté turns and further jumped tours à la seconde. Finally, he bounds through another double tours en l'air that folds once more into a kneeling pose that arises, at the last second, into a tendu-braced standing pose, finished by arms postured between gracious salute and personal celebration.

The coda ensues as the music heats up and accelerates. Lise takes off into a sequence of steps and moves that sometimes mirror those of Colas: grand jeté, coupé-jeté, sauté-grand battement en cloche. In Lise's case, however, the jumps are more darting, the turns more delicate, and the swinging, leggy moves more quicksilver. Interestingly, except for a brief, momentum-gathering length of chaîné turns, which may be an embellishment of Collier's own (the recorded Nerina performance does not include them), the solo is worked exclusively without full-pointe positions. Just before these spiraling chaînés, you might be interested to note true *jeté en tournant* steps, which as you can see are quite different from the grand jeté en tournant sometimes misidentified as "jeté en tournant."

A happy, grand jeté pas de chat, which lands, in such a way to direct Lise's attention to the other side of the "field," cues Colas's next entrance. He flies on from the wings, sailing through a path of tour-jetés into a set of quickly pumped single pirouettes, multiple pirouettes, a multiple fouetté turn, tours en l'air, and then more of the same. A trilling musical passage follows for Lise, traveling on a diagonal at once demonic and demure. As Collier delicately holds her skirt out to the side as if she were preparing to curtsy (Nerina apparently only held her hands over her head), she repeatedly fires her pointes in rapid walking steps that work her toes like a sowing/sewing machine. As this sharp yet soft effect continues, the picnickers snap their fingers in encouraging accompaniment. (Ashton lore tells us the choreographer took inspiration for this *tacqueté* effect from seeing Soviet Georgian *male* dancers moving forcefully on their toes in their traditional, soft leather boots.)

After lifting Lise in one more joyous, split-leg position high over his head, the couple twirls through matching chassé-tours in and out of flourished postures and then link hands—like Blue Bird and Florine—and beetle down a diagonal where their legs scissor smartly against the turning of their heads. The final stroke of the lovers' pas is a proud and brazen "chair" lift. "Sitting" on the palm of Colas's hand, raised at arm's length over his head, Lise outstretches her arms above her in a carefree manner.

In spite of her friends' desire to hide Lise from view, her mother does see her and proceeds to reprimand her for dallying with Colas (in a brief transition called "Simone"). A convenient distraction immediately intervenes. After being briefly coaxed to dance herself—the mime is the sign for "dance"—Simone more or less leaps at the chance. As soon as she is fitted with her "sabots" or wooden shoes (clogs), she hies to the "Clog Dance."

Though the clog shoe has a definite, and apt, French connection, the dance in Ashton's ballet has clear English roots. Stanley Holden, as Ashton's original Simone, brought to the choreographer a knowledge of Lancashire clogging (an English dance form that was one precursor of American tap dancing). Lanchbery's music for Madame's "turn" is his most direct borrowing from the short-lived Hertel score from 1864 for Paul Taglioni's *Fille*. With a stomping of her clog-shod foot and swish of her skirt, she's off and clogging. After some heel-toe scuffing and bell-clapper kicking, Simone is in the thick of her dance, all the while genteelly holding her skirt out to each side. Soon she's joined by four of Lise's girlfriends, who manage to rise and pick around on the "pointes" of their clogs. Simone's attempt to match this is crude to say the least. Open-close, heel-toe fanning and gliding steps add further variety. Simone's sliding variant turns into a braked skidding move. After leading the line of friends as a kind of little train, Madame launches into a "hoofing" segment that soon finds her on weak ankles and fatigued feet. After letting her clogging do the talking (she mimes listening to the friends' "reply" with their tapping toes), Simone fits herself in the middle of their lineup. Their finale finds Madame duly supported by two friends on each side as she hoists herself off the ground to perch at the center of their grouping.

A "Maypole Dance" follows. The men bring on a barrel stuck with a tall pole, streaming with ribbons. Also English in tradition, this one-time fertility rite involves the weaving and unweaving of ribbons around a pole as the individuals circle the pole holding the ribbons' ends. The "traveling" music that accompanies Ashton's maypole dance comes from Hérold's originally intended "Divertissement" pas, a folk tune that Lanchbery recycled for the beribboned pole number. After ringing the pole and dancing round and round each other for starters, the men and women eventually crisscross one another as the one group travels clockwise and the other counterclockwise. In the process they prettily and precisely weave their ribbons into a colorful braid around the pole. Then, just as clearly, their dancing unweaves the pattern and takes the pole back to its starting point. (For a pale and almost thoughtless rendering of this same ritual, see the *Swan Lake* staged for American Ballet Theatre and recorded on video. Oddly, this other maypole dance, which amounts to very little theatrically, was arranged by none other than Ashton's first Colas, David Blair.)

The slight uneasiness rumbling in the music as the maypole dance loses itself in circles becomes prominent just as the pole has been unwound of its ribbons. Lightning flashes in the background and thunder bellows. Themes borrowed from Rossini's *La Cenerentola* (Cinderella) give the storm its "music." Ashton stages it with leanings this way and that as if the men, women, and maypole were all being buffeted by the winds. Alain's bright red umbrella makes a nice try at protecting him and his mother, but all it really does is help dramatically show the forceful way the winds are blowing.

After everyone gets momentarily blown out of sight, there comes a respite in the hurly-burly. The music sweetens and turns calm and Lise and Colas are found momentarily alone together. Lise mimes that the rain has stopped and then draws an arc tracing a rainbow. She reminds Colas, who seems eager to embrace her, that they should give a prayer of thanks in light of the heavenly symbol. He agrees and sidles up to snuggle near her. No sooner is their prayer done than the storm resumes. As if blown back into the field by the winds, the field workers go back and forth in neat groupings complete with grand jeté and saut de basque jumps and ciseau kicks. As the workers disappear once more, we see Thomas and Simone collide, and Lise and Colas reappear, along with Alain. In the confusion of racing around for cover, Alain gets taken up into the air, riding his turned-inside-out umbrella as flying steed. (The flying effect for Alain on wires goes back at least as far as the early nineteenth century.)

Act 2: Interior of the Farm

Lanchbery's overture briefly restates the tunes he borrowed from Hérold and worked as little motifs throughout the first act. After being played before the title-inscribed front curtain, the musical introduction segues into a scene called "Lise and Simone."

Now we find ourselves in the large room of Simone's farmhouse. To slightly bumbling music, mother and daughter come in after being rained on. Their heads balance sheaves of grain, which they had hoped would provide some protection from the elements. The scene is all pantomime. Lise puts some bits of clothing near the fireplace to dry and Simone procures some neck scarves to keep them warm. After deciding that the pink one suits her better and that Lise should wear the yellow one, Madame indicates it's time for some spinning. First, however, she confidently locks her door and puts away the key. Lise indicates that she's chilly, so she and her mother exchange gentle massaging, warming-up gestures. In the process, Lise tries to filch the key. Madame notices and reacts with a firm slap on Lise's wrist. Now it's spinning time.

Like the preceeding action, "Spinning" and its ensuing dance scene come essentially from the 1789 score. To the music's charming illustration of delicate busywork, Simone pumps her spinning wheel and pulls the thread coming off the distaff held by Lise. Soon her daughter is dancing, cued by the flute piping into the musical mix. First, it's a padding around in place, with Lise variously rising to and descending off pointe. When she makes a circuit of the spinning wheel by way of other pointe steps, she inadvertently catches and winds the yarn about her mother's neck. She ultimately comes back to where she started and in a series of little jetés and relevé-petit battement moves, she finds that her soothing music and her soft dancing has sent her mother off into a little nap. Lise unsuccessfully tries to take advantage of the snooze and retrieve the key from Simone's pocket, but she manages only to prod the sleeper to start snoring. We hear Simone's funny breathing in the music, a fine cranking effect similar to that we heard more forthrightly for nutcracking in *The Nutcracker*. All this comes to a thumping end when Lise awakens her mother as she tries to stop her snoring.

A startled Simone looks puzzled as Lise pretends she has just caught a pesky fly. After miming her swatting and squashing of the troublesome insect, Lise follows Simone to a chest of drawers from which her mother retrieves a tambourine. We have come to "Tambourine Dance," the last of this segment's direct quotes from the ballet's original score. With Simone seated as accompanist, Lise stands apart and dances a folkish solo. Lanchbery's music is mostly for reeds (we hear an oboe and a bassoon), with Simone's actual tambourine taps adding their own tinkle. Lise starts out in place, gradually working from accents à terre to moves that open out with extensions and steps en l'air. She even includes some turn-in/turnout steps reminiscent of Simone's "clogging" steps.

As Simone's tambourine playing gets bolder so does Lise's dancing. Bolder, faster, and more detailed. Lise holds out her skirt in a gesture of prettiness and pride. She even takes a stab at thumping Simone's tambourine herself. Eventually the music's texture lightens and its volume diminishes, as does Lise's dancing.

A woozy, feather-light interlude follows. Lise looks longingly at the locked door, wondering about her beloved Colas and life outside. No sooner has she climbed the stairs to look out the door's window, when the door's top half swing open to reveal the face of her swain. He fixes himself so that the door frames his upper body. Lise runs to him as if on air, and he picks her up in his arms. From our angle, and to the interlude's lullabylike quality, we see Lise swing dreamily, like a pendulum on a heavenly clock. There is precedent for this arrangement in *Fille*, as it came out of Russia, partly through Nijinska, but Ashton elaborates what was a simple appearance of Colas in the frame of the half-door into a full configuration for the couple as they perform a brief supported adagio.

When Colas lowers his belle to the floor, he begins to partner Lise inside her room from his odd position outside it. Interweaving his support for her various pointe moves made up of développé-rond de jambe to arabesque with tender kisses to her hands, Colas partners from on high. The "stolen" adagio builds to a set of finger turns, one variation of which makes us think of Lise being supported en promenade by her ribboned "carousel." Just as the lovers again embrace and find time for another kiss, the mood is abruptly shattered.

Simone wakes with a start rudely announced in the music. This scares Lise and sets her off in a dopey reprise of her dance to Simone's tambourine. After staring quizzically at her daughter's automatonlike behavior, Simone goes with the flow and eagerly dances around Lise. A rumbling in the score's percussion signals knocking at the door, and after a hurried tidying-up, Simone opens the door to admit the male field workers bearing their sheaves of grain.

Now comes the "Harvesters" scene. After they pile up their bundled crop, the men go to Simone, from whom they receive their almost grudging payment. In an act of celebration, the young men surround the fruits of their labors and begin a ring dance. This takes the form of a "Stick Dance," which has roots in English folk dancing. Some of Ashton's choreography takes specific inspiration from the ensemble aspects of England's morris dancing, which is brightly paced work for groups of men. The sticks, something like children's rhythm sticks, are used as percussive musical instruments and as relay-race batons to link their line and ring formations as they prance brightly around the room. Amid all his folkloric touches Ashton reveals plain ballet ones, such as double tours en l'air.

In a wrap-up mood, the twelve young men configure a kind of parade float with their bodies, limbs, and sticks. They then triumphantly carry Lise atop their "structure" like a beauty queen in a parade. She has hopes of slipping out of the house in this moment of giddy playfulness, and Simone briefly gets caught up, too, happily saluting her celebrated daughter. But, not for long. Presently she sends the men on their would-be clever way and reconfines Lise to the house. Once Simone realizes that she has an appointment (the clock shows six, which she registers in a six-finger mimetic sign as the music sounds like the mechanisms of a clock), she sets off leaving the unhappy Lise locked in the house.

Once the "Harvester" music diminishes, we're into a scene the score calls, " 'When I'm Married.' " Its music is largely based on a Rossini aria "Bell'alme generose." After pouting and feeling sorry for herself, Lise gets distracted by her daydreams. As the lyrical strains of a flute lightly float in the air, she begins imagining her future. The pantomimic text of her mental images comes directly from the ballet's Russian past as given to Ashton by Karsavina. We see Lise ponder her wedding day, complete with luxurious dress, delicate veil, sweet-scented flowers, and loving bridegroom. Then we follow her to imagine herself bearing a child, finally having three to raise. As a mama, she plays how she'll help with lessons and how she'll react, with a firm, spanking hand, when lessons get careless; then, how she'll show compassion when another little one needs consoling.

In the midst of her demonstrating tender loving care for her littlest one, Lise moves near the piled-up sheaves as if to place her babe on their soft surface. However, just as she gestures the bedding-down of her treasured child, the pile of bundles erupts at the center. Popping out as if from a specially baked cake, Colas reveals himself to a somewhat frightened Lise. Unbeknowst to her (and to us as well), Lise's beau was in hiding all the while the grain had been sitting in the house. Lise's fright shortly turns to embarrassment and then anger at being watched in her daydreaming. (A different song, one from the late eighteenth century called "La Jeune et Gentille Lisette," accompanies this segment of the scene.)

But when the Rossini-based air surfaces once more, as Colas inches his way up Lise's arm with gentle kisses, the mood becalms. Seating himself beside Lise on some of the sheaves, Colas wipes his sweetheart's weepy eyes and nose with his scarf. They perform a little ritual of exchanging neck scarves, which they seal with a more prolonged kiss.

Bellowing, thumping, and almost mocking music, "Simone's Return," halts Lise and Colas in their billing and cooing. In a silent-movie mad dash the two look in all the wrong and absurd places—a shallow drawer, a hot fireplace—for somewhere Colas can hide. Finally Lise shuts him into her own room, and, to the music's note of false calm, commences looking busy with a broom. Simone finds the sight of an industrious Lise almost alarming, and mimes the need for her daughter to change her clothes in her room. When Lise looks apprehensive and tries to dissuade her mother from this idea, Simone notices that Lise is wearing a scarf different from the one she chose for her earlier. After making a few suspicious checks of a potential hiding places, she pulls her panicked daughter by the hand and shoves her into her room, locking the door for good measure.

A rumbling, anticipatory musical moment that tells of someone knocking at the door introduces "Thomas, Alain, and the Notaries." Simone opens her doors to a dressed-up Thomas and two legal officials. After the two parents finish inking marriage documents and drinking a toast, lines of Lise's and Colas's friends chain into the room. Just as the fellows finish clearing away the sheaves of grain, a spiffily dressed Alain slips through the door. He's holding a huge "rock" of a wedding ring in his hand in an absurdly formal and awkwardly stiff manner. After looking and acting puzzled about what to do with the ring, he attempts a retreat as if in the wrong place. Thomas hauls him back and, in a variation on his original solo music, all but Alain join in a little dance. Alain himself picks up the festiveness and prances and skids through a brief solo of his own. Everyone else stands back and watches the spectacle, which leads Simone to present the fiancé with the key to Lise's room.

"Consternation and Forgiveness" comes next. When Alain finally undoes the lock in question, the door opens to reveal Lise and Colas in an embrace. The sight sends Alain slipping backward down the stairs to the room and causes Simone to faint. The music sounds a little like a sudden Rossinian storm, and Thomas takes his victimized son by the hand and tries to console him. In contrast, the air fills with restatements of the tune announcing the love and rapport between Lise and Colas, as the couple sweetly moves to the center of the scene.

Lise kneels lovingly at her mother's feet, indicating her strong love for Colas, and confuses Simone further still. The notary sees this as evidence of the lack of validity in the signed contracts, and tears up the documents in favor of the truer bond evident between

Lise and Colas. He points out these facts to Simone, who finally acquiesces and blesses Colas's hand in Lise's. Stormy consternation surfaces once more. Thomas blusters about as all back away, leaving the spurned father and forlorn son to gesture sadly about their turn of fate. Finally the angered father leaves, dragging along the jilted bridegroom. They quit the scene with a bang.

A lyrical interlude introduces the "Pas de Deux." First Colas gallantly shows his affection toward Simone, then he escorts Lise to the center of the room for their first dance in Simone's approving sight. A flute and harp initiate the dance's music. The tune is the one we heard in "When I'm Married," based on the Rossini aria. It begins with a variety of floating and turning lifts—freer, more filled-out versions of the rapturous moments Lise had in the duet at the Dutch door. After a delicately dramatic unfolding to arabesque balance on pointe, Lise remains poised for Colas to turn her slowly in place, with enraptured pauses for both lovers to drop back and nod their heads forward in a kind of braiding image. Two creamy and elaborate supported pirouettes lead to three seamlessly graded lifts that float Lise through grand jeté in attitude positions. Three supported piqué-arabesque moves occur, with each changing dramatically from on- to off-pointe position with delicate theatrical suddenness.

From there, in a diagonal delicately reminiscent of the "fish-dive" sequence from the "Wedding Pas de Deux" in *The Sleeping Beauty*, Colas prepares, through pliant chassé-tour movement, to await Lise's next move. Each time he prepares, she slips into his embrace. Twice she skims through tiny pas de bourrée to entwine her arms and rest her head in his arms. (The configuration of their arms, hands, necks, and heads makes yet another kind of lovers' knot, established by Ashton's use of ribbons.) A third time he swirls into position by way of chaîné turns and, after following similar suit, she finds herself in a big arched-back lift. Three more piqué-arabesque penchée moves follow with one arm dramatically free for both Lise and Colas to embellish the sequence with a simple flourish. Two more joyous lifts follow, in which Colas lightly tosses Lise in the air to shimmering cymbal crashes. A final lift for Lise sitting calmly on Colas's shoulder caps the duet, which sighs to a close as the bride slips softly to kneel at her groom's feet. Their final, still pose, with Colas hovering happily and protectively over Lise, cues the "friends" to celebrate the couple with a shower of flower petals.

When our field worker/flutist takes up his flute and pipes his "field dance" air in Simone's ear, the "Finale" begins. Lanchbery modeled his on one of two he found in the Hérold score. The flute playing lad then moves center stage, and with steps reminiscent of his previous solo, he slowly encourages dancing from all those around him. After the weaving and circling of village men and women, Lise whisks through on fleet feet, throwing off clean little jetés and simple saut de basque moves. After her eight friends spell her a bit, she takes their direction and leads them in a little ensemble moment that features a repeated sequence of small pointe steps and smartly curled arms and hands on hips. In Ashton's catalogue of works, this specific combination is know as the "Fred Step" because Ashton used it, almost without fail, in every one of his ballets. Based on a sequence Pavlova used in a famous "Gavotte" of hers, its sequence of arabesque-piqué/coupé/développé/pas de chat pleased Ashton and became a kind of good-luck charm in his career. He varied it greatly from one use to another—this one is small and fast. Another lightning set of flashing fine footwork follows for Lise, zigzagging on pointe (Collier throws in swift, side-to-side pas de chat jumps) as she lifts her skirt to help accentuate her "ecstatic" feet.

Colas gets his turn to come front and center, and there he turns and turns and turns, executing a series of grand pirouettes. Coleman's personal success, especially with his climactic, septuple spin, gets the dancers rhythmically clapping, encouraging Madame to kick up her heels. This she does eagerly, scuffing about before clicking her heels side to side like the clapper of a bell. Three concentric rings of dancers now revolve, with the tiniest, central one providing support as it raises up our happy protagonists one by one. First Simone, then Colas, and finally, Lise.

As our heroine is raised up for us, the circling lines link into one spiral and start to curl out through the front door. As the assembled do so they begin to sing a little "La, la, la" lyric as they go. (This "song and dance" reclaims a moment from Dauberval's staging when his cast sang the lyrics of the folk song from which the original title was taken: "Il ne faut désespérer de rein / Il n'est qu'un pas du mal au bien." "It's unnecessary to ever despair / It's only a short step from bad to good.") Lise and Colas trail at the tag end of the snaking line, and in what looks like an ending, the happy young man sweeps his bride into his arms and plants a loving kiss on her lips before carrying out the day.

But wait, someone's at the window. It's Alain, still in his cutaway frock coat and top hat. He moves with stealth and looks around somewhat anxiously. The music's mood is pussyfoot in tone until the little guy points with satisfaction to what he's seeking. It's his red umbrella, which he retrieves from the table and, as his music turns to more elated "traveling music," scuttles out, almost as if pedaling on air as he hugs his beloved brolly.

Chapter 12

ROMANTIC: SMALL "r," BIG EMOTIONS

Romeo and Juliet

• • •

Choreography by Kenneth MacMillan
Music by Sergei Prokofiev

If you've been watching ballet for more than five minutes and have been hearing about it for more than two, you've probably come across a production of *Romeo and Juliet.* If *Swan Lake* comes to most people's minds first when ballet gets mentioned, *Romeo and Juliet* is not far behind. (*The Nutcracker* is certainly high up in the popularity stakes, but as we've seen, it has become something beyond a ballet or even indeed ballet itself, and taken on an aura of generic holiday spectacle.) *Romeo and Juliet* comes to mind mainly as a "romantic," small "r" (for lovers' romance) tragedy told in the form of ballet theater. Just as the 1595 Shakespeare play that gives this ballet its scenario has precedents in earlier Italian literature dealing with similarly fated young lovers and surroundings, so our *Romeo and Juliet* choice has related precedents. Here is a case, incidentally, when I have decided not to go with my own personal favorite rendering of this material, but with what appears to be the world's current favorite.

Kenneth MacMillan's *Romeo and Juliet* dates from 1965 and his choreography qualifies in no sense as "a first." The Prokofiev score is but one of several composed for this ever-popular Shakespeare narrative, and had been choreographed several times before MacMillan tried his hand. (Prokofiev's score had its first staging in 1938.) Many of those that preceded MacMillan's have continued to be shown in repertory. But, due to both the frequency with which MacMillan's ballet continues to appear in the Royal Ballet repertory, as well as numerous subsequent productions of it, say *Romeo and Juliet* to balletomanes and they'll likely see MacMillan's.

The video accompanying our discussion originally appeared as a "feature-length motion picture." The fact that a budget big enough to fund this kind of project was available for the specialized art of ballet testifies to the popularity and commercial potential of the product. The presence of Margot Fonteyn and Rudolf Nureyev in the film's leading roles accounts in good measure for the movie's being made on a large scale. At the time, the Fonteyn-Nureyev partnership was being widely heralded in terms of superstardom. Although neither represented the ballet's true first cast as far as its choreographer was concerned, pressures from outside influences, namely the number-one U.S. ballet marketing stragetist and impresario Sol Hurok, were brought to bear and MacMillan let a ballet he had created for two other, younger dancers (Lynne Seymour and Christopher Gable) become identified with artists whom he viewed more as a second cast.

About this video:

> *The Royal Ballet with Rudolf Nureyev and Margot Fonteyn in "Romeo and Juliet,"* with David Blair, Desmond Doyle, Julia Farron, Anthony Dowell, Michael Somes, 1966, 124 min., Color.
>
> Filmed only a year after its premiere performance, the movie, now transferred to video, records most of the dancers (beyond the abovementioned leads) for whom MacMillan created his choreography. Filmed to simulate the actual stage performance (by Paul Czinner, who worked consistently in England to honor the stage performance in the medium of film), this Royal Ballet *Romeo* remains a triple-whammy document of a ballet, of a newsworthy partnership, and of a noteworthy company.

After the story of *The Sleeping Beauty*, probably the next best known of all narrative ballet plots is that of *Romeo and Juliet*: Boy from one good family (Montague) meets girl from another good family (Capulet) and they fall in love, even though there is much bad blood between their elders. After secretly marrying Juliet, Romeo finds himself amid the dueling families and ends up killing Juliet's cousin, Tybalt. After Romeo is banished, Juliet takes part in a scheme that involves feigning death, which Romeo fails to realize is simulated. After the distraught young man kills himself in grief over the "death" of his bride, she awakens and then joins him in death by her own suicide.

Love stories with tragic endings, often specifically involving suicides (see *Swan Lake*, *Giselle*, etc.), are not unknown to ballet history. But MacMillan's rendering of the fairly standard material goes in a somewhat unusual direction. If I may borrow a term from opera history, I'd label MacMillan's work *verismo*. In opera terms the designation identifies melodramatically themed works that accentuate violent plots and intense emotions, all presented with a kind of realism that departs from opera's standard, formal conventions. (The root of *verismo* is *vero* meaning "real" or "true.") As we shall see, MacMillan's ballerina heroine will wear pointe shoes, but no tutu. She will die a theatrical, but not a Gautier-style "pretty" death.

The major Soviet precursor to MacMillan's *Romeo and Juliet* is Leonid Lavrovsky's 1940 Leningrad Kirov Ballet's. Its realism, however, was more in the vein of Social Realism than a *verismo* realist one. Soviet Social Realism had an agenda that accentuated the corrupt or negative aspects of merchant and aristocratic characters while promoting the goodness and purity of innocent common folk. (For a specially filmed Bolshoi Ballet staging of this production see either *Romeo and Juliet* with Galina Ulanova, 1954, 95 min., Color, or *Romeo and Juliet* with Natalia Bessmertnova, 1975, 108 min., Color.) MacMillan's realism accentuates the emotional dimension of his characters with regard to the particulars of plot, regardless of their class. Lavrovsky's *Romeo* was interested in approved behavior by one class versus another; MacMillan represented his interest in "real people," whatever their background.

Physically and spiritually, MacMillan's *Romeo* owes something to Lavrovsky's way with ballet. By 1965, Moscow's Bolshoi Ballet had toured the West with its staging of Lavrovsky's ballet and impressed audiences with its acrobatic aspects, especially with regard to partnering and lifts, as well as regarding such simple, forthright features as how ballerinas ran and leapt. Still, there was a chasteness and a kind of formal reserve in the fabric of Lavrovsky's aesthetic that MacMillan chose to bypass in favor of a more nakedly emotional effect.

It wasn't only from aesthetics bred behind the Iron Curtain that MacMillan departed. His ways of conceiving and working ballet theater also went in a direction different from that of his own mentors and predecessors in England, primarily Ashton. As we shall see, MacMillan's realistic interests didn't prevent him from having his dancers get literally if not figuratively "down and dirty" with their dancing. His lack of reticence about letting his ballerina/heroine get dragged along the floor in moments of fulsome emotion prompted some naysaying along lines such as: "In ballet, people make love on their feet, not on the floor."

In MacMillan's *Romeo and Juliet*, for example, his young lovers will kiss each other in a display of intense passion. In the Lavrovsky prototype of this ballet, the lovers kiss each other more sedately, often limiting acting on their amorous passions with a tender caress of Juliet's hands to Romeo's face and saving their extravagant physical displays of emotion for more formal dance moves, such as big, acrobatic-styled lifts.

Our tape begins with Prokofiev's "Introduction" played before a normally closed stage curtain, here it accompanies informative illustrated, on-screen synopses of the various scenes making up Act 1.

Act I, Scene 1: The Market Place

Czinner's cinematic style, described in an on-screen introductory note, works to preserve a sense of being in a theater. At the ballet's "curtain up" we see the red plush curtains of the Royal Opera House at Covent Garden part as they would in the theater. Prokofiev calls his first scene "Romeo," and MacMillan stages Romeo's appearance immediately and delicately. He has the lute-carrying young man, swathed in his cape, amorously trail behind Rosaline. The measured encounter, overseen by Rosaline's bodyguard and Romeo's sidekicks, takes place on a simplified and pared-down piazza fed by a colonnade and sweeping staircase.

The ballet's designer is Nicholas Georgiadis, a longtime MacMillan collaborator. I mention him specifically because MacMillan does not follow the tradition of reconceiving the scenic and costume designs for ballets, such as *Swan Lake* and *Nutcracker*, that are restaged after their premiere performances; MacMillan's *Romeo* is more in line with the *Gesamtkunstwerk* (or "total work of art") tastes in Diaghilev's legacy. You are more likely, in this case, to find the same Georgiadis designs in place for subsequent stagings of MacMillan's *Romeo* than you might for numerous other "standard" ballet stagings.

Romeo's gallant and sweet resignation toward his thwarted attempt at wooing Rosaline helps wrap up the scene's first episode. Nureyev's smiling swain shrugs off the unfinished business of courting as he moves aside with his companions, Mercutio (David Blair) and Benvolio (Anthony Dowell). Now, in a scene called "The Street Wakens," the marketplace stirs with life. Antagonistic members of the Capulet household, townspeople, merchants, beggars, and harlots fill the scene. MacMillan's "bustle," for all its variety of naturalistic (howdy-do mime) and dance-step dimensions (grand jeté-ing swordsmen and soutenu-ing townswomen sweeping with brooms) occurs specifically on musical cues. We see ballet steps peeping through the "street activities" but not ballet pointe shoes. While the leading men wear regulation ballet slippers, everyone else wears some kind of character shoe—boots or heeled slippers. Even the semiprominent harlot characters execute their ballet steps in heeled pumps.

"Morning Dance" follows when a gold-dressed harlot (Monica Mason) entices Romeo to dance with her. Soon Mercutio and Benvolio are up and dancing with harlots (Deanne Bergsma and Carole Needham) as well. The swing-your-partner maneuvering has the look of a social dancing couple displaying ballet's artful legs, feet, and other strengths. As the dance music grows more vivid, the couples separate into happy, jumping individuals (successive, crisscrossing paths featuring grand jeté pas de chat); then, into individual couple dances. The women, who dance in heeled pumps, leave it to the leading men, in their ballet-slippered feet, to display ballet's "truest" line. We see this in the arabesques Nureyev's Romeo releases as he swings his partner around and in the sauté-passé steps and the relevé-grand battement moves Dowell's Benvolio flashes.

The dance ends with a succinct "button," as the women fall back with abandon in their partners' arms. But the slight uneasiness we noticed in the townspeople's occasional miming of disapproval and displeasure at the harlots' behavior now magnifies. We have come to "The Quarrel," instigated and led by swordsmen of the Capulet family. Their instigator is the red-clad Tybalt (Desmond Doyle) and the musical scene rumbles with foreboding. A more chipper theme accompanies the teasing appearance of Romeo and his fellow Montagues. Holding their swords rather elegantly, the young men file on with sauté-balloné steps and bow somewhat mockingly to the troublemakers.

Teasing and taunting actions ensue, all timed to specific musical cues, as Montague swords flick "love taps" at Capulet weapons. "The Quarrel" becomes "The Fight" as Prokofiev's strings create a buzz describing the whirring of fine metal swiping the air, and mostly smiling Montagues conduct swordplay, in earnest, with humorless Capulets. Tybalt, near the center of the fight, is the most ill-humored of all. Individual townspeople enter the fray, especially some women, who take off after the harlots. Eventually, anyone with a sword is doing battle with some adversary as the scene becomes awash with flashing blades. The Montague trio keeps smiling; Nureyev's Romeo even spins a pirouette out of one of his sword strokes.

As the music grows foreboding and denser in texture, Lord and Lady Capulet (Michael Somes and Julia Farron) and Lord and Lady Montague (Christopher Newton and Betty Kavanagh) enter. The ladies sweep aside to provide moral support or buffer zones for their het-up husbands, who perform ritual-like battle with heavy, broad swords. Chimes then start to clang through the musical fray. After the instigators all pull away, baring a body-strewn plaza, the stage picture freezes.

Down the stairs comes a stern Escalus, Prince of Verona (Leslie Edwards). Blustering and bellowing music accompanies the mimetic scene, "The Duke's Command." He makes a spectacle of the heap of casualties and demands a putting down of swords, which gets done with some reluctant ceremony. The feuding lords and ladies obey their duke and grudgingly pay homage to one another, as Capulet and Montague foes stand off and apart, all with their hands arrogantly placed on their hips.

Act 1, Scene 2: Juliet's Anteroom

In the theater, an interlude would follow to cover a scene change. In our film we segue directly into Juliet's anteroom, for "Preparations for the Ball" and "The Young Juliet," which follow succinctly one after another. The scene begins with Juliet's entrance: a running one on suitably skittering music. The young woman (Fonteyn at forty-five), loose hair streaming behind her, scurries over to a chair filled with her napping nurse (Gerd Larsen). She wears a Renaissance-cut, high-waisted dress, and pointe shoes. A somewhat sylphlike kiss, delivered after a joyous arabesque-piqué balance on pointe, awakens the older woman, as Juliet takes off into her music's frolicksome mood with her doll. "Catch me if you can" becomes the name of the game as the toy is tossed about. Some darting coupé-jeté moves and delicate swings into arabesque-piqué dot Juliet's playfulness. The soft chords of Prokofiev's Juliet music have been compared to clapping hands.

When Lord and Lady Capulet enter with noble Paris (Derek Rencher), the mood shifts. Juliet becomes sedate and shy as her mother introduces her to the man she is to wed. After her father does the formal honors, joining Juliet's hand to that of Paris, the thoughtful daughter slips apart, striking more careful arabesque poses. Each of the moves and poses she renders on pointe help put her on a plane separate from that of the surrounding characters. She skims in pas de bourrée couru and turns through a couple en dedans arabesque tours as if demonstrating her poise and gracious manners.

Her various relevés onto pointe or pointes take on a genuinely singular quality that dramatizes the character's special dimension. When she finishes by circling her nurse like a kitten would its mother, Paris makes a bow of pleasure and Juliet a curtsy of respect. As soon as the suite departs, the would-be shy young woman resumes her teasing, playful game of catch-me. As the music grows more somber, the nurse does, too. The "curtain line" is a gesture directed toward Juliet's budding womanhood. The nurse's hands on the young woman's breasts give even the spritely Juliet pause to reflect.

Act 1, Scene 3: Outside the Capulet House

Now we come to another transitional scene, the "Arrival of the Guests." This takes place at the gates to the Capulets' residence. Couples of men and women parade by, many wearing masks. The sense of a courtly minuet remains in the background as the scene's undercurrent. Included among the masked arrivals are Romeo and his companions, swathed in billowing capes. Prominent among the guests is Rosaline, who arrives in a sedan chair. Tybalt and Lord Capulet are on hand to usher in the special arrivals. Rosaline gets a rose from Tybalt, and the host personally greets Paris. The mischievous male threesome, led by Romeo, mostly enjoys paying homage to Rosaline.

After all the official invitees enter, a rustle of snare drums cues "Masks," a jubilant pas de trois for Romeo, Mercutio, and Benvolio. It's a jaunty number filled with turning moves. En dehors relevé-attitude turns dominate the start, with Romeo as a kind of centerpiece. Sharp and softly emphatic développé extensions à la seconde keep acting to charge, recharge, and trigger the turning moves. After dancing through travels that involve grand rond de jambe accents and croisé extensions front, the men reposition themselves side by side and take off into a set of sauté-grand battement (à la seconde) moves that lead to a series of various en dedans turns. Some of their relevé-rond de jambe en l'air and related moves have a sense of swordplay about them. Benvolio and Mercutio even play with their respective port de bras and leg work as if they were fencing partners. Finally Romeo leads the way, turning through almost giddy en dedans turns and leading the trio in a series of swings into relevé-poised arabesques. As the number's music subsides, they wrap themselves in their capes, take up their lutes, and slip into the palace.

Act 1, Scene 4: The Ballroom

Now, in the Capulet ballroom, a "Dance of the Knights" follows. Interestingly, we find the new location more impressive in the theater than we do on film. The sudden sight of the gathering's lords and ladies instantaneously appearing and advancing toward us in their stately court dance, all due to a simple, sudden full-lighting cue, is a kind of coup de théâtre. Front-to-back lines of men, prominently led by Paris, Tybalt, and Lord Capulet pace through striding, marking-time, and "dragging" steps. Eventually the court women advance to accompany the men. The women's streaming trains and pelvis-forward posturing recalls images captured in Renaissance prints of dancing at Italian *ballos*. Prokofiev indicated this as a "pillow" or "cushion" dance, meaning the women carried pillows, which they artfully dropped so they could kneel in moments of embrace with their men. (See the 1975 Bolshoi Ballet video listed above.) MacMillan found the image not to his liking.

During the obviously practiced and schooled ballroom dance, Romeo and his party enter in the background. So, too, finally, does Juliet. A mild fanfare of mellow brass cues Juliet's arrival amid the court dance. She greets Paris with some girlish shyness and pays honor to her parents. Simultaneously Romeo tries to distract Rosaline with his attentions, as the court dance resumes and comes to further pause.

Another interlude follows. It accompanies a specially featured couple dance for Juliet in which the young woman's intended husband partners her in a more elaborate, ballet-styled rendering of a ballroom dance. Simple sweeps to arabesque and demure piqué steps releasing rond de jambe en l'air accents fill out her special moment. Gently jumped lifts and delicate swoons into Paris's arms also figure in the vignette. Just as Juliet's danced interlude is about to conclude, and her elders' dance resumes, the young woman's eyes meet those of Romeo behind his mask. As he takes his place across the crowded room, the two savor their "meeting" in private reflection.

With his ballet's eponymous lovers now "connected," MacMillan makes a slight rearrangement of Prokofiev's score. He wants to focus the action—the dancing—on the protagonists, so he amplifies the score's next segment, "Juliet's Variation," with a danced appearance for Romeo. (Interestingly, the variation for Juliet now part of the score was added by Prokofiev at the specific request of Lavrovsky.) Therefore, after Juliet's variation is introduced, MacMillan interpolates Prokofiev's "Aubade" (a "morning dance," originally meant to accompany a dance for Juliet's friends in Act 3, scene 3). This will be an occasion for Romeo to dance for Juliet, as well as for us.

The introduction cues Juliet to take a mandolin from her friends and accompany them in their dancing. Now, to the interpolated "aubade" Juliet's six girlfriends dance. Like Juliet, they dance delicately, on pointe (the only ones who will do so besides Juliet). As their gentle pas de six honors their friend and delicately perfumes the air of the ball with pretty posturing, skimming, and stepping on toe tip, a beguiled Romeo takes to dancing a seemingly improvised solo in their midst. They scurry aside, as if giggling, while Romeo steps into a series of happy turns, telling, perhaps, of his deliriously happy infatuation with the young woman playing her mandolin. En dedans turns (one set in arabesque before a wrap-up one in passé position) begin Romeo's show of finesse.

Then he spins into a series of en dehors turns. As he dashes over to present himself more directly to Juliet, her friends scurry in the opposite direction and he positions himself to perform another diagonal of turns for her amusement. For her part, Juliet looks partly flustered, partly intrigued, and partly tickled. More en dedans turns follow, slowed into attitude poses through start-stop fouetté moves. After some turns and poses that accentuate extensions à la seconde and arabesque, Romeo throws in a couple of sissones and turns that open out through développé to extension. Soon, one brave friend of Juliet's joins him, playfully mirroring his steps with hers.

On yet another of the music's repeats, he dances solo again launching into a further set of turns as Tybalt begins to get restive at the sight of impromptu spectacle. Romeo keeps returning to a diagonal line away from Juliet so he can keep traveling back in her direction. Now his approach is set with lightly beaten cabriole jumps to the back. (Or at least Nureyev's is in our film. MacMillan, who devised Romeo's choreography for English dancer Christopher Gable, included more English-school moves here, a kind of neatly crisp extension move to arabesque from passé-back position, which the Russian-schooled "jump-happy" Nureyev substitutes with cabrioles.) A most joyful set of sauté-fouetté moves take him upstage once more so he can spin back downstage toward Juliet, which he does with pirouettes and a string of chaîné turns.

While the ballroom stirs with bewilderment at the identity of the masked dancer who has taken himself to kneel at Juliet's feet, Paris is encouraged to escort his fiancée into her own solo. Now, the score returns to where it was before the interpolation, and we're back with Juliet's variation. This takes place as all eyes watch the Capulet daughter, none more intently than Romeo's. He has taken up a position similar to Juliet's during his dance. Most of her dance steps are piqué ones, as she turns demurely in demi-arabesque, and more brightly in passé position. When her eyes meet Romeo's, and the music—dominated by flute and strings—begins to quicken, she backs away fixed on Romeo by means of moves that sweep through grand rond de jambe en l'air to paused arabesque. A circuit of light jumps and piqué steps grow out of the music's even brighter quickening of pace.

As Romeo stations himself directly in her sight, she seems to take energy from his attention and moves away in steps that keep turning back to face him by way of soft fouetté maneuvers and easy en dedans turns. Consistently, her dancing takes her arabesque poses facing Romeo. After three beguilingly soft approaching steps through arabesque-piquée, in which she seems to become lost in her own daydreaming flight, Juliet finds herself in Romeo's grasp. As the music starts to pulse with only high-pitched strings, Romeo guides Juliet through a manège in which she looks out rapturously as she skims on her pointes and he guides her in looping, hovering lifts.

The circuit comes to a soft and unemphatic ending when a quizzical Paris approaches the couple, standing face to face at the end of their manège. As the music winds to a transitional mode, Juliet makes a delicately hasty exit, followed more summarily by her parents and Paris. Seeing the confusion his friend has caused, Mercutio decides to become a distraction and diversion. The score's "Mercutio" segment cues a solo for the character of the same name. It's a teasingly mocking and driven display, with Mercutio loping, hopping, and spinning through a manège of continuously cocky moves. He all but jogs into action. After circling the room twice over with successive turns à terre and en l'air, he spins through a diagonal of further revolutions that change position, change feet, and change "rotational" emphasis en dedans turns alternating with en dehors turns.

With a smiling flourish toward Benvolio, Romeo's other companion enters the dance. As a bassoon lightly bellows to the musical surface, a teasing Benvolio strides and snakes about the room, sometimes with *sauté-enveloppé* moves. (These have accents opposite those of developpé moves; they bring the extended leg into closed tight position, rather than open extended position, by way of successive incremental movements.) In contrast to Mercutio's whirlwind turning foray, Benvolio's is mostly a jumping circuit of the room. In between his smiling, artful bounding about, he acts as a wily interloper, intermittently slipping between linked couples as if he were bursting through a garden gate.

Benvolio's grand jeté exit leaves an annoyed Tybalt in his wake, all of which seems to cue Mercutio to resume his almost breathless string of traveling turns. A set of en dedans compass-point spins (with his working leg à la seconde) into a plainer en dedans pirouette are elaborated by a kind of "in your face" hand gesture. Finally, the distraction of dizzying turns comes to a close with a semi-lunge position with a hand-to-sword gesture as a final taunt to a poker-faced Tybalt.

Between them, Benvolio and Mercutio have cleared the room with their teasing dances; only the extra-suspicious Tybalt has stayed to the last. After the annoyed Capulet hies after Mercutio, the ballroom stands empty. Now, to a more serene "Madrigal"—all strings (violins and violas), no blaring horns—Juliet enters alone, seemingly lost in thought. Almost immediately, Romeo appears and, after a brief moment of intimacy, slips away at the sound of someone's approach. It's Juliet's nurse, who is sent away after her charge indicates she has a headache. When her intriguing, masked young man reenters, Juliet delicately sweeps to an arabesque pose on pointe as Romeo holds her by the waist. She backs into the pose successively and then slips forward similarly, each time in arabesque-effacée, sometimes indicating a desire to remove his face mask.

When Lady Capulet arrives with Paris, Juliet again feigns indisposition. Tybalt uneasily notes Juliet's dismissal of her mother and suitor and follows them out. As the music now swells and blossoms more fully, Romeo reenters once more. After throwing off his mask, he stands while Juliet rushes to his arms. In his embrace, Juliet strikes an arabesque-penchée, which Romeo lovingly promenades. When his partner returns to her vertical axis and leans her torso back in another arabesque variation, Romeo slides her backward with equal tenderness. As their music soars higher still, so does their doublework. A high lift in arabesque changes to a kind of stag-leg position where Juliet seems to float, as if riding some magic carpet.

When he sets her down, and she swoons over his supporting arm, their rapturous coupling continues to swirl into a face-to-face promenade of Juliet posed in arabesque-fondue. They briefly separate and, to musical reminiscences of Juliet's variation, they dance happily side by side, accentuating temps levé-rond de jambe en l'air moves. All of which comes to an abrupt end, when almost rude horns sound and Tybalt reenters.

"Tybalt Recognizes Romeo" becomes an emotionally reined-in scene of confrontation. Juliet tries to placate her cousin, while he insists on looking the now-unmasked intruder in the face. Tension mounts and peaks when Tybalt pulls Romeo's hand from shielding his face. It builds further when, instead of leaving immediately as Tybalt directs, Romeo goes to kiss Juliet's hand. Lord Capulet, heading the return of the rest of the guests, tries to make peace, as directed by Escalus. Romeo seems more willing to comply than Tybalt.

With everyone once more in dancing places, the ball's "Gavotte" begins. Seven trios form, with Juliet and her friends on the "outside hands" of the men involved and the more mature court women on the "inside hands." Rearrangements of the configurations in the course of the dance put Juliet and Romeo together momentarily. They remain paired until Tybalt intervenes, and the Mercutio and Benvolio persuade Romeo to depart.

Act 1, Scene 5: Outside the Capulets' House

Our tape cuts the "Gavotte" at this point, with the Montagues' exit from the ballroom. (In the theater, the scene segues into a general departure of guests outside the palace gates.) There we see Romeo wrap himself in his cape and slip away unattended. Meanwhile, the courtly guests leave in various states of decorum and inebriation. Mercutio and Benvolio delay their exit long enough to flirt with the guests who interest them most. Tybalt finds their presence annoying and tries to send them on their way with the point of his sword. In a parting shot, the prankish Mercutio returns swordplay by producing his mandolin as a weapon. Lord, and especially Lady, Capulet try to calm their cousin and call it a night.

Act 1, Scene 6: Juliet's Balcony

Prokofiev's "Balcony Scene" title borrows the world's most ready association with Shakespeare's play. When the front drop rises on the stage, we see what looks like the secluded wing of a palazzo with a little balcony fixed at about a first-story level. To dreamy, contemplative music, Juliet comes onto her balcony. Essentially she stands taking in the night air, lost in thought; Fonteyn's stole slips absentmindedly from her shoulders. The moment remains slightly ad lib allowing Juliet to be lost in thought in her own way. Some Juliets will seem to sigh or rest blissfully on the balcony's balustrade.

As an interruption of the music's floating calm occurs, a cloaked figure enters on the ground below the balcony. His shadowy appearance and stealthy gait distract Juliet. When Romeo, the "intruder," turns to face the balcony, the music starts to build and swell, while he remains perfectly still fixed on Juliet, who remains similarly immobile. (MacMillan will work with the dramatic contrast between "big" musical effect and "frozen" dance effect at select moments in his ballet. This is the first.) After moving to another vantage point, Romeo fixes his gaze on Juliet in one more moment of pointed stillness, which leads to the transfixed woman's descent to the "garden." Their meeting maintains something of their mesmerized stillness. As the two stand hand in hand, Juliet takes Romeo's free hand and presses it to her doubtlessly fast-beating heart.

With an immediate, deep musical surge, we move to "Romeo's Variation." After taking what looks like a nearly standard preparation stance, croisé-pointe tendu (as if he were to launch into classroom exercise "en diagonale"), Nureyev's Romeo lauches into an ecstatic solo. Lush renversé turns make the impassioned young man look proud as a peacock and lead him to more dizzying en dedans spins and soaring jumps, some with batterie details that make him hang momentarily at their crest. The "Romeo shirt" that he wears, no longer covered by an outer tunic, fills with the air of his billowing moves.

A manège of leaps (coupé-jeté en tournant) that alternately cut through split-leg arabesque line and through tours à la seconde takes Romeo into further fancy flights. For her part, Fonteyn's Juliet rushes from one side of the space to another to admire and help demarcate the rush and flow of his space-eating moves. Indeed, the particular kind of jumps and turns displayed by the then recently arrived Soviet-school dancer contrast with the English-school details MacMillan had worked into his Romeo choreography. Like the idiosyncracies Nureyev displays in his ballroom solo, the steps he does near the balcony are somehow his own. English Romeos are called upon to do fewer open-leg turning jumps and beaten big jumps. Their manèges include more repeated double saut de basque and more of that developpé-to-arabesque move that was part of the "aubade" ballroom solo.

Finally, Juliet joins Romeo for what Prokofiev calls "Love Dance." After what should be an abandoned supported pirouette into grand rond de jambe en l'air into headlong arabesque-penchée, more swirling double work evolves. (I said "should be" to indicate that Fonteyn's inimitable reserve throughout this almost liquidly fluid duet are in part due to her individual way with ballet dancing and to her aging body. Lynne Seymour, the young ballerina on whom MacMillan shaped his choreography and who is not recorded on video, displayed the choreographer's desired aesthetics more clearly.) A turning lift and a multiple supported pirouette each finish with Juliet in calm first arabesque on pointe in Romeo's arms. Two swoons, one this way, one that way, follow. Tremulously, Juliet skims apart from her partner, only to be taken up in his arms again and turned around in épaulé-arabesque-line lifts. Further pirouettes spin into demi-arabesque postures for Juliet to hold while Romeo rotates her in her serene pose. All the lifts remain low, with Juliet taken to about Romeo's chest height, until out of one en dehors promenade and double pirouette the elated woman is held at a soft angle, with her legs high above her partner's head. The demi-arabesque line of her legs is a favored position with MacMillan. It has something of a fish-tail silhouette and character.

After a moment of tender, low-key intimacy that includes Romeo's caressing of the hem of his beloved's shift, Juliet strikes further plain yet exultant arabesques, which Romeo embraces and partners into swooning lifts, high and low. On one of the harp's glistening embellishments, Juliet gets held high, in a swept-back vertical posture, with one épaulé arm raised higher still, like a spout of clear water. When Romeo kneels and salutes Juliet with open arms, she rushes to him, where she's caught in an ecstatically arched position as if swimming in the air. For his part, Romeo sinks down and rises up in his kneeling position as if in some sort of prayer. After twining their arms like mating tendrils, the two change modes. Romeo settles back into a semi-reclining position as Juliet takes off into a solo flight of her own. She skims apart, softly striking arabesque-épaulée, before spiraling through more turns and skimming through more runs on pointe. Tickled by the sight, Romeo arises and then settles back once more as Juliet shows her excitement and rapture in light, galloping runs and smoothly struck arabesque-piqué balances on pointe.

In a "choreographic remembrance" of her arched posture caught as Romeo kneels with her in his arms, Juliet leans into her partner's arms as he sinks back and rises from his knees, allowing her arabesque pose to melt forward and to expand again into the pose's more open and vertical line. A momentary moving apart reverses to a dramatic coming together, with Juliet "caught" in a high, swept-back lift that has her changing arm and leg positions as she's carried ecstatically in the air. When she runs away, as if deliriously happy, Romeo follows her and takes her by the hand. Their music now slowly subsides, as face to face, Romeo takes Juliet into his arms for an impassioned kiss. The prelude to their kiss is Juliet's rising to pointe. Though Czinner's film framing does not show us this specifically (Fonteyn's feet are out of the picture), we see her "grow" taller in his embrace and sense her delicate base of balance as she floats gracefully in Romeo's arms.

As if pulled magnetically back to her balcony, Juliet slips out of the arms holding her and turns to run up the strairs to the porch of her room. The scene's final musical sigh has the two individuals reaching across the gulf of night air separating them. Lunging from his same downstage position, Nureyev's Romeo remains in fixed position, opening his chest as if to offer Juliet his heart. Fonteyn's Juliet almost hypnotically stretches her upstage arm like a soft laser beam in the direction of her suitor. Some of this is ad-libbed as well; sometimes MacMillan's Romeo will approach the balcony and reach his hand as close as possible to that of the reaching Juliet. (Our video provides a medley of Prokofiev's score as an intermission and to underscore the helpful synposes shown on screen of the upcoming scenes.)

Act 2, Scene 1: The Market Place

This act begins without ceremony in our video. The curtain rises on the very first blaring notes of Prokofiev's "Folk Dance." The Lavrovsky (see video listed above) and John Cranko versions of the ballet treat the dance as a recognizable folk-dance. MacMillan uses it more as a kind of "general dance" d'action, which is to say a scene-setting dance detailing some of the aspects of the world we've been introduced to so far. The cheeky and saucy harlots figure prominently. Their street dancing acts mostly to tease and flirt with the menfolk and to annoy and put off the womenfolk. Front and center, a dark-haired harlot (Needham) flashes through a bucking sissone jump.

There are a good many leg-front steps—pas emboîté and pas ciseau—as if wanting to kick at the upstarts. The happy-go-lucky men and harlots prance and twirl through the piazza over and over, sometimes with twisting and dipping torsos atop chassé-tours. Intermixed with kicking, prancing, and twirling steps are mimetics show-

The head mandoliner (Keith Rosson) tosses his instrument to Mercutio after swaying through the first few rocking steps of the dance. Once Prokofiev's bleating horns enter the mandolin-sounding strings making the dance's music, Rosson is spinning and jumping with a softly punchy force. Double en dedans saut de basque jumps pop up early in the dance, which have the effect of obeying the music's consistently pungent pulse. A spiraling path of piqué steps with grand battement-rond de jambe keep upscaling the dance's momentum. So do elaborately finished grand jeté en tournant steps, as well as jumped fouetté turns.

In order to give the hard-dancing head troubadour a rest, the attendant quintet spells him. Now that they've handed off their mandolins, they spin and bow *en face* toward the audience. On their return path, they throw in a series of handstands, with their legwork upending them as if they were playful bucking broncos. Turning jumps and jumped turns related to those executed by their "leader" wrap up this part of the quintet's dance. The lead mandoliner comes back, full force. After spinning through a set of knees-up grand jeté en tournant flights, he leads two of his fellow dancers in a bounding series of sauté-arabesque and sauté-balloné-front steps, which the three remaining mandoliners pick up on the opposite diagonal.

In the space they've all left clear, the main mandolin man spins and bounces through a continuously varied series of grand pirouettes, "sauté-ing" his standing leg for extra virtuoso measure. This briefly "inspires" the fivesome to emulate these fancy steps, which they cap with froglike soubresaut leaps. Soon, however, the "inspirer" is back, front and center, leading his men in one final burst of hopping and/or whipping turns, all of which end with everyone sedately landed in half-seated, half-kneeling positions on the floor. When MacMillan staged his 1965 ballet for ABT in 1985, he increased the complexity of the lead mandoliner's dance and gave the solo to Mercutio.)

Now, to more incidental and low-profile music, we come to a scene called "The Nurse," which is essentially an all-mime sequence. Juliet's nurse carries a note meant for Romeo and, hoping to make light of her not knowing precisely which one is the Capulet son, the people of the Market Place play into her confusion. The three Capulets put on their masks and "pass the buck" of which one is actually Romeo from one to another. The harlots brazenly present themselves to her as an alternative. (In current stagings their reaction is to lewdly pick up their skirts to shock the older woman, but the original staging included no such vulgarity.) Next, the Capulet threesome does a kind of ballet-styled soft-shoe "truckin' " routine to tease the nurse further. But, soon enough, after being alternately escorted and pinched, the message bearer takes an "if you can't beat 'em, join 'em" tack and lets the three young men dance with her. When they repeatedly peck her with kisses, she all but faints, overwhelmed. One last witty, pussyfooting dance for the trio, in a neat little row, leads to a willing unmasking of the jokesters and the placing of the envelope in Romeo's own hands.

"The Nurse and Romeo," a scene underscored by happy, agitated music, brings an ecstatic expression to Romeo's face. None of his male and female companions can see what he's been told, even though they try to gain a peek at his missive. Mercutio and Benvolio circle their friend with familiar dance steps and Romeo unspools energetically away from them, in a dizzying arc of excited chaîné turns to wrap an excited hug and plant a juicy kiss on the bearer of the glad tidings.

Act 2, Scene 2: The Chapel

MacMillan has cut the score's next scene, "Romeo at Friar Lawrence's," probably because it does little more than duplicate the scene following, where his ballet continues, "Juliet at Friar Lawrence's."

As a flute calmly pierces through a contemplative opening, we see Friar Lawrence (Christopher Newton) with a prayer book, walking in reverent supplication. We are in a rough-hewn, shallow space (forward of the first wing) frescoed with icons. Romeo enters first, and after paying obeisance to the friar, shows him the nurse's note about arriving for a secret marriage to Juliet. While the holy man shows his misgivings, the nurse enters and presently directs the friar's attention to the prospective bride. After paying her respects to the monk, Juliet fixes her gaze on Romeo as he does on her. As the music swells with the sound of muffled horns, the two lovers kneel to have the friar join their hands and bless their union. They stand and kiss as passionately as they might in this holy and non-private surrounding until the nurse urges Juliet away and Romeo exits opposite.

During this ballet's heyday with this super-stellar "first cast," diehard Fonteyn fans could be heard proudly announcing that they skipped Act 2 because "Margot only gets married in it," and they were saving their concentration and energy for the acts in which she has more acting and dancing to perform.

Act 2, Scene 3: The Market Place

With the simple raising of the chapel "wall," we return to our previous street scene. Prokofiev's "Public Merrymaking" is based on a bright and frenzied tarantella, the dance from southern Italy said to drive away the ill effects of a spider's sting. After some generic milling about of all those in the scene, the harlots begin to lead a general dance. Mercutio, Benvolio, and the lead mandoliner each link criss-crossed hands with one of the harlots and off they go into the dance's increasing energy and volume. (Czinner's camera closes in momentarily on a very unmerry Tybalt, who looks down disdainfully from the colonnaded upper level.) Soon the rest of the pedestrians pair up and join the jaunty dance: head-tipping chassé steps, sauté-arabesque moves, and partnered, twirling tours-jetés. After three advancing lines of four couples each, the stage fills with swing-your-partner dancing, in counter-revolving concentric circles and, eventually, a snaking line (eighteen couples strong) led by the newlyweds from the first scene.

After the happy-go-lucky reveling couples pause in a punctuational bow, the mood changes. (MacMillan cuts the full score's next scene, "Further Public Festivities," probably because of its similarity to the previous scene.) We have come to the "Meeting of Tybalt and Mercutio."

The surly Capulet cousin flashes his sword in the midst of the crowd and scatters it to the sidelines. Mercutio, however, is all smiles and brazen teasing. He flicks his swords, one in each hand, at those Tybalt wields. Music at once ominous and mocking underscores their standoff. A dreamy interlude, for an unhurried horn, interrupts the storm of agitation, giving a reflective Romeo an entrance. His far-off expression soon turns to worry as he sees his new cousin at swords drawn with his best friend. His desire to make peace with Tybalt falls on deaf ears with the Capulet and on the angry bewilderment of Mercutio.

"The Duel" (or "Tybalt and Mercutio Fight") begins. With the onlookers pulled back and Romeo restrained by Benvolio from intervening any further, the Montague cohort and Capulet cousin engage earnestly in swordplay. The music provides a strongly voiced, back-and-forth repartee to mirror the sword-to-sword confrontation. The jocular Mercutio gives a confident show of having the upper hand, pausing between parries to give and or get a good-luck kiss from his favored harlot or to grin a confident smile. The duel's climax occurs just after a seemingly unbeatable Mercutio gallantly returns to Tybalt the sword he momentarily dropped. As Mercutio steps aside to gloat over his success with Romeo, Tybalt takes advantage of his adversary's turned back and plunges his sword blade into his side.

A melodramatic turnaround in the score, from the duel's thrust-sword punctuation to a stunned tremulousness, takes us to the "Death of Mercutio." As the music wails on one level and pulses with a loss of vitality on another, Mercutio holds his side in disbelief. Some mockingly jocular music cues the wounded Montague to mime laughing at his condition. (The film adds a touch of verisimilitude by showing a blood smear on his palm. No such details occurs in the theater.)

To a halting and woozy rendering of some previously animated music, Mercutio takes a sword in his "unbloody" hand and lamely proceeds to stab the air in the direction of Tybalt. Then, treating his weapon as a kind of musical instrument, he pretends to play it as if had strings to strum, and staggers to a once playful tune now played like a dirge. Benvolio and one of the harlots come to their friend's side when he falters. When Mercutio collapses to the ground, Benvolio offers him a cup of drink, which he gallantly toasts in the direction of his favored harlot. His final acts are to send hexlike gestures in the direction of both Tybalt and Romeo—making physical Shakespeare's "a plague on both your houses"—before collapsing into his own death. Prokofiev's sound effects here, cello tremulos, have the character of death rattles.

With Mercutio lifeless and flat on his face, the whole stage remains still as one anonymous townsman makes the sign of the cross. The silence and stillness are broken as the score heats up again and the assemblage crowds around the corpse. "Romeo Decides to Avenge Mercutio's Death" follows. As Benvolio gets the townspeople away from Mercutio's body, Romeo rushes to it. To music that swells, bellows, and races like the emotions and blood pulsing through Romeo, the Montague lets go his hold on Mercutio and takes hold of his sword. He then tears into a sword fight with Tybalt, who's been aching for such a match since he arrived on the scene. To a frenetic surge of strings that sounds like a horde of rabid locusts, the fight proceeds with a fiery Romeo like an attack dog against a smugly confident Tybalt. Ultimately their duel comes to a few wild strokes of Romeo's blade against Tybalt's, with a final one skewering the Capulet's torso.

Though the death of Tybalt merely occupies the closing moments of the "Romeo Decides to Avenge Mercutio's Death," it stands apart from the scene musically and dramatically. Fifteen sure, separated, and insistent thumps on a kettle drum accompany the lurching Tybalt's death throes. The moves are not set; each different Tybalt staggers, writhes, and lashes out to his own drummer, so to speak. Some time their convulsions to unintended comic effect.

A screeching, wailing passage grows out of the drummed death, as the townsmen and women press around the dead and reviled Tybalt. The "Finale" has begun. Romeo, realizing what he's done to Juliet's cousin, reveals his anguish and panic, while Benvolio tries to comfort him. Slowly making her way through the crowd, which she summarily shoves aside, Lady Capulet comes in horror to lament the loss of her cousin. At moments swooning and demonstrably grieving, the distraught woman (Julia Farron) presses herself onto Tybalt's fallen body and cradles it before getting up to hurl herself in Romeo's direction. All this, unlike the agonies of Tybalt, is set specifically on the boisterously sorrowful music. After Benvolio restrains Juliet's mother from attacking Romeo, she takes up Tybalt's sword with a mind to slaying his slayer.

Restrained once more, she stands frozen in anguish as Romeo falls, pleading for forgiveness at the hem of her dress. But she moves away from his gesture in disgust and beats at herself in mourning. Benvolio takes the opportunity to hustle Romeo away. A heavy tread of further drumming underpins the whole of the moaning music. After throwing herself once more on Tybalt and then onto the floor in agonized rolling, Lady Capulet turns to the stunned assemblage and gestures for their show of sympathy. Slowly the entire stage empties. In the end, having seen her husband arrive, she drags Tybalt's lifeless body onto her lap as a stricken Lord Capulet grieves in the background. Crashing chords bring down the curtain.

Act 3, Scene 1: The Bedroom

Our film omits the orchestral introduction Prokofiev wrote to open Act 3, but it remains part of MacMillan's ballet in the theater. Thematically, the somewhat sour and lachrymose sounds restate the reproving mood heard in the music motivating Escalus's quelling of the feuding families' brawl in Act I.

Instead, Czinner's film opens the act with "Romeo and Juliet," an interlude-length scene that begins with a flute sounding like a morning lark's song. (During the Lavrovsky production preparations, this was known as the "Lark Scene," recalling Shakespeare's text in which Juliet tries to persuade Romeo that it was a nightingale, not a lark, they were hearing.) With both individuals on Juliet's canopied bed, Romeo is the first to arise. We are now at the start of Prokofiev's "Romeo Bids Juliet Farewell." Romeo takes his cape from a chair and opens the room's curtain, letting in the strong light of morning, all of which causes Juliet to stir. She arises and runs into Romeo's arms. In the theater, MacMillan's staging calls for Romeo to enfold Juliet in his cape as he wraps her in his embrace. But Nureyev leaves his cape at the window, wrapping Fonteyn with his cape-free port de bras.

After the distraught lovers alternately rest their heads on each other's shoulders, again and again, the music swells as Juliet moves away in a kind of desperation, only to sweep into Romeo's arms for a pas de deux telling of their sorrowful situation. Juliet keeps reaching into arabesque poses. Juliet's arabesques—or to be specific to a MacMillan preference, demi-arabesque poses—consistently yearn away from her present circumstances while Romeo keeps supporting her steadying grasps and comforting lifts. Details such as epaulé port de bras and downcast angles for her head, variously shield her face from our view, shade the often automatically exultant arabesques in a more somber key. Certain lifts and turns end with Juliet casting her head back, out of a deeply arched torso. Supported turns and arabesques finish not presentationally, but in poses like clinging embraces or in lunging pauses that have the feeling of holding one's head in one's hands and telescope the unhappiness of the situation.

As the unhappy and uncomprehending Juliet keeps running away from her lover's arms in distracted desperation, he keeps enfolding her in partnered moves such as lifts and secured balances. By now their music has begun to recall the raptures heard in the "Love Duet" of the "Balcony Scene." Sometimes she spins like a slippery fish in his embrace only to bend like a weeping willow branch over his arm at the spiral's ending. Both run momentarily away from each other to rejoin, coupled with Juliet bent forward over Romeo's arm, with her head and hair hanging down like falling tears. Their partnered positions are as often back to front as face to face. In a move that echoes the crescent shaped lifts of the "Balcony Scene," Romeo lets Juliet repeatedly fall forward into his arms as he sits on the floor and her demi-arabesque positions arc, briefly backward, only to fold forward and close on the floor before him.

When the music's churning tread undoes the reveries reminiscent of the "Balcony" duet, Juliet sweeps aside, through a tour-jeté, and buries her face in her hands. After he goes to draw the curtain Juliet opened in a moment of desperation, Romeo goes to Juliet, also by way of a tour-jeté. She mirrors the music's agitation and keeps pulling way from his embrace. She undoes his embrace on her waist and runs into arabesque-piqué poses with imploring arms. After three such pullings-away, she goes into another tour-jeté that finishes collapsed to the floor. After a moment of passionate and somewhat hysterical kisses from Juliet, Romeo holds her head and more calmly seals the embrace with a long, passionate kiss as Juliet stands almost frozen in her thoughts. She remains so, standing almost in a trance, as her lover takes up his cape and exits by the window. Plucked strings tell of his stealthy departure as well as of Juliet's aching heart.

While Juliet looks longingly from her window in the direction of Romeo's route, we hear a gentler, more carefree tread in the music. The "Nurse" scene begins as the forlorn young woman returns to her bed to feign sleep. We hear a brief recollection of Juliet's earlier playful moods and see the bereft bride absentmindedly arise and loosen her wrap as her nurse tries to ready her for greeting her parents. Lady Capulet enters first, lifting her mourning veil as she approaches her daughter. Lord Capulet follows, embracing and kissing his daughter and making another introduction of Paris, who enters last. These entrées occur on music recalling the arrival of guests to the Capulet ball. The scene comes to its end as the larklike flute cues Paris to pay his repects to his promised bride, who slips away from the attempt, seeking emotional support from her nurse.

Paris's further attempts lead to the next segment, "Juliet Refuses to Marry Paris." It begins on decidedly more agitated music. Juliet brusquely pulls away from her intended. She appeals to her mother and to her nurse, who show their powerlessness at intervention. Juliet's pleas to her father, on her knees, obtain an angry rebuke that results in her being shoved prone to the floor. Paris's attempt at comforting her sends Juliet to her bed, where she hides under the covers. By now the music is further agitated and layered, sounding like so many angry arguing voices sounding all at once. After circling their daughter with gestures hoping to talk sense into her, the parents pause on Lord Capulet's command.

To ominous reed sounds, Juliet pulls away and walks like a zombie toward Paris. When he tries to take her hand, she rises to her pointes and backs off in even more hypnotic pas de bourrée couru. "Serious" sounding, bellowing music sends Lord Capulet striding to confront his obstinate daughter. Her steadfast refusal to acquiesce further arouses his ire, and all pleas on her behalf, especially those from her nurse, are angrily dismissed.

Juliet is thus left collapsed on the floor, shuddering with sobs. Now we hear "Juliet Alone." She rises, collapses, weeps, and returns to her bed while reaching in the direction of Romeo's departure. All the time her music slowly builds, as if she were collecting her desperate thoughts. When she comes to rest on the forward edge of her bed, her thinking starts to crystallize.

Like a gathering storm in billowing, rolling clouds, Prokofiev's surging tempest of sound pours forth. We have come to the composer's "Interlude" and to the choreographer's next big moment of dramatic stillness. In our film Fonteyn sits in front of her bed, her formerly downcast face looking up and out. In the theater MacMillan's Juliets sit on the bed flatly staring forward, back ramrod straight, and feet propped on pointe in parallel first position. Thus as the music swells toward some of its grandest volume and density, we see nothing but an intensely thoughtful young woman amid her swirling thoughts and approaching resolve. When the musical interlude recharges itself, Juliet, still keeping her sights and head high, takes her cloak and makes a running circuit of the room before exiting with her silk wrap trailing in her wake.

Act 3, Scene 2: The Chapel

Now familiar music associated with the story's friar returns us to the holy man's chapel for "At Friar Lawrence's Cell." The all-mime scene reveals Juliet's distress as she rushes and kneels at the friar's feet. After general and not overly detailed gestures, the monk momentarily leaves and returns with a small vial. After presenting it to Juliet and signing hypnotically over her head, as she reels in time with the woozy music, the frightened woman takes and then gives back the container of potion. The two kneel in prayer, which ends when Juliet extends her hand to take back the potion that will drug her into a deathlike sleep. MacMillan cuts some of the scene's music here, and with an exit from the friar's cell, and a lifting of the cell's setting, we are back in Juliet's bedroom as she enters.

Act 3, Scene 3: The Bedroom

Prokofiev's "Juliet's Room" accompanies the Capulet daughter once more in her own room. Bellowing horns tell of approaching heavy, implacable footsteps, and Juliet quickly closes the curtain to "Romeo's window." After seeming to come from bed, she allows her nurse to attend her in advance of the Capulet patriarch's arrival. As the stern man approaches her, she makes one more plea for help to her mother, who's accompanied by Paris. Then, with her father's determined gesture, she is once again presented to Paris.

Presently, the Capulet daughter is led into a duet of sorts with Paris. This takes shape as Juliet moves mechanically and stiffly through some motions for a kind of minuet with her fiancé. We hear musical reminiscence of the happier, more innocent minuet of the betrothal ball. She approaches him in stiff walking steps on pointe, and alternately moves rigidly aloof and limply downcast. She makes no eye contact with her dance partner and looks numbly away from him at every opportunity. When she tears herself away in almost violent animation, as her music indicates some fight left in her, the young man attempts to tussle with her himself. The following choreographic and musical passage dramatizes that tension. Juliet pulls away from Paris in one arabesque-effacé moment and drops into a swooning back-fall in another.

After squirming out of his embrace and making one more beeline for her Romeo window, she stands frozen and emotionless again. After Paris joins her and kisses the hem of her shift, she returns to her stiff acquiescent mode. More of the one-sided minuet recurs, with Juliet looking out from her dancing with Paris for parental understanding of her wishes against the marriage. Finding no such sympathies, she draws away to an oboe recalling the lark's song, and finally curtsies in a brief, formal, low-key acceptance of Paris's hand. His response, attempting to kiss her hem once more, causes the "accepting" Juliet to rise almost hypnotically again to her pointes and to bourrée as if floating away in her own world.

Staccato, nearly sour, chords introduce another musical scene called "Juliet Alone." The enervated daughter moves like an automaton around her bed. Then, to suitably dark and foreboding sounds, she retrieves the vial from under her pillow. Her moves and gestures telescope hesitation and indecision. After pitching the potion container to the floor, she backs leerily away from it, and when her music restates the swirling theme first heard in the friar's scene, she approaches the discarded drug as one might an unpredictable animal. The plucked strings define a delicate tread that she follows precisely in demi-pointe approach to the dreaded item. A restatement of some of the Balcony Scene's "Love Duet" raptures sends her to prayer at the little shrine to the Madonna in her room.

With that former blissful moment filling the air musically, Juliet runs to the apothecary vial, unstops its cap, and drinks the contents. The higher-pitched music now slides to a lower pitch, as if following the trickle of a drug slipping into her body. Her hands, drawn down her torso's front, also indicate the mixture's path. More of the woozy-headed state rises from the music as Fonteyn reels and staggers and contracts her torso forward. (Some Juliets take the trilling and tremolos heard in the music to indicate a spasm to throw up the liquid, but Fonteyn does not get this realistic.) Slowly, and in varyingly weak states of energy, she crawls, somewhat like a heroic wounded animal, onto her bed. After reaching one last arm toward the Romeo window, she falls back onto her pillow, seemingly lifeless.

Next should come Prokofiev's "Aubade," but as we've seen, MacMillan moved this number to the ballroom scene, so our action segues into the "Dance of the Girls with Lilies." These specific wedding talismans are dispensed with by our choreographer, who offers a lighthearted dance for Juliet's six friends. The first three arrive in fleet shimmering runs. As they unfold gentle grand battement développé steps toward Juliet's bed, three more of their number arrive with bouquets of roses, which they place about the bed. The delicate music and their piqué step dancing has the tone of whispered celebration, so as not to awaken the bride rudely. It's a toe dance with an added tiptoeing dimension.

After the music and "friends" stop telling of tiptoes, what Prokofiev calls "Juliet's Funeral" begins. The elated young women approach the bed of their friend and try to rustle her awake from her sleep. As the prodding and touching of one of the six finds no animation in Juliet, they pull away to ominous music. Then the nurse's now familiar jolly and chipper music intervenes, and it brings her waddling on, carrying Juliet's wedding dress in her arms. When the sight of the garment falls on stunned and frightened eyes, the friends back away from even touching it, and the nurse rushes to the bed. She expresses horror when she finds no life in Juliet's reclining body.

While the music seems seared with growing grief, it begins to wail as Lord Capulet, followed by Lady Capulet, enters. Juliet's father finds no more life in her than did her nurse. Each time her torso gets lifted or her arm raised it falls back to the bed. All bow their heads as the scene closes: Juliet's friends off to the side, at a distance, her father over her, stock-still, her mother with her face buried in the bedcovers, and her nurse prostrate at the bed corner, beating her fists on the floor to demonstrate her shuddering sobs.

Prokofiev calls his closing scenes Act 4, but MacMillan attaches them to his third act.

Act 3, Scene 4: The Capulet Family Crypt

Now familiar music pierces the air as the scene changes to Juliet's burial place. A second scene the composer calls "Juliet's Funeral" begins. When all is in place, a stone-walled space dominated by two weather-worn, angel sculptures turn what was Juliet's bed into her tomb. (Quite literally so, in terms of stagecraft: upon removing the covers, frame, and bolster from Juliet's platform bed, the scenic elements transform from mattressed bedroom fixture to stone-slab, mortuary surface.) A solemn procession of candle-bearing monks enters as parents, nurse, and Paris pay their final respects. Unnoticed by them, one monk, carrying no taper, draws up the rear of one line and lingers behind one of the side tombs. (Shrouded bodies lie on the tombs flanking Juliet's, one presumably Tybalt's.)

When all leave, with Paris lingering for a moment, the monk reveals himself to be Romeo in disguise. (Although Shakespeare's play and Lavrovsky's staging indicate that attempts to inform Romeo of Juliet's feigned death are foiled, MacMillan's staging makes no asides to demonstrate this. We must read in the program notes that Romeo has failed to receive a message from the friar regarding the staged death.) Being quickly noticed by Paris, Romeo goes on the attack and dispatches the nobleman with a knife in the abdomen. Without ceremony, the grieving young man hops up onto Juliet's tomb and desperately tries to embrace and hold her. He finds her arms slipping out of his, and when he carries her off her bier she remains ramrod straight in his grasp.

As their music swells, blares, and groans, Romeo lifts and carries his new bride while she folds up and her limbs hang like a rag doll's. Twice she slumps backward out of his arms. In the latter case, Romeo's grief takes the form of dragging Juliet's supine body by one limp arm. These moments are MacMillan at his most *verismo*. (His later ballets evolve such "realistic" or "truthful" effects to even greater and more pervasive degrees.) After trying yet again to revive his Juliet by clinging to her with smothering caresses and kisses, Romeo again raises her up in lifts that resemble a parent's of an adored child. Each time, on music that surges up then slides back down again, the inert woman falls, first to the ground and then into his arms.

It's in this awkward position that Juliet remains while Romeo places her once more on her bier. Facing her in anguished determination, he grabs hold of the container of potion he carries. Moving aside, he imbibes it. Shadowy tremolos cue his cramped movements back to Juliet. Sweeter-voiced and higher-pitched strings accompany his shuddering death throes and begin the ballet's final musical scene: "Juliet's Death." Weakly, Romeo enfolds Juliet in one more embrace, and during a last kiss falls backward alongside the bier. As he lies lifeless, a new musical motive wells up.

High-pitched strings pierced by higher flutes, give the effect of a wakening. Juliet's torso—breastbone, shoulders, and arms—begins to heave with air. She gropes about, realizing she's on cold stone and gets up with a start. After running to one side and then another, she finds one deadly sight after another: a shroud-wrapped body, a dead Paris, and another mummylike body. Then in dazed confusion she turns and catches sight of the reclining Romeo. She freezes momentarily, for the third of the dramatic stillnesses MacMillan marked in his ballet. With her music swirling about her, Juliet stares wonderingly at the vision of her beloved Romeo. As if coming to life a second time, she goes to him and cradles his head in a moment of embrace and kisses. Presently, her ecstasy turns to horror. She touches the "feel" his lips have left on hers: bitter and chill. Next, kissing his hand, she starts to sense the lifelessness of his limbs and torso. In direct, steady, and unswerving paces, she walks to the dagger that Paris had dropped. And, with little hesitation, the uncomprehending woman aims the dagger at her chest, and using both hands on its handle, plunges it into her heart.

As the music floats an air at once like the voice of a lark and a nightingale, the wounded Capulet crawls up onto her stone "bed." In weakness and agony, she reaches its other side, and after drawing Romeo's limp arm and hand to her lips for one more kiss, the lifeless limb falls back to its lifeless body as her own body drains of all its life and animation. The final tableau, especially as configured by Fonteyn, shows the Capulet daughter swooned backward over the tomb's stage-right side. The "design" of limp nightgowned woman spilling lifelessly off her pallet closely resembles the seemingly boneless female figure pouring from her bed in Johan Heinrich Fuseli's pre-Surrealist *Nightmare* painting from 1781.

Curtain

After this film of *Romeo and Juliet* was made, it became something of a tradition in the theater to close the curtain on the dead lovers' tableau and then bring it up again on that scene. The first curtain call then went to the lovers alone, with the dancers in the other leading roles, Lord and Lady Capulet, Tybalt, Mercutio, Benvolio, and the Nurse, coming on for bows afterward. In the tradition of the Covent Garden Opera House, the bows take place in front of an intermediate curtain just behind the parted house curtain. All that's missing from the traditional bows recorded in Czinner's film is a flower throw, which, very likely, Fonteyn and Nureyev inspired more readily than any other partnership of dancers.

Chapter 13

PUSHING AND SHOVING BALLET A BIT

Push Comes to Shove

• • •

Choreography by Twyla Tharp
Music by Joseph Lamb and Franz Joseph Haydn

There were other experiments by non-mainstream ballet choreographers before Twyla Tharp's *Push Comes to Shove*. Indeed, there were other experiments by Tharp herself before this one at American Ballet Theatre. But this one stuck. The fact that the leading role was fashioned for the super-stellar Mikhail Baryshnikov undoubtedly had something to do with the staying power of *Push*, so too did the performance Baryshnikov gave in his "experimental" role. So-called crossover ballet came into new prominence with Tharp's first work for ABT.

One indication of the prominence of *Push* comes in the knowledge that none of the other, previous crossover ballets found their way to videotape. (As we'll see further along, *Push* was also televised in an earlier guise.) My choice for our video companion isn't really a choice, as there are no other versions available on the market, but it might well be a choice in any case. While this video hardly records Tharp's original cast, it does include one member of that roster, who turns out to be the most crucial: Baryshnikov himself. The tape that includes *Push* also includes two subsequent Tharp works for ABT.

About this video:

Baryshnikov Dances Sinatra and More . . . With American Ballet Theatre, including *Push Comes to Shove*, 1984, 60 min., Color.

Here's another example of a tape that changed identities during its life on the market, in this case, the tape was renamed. Originally aired as a "Dance in America" telecast and marketed as *Baryshnikov by Tharp*, you may already own this very cassette. Always check the personnel and dance titles on a cassette before purchasing it. Accompanying *Push* are *The Little Ballet* (formerly called *Once Upon a Time*) and *Sinatra Suite*. Interlinking all three Tharp creations is a "Ballet Alphabet" written especially by Tharp to accompany her ballets, with Baryshnikov demonstrating and narrating her lexicon. When you come to this volume's Glossary, you might like to refer again to this tape in the instances of those items that Baryshnikov demonstrates.

Push Comes to Shove was created in a spirit of experiment and risk. Baryshnikov, living in the United States on a special visa, had been in the country only a little longer than a year when he began to work with Tharp on *Push*. Her ways were experimental; she occupied a solid place in a third-generation American modern dance lineage. (To put it perhaps too simply, she came out of the company of Paul Taylor, who had come out of the fold of Martha Graham.) Baryshnikov's roots were largely traditionally classical, out of the St. Petersburg traditions that proceeded from the nineteenth-century heyday of Marius Petipa into the pedagogy of Soviet ballet in Leningrad.

Tharp's ABT commission came on the heels of two successful creations for the Joffrey Ballet in 1973, *Deuce Coupe* (to the recorded pop music of the Beach Boys) and *As Time Goes By* (to Haydn). Though she had her interests and her own background in ballet, she hadn't made her career in the ballet world per se. Her own chamber-size troupe did not strictly subscribe to the ways of the danse d'école. For lack of an existing label, she chose "complex movement" to identify her preferred way of working, which tended to include her personal blend of jazz dance, modern dance, and the danse d'école.

When Tharp began working on her untitled, libretto-less ballet, her chosen music was Johann Sebastian Bach's Partita no. 2 in D minor for Solo Violin. Her dancers at the time were mostly Baryshnikov and, partly, Gelsey Kirkland. As she worked with her "clay," she found great satisfaction in Baryshnikov's ways of working and less with Kirkland's. Eventually the latter dropped out of the project, and Tharp replaced her, adding other dancers, even changing her music.

Firstly, she thought better of her baroque Bach and decided on some rococo Haydn. Then, to enrich the arrangement, she tagged on yet more music, this by a different composer. With thoughts of Baryshnikov's foreign classical background motivating her in part, she decided on some native classicism to set the whole thing in motion. If jazz was American classical music, then its precursor, ragtime, was America's early classicism. Having recently blended Wolfgang Amadeus Mozart with Scott Joplin in a cagey creation called *The Raggedy Dances* for her own non-ballet ensemble, Tharp chose to open her ABT ballet with a casually cool and witty American rag from 1919.

Along the way she worked unofficially and nonspecifically with a kind of libretto. Her ballet would focus on Baryshnikov in a conflict concerning two (musical) worlds and two (ballet-world) women, one tall and one short, all amid a bevy of other ballet women interspersed by a few ballet men. None of this was to be spelled out in the program, or anywhere else for that matter. The one-act ballet's sections would be identified only according to their music, which eventually included the addition of a ragtime piano piece (by Joseph Lamb). ABT watchers in particular and ballet lovers in general might or might not pick up on the subtle references to ballet repertory in general and to ABT's internal goings on, per se. In the end Tharp's ballet in four movements with prelude, was created "about" its music and its performers.

The ballet's credits are as follows:

Choreography by Twyla Tharp
Music by Franz Joseph Haydn (Symphony no. 82)
and Joseph Lamb (Bohemian Rag, 1919)
Arranged by David E. Bourne

Costumes by Santo Loquasto
Lighting by Jennifer Tipton

As indicated above, *Push* was telecast, in part, during its premiere year. For a television series called *In Performance at Wolf Trap*, the ballet's prelude and first movement were taped with the original cast. Unfortunately the cassette since marketed as *Baryshnikov at Wolf Trap* does not include the excerpt of *Push*. But if you can find a copy of the original telecast in a dance archive collection, you can see the ballet's first two segments in something like their original manifestations.

Our tape starts immediately with a casual-seeming guy (Baryshnikov) stepping into a conelike shaft of light in a black void. The leading dancer has entered in front of a black velour drop masking the full depth of the stage to put the prelude "in one"—that is, in the stage space defined by the first wings. As we've seen before, this device helps keep shows going in limited stage space while scene and/or cast changing takes place behind the dropped curtain. A delicately blaring intro from a trumpet alongside some rattling drums clears the way for the man's dance to the rag's slouching and teasing music.

Dressed in a loose satin top and high-water pants with ankle warmers, the man of *Push* also sports a bowler (or derby) hat. On our tape it's toast-colored; in the theater, it's traditionally black. The change to the unusual color was motivated, no doubt, by wanting it to "read" easily against the dark background on the television tube. In the main, the costume resembles a dancer's casual practice wear. (Its most direct reference goes to a costume Loquasto designed for Tharp in her "swing-time" dance called *Sue's Leg*.) In its way, this male solo invites its dancer to ape Tharp in one of her typically sly, slippery, and introspective modes.

The articulation is often close into the body. When it's not, its openness is deftly yet oddly timed. Much of the physical accent has the sense of "going behind the back" of the obvious musical accents. If *rubato* timing in dancing "robs time" along its way by dragging here and catching up there as the individual dancer sees fit, Tharpian timing more or less is fixed to tease and contradict musical time. The result remains marvelously musical, because the witty play around, against, or through the musical material never ceases to reinforce the music itself. With the bowler pulled down to shade the dancer's eyes, the whole is a teasingly private display.

Some of the arm and hand "jive" has a finger-snapping edge to it. On a rolling, musical whirl, a sassy young woman twirls on. Here she enters from the left of our television screen; in the theater she "announces" her arrival by slipping one pointed leg out from the wing before making her full entrance. (Elaine Kudo on our tape; Marianna Tcherkassky, originally, replacing Kirkland.) On pointe and off, mixing pointed and flexed footwork, she vamps and circles around the male dancer, whose looks tell more of a competitive than an "interested" air.

As the two dancers engage in spurts of partnered moves that more resemble his dancing meshing with hers than consciously coordinated double work, a second woman twirls on. (Susan Jaffe here; Martine van Hamel, originally.) She too sneaks her leg into view first in the stage version, before spinning on in chaîné turns on pointe. In Tharp's unspecified scheme of things, the second ballerina defines the tall-girl ballerina "type." (In simplistic terms, the shorter ballerina represents the Giselle-type danseuse; the taller one, the Myrtha type.)

The "little" ballerina vamps and circles close to the short, shy virtuoso. Sometimes she finds herself "partnered" in his arms, but essentially the two remain in a kind of coy competition. Or is it a flirtation, with a veneer of acting blasé? When Kudo is scooped into Baryshnikov's arms, it's more as an automatic reflex than a gallant show of deference: she knows what his job entails and he knows he must fulfill his function. After he tosses his bowler to the "tall" ballerina, he links up with his similarly sized partner and they play doubly cool with each other. All three dancers (the couple off to our left and the lone woman to our right), pace through moves involving hand and foot jives as well as slinky kicks and teasing shoulders.

When Lamb's rag segues into what sounds like typical traveling music, the three move in a line toward the opposite side of the space.

All the while, the hat becomes a kind of "relay race baton" prop. Once the music sounds as if it's regathered momentum and is ready to take off in a new, slouching direction, the guy in the hat offers one arm to each of the women so they can proceed suavely, arm-in-arm. More hat-play and more slinky behavior follows. Soon the women duck out on their partner as he's left to snag his hat one more climactic time from its toss in the air.

The final hat catch sends the male dancer scooting into the wing where the women exited. Thus Tharp's introductory dance number "in one" has neatly passed from our left to our right, somewhat like a sentence for us to read. Before his exit, for the camera's and the tape's sake, Baryshnikov smiles slyly and tosses his hat high in the air to cue the beginning of the first movement of "The Bear," Haydn's Symphony no. 82 in C Major from 1786. Behind the symphony's beginning, the tape offers a rundown of the ballet's credits and cast, rather like movies that delay credits until after a taste of the movie occurs. Besides the names we've already mentioned, the prominent dancers include Cheryl Yeager and Robert LaFosse.

The applause and laughs we hear on the tape are in the "laugh-track" mode of sitcom television series. Ironically, these particular reaction "takes" come from ABT's then current performances of *Push*, which were led not by Baryshnikov but by ABT principal dancer Danilo Radojevic, whom Tharp cast during Baryshnikov's tenure directing ABT. What their enlivening element proves is that Tharp's sight gags and witticisms don't necessarily depend on the idiosyncratic timing of virtuosos like Baryshnikov. The same 1984 season that *Push* was in active repertory at ABT also marked the season of Tharp's newest American Ballet Theatre commission. Called *Bach Partita*, it used the same Bach music Tharp originally toyed with when she began working out the solo choreography for the Baryshnikov role in *Push*.

Soon the stage is bared to its fullest depth, a hot-keyed cyclorama acts as background and frames the now familiar male dancer, whom we just watched ooze with such cool and ease to Joseph Lamb's rag. Only now he's standing casually still, sunk on one hip and seemingly deep in thought. On tape, Baryshnikov is caught in close-up, pondering the music swirling and surging around him. Hadyn has written it "Vivace assai" (rather vivacious). From his pensive, inert stance, the leading male dancer moves into his first extended solo. His initial movements are nonchalant, natural ones. They are, in fact, Baryshnikov's most natural and frequent tics, such as running his fingers through his hair and folding his arms in front of his chest. But as the flutes pipe up, he starts to enter into his music's energy. He plumps a foot down as if to begin a turn and then turns on the *other* foot, leaning wittily backward.

He then launches into a set of pivots and spirals, kicks and jumps that alternately appear to be driven by the music and chasing it. Some of his arm and hand moves have an air of toying with the music in a "let's play conductor mode" or of poking at and hitting its most obvious accents. He works start-stop moments into the mix, holding little stillnesses as counterpoints to the musical rush. A wildly launched tour-jeté hangs almost still in the air during its battu embellishment. Upon landing, the lush jump torsions into further embellishments made by a back-bent renversé swirl. A grand pirouette starts more or less formally enough, then gets fancied up as if the musical impetus was dogging him to continue in alternately changed directions with a brisé step here and pivot step there. (Sometimes when George Balanchine was asked to name a particularly dazzling move, he'd indicate that it didn't have a danse d'école name because it wasn't "school," it was "choreography.")

After nonchalantly smoothing his fingers through his hair yet again, *Push*'s male dancer opens a cool développé extension à la seconde, and then, on three direct string-stroking stresses in the music, he tips forward into teeter-totter arabesques-penchées. Unhurried, cooler moments of deadpan contemplation follow as if stopping on a dime, and more flights of fancy ensue. More hitting-at-the-air gestures follow, as if the music's accent makers were there, waiting to be acted upon. Delicate, offhand, eccentric accents, almost like tics, keep the choreography going at an intimate and zany level. We see the dancer sink introspectively into what he's doing. His moves include restively folding his arms and twitching with somewhat mocking gestures. One of these blithely and briefly "throws a fig," in the Italianate gesture that says, "Blank this!" in so many words.

When the music gets skittery again, it inspires the dance to get bigger and more daring. More brisés fly out from his feet, and his legs swing, in *en cloche* (bell-like) arcs dominated by kicks that appear to turn the teeter-totter penchées upside down and inside out. Light, floating, and expansive coupé-jetés pop out from the mix until the music quickens and inspires demonic *emboîté* steps that tell of a spinning run accomplished by kicking up one's heels. More would-be frenzied embellishments color and characterize the dancer's seemingly hasty travels. And, finally, after beating his working leg in and around his supporting leg, he bolts out as if the extra and excessive accents have cocked a gun that finally shoots the dancer, by way of a skidding kick, out of the action (and into the wings). (All of Baryshnikov's opening solo from the 1976 Wolf Trap telecast is included in *Twyla Tharp Scrapbook*, a 1982 videotape that Tharp produced and that has sometimes shown up on television, and perhaps may one day show up on the commercial market.)

While we assume the male dancer takes a bit of a breather, the tall ballerina slinks on. She follows the music's daintier texture with somewhat grand posturing and moves embellished by arms outstretched with winglike arms. When our male soloist sashays back on stage he positions himself next to his "ballerina competition." Her "knuckle-cracking" linked hands and arm flexions make her look something like a baseball pitcher warming up. On our tape, after she appears to release an object into the air, Baryshnikov does a double-take to see what flew by, and she goes back about her twirling dance business.

Once the music recapitulates its former het-up mood, the ballerina darts this way and that in grand jeté pas de chat, and funked-up slinking moves that include miming the wearing of trying on the bowler hat. The danseur goes about his own business, recapitulating, with casual variation, his previously executed steps. When both dancers pause, as if frozen by the music's cadence, the shorter ballerina enters. Her mood, musically and choreographically, has her demurely chasing things—tremulous notes as butterflies, perhaps. She dances in her own little world as the male dancer watching her stands off seemingly bored as she wraps up her airy-fairy reverie.

The shorter ballerina, in a golden-colored dress lighter in texture and easier of cut than the taller ballerina's light blue dress, dances with a similar, contrasting lightness. If her sister ballerina smoothly flaps her arms and unfolds her legs with a majestic tone, she floats her arms shaping curlicues while delicately extending and working her pointes to a lighter degree. If the blue-dressed woman moves like a benign bird of prey, the golden-dressed one resembles a more fragile insect.

Thumping tympany cues the male dancer to break his lackadaisical mood and recharge his motor energy. He paces more deliberately and calmly through moves we've already seen, retarding and actually pausing at points to dramatize the music's pull, push, and shoving energy. A quickening in the score drives him to faster action and gives him pause, literally in dead-stops, to resist and/or ponder its rush. Back and forth he goes, spiraling this way and that, kicking in one direction and recovering to twirl in another. Some of the insistent direction changes have the witty look of indecision. Others have the thrust of wit: "Fooled ya, didn't I? You thought I was going the other way."

Some of the teasing timing is concerned with stopping still, like a gathering storm, before plunging on ahead with new bursts of energy and articulation. Out of one seemingly casual relevé en dehors turn in demi-arabesque comes an oddly torsioned en dedans turn, wheeling widely with the working leg in a grand rond de jambe en l'air and the torso at a seemingly exhausted cant. Another driven foray unspools and another pause follows it.

The laughs that come are not unexpected, but neither are they played for. The dancer goes steadily at start-stop mode and his casual gesture versus driven danse d'école moves occur without direct regard for their immediate effect on the tickled audience. The gags, witticisms, and surprises come out of and into the music, with no room left for self-aware acknowledgement of the public's response. The final burst of dance business comes out of another port de bras sequence that looks more like a pitcher's windup.

With another stroking of his fingers through his hair and a kind of wiping of his hands on his trousers and a final flexion of his leg to the side and then to the back, the danseur prepares for one more multiple pirouette. As Haydn's final fanfare brings this movement to a close, the dancer spins, and spins and spins, through a multiple en dehors pirouette. The septuple convolution spins potently through the music's final cadence and beyond. He keeps spinning clearly into the silence that marks the symphonic movement's ending.

Baryshnikov's finishing pose, a pliant, crystalline fourth position croisé lunge, takes shape out of a suspended pause in relevé-passé stance. The wild applause that Tharp expects for her showcasing of a dancer's skill comes here almost as if it were part of the score/scenario. Baryshnikov bows to his audience coolly, neither ungracious nor servile in mood. But his coming out of the ballet's time into the audience's time and place is short-lived. As soon as he's finished bowing, which is not coincidental with the finish of the applause, he retakes his previous lunge position.

As the interval of silence from the orchestra lengthens, Baryshnikov finds himself joined by two corps de ballet women. Immediately, he takes a cue from their dancing, as, during the silence, they "pick up on" the steps and moves made earlier by the two ballerinas. He now repeats some of his previous moves and finally hurls himself offstage (stage right) in a wild *tours de rein*. The explosive power and expansive scale of his exit invariably recues the audience to resume its vociferous applause.

As the applause dies down, an ensemble of women, clad similarly to our short ballerina, takes its place on the stage. They lead off the symphony's (and ballet's) second movement. It's a slower movement, designated "Allegretto" and composed as a set of variations. It takes choreographic shape as a leader-and-followers scheme. Kudo remains front and center as her eight "friends" back her up with related moves. Their movement vocabulary includes most of the steps and gestures the little ballerina demonstrated earlier.

In ballet history, the shorter, "soubrette" ballerina is often associated with the role of Swanilda, the clever village lass who dominates *Coppélia*, Arthur Saint-Léon's 1870 ballet (to Delibes) about a female automaton, whom Swanilda resembles (based on an E. T. A. Hoffmann story). In their *Push* material, these nine dancing women intermingle the carefree qualities of a Swanilda and the mechanical moves of a Coppélia. Their display of dance and variations responds noticeably to Haydn's display of musical variations. To a kind of meowing sound, the lead ballerina flicks her clawed hands out in the air with scrappy, catlike playfulness.

While the first of Haydn's two variations winds down through another of its many repeats, a contingent of "blue" women walk on and take the places of the "golden" women. When they are all in place and their counterparts have exited, *their* leader appears. (Originally Christine Elliot, here Yeager.) The "blue" variation is more high-pitched and high-strung. Yeager's dance appears more driven. At one pronounced point along the way she folds forward in a comic collapse of exhaustion. Her sister dancers go more calmly and demurely about their dancing, while our leader chases hers.

By the time the "golden" team's variation recurs, the golden ensemble has joined the blue. Both themes include "call and response" modes in their structure, and the conversing mode that we hear becomes aptly animated for our eye. The tape's camera work seems motivated to put us on stage with these teams of women, rather than stay back and show us their gestures, moves, and formations. In her way, Tharp acknowledges ballet's inimitable geometry in her "design" and disposition of the groupings, all the while she shows her own iconoclastic and potpourri interests in "pushing and shoving" ballet's standard moves with unorthodox ones from outside ballet's classroom. Turn-in works against turnout, pointe work segues into flat, flexed, and shuffled footwork. All of which gets becalmed by plain pauses in arabesque-allongée.

Around about this point the busily working and intermingling "teams" add a head-waggling detail to their moves. The cat-clawing moves look even more zany connected to their bobbing heads. When the two leaders cut down the center of the eighteen-strong formation, they arrive just in time for a recurrence of the first variation, associated with the golden gals. As the golden and blue leaders "converse" back and forth with their accented arm and leg work, the two teams echo "conversations" of their own. When the leaders claw their "cat" hands back and forth at each other, the funny gesture becomes funnier and more of a gesture. The blue ballerina's folding up into another deep breath draws as much or more laughter a second time.

What our video does throughout this movement is take us nearly to the middle of the lined-up and intermingled forces that Tharp has worked out. In the theater, depending upon your particular seat, you'll see the sweep and the easy, geometric formations of Tharp's grand plan. X's and crosses formed by the different ensembles take shape, move, or wheel over the stage as they evolve. We can't really see these aspects of Tharp's choreography because the camera takes us almost inside each formation. Instead we feel giddily lost in the "traffic" of the ensembles. Another giddiness pertains when we watch the traffic flow from afar.

Just before what looks and sounds like a lilting ending to the leaders-and-teams episode, Kudo goes to the side and brings Baryshnikov onstage. After calmly coupling with her partner, the golden ballerina finds him and the music racing off in a new dimension. But serenity returns once more as they dance slowly à deux. The music subsides and ends just before their dance phrase does, displaying his croisé-extension front aligned as an echo of her effacé-arabesque-penchée. The two leading dancers take themselves into side-by-side lunge positions, facing upstage, as the teams make a cool, walking exit. But to keep the surprises coming, Tharp cues the leads to break their posing momentarily and bow gravely to the audience. At the same time, the exiting ensemble women similarly pause and bow at the same time the leading dancers do.

Left alone in silence, the shorter ballerina and her male counterpart pace through some of their already familiar "partnered" maneuvers, only here the timing is all their own. The moves are executed in uncharacteristic silence and their frenzied and/or lethargic pacing makes them doubly eccentric and funny. Just before the two end their cutting up and exit, a new, smaller ensemble appears. This one includes four men, dressed similarly to our solitary male lead, and four women, dressed in a look that differs from that of both the short and tall ballerina. The new ensemble women wear slinky, long jersey dresses, with their heads wrapped in turbans. (Coiffeur-wise, the short ballerina sports a "bun-head" hairstyle, reminiscent perhaps of Giselle in the second act of the ballet that bears her name. The tall ballerina has her hair done in a fairly contemporary style, fluffed out and sprayed to look soft and loose.)

With the soubrette ballerina shown off to the symphony's second, and slow, movement, the taller, statelier ballerina gets the third. It follows a "Menuetto" (*sic*) form, marked "un poco allegretto." The form being invoked is the minuet, the most elegant and refined of French court dances, sometimes misspelled by composers such as Haydn, likely because its root French word is *menu* meaning "small," with regard to the dance's dainty and measured steps.

There is little that is dainty about Tharp's reading of Haydn's minuet variation. The blue ballerina enters with her own partner in attendance as an unknown "cavalier." (There are echoes in his anonymous identity to the partner-cavalier attending the Sugar Plum Fairy in the pas de deux of *The Nutcracker*.) Here the dancer is LaFosse; originally it was Clark Tippet. The first of the symphonic movement's themes gets danced by the tall ballerina and her own sidekick/partner. Actually, he doesn't partner her at all during this segment. At a suitably stately and gracious pace, the two directly heed the music's call. Her dancing is made of already familiar moves from her earlier appearances. His is extra presentational, as if he were bowing variously to his ballerina and to the public. Initially he appears to shadow his aloof and independent partner's. Eventually her moves take on the presentational nature of his, and his take on the academic geometrics of hers.

Some of the new ensemble backs up the leading dancers with swirling steps and postures that echo those of the blue ballerina and her partner. In the ABT world that experimentalist Tharp entered to make her ballet, such background "courtiers" regularly framed the stage and the drama of narrative ballets. With regard to partnering, all that happens in this area concerns brief moments when the ballerina leans, matter-of-factly, on her cavalier to gain ballet-barre-like support for some of her moves. By the wrap-up of the first musical theme's exposition, the blue ballerina and her mate are dancing in casual unison. Their activities recall those established by the ballerina's earlier moves, as well as those of the leading male dancer. As the theme presses on plainly to its conclusion, one of the male "courtiers" stations himself strategically to lift and toss the ballerina climactically into her cavalier's arms.

The second musical theme begins by motivating the courtier

group into further action. When the music continues at a witty and almost teasing pace, the ballerina and her escort do a kind of arms-akimbo chicken walk. Squint and you can see a moment of Ashton's *Fille* chickens, out of their feathers and in their dress-up clothes. They proceed from stage left to stage right in profile positions that dramatize the neck-jutting articulations of their moves. Soon their gawky moves melt and they bend and lilt into the music's increasingly floating quality. They soon arrive at a more emphatic and boisterous musical passage. After "catching" his ballerina in big arabesque balance on pointe, the cavalier lifts her by the waist and tosses her into a grand jeté pas de chat.

His own brief set of jumping brings him to stand behind the ballerina, who assumes a "partner me" stance. Now the Myrtha-like ballerina smilingly plays a bit of Giselle, while her would-be Albrecht keeps sneaking and holding attention-getting postures blatantly behind her back. A seemingly spontaneous accentuation and manipulation of limbs by the cavalier of his ballerina indicates, with deadpan humor, a desire to spoof the music's character with step-for-note obviousness. As the ballerina continues on her way, in her own world of dancing, her cavalier interacts with the courtier dancers by way of vestigial pantomime that indicates a mix of questioning wonder at the sight and behavior of the ballerina and gracious "toasting" of her with mimed goblets.

Now, the cavalier has joined with his fellow dancers. Together, these like-minded men and women form a neat group engaged in stately yet lively unison dancing. Most of their moves restate those earlier introduced by the cavalier. The ballerina dances to her own drummer, in front of their background dancing. A scurrying and changing of places within the ensemble's formation amuses the audience and distracts the ballerina as she catches the "adjustment" of a "mistake" out of the corner of her eye. Some tit-for-tat shifting of heads and glances as the music shifts similarly, causes some laughter (on the soundtrack), but as with the symphony's second movement, the camera takes us so clearly into the midst of the confusion that the back-and-forth jokiness gets somewhat lost. An obvious repeat of the movement's earlier detail of tossing the ballerina into the air to land alongside her cavalier is not lost on anyone.

With the ballerina thus landed and her cavalier thus becalmed, the ensemble does a hat-passing routine that brings the derby back into the action. It rests in the hands of the blue ballerina and she toys with it as she dances. In a typically Tharpian mode, the symphony's final movement is introduced by an added musical moment. A percussion stick tick-tocks a rhythm all its own, like an eccentric metronome's. Ensemble member Gil Boggs (originally Kenneth Hughes) leads the warm-up fray with slinky jumping and teasing batterie as the four men, plus the tall ballerina, all appear to dance to his or her own drummer, as heard in the tick-tocking accompaniment. Before this interlude is ended, the men have scooted off, leaving the ballerina to her own last "word" before she exits.

Haydn's "Finale" movement now begins, "Vivace assai" (extremely lively). Its sweetly growling start, in which we probably hear the "bear" of Haydn's 82nd symphony, cues the reappearance of the Baryshnikov dancer. With the "bear" motive stated three times in succession, one wonders if Haydn knew the bedtime story of the three bears. (Coincidentally, around this time a clever teddy-bear manufacturer came out with a Bear-ishnikov item.) The derby-sporting stellar dancer enters and instantly vaults into a double saut de basque, before slipping forward to take off his hat and open his arms to a warm welcome. With his arms graciously spread, he keeps getting teased choreographically. First a corps de ballet female courtier joins him and then slips away; next a member of the soubrette corps takes the derby out of his hands.

Now the dancing and the music heat up further. A trio dances downstage while the derbyless danseur does so upstage. He manages to snatch back his hat, and soon finds each of the two soubrette women being thrust into his arms. When he jumps sideward, near the wings, by way of pas de chat en tournant, he meets up with a larger contingent of the soubrette corps. The strength of their numbers slightly overwhelms him and, with his bowler pulled down to his eyes, he appears lost among them as if their lineups amounted to so many revolving doors. Even trying to entice the women randomly with opportunities to try on his hat does not help stem the tide of their milling about.

When the blue ballerina slips onstage and passes through escorted by her cavalier, she remains oblivious to the attention and gracious bowing shown her by the derby-wearing dancer. As the section's opening strains are restated all the prominent and semiprominent dancers—the blue and yellow ballerinas, the blue ensemble leader, the cavalier, and the "metronome" man—take center stage and catch derbies pitched from offstage as they slink and grind through their own "bear" dance. When the original derby-wearing danseur joins them, they acknowledge his presence only so far as they hand him their hats individually. Loaded down with his hands full of hats, and with no one and nowhere to pass them off to, he blithely tosses them into the air (in the theater this would mean into the wings).

The growling "bear" theme comes back yet again, and the central danseur is alone once more, hatless and vaulting through big jumps (more double saut de basque) and spiraling and torsioning through variations on moves he's done earlier. Soon he's concentrating on a rich variety of turning moves, including a fouetté-embellished one that gets charged up, mid-revolution, by a daring hop of the supporting leg. The effect of all this turning becomes increasingly forceful. Eventually the force is so great that, as if he is a whirlpool, the dancer appears to be drawing all the other participants back into the ballet.

Initially, the female corps de ballet in their lighter dresses surrounds the lone male dancer. As he dances amid their choreographed motions, he passes through the other dancers' formations and through the music's textures, embellishing his steps and slinks with more arm foldings and a running of fingers through his hair. Eventually he comes to acknowledge a strong, climactic musical accent by once more "throwing a fig" into the mix. This is followed by another Swanilda entrance by our golden ballerina. Once she meets up with our leading man, they recapitulate some of their familiar double work, complete with eccentric accents seemingly oblivious to the music's harmoniousness.

Meanwhile, almost subversive to the prominence given to the Baryshnikov role, the ensemble performs as if slyly doing so "behind his back." Some of their performing involves taking bows as if the moments were theirs and theirs alone. With everyone now back on stage, each unit—the principal players, the soubrette ensemble, the courtier group—recapitulates its own dance business, all somehow oblivious to their fellow units and yet in phase with their common musical accompaniment.

A drum-roll preparation for the finale's actual finale cues a lift/flip of the golden ballerina by Baryshnikov. She ends up in a split position on the floor. From this funny physical marker, the ballet's final strokes come in quick and sharp succession. Tharp accents each one of Haydn's thumping finishes toward final punctuation with little "holds," stillnesses that freeze the stageful of dancers into snapshot groupings.

Tharp's ultimate stroke is as teasing as Haydn's. Her visual punctuations make her clap-happy audience giddier in their eagerness to applaud what they see. Each preparatory pause establishes a would-be climactic pose. Three occur before the really final one. And, in a witty Tharpian twist, the last one looks less at rest and fixed than the premature ones. This comes partly from the fact that some of the dancers, including the golden ballerina, freeze mid-gesture rather than settle into secure pose. It also partially flows from the fact that, as the dancers remain frozen in their places, the derbies—two in the stage version, nearly a half-dozen on our tape—fly into the air, released by the dancers who held them and wore them earlier.

Our videotape adds a freeze-frame that catches the hats in suspended animation. In the theater the curtain comes down as the hats fly upward. All at once, then, *Push Comes to Shove* comes to an end, the dancers stay stock-still, and the ballet's derby hat emblem just keeps on going.

GLOSSARY OF BALLET TERMS AND PHRASES

Dancers mostly speak with their bodies, but, like us, they also speak with their tongues. The "tongue" of ballet is like the language of any specialized field. It uses a good many of our own everyday words but often gives them their own ballet spin, so to speak. The language of ballet teaching is French, but often the "pure" French word takes on a less than pure anglicized meaning when spoken by English-speaking dancers and dance watchers. Some of the terms offered here really qualify as "Franglais," which is French given a kind of English-language logic. Other terms here qualify as English, but have a particular ballet logic and a particular meaning.

• • •

ADAGIO is a term borrowed from music, where it means "at ease" or "slow" and sometimes names a movement or section of a musical composition. In ballet, it means slow and sustained movements. In a traditionally structured ballet class, the adagio segment comes mid-lesson, for "center work," the part of the practice that takes place in the center of the classroom, as opposed to at the barre. Sometimes adagio is short for "supported adagio" or "double work," meaning the practice of the one dancer, traditionally female, working with another, partner dancer, traditionally male. Supported adagio took its part in the formula of the classical Petipa pas de deux during the latter part of the nineteenth century. Suitably "adagio" music traditionally accompanies adagio dancing. In Petipa-era ballets we find various examples of such adagios: in *The Nutcracker*, in the climactic second act; in *Swan Lake*, in the pas de trois of the first scene and two grander ones in each of the successive scenes; and in *The Sleeping Beauty* the title ballerina has an adagio in each of her three acts. In *Giselle*, we find not only a supported adagio for the title figure and her partner but a solo adagio for her that resembles in good measure a "center work adagio" in a rigorous ballet class.

ALLEGRO, the opposite of adagio, also borrowed from music, indicates "merry" or "quick and lively" tempo. Often the "allegro" is qualified as *petit* or *grand allegro.* The former "little" designation usually refers to small-scale, fast footwork, usually animated by brightly worked batterie. The latter "big" distinction has to do with larger-scaled moves that entail eager and expansive moves. In the "Elssler Pas de Deux," discussed in the chapter on Ashton's *La Fille Mal Gardée*, both Lise and Colas have opportunities to display petit and grand allegro dancing.

ALLONGÉ, "elongated," describes poses, usually arabesques, that actively reach longer and farther away from their center. The arabesque repeatedly struck by the "Shades" in the "Kingdom of Shades" in *La Bayadère* illustrates *allongé* accent. Frequently, the standing leg for such positions involves a plié action, a quarter plié (plié à quart) in the case of the Shade's arabesque. The participation of plié softens and buoys the extending limbs and the torso so the "working" elements, the extended arm(s) and leg can "float" more pliantly and reach longer than in still or held poses.

ARABESQUE names a position for the body balancing on one leg (straight or bent) while the other is extended away from the body's center, and the torso, arms, hands, neck, and head are artfully held in harmony to the standing and working legs. The term is borrowed from the scrolling, tendril-like tracery prevalent in Islamic visual art, sometimes called Moresques. The standard ballet detail for a wide variety of arabesque poses is an extended leg, almost always to the back of the dancer, with a "straight"—as opposed to firmly flexed or bent—knee. Since the name arabesque comes from visual designs based on decorative curves, it's important not to let the straightness of the extended leg lead to imagining a posture of flat and plain lines. The signature extended leg of arabesque positions dominates the idea of arabesque in most people's minds, but that detail merely completes and elaborates the source of the pose concentrated in the dancer's torso. Besides a specific variety in technique within the different schools of ballet for the working and standing leg and for the disposition of the arms and head, all usually designated by numbers—first arabesque, etc.—further details also pertain. For example, the Russian-Soviet school countenances a slightly flexed or relaxed knee in its arabesque positions, while other schools, emanating from the Italian, stress a "stretched" straightened knee. Also, the "height" of the extended leg is varied with regard to various aesthetic preferences. Extending the leg to a height higher than hip level, more or less the ultimate height during the nineteenth century, has become standard in the late twentieth century. George Balanchine was instrumental in advancing this preference over the more demure, conservative hip-level arabesque. With regard to certain "extension" poses, the arabesque has been identified as the "signature" pose of the 1895 Petipa-Ivanov *Swan Lake*, while the attitude pose (see next entry) has been seen as the identifying pose of Petipa's 1890 *Sleeping Beauty*.

ATTITUDE names a leg-extension pose of the body, related to that of the arabesque, where the extended leg is distinctly bent at the knee. The term derives from a description by nineteenth-century Italian ballet master Carlo Blasis of a pose made famous in a famous statue of Mercury by the sixteenth-century sculptor Giambologna. The sculpture shows Mercury balanced on one leg, the other artfully crooked and elevated behind him. The nature of the "crook"—that is, the angle defined by the relationship of the raised thigh to the extended lower leg—and the height of the knee vary somewhat from one ballet school to another. The extremes in prescribed attitudes are defined by the Russian and the Italian schools. Russian-Soviet schooling prefers a less than 90-degree flexion to the knee and alignment that holds the foot higher than the knee, which is held slightly higher than the level of the hip joint. The Italian school, as promulgated by Cecchetti's teaching, aims for strict 90-degree flexing at the knee, and alignment consistently out of the hip so that the extended knee and foot remain in a fairly consistent line with the hip. Balanchine's Russian references depart here; his attitude aims more for Italian-school dimensions. Sometimes the alignment holds the knee just slightly below the hip level and the foot just slightly below that. Attitudes are usually defined as extensions "back," with various disposition of the arms and torso. But sometimes the attitude is extended "front," in which case the alignment is more consistent from school to school. In the attitude-front, the knee is usually held slightly lower than hip level and the foot slightly lower than the knee level.

Additionally, the leg of attitude-front (or *devant*) is less firmly turned out than the leg of attitude-back (or *derrière*). The famous pose of the *Les Sylphides* danseur supporting two ballerinas by steadying each one's upraised hand in his own upraised hands shows flanking or framing attitude-front positions on the part of the ballerinas. The signature pose for Aurora in the "Rose Adagio" of *The Sleeping Beauty* is attitude-effacé. Like arabesque poses, attitudes can be positioned effacé or croisé. In isolated cases, often to simulate Asian or other "ethnic dance" plastique in which the traditionally stretched and pointed foot is flexed, attitude extensions can be held to the side (à la seconde).

BALLERINA, technically this term describes a female expert in the art of ballet. Its origin is Italian; the proper French equivalent is *ballerine*, though ballerina is used today in any culture where ballet is practiced. Even though the designation "principal dancer" suffices and the title "ballerina" is rarely to be found among company rankings, the term is widely used, in conversation and in print. Balletomanes will argue unendingly about legitimate or "true" ballerinas—those who qualify as technically and spiritually superior to others; and just-plain ballerinas—those who hold the rank simply by being placed at the top of their company's roster, where they perform principal dancer roles. There are no consistently set rules to ballerina status. One balletomane suggested to me that standard leading female principal dancers present themselves to us *a* woman, whereas rare and incomparable ballerinas represent womankind or the "eternal feminine." Some balletomanes look for an essence they call "B.Q." for "Ballerina Quality" or "Ballerina Quotient," and as they watch young female dancers grow and approach the peak and maturity of their careers, they assess the the presence and degree of B.Q. Alexandra Danilova identified the essence of the ballerina as "perfume," by which token the average leading female dancer is said to have "no perfume" while the "ballerina" is spoken of in terms her unmistakable "perfume."

BALLET BLANC, literally "white ballet," comes out of ballet's Romantic era ("Ballet of the Nuns" in the opera *Robert Le Diable*, to *La Sylphide* and after), with its then requisite scene of white-clad female spirits or visions who have occasion to group, regroup, and dance for some protagonist or even antagonist in the ballet's narrative. Sylphs, Wilis, Sprites, Nymphs, Shades, Swan Maidens, all these "characters" had occasion to perform intricate group dances for some plot turn or twist. Often these gatherings of tulle-beclouded female dancers took place in moonlit nighttime scenes. By the early twentieth century, Fokine took this formerly standout scene from the narrative ballet and made it stand alone. With his *Chopiniana* renamed *Les Sylphides*, the all-dancing ballet scene in misty, moonlit and white costuming became all of the ballet. The true ballet blanc is not just any dressed-in-white one-act ballet or isolated scene in a multi-act ballet; it is a ballet scene, danced by any number of women (ensemble plus leading dancers) on pointe, for the pure pleasure that lyrical ballet dancing offers. The ballet blanc contrasts with the "national dances" and other pantomime or danced activities that occur elsewhere in the course of a multi-act narrative ballet. Balanchine's 1935 *Serenade* became a ballet blanc, but one that takes place at what the French call *l'heure bleu*; that is, at shadowy twilight as opposed to shimmering moonlight.

BALLET D'ACTION, variously called *ballet en action*, *ballet pantomime*, and *ballet héroïque*, came into usage during the mid-eighteenth century. Today the term simply means a ballet that relates a story or narrative. The *action* in the designation is not physical activity—all ballet dancing involves bodily action—but rather dramatic action or activity meant to convey specific drama or character portrayal. The form evolved by adapting pantomime—or silent gestural acting—to the dancer's vocabulary. Prior to the development of ballet d'action, *le ballet* or *le ballet à entrée* meant a theatrical presentation of ballroomlike dancing—fancy, stately, or diverting dancing of a decorative nature that climaxed by way of "celebration" a theme or text previously told in music, song, or poetry. *Divertissement* (see below), or a diversion of dancing, also contrasted with dancing that told stories. In late nineteenth century "narrative ballets" that tell stories, divertissements occur, pausing or breaking the plot's momentum, but the "action" eventually resumes and moves toward its conclusion.

BALLET MASTER comes from the French *maître de ballet,* and the German *Ballettmeister.* In ballet's historical past, the "dancing master," a variation on ballet master, was the person who arranged the dances. "Choreography" referred to the writing down of the dance patterns and arrangements. Thus, by default, the related term "choreographer" would mean the individual who does the writing down, or notating, of the particulars of a given dance. As we have seen in our century, the terms "choreography" and "choreographer" have come to identify, respectively, the creation of dances and their creator, who is sometimes also called a Ballet Master.

BALLETOMANE refers to a self-motivated and self-taught devotee with a *mania* for ballet watching. The appearance of the term and the type of individual it identified, then invariably male, dates from the nineteenth century and the milieu of Russian ballet. When these individuals behaved badly, sometimes causing noisy demonstrations—both pro and con—during performances and when they attempted to meddle with or influence the artistic policies of the ballet's professionals, they became anathema to the ballet company directors and ballet masters. In France the wealthy and often influential *abonnés*, or subscription ticket holders, became the counterpart to balletomanes in Russia. The negative, haughty, and destructive side of balletomanes in their rabid mania, inflamed American ballet champion Lincoln Kirstein enough to coin the pun "balleptomaine" (a wordplay on ptomaine, a putrid bacteria associated with food poisoning). Balletomanes also have their endearing and invaluable side. They follow the ins and outs and the whys and wherefores of ballet, like committed fans of any subject, and they are part of the specialized experience. Novice balletgoers stand to learn more quickly when knowledgeable balletomanes are part of the audience. Even if you don't agree with their expressions of approval or disapproval, their intensity and eagerness make you regard what's taking place all the more keenly.

BALLON, the French word means a "hard ball" or "(child's) balloon." The eighteenth-century French court dancer Monsieur Claude (or Jean) Balon (or Ballon) is sometimes said to be responsible for the term's application to ballet technique. A little like "line" (see below), *ballon* is tricky to define in words, yet fairly easy to recognize in action. The quality of *ballon* is impressively present in ballet's *temps d'élévation*. Not to be confused with quantitative elevation (see below), *ballon* has to do with a quality of lightness of spring, with a suspension of shape and form in the air of "jumped" steps, and with a softness in landing. When you see a dancer take off, hover, and alight with a pliancy and smooth and unstrained coordination, you are seeing a dancer to whom aerial moves come almost naturally. No dancer, to be sure, jumps brilliantly without careful schooling and practice, but to some dancers the skills of *temps d'élévation* come more naturally than others. Good *ballon* can be taught, practiced, and honed; great *ballon* probably comes from nature. Watch dancers jump, and take in how some strain or push to get off the ground and stay in the air, and how others seem to get up and stay airborne as easily as most of us walk. *Ballon* allows jumps to float and hover no matter how far off the ground.

BARRE, literally "bar," refers to the horizontal pole affixed to the wall of the ballet classroom or, in the case of space-saving compromises to accommodate overcrowding, set up freestanding in the middle of the room. Traditionally made of wood, freestanding barres are nowadays also made of aluminum. The barre's purpose is to give the dancer a support on which to hold, at about waist height, while exercising one side of the body at a time. Scholars assume that a bellpull-like rope, once held on to by courtiers practicing their ballroom dancing, prefigured the ballet classroom's barre. "Barre" is also the name given to the beginning warm-up part of a standard ballet class. Sometimes the dancer faces the barre and works with both hands on the support. These "facing the barre" exercises can benefit especially young pupils who need extra support—beginning pointe-work students, for example, or dancers who want to work extra forcefully to the back while they hold on to something firmly to the front.

BATTEMENT, literally "beating," this refers to moves in which the foot or leg beats the air or space around it. Like allegro, battement is strictly divided into grand and petit accents. In its grand form the leg moves noticeably far away from the starting or beginning position. The common *grand battement* is simply a large, kicked move, sweeping the leg from a closed or à terre position through to a wide open, far-reaching, open position. For example, the grand battement à la seconde has the dancer sweeping his working leg from fifth or first position high into the air of second position, as high in the air as physical strength, muscular stretch, and given musical cadence allow. *Petit battement* would move the working leg, guided by the working foot, less far away from the standing leg and foot. The basic *battement tendu* exercise of elemental ballet classes stretches the working leg and foot à terre away from the standing leg and foot only to the full stretch of the working limb. Battement tendu falls into the petit battement category and has, perhaps, the dimension of extending a hand for the purposes of a handshake. Grands battements have the air of throwing up one's hands and arms in gleeful, abandoned celebration.

BATTERIE, a term related to *battement* (see above) identifies "steps beaten." Unlike battements, which tend to work one leg against its standing counterpart, batterie involves the beating or crossing of one leg against the other in equal measure. *Changement de pied* or just plain *changement* is the simplest version of a batterie move: the feet simply move up into the air from being crossed in one way—say, right foot in front of left—to finish being crossed in the opposite way—left in front of right. When the feet cross twice in the air, the entrechat becomes quatre because each of the feet cross or change twice. When the change happens three times over, the move qualifies as entrechat-six. Entrechats fall into the category of petit batterie, so do the brisé (see below) moves in the "Blue Bird Pas de Deux" in *The Sleeping Beauty*, for example. *Grand batterie* involves beaten moves combined with jumps of grand jeté elevation. Cabrioles (see below) qualify as grand batterie moves.

BOURRÉE is short for *pas de bourrée* or *bourrée step*. The Bourrée was originally a folk dance from central France that was adopted to court dancing. A specific bourrée musical form accompanied the dance of the same name. Ballet today has a wide variety of bourrée-designated steps, with various up-versus-down sequencing to its three-part formula. Up/up/down is a familiar sequence of pas de bourrée accents. In everyday ballet shorthand, however, bourrée almost always refers to the step variously known as pas de bourrée-couru or-chaîné, or-suivi. These are the tiny, linked traveling steps, primarily executed on pointe, as ballerinas skim across the stage. Myrtha the Queen of the Wilis in the Perrot-Coralli *Giselle* has a famous sequence of these steps for her entrance. Likewise, in the Petipa-Ivanov lineage for *Swan Lake*, Odette makes her exit from the first lakeside scene by means of these steps. Frequently the ballerina's legs work through these bourrées in fifth position.

B-PLUS is a nickname for an *attitude à terre* pose in which the dancer stands on one braced, straightened, turned-out leg, usually *en face* (see below), while the other is lightly flexed and gently crossed behind the standing leg, something like a fishtail. The foot of the flexed leg rests on the floor by making contact with it on the tops of toes, or more likely on the top of a toe shoe's or slipper's vamp. Legend has it that Balanchine's name gave the pose its B, because he had preference for this contrapposto stance. B-plus stances work to soften and make extra interesting the normally strict, dry, and formal geometry of en face positions.

BRISÉ designates a step in the petit batterie category. The English translation, "broken," seems a little harsh for the effects of such steps—"flutter" would seem a more apt description. In brisé steps the dancer gently shoots a foot in the direction of travel and then brings the other up to meet the first and crosses/beats the two at the moment of meeting, before landing on one of the two feet. Repeatedly executing brisé steps to the front and to the back in the step known as *brisé volé* (broken/flying) can give the effect of flutter and hovering flight, as seen in the "Blue Bird Pas de Deux" from Petipa's *Sleeping Beauty*.

CABRIOLE belongs to the category of steps of elevation (see below) as a "capered" jump in which the dancer beats his legs, making calf-to-calf contact once, twice, or perhaps three times. The rebound of the beat, or contact made by the one leg with the other, should send the uppermost leg clearly away from the other as it "lands" the jump. Though they usually have a grand jeté emphasis and scale, when they technically qualify as *grandes cabrioles*, they can also involve less elevation, as *petites cabrioles*. They beat the legs in front of, behind, or to the side of the dancer's starting point. Cabrioles "to the front" can make the dancer look like he's sitting in the air; those "to the back," as if he were floating in the air. Their usual, clean-line, pointed-feet look can be executed with bent knees and flexed feet. In these cases, the beat is not calf-to-calf, but heel-to-heel, and the step can be called a "character cabriole."

CAMBRÉ, meaning "arched," is the opposite of *penché* (see below). While the arched-from-the-waist accent can take the torso, led by the head, backward or sideward, the more frequently seen cambré accent is to the back. Sometimes referred to as a backbend or a fully arched torso, cambré position leans lushly backward. In the long, slow entrance for the corps de ballet in *La Bayadère*'s "Kingdom of the Shades," the white-clad female dancers step into arabesque-allongée out of contrasting cambré stances in a pointe-tendu–front position.

CARACTÈRE, meaning "character," refers to ballet dancing that aims to represent specific, often ethnic characters. *Demi-caractère* dancers tend to be shorter and have bulkier muscles than classically noble dancers; their dancing tends to be more athletically showy and emotionally animated than that of their more staid or *sérieux* counterparts. Character dancers tend to be largely mime performers, their portrayals in the "rustic" or "grotesque" vein. The wicked fairy Carabosse in *The Sleeping Beauty*, the strong-willed widow Simone in *La Fille Mal Gardee*, and Hilarion in *Giselle* are all character roles. The first of these is often treated as a travesty (see below) role; the second, in Ashton's ballet, is always so treated.

CAST, the players performing a theatrical work, refers in ballet to the dancers involved in a given performance. The term "first cast" refers specifically to those dancers on whom the choreography was fashioned. Knowing something about the dancers who created the roles of a ballet in question can illuminate our understanding and expectations of those roles. In a given season, a ballet will sometimes be performed with a "second" and/or "third" cast, which have the task of making their own, the parts that were tailor-made for the first cast dancers. In some cases, choreographers or ballet-masters will alter steps to suit subsequent casts. Still, especially in cases of touchstone or legendary choreography, future casts feel compelled to work scrupulously to relive or repeat steps and moves that were made famous over the years in a ballet. The fouettés for Odile in the "Ballroom" scene of *Swan Lake* are but one case in point. Many a ballerina to whom fouetté turns do not come easily has dutifully ground through the "Black Swan" sequence, simply because she didn't want to be accused of not doing the "original" choreography.

CAVALIER, which comes from the French *chevalier*, meaning knight or courtly gentleman, as well as woman's escort or dancing partner, has today become synonymous with partner of the ballerina in a pas de deux. The term has strong links to the repertory of ballets created by Balanchine. In some cases, where the male dancer has no specific character name in the context of a classical narrative ballet, Balanchine identifies him specifically as a "cavalier," such as the Cavalier to the Sugar Plum Fairy in *The Nutcracker* or the Cavalier to Titania in *Midsummer Night's Dream*. But the roots are probably in the ballet of Balanchine's Russia. In her memoirs, ballerina Ekaterina Vazem, the first Nikiya in Petipa's *La Bayadère*, uses the term "cavalier" to refer to an 1870s partnering role for Lev Ivanov (Petipa's collaborator on *Swan Lake* in 1895).

CHAÎNÉ, which means "chained," as in "linked like a chain," is shorthand for the most frequently seen and used chaîné move: chaîné turns, or *tours chaînés deboulés*, or "chained turns rolling like a ball." Each full rotation of such turns is made by stepping into two half-turns on alternate feet. The turns can be done on demi-pointe or full pointe. Special "twist" variations are done on the heels of feet flexed upward, but the most standard and frequently seen chaîné turns are those on pointe for women and on demi-pointe for men. In consummate control, ease, and force, they can give the dancer the look of being driven (or actually, driving) a benign tornado.

CHOREOGRAPHER, originally "one who writes dances," now the one who invents and arranges them. The term is interchangeable with ballet master, formerly dancing master. In the days when dance was taking root in U.S. theater, the individual responsible for creating the dances would have the credit "Dances arranged by." Eventually "Choreography by" became the credit line and the person responsible was the choreographer. When a choreographer works out the particulars of a piece of choreography on his chosen dancers, they become identified as the ballet's "first cast" (see "Cast"). Knowledge of the particular strengths or weaknesses of the first-cast dancers helps us understand the essence of the choreography. In the States, first-cast dancers tend to say that their roles were "created *for* them"; in Britain, such dancers would note roles that were "created *on* them."

CLASS is the daily regimen dancers perform, in their classrooms, with their teachers, to learn their craft and keep that craft (and their physiques) in workable shape. After "taking class" in grades and stages, each according to the particularly prescribed process of individual institutions, professional dancers continue to take class. I say "take," because that's the usage style in the States; in England, they say "do" class. "Taking the class" in England means teaching it, as in taking charge of its instruction. The instructor of U.S. ballet classes is said "to give" the class. When dancers reach the highest ranks of their companies, the special classes given to those levels are sometimes referred to as the "Class of Perfection," from the longstanding French designation, *classe de perfectionnement*.

CLASSICAL BALLET is a tricky and slippery category. To many people it's a specific era of ballet history. Unlike many other theatrical dance eras, this one does not coincide with its like-named musical era. Late seventeenth- through early eighteenth-century Baroque music, for example, corresponds with a similarly named Baroque dance period. The same goes for a period of Romantic music and for Romantic ballet, the early to mid-nineteenth century. But the late-nineteenth-century period of "classical ballet" does not coincide with a related period of classical, Mozart-era music, which is post-Baroque and late eighteenth century. The ballet structures and formulas of Marius Petipa in imperial Russia stand for many as hallmarks of the ballet we today call "classical." With their shorter, stiffer tutus and the variety of foot- and leg work exemplified by the tour de force aspects of Italian virtuoso technique, the ballerinas in Petipa's ballets reigned supreme in their ballets' choreography. If the effect of the earlier named Romantic Ballet (see below) was one of luminous pearls, the physical, visual effects of Petipa's classicism were those of sharply facetted gemstones. The problem and limitations of this view of classical ballet rest in thinking that the era closed with Petipa's death. Many people prefer to define what happened in a related vein after Petipa as "neoclassicism." Some post-Petipa experiments (accent on experimental, modernist thinking) fit such a bill. However, if the post-Petipa choreographer displays the dancer's skill in a similarly sharp and clear manner while taking into account the dancer's contemporary physique and evolving strengths, the result can rightly be viewed as classical. Essentially, most people mean the classical tutu (see "Tutu") ballet when they refer to classical ballet. Without strict and universal parameters you'll have to shade the definition yourself.

CODA, an Italian-language musical term meaning "tail," which ballet borrows for the finishing segment of a formal pas, such as a grand pas d'action or a pas de deux. The structure, as we've seen in highlighted pas de deux from ballets such as Petipa's 1890 *Sleeping Beauty*, Balanchine's 1954 *Nutcracker*, and Ashton's 1960 *La Fille Mal Gardée* goes as follows: entrée, adagio, (man's) variation, (woman's) variation, coda. The capstone segment, traditionally the most animated, forceful, and quick-paced of all the segments, brings all the dancers involved in the pas together to finish in coordinated harmony.

CORPS DE BALLET, literally "body of the ballet," meaning largest body of dancers in a given troupe. In the Paris Opera Ballet, "corps de ballet" refers to the entire company. Early on the dancers of the ensemble were known as *les choristes dansantes* (dancing choristers). Normally ballet companies list the basic ensemble as corps de ballet, which comes last in its hierarchy, unless the troupe includes apprentices or aspirants, in which case those individuals come last. Depending upon company tradition and/or union stipulations, the male and female dancers may be listed as one corps de ballet or as separate ranks (all the men followed by all the women, or vice versa). Sometimes simply called the "corps," these dancers tend to work in groups or ranks. Depending upon union rules and/or tradition, individual members of the body of dancers may or may not be used in prominent or solo capacities. European dance traditions tend to hold ranks firm, and pool only upper levels of dancers for prominent or solo dance parts. American companies tend to be more fluid in function, and may give a corps de ballet dancer a solo or even a leading-dancer role in the course of a season. Some troupes have strong and revered traditions for uniformity of size and regimentation of corps de ballet dancing. Others are less concerned or strict with regularity of presentation.

CORYPHÉE, a word with roots in the ancient Greek theater where a similarly named individual, a *koryphaios*, was the leader of the chorus. In ballet the ranking names the level above corps de ballet. In companies where the rank still exists, mostly European ones, the designation stands for "little soloist," since these dancers may be offered roles with more prominence than those of the corps de ballet.

CROISÉ means "crossed" and refers to one of the specific positions (or directions) of the body framed by the proscenium stage. In croisé positions, the dancer faces one of the corners of the stage while his downstage leg is positioned and/or extended so that its line crosses in front of the upstage leg. As with écarté and effacé positions (see below), croisé "shadings" consistently display the dancer's physique to the audience watching from the front defined by the proscenium stage. Individual schools of ballet practice specific ways for the upper body, arms, and head to be held in its various croisé positions. If you want to define a position as croisé, effacé, or écarté, look to the legs. If the leg nearest you is aimed, angled, or "held" in front of the upstage leg, the dancer is in some croisé position.

CROSSOVER BALLET was coined in the United States in the 1970s when choreographers from modern dance, an area once antagonistic toward the principles and means of ballet, began to create dances for ballet companies. (Twyla Tharp's *Push Comes to Shove* is an example.) The experimentation that results can be refreshing or it can be stalemating, depending upon the openness of both the modern dance choreographer and the ballet dancers. The biggest challenge to the non-ballet choreographer is the dimension of pointe work. Along the way of working creatively with the ballet dancer's skill, the choreographer from outside ballet must experiment deftly so as to maintain the integrity of the feet, the safety of the dancer.

DANSE D'ÉCOLE, literally "dance of the school" (or academy), applies to any ballet that is based on the established inventions of ballet dancing evolved since its beginnings in France in the mid-seventeenth century. In the name of experiment, especially in crossover ballets (see above), some choreographers choose to abandon or downplay the accumulated vocabulary of ballet technique. Those who accept and work with that recognizable vocabulary, even as they hope to experiment and extend the means, can be said to honor the danse d'école.

DANSEUR is often used to describe the male dancer, often the most prominent male dancer in a given ballet. The Italian-language male counterpart to ballerina is ballerino, but this term has not caught on in daily usage, either written or spoken. Sometimes danseur usage implies *danseur noble*, an exponent of the longstanding "noble" or "serious" genre of ballet-dancer types. Sometimes "noble" is used by itself to define the same category. These individuals are traditionally tall, long of limb, and slender of musculature. Because there is physically more of them to put in space, the noble male dancer sometimes finds himself in a repertory of "partnering" or "cavalier" roles, with dancing that demands more control and poise than fiery energy and athleticism.

DEDANS, EN, meaning "in an inward direction," refers to the direction and impetus the dancer's working gives to a turning move. It doesn't matter which leg or what position the leg works from, all en dedans turns spin "inward"—in a direction that aims toward the standing leg. "En dedans" turns give the impression of wrapping things up, of spiraling inward, with a effect of tightening a screw.

DEHORS, EN, meaning "in an outward direction," describes the direction and impetus of turns that seem to grow out from the axis of the standing leg. If en dedans turns have the effect of wrapping up as they spin, en dehors turns have the effect of opening out as they revolve. If you want to note the identity of the inwardly versus outwardly impelled turns, look carefully at the standing leg. Pirouettes (or tours) in passé (see below) position or à la seconde extension are fairly easy to identify. Turns in arabesque and attitude are less easy, but the same "key" holds: Look at the standing leg, if the turn rotates in a direction toward the standing leg's axis, it's en dedans, if it's away it's en dehors.

DÉVELOPPÉ, literally meaning "developed," is often used synonymously for "extension." Dancers who are described as having "big développé" are those who display a fluid flexibility that results in holding an extended leg impressively high in the air (extension). Mechanically, the développé movement starts in the foot of the working leg, which is drawn precisely up the front, back, or side of the standing leg (depending upon the prescribed technique of the school in question) and then moves away from the standing leg, usually after the working foot reaches the standing leg's knee, by unfolding and extending itself, fully stretched in a given direction. Extensions can reach to the front, side, or back of the dancer. As we've seen, the leg extended fully to the back is called an arabesque. Extensions to the front, less common in occurrence, are usually called "extensions front." But the leg extended to the side, à la seconde, is the one usually termed "développé." In the twentieth century, the height, rake, and reach of the extended leg à la seconde has grown in scale due to freer costuming and more pronounced flexibility. Time was when the leg was held in clear alignment with the level of the hip—the working/extending foot held the leg at the quarter of or quarter after six o'clock position, and the standing leg aimed the torso to the clockface's six position. Today the working foot points and takes the working leg high above hip level, to the five to six o'clock position, or, five after, depending on which is the working and which the standing leg. In extreme cases—extremely flexible hip joints and lithely stretched legs—the développé move can point to the positions indicating one or two minutes before (or after) six. The "big développé" has lately gotten about as big as it can get without becoming a contortionist's deformation.

DIVERTISSEMENT, meaning "diversion," refers to a dance number offered to divert the audience's attention with momentary entertainment. Such displays of dancing for the sake of dancing, rather than for the sake of narrative or dramatic effect, came into ballet history out of the entrées that were part of ballet de cour (court ballet) and opera ballet (spectacles intermixing song and dance). Divertissement became separate from the categories ballet pantomime and ballet d'action (see above). Once the ballet d'action evolved into the multi-act narrative ballets devised by Marius Petipa, the divertissement became a usual part of those ballet's plan. In the traditions established by Petipa, divertissements became part of his climactic and often celebrational last acts. Sometimes these separate little diversions made up a suite, as in the suite of national dances in the ballroom scene of *Swan Lake* or in the suite of fairy-tale character numbers in the wedding scene of *The Sleeping Beauty*.

ÉCARTÉ means "separated" or "thrown wide open" and names another specific position or direction of the body on ballet's proscenium stage. As in the case of croisé (see above) and effacé (see next entry) positions, écarté positions involve the dancer in a stance aligned along one of the stage's corner-to-corner diagonals. Thus stationed, the dancer is in écarté position when the working leg extends (à terre or en l'air) to the side, while holding his head in profile to his torso. The arms framing the profile and the angle of the dancer's gaze vary according to different systems of ballet teaching, but écarté positions consistently show the legs in a variant of seconde position while the dancer's torso faces one of the stage's corners. In the end, the telltale legs of this ballet position give it away, as the turned-out foot of the standing leg points toward one corner of the stage, while the turned-out foot of the working leg points toward the opposite corner.

EFFACÉ, meaning "shaded," identifies ballet positions or body directions that contrast directly with croisé positions. Effacé is sometimes mistakenly translated as "open," since the telltale leg positioning that distinguishes the effacé pose qualifies as open when compared with the crossed disposition of the legs for croisé. In fact, the French school calls its related position *ouverte* (open). As in croisé positions, the dancer faces one of the stage's corners, but instead of extending (en l'air or par terre) his downstage, working leg across the line of his standing leg, he extends it away from his standing leg's line. Thus, while not crossing his standing leg, he *shades* it, or perhaps casts a shadow on it. As in the other specific body positions (or directions), various pedagogies specify various ways for holding the arms, torso, and head for effacé poses. Effacé poses, whether held or momentary, show off the dancer's full figure more plainly and expansively than "croisé" poses. Sometimes choreographers show a preference for the one over the other. My own observations, full of exceptions to be sure, find that Balanchine had a preference for effacé positions, Ashton for croisé.

ÉLÉVATION sounds different in French but in ballet it means the same thing it does in English: the height to which something is elevated or to which it rises. Talk of a dancer's elevation refers to the height of his jumps, the dancer's ability to attain height in the air. It differs from *ballon,* which in contrast might be said to concern the dancer's ability to *sustain* height in the air. The effect of pas (or temps) d'élévation meet the eye most readily in terms of the aerial aspects, but in fact all jumps and jumped steps depend to a fine degree on the demi-plié takeoff and the landing that frame the jump's crest or airborne moments. Male dancers are frequently more praised for their remarkable elevation than female dancers, though certain female dancers gain such praise as well. Female dancers schooled in the Russian or Russian-based ways of ballet frequently command attention for their impressive jumps with regard to quantity of elevation.

ENTRECHAT is a specific dance term that entered the French language in the early seventeenth century. It derives from the Italian *intreciarre*, which means to braid or interweave. In this case, the braiding image results from the activity of the dancer's lower legs' crossing and recrossing a given number of times after he springs into the air off two feet before landing again. Entrechats come in odd- and even-number variants. The odd-numbered ones, which span from number three to nine—entrechat-trois through entrechat-neuf—land on one foot with the other raised slightly off the floor (in a position known as *sur le cou de pied,* or "at the neck of the foot"). The usual even-numbered entrechats—two through ten or entrechat-deux to entrechat-dix, rise from two feet and land on two. Entrechat-deux, a variation on ballet's changement de pieds, is also known as entrechat royale, because it is said to have been done originally by King Louis XIV. Entrechat-dix is now "off the charts," and seems to have been ever since it was put there, according to legend, by the legendary Vaslav Nijinksy. As noted in this text, entrechats can have the effect of fluttering flight, thus their prominence (as entrechat-six) in the Petipa-heritage choreography for the "Blue Bird" in *The Sleeping Beauty.*

ÉPAULÉ literally means "shouldered," and comes into play as an upper-body "shading" of various body positions (or directions; see Croisé, Effacé). "Shouldered" positions come into being by means of épaulement, or "shouldering" moves and/or shifts. These accents occur when the downstage arm of a dancer in profile, or on a diagonal stage line, reaches long, ahead of the torso, so as to draw the shoulder forward and elongate the upper part of the back and torso. The épaulé angle of the torso is the detail that distinguishes most second arabesque poses from first arabesque positions. In the repeated exits of the ballerina performing the "Mazurka" in *Les Sylphides*, the épaulement acts as an artful afterthought to the striking of her climactic arabesque pose.

EXTENSION is an English language term that identifies the often dramatically or climactically extended leg out of some preparatory move, such as développé or grand battement. The most dramatic and/or spectacular nowadays is the extension à la seconde, since it's in this position that the leg is most inherently free to extend out of the hip joint.

FACE, EN, sometimes known as *de face,* meaning "to the front" as in "face front," this direction is the plainest, most direct angle for presenting a dancer to his audience. Balanchine is said to have called the position the most difficult to make interesting because the dancer had no "seasoning" ingredients, such as croisé, effacé, or épaulé adjustments, to enrich the standing figure. He also said it was an important direction to practice and perfect, so that its purity and simplicity could shine and indeed prove interesting visually. Oftentimes, grandes pirouettes, tours en l'air, and fouetté turns (all defined below), take their preparatory moves in en face position.

FINGER TURN *See Fouetté*

FIVE (BASIC) POSITIONS OF THE FEET. The five ballet positions for the feet and legs evolved from ballroom dancing skills. Since the eighteenth century, these first through fifth have remained remarkably consistent, with the odd-numbered ones being "closed" or *fermé* positions and the even-numbered ones "open" or *ouverte*. Probably the most frequently seen on stage is the tightest, tallest, and most centered of the five: fifth or cinquième position. The science of the sequence of the positions is based on each dancer's own measure: the space separating the feet for each of the open positions is the length of the dancer's own foot. Interestingly, alongside these five "true" positions there were five others, the so-called false positions, which were reserved for the vocabulary of the grotesque or comic genre dancers.

FOUETTÉ, which simply means "whipped," is an action that can apply in numerous ways to ballet moves. However, for all of the ballet world the term is shorthand for *fouetté rond de jambe en tournant*, or a "fouetté turn." This names the usually successive turns done with impetus from a fouetté move combined with a rond de jambe (see below) move. A slow version of this fouetté-propelled turn is the "finger turn," in which the dancer, traditionally a female dancer on pointe, takes support from the finger that her partner, traditionally a male dancer, holds over her head to grasp as she gently pushes off her partner's extended arm and lets her fouetté rond de jambe leg movement propel her into a spin. This "supported fouetté" can be seen near the end of the traditional Ivanov version of the "Love Duet" in the first lakeside scene of *Swan Lake*. The unsupported and rapid-fire version of successively executed fouetté turns are also usually seen in *Swan Lake*, in this case in the internationally famous Petipa choreography for Odile in the "Pas de Deux" of the "Ballroom Scene."

JETÉ means "thrown," and has become a catch-all term meaning "jump" to ballet watchers. For the record, the everyday French for "jump" is *saut* as a noun and *sauter* as a verb. The jeté category technically defines only jumps that take off from one foot and land on the other. Jetés are variously named and often qualified according to scale, conveniently identified as *jeté* or *grand jeté*. Some of these involve turning moves, in which *tournant* becomes part of the name, others involve beats, in which case *battu* becomes a qualifier, and still others include whipped changes of direction or sharp, "cutting" changes of feet, in which cases *fouetté* is part of the whipped jeté's name, and *coupé* becomes part of the foot-cutting variety. Jeté moves also vary according to direction of travel; that is, moving forward, often called *en avant* or backward, as in *en arrière*, or sideways, either *de côté* or *à la seconde*. Jumps specifically categorized as *sauté* moves, differ from jetés in that they involve the dancer moving from one foot to the same foot. Essentially these jumps are hops. Jumps done from two feet to one foot come under the category of *sissone*, a move named for its probable originator, one Comte de Sissone, but also reminding some of the delicate scissoring aspect of the jump's action. (Never mind that *ciseaux*, the actual French for "scissors" is a specific kind of jump from two feet to two feet—see ahead—Franglais has its own cockeyed logic.) Jumps from two feet to two feet are in the jump category as well. Some of these qualify as *soubresaut* moves, meaning "sudden leap or bound"; others, as indicated above, qualify as ciseaux moves, in which case a soubresaut jump involves the opening out of the legs, symmetrically and widely, before landing on two feet. The term *tour jeté* is a shorthand corruption of *grand jeté dessus en tournant*, "large jump, turned over." *Jeté en tournant* is a more delicate, small-scaled, fleet jump, with effects all its own. See Ashton's *La Fille Mal Gardée* for examples of both kinds of turning jumps.

LEOTARD, a one-piece torso-covering fitted garment of light fabric, was named after the French circus performer who devised it. Once considered a garment for dancers to wear for class or rehearsal, now, in part due to the aesthetic preferences of Balanchine, who created what became known as "leotard ballets," the garment is uniform costuming. Colors and the cut of the top may vary, but the leotard essentially acts to clothe the dancer in a simple second-skin covering. Traditionally, female dancers wear their leotards over their tights, while male dancers tend to wear their tights over their leotards. In a corruption of "leotard," the term "unitard" has come into parlance. These "all-over tights," as they are sometimes called in Britain, name a garment that covers not just the dancer's torso, but his legs and feet as well. Also called a "body suit," a unitard is worn similarly by both men and women. They vary in the cut and kind of top—long, short, or no sleeves—as well as in kind, color, and/or coloring of fabric.

LIFT, rather rarely known as *enlèvement* (carrying off), refers to the effort and effect of one dancer, traditionally male, as he takes in his arms and raises above the stage another dancer, traditionally female. Lifts can take the lifted dancer slightly off the ground or high in the air, depending upon the desired choreographic effect. Late-twentieth-century ballet acknowledges the art of Russian-Soviet ballet as the "source" of many lifts now in standard use around the world. The heroic emphasis in Soviet ballet's socialist realist aesthetic doubtlessly led to a whole repertory of such "stunts." Modernist experimentation with geometric patterns and with acrobatic elements infused ballet's theatrics in the post-imperial age. Outside Soviet Russia, choreographers experimented with lifts as an elaboration of the art of the pas de deux (see below). Both Balanchine and Ashton seem to have become interested in "carry lifts" around the same time. These lifts hold and carry the ballerina so that she seems to float and skim the ground on which her partner stands. Bigger, more acrobatic and emphatic lifts became part of the Soviet choreographic canon. One-handed lifts with the ballerina held at arm's length above her partner's head came into common parlance. In Russian the word *stulchik* (little chair or stool) names a lift in which the ballerina sits on the upraised palm of her partner's (see "Cavalier") hand. We saw this lift at the end of the "Elssler Pas de Deux" of Ashton's *La Fille Mal Gardée*. Sometimes the acrobatics of Soviet-styled lifts include tossing the ballerina in the air and catching her dramatically, in which case the lift is called a "throw." When the ballerina is held at arms' length in both hands of the partner while she seems to float supine overhead, the lift is called a "bird." When the ballerina is lifted from standing in front of her partner to end sitting prettily on his shoulder, the lift is called a "shoulder sit." No matter how simple or complex the lift looks, its success is much more a matter of coordination between dancers than it is the sheer strength and suitable weight of the other. Timing and a careful working together make for graceful, smooth, and strong lifts. If, for example, the ballerina doesn't prepare with a jumped uptake at the start of a lift, mere physical strength will not accomplish the task. American Ballet's Jerome Robbins became a proponent of gracefully fanciful and acrobatic lifts.

LINE, which is English for *ligne,* is one term in the English-speaking ballet world that does not co-opt French-language spelling. A little like *ballon* (see above), "line" is a ballet element more people can readily see than precisely define. A dancer's "line" rests in the harmonious alignment of the various parts of his body. "Line" essentially emanates from a dancer's center, which is located in some theoretical central internal point demarked by the dancer's waist. Sometimes the center seems fixed at the base of the spine, in the lower back. The svelte shape and clear proportions of the dancer's physique have a strong effect on his line. But a pretty or impressively lithe body does not guarantee strong or true ballet line. What's important for clear, clean, pure line is that, as the eye follows and takes in the shape held, however momentarily, by the dancing dancer, it find a totality, a continuity of energy and form without noticeable disruptions, snags, or breaks. To maintain and dramatize his line, a dancer needs to be coordinated to the nth degree. Everything a teacher's eye and tutelage has given a dancer to think about and work at must be subconsciously heard and obeyed as the dancer dances and poses. Any forgetfulness or laziness of detail will take its toll and spoil the dancer's line. Adagio movements and the poses these moves methodically go through are meant to display a dancer's line. But allegro moves (see above) also demand harmonious line, and any break in it, however brief, can act like grit in the eye of beholder, just as a distortion or interruption of line in adagio circumstances can seem to warp or crease the otherwise smooth and continuous surface of a radiant picture. One aspect of line is its unending harmoniousness; it leads the viewer simultaneously to fix on the dancer's physical design in space as well as to follow the performer's energy as it radiates beyond its actual physical limits. Line doesn't outline or contain the dancer's presence in space, it continues it. For this reason, the pointed foot, completing the artful length of the dancer's longest limb, his leg, must never be what ballet lingo calls "sickled." Sickled feet break the line of the leg by stopping the outward, continuous flow of the limb and derail it by turning the dancer's line back on itself. Unstretched or unsupple muscles and unaligned or tight joints can also interrupt the free and continuous flow of a dancer's line. The entrance of the Shades in *La Bayadère* is a good opportunity to observe what the Russians specifically call *cantalena* (or "singing") line.

LOST BALLET. *See* Reconstruction.

MANÈGE, EN. *See* Tour.

MIME, short for "pantomime," comes from the Greek for "all acting." In ballet, the gestural art of "signing" emotions and narrative details, separate from "pure dancing," evolved out of a largely Italianate art form. For a long period of ballet's development in the nineteenth century, certain dancers were classified as *Italien* to signify their excellence and speciality in mime roles. (Those classified as *Français* excelled and specialized in pure-dancing parts.) Mime carried forth the storyline of all nineteenth-century narrative ballets. Ballet scores made allowances for mime scenes, often labeled *scène* by the composer, that were separated from dance passages, variously named *danse* or *pas*, etc., in the score. Mime can be declamatory, as when a character tells his story directly to the public, like a soliloquy, or it can be conversational, as when characters communicate with one another. Examples of declamatory mime can be found in most traditional stagings of *Coppélia* (1870). Examples of conversational mime can be found in stagings of Bournonville's *La Sylphide*, particularly in the exchanges between a bewildered James and a beguiling Sylph. Mime is largely an art of the upper body, particularly the arms, hands, and face. Since it is a "mute" art, the miming dancer should not move his lips and/or open his mouth when signing. Ballet mime differs from generic or standard mime in its relationship and dependence on accompanying music. In the word of the French ballet world that Italianate mime became part of, the gestural art was *mésuré*—that is, specifically structured to music. If you have a phobia for whey-faced, sad-eyed mimes, don't let your fear of mimes prevent you from admiring and paying attention to the mime passages of narrative ballets. Mime becomes unique in the context of ballet plot and ballet music.

NOTATION refers to dance moves and choreographic patterns written down on paper for others to follow in their efforts to stage the dance in question. Originally our now familiar word choreographer identified not the person who devised the dance moves and patterns for a certain dance, but the person who wrote on paper the dance master's designs in space. Various forms of notation have been proposed and utilized since ballet's beginnings, but none has become as standard and international as musical notation. Today, the Benesh Notation (also called "Choreology") and Labanotation systems have become prominent, and adherents to both methods work worldwide, recording new stagings in their methods and reading existing notations to put notated ballets in the bodies of new dancers and back onstage. In the late twentieth century the use of videotape has become a pervasive tool for recording and, as a result, for restaging dances. Though more readily available and accessible than written notation, video "notation" is trickier to read and to work with than carefully written symbols. On videotape, details can become lost or fuzzy and what gets recorded can be more an individual and perhaps idiosyncratic performance than the essentials of the choreographic intention.

PANTOMIME. *See* Mime.

PARTNERING, sometimes called double work, refers to the working together of two or more dancers for a singular purpose. The art of couple dancing in ballet dates from the ballroom dances done at the courts of Italian, French, and English monarchs. But the art of the male partner working with his female counterpart essentially matured into the form we see today during the nineteenth century, once the ballerina began working on her pointes. Partnering makes the pas de deux (see below) more than the sum of its two-dancer parts. The double work performed by the partners can be simple and delicate or complex and emphatic. Sometimes the partnered ballerina works with her partner almost as if he were a barre, available to provide steadying support. In partnering a ballerina's multiple pirouettes on pointe, for example, the partner seems to do no more than hold his hands as a kind of a loose belt around the spinning dancer's waist so she can be kept delicately centered and on balance as she turns. (Actual pushing of the turn, as if the ballerina's torso were a cylinder rolled in the hands, is a recent phenomenon that hints at uncalled laboriousness on the danseur's part and laziness on the ballerina's.) Some partnering is more physically active. Lifts (see above) obviously involve much more work, strength, and carefully coordinated timing. So do the "catches" that sometimes result from "throw lifts." In *The Sleeping Beauty*, "fish dives" concern catching the ballerina out of an en dedans pirouette and holding her in a pose that makes her look as if she's curvetting like a fish sprung out of water. When a partner steadies a ballerina by the waist and turns her around in place (on pointe, or off-), he is said to *promenade* her. Sometimes all he need do to offer support is kneel or lunge with an arm outstretched, where the ballerina can lean, as if on a barre, and stretch herself into any variety of extension poses. Often partnering consists of one dancer offering a hand to another for sustaining support. With the four cavaliers attending the Princess Aurora, the pas d'action ("Rose Adagio") of *The Sleeping Beauty* includes a wide variety of partnering maneuvers, including supported pirouettes, promenades, lifts, and steadying moments of escort.

PAS, meaning "step" or "dance" is used variously in ballet lingo. It is almost always combined with some modifier to identify what kind of step is meant (see various examples that follow). Sometimes a solo, for example, can be called *pas seul* (a dance alone).

PAS D'ACTION refers to a "dance of action" in the sense of dramatic action in a narrative context. In this case "dramatic" does not necessarily mean heavy or melodramatic emotion, it means dramatic, in contrast with purely decorative. A pas d'action is the opposite of divertissement (see above). A pas with action works through dancing to advance the dramatic line of the ballet. The

"Rose Adagio" in *Sleeping Beauty* is a pas d'action, because in the process of dancing with her four suitor-princes the Princess Aurora tells us something about her skill, about her obedience to her parents, about her aplomb (literal and figurative) in social situations, and about her gracious lack of favoritism.

PAS DE CHAT literally means "step of the cat." There are two prominent variants on the step in danse d'école teaching. One is often referred to as Cecchetti pas de chat because it comes to us by way of the teaching of Enrico Cecchetti. It has the dancer look as though he's gamboling to the side by smartly lifting the knee of the leg leading the sideward step and then by having the "following" leg its knee. Each lifted foot aims for the other leg's knee before the step closes in the fifth position, from which it started. Russian-school pas de chat looks frisky in a different way. Instead of loping sideward with sharply raised knees, the Russian variety travels lightly forward as the legs kick up to the back with lightly flexed knees. The Cecchetti step is more angular; the Russian more arced. A clear example of the former is in the "Dance of the Little Swans" in *Swan Lake*. Examples of the latter in divertissement for "Puss in Boots and the White Cat" is in most Russian company versions of *The Sleeping Beauty*.

PAS DE DEUX means "dance for two," and has, since the nineteenth century, become one of ballet's most expressive forms. Sometimes called "supported adagio," pas de deux became the pièce de résistance of the ballet structure in the classical ballet age of Petipa. This formal coming together of a ballet's leading male and female "characters" grew into a formula. This involved, in order, an entrée (for both dancers), an adagio (for both working together), solo variations (for each of the duet's participants), and a coda (a climactic, lively coming together for the two to finish as a couple) (see above). The pas de deux proper, or the actual duet, involved extensive partnering (see above). Almost all the ballets focused on in this book have prominent pas de deux.

PASSÉ, meaning "passed," has become shorthand for a position in which the dancer holds his working leg so that the thigh is held turned out and in seconde position while the lower leg, out of a bent knee, aims to place the pointed toes of the working foot at the knee of the standing leg. Sometimes the passé position is known as *retiré* (withdrawn); other times the term *raccourci* (shortened) is used synonymously with passé. When a dancer executes certain moves, développé, for instance, the term passé refers to the *action* of moving the working foot past the knee as it goes to its ultimate position. At its most familiar as a pose, "passé" position presents the dancer's legs in pennantlike configuration: the bent, working leg creates a triangular space alongside the half of the standing leg, which may be balanced on flat, demi-, or full pointe.

PENCHÉ, meaning "inclined," describes all ballet poses in which the dancer inclines and leans his torso forward in direct proportion to the rising ascent of an extended leg. The moves can be done on flat, demi-, or full-pointe positions. Probably the most familiar is *arabesque-penchée*, commonly called *penché arabesque*. Note: "*Arabesque-penchée*" is French, thus the "inclined" or "leaning" modifer needs to agree with the fact that "arabesque" is a "feminine" French noun; "penché arabesque" is Franglaise, i.e. Anglicized French, which pays only casual attention to French grammar rules. Sometimes the descent is sharp, immediate, and dramatically sudden, such as when a ballerina springs (through rélevé) into penché arabesque on pointe. Other times it can be slow, deliberate, and dramatically controlled, such as when Myrtha, *Giselle*'s Queen of the Wilis, performs penché arabesque to one side and to the another, in a mood of incantation. Sometimes the penché arabesque or penché attitude posture is held by the ballerina while her partner "promenades" her either slowly in adagio tempo or briskly in allegro.

PIROUETTE literally means "whirligig" and probably comes from *pirouelle*, a Burgundian word for child's top. In ballet the term has come to mean a spin or a whirl. Pirouette defines any of a variety of turns in which the standing leg centers and defines a gyroscopic central axis while the working leg is held in a way that cooperates and complements the turn's shape and momentum. The most common pirouette is an en dehors (see above) spin triggered out of a demi-plié (see below) two-foot position, into a passé (see above) position on pointe or demi-pointe. Pirouettes may also be executed en dedans (see above), and may be done in any number of poses. Multiple pirouettes refer to turns that make more than one complete revolution, in which case they can be specifically known as double, triple, or quadruple pirouette, etc. Some turns are qualified as adagio turns, meaning they revolve with deliberate slowness. Most pirouettes involve an action known as "spotting." This term and its root form, "to spot," refers to the act of a dancer's fixing his focus on some stationary point in front of him and bringing his head around to see that "spot" at the end of a 360° revolution. This consistent focus on a focal point keeps the pirouetting dancer from getting dizzy. Adagio turns, often in the form of attitude or arabesque turns, do not use the spotting action. The aim of such turns is serenity and unshakable calm, which would be broken by the spotting "snap" of the dancer's head. Supported pirouettes refer to turns executed with assistance from a partner.

PLIÉ, meaning "bent," comes into ballet as one of its most basic elements. The bending of the dancer's legs at the knee as he stands at barre or in the center of class helps keep his muscles limber and his tendons and muscles supple. Demi-and grand-plié exercises and positions work respectively with a half-bend of the knee and a full bend of the knee. Most ballet steps and weight-changing moves begin and end in demi-plié positions. The former helps give the move impetus and spring, the latter gives it cushion and/or rebound. A well-calculated and timed demi-plié landing allows jumps to land softly and noiselessly. Perfectly timed demi-plié moves are almost invisible to the average eye; they set up and recover a wide variety of steps, moves, and poses that seem to come from nowhere and, when finished, make us remember their climactic shape more than their shock-absorber landing.

POINTE, literally "point" or "tip," the ballet term evolved to this single word from *sur la pointe* (on the [toe] tip) or *sur les pointes* (on the [toe] tips). Pointes have variously and poetically been called "arrows" or "steel toes." The expertise for balancing and variously stepping or working on the tips of the toes evolved during the nineteenth century in the dancing of the so-called Romantic ballerina. At first specially treated shoes, with idiosyncratic details of darning and stiffening, helped give added support to the ballerina's foot. Eventually, specially "blocked" (or stiffened) pointe- or toe shoes were devised, at first mostly by Italian shoemakers. Isolated and dramatic examples of men working on pointe have surfaced over the years, but essentially ballet tradition has isolated this specialty for the female dancer. The term is often qualified according to the incremental amounts of "lift" made by the heel off the floor. Thus the terms, quarter-, half-, and three-quarter pointe, all defining an area between full-or flat-foot positions on the floor and full-pointe position. Often any foot position that is not fully flat on the floor or fully poised on toe tips is known as *demi-pointe*. Full pointe is the smallest base of balance a dancer can work and still be considered to be working "à terre." After that the dancer is working en l'air.

PORT DE BRAS, literally "carriage of the arms," refers to set positions and/or movements of the arms in the ballet lexicon. All the set positions of the body in space—croisé, effacé, etc.—have specific ports de bras to complement the positioning of the legs, according to the various schools of ballet. The same is true for set arabesque positions. In the choreography for the "Poet" of Fokine's *Les Sylphides*, we see the arm position known as *en couronne*, meaning "in the shape of a crown," and shaped with the arms curving upward to frame the face and the hands as if they were about to place a crown upon the dancer's head. The role of Giselle has repeated moments for her arms to be held *à deux bras*, which means her arms are held in front as she's seen in profile, with the upstage arm higher and the downstage one lower. The amount of straightness and/or curve or softness at the wrist and elbow joints also varies according to the dictates of the various schools. Very often the carriage of the arms involves épaulé (or shouldering) positions as well.

PUFF is contemporary dance-speak for a role that can easily make a dancer winded. A puff is aerobically challenging—such roles likely involve a good deal of jumping and keep moving at a brisk pace. In order to gather energy for a puff solo after partnering a pas de deux, such as that at the end of *The Sleeping Beauty*, a male dancer might graciously keep calling back his partner for a bow, so as to lengthen the time between his rigorous partnering duties and the even more rigorous demands of his upcoming solo.

PURE-DANCE/ABSTRACT/PLOTLESS BALLET are twentieth-century terms for ballets without particular stories or narratives. Petipa, the grandfather of large-scale narrative ballets—grand ballets, ballet-féeries, or ballet pantomimes—also showed the way to non-narrative by way of the self-contained divertissements he devised for the celebrational climaxes for his story ballets. Those ballets-within-narrative-ballets were sometimes inspired by an ethnographic theme, such as the *pure* "Grand Pas Hongroise" that caps his *Raymonda* or the "Grand Pas Classique" capping his *Paquita*. In the twentieth century, especially with the taste engendered by Diaghilev's one-act ballets, the pure-dance or abstract ballet became a genre all its own. Fokine's famous "ballet of mood," *Les Sylphides*, inspired by the music of Chopin, led to other ballets inspired solely by their music. The term "abstract ballet" for the plotless, non-narrative, or non-literary-based ballet came into twentieth-century usage with a term borrowed from modernist painting. Massine's "symphonic ballets," ballets meant to visualize the music of grand symphonic compositions, were called "abstract." So too were Balanchine's music-inspired works, such as *Serenade*. But Balanchine balked at the aptness of "abstract," which conjured up the non-figurative elements of abstract painting. Claiming any work of art that dealt with the non-abstract human figure, which dancers certainly represented, could not ever be considered abstract in the plastic art sense, Balanchine preferred "storyless" as a label for his pure-dance explorations. Today the ballet without a story is more often the norm than that with the story, reversing the situation that existed to give rise to the special distinction of pure-dance or abstract ballets.

RACCOURCI. *See* Passé.

RECONSTRUCTION refers to the process of bringing back to the stage "lost" ballets, those works with a significant gap between their last performance and contemporary efforts to restage them. This gap is usually measured in decades, but there is no hard and fast rule. The gap becomes a formidable lapse when the individuals who knew and/or danced the ballet in question are no longer alive or no longer actively performing. Unlike usual restagings, which can mean a bringing together of the dancers and the choreographer involved in the original creation of the ballet, reconstructions take more concerted efforts of research and often educated guessing. More often than not these acts of "reclamation" involve not only ballet's usual oral tradition (the handing down by word of mouth from one generation to the next a ballet's nuts and bolts) but also library research that pieces together evidence from pictorial and written documentation. Motion- and still-picture evidence makes up the former; reviews, reportage, and related writings constitute the latter. The educated guessing comes in whenever no specific evidence can be found or when there are conflicting amounts of evidence. In the end, the result tends to be judged with as much instinct as played a part in the act of retrieval itself. Soundly educated and thorough individuals are best equipped to reconstruct lost ballets, just as equally enlightened individuals are best at assessing the results in performance.

RELEVÉ, or "raised," concerns the raising of the heel from the floor so that the dancer stands on some part of the front of foot. It is this raising of the heel that makes for various relevé moves. (*See* Pointe.) The relevé stance or base of balance minimizes the amount of contact the foot makes with the floor, thus facilitating the mechanics of turning out and elongating the look of the leg. Various turns and poses employ the relevé position of the supporting foot. Arabesque poses *en relevé*, for example, make the given arabesque look longer, lighter, and leaner. Most grounded (*à terre*) turns work on some kind of relevé base of balance. Various schools or theories of ballet technique specify relevé positions in their own way. Some prefer a slight lift of the heel for certain turns or balance positions, sometimes called quarter-pointe (or *pied à quart*), other times low demi-pointe. Other theories prefer a higher lift to the heel, sometimes called three-quarter pointe (or *pied à trois-quart*), also known as high half-toe or high demi-pointe. The ultimate or maximum relevé position is full pointe or *sur la pointe*.

RETIRÉ. *See* Passé.

RÉVÉRENCE literally means "curtsy," but has come to mean bow in the ballet world. The act of deference to the public begins in ballet classes with pupils making polite shows of gratitude to the teacher as the classes end. Women traditionally execute a "proper" curtsy, which is a bowing of the head coordinated with a sinking into both knees with one leg clearly in front of the other. Men traditionally bend forward from the waist and lower their heads, sometimes after gesturing with an arm in the direction of the public being saluted. The post-performance display of the révérence is generically referred to as a "curtain call."

REVIVAL refers to a ballet that returns to the stage and repertory after what might be called a rest. This means that after being performed regularly by a certain company and then going out of circulation, the ballet in question returns to repertory. The hiatus between the previous performance and the current one tends to vary but not to a degree that would take reconstruction (see above) research to put it back on stage. Revivals of formerly popular ballets often become part of a company's selling point. Sometimes revivals have the added novelty of offering popular, older ballets with brand-new visual designs, such as costumes and scenery. The cast of the revival is also an important feature. Audiences with fond memories of the revived ballet's former casts can sometimes have trouble seeing the individuality of the current cast. Revivals might be seen as akin to taking a garment that once belonged to an older relative and wearing it in front of those who knew the original owner. Reconstructions are akin to carefully researched remakes of garments from a bygone era, made to be worn by individuals in the present era.

ROND DE JAMBE, literally meaning "circle of the leg," comes in two separate varieties: *rond de jambe à terre* and *ronde de jambe en l'air*. The former traces a circular path on the ground with the dancer's working foot; the latter traces circular paths in the air. Those à terre are mostly, though by no means exclusively classroom moves that work the whole length of leg to strengthen the ease and facility of that leg out of the hip socket. In fact, the circle made in rond de jambe à terre is a half-circle, often practiced at the barre, beginning in fourth position front and sweeping in a semicircular path to fourth position back, or vice versa. Rond de jambe en l'air movements work from the knee down to toe tip with the leg lifted off the ground, tracing what are in fact ovoid paths in the air. Grand rond de jambe en l'air indicates a semicircular sweeping of the full and stretched leg out of the hip as the working leg is lifted off the ground. French and French-inspired Danish-school dancing includes a good many rond de jambe en l'air moves (as in Bournonville's and Taglioni's *La Sylphide*). Sometimes these moves, which can look like a stirring or mixing mode of the lower leg in the air, can be executed at the peak of a sauté move, in which case you are seeing a sauté-rond de jambe en l'air.

SAUTÉ. *See* Jeté.

SEVEN (BASIC) MOVEMENTS OF BALLET. Ever since the eighteenth century, ballet has been seen in terms of five positions of the feet (see above) and seven movements, or steps. Though the names of the seven movements have varied to some degree regarding this or that step, a consistency has prevailed. Dancer and teacher Enrico Cecchetti specified a still useful set of "seven." They are : *plier* (bend), *étendre* (stretch), *rélever* (rise), *glisser* (glide), *sauter* (jump), *tourner* (turn), and *élancer* (dart).

SPOT. *See* Pirouette.

SUPPORTING LEG, sometimes called "standing leg," refers to the leg on which the dancer stands and balances while his other leg executes some more active work. The supporting leg can be straight at the knee or bent, while it centers the dancer's weight and keeps his balance. It can lend its support variously. In "flat" or full-foot contact with the floor, or in full- or demi-pointe positions. When dancers work in class at the barre, the supporting or standing leg is the one nearest the barre.

TERRE À TERRE, literally meaning "ground to ground," refers to dancing that emphasizes the "tracing" or accenting of steps that consistently remain grounded. The opposite of terre à terre dancing is dancing that emphasizes moves of elevation—jumping steps. In ballet's Romantic era rival ballerinas Marie Taglioni and Fanny Elssler were sometimes contrasted as creatures of the air and the earth, the former an aerial dancer, the latter a terre à terre ballerina.

TIGHTS refers to the tight-fitting leg and pelvis-covering garment that has been part of ballet costume since at least the early nineteenth century. The word *maillot*, which the French use when referring to tights, is said to come from the family name of the garment's manufacturer in Paris, but words of a similar form predate this period. Traditionally, the hose, or what Americans call "panty hose," came into use when ballet costumes grew translucent. Victor Hugo referred in the mid-1800s to women dressed in "pink maillot and a gauze skirt." Men as well as women eventually began wearing tights as a normal part of ballet costuming. As noted in connection with the leotard (see above), when tights and leotard are worn together, female dancers wear tights under their leotards, while men wear them over. Essentially the finely knitted leg covering, originally made of silk, now from various synthetics and other fibers, acts to define, harmonize, and reveal the "look" of the leg without actually baring it.

TOUR, meaning "turn," is often interchangeable with pirouette (see above). Generally, tours tend to revolve or spin (on the ground or in the air) out of their initiating impetus sometimes with, and sometimes without involving the "spotting" action (see "Spot") associated with pirouettes. Piqué turns, executed atop a sharply struck (piqué) pointe or demi-pointe of the supporting foot, involve the spotting action. Turns in arabesque or in attitude revolve without employing spotting. Steps that involve turning with other emphasis are said to be *en tournant. Tour jeté* is a shorthand way of defining *grand jeté en tournant* (See "Jeté.") Sometimes when steps follow a sweeping, circular path around a given dance space or classroom, they are said to go *autour de la salle* (around the room) or *en manège* (roundabout). Many solo dances travel en manège—around the stage of the ballet in which they are featured.

TOUR EN L'AIR, literally a "turn in the air," is but one form of tour, but is singled out here because it remains a specially pronounced part of the male dancer's vocabulary. These jumped turns spring from two feet in fifth position and take the dancer around once, twice, or three times before landing back in fifth position or in some other pose, say an arabesque-allongée. Sometimes called double tours (franglais for *tours en l'air double*), these neat, rocketing, revolving moves can climax or wrap up many a male solo (variation) in a formal pas de deux. The Russian school often prefers the dancer to lift his working leg into passé position during the revolving part of the step, whereas other Western ballet schools specify that the dancer's legs be held taut, in tight fifth position from preparation through execution to finish—the landing of the move. Double tours are the most common, though a few dancers find three actually easier to execute than two. Women tend not to practice or perform tour en l'air, though there may be exceptions to this rule for given dancers and given roles.

TRAVESTI, EN, French for "in disguise" or "masked," refers theatrically to roles of one gender played by a performer of the opposite gender. Widow Simone in *La Fille Mal Gardée* can be played by a man. In the latter part of the nineteenth century, male roles such as the hero-swain in Arthur Saint-Léon's *Coppélia* were played by women. The female dancer playing a male part was said to be *en travestie*. (In opera when female singers take on the parts of male characters these are known as "trouser" or "pants" roles.) The expressions "drag" and "transvestism" are sometimes used by American journalists to refer to "travesty" ballet performing. Similarly the British terms "cross-dressing" and "dressing up" also appear in reportage on travesty performing. "Pantomime dame" has become a specifically British term identifying men performing as women in so-called pantomimes, theatrical "dumb shows." In Frederick Ashton's *Cinderella*, for example, the roles of the ugly stepsisters are choreographed for male performers and are sometimes referred to as "pantomime dames."

TURNOUT, or "turn-out," may be the singlemost distinguishing characteristic between ballet and other forms of theatrical dance. The term refers to the outward, 90-degree rotation—en dehors—of each leg in its hip socket. Together the fully turned-out legs of the dancer in first position display a 180-degree openness. This extreme accenting of the leg out of its hip holds the leg in profile view for the audience. It also keeps the dancer on a strong and concentrated base of support and holds his legs ready to move out without further adjustment into any desired direction, to the front, side, or back. Turnout came into ballet from courtly ballroom dancing where similar, though less extreme leg positioning prevailed; 45-degree rotations of each leg marked the stance of the courtier dancer. During the eighteenth century a device called *tourne hanche* (hip turner) was employed to force the legs and feet to turned-out positions. When the results of this torture-chamber machine were seen to do nothing for the hips and to deform the ankles and knees, it was done away with. By the time of Carlo Blasis in the early nineteenth century, the full 180-degree turnout was deemed a desirable goal that needed to be carefully attended to in rigorous classroom exercises. Today 180-degree turnout remains the ideal way of standing and working for the ballet dancer.

TUTU, an early nineteenth-century word probably based on the French baby-talk *cul-cul*, meaning "bottom" or "backside," is the term that now universally describes the ballerina's starchy, layered skirt of tarletan or tulle. (Some suggest the word's origin comes from "tulle.") In Paris, the term *juponnage* was sometimes used for the same skirt, because *jupon*, meaning "petticoat" or "slip," kept the reference to the "underskirt" quality of the garment. Different degrees of gathering, stiffness, and length separate tutus into distinct subcategories. Longer, softer, bell-like silhouettes have become known as "romantic tutus," acknowledging the origins of the skirt's prototype on Marie Taglioni in *La Sylphide*. Shorter, stiffer, more leg-revealing tutus have become known as "classical tutus," which Michel Fokine once unfavorably likened to the look of an "open parasol." The separately constructed but aesthetically coordinated bodice of the tutu completes the ballerina's tutu costume, whether classical or romantic length. The "building" of the trim, fitted bodice is as important as that of the skirt, which traditionally sits down on the hips rather than directly at the waist. Ukrainian-born Barbara Karinska, the longtime artistic collaborator and costumer for George Balanchine, did groundbreaking work in the twentieth century toward making the tutu bodice workable, comfortable, and pretty.

UNITARD. *See* Leotard.

VARIATION, a term borrowed from musical composition where it constitutes a varied working of some theme material, refers in ballet to a solo dance. As we have seen in the formal pas de deux (see above) formulated in the nineteenth century, the variations of the ballerina and her danseur partner come after the adagio (see above) of the duet's sequence.

WORKING LEG refers to the leg the dancer works while supporting himself on a stabilizing standing or supporting leg (see above). In classroom work at the barre, the working leg is the outside one. The "work" can be as simple as a foot-pointing stretch or as elaborate as a sweeping, sky-reaching, or unfolding move. In any case, the working leg is the one in action, which contrasts with the inactive or less active standing leg.

VIDEOGRAPHY

Ballets

NTSC-format Video-recorded ballets are listed here by title, followed by identification of choreographer and composer (separated by slash, in parenthesis), followed by company and/or featured dancers. Additional information includes the names of company, cast, and other pertinent information, such as date of filming or of video release, and comments on the performances. The date at the end of the entry's basic information, and before the commentary, gives the year the video was produced; any dates in parenthesis earlier in the entry, following the names of the individual dancers, gives the date the performance was filmed when that year differs from the date of the video itself. In the case of more than one video of the same work, the commentary text will follow the final item of the series. Technological advancements occur steadily, yesterday's film reel has become today's videocassette, which may be tomorrow's laser disc and the future's digital video disc. For this reason this list will focus on ballets by name, by company, and/or featured artists. Distributor labels may change as might video format. A listing of distributors that feature ballet tapes appears at the end of this section. All these organizations have catalogues and current title lists available on request.

Adagietto, (Béjart/Mahler), on *The Art of the 20th-Century Ballet*, featuring Jorge Donn. 1985.

This solo, to the widely popular fourth movement of Mahler's Fifth Symphony, is a storyless "journey of man" episode. Béjart's choreographic moves alternately harmonize and oppose Mahler's "romantic" mood. One needs to be a big fan of Béjart, Donn, and Mahler to make this journey happily.

Agon, (Balanchine/Stravinsky), excerpts—First Pas de Trois: Sarabande; Seconde Pas de Trois: Bransle Simple; Pas de Deux in *Balanchine Celebration*, pt. 2, selection of the Balanchine Library, with New York City Ballet, featuring Peter Boal, Zipporah Karz, Kathleen Tracy, Wendy Whelan, Albert Evans, Arch Higgins, Darcey Bussell, Lindsay Fischer. 1993.

This post-Balanchine performance is reliable if not inspired, with the Royal Ballet's Bussell taking a striking if rather English approach to what represents American classicism.

Anastasia Pas de Deux, a.k.a. "Pas de Deux Imperiale" and "Kschessinska Pas de Deux," (MacMillan/Tchaikovsky), on *Gala Tribute To Tchaikovsky*, featuring Viviana Durante, Bruce Sansom. 1993.

Set to the second movement of Tchaikovsky's Third Symphony, the pas is a self-contained classical duet amid the second act of MacMillan's narrative ballet *Anastasia*. More neoclassical than pastiche classical, the duet has its technical difficulties, and not so many visual rewards. Both Durante and Sansom give it their all, though the full value is less rewarding than they deserve. The music, incidentally, is the same as that for the female corps de ballet segment that opens Balanchine's "Diamonds" in *Jewels*.

Apollo, (Balanchine/Stravinsky). *See Apollo* chapter.

Après-midi d'un Faune, L' (Nijinsky/Debussy). *See* chapter on Diaghilev's Triple Bill.

A good reconstruction of an atmospheric ballet, especially strong on visual elements. Since this video was made scholarship has come up with a differently detailed and more authentic version of the ballet according to Nijinsky's own notation. A videocassette of student dancers from New York City's Juilliard Dance Division performing this staging accompanied *Choreography and Dance* 1, pt. 3, 1991. An academic journal series published and distributed by Harwood Academic Publishers.

Aurora's Wedding. See *The Sleeping Beauty*.

Bayadère, La, (Petipa/Minkus). See *La Bayadère* chapter.

———, with the Bolshoi Ballet, featuring Nadia Gracheva (a.k.a. Nadezhda Grachova), Alexander Vetrov. 1992.

Filmed in Moscow's Bolshoi Theater with stage lighting (rather than adjusted-for-camera brighter light), the performance can get lost in the darkness of long shots. The full vista of the "Entrance of the Shades" on the deep and wide Bolshoi stage illustrates the choreography's clear debt to the Doré-inspired image of angels chaining into the netherworld. The leading roles are performed vividly if at times a touch too "Bolshoi" in its exaggeration and a penchant to lard mime scenes with gratuitous dance steps. All of the secondary roles go unidentified. Marina Bylova, Yuri Vetrov, and Yuri Klevtsov perform as Gamzatti, the High Brahmin, and the Little God (or Bronze Idol), respectively. Unlike the Kirov staging detailed in our *Bayadère* chapter, this Russian production indicates the ballet's cataclysmic ending in telescoped and somewhat perfunctory form. F.Y.I.: Keep a lookout for NTSC (American system format) release of a video of Rudolf Nureyev's production for the Paris Opera Ballet, first presented there in 1992, with Isabel Guérin, Laurent Hilaire, Elizabeth Platel. *See also* "The Kingdom of the Shades."

Billboards, (Arpino, dir./Prince), Laura Dean, Charles Moulton, Margo Sappington, Peter Pucci of the Joffrey Ballet, featuring the Joffrey Ballet. 1993.

Perhaps the ultimate excursion in crossover ballet, the four ballets' "billboard" structuring offers a succession of dances made for a ballet company by primarily non-ballet choreographers. The fancy filming and sometimes florid effects, some reproducing the ballet's stage effects, others specifically devised for video, make the dance itself somewhat hard to follow but point to the self-conscious aim of making ballet mirror pop culture.

Blue Angel, The, (Petit/Bruder), with Ballet National de Marseille, featuring Dominique Kalfouni, Roland Petit, Jean-Pierre Aviotte. 1988.

A late example of the kind of ballet Petit made in his attempts to "modernize" France's seemingly staid ballet traditions. Originally made for Natalia Makarova in 1985 as "Professor Unrat," here the ballet, based on a famous cinema classic of the same name, gets a dutiful performance.

"Blue Bird" Pas de Deux from The Sleeping Beauty, on *Pas de Deux*, with the Los Angeles Ballet, featuring Nadezda Zybine, Luis Astorga. 1984.

This famous excerpt from the fairy-tale divertissements of *Sleeping Beauty* is surprisingly rare on commercial videos. This is partly so, no doubt, because the choreography is so demanding, especially in the case of the male "Blue Bird" part. Though the dancers here are hardly well-known names, they dance with reliable skill, and Astorga as the "Blue Bird," while no monster of perfection, dances with gratifying ease and spirit, soaring and bounding through the choreography's tricky circuit of steps with impressive flair. Balanchine-trained artistic director John Clifford, who hosts this program of duets, is very likely responsible for the grace-note transitions that enliven the Blue Bird's choreography.

Boléro, (Béjart/Ravel), on *Ballet of the Twentieth Century*, with Ballet of the Twentieth Century, with Jorge Donn and forty members of the male corps de ballet. 1989.

Originally conceived for a lone female dancer and forty male dancers, Béjart first recast his work, reminiscent of a Marseilles social ritual where the men surround a woman dancing on a table, into a ritual of a man dancing on a table surrounded by forty women. Here he casts it for all men. Fancy filming, close-ups, and dramatic overhead shots complicate the mix on this video.

Carmen, (Petit/Bizet), with Ballet National de Marseilles, featuring Zizi Jeanmaire, Mikhail Baryshnikov, and Denis Ganio. 1980.

Another example of Petit's modernism, an antidote to the standard classical modes of French ballet. At the ballet's 1949 premiere Petit himself danced Don José to Jeanmaire's Carmen. Approximately thirty years later, an expatriate Russian, with fond memories of Petit's innovations, dances with the ballet's original Carmen, the seemingly ageless "Zizi."

Carmen Suite, (Alberto Alonso/Bizet, arranged by Shchedrin), on *Carmen*, with the Bolshoi Ballet, featuring Maya Plisetskaya, Nicolai Fadayechev, and Sergei Radchenko. 1973.

This is Bizet rearranged for Soviet ballet purposes, with the irrepressible Plisetskaya, for whom the ballet was created by Cuban choreographer Alberto Alonso. Soon after, the choreographer mounted his "spin" on Petit's ballet for Alicia Alonso in their native Cuba. (See below.)

———, on *Alicia: A Portrait*, with National Ballet of Cuba, featuring Alicia Alonso and Azari Plisetski. 1968.

Filmed a year after its premiere performances in Moscow and Havana, this ostensibly socialist realist ballet on the corrupt wiles of a headstrong woman, shows itself off with a winking smile and switch-blade legs.

Chaconne, (Balanchine/Gluck), on *Choreography By George Balanchine: Chaconne, Prodigal Son*, selection of the Balanchine Library, with New York City Ballet, featuring Suzanne Farrell and Peter Martins. 1978. [The Balanchine Library is a trademark of the George Balanchine Trust and marketed by Nonesuch as an on-going series of releases concentrating on Balanchine's ballets and ballet teaching.]

This is most of Balanchine's 1976 staging of an opera ballet he made in 1963. It features the two dancers for whom the choreographer remounted his work. With filming that accents the ballet's otherworldly realm in contrast to scenes of earthly love, the video lovingly records Balanchine's last great "muse," Farrell, in near-full glory, and Martins, one of his last great noble danseurs, at the peak of his power. The video omits three intermediate divertissement dances—a trio, a pas de deux, and a female pas de cinq—otherwise it records the ballet faithfully, though for filming purposes to introduce the dance by way of its hero and heroine, Balanchine reverses the structure of his "Dance of the Blessed Spirits." Here he opens with the duet for his Euridice and Orpheo and closes the segment with a dance female corps de ballet. In the stage version, the opposite order occurs.

Checkmate, (de Valois/Bliss), with the Sadler's Wells Royal Ballet, featuring Margaret Barbieri, David Ashmole, and David Bintley. 1982.

A look at what early British ballet was like. The video's narration sets the scene, identifying the figures of Love and Death and alerting us that their chess game represents a fight for the lives of the subjects. Somewhat heavy of costume, decor, symbolism, and music, the ballet nevertheless reveals a certain nicety of dance steps.

Chopiniana, (Fokine/Chopin, orchestrated by Glazunov, etc.), on *The Maryinsky Ballet*, with the Kirov/Maryinsky Ballet, featuring Altinai Asylmuratova, Konstantin Zaklinsky. 1991. (*See Les Sylphides.*)

A good performance of what has come to be a more gloomy mood ballet in the West. Still performed in front of a bucolic landscape, according to Soviet Leningrad/Petersburg traditions, the reverie floats finely on the screen. The subsidiary and corps de ballet sylphs shimmer in the amber light, and the minxlike Elena Pankova is a special delight.

———, Pas de Deux excerpt opening Nocturne, and closing Valse Brillante (1978), on *Classic Kirov*, featuring Galina Ulanova, unidentified partner, Xenia Ter-Stepanova, Vadim Gulyaev, Olga Likhovskaya. 1992.

These three excerpts from different Kirov eras offer further glimpses into a ballet long associated with this troupe. The earlier footage presumably shows the legendary Bolshoi "prima" Galina Ulanova before she made her move to Moscow from Leningrad, and here she dances with a refreshing freedom not associated with this "moonlit" ballet. The later, longer excerpt, is unfortunately sometimes lost in pockets of dim stage light, but it shows a company cohesiveness not easy to come by.

———, Valse Brillante, on *White Night of Dance in Leningrad*, with the Kirov, featuring Elena Evteyeva, Olga Likhovskaya, Elena Pankova, Kirill Melnikov. 1987.

Filmed on a platform set up in a Russian park—Petersburg's Summer Garden—the ballet blanc finale loses a little something in so naturalistic a setting. (The occasional car cruising by in the distance doesn't especially add to the ballet's contemplative atmosphere.) Still, the performances are good, especially the lyrical, elegant Melnikov.

———, Pas de Deux, on *Russian Ballet: The Glorious Tradition vol. 3*, featuring Natalia Makarova and Vitaly Onoshko (1965). 1993.

A somewhat grainy telecast of the soon to be internationally famous Makarova. Here, ably supported by a little known Kirov dancer, the ballerina can be seen in her pre-Western phase, the same, yet different as it turns out.

Cinderella, (Marin/Prokofiev), with the Lyon Opera Ballet, featuring Françoise Jouille, Dominique Laine, Jayne Plaisted, Daniele Pater. 1990.

A dollhouselike, postmodernist rendering of the story that streamlines the score and gives ballet dancing a minimal part in the overintellectual mix.

———, (Zhakarov/Prokofiev), with the Bolshoi Ballet, featuring Raisa Struchkova, Gennadi Lediakh. 1960.

One of the grandparents of late-twentieth-century Cinderella ballets, this one has the enchanting presence of Struchkova to override some of the more heavy-handed touches of Soviet ballet characterization. Some sparkly pointe shoes accent some sparkling pointe work, specially filmed to accentuate its speediness and flair.

Configurations, (Goh/Barber) on *Baryshnikov: The Dancer and the Dance*, with American Ballet Theatre featuring Mikhail Baryshnikov. 1983.

A documentary about and performance of a ballet by a then popular choreographer in smooth, post–modern–dance ballet language. Baryshnikov soars above any potential compromise of ballet's rigors.

Coppélia, (after Petipa/Delibes), with Ballets de San Juan, featuring Fernando Bujones and Ana Maria Castanon. 1980.

———, (Vinogradov/Delibes), with the Kirov Ballet, featuring Elvira Tarasova, Mikhail Savialov, Irina Shapshitz. 1993.

It's too bad there aren't more reliable versions of this ballet on the market. The Bujones tape is not quite professional enough, and while the Kirov recording is sharp and colorful, Vinogradov's choreography is largely grotesque and incoherent. Still, in both cases, many of the performances are worthy and strong.

Corsaire, Le, (Petipa and others/Adam and others), with the Kirov Ballet, featuring Alitnai Asylmuratova, Elena Pankova, Konstantin Zaklinsky, Evgeny Neff. 1989. (*See also* "Jardin Animée, Le" and "Pas d'Esclave.")

For years all most of the ballet world outside Russia knew about *Le Corsaire* was a single, flashy pas de deux. Then the Kirov came out of Russia with this full-length production about abductions, rescues, more abductions, and more rescues. The story, loosely based on Lord Byron's lyric poem of a "dangerously" exotic pirate world, is nearly unfollowable. Still, the performances are nearly all enchanting and ballet steps come shining through at some of the least likely moments.

[Le] Corsaire Pas de Deux, (after-Petipa/Drigo), on *An Evening with the Royal Ballet*, featuring Margot Fonteyn and Rudolf Nureyev. 1965.

———, on *Ballet Legends*, with Ninel Kurkapkina and Vadim Budarin (c. 1970). 1993.

———, on *Pas de Deux*, with Marielena Mencia and Yanis Pikieris. 1986.

———, on *The Magic of the Kirov*, with Tatiana Terekhova and Farukh Ruzimatov (1986). 1989.

———, on *Maryinsky Ballet*, with Lubov Kunakova and Farukh Ruzimatov. 1991.

———, on *Essential Ballet* and *Welcome Back, St. Petersburg*, with Margarita Kulik and Farukh Ruzimatov. 1993.

As far as Western ballet is concerned the most emblematic of all these performances is the oldest one, the 1965 rendering by Fonteyn and Nureyev. According to the source from which Nureyev's influential staging comes to us—the Kirov Ballet (see *Corsaire* above)—this pas de deux is really meant to be a "pas de trois" (the "slave partner" is nothing more than a convenient *porteur* or "carrier", to help the ballet hero out with his partnering). But Nureyev, initially with Fonteyn, made the number very much a pas de deux. Fonteyn's somewhat prim and precise quality is at odds with most of the other ballerinas in these duets (in the role of Medora). Nureyev, and likely Vakhtang Chabukiani who inspired him, set the male scene-stealing standard that seems to motivate all these performances, but Terekhova certainly does her level best to steal the show when she can.

Creole Giselle. See *Giselle*.

Robert Schumann's Davidsbünlertänze, a.k.a. ***Davidsbünlertänze***, (Balanchine/Schumann), selection of "Balanchine Library," with New York City Ballet, featuring Suzanne Farrell, Karin von Aroldingen, Jacques d'Amboise, Peter Martins (1981). 1995.

This specially filmed-for-television performance of a late Balanchine ballet—one that inspires much thinking that Balanchine, who would die two years hence, was himself thinking about death—includes almost the entire first cast for whom the choreographer created his ode to Schumann. (Only Leland, who dances the part created for Kay Mazzo, is not from the original cast.) The perfumes are pungent throughout the episodic work, and some who closely watched and especially adored Farrell, Balanchine's last muse, find this video the one that best captures her special spontaneity and prodigious gifts.

Diana and Actéon divertissement, (Petipa/Drigo), on *Kirov Ballet: Classic Ballet Night*, with the Kirov Ballet, featuring Tatiana Terekhova and Sergei Berezhnoi, and 12 women. 1982.

———, Pas de Deux, on *Essential Ballet* and *Welcome Back St. Petersburg*, featuring Larissa Lezhnina, Farukh Ruzimatov. 1992.

———, on *Kirov Soloists: Invitation to the Dance*, featuring Tatiana Terekhova and Nikolai Kovmir. 1982.

This daring and vivid pas de deux with sometime backup from a women's ensemble, is probably the creation of Agrippina Vaganova, the great Leningrad teacher who acted as ballet mistress to the post-imperial ballet. Watching Terekhova let fly with her potent and whirlwind dancing, you can see why she was cast so often in the part of Diana, as well as why eager, proud firebrands such as Ruzimatov, would give the dancing of Acteon their all.

Divertimento No. 15, (Balanchine/Mozart), "Andante" movement on *Choreography by George Balanchine: Tzigane, Andante from Divertimento No. 15, The Four Temperaments*, with the New York City Ballet, featuring Merrill Ashley, Maria Calegari, Susan Pillare, Stephanie Saland, Marjoire Spohn, Tracy Bennett, Victor Castelli, Robert Weiss. 1977.

Filmed when Balanchine was very much in charge, this segment of his sublime Mozart masterwork shows his company in a kind of transition. Most of the dancers are young and on the rise, what you lose in maturity and fullness of dancing, you get in freshness and eagerness of performing. The central focus on the just-named principal dancer Ashley is apt, and shows the world why Balanchine was promoting her and what she could do to promote the rigors and beauties of ballet dancing. A young Calegari is also a special pleasure.

Don Quixote, (Petipa/Minkus), with Russian State Perm Ballet, featuring Alexander Astafiev, Nina Ananiashvili, Alexei Fadeyechev. 1992.

———, with the Kirov Ballet, featuring Vladimir Ponomaryov, Farukh Ruzimatov, Tatiana Terekhova. 1988.

———, (Baryshnikov, after Petipa and Gorsky), with American Ballet Theatre, featuring Richard Schafer, Mikhail Baryshnikov, Cynthia Harvey. 1984.

———, (Nureyev, after Petipa), with the Australian Ballet, featuring Robert Helpmann, Rudolf Nureyev, Lucette Aldous. 1972.

All of these *Quixote* productions emanate from the Petipa-Gorsky lineage kept alive in Soviet Russia. Each includes the Petipa "Dream" scene, though not always at the same part of the action. Baryshnikov's production is the most streamlined; Nureyev's the most boisterous. The Soviet state productions are fairly consistent regarding structure and choreographic elements. Unfortunately the greatest Kitri and Basilio team of all, Maximova with Vasiliev, is not recorded in any full production (see *Don Quixote Grand Pas de Deux* below), but Baryshnikov and Nureyev both give distinct portrayals and offer distinguished dancing. Terekhova is an especially vibrant Kirti and Ananiashvili an especially sweet one.

———, (Gorsky, Ponomoraev/Minkus), excerpts on *Classic Kirov*, featuring Ninel Kurkapkina and (unidentified Nikolai Kovmir [?]). 1980.

———, (Petipa/Minkus), on *Russian Ballet, The Glorious Tradition*, vol. 3, featuring Maya Plisetskaya and Yuri Kondratov (1954), Mikhail Baryshinkov (1969), Mikhail Lavrovsky (1974), Irek Mukhamedov (1988). 1993.

The earliest black-and-white film footage of Plisetskaya records what probably qualifies as the ballet's most important revitalization in the twentieth century, comparable, one suspects, to Maria Callas's "reawakening" of various bel canto operas. The three male solos, all from the Act 3 pas de deux and duly dated, provide glimpses of a neat array of Soviet ballet hall-of-famers.

Don Quixote Grand Pas (after Petipa and Gorsky/Minkus), on *Nina Ananiashvili and International Stars*, vol. 2, featuring Nina Ananiashvili and Farukh Ruzimatov, with Irma Nioradze, Rose Gad. 1991.

This pas de deux plus female ensemble has become a traditional Soviet-styled way of excerpting *Don Q* or *Don Quichote*, as the Russians say. Sometimes the female soloists are known as "Flower Girls," sometimes merely *pas classique* soloists. For an even more lavish suite form of the same ballet, see next entry.

———, Suite, on *Nina Ananiashvili and International Stars*, vol. 4, featuring Nina Ananiashvili and Aleksei Fadeyechev, with several unidentified dancers, and Tatiana Terekhova, Darci Kistler, Zhanna Ayupova, Inna Dorofeeva, Elizabeth Platel, Rose Gad, Nicolas Le Riche, Igor Zelensky, Vadim Pisarev, Alexander Kølpin, Yuri Posokhov, Andris Liepa. 1993.

A more elaborate conflation of *Don Quixote* dancing shows itself here as one-time gala fare. Ananiashvili's special-event arrangement offers bits of "Don Q" dancing to all the dancers participating in her gala tour as a full-out program closer. There are bits from all over the ballet's three-act scheme here, including doubling and sextupling up of some solos to make for extra-festive presentation.

Don Quixote [Grand] Pas de Deux, (Petipa etc./Minkus), on *Baryshnikov at Wolf Trap*, featuring Mikhail Baryshnikov and Gelsey Kirkland. 1976.

———, on *Erik Bruhn Gala*, featuring Earl Pickford and Viviana Durante. 1988.

———, on *Essential Ballet* and *Welcome Back St. Petersburg*, featuring Kader Belarbi and Nina Ananiashvili. 1993.

———, on *Kirov Ballet in London*, featuring Tatiana Terekhova and Makhar Vaziyev. 1988.

———, on *Magic of the Bolshoi*, featuring Vyacheslav Gordeyev and Nadezhda Pavlova, and Vladimir Vasiliev and Ekaterina Maximova. 1987.

———, on *Magic of the Kirov*, featuring Farukh Ruzimatov and Tatiana Terekhova. 1988.

———, on *Nina Ananiashvili and International Stars*, vol. 4, featuring Aleksei Fadeyechev and Nina Ananiashvili. 1993.

———, on *Pas de Deux*, with Tetsutaro Shimizu and Yoko Morishita. 1986.

———, on *Russian Ballet: The Glorious Tradition*, vol. 1, featuring Ludmila Semenyaka and Mikhail Baryshnikov (1971). 1993.

As one of the ballet circuit's most popular items, this pas de deux, which Balanchine sometimes classed in an "old lady" category, rarely fails on its flash level. Baryshnikov is recorded at different points in his career pouring forth especially potent dancing. Likewise, Vasiliev, whom Baryshnikov readily looked to for inspiration and who is partly responsible for the choreography of the Petipa solo, dazzles in his performance. His fellow Soviet dancers in the leading role of Basil, especially the dashing Fadeychev, and the sublime Gordeyev make their own distinctive marks. Of the ballerinas in the female lead of Kitri, Maximova, Terekhova, and Pavlova, for their respective Soviet generations, each grab your attention with their individual flair.

———, (d'Amboise, after Petipa), on *Firestone Dances*, featuring Melissa Hayden, Jacques d'Amboise (1963). 1995.

Though all these "Don Q" pas de deux have their variants, this one, by NYCB favorites (and products of Balanchine's tutelage) strays the most from tradition. As we see with the presence of two other famous Balanchine dancers in the traditional *Nutcracker* pas de deux (see *Nutcracker* below), Balanchine's dancers still manage, even outside the ballet master's own choreography, to honor his aesthetics. Thus, here, Hayden and d'Amboise soar, spin, and "show" their steps in a recognizably Balanchinian light, and lightness. In the end the whole of this duet is a study in subtle contrasts to the others listed above.

———, Kitri's solo, on *That's Dancing*, featuring Tamara Toumanova (c. 1950). 1985.

This clip of the solo from the Act 3 pas de deux of "Don Q" shows a confident and accomplished Tourmanova. The "toe-tapping" variant that "the black pearl of Russia" brings the final diagonal of hops on pointe is unique to her, and ready to be stolen by any ballerina who cares to add such a personal touch of virtuosity to her tired *Don Quixote* soloing.

"Pas d'Esclave" from *Le Corsaire*, on *Nina Ananiashvili International Stars*, vol. 1, with Inna Dorofeeva and Vadim Pisarev, 1991.

This duet qualifies as the "other" pas de deux sometimes excerpted from *Le Corsaire*, though not nearly as often the one commonly known as *Le Corsaire Pas de Deux*. The action here is rather more dramatic, as its dancers represent a slave merchant and the slave woman he's trying to sell. Most of this is indicated delicately and decorously—the tutu-wearing ballerina (slave woman) is prettily unwrapped from a gossamer fabric, by her proudly smiling partner (slave merchant). Her consternation is shown in graceful gestures of standoffishness. At the end of the duet with variations and coda, the merchant catches a bag of coins tossed from the wings. Dorofeeva is suitably tremulous; Pisarev, suitably cocky.

Dying Swan, The, a.k.a. ***The Swan***. *See* "Postscript" in chapter on *Swan Lake*.

———, on *The Bolshoi Ballet*, featuring Galina Ulanova. 1956.

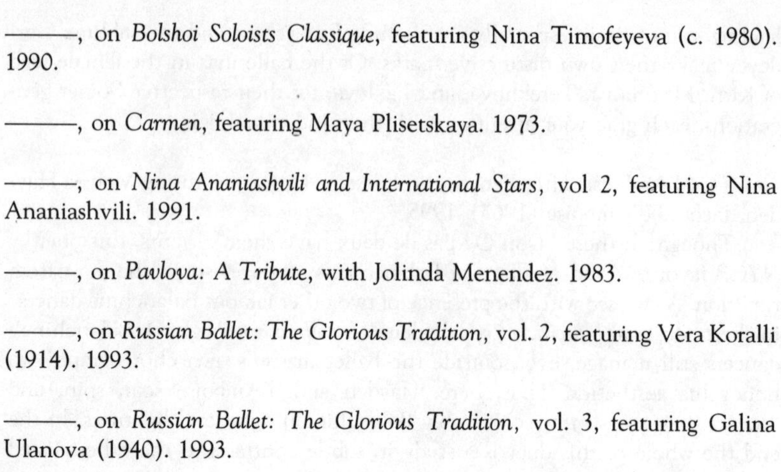

———, on *Bolshoi Soloists Classique*, featuring Nina Timofeyeva (c. 1980). 1990.

———, on *Carmen*, featuring Maya Plisetskaya. 1973.

———, on *Nina Ananiashvili and International Stars*, vol 2, featuring Nina Ananiashvili. 1991.

———, on *Pavlova: A Tribute*, with Jolinda Menendez. 1983.

———, on *Russian Ballet: The Glorious Tradition*, vol. 2, featuring Vera Koralli (1914). 1993.

———, on *Russian Ballet: The Glorious Tradition*, vol. 3, featuring Galina Ulanova (1940). 1993.

———, slightly abridged on *Classic Kirov*, featuring Anna Pavlova (1925). 1992.

The abridged version of Pavlova, which cuts off just before the ending, is where to begin any concentrated look at this trifle of a number. Common knowledge has it that Ulanova and Plisetskaya made something of the Pavlova-tailored vignette, and that all other "takers" miss on this or that account. Still, these two ballerinas did make their marks in this stream-of-whiteness solo well after Pavlova's death, so the chance exists that a new "definitive" interpreter may well yet come along. Look at them and take the measure of their movement and of your being moved.

***Esmeralda* Pas de Six** (Perrot, Petipa, Vaganova/Pugni, Drigo), on *Classic Kirov*, featuring Altinai Asylmuratova and Kyril Melnikov. 1992.

———, on *Kirov Ballet: Classic Ballet Night*, featuring Gabriela Komleva and Vitali Afanoskov. 1982.

———, on *Kirov Ballet in London*, featuring Elena Evteyeva and Eldar Aliev. 1988.

This dramatic pas d'action from a dramatic moment in the multi-act *Esmeralda*, tells of the ballet's eponymous street-dancer heroine, who realizes as she arrives to entertain a wedding couple that the bridegroom is the man she truly loves. Gypsy coins and tambourines jingle among the heartbreaking sighs and yearnings that fill out the distressed ballerina's dancing. In the three videos listed, the beauteous Asylmuratova, with the truly innocent Melnikov, makes the most potent impression. Second best is Evteyeva, movingly partnered by the intensely attentive Aliev.

Fairy Doll, The, a.k.a. ***Puppenfee***, (Legat/Drigo, misidentified as Bayer, composer of original *Die Puppenfee*), on *The Maryinsky Ballet*, with Larissa Lezhnina, Dmitri Gruzdev, Yaroslav Fadayev. 1991.

This 1903 pas de trois is unusual in that it is set for two men and one woman. Originally the men were the Legat brothers, Nikolai and Sergei, dancer-choreographers at the time in St. Petersburg. The ballet is associated with Vienna, where it was first given, and with Anna Pavlova, who toured a version choreographed for her by Ivan Clustine. This one became a Standard Soviet divertissement. This performance is as sweet, or as cloying, depending upon your taste, as can be.

Fall River Legend, (deMille/Gould), on *Dance Theater of Harlem*, featuring Virginia Johnson, Stephanie Dabney, Hugues Magen, Lorraine Graves, Lowell Smith. 1989.

This is the only available record of de Mille's post-Tudor cum post–Martha Graham dance. The Harlem dancers give it their ever remarkable all, but you have first got to like this kind of axe-murderer dumb show.

La Fille Mal Gardée. See *La Fille Mal Gardée* chapter.

Firebird, The, (Grigoriev and Tchernicheva after Fokine/Stravinsky) on *The Royal Ballet*, with The Royal Ballet, featuring Margot Fonteyn and Michael Somes. 1960.

This truncation of the Royal Ballet's Fokine-based *Firebird* had the great benefit of coaching by Tamara Karsavina, Fokine's original Firebird ballerina. Fonteyn remains Fonteyn, all the while vividly taking into account Karsavina's counsel. There is a *farouche* (wild) quality to her portrayal that jibes well with the ballet's lore. It's interesting to see how much of this exotic-bird character Fonteyn grafted onto her Odette/Odile characterizations for *Swan Lake* (for which see below).

———, (Tetley/Stravinsky), with the Royal Danish Ballet, featuring Mette Hønnigen, Torben Jeppesen, Lars Damsgaard. 1982.

Like most Tetley ballets, this has one foot in the world of modern dance, all sleekly dressed in unisex unitards.

———, Firebird-Ivan Pas de Deux, on *Essential Ballet*, featuring Ilse Liepa, Andris Liepa. 1992.

This records some of Andris Liepa's earliest efforts to bring Fokine's Diaghilev-created ballets to his Russian homeland. Here the Fokinesque choreography includes a ballerina/firebird dressed, not in a now traditional tutu, but in a chemiselike costume vaguely approximating the Oriental garb originally worn in 1910. The result, both in choreography and design, remains dubious, but Andris Liepa's passion to bring this work back into his life and world are palpable, even as Ilse Liepa's dancing fails to grip the viewer.

Flames of Paris, (Vainonen/Asafiev) abridged on *Stars of the Russian Ballet*, featuring Vakhtang Chabukiani, Maria Gottlieb. 1953.

A vividly overacted socialist realist ballet tract about the decadence and oppressiveness of an effete monarchy and the goodness and heroism of the "people," in this case the citizens of the French Revolution. No matter, a hero is a hero, and the winning Chabukiani is perfectly charismatic. In an era when Moscow's Bolshoi Ballet excelled in character dancers and dancing, the ballet is full of individually detailed performances. More heeled shoes and boots than toe shoes show up in this silent movie of a ballet. Sometimes just running—see the "Marianne" figure with her tricolor flying in her wake—can be more thrilling than self-consciously rendered virtuoso pyrotechnics; the actual pyrotechnics by the likes of Chabukiani give high standards a run for their money.

———, Pas de Deux, on *Stars of the Bolshoi*, featuring Ekaterina Maximova, Gennadi Lediakh (1959). 1987.

This pas de deux was once a warhorse of the "highlights" programming popularized by the Bolshoi. This is the only one so presented on video at present, but with Maximova as Jeanne, the ballet's innocent, good, and down-to-earth heroine, this single entry would be hard to beat. Watch for various ballet competition compilations and the like; this duet might well show up as a flashy number.

Flower Festival at Genzano Pas de Deux, (Bournonville/Helsted), on *Kirov Ballet: Classic Ballet Night*, featuring Natalia Bolshakova, Vadim Gulyaev. 1982.

The oddity here is less seeing Russian-schooled dancers trying to honor the French-Danish traditions in this pas and more seeing a backup ensemble of six women framing the duet. Bournonville stager Elsa Marianne von Rosen arranged the dance, elsewhere given nowadays only as a pas de deux, to include the six ensemble women. Scholarship has proven that the pas de huit is legitimate, and even that the dance may not even be the work of Bournonville, but the Russians give it their own presentational and physical spin in any case. (For less eccentric versions, see below.)

———, on *Nina Ananiashvili and International Stars*, vol. 1, featuring Rose Gad, Alexander Kølpin. 1991.

———, on *Pas de Deux*, featuring Linda Hindberg, Arne Villumsen. 1884.

Essential viewing for diehard fans of the Royal Danish Ballet and especially of the Bournonville repertory. The two preceding performances listed of this pas, arguably the most famous of Bournonville's on the concert-competition-gala circuit, both show Danish dancers in their element. Personal preferences always take precedence, and mine for Villumsen's sublime gifts make me single out him, even if his performance was filmed under far less agreeable performances than the other. Both, however, still render the "text" of this pas, whoever its choreographer might be, with reliable ability and tone.

Forgotten Memories, (Anastos/Tchaikovsky), on *Ballets Russe, A Comedy on Pointe*, featuring Melanie Wright, Ronald Shepherd, Allison Saracchi, Dieter Riesle. 1988.

In the decade before he made this ballet parody, Anastos was a founding director of, arguably, the most famous ballet spoof troupe in the world, Les Ballets Trockadero de Monte Carlo. That company doubled the weight of its wit by being a (nearly) all-male travesty company. This ballet is not performed by a travesty company, but by the choreographer's "legit" troupe, the Garden State Ballet. Primarily a pastiche of an Antony Tudor ballet, this crisscrossing foursome of faithless lovers is set in its own era. The video is fancied up as if it were a telecast with news and commentators breaking in, but the jokes are still in place and still funny. (See *Yes, Virginia.*)

Fountain of Bakhchisaray, The, (Zakharov/Asafiev) excerpts on *Stars of the Russian Ballet*, featuring Galina Ulanova, Maya Plisetskaya, Pyotr Gusev. 1953.

A stirringly danced and filmed encapsulation of this socialist realist rendering of a Pushkin Romantic poem dwelling on female rivals and barbaric abductions. Made before the Bolshoi first appeared in the West, the film came to be seen as a golden document of the Soviet Bolshoi's golden age. The Leningrad/Petersburg-schooled Ulanova contrasts temperamentally, physically, and technically with the Moscow-trained Plisetskaya. Silent-movie emotions in full color.

———, excerpt on *Russian Ballet: The Glorious Tradition*, vol. 3, featuring Ekaterina Maximova and Alexander Bogatyrev (1977). 1993.

This is an excerpt of the "Polish" scene, in which the heroine, Princess Maria, celebrates with her court, attended by her gallant lover, Vatslav. Differently excerpted on the above more extensive encapsulation of the ballet, this one shows a radiant Maximova (a protégée of Ulanova's) in solo and pas de deux moments, ably supported by Bogatyrev's harp-playing and elegant suitor.

———, excerpt on *Classic Kirov*, featuring Alla Sizova, N. Ostaltsov, L. Galinskaya. 1981.

The somewhat darkly filmed scene from the ballet's final act shows the scene between the emotionally wounded Zarema and the captive Polish princess, Maria. The woman-to-woman confrontation (as in *La Bayadère*), ends with the spurned woman stabbing her innocent rival to death. All wide-eyed and open-armed pleas and sorrowing submissions, the scene has much more acting than dancing.

Four Temperaments, The, (Balanchine/Hindemith), on *Choreography by George Balanchine: Tzigane, Andante from Divertimento No. 15, The Four Temperaments*, Balanchine Library, with New York City Ballet, featuring Bart Cook, Merrill Ashley, Daniel Duell, Adam Lüders, Colleen Neary (1977). 1995.

This represents Balanchine's earliest efforts in participating in PBS's *Dance in America*. The 1977 cast and camerawork of his 1946 ballet were both personally supervised by the choreographer. He had only recently brought his influential ballet back to the stage for his ballet company, which until his death, remained the only company performing this work. A few years after its premiere, he discarded the fanciful and cumbersome costuming and decor that cluttered the "look" of his ballet, and *The 4 T's*, as the work came to be nicknamed, helped establish the "black-and-white" look of certain modernist Balanchine ballets. (See the 1957 *Agon* for future such examples.)

Gaîté Parisienne, (Massine/Offenbach, arr. Rosenthal), with Ballet Russe de Monte Carlo, featuring Alexandra Danilova, Frederic Franklin, Leon Danielian (1940s). 1979.

This black-and-white footage was made surreptitiously over a period of years in short takes of silent film. In the 1970s, the filmmaker, Victor Jessen, added post-synchronized sound to the spliced-together film. His focus was Danilova, who remains consistently documented throughout the film. Most of the other dancers vary somewhat, since the casting of the other roles changed over the years. The final result is both choppy and charming. The character-ballet quality of works like this comes through as quaint and clear. If this ballet suits your fancy, be on the lookout for possible video release of a 1941 film condensation of the ballet made by Warner Bros.

Gayne, (Anisimova/Kachaturian), variation on *Firestone Dances*, featuring Rudolf Nureyev (1963). 1995.

This is a brief but tantalizing look at the young Nureyev as he made one of his early appearances in the United States. Filled with fire and folkloric detail, this ballet dance for a youthful, boot-wearing, elegant warrior is enlivened by the dancer's fun-loving facial expressions as he revels in his spotlight.

Giselle, (Coralli, Perrot, Petipa/Adam). *See Giselle* chapter.

———, with American Ballet Theatre, featuring Carla Fracci, Erik Bruhn, Toni Lander. 1969.

This records what was during its time one of ballet's most popular and heralded *Giselle* partnerships. Rule of thumb: The hype has to be pretty high for a major motion picture–style production of a ballet to get made. Unfortunately, such big-time extra care and attention can sometimes get too fancy, losing the ballet amid cinematic bloat. This somewhat happens here, with big-screen close-ups, busy camera work, frenetic editing, and arbitrary cuts disturbing the logic and focus of the ballet master. (Ironically, ballet master Blair has co-directing credit.) In any case, Bruhn and especially Fracci are both rarefied tastes, though the former's prowess as a classical technician is legendary and well founded and the latter's screen-actress presence is undeniable. When the camera remains at decent length on the dancing, it records some textbook-clear and exemplary dance details from both Bruhn and Toni Lander (Myrtha), whose batterie is exemplary. For a shining example of cabrioles to the front and to the back, see Bruhn's solo dances in Act 2. For ideal examples of entrechat-six, see any example offered by Bruhn or Lander. Fracci's strong suit remains in petit allegro moves, such as entrechats and ronds de jambe en l'air. And, while some of the production's realistic touches are distracting and anomalous, there is solid historical precedent for the live horses in the hunting party scene.

———, with Ballet Teatro Municipal de Rio de Janeiro, featuring Ana Botofogo, Fernando Bujones, Simone Ferro. 1984.

Only Bujones's fans will treasure this record of this ballet. Bujones brings his inimitably sleek and eager dancing to bear on a standard production (staged by Britain's Peter Wright), which has little else to recommend it. Most often the stage picture is thin on production values and dim with unremarkable dancing.

———, with the Bolshoi Ballet, featuring Natalia Bessmertnova, Mikhail Lavrovsky, Galina Kozlova. 1979.

This is a rather wispy-looking film, a vista of pale colors and gauzes. Still, even in the slightly tricked-up staging that is the mark of Bolshoi artistic director Yuri Grigorovich, the "text" is a sound record of Soviet-Russian *Giselles*, and Bessmertnova in the title role is her sublimely fragile self. Bolshoi Wilis are always hard to beat.

———, abridged on *The Bolshoi Ballet*, featuring Galina Ulanova, Nicolai Fadeyechev, Rimma Karelskaya. 1957.

This film comes from an era in the West when certain Russian-Soviet ballet influences were being felt for the first time. The slightly sympathetic spin on Hilarion (good peasant wronged by philandering aristocrat) would have its effect on productions thereafter, as would the vividly strong and cohesive dancing of the Wilis. The rapport and coordination between Fadeyechev and Ulanova is beautifully honed, as is her finely detailed dancing and acting.

———, with the Kirov Ballet, featuring Galina Mezentseva, Konstantin Zaklinsky, Tatiana Terekhova. 1983.

A historically reliable staging of the ballet as it has come down to us through the emendations and upgradings of Petipa. As usual with Petersburg tradition, the aristocratic texture of the ballet gets confidently stressed, no scene stealing and vernacular peasant shenanigans here. The ensemble's work as both villagers and Wilis is beautifully consistent; the leads are all reliable and, in descending order, impressive: Terekhova's icy, macabre queen, Zaklinsky's sweet-natured Albert (as the Soviets tend to call the young Duke), and Mezentseva's overarticulated and overattenuated Giselle.

———, (Alonso, after Coralli), with the National Ballet of Cuba, featuring Alicia Alonso, Azari Plisetzky, Mirta Pla. 1964.

After a career made famous in part from her portrayal of Giselle, Alonso staged her own version for her Cuban troupe. Traditional in basic outline, the resulting production is particular in acting and danced details. A kind of realism overrides the two acts, and Alonso gives it her inimitable all, at once austerely academic and floridly presented. Plisetzky, brother to ballerina Maya Plisetskaya, is a fair foil for this *Giselle* that's continually about Giselle. Equally bold yet academic dancing comes from the supporting cast, especially the almost rabidly performed Wilis. (Filmed in black-and-white.)

———, with Russian State Theater Academy of Classical Ballet, featuring Ludmilla Vasileva, Vladimir Malkahov. c. 1990.

Spread out on the vast stage of Moscow's Kremlin Palace, this standard Soviet-era staging has sound problems and some odd camera work. It also has rather incomplete credits, with only two leading dancers named. Still, one of these is the incomparable Vladimir Malakhov, and for his deservedly numerous fans the tape is a worthy look at this beautifully committed artist near the beginning of his formidable career.

———, excerpts from Act 1 "Mad Scene" and Act 2 "Pas de Deux" on *Bolshoi Ballerina Ludmila Semenyaka*, with the Bolshoi Ballet, featuring Ludmila Semenyaka, Andris Liepa. 1989.

Little more than snippets from Acts 1 and 2, these excerpts give teasing samplings of Semenyaka in a part for which she was rightly well known. Neither excerpt, however, proves substantive enough to give a fair picture of her "feel" for this classic romantic role.

———, Act 2 Pas de Deux on *Essential Ballet*, featuring Carole Arbo and Kader Belarbi. 1992.

———, on *Nina Ananiashvili and International Stars*, vol. 2, featuring Irma Nioradze, Yuri Posokhov. 1991.

———, on *Nina Ananiashvili and International Stars*, vol. 4, featuring Rose Gad, Alexander Kolpin. 1993.

———, on *Russian Ballet: The Glorious Tradition*, vol. 1, featuring Nadezhda Pavlova and Vyacheslav Gordeyev (1976). 1993.

The preceding tapes offer an array of the variations on the Franco-Russo traditions that are part of this adagio in macabre moonlight. The French and Danish dancers perform the specially designated pas de deux, while the Russian couples combine the duet from the "Apparition of Giselle" with parts of the pas de deux proper. The French dancers—Arbo and Belarbi—tend to be mundane; the Danes—Gad and Kolpin—dutiful. The Russians are far more vivid, with the exception of Nioradze, who delivers only a workaday performance. Posokhov, unfortunately often framed black-on-black, is wonderfully impassioned; the then-budding partnership of the superb Gordeyev and the rapturous Pavlova reveals much about what made these youngsters a glorious team of magisterial dancers.

Giselle and The Wilis, The Making of, (Haydee/Adam), mini-documentary, with the Stuttgart Ballet, featuring Birgit Keil, Tamas Deiter, Melinda Witham. 1989.

This retelling of the nineteenth-century ballet in convoluted twentieth-century terms is called *Giselle and the Wilis*. An island replaces the Rhineland vineyard, and new characters mix with old. A clown and his family enter into the narrative. This video talks through the new concepts, while interspersing scenes of the ballet's creation and rehearsal with some of the performance.

Golden Age, The, (Grigorovich/Shostakovitch), with the Bolshoi Ballet, featuring Irek Mukhamedov, Natalia Bessmertnova, Gedeminas Taranda, Tatiana Golikova. 1987.

This piece of nouveau Soviet socialist realism (1982) reworks a classic piece of 1930 Socialist propaganda. It's in Grigorovich's theatrically driven mode, big on caricature in this case. Still, the performances are bigger than life, with a young and impassioned Mukhamedov, a tremulous Bessmertnova, a wildly debonair Taranda, and a minxlike Golikova.

Grand Pas de Quatre. *See Pas de Quatre.*

Great Galloping Gottschalk, (Corbett/Gottschalk, arr. Bond), on *American Ballet Theatre in San Francisco*, featuring Elaine Kudo, Susan Jaffe, Robert LaFosse, Deirdre Carberry. 1985.

A crossover ballet suite to the music of one of America's most dazzling piano virtuoso composers. Filmed onstage with the original cast, the often jokey display comes off as a pajama party romp for some young and eager ballet dancers. The cast represents a good sampling of the dancers brought along early by Baryshnikov as ABT artistic director. Ribbon candy for the eyes.

Grand Pas Classique, (Gsovsky/Auber), on *Nina Ananiashvili and International Stars*, vol. 3, featuring Elizabeth Platel and Nicolas Le Riche. 1993.

———, on *Paris Opera Ballet: Seven Ballets*, featuring Sylvie Guillem and Manuel Legris. 1985.

———, on *Russian Ballet: The Glorious Tradition*, vol. 3, featuring Gabriela Komleva, Yuri Soloviev (1974). 1993.

These three performances of a self-consciously bravura showpiece are each neatly separated by a decade. The earliest has especially splendid dancing by Leningrad's legendary Soloviev, whose world-famous Blue Bird (in *The Sleeping Beauty*) is not reliably recorded on tape, but whose shining batterie and wondrous elevation here give a sense of what made his Blue Bird so famous. The extremely talented Legris and the plainly extreme Guillem lead the same dance for the 1980s with variously impressive and indelible details. For the 1990s, the whistle-clean Platel and the pliant, fleet Le Riche do the honors, with flying colors.

Hamlet, (Rizhenko/Tchaikovsky), on *Shakespeare Dance Trilogy*, featuring Vlastinil Garallis, Nikita Dolgushin, Svetlana Smirnova, Gabriella Komleva (c. 1988). 1993.

Hamlet Ballet, (unidentified/Shostakovitch), featuring Vladimir Malkahov. c. 1990.

The two "fantasies" on Shakespeare's *Hamlet* listed come from late Soviet ballet, just prior to perestroika in the case of the former, and just before the union's disintegration, in the case of the latter. Both are fanciful expositions of the play's action in plain ballet terms. The earlier one, with the grave and dignified Dolgushin as a standout Claudius, is filmed in a realistic setting and performed as if by a troupe of traveling players. The later one, with the insectile Malakhov as the title figure, is filmed with much trick camera work and variously flapping costumes. Neither tells much noteworthy about Hamlet, but both tell a good deal about Soviet Russian notions of modernist ballet.

Harlequinade Pas de Deux, (after Petipa/Drigo), on *Ballet Legends*, featuring Ninel Kurgapkina, Nikolai Kovmir. c. 1972.

———, on *Russian Ballet: The Glorious Tradition*, vol. 2, featuring Ninel Kurgapkina, Nikolai Kovmir (1974). 1993.

Similar performances come in these two listings; the former shot in color; the latter in black-and-white. In both, Kurgapkina plays a delicate and shimmering Columbine, with Kovmir an elegant scamp of a Harlequin. The choreography for ballerina's solo is sometimes found in a pas de deux attributed to Gorsky from his *Fille Mal Gardée*. FYI: Be on the lookout for potential marketing of *Baryshnikov at the White House*, a specially telecast program of ballet from 1980 in which Baryshnikov dances Harlequin opposite Patricia McBride's Columbine (in a role she created for Balanchine), all of which is framed by some of the children's dances Balanchine made for his two-act *Harlequinade*.

Ivan the Terrible, (Grigorovich/Prokofiev), featuring Irek Mukhamedov, Natalia Bessmertnova, Gedeminas Taranda. 1990.

———, abridged, with the Bolshoi Ballet, featuring Yuri Vladimirov, Natalia Bessmertnova, Boris Akimov (1977). 1988.

———, Act 1, on *Bolshoi Prokofiev Gala*, with the Bolshoi Ballet, featuring Alexander Vetrov, Maria Bylova, Gediminas Taranda. 1991.

Grigorovich's 1975 epic-scope multi-act ballet followed his earlier *Spartacus* (see below) as a sweeping and thundering picture of the life and times of a troubled and troubling hero. The earliest of these three videos captures the original cast and is rather lavishly filmed for the movie theater. The 1990 tape, with a young and vivid Mukhamedov as the eponymous tsar and an intensely dark and dashing Taranda as the dangerous lieutenant, is a more straightforwardly filmed stage performance, on the boards of the Bolshoi Theater. The 1991 recording is quite similar, though less crisply filmed. All are well-done documents of a rather unsubtle spectacle of nearly one-note ballet theater.

"Jardin Animée, Le" from *Le Corsaire*, (Petipa/Délibes), on *The Kirov Ballet in London*, with the Kirov Ballet, featuring Yulia Makhalina, Lyubov Kunakova, Altynai Asylmuratova, Farukh Ruzimatov. 1988.

This presentation of the ballet's "garden of femininity," featuring the female corps de ballet impressively led by a regal Makhalina and a confident Kunakova, includes the scene's vivacious pas de trois, sometimes referred to as the ballet's "classical trio" or as its "odalisque pas de trois." Additionally, it has the unusual interpolation of the ballet's famous pas de deux, which is meant to come in the ballet's previous act (see *Le Corsaire* above). Here it is danced by an iridescent Asylmuratova and a fiery Ruzimatov. The female corps (30 strong beyond its two leading ballerinas), comes back with their arches of flowers and their fragrant dancing to frame and close the pastel pink and blue stage picture on a sweet and large-scale note.

Jardin aux Lilas, Le, (Tudor/Chausson) on *American Ballet Theatre in San Francisco*, featuring Leslie Browne, Robert LaFosse, Martine van Hamel, Michael Owen. 1985.

One of the so-far rare commercially available records of a Tudor masterwork. The choreographer himself chose and prepared this cast. The filming is somewhat long range and clinical, but it presents the ballet's sense of atmosphere, architecture, and intimacy in reasonable order. For snippets of other productions and explications on the ballet's movement vocabulary, see a 1985 (released 1992) video documentary Tudor made for Swedish television called *Antony Tudor*. Also, look for potential release of a *Dance in America* telecast called *A Tudor Evening with American Ballet Theatre* from 1990.

Jazz, (Martins/Marsalis), on *Accent on the Offbeat*, with New York City Ballet (and the Wynton Marsalis Ensemble), featuring Jock Soto, Heather Watts, Albert Evans, Nilas Martins, Melinda Roy, Nikolaj Hübbe, Wendy Whelan. 1994.

A performance of the complete *Jazz*, filmed during its premiere season, follows a documentary about the ballet's creation (and the choreographer's collaboration with the composer), which includes excerpts of the ballet performed in rehearsal and onstage. The "working session" part is the stronger segment of the cassette, particularly because musician Marsalis is so fascinating to see and hear on tape.

Jewels, excerpts "Emeralds" and "Diamonds," (Balanchine/Fauré, Tchaikovsky), on *Choreography by George Balanchine: Selections from Jewels and Stravinsky Violin Concerto*, featuring Merrill Ashley, Gerard Ebits, Karin von Aroldingen, Sean Lavery, Suzanne Farrell, Peter Martins (1977). 1996.

For some reason, the pas de deux from "Rubies," the Stravinsky segment that comes second in the three-act *Jewels*, was excluded from this marketed version of the original *Dance in America* telecast. Both other segments, however, the opening "Emeralds" and the closing "Diamonds" remain as taped. The former is the most extended excerpt, missing only a solo here and pas de deux there, but including the pas de trois and the additional pas de sept Balanchine added nearly ten years after his ballet's premiere. "Diamonds" is represented only by the segment's magisterial pas de deux, but what a jewel this pas is. Unlike "Emeralds," which includes none of its original cast members, "Diamonds" is recorded with Farrell, for whom Balanchine made his sublime Tchaikovsky dance, and who dances as sublimely as can be expected for a ballerina who gloried in performing for live audiences.

"Kingdom of the Shades" from *La Bayadère*, (Petipa/Minkus), on *The Kirov Ballet in London*, with Olga Chenchikova, Konstantin Zaklinsky, Margarita Kullik, Irina Sitnikova, Zhanna Ayupova. 1988.

More plainly filmed in terms of camera work and stage setting than the same scene in the context of the entire ballet with full narrative, this video records the ballet blanc as the self-contained entity it popularly became in the late twentieth century. Compare, if you like, the Kirov's strengths and weaknesses as they meet your eye here, some ten years after the earlier filmed, full-ballet version.

———, on *The Magic of the Kirov*, featuring Gabriela Komleva, Rejan Abdeyev. See chapter on *La Bayadère*.

———, "Entrance of the Shades," (a.k.a. "Les Ombres") on *White Night of Dance in Leningrad*, with the Kirov's corps de ballet. 1987.

As with all examples on this tape, this one takes place in a picturesque spot in Leningrad/Petersburg, in this particular case, as in others here, outdoors. The effect of the northern summer night light is magical on this would-be moonlit scene of spectral maidens, but the real night air and ambience also cut into the formal, hothouse beauty of the corps de ballet's pellucid dancing.

———, abridged excerpt from (a.k.a.) *Bayaderka* on *Classic Kirov*, with the Kirov Ballet, featuring Natalia Dudinskaya, Vakhtang Chabukiani (1940). 1992.

———, on *Russian Ballet: The Glorious Tradition*, vol. 2, with the Kirov Ballet, featuring Natalia Dudinskaya, Vakhtang Chabukiani (1940). 1993.

Put these two taped excerpts together—each is a different excerpt of the same film—and you have all of the Hollywood movie–style "Shades Scene" the Soviets produced for this mid-century film. Down a sleek staircase and onto a mirror-glossy floor come the reduced complement of Shades and a fluffy-tutued Dudinskaya pursued by a Douglas Fairbanks-like Chabukiani. The whole slick production, though, is happily effective. The female corps de ballet makes a Busby Berkeley chorus look lame, while Dudinskaya cuts through space like a marble goddess and Chabukiani cuts through the air like an unstoppable zephyr.

L'Après-midi d'un Faune. See *Après-midi d'un Faune*.

Leaves Are Fading, The, Pas de Deux, (Tudor/Dvorák), on *Erik Bruch Gala*, featuring Rose Gad Poulsen, Lloyd Riggins. 1988.

———, on *Essential Ballet*, featuring Altynai Asylmuratova, Konstantin Zaklinsky. 1992.

There is no commercial video of this Tudor ballet complete, though a performance by American Ballet Theatre, the company for whom Tudor created his elegiac reverie in 1975, was telecast in Japan in the 1980s. Neither of the two *Leaves* pas de deux on tape shows performers who worked directly with Tudor; the former of these two comes from a ballet competition by two dancers from the Royal Danish Ballet; the latter, from a gala performance by two dancers from Russia's Kirov Ballet. Both couples look like "foreigners" to Tudor's English-American way with ballet, but the ballet's lyricism and twining plastique come across well enough to tell of the choreographer's intentions.

Legend of Love, (Grigorovich/Melikov), part of *Bolshoi at the Bolshoi* series, with the Bolshoi Ballet, featuring Marina Bylova, Alla Mikhalchenko, Irek Mukhamedov, Gedeminas Taranda (1989). 1990.

Grigorovich's telling of a fanciful Middle Eastern tale ostensibly looks to the world of Persian miniatures, but the finesse of those images is largely overwhelmed here by what Soviet ballet calls "big poses" and declamatory posturing. No onscreen synopsis provides a clue to the intended meaning of the choreography's often opaque activities. Still, with the exception of weak performing by Mikhailchenko as the heroine Shirin, the performances tend to be impressive, especially the impassioned portrayals of the men—Mukhamedov as the poetic hero and Taranda as the sinister anti-hero. The filming, done by a scrupulous Japanese team working with the aid of digital technology, results in crisp and clean images, though the stage lighting on the Bolshoi's enormous stage has its patches of heavy darkness.

———, excerpt on *Bolshoi Ballerina Ludmila Semenyaka*, with Bolshoi Ballet, featuring Ludmila Semenyaka, Vyacheslav Gordeyev. 1989.

This excerpt from the ballet's second act shows Semenyaka's Shirin with her "Persian sisters" and then entwined in a duet with her painter-lover Ferhad. Though she brings honor and dignity to her role, the ballerina is not seen at her best. In the duet's couplings she's more impressive, and Gordeyev is his elegant and lyrical self.

Little Ballet, The, (Tharp/Glazunov), on *Baryshnikov Dances Sinatra, and More* (a.k.a. *Baryshnikov By Tharp*), with American Ballet Theatre, featuring Mikhail Baryshnikov, Deirdre Carberry. 1984.

Originally entitled *Once Upon a Time*, this reverie for a lone male dancer in shirt and trousers shows Tharp taking an American crossover look at the nineteenth-century ballet world that dominated the schooling of Baryshnikov and his fellow Russian dancers. The music is from Glazunov's 1898 *Raymonda* (see below), which came into ballet history by way of Petipa, and some Hungarian-flavored classical dancing. Also part of this music's past is *Raymonda Variations* (1961), Balanchine's delectable, nearly exclusively female garden of ballet delights, in a nouveau nineteenth-century mode. Tharp's eye looks back to all these *Raymondas* and ahead to the dreams of 1980s ballet dancers in the West. Baryshnikov remains happily lost at the center of all these focal points.

Little Humpbacked Horse, The, (Radunsky/Shchedrin), with the Bolshoi Ballet, featuring Maya Plisetskaya, Vladimir Vasiliev, Alexander Radunsky. 1961.

With substantial narration and some cartoonlike animation, the film makes its fairy-tale subject quite clear. Another of Soviet ballet's carefully and specially filmed versions of a ballet, the production is colorful and delightfully performed. All of the Bolshoi's strong wing of character performing comes into play, yielding a rich gallery of earthy peasants, pompous nobles, fantastic bird and animal creatures, and beautiful maidens. Vasiliev's "simple Ivan" is all innocence, sweetness, and savvy; Plisetskaya's princess all regal majesty and eloquence.

Macbeth, (Vasiliev/Molchanov) with the Bolshoi Ballet, featuring Alexei Fadeyechev, Nina Timofeyeva. 1984.

Fraught with what an isolated faction Soviet ballet desperately hoped would pass for the latest, twentieth-century modernism and still pass muster with Soviet censors, this highly stylized playing out of Shakespeare's tragedy in ballet terms is mostly heavy-handed and clichéd. The witches are danced by men on pointe, and most of the choreographically dramatic gestures are punched hard. But, Fadeyechev brings much dignity and nuance to the few-note title role, and Timofeyeva, impassioned as the wicked Lady Macbeth, is seen here slashing through high-kicks of anger and flashing through various, huge leaps telling of unstoppable royal power.

Mademoiselle Fifi, (Zolov/La Jarte), featuring Alexandra Danilova, Roman Jasinsky, Michael Maule. 1955.

A black-and-white kinescope of the legendary Madame Danilova, made late in her illustrious career. Except for the makeshift filming of *Gaîté Parisienne* (see above), this is the only readily available record of Danilova's dancing. The French-language commentator refers to the *caractère piquant* that Danilova presents as Mlle Fifi. The setting is backstage in a dressing room, the situation one of post-performance flirtation between an adored ballerina and her adoring suitors—a father and his son, it turns out. Still, there is more beguiling animation, academic dance geometry, and vivid characterization here from La Danilova than from many "serious" and lengthy ballets of the late twentieth century.

Manon, (MacMillan/Massenet), with the Royal Ballet, featuring Jennifer Penney, Anthony Dowell, David Wall. 1982.

Note: A nicely filmed version of MacMillan's three-acter based on *Manon Lescaut*, of novella and, subsequently, opera fame. Using none of Massenet's music from his opera of the same name, MacMillan's ballet tells the same story, with slight adjustments for the ballet medium. This tape, which records both of the dancers who created the roles, gives a good picture of English ballet dancing as MacMillan helped breed it. Though the eponymous lead, Penney, didn't "create" the original character of Manon (Antoinette Sibley did), she was partly responsible for the role's "shape" since MacMillan worked with her a good deal when creating his work, because Sibley was partly indisposed. Since its 1974 premiere, the ballet has gained wide popularity and has become part of numerous companies' repertories.

Marguerite and Armand, (Ashton/Liszt, arr. Searle), on *I Am a Dancer*, with the Royal Ballet, featuring Margot Fonteyn, Rudolf Nureyev, Michael Somes. 1973.

Ashton's *evocation poètique* showcases the individual talents and the celebrated partnership of Fonteyn and Nureyev in a lushly romantic chamber ballet of the Lady of the Camellias of literature and opera fame. This specially filmed and, in part, narrated version is an abridgement of the full ballet. The May-December aspects of the source material find related dimension in the careers of the two featured dancers. For the full, unabridged version, be on the lookout for "Out in the Limelight; Home in the Rain," the final segment of "The Magic of the Dance," a historical dance series that Fonteyn devised and narrated.

———, on *Fonteyn and Nureyev: The Perfect Partnership*. 1985.
An excerpt of the same abridged version mentioned above.

Markitenka, (Saint-Léon/Pugni). See *Vivandière, Pas de Six*.

Mayerling, (MacMillan/Liszt, arr. Lanchbery), with the Royal Ballet, featuring Irek Mukhamedov, Viviana Durante, Leslie Collier, Darcey Bussell. 1994.

The choreographer himself supervised the scrupulous revival of his 1978 three-act ballet based on the historical events surrounding the last of the Austrian, Hapsburg dynasty. The cast on tape represents, almost to a dancer, those chosen and personally rehearsed by MacMillan. The clearly and caringly filmed tape is splendid record of a ballet about decadent splendours. As the impassioned and driven, near-diabolical crown prince Rudolf, Mukhamedov is especially superb.

Merry Widow, The, (Page/Lehár), with the Chicago Opera Ballet, featuring guest dancers Patricia McBride, Peter Martins, George de la Pena. 1983.

Page's ballet-shaping of a once popular operetta is typical of her work, dutiful and literal. The filming of the 30-year-old ballet is fairly clear and the cast is largely made up of dancers moonlighting from New York City Ballet. Martins is a dour prince, de la Pena a soigne count, and McBride a sweet-faced widow.

Napoli, (Bournonville/Helsted, Rossini, Lumbye, Gade, Paulli), with the Royal Danish Ballet, featuring Arne Villumsen, Linda Hindberg (1986). 1987.

As with the royal Dane's *La Sylphide*, this multi-act nineteenth-century narrative ballet is a treasure from the past. Lovingly preserved and handsomely presented, the Danish-told tale of Neapolitan life unfolds in simple yet remarkable happenings that tell of young love amid the dark forces of the underworld succumbing to the light powers of Christian belief. The overall casting is very good; that of Villumsen as the essentially calm, momentarily derranged and finally serene hero, is just about perfect, as is his performance.

Narcisse, (Goliezovsky/Tcherepnin), on *Russian Ballet: The Glorious Tradition*, Vol. 1, featuring Vladimir Vasiliev (1971). 1993.

The Soviet experimentalist choreographer created this vignette about a classically beautiful and vain young god in 1960 for the classically superb Vasiliev. More than ten years later the dancer is seen performing his part with intense passion and freedom, presenting the mythological character's naked self-absorption with innocence and finesse.

Noces, Les (Nijinska/Stravinsky). See chapter on Diaghilev Triple Bill.

Nutcracker, The (Balanchine/Tchaikovsky). See chapter on *The Nutcracker*.

———, (Baryshnikov/Tchaikovsky), with American Ballet Theatre, featuring Gelsey Kirkland, Mikhail Baryshnikov. 1976.

Unlike the Balanchine version that looks to *Nutcracker*'s 1892 beginnings in Petipa and Ivanov's scheme, this staging rethinks the original libretto and owes a strong debt to Soviet ballet's influential 1934 choreography by Vasily Vainonen. Specifically, the production includes Vainonen's tutued "Waltz of the Snowflakes," laced throughout with Soviet-styled jumps, big and small. In addition to showing Baryshnikov in peak form, this specially filmed performance documents the dancing of Kirkland, a much heralded ballerina of her generation who is not widely recorded on video.

———, (Grigorovich/Tchaikovsky), with the Bolshoi Ballet, featuring Natalia Arkhipova, Irek Mukhamedov. 1989.

———, featuring Ekaterina Maximova, Vladimir Vasiliev, Nadezhda Pavlova, Vyacheslav Gordeyev. 1978.

———, featuring Ekaterina Maximova, Vladimir Vasiliev. 1984.

After Vainonen's *Nutcracker*, Grigorovich's 1966 production has had the most influence on Soviet *Nutcrackers*. As with Vainonen, the children's roles are performed by short-statured adult dancers. The first act's "little girl" thus "matures" to the second act's ballerina/heroine. Of the three versions on tape listed here, the Arkhipova-Mukhamedov is the most clearly filmed, but the other two include the more dazzling performances. The major difference between the two videos concerns the change of lead casts from Act 1 to Act 2, which was necessitated during the "live" 1977 telecast because of an injury to Vasiliev. The then-blossoming partnership of the prodigious Pavlova (just watch her unfold and extend her leg à la seconde in the pas de deux) and the glorious Gordeyev makes a dazzling counterpoint to the fully matured one demonstrated by the radiant and magisterial Maximova and Vasiliev.

———, excerpt, Act 2 Pas de Deux, on *Bolshoi Ballerina Ludmila Semenyaka*, with the Bolshoi Ballet, featuring Ludmila Semenyaka, Mikhail Lavrovsky. 1989.

Though in the twilight of her career, Semenyaka, in the ballerina/Masha role, brings an unmistakable grandeur to the ballet's climactic scene. Surrounded by the large and expert Bolshoi ensemble, the ballerina positions Masha as if she were a crystalline jet of pure water. Lavrovsky attends her with similar dignity and decorum, like the good soldier the role calls for.

———, (Kasatkina and Vasiliov), with the Russian State Theater Academy of Classical Ballet, featuring Ludmilla Vasileva, Alexander Gorbatsevich. 1995.

The inspiration for this post-Soviet *Nutcracker* seems to be a conflation of Vainonen and Grigorovich *Nutcrackers*. The Vainonen Snowflakes are here in their standard choreography, as well as the same choreographer's four extra cavaliers. A few real children appear in the party scene, and the disruptive fizz of clicking camera shutters tell us this was filmed at a photocall. The actual videocamera work is choppy to say the least, given the often confused stage pictures and relentlessly busy choreography. Still, some nicely skilled and schooled Russian dancers appear all through this derivative staging. (The male choreographer, by the way, Vladimir Vasiliov, sometimes spelled Vasiliev, is not *the* Vladimir Vasiliev of Bolshoi fame, though many sources understandably confuse the two identically named men.)

———, (Nureyev/Tchaikovsky), with the Royal Ballet, featuring Merle Park, Rudolf Nureyev (1968). 1997.

———, with the Paris Opera Ballet, featuring Elizabeth Maurin, Laurent Hilaire. 1988.

Like Baryshnikov and Grigorovich, Nureyev looks to Vainonen for his *Nutcracker*'s inspiration. And like his two fellow Russians, he adds frequent touches all his own, including the concept of having eccentric Herr Drosselmeier performed by the same dancer playing the heroine's prince. And, as Baryshnikov would do after him, Nureyev pays specific homage to Vainonen by including his Snowflakes choreography. This big ensemble number displays particular grandeur in the Paris Opera production. The earlier Royal Ballet tape records Nureyev's dancing and acting skills at the beginnings of his maturity as a dance artist in the West.

———, *Nutcracker: The Motion Picture*, (Stowell/Tchaikovsky), with the Pacific Northwest Ballet, featuring Patricia Barker, Wade Walthall. 1983.

Maurice Sendak, the celebrated illustrator, is responsible for the scenic and costume designs of this production. The film was released partly on the strength of Sendak's name, and partly because its director Carroll Ballard had previously directed *The Black Stallion*, a children's movie classic. The film is big on filmic effects, much of them adding to the production's opulence and energy. Even usually annoying cuts that close in on dancer's isolated limbs or features are deftly done and neatly woven into the choreography's architecture. Sendak's costumes and scenic effects intermix stage scale with special effects movie magic.

———, (Vainonen/Tchaikovsky), with the Kirov Ballet, featuring Larissa Lezhnina, Victor Baranov. 1994.

Some sixty years after its influential premiere, Vainonen's ballet comes to the video screen. The Kirov production is obviously an update of the original, as is the choregraphy in some measure. But the influences gathered up by Grigorovich, Nureyev, and Baryshnikov are all here in place. Overall, the performance, led by a sweetly pretty Lezhnina and a sweetly handsome Baranov, radiate with a winning Kirov air of unhurried energy and unaffected elegance.

———, (Wright, after Ivanov/Tchaikovsky), with the Royal Ballet featuring Leslie Collier, Anthony Dowell. 1985.

———, with the Birmingham Royal Ballet, featuring Miyako Yoshida, Irek Mukhamedov. 1994.

Peter Wright's British productions looks not to Vainonen's legacy, but to Petipa's and Ivanov's. In the case of the older of these on tape, the dance historian and scholar Roland John Wiley acted as advisor, helping provide notes on the ballet's original 1892 staging. Both efforts end up being rather heavy on the eye and perhaps overpunctilious in detail. Still, Dowell is a charming prince in the earlier version and Mukhamedov an impassioned one in the latter.

Nutcracker Pas de Deux (after Grigorovich—misidentified on tape as Petipa/Ivanov, on *Nina Ananiashvili and International Stars*, vol. 2, with Inna Dorofeyeva, Vadim Pisarev. 1991.

A fairly standard rendering of a Soviet-styled grand pas de deux.

———, (after Ivanov), on *Gala Tribute to Tchaikovsky*, featuring Leanne Benjamin, Tetusu Kumakawa. 1993.

This is the same choreography included in Wright's production for the Royal Ballet (see above). These smaller, younger dancers lack something in grandeur next to those of Collier and Dowell, though Kumakawa throws in a few bravura embellishments of his own in his "Tarantella" solo.

———, on A *Tale of Christmas: The Bell Telephone Hour*, featuring Violette Verdy, Edward Villella. 1961.

Though both these famous dancers are associated with New York City Ballet and the choreography of Balanchine, here they perform in their "guest artist" mode, appearing on a television show as a "ballet act." They dance a variation on what has passed for the standard Ivanov choreography in the States since the 1940s. Villella dances a solo to music from the ballet's general coda; Verdy does the Ivanov-tradition "Sugar Plum" solo. Both dances include touches of Balanchinean details, as does the pas de deux itself. Villella's entrechat-six sequence and Verdy's successive fouetté turns both stand out as dazzlingly clear examples of their kind.

———, (Vainonen), on *Classic Kirov*, featuring Irina Kolpakova, Vladilen Semenyov (c. 1970). 1992.

———, on *Russian Ballet: The Glorious Tradition*, vol. 1, with Larissa Lezhnina, Igor Zelensky (1990). 1993.

The first of these Vainonen excerpts includes only the climactic pas de deux, which the choreographer has devised as a pas de deux à six by adding four *Sleeping Beauty*-style cavaliers to attend the prince's partnering; that is, no variations or coda. Though it's filmed on a movie sound stage in black-and-white, albeit with especially luminous lighting, the performance radiates with a rosy glow emanating from Kolpakova's beauteous dancing. The later pas, filmed on a fully set stage, in color, does include both dancers' variations and their coda. The special pleasure here is not the Masha (or "Sugar Plum" ballerina) but the prince, danced with inimitable dash and expansive breadth by the part-sullen, part-sweet Zelensky.

Ondine, (Ashton/Henze), abridged, on *The Royal Ballet*, featuring Margot Fonteyn, Michael Somes. 1959.

One of the too few Ashton ballets carefully captured on video. In one of her most celebrated parts, Fonteyn is nicely recorded here, in all aqueous fluidity that Ashton encouraged and stressed in ballet dancing. Most of the story, about a sea sprite beguiling a very human young man, remains intact. Many of the obviously magical stage effects are here as well, including the sense of being aboard a ship on a tossing sea. Underwater as well as aboveground activity inspire Ashton to create some of his most enchanting ballet theater.

Onegin, with National Ballet of Canada, featuring Frank Augustyn, Sabina Allemann, Jeremy Ransom, Cynthia Lucas. 1986.

An adapted-for-television record of John Cranko's arguably best-known ballet, danced in this case with suitable strength if not undue flair.

Papillon, Le Pas de Deux, (Lacotte, after M. Taglioni/Offenbach), on *The Kirov Ballet in London*, featuring Irina Kolpakova, Sergei Berezhnoi. 1988.

———, on *Kirov Soloists*. 1982.

This 1976 duet comes from the educated guessing of Lacotte (see *La Sylphide* chapter), a choreographer highly educated in historical dance. The complete ballet's original inspiration and interpreter was Emma Livry, whose tragic death from burns incurred onstage (during a rehearsal of *La Muette de Portici*) profoundly connected her to the butterfly subject matter in Taglioni's choreography. Kolpakova, ably attended by Berezhnoi, is sublimely fragile, darting and fluttering with delicate precision. The special reason to look at the earlier tape listed is its inclusion of the solo passages, not included on that later tape. Kolpakova presents a perfect example of the French term *tacqueté*, which freely translated refers to "making lace with the feet."

Paquita, Grand Pas [Classique], including the "Golden" *Pas de Trois*, (after Petipa, etc./Minkus), on *The Maryinsky Ballet*, featuring Yulia Makhalina, Igor Zelensky, five additional female soloists. 1991.

This is the only "Grand Pas" now on the market that includes the "Pas de Trois," both of which Petipa added to his pantomime ballet in 1881. Over the years, the classical Spanish-flavored divertissement has become a kind of miniature gala performance, with its array of solos lining up a string of ballerinas. This one has five solos preceding her climactic one for Makhalina's ballerina "turn." Since the pas de trois is danced in the midst of the grand pas, the ballerina's partner cannot dance an interpolated solo from the music of the pas de trois, as is sometimes done, so the athletic and intense Zelensky dances one to music interpolated from Delibes's *La Source* (the same music used by Balanchine for an interpolated male solo in Act 1 of his production of *Coppélia*.)

———, on *American Ballet Theatre at the Met*, featuring Cynthia Gregory, Fernando Bujones, four additional female soloists. 1984.

This is Makarova's staging of a ballet from her Leningrad days. She includes four soloists, besides the ballerina: a forthright Leslie Browne, a sly Susan Jaffe, a fine-spun Cyntha Harvey, and a dynamo-driven Deirdre Carberry. Bujones dances a solo taken from the pas de trois. Gregory dances the "flute" variation, introduced by a ballerina-heralding harp arpeggio, and embellished with more from the harp. She "swims" through the choreography with her inimitable aplomb and unshakable confidence.

Pas de Quatre (Dolin/Pugni) on *Kirov Ballet: Classic Ballet Night*, featuring Irina Kolpakova, Gabriela Komleva, Elena Evteyeva, Galina Mezentseva. 1982.

———, on *Nina Ananiashvili and International Stars*, vol. 3, featuring Nina Ananiashvili, Rose Gad, Darci Kistler, Tatiana Terekhova. 1993.

———, Cerrito's Variation on *Firestone Dances*, featuring Carla Fracci (1962). 1995.

Anton Dolin's pastiche choreography for Perrot's 1845 ballet event owes little to historical accuracy. Though these records steer somewhat clear of the trap, an oppressively camp aura often surrounds performances of the ballet. Of the two renderings, the Kirov staging has more "seasoned" weight to it—Dolin himself staged the work for the company when some of these dancers were involved with the company. The other is fairly agreeable, nevertheless. The Fracci solo offers, in isolation, a performance the same ballerina gives on a currently unavailable tape called *Romantic Era*. There the full ballet is led in traditional order by Ghislaine Thesmar as Grahn, Eva Evdokimova as Grisi, Fracci as Cerrito, and Alicia Alonso as Taglioni.

———, undated, black-and-white excerpt on *Alicia*, with Alicia Alonso and unidentified dancers. 1976.

Though a touch of camp creeps into this performance, it includes a look at what the legendary Alonso stressed in her own dancing and in that of her pupils. The segment includes the opening and closing dances for the quartet of women and the Taglioni solo danced, of course, by Alonso herself. Clean footwork, wryly held perfectly still balances, and crisp petit batterie distinguish the dancing overall, and Alonso's in particular.

Petrouchka (Fokine/Stravinsky), on *Paris Dances Diaghilev*, with the Paris Opera Ballet, featuring Thierry Mongne, Monique Loudières, Jean Guizerix. 1990.

Of the various stagings, this one put on by Nicholas Berisoff is at variance in parts with other "Fokine" versions around the world. The most reliable staging, so far as Fokine's text is concerned, is that put on by the Joffrey Ballet in 1976. A video record exists in PBS's *Dance in America* archives, starring Nureyev. (Watch for its possible release.) The Paris stage picture is richly detailed, with a working Ferris wheel and merry-go-round in the fair scene. Unfortunately, the portrayals are somewhat lacking in dramatic and choreographic detail and, with the notable exception of Guizerix as the Moor, most tend to be blandly yet obviously playacted.

———, (Vinogradov), on *The Maryinsky Ballet*, with the Kirov Ballet, featuring Sergei Vikharev. 1991.

This naively modern production reduces the original Fokine-Stravinsky-Benois scenario to a theme of innocent artistic underlings squelched by oppressive overlings. The lithe and supple Vikharev, with reddish puppetlike hair, keeps trying to exert himself as a free spirit and creative light while his fellow citizens back him up with similar behavior. Thuggish, masked, and padded characters acting as police and political bosses keep thwarting and/or torturing the Petrouchka figure. In the end, after being beaten down one final time, he's held up in a cruciform lift, as a sacrificial lamb, with perhaps only one female counterpart feeling the true loss of her fellow "artist." The whole of the rather monotonous affair owes something to the "Red Shoes" ballet from *The Red Shoes* film (see below) and something more to a Soviet cartoon.

Prince Igor: Polovtsian Dances, (Fokine/Borodin), on *Classic Kirov*, with the Kirov Ballet, featuring Yuri Goumba, A. Kashirina (1983).

Fokine made this opera ballet into a one-act ballet for Diaghilev's 1909 Paris season. The Kirov staging still employs the chorus that was eventually dropped from the ballet version. The "mysterious" East, as seen by the cosmopolitan Eastern European, undulates forth from the chains of veiled dancing maidens and from the bold leaps of bow-wielding warriors. The Kirov gives this atmospheric interlude all the depth and texture it asks for, and more.

Prince of the Pagodas, The, (MacMillan/Britten), with the Royal Ballet, featuring Darcey Bussell, Jonathan Cope, Fiona Chadwick. 1990.

MacMillan's last multi-act narrative ballet (1989) was recorded a year later with nearly all of its original cast. Clearly and agreeably filmed on the Covent Garden stage, the three-act work has handy onscreen plot synopses, which help in following the complicated scenario. The best reason to see the less than satisfying spectacle is for the daring, dazzling, and unaffected dancing of Bussell, who was only nineteen when MacMillan made her into the star of his ballet as the Princess Rose. The convoluted tale, part *King Lear*, part *Beauty and the Beast*, is unconvincingly set to the atmospheric music of Britten, but there is nothing unconvincing about Bussell or, for that matter, Cope as her loving, warm salamander of a prince. The final scene, a sparkling bright divertissement, could well stand on its own as a separate ballet when the likes of Bussell and Cope lead the event.

"[La] Princess Zenobia Ballet" from *On Your Toes*, (Balanchine/Rodgers), pas de deux excerpt on *That's Dancing*, with Vera Zorina, Charles Lasky (1939). 1985.

This outtake from the *Schéhérazade* pastiche Balanchine made in an era when *Schéhérazade* was still a highly popular ballet, shows Balanchine being Balanchine all the while winking in the direction of Michel Fokine. Zorina is made to look luminous, glamorous, and strong, while her partner looks solicitous and secondary.

Puppenfee, Die. See *Fairy Doll, The*.

Push Comes to Shove. See chapter on *Push Comes to Shove*.

Rake's Progress, The, (deValois/Gordon), with the Sadler's Wells Royal Ballet, featuring David Morse, Nicola Katrak, Kim Reeder, David Bintley. 1982.

Like *Checkmate* (see above), this ballet comes marketed under a subheading called: "Masterpieces of British Ballet." Whether it's masterly or not time and your own feelings will tell, but the choreographic rendering of a series of narrative paintings by England's revered William Hogarth has a good deal of historical weight to it. The black-and-white filming of the ballet is good and the performances true. More mimetic still in scope than *Checkmate*, the work shows the English interest in narrative ballet in an early (1935) example.

Raymonda (Grigorovich, after Petipa, Gorsky, etc./Glazunov), with the Bolshoi Ballet, featuring Ludmila Semenyaka, Irek Mukhamedov, Gedeminas Taranda. 1987.

———, *The Bolshoi at the Bolshoi* series, featuring Natalia Bessmertnova, Yuri Vasyuchenko, Gedeminas Taranda. 1989.

These two videos record the same 1984 staging of an 1898 Petipa concoction about a Hungarian princess, her shining-knight fiancé, and a handsome Saracen stranger. The 1989 video is more handsomely filmed, the 1987 more beautifully performed. Though Grigorovich mounted his restaging for Bessmertnova, Semenyaka, in the earlier tape, dances as if the work had been made especially for her. Both are good records of this production, with reasonable links to its Petipa and Gorsky heritage. Mukhamedov is the more dashing hero, but Taranda is equally vivid and captivating in both tapes, proving yet again that sometimes the baddies are the most interesting of characters in fiction.

———, (Sergeyev, after Petipa), "Pas de Dix and Variations" on *Russian Ballet: The Glorious Tradition*, vol. 3, featuring Irina Kolpakova, Vladilen Semenov (1976). 1993.

This specially filmed footage comes from the Kirov Ballet's beautifully staged version of the complete three-act ballet. (Some day, perhaps, the complete ballet will be released on video, since it was televised in 1980 on the BBC, with Kolpakova and Sergei Berezhnoi.) In her tutu and little hat, with its egret-feather panache, Kolpakova is a dream of a Raymonda, even outside the ballet's official "dream scene." (See the especially well-filmed dream episode in Bessmertnova tape above.)

———, excerpts on *Classic Kirov*, featuring Natalia Dudinskaya, Konstantin Sergeyev. c. 1955.

This series of dances and scenes from the ballet's three acts gives a sense of the production's opening, dream, and final scenes. The production values are high, in both detail and grand scale. The performances are all suitably vivid and generous, including the "character" Spanish number. As a record of Soviet ballet, it fills out the picture of what virtuosity was like in the early 1950s behind the Iron Curtain—Dudinskaya's steely points and Sergeyev's liquid turns with little emphasis on "clean" form.

———, "Pas de Deux," on *Nina Ananiashvili and International Stars*, vol. 3, with Nina Ananiashvili, Aleksei Fadeyechev. 1993.

This is the central pas de deux from the ballet's climactic "Grand Pas Hongroise" of the Bolshoi Ballet's Grigorovich production mentioned above, which both these dancers performed when they were with the home company. Each dancer performs impressively, with the ever-knightly Fadeyechev making a most profound impression.

Red Shoes, The, (Helpmann and Massine/Easdale) feature-length motion picture featuring Moira Shearer, Leonide Massine, Robert Helpmann, Ludmilla Tcherina. 1948.

This item should perhaps be included in the historical section of this appendix, but since there was a stage version of the film that included a self-contained ballet called "The Red Shoes" (with choreography by Lar Lubovitch), it can be listed with other individual ballets. Though the musical-theater rendering of the film failed at the box office, the ballet itself found a brief life of independence at American Ballet Theatre. The "ballet within the ballet film" is partly dependent on filmmaking techniques, and shows the beauties of Shearer's person and dancing. The surrounding story, with its snippets of then-popular ballets, is of some interest historically, presenting as it goes, with frequent poetic license, the career of Serge Diaghilev.

Romeo and Juliet, (Grigorovich/Prokofiev), with the Bolshoi Ballet, featuring Natalia Bessmertnova, Irek Mukhamedov. 1989.

———, Act 2 on *Bolshoi Prokofiev Gala*, with the Bolshoi Ballet, featuring Ludmila Semenyaka and Yuri Vasyuchenko. 1991.

This choreographic rendering of Soviet Russia's arguably most famous ballet score is not likely to last long on the boards of post-Soviet ballet theater. Detailed with Grigorovich's signature conceit for all-dance (no pantomime) storytelling action, this three-acter can be hard going for both overwrought dancer and bewildered viewer alike. Still in the complete record of the ballet, Bessmertnova's willowy Juliet and Mukhamedov's buoyant Romeo bring further honor to both these artists' careers. In the isolated second act, the filming is a little dark and overwhelmingly red, but most of the performing is better than average, and more coherent than some of the choreographic conceits, though Vasyuchenko's Romeo is not especially distinguished.

———, (Lavrovsky/Prokofiev), with the Bolshoi Ballet, featuring Natalia Bessmertnova, Mikhail Lavrovsky. 1976.

———, abridged, featuring Galina Ulanova, Yuri Zhadanov. 1954.

These two videos of the Bolshoi Ballet's staging of Lavrovsky's influential version of this widely popular ballet score are separated by more than twenty years. The earlier record, with Ulanova, for whom Lavrovsky created his Juliet, is a lushly filmed production. Outdoor locations and other details take the ballet well beyond the walls of a staged production. Both the delicately impassioned Ulanova and the radiantly handsome Zhadanov mesmerized the camera and the viewer. The colorful performing of the surrounding characters, including a wild-eyed Aleksei Yermolayev as Tybalt, that frames the central roles shows the Bolshoi performing ensemble in one of its richest periods. To get a clearer sense, however, of the ballet as stage spectacle, the later tape listed above does the job. Bessmertnova is a tremulous, reedy heroine, and Mikhail Lavrovsky, the choreographer's son, is a steadfast hero. Though it isn't quite the great outdoors, the Bolshoi Theater stage is higher, wider, and deeper than almost any other opera house space where this ballet might be performed.

———, brief "wedding" excerpt on *Classic Kirov*, featuring Galina Ulanova, Konstantin Sergeyev. 1940.

———, "bedroom" excerpt, pas de deux, on *Russian Ballet: The Glorious Tradition*, vol. 2, featuring Galina Ulanova, Mikhail Gabovitch (1951). 1993.

These two excerpts predate the more extensive, if truncated, film of Lavrovsky's ballet with Ulanova. Still, they are both of interest, the older black-

and-white clip because it documents the ballet's beginnings as a Leningrad (Petersburg) production, here with the original Romeo, Konstantin Sergeyev, and because it shows the young Ulanova in her Leningrad (Petersburg) years. Furthermore, the wedding-vow choreography reveals some of the choreography's most lyrical plastic images. The later "bedroom duet" shows Ulanova in her Bolshoi period with a different Romeo, and frames her in a more stagelike space.

———, (MacMillan/Prokofiev). See chapter on *Romeo and Juliet.*

———, with the Royal Ballet, featuring Alessandra Ferri, Wayne Eagling. 1984.

This video records MacMillan's ballet onstage, in performance before a live audience. Ferri, like Bussell (see *Prince of the Pagodas* above) was a special protégée of MacMillan's, and you can see why from her impassioned performing in this video. The rest of the cast is unfortunately somewhat less impressive, with the slight exception of Stephen Jeffries as Mercutio. Be on the lookout for a performance of the ballet with American Ballet Theatre, led by Natalia Makarova and Kevin McKenzie, which was telecast live and made slightly infamous by the fact that McKenzie's Romeo performed the tomb scene in his warm-up pants, which he'd forgotten to remove before coming onstage for the ballet's final scene.

———, (Rizhenko, Smirnov-Golovanov/Tchaikovsky), on *Shakespeare Dance Trilogy*, featuring Alexander Sememchukov, Svetlana Senonova, Nikita Dolgushin (c. 1988). 1993.

Like its companion Shakespeare ballet, *Hamlet*, this Soviet-Russian one-act ballet is a fantasy on the themes of its subject. The music is Tchaikovsky's own "Overture-Fantasia," and the ballet plays like a dream encapsulation of the narrative's leading characters, with Friar Lawrence standing in for all the others of the drama. Dolgushin is as dignified as ever; the protagonists young and appealing; the choreography general and airy; the outdoor setting awe-inspiring and a little overwhelming.

"Romeo and Juliet Ballet" from Goldwyn Follies, (Balanchine/Duke), on *Goldwyn Follies*, featuring Vera Zorina, William Dollar. 1938.

This urban reworking of the warring Capulets and Montagues precedes *West Side Story* by more than a decade. Only in this case the "gangs" are tap-dancing Capulets against ballet-dancing Montagues. Lines of laundry and the "line" of ballet dancing intermix in a witty yet serious attempt to put choreography into Hollywood filmmaking. Unlike the "Water Nymph Ballet" (see below), this one is not strictly self-contained, but plays a part in the movie's plot.

Ruslan and Ludmila, Act 3 dances, Naina's maidens (after Fokine/Glinka), on *Classic Kirov*, with the Kirov Ballet, featuring Gabriela Komleva (c. 1975). 1992.

This opera ballet elaborates a scene of enchantment and enticement worked by a sorceress over the opera's hapless hero. How the Soviets kept this as Fokine's work when he remained outside the country for most of his mature career is another of the mysteries of Soviet ballet. In vague outline, the leading ballerina, attended by two solo ballerinas and framed by an all-female ensemble of twenty, might be seen as *Chopiniana* without the youth/poet present. Still, this tape shows something specifically Soviet about the ballet, and it preserves the same music Balanchine used for a rarely seen "Pas de Trois," often called "Glinka Pas de Trois."

Russian Dance, (Gorsky? or Goliezovsky?/Tchaikovsky), on *Essential Ballet*, featuring Olga Chenchikova. 1992.

This solo for a ballerina costumed à la russe in beaded *sarafan* (shift) and *kokoshnik* (elaborate diadem) takes its inspiration from an interpolation made early on by Tchaikovsky into his *Swan Lake*, and today not often played in that ballet. (It was written as the ballerina's Odile solo in the "Ballroom Scene.") The music is a marvelously lush, intense violin composition and this dance is both simply choreographed and deeply felt. The seemingly elemental folkloric material takes the ballerina on a large and easy circuit of the stage, eventually accelerating to a theatrical near-frenzy. The delicate use of handkerchief—perfumed we presume—helps cap the dance. Chenchikova performs well, but look for the video release of a film called *Katia et Volodia*, in which Ekaterina Maximova dances the same solo even more sublimely, looking for all the world like a palace porcelain figurine.

Sacre du Printemps, Le (Béjart/Stravinsky), closing dance on *The Art of the 20th-Century Ballet*, featuring the Ballet du XXe Siecle, with Eric Vu An, Grazia Galante. 1985.

This excerpt of the most well-known of the late-twentieth-century *Sacres* (or *Rite of Springs*), is brief, about five minutes long, but it shows something (if not the most memorable of Béjart's modernist moments) of his popular "unitard" rendering of pagan Russian rites.

Satanella Pas de Deux, (after Petipa/Pugni), on *Nina Ananiashvili and International Stars*, vol. 3, featuring Inna Dorofeyeva, Vadim Pisarev. 1993.

This divertissement pas de deux, with tenuous links to a narrative ballet formerly known as *Le Diable Amoureux* and sometimes known as "Satanilla" or "Carnival de Venise" is a flamboyant little showpiece. This performance is suitably showy. For more about this less-than-well-known ballet, see *The Children of Theater Street*, a 1978 documentary film now on video.

Scherzo à la Russe, (Balanchine/Stravinsky), on *Balanchine Celebration*, pt. 1, "The Balanchine Library," with New York City Ballet, featuring Helene Alexopoulos, Diana White. 1993.

Of the eleven ballets shown on this two-part program, only this one is offered complete. In their theatrically Russian sarafans and kokoshniks, the all-female ensemble and leading ensemble dancers perform a kind of greeting ceremony in the process of their folkloric ballet dancing. In the end, it's all fluttering ribbons, kicked-up heels, and gracious, courtly Russian bows.

Sinatra Suite, (Tharp/Sinatra Songs), on *Baryshnikov Dances Sinatra, and More*, with Mikhail Baryshnikov, Elaine Kudo. 1984.

This is a customized reduction of Tharp's *Sinatra Songs*, a post–modern dance suite of duets inspired by ballroom dancing. Baryshnikov dances in a tux; Kudo in "little black dress" and heeled pumps. The honey-voiced Sinatra pours forth in recorded song as the sometimes combatant couple of dancers body through Tharp's sometimes lyrical, sometimes quirky, sometimes athletic choreographic inventions.

Sleeping Beauty, The (Petipa and after/Tchaikovsky). See chapter on *Sleeping Beauty*.

———, with the Kirov Ballet, featuring Altinai Asylmuratova, Konstantin Zaklinsky, Lubov Kunakova. c. 1990.

———, featuring Irina Kolpakova, Sergei Berezhnoi, Lubov Kunakova. c.1980.

———, featuring Larissa Lezhnina, Farukh Ruzimatov, Yulia Makhalina. 1989.

The three videos listed above all record the longstanding Kirov production of *Sleeping Beauty* as revised during the 1950s and the 1980s by Konstantin Sergeyev from the troupe's direct links to Petipa's original production. The one led by Kolpakova, who has the closest links to Sergeyev's work, is handsomely filmed on the Maryinsky stage, on which Petipa's original *Beauty* was born. The one led by Lezhnina was filmed on tour, in Montreal; the one with Asylmuratova, on the stage of Moscow's Bolshoi Theater. This last-named venue, the biggest of the three, sometimes engulfs the action in undue darkness. Each video, however, has things to recommend to the viewer. The innumerable delicacies in Kolpakova's performance are a special pleasure of the earliest of these video records, as is the good dancing of Berezhnoi. In the Canadian video, the radiant Yulia Makhalina stands out as a beguiling Lilac Fairy. The Asymuratova-Zaklinsky performance has the unusually tall and marvelously lyrical Kyril Melnikov as "Blue Bird" alongside the minxlike Elena Pankova as Princess Florine. Unfortunately all are fairly bereft of standard pantomime, a particular loss in the scenes with Carabosse, especially in the overkill use of a child stand-in to enact the demise of the young princess. Two of the three Carabosses are performed by male dancers; the third, in the Asylmuratova video, may be a woman, but the lack of credits and packaging notes makes this hard to say for certain.

———, with the Royal Ballet, featuring Viviana Durante, Zoltan Solymosi, Benazir Hussein. 1994.

This is a rather controversial staging because of the wierdly angled architecture indicated by Maria Bjørnson's set—she who designed Broadway's *Phantom of the Opera.* The costumes, about as fanciful as a Hollywood period picture from the 1930s, are also hardly traditional in mode. Still, the choreography is fairly standard British-Russian and the performances are all solid: an unshakably confident Durante, a rapturous and elegant Solymosi, and distinguished Hussein. As the wicked fairy Carabosse, Dowell is masterly, glamorous, and venomous all at once.

———, abridged, with the Kirov Ballet, featuring Alla Sizova, Yuri Soloviev, Irina Bazhenova. 1964.

———, (Nureyev, after Petipa) with the National Ballet of Canada, featuring Veronica Tennant, Rudolf Nureyev, Christine Soleri. 1972.

Both of these videos clock in at about 90 minutes (More complete versions go about two hours). Each has its merits and individual pleasures. The Kirov record shows a glorious Sizova and an amazing Soloviev, who was, it turns out, even more renowned for his Blue Bird. The Blue Bird in this film is Valery Panov, paired with Natalia Makarova as Princess Florine. (Unfortunately, their divertissement is severely cut, leaving little of their dancing in the final cut.) Each of these truncated *Beauty*s offers an unusual take on one of ballet's crucial roles. The Kirov has a woman, the distinguished ballerina and teacher, Natalia Dudinskaya, performing her role on pointe. The NBC version has the Lilac Fairy in a big, hoop-skirted garment, parading through the proceedings exclusively as a mime artist.

———, Act 3, a.k.a. "Aurora's Wedding", on *An Evening With the Royal Ballet*, featuring Margot Fonteyn, David Blair. 1963.

For years in the West, with isolated exceptions, *The Sleeping Beauty* was known primarily from this excerpt based on the ballet's last act. Here is the last act of the Royal Ballet's full-length production, excerpted for film purposes. It documents a *Beauty* tradition fairly untouched by the pervasive Russian-Soviet influences that would soon affect the ballet in the West. The prince's solo, as danced by Blair, shows none of the Nureyev influence that would soon affect it in the West. In fact, the driving force of Ashton, the company's most important choreographic voice, can be felt in this staging almost as much as that of Petipa's choreographic designs.

———, excerpt from the "Vision Scene" and solos and coda from Act 3 Pas de Deux, on *The Magic of the Kirov*, featuring Irina Kolpakova, Yuri Soloviev (1976). 1989.

Recorded on the Maryinsky stage, this video documents the Kirov production and Kolpakova, a few years earlier than the complete version listed above. Soloviev repeats the role he performed alongside Sizova some ten years earlier (see above). Though he looks less streamlined than in the 1964 film, Soloviev dances with his exceptional and remarkable lightness and ease. Kolpakova remains her shimmering, radiant self.

———, Act 1 "Rose Adagio," on *Bolshoi Ballerina Ludmila Semenyaka*, featuring Ludmila Semenyaka. 1989.

Framed by Grigorovich's production of the 1890 Petipa ballet (see *Sleeping Beauty* chapter), the Leningrad-trained Semenyaka brings to Moscow her own traditions. Ably supported by four elegant cavaliers, the confident and clear ballerina gets through the rigors of this endurance test well, if not as superbly as she did when she first took on the part years earlier. Of all the Soviet interpreters of Aurora, Semenyaka takes most readily to the detail of holding and sustaining her unsupported balances in efface attitude. Still, these *equilibres* really are not the province of Soviet ballerinas.

———, Act 3 Pas de Deux, on *Gala Tribute to Tchaikovsky*, featuring Leslie Collier, Irek Mukhamedov. 1993.

———, on *I Am a Dancer*, featuring Lynn Seymour, Rudolf Nureyev. 1973.

———, on *Ballet Legends: Ninel Kurgapkina*, featuring Ninel Kurgapkina, unidentified partner (c. 1970). 1993.

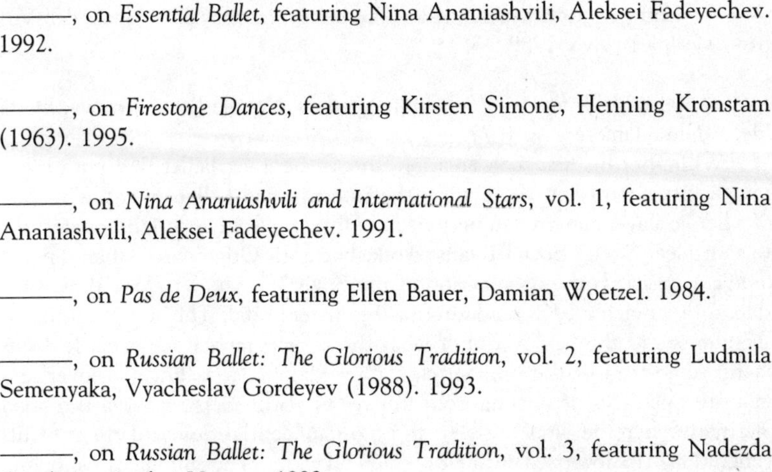

———, on *Essential Ballet*, featuring Nina Ananiashvili, Aleksei Fadeyechev. 1992.

———, on *Firestone Dances*, featuring Kirsten Simone, Henning Kronstam (1963). 1995.

———, on *Nina Ananiashvili and International Stars*, vol. 1, featuring Nina Ananiashvili, Aleksei Fadeyechev. 1991.

———, on *Pas de Deux*, featuring Ellen Bauer, Damian Woetzel. 1984.

———, on *Russian Ballet: The Glorious Tradition*, vol. 2, featuring Ludmila Semenyaka, Vyacheslav Gordeyev (1988). 1993.

———, on *Russian Ballet: The Glorious Tradition*, vol. 3, featuring Nadezda Gracheva, Andrei Uvarov. 1993.

This pas de deux is a "greatest hit" excerpt performed frequently in galas and in competition settings. The range of quality and quantity is wide on the tapes listed above, from a green and agreeably cocky teenaged Damian Woetzel to a golden mature Fadeyechev, with a wondrously elegant and noble Kronstam in-between, showing his inimitable mix of Danish mimetic warmth and purest classical cool. It's also interesting to note the details stressed by the mature English Collier and the mature Soviet Semenyaka. Or to note the accents made by two former Soviet-trained Tartars, Nureyev and Mukhamedov, or the unfailing elegance, ease, and nobility of Fadeyechev. Given the vagaries of Kurgapkina's partner/prince, perhaps his name was left off the credits for good reason.

———, (prince's act 3 variation), on *Firestone Dances*, featuring Rudolf Nureyev (1963). 1995.

A companion to the *Gayne* solo (see above) this young, eager, and already golden dancer was "turning out" to his adoring and growing public in the States. Nureyev's presentation of the solo would become the standard by which all "Sleeping Beauty" princes would match themselves for the rest of the century. Interestingly, Nureyev hadn't yet inserted his soon-to-be-signature, emphatically if nonchalantly closed fifth position as the dance's final punctuation mark.

Spartacus, (Grigorovich/Katchaturian), with the Bolshoi Ballet, featuring Irek Mukhamedov, Natalia Bessmertnova, Mikhail Gabovich, Marina Bylova. 1984.

———, featuring Irek Mukhamedov, Ludmila Semenayaka, Alexander Vetrov, Marina Bylova. 1989.

———, (abridged), featuring Vladimir Vasiliev, Natalia Bessmertnova, Maris Liepa, Nina Timofeyeva. 1977.

While not his first such creation, this is the 3-act ballet that put Grigorovich prominently on the map of the international ballet circuit. This tale of a heroic slave, martyred in his pursuit of freedom from imperialist oppressors, was an ideal Soviet Social Realist work, but until Grigorovich's handling, it didn't quite catch the imagination of the Soviet people, let alone those outside. Grigorovich's 1968 rendering of the material did. The slightly trimmed '77 film is still the best record of what the choreographer achieved. It documents almost all of the original cast; only Maximova as Phrygia, lover and mate to Spartacus, is missing from this record. Still, Bessmertnova is a good alternative heroine, and Vasiliev, the most influential Soviet danseur of his generation, is showcased in all his splendid glory. The filming is calibrated with fine special effects, even the slow motion moments somewhat dramatize the ballet's vividness. The other videos more carefully record the ballet's shape on a stage, and Mukhamedov is a worthy successor to Vasiliev. Timofeyeva as an unstoppable Aegina and Liepa as a venomous Crassus also stand as near-impossible acts to follow, though the subsequent casts recorded here do well with their tall orders.

———, excerpt, Act 2 Phrygia-Spartacus adagio, on *Bolshoi Ballerina Ludmila Semenyaka*, featuring Ludmila Semenyaka and Mikhail Lavrovsky. 1989.

Performed as a self-contained acrobatic adagio number on a stage set with an indication of the complete ballet's production values, Semenyaka is ably supported in all the duet's contortionist oddities. She gives the would-be introspective and melancholy number all the passion it asks, and more.

Spectre de la Rose, Le, (Fokine/Weber). *See* chapter on Diaghilev Triple Bill.

———, on *Baryshnikov at Wolf Trap*, featuring Mikhail Baryshnikov, Marianna Tcherkassky. 1976.

———, on *Nina Ananiashvili and International Stars*, vol. 1, featuring Farukh Ruzimatov, Nina Ananiashvili. 1991.

Both of these stagings have a slightly makeshift air with regard to the Bakst setting that traditionally goes along with Fokine's choreography. Baryshnikov's version of the choreography comes through a link to Andre Eglevsky, a dancer who had been coached by Fokine himself in the role. Ruzimatov's comes from less direct sources, and it shows.

Spring Waters, (Messerer/Rachmaninoff), on *The Bolshoi Ballet*, featuring Ludmila Bogomolova and Stanislav Vlasov. 1957.

One of Soviet ballet's self-styled "concert numbers" (isolated, nonnarrative show pieces) this spring-green, daredevil romp of a duet is one of the grandparents of numerous show-stopper dances that followed. Messerer, as both dancer and choreographer, helped give a new dimension to the acrobatic nature long associated with the Soviet Bolshoi Ballet. The two pros performing here come from an especially strong generation of wonderfully flamboyant and grand dance artists.

Square Dance, (Balanchine/Corelli), excerpt, male solo, on *The Balanchine Celebration*, pt. 1, featuring Manuel Legris. 1993.

Balanchine's homage to the American square dance came in 1957; all that's officially on the video market is the male solo (made for Bart Cook), a "sarabande" that the choreographer added when he revived his work in 1976. Here one of the finest Paris Opera dancers, Legris, does his best with this "foreign" material. The dance puts an island of melancholy and reverie into the more outgoing, bright-eyed mix. Isolated here, the contrast is gone, but the beguiling mysteries of the choreography still rise to the surface of Legris's beautiful dancing.

Stars and Stripes, (Balanchine/Sousa, arr. Kay), fourth and fifth "campaigns," on *The Balanchine Celebration*, pt. 2, with New York City Ballet, featuring, Margaret Tracey, Damian Woetzel, Katrina Killian, Gen Horiuchi. 1993.

The final two segments of Balanchine's strutting and saluting Sousa ballet kick off with "Liberty Bell and El Capitan," the ballet's showy pas de deux (in the manner of that from *Le Corsaire*). After the teasing and grand duet with formal variations and coda for the military-costumed ballerina and her partner comes the climactic "title" movement: "Stars and Stripes" for all the leading dancers and "regiments" that make up the ballet's first three movements (not given in this tape). A big brass marching band atmosphere, complete with stars and bars rising from the ground to the skies, caps the whole affair with a stageful of dancing majorettes and dress-uniformed men.

"Still Life" at the Penguin Cafe (Bintley/Jeffes), with the Royal Ballet. 1989.

This multilayered and variously sectioned ballet takes on the issues of endangered species and shapes itself loosely as a tea dance taking place in a palm court setting. The dancers sometimes appear to be wildlife, fitted with animal or bird heads or costumed as if all animal. The setting sometimes changes as well to take us to the natural habitat of some of the animal life in question. Playful here, pointedly "meaningful" there, the mix is strange; the impact, mixed.

Stone Flower, The (Grigorovich/Prokofiev), with the Kirov Ballet, featuring Anna Polikarpova, Alexander Gulyaev, Tatiana Terekhova. 1991.

———, Act 2, on *Bolshoi Prokofiev Gala*, with the Bolshoi Ballet, featuring Natalya Arkipova, Nina Semizorova, Yuri Vetrov. 1991.

———, excerpt, "Fair Scene", on *Bolshoi Ballet*, a.k.a. *Bolshoi Ballet 1967*, with the Bolshoi Ballet, featuring Raissa Struchkova. 1966.

This is the ballet that made Grigorovich's name (in 1957). Though the three-act work was made for the Kirov Ballet, the record of the complete ballet with the Kirov company was made when the choreographer was long gone from working directly with Kirov dancers. Compared to the Bolshoi excerpts on the other tapes listed above, the Kirov version looks almost overbred, though the leading dancers are all pleasing to behold. The older Bolshoi excerpt makes one wish it were longer so there could be more extensive examples of the dancers of this period. The more recent Bolshoi tape is very much a Grigorovich company piece.

Stravinsky Violin Concerto, (Balanchine/Stravinsky), on *Choreography by George Balanchine: Selections from "Jewels" and "Stravinsky Violin Concerto,"* with New York City Ballet, featuring Kay Mazzo, Karin von Aroldingen, Peter Martins, Bart Cook (1977). 1996.

Though Balanchine made slight adjustments in his 1972 choreography for the 1977 television cameras, his plainly dressed "black and white" ballet remains faithful to his original version on stage. With the exception of Cook, who takes on a role created for Jean Pierre Bonnefous, the video shows Balanchine's dance with his specially chosen dancers. The duet with Martins and Mazzo will show anyone eventually following Martins's own choreography where many of his choreographic preferences come from. With so few of Balanchine's influential black and white ballets on video, this complete one gives a fair look at the essential aesthetic interests of the peerless master of nonnarrative, plotless, but not meaningless ballet.

Suite Grecque, (Béjart/Hadjidakis, Theodorakis), on *White Night of Dance in Leningrad*, with the Ballet du XXe Siecle, featuring Phillipe Lizon, Michel Gascard. 1987.

Filmed with Leningrad's Neva River, its bridges and facades in the background, this folkish, modernist exercise in male dancing à la grecque, is a fair sampling of Béjartian calisthenics.

Swan Lake, (after Petipa and Ivanov/Tchaikovsky). See chapter on *Swan Lake*.

For another Makarova performance, be on the lookout for the re-release of American Ballet Theatre's David Blair staging, which closely follows extant Petipa-Ivanov traditions in the West. Makarova is paired in this 1980 video with Ivan Nagy, for years her peerless partner-prince. The video record was made, and telecast, "live" at Metropolitan Opera House in New York City.

———, (after Petipa/Ivanov/Gorsky), with the Kirov Ballet, featuring Galina Mezentseva, Konstantin Zaklinsky. c. 1985.

———, with the Kirov Ballet, featuring Yulia Makhalina, Igor Zelensky. 1990.

This production stands among those currently available on video as a good approximation of the ballet's hallowed and popularized 1895 scheme. Both are filmed on the Kirov's Maryinsky stage, where the ballet first appeared. Makhalina's Swan Queen is more deliquescent; Mesentseva's more emotive. Both princes are remarkable, Zaklinsky's for his innocent charm and freshness; Zelensky's for his fervor. The latter is the more powerful dancer, and, owing to his eagerness and expertise as a classical stylist, he also performs the male part of the pas de trois normally given to a separate solo dancer. The "swan corps" is superb.

———, excerpt, first Odette-Siegfried pas de deux, on *The Kirov Ballet in London*, featuring Natalia Makarova, Konstantin Zaklinsky. 1988.

This excerpt from what is often called Act 2 of what is often called the "White Swan Pas de Deux" shows Makarova late in her career. But the event is fraught with emotion, since the ex-Kirov ballerina was dancing for the first time since her 1970 defection with her home company in the city where she bolted from the troupe. Zaklinsky partners with superb attentiveness and loving sensitivity, and Makarova dances with great spirit, if under her former strength. The Kirov swan maidens' corps de ballet provides a perfectly apt background for the event's emotional element. The wonderfully lustrous lighting also adds to the glow.

———, (Grigorovich), with the Bolshoi Ballet, featuring Natalia Bessmertnova, Alexander Bogatyrev. 1984.

This video of the Bolshoi Ballet's artistic director and chief choreographer comes in two slightly different versions. One, entitled *The Ultimate Swan Lake*, is the very same performance listed here, but includes a narration by Gene Kelly, sometimes as a voice-over atop the dancing. The other, called simply *Swan Lake*, has no such intrusiveness. Those looking for a traditional staging of this most popular of ballets which reclaims its 1895 workings will have to look to other productions. Grigorovich's includes various original conceits, such as having the genie Rothbart played as a dark-toned counterpart of the young prince himself. Additionally, all the "character" divertissements in the ballroom scene are performed as recognizable ballet dances, with the women on pointe. Still, Bessmertnova, nearing the beginning of the end of her career, shows fine poetic moments, and Bogatyrev comes off with a princely gentleness. Additionally, the Bolshoi's corps de ballet, especially the women as swan maidens, remain very impressive.

———, featuring Alla Mikhailchenko, Yuri Vasyuchenko. 1989.

Yet another record of Grigorovich's eccentric production, this nicely filmed, clear-resolution video comes from the scrupulous *Bolshoi at the Bolshoi* series. Too bad the cast is less stellar than it might otherwise be.

———, Odile-Siegfried duet, on *Bolshoi Ballerina Ludmila Semenyaka*, featuring Ludmila Semenyaka, Aleksei Fadeyechev. 1989.

This concert-number rendering of the "Black Swan Pas de Deux" shows Semenyaka full of daring and spirit, if somewhat lacking in precision. As her adoring prince, Fadeyechev is all good manners and perfect grace; his elevation in the jump-happy solos dancing he's asked to do is astounding, to say the least.

———, (Makarova, Petipa, Ivanov, Gorsky, Ashton), with London Festival Ballet, featuring Evelyn Hart, Peter Schaufuss. 1988.

Something of a hodgepodge of *Swan Lake* productions past, the overriding scheme comes from the projections and settings by opera designer Gunther Schneider-Siemssen. Neither the staging nor the performing proves especially successful.

———, (Nureyev), with the Vienna State Opera Ballet, featuring Margot Fonteyn, Rudolf Nureyev. 1966.

This is a grandly filmed but rather airless studio-recorded video—there are no ambient audience reactions. The reasons for watching have less to do with *Swan Lake* history (Nureyev's original touches often have a touch of absurdity about them) than with the history of the partnership of these historic dancers. The film reliably captures much of what Fonteyn brought to a role she had made famous over a thirty-year period. (*See also* Act 2, abridged, below.) Additionally, Nureyev, barely five years outside the Soviet Union, is here in all his early, indelible glory. The ensemble support is more stolid than inspired.

———, abridged, (Lavrovsky after Petipa/Ivanov/Gorsky), with the Bolshoi Ballet, featuring Maya Plisetskaya, Nicolai Fadeyechev. 1957.

———, abridged, (Sergeyev after Petipa/Ivanov/Gorsky), on *Stars of the Russian Ballet*, featuring Galina Ulanova, Konstantin Sergeyev. 1953.

These 1950s recordings of Soviet *Swans* show the company performing in its bubble of blissful isolation from the world outside. Partly old-fashioned and partly charmingly innocent, these films document the kinds of dancers and dancing that first wowed the West when Soviet ballet, post-Stalin, began to tour. The 1953 onc has an overriding Leningrad (Petersburg) pedigree: Ulanova (now Bolshoi, formerly Kirov) shares the Swan role with the Kirov's Natalia Dudinskaya, who performs a bold Odile to Ulanova's lyrical Odette. The 1957 tape, with the emphatic and mold-breaking Plisetskaya as Odette/Odile, is Bolshoi through and through, complete with scampish jester and fearless character dancing. Fadeyechev is the picture of courtly, princely warmth and decorum, complete with heeled pumps in Act 1. The winged Rothbarts both lose their lives in mortal combat with Siegfried, thus permitting the "happy ending" resolutions prescribed by Soviet censors. The Leningrad Rothbart is thrown, for cinematic purposes, into the sea; the Moscow one fatally loses one of his wings. Both films record strong corps de ballet swans, all sporting enormous tutus with richly ruffled skirts.

———, Act 2, abridged, (Ivanov), on *The Royal Ballet*, featuring Margot Fonteyn, Michael Somes. 1959.

This is Fonteyn's Swan Queen before she met the Prince Siegfried of Nureyev. It's more than five years earlier, but somehow not necessarily five years younger or more vivid. The precise and attractive dancing of the Royal Ballet corps of swans is quite noteworthy. Historically, this staging records the active presence of Benno, the prince's friend who came into the 1895 staging of the ballet as a partner in the "Love Duet" between Odette and Siegfried, making it a pas de deux à trois.

———, excerpts on *Russian Ballet: The Glorious Tradition*, vol. 2, featuring Marina Semyonova (c. 1940), Maya Plisetskaya, Valery Kovtun (1974). 1993.

These *Swan* moments include the legendary Semyonova in a late phase of her career, heroically performing Odette's solo dancing, and the more recently legendary Plisetskaya nearing the final phases of her renowned career. The latter is seen more extensively, performing, in special television setting, the pas de deux that Odette and Odile each have in the course of *Swan Lake*'s four sections. Both ballerinas make the roles their own. Too bad Semyonova wasn't filmed somewhat earlier.

———, excerpts, Odile-Siegfried pas de deux, and swan dances of final scene, with the Kirov Ballet, featuring Galina Mesentseva, Konstantin Zaklinsky. c. 1985. See complete record of their performance above.

———, Odette-Siegfried pas de deux, with the Kirov Ballet, featuring Yulia Makhalina, Andris Liepa.

———, on *Nina Ananiashvili and International Stars*, vol. 1, featuring Irma Nioradze, Yuri Posokhov. 1991.

———, Odile-Siegfried pas de deux, featuring Tatiana Terekhova, Yuri Posokhov. 1991.

The first of these duet excerpts has backup from a swan corps de ballet, reinforcing the Petipa-Ivanov-Gorsky touches to the ballet's distinctive "symphonism." In the Kirov sampling, Makhalina remains luminously and voluptuously inside her dancing. The intense and eager Bolshoi-bred Posokhov makes his Siegfried come to life as both dancer and character, while the ever-eager Terekhova, here just past her prime, seems to be supporting the sometime tradition that casts one ballerina as an apt Odette and a different one as contrasting Odile.

Sylphide, La (Bournonville/Løvenskjold). See chapter on *La Sylphide*.

———, Act 2 pas de deux, on *Nina Ananiashvili and International Stars*, vol. 2, featuring Rose Gad, Alexander Koplin. 1991.

This is not an easy pas de deux to excerpt, but various dancers on various occasions try. These two Royal Danes accomplish the task about as well as can be expected, bringing to their isolated coming together and dancing together a sense of the narrative's surrounding details. As history tells us, the male role was especially devised by its choreographer-dancer creator to include substantial dancing for the male lead. Kolpin meets the challenge with easy strength and sureness of touch.

———, (Lacotte, after Talgioni/Schneitzhöffer). See chapter on *La Sylphide*.

———, Act 2 pas de deux, on *Pas de Deux*, featuring Ghislaine Thesmar, Michel Denard. 1984.

These are the same dancers recorded on the film of the full ballet more than ten years earlier. Both still dance with precision and ease. There is much complex footwork to admire, even if some of the athleticism for the male dancer seems out of place historically in this pastiche of early-nineteenth-century dancing. However gracefully and deftly the handsome and fleet Denard lifts the light and shimmering dancing figure of Thesmar, the very fact that the character of James holds his sylph so frequently and firmly weakens the libretto's premise of elusive spirit and questing Scot. Still, both these French-schooled dancers do some impressively fancy dancing, authentic or not.

Sylphides, Les. See Chopiniana above and chapter on *Les Sylphides*.

———, on *Bolshoi Ballet: Les Sylphides (Chopiniana)*, featuring Natalia Bessmertnova, Alexander Bogateryev, Galina Kozlova, Irina Kholina. 1986.

———, (Grigoriev and Tchernicheva after Fokine) on *An Evening with the Royal Ballet*, featuring Margot Fonteyn, Rudolf Nureyev, Merle Park, Annette Page. 1963.

Of these two videos, the earlier one, with the "after Fokine" staging shows a fuller stage picture; the Bolshoi performance takes place in a void painted inky midnight blue. Both include the "slow mazurka" male solo, which differs from the mazurka Fokine staged in the West. Fonteyn and Nureyev lead their performance with more of their ying/yang complementary harmony; Bogatyrev and Bessmertnova, with their shared schooling, blend into a lovingly coupled unit.

Sylvia Pas de Deux, (Balanchine/Delibes), on *American Ballet Theatre at the Met*, featuring Martine van Hamel, Patrick Bissell. 1984.

This performance of a showpiece Balanchine pas de deux dazzles and shimmers and breathes with a grandeur that only artists as large scale and large spirited as these two can muster. Originally made for Maria Tallchief and Andre Eglevsky, the lustrous duet was one of the Balanchine pas de deux to be seen outside his home company, due in this case to Eglevsky's stewardship of the choreography. With van Hamel and Bissell the pas de deux looks fresh and new.

Tales of Beatrix Potter, (Ashton/Lanchbery), with the Royal Ballet, featuring Alexander Grant, Leslie Collier, Wayne Sleep, Ann Howard, Michael Coleman, Frederick Ashton. 1971.

You'll have to be good at recognizing a dancer by his or her feet here, because all these Royal Ballet dancers wear amazingly realistic and effective animal-head masks. The delights of Ashton's choreography, including some for himself as Mrs. Tiggy-Winkle, are unending. For those who love Petipa's *Don Quixote* you're in for a treat, as the animals dance to the "Dream Scene" music that Lanchbery pinched for his patchwork score. You'll have to decide for yourself whether it's mice or pigs or geese who look most "natural" dancing on their "pointes."

Talisman Pas de Deux, (after Petipa/Drigo), on *Nina Ananiashvili and International Stars*, vol. 4, with Tatiana Terekhova, Yuri Posokhov. 1993.
———, abridged, on *Bolshoi Ballerina Ludmila Semenyaka*, featuring Ludmila Semenyaka, Alexander Vetrov. 1989.

In one of its earlier manifestations this little-known ballet provided Nijinsky with a plum part playing a young god of wind. As it has come to us of late from Soviet ballet, the acrobatic duet, with Grecian details in the young woman's costuming, bears a striking resemblance to *Diana and Actèon*. Of these two videos the Terekhova-Posokhov is the more impressive, especially for the zephyrlike Posokhov.

Tchaikovsky Pas de Deux, (Balanchine/Tchaikovsky), on *Firestone Dances*, featuring Melissa Hayden, Jacques d'Amboise (1962).

———, on *Gala Tribute to Tchaikovsky*, featuring Darcey Bussell, Zoltan Solymosi. 1993.

———, on *Pas de Deux*, featuring Patricia McBride, Reid Olson. 1984.

This duet made by Balanchine as a showpiece in 1960 surprisingly has been recorded commercially only once, in a black-and-white *Firestone* kinescope, with a cast of dancers who worked closely with Balanchine. And the connection shows through radiantly, with a flush of energy, a tingle of daring, and a glow of confidence. Still, the sublime English ballerina Bussell and the dashing Hungarian Solymosi give the duet a full, rosy blush of life. Opposite Olson, McBride, a renowned ballerina who worked all but exclusively with Balanchine, is not quite at her best, but the partnership for this occasion works well enough. F.Y.I.: The Balanchine Library is promising release of another *Choreography by George Balanchine*, which should include a 1979 performance of this duet overseen by Balanchine himself, in which McBride is paired with Mikhail Baryshnikov.

Theme and Variations (a.k.a. "Tema con Variazioni" from Tchaikovsky Suite no. 3), excerpts, pas de deux and finale, on The Balanchine Celebration, Pt. 1, with New York City Ballet, featuring Darci Kistler, Igor Zelensky. 1993.

This is technically the climax of an entire orchestral suite of Tchaikovsky which Balanchine choreographed in 1970, though he previously used this musical segment for a 1947 (American) Ballet Theatre work called *Theme and Variations*. Here the duet is somewhat cautiously danced by Kistler and strongly supported by Zelensky. The thrilling finale, complete with courtly polonaise, follows the pas in most of its sweeping and geometric glory. (Perhaps someday we will see the release of the *Live from Lincoln Center* telecast in which Gelsey Kirkland and Mikhail Baryshnikov led the ABT staging.)

Triad (MacMillan/Prokofiev), on *American Ballet Theatre at the Met*, with American Ballet Theatre, featuring Amanda McKerrow, Robert LaFosse, Johann Renvall. 1984.

MacMillan's "mènage a trois" is without scenario or program notes, but reportedly concerns two brothers loving the same woman. The ballet was made for Britain's Royal Ballet, and was transferred to ABT while MacMillan served there in an artistic advisory capacity. It's a "unitard ballet," with a minimal setting; the "brothers" and the lone woman twine, float, and streak their ways through the atmospherics created by Prokofiev's plaintive violin concerto (no. 1).

Troy Game, (North/Downes, arr. Keliehor), on *Dance Theater of Harlem*, featuring the male ensemble of Dance Theater of Harlem. 1989.

This mostly tongue-in-cheek display of athletic men behaving athletically takes its inspiration from some kind of ancient sport occasion. The men of this company respond to North's witty physical "commentary" with physical expertise and personal distinction. (The work was originally made for the modern dancers of London Contemporary Dance.) In effect, it harks back not only to athletic contests and preparations of classical Greece but also to the physical theater offered by troupes of acrobatic performers in seventeenth-century Europe.

Tzigane, (Balanchine/Ravel), on *Choreography by George Balanchine: Tzigane, Andante from Divertimento No. 15, The Four Temperaments*, with New York City Ballet, featuring Suzanne Farrell, Peter Martins (1977). 1995.

This "gypsy violin" number is a musical jeu d'esprit as well as a choreographic one. Farrell created this part soon after she returned to Balanchine's company after a strained absence. With it she regains her position as the choreographer's primary muse. Martins is a perfectly cool foil to her perfectly enticing airs. Amid all the abandon and playfulness there is delectable incidence of man-to-woman rapport, all of it told in terms of ballet's own vocabulary. Farrell is seen to good, if not her best, advantage during this period; Martins is at the top of his formidable form.

Union Jack, (Balanchine/Kay), "The Royal Navy", on *The Balanchine Celebration*, Pt. 1, with New York City Ballet, featuring Michael Byars, Yvonne Bouree, Jeffrey Edwards, Damian Woetzel, Katrina Killian, Tom Gold, Roma Sosenko, Leonid Kozlov, Maria Calegari. 1993.

Balanchine created this spectacle paying homage to British parades and military formations as a U.S. bicentennial offering. This segment is the culminating one—Scottish tattoos and an English music hall number precede it in the complete work. Here the ballet company's male and female dancers disport themselves as hornpipe-dancing and teasing sailors and sailorettes. As a pendant piece to his *Stars and Stripes* (see above), *Union Jack* ends its frolicking mood with a raising of a flag, in this case the Union Jack, as the assembled "sailors" semaphore a message that says, "God Save the Queen."

Vestris (Jacobson/Banchikov), on *Baryshnikov at Wolf Trap*, featuring Mikhail Baryshnikov. 1976.

———, excerpt and rehearsal, on *World's Young Ballet*, featuring Mikhail Baryshnikov. 1969.

The two tapes listed dovetail nicely regarding this solo, which was specially choreographed for Baryshnikov as a vehicle for his participation in the 1969 Moscow International Competition of Ballet Artists. The Wolf Trap tape shows the work performed in its entirety more than seven years after its creation and premiere. The choreographer, Leonid Jacobson (sometimes spelled Yakobson), was known to be something of a experimentalist in the Soviet Union, where he favored what were known as "ballet miniatures"—neither multi-act spectacles nor one-act affairs, but briefer ballet sketches. The subject of Jacobson's ballet miniature for Baryshnikov was the eighteenth-century career and artistry of Auguste Vestris, the legendary French virtuoso. Mercurial mime and physical virtuosity intermix to encapsulate the dance arts of yesteryear in a prodigy of a new era. The earlier snippets, which show Jacobson coaching some of the miming, prove fascinating companions to Baryshnikov's later maturity.

Vienna Waltzes, excerpt, first suite of waltzes from *Der Rosenkavalier*, (Balanchine/Richard Strauss), on *The Balanchine Celebration*, Pt 1, with New York City Ballet, featuring, Stephanie Saland, Adam Lüders, Kyra Nichols, Lindsay Fischer, Heather Watts, Jock Soto, Simone Schumacher, Alexandre Proia, Maria Calegari, Erlends Zieminch. 1993.

This is the closing segment of the five-part suite. On this occasion, midway on a two-part performance day, Saland, in the central role of the *Rosenkavalier* waltzes was making her farewell appearance with the company. The full sweep of the waltzing masses, which look fifty couples strong when the twenty-five couples are reflected in the scenery's mirrors, is hard to capture with a single camera lens on a small screen, but even the reduced effect is potent. Both Saland and Lüders perform the central roles effectively, especially Lüders as the phantomlike escort to the ballroom's "empress." F.Y.I.: Be on the lookout for potential release of *New York City Ballet Tribute to George Balanchine*, a 1983 *Live from Lincoln Center* telecast documenting the complete ballet, with nearly all of the original cast.

[La] Vivandière Pas de Six, a.k.a. *Markitanka* or *The Canteen Keeper*, (Saint-Léon/Pugni), on *Kirov Ballet: Classic Ballet Night*, with the Kirov Ballet, featuring Alla Sizova, Boris Blankov (c. 1978). 1989.

———, on *The Kirov Ballet in London*, featuring Elena Pankova, Sergei Vikharev. 1988.

This buoyant 1848 dance comes to our stages from an early piece of dance notation (or "choreography" in its most literal sense). "Sténochoréographie" was devised by Arthur Saint-Léon, the creator of this pas. Both of the performances recorded on these videos are by the Kirov Ballet, from its readings of Saint-Léon's 1852 notation. (The reading of all bygone notation takes some educated guessing.) Both these performances are stirring and vivid. The older 1978 one is led by Sizova with amazingly open and large-scale dancing that misses no small detailing along the way. The second is dominated by Pankova with almost wild abandon and rich plasticity. Both the solo men do well, with Vikharev making the somewhat finer showing. It is interesting to compare this sampling of French-school dancing and choreography to that of the similarly influenced Danish school as exemplified in the canon of August Bournonville.

Walpurgis Night, (Lavrovsky/credited Gounod, probably Delibes), on *The Bolshoi Ballet*, with the Bolshoi Ballet, featuring Raissa Struchkova, Alexander Lapauri. 1956.

———, a.k.a. *Faust: Walpurgis Night*, on *Russian Ballet: The Glorious Tradition*, vol. 2, with the Bolshoi Ballet, featuring Ekaterina Maximova, Stanislav Vlasov (1978). 1992.

This bacchanal à la russe is awash with undulating arms, sideward glances and smiles, all punctuated with flamboyant lifts and daring acrobatics. The older generation led by Struchkova is full of the daredevil dynamics; the younger, headed by Maximova, plays up the relish a little less and clarifies the actual dancing a little more. Maximova's legs and feet glow with power and finesse, while setting high standards for their wondrous shape and beauty.

Walpurgisnacht Ballet, (Balanchine), abridged on *The Balanchine Celebration*, Pt. 1, with New York City Ballet, featuring Kyra Nichols, Ben Huys, Nicole Hlinka. 1993.

Unlike the abovementioned Bolshoi version of this celebrated "Witches Sabbath," Balanchine's is not an orgy with a few "nymphs" lost among a horde of satyrs, fauns, and frolicking maidens. Instead it's a garden of feminine beauties, led and dominated by one of their own, who has her own personal partner for some of her forays. Too bad the little ballet is not complete here, though what's left is a significant portion of the brief one-acter. Nichols is the picture of a Diana the huntress in strength and beauty; her "sisters" make a suitable surround. Huys is a gallant cameo escort, and when all the women reenter the picture for the frenetic finale, their hair is undone, making for a simple but wildly abandoned picture and event.

"Water Nymph Ballet" from Goldwyn Follies, (Balanchine/Duke), on *Goldwyn Follies*, featuring Vera Zorina, William Dollar. 1938.

This quintessential "movie ballet" has a ballerina/nymph arise majestically from a pool of water and a storm scene blowing streams of tulle across the porticoed landscape. Zorina is her enigmatic goddess self, and the choreography sound as ballet and full of cinematic surreal imagery.

Western Symphony, (Balanchine/Traditional, arr. Kay), "Rondo"/Fourth Movement, on *The Balanchine Celebration*, Pt. 2, with New York City Ballet, featuring Susan Jaffe, Nikolaj Hübbe. 1993

To close his homage to popularized cowboy entertainment, Balanchine created a suite of ballet dancing for "dance hall girls" and "cowpokes." The final movement, offered here with strains of "Golden Slippers" in the musical mix, is led by a leggy Jaffe (guest from ABT) and a jaunty Hübbe (a "Royal" Dane who expatriated to NYCB). The final moments of the near-breathless finale offers up a happy block of dancers (32 strong) snapping through repeated pirouettes (from fifth position) as the curtain descends. (Originally, Balanchine would raise and lower the curtain as the pirouettes poured forth, but that fillip is no longer being done at NYCB.)

Who Cares?, (Balanchine/Gershwin, arr. Kay), selections on *The Balanchine Celebration*, Pt. 2, with New York City Ballet, featuring Jeremy Collins, Viviana Durante, Judith Fugate, Robert LaFosse, Lourdes Lopez, Elizabeth Loscavio, Ronald Perry, Melinda Roy, Jock Soto, Heather Watts. 1993.

Balanchine's suite of dances to eighteen Gershwin songs (without the words) builds to a set of pas de deux and solos, capped by a finale. That's the part this video focuses on. Four of the featured dancers appeared with NYCB as special guests for this "Celebration" occasion. Most do well, in some cases outdancing some of the "Home Team," especially San Francisco Ballet's Loscavio. F.Y.I.: Be on the lookout for release of a 1983 telecast of the complete ballet: *Live from Lincoln Center: New York City Ballet Tribute to George Balanchine*; or better still, a 1971 CBC kinescope of the nearly original cast, only Jacques d'Amboise is missing; Jean Pierre Bonnefous dances the leading male role.

Winter Dreams, (MacMillan/Tchaikovsky), with the Royal Ballet, featuring Irek Mukhamedov, Darcey Bussell, Viviana Durante, Nicola Tranah, Anthony Dowell. 1992.

This one-act ballet based on Chekov's *Three Sisters* began life as a pas de deux (entitled "Farewell Pas de Deux"), which is now the ballet's central duet. The leading characters of Vershinin and Masha are danced, respectively, by Mukhamedov and Bussell. The video version of the complete ballet, which was filmed under MacMillan's supervision, is more elaborate than the stage version and more realistic in setting. The performances here, all first cast, are beautifully done and handsomely recorded. The story might not be easy to grasp if you don't know the play, but the dancing, especially that of Bussell and Mukhamedov, needs no outside information, it "sings" compellingly from deep inside each of these ballet artists. Dowell's partly mimetic solo dance is also a wonder to behold, even as his character goes through the torments of betrayed love.

Yes, Virginia, Another Piano Ballet, (Anastos/Chopin), Mazurka and Etude, on *Ballet Russe: A Comedy on Pointe*, with the Garden State Ballet, featuring Kirsten Long, Oswaldo Muniz, Mary Ann Orbe, Julie Sorrentino, Elie Lazar, Keith Southwick. 1988.

These two numbers from Anastos's wickedly witty look at ballets danced to solo piano music (specifically Jerome Robbin's *Dances At a Gathering*) only make one hungry for more of this kind of dancing and humor. All the eccentric and "Mickey Mouse" responses to the music's moods and colors make for dancing that's as funny as it is rich.

"Zenobia Pas de Deux." See [La] *Princess Zenobia Ballet*.

Ballet History and Technique Videos

Some videos dwell on surveys of ballet's history and explications of its schooling. Some of these are listed here.

BALLET HISTORY

Ballarino, Il, "The Dancing Master"; "The Art of Renaissance Dance," with Julia Sutton of the New England Conservatory of Music, with Patricia Rader, Charles Perrier. 1991.

This is essentially a pre-ballet explication of sixteenth-century Italian court dancing, dwelling on ballroom dances of Caroso and Negri, notated in the era under discussion and demonstrated for the camera. One duet, which translates as "I Know Who Is Having a Good Time," is demonstrated in a rehearsal format followed by performance. Superimposed titles are sometimes used to define the individual elements of the dance being shown.

Early Dance, Part 1: From the Greeks to the Renaissance, produced by Isa Partsch-Bergsohn, directed by Harold Bergsohn. 1995. See next note.
Early Dance, Part 2: The Baroque Era, produced by Isa Partsch-Bergsohn, directed by Harold Bergsohn. 1995.

This two-part series is an illustrated lecture of pre-ballet history, sometimes with reconstructed period dancing, other times with appropriate graphics from the eras being discussed. Besides period illustrations of the ballet's various "positions of the body," the tapes offer a dancer demonstrating similar positions. A related treatment shows the established positions of the feet. Not all the demonstrations of period court dancing are finely filmed, but the demonstrating dancers are finely skilled.

BALLET TECHNIQUE

Balanchine Essays: Analysis and Aspects of Balanchine Technique
"Arabesque," with Merrill Ashley and Suki Schorer. 1995.

———, "Passé and Attitude," 1996.

———, "Port de Bras and Épaulement," 1996.

This series intends to grow beyond these three installments. So far the School of American Ballet teacher Schorer and New York City Ballet principal dancer and teacher Ashley have completed explications on the areas of ballet technique listed above as they understand them according to the dictates and teaching of Balanchine. The tapes contain teaching demonstrations concentrating on their specific areas of ballet technique, with samplings from the repertory of Balanchine's choreography where the physical details are variously and prominently displayed.

Bournonville Ballet Technique: Fifty Enchaînements, selected and reconstructed by Vivi Flindt, Knud Arne Jürgensen, featuring Rose Gad, Johan Kobborg. 1992.

A nicely filmed demonstration of fifty "combinations" from the notebooks of Denmark's most influential ballet master, August Bournonville. The studies were notated in 1893 by an important artistic heir of Bournonville's, Hans Beck. They give us not only a sampling of the dancing that Bournonville practiced in nineteenth-century Copenhagen, but also a link to the French-school moves that his master learned from one of his most revered teachers, the legendary Auguste Vestris. Included are actual solo segments from *Konservatoriet*, the choreographer's ballet, honoring his French teacher and French schooling.

Cecchetti Method, Classical Ballet, Elementary Syllabus, with artistic directors Victoria Chappell, Sandra Powell, featuring Jessica Clarke, James Bailey. 1994.

This is a careful and well-organized look at the training prescribed by the Cecchetti Society. The progression of exercises from barre through center to specific exercises for male and for female dancers (on pointe) is graded as it would be in a Cecchetti-method class. The focus on the male and the female dancer is fairly equal of balance. Though the musical accompaniment is specific and clear it's not so strongly tracked as it might be. It would be interesting to compare this to the Bournonville and Balanchine tapes.

Video Dictionary of Classical Ballet, double-cassette package running approximate four and a half hours, featuring Merrill Ashley, Denis Jackson, Kevin McKenzie, Georgina Parkinson. 1983.

This demonstration of ballet schooling attempts to demonstrate positions, poses, steps, and moves according to their sometimes varied names in different "schools" or "theories" of technique. A plus of the format, with demonstrations by both male and female dancers, is the repeat of moves in slow motion. A minus is the lack of specific musical accompaniment and timing, for the individually demonstrated steps. A handy card inserted with the cassettes spells out the items in order of their presentation on the video, with section and subsection tape times for easily returning to an element of specific interest.

A Note on Acquiring Videos

As mentioned earlier, distributors can change from time to time regarding ballet video titles, as can the format: laser disc, videotape, and soon digital video discs.

Following is a list of distributors who specialize in dance videos. If you are having difficulty obtaining videos you might call them for their individual catalogues and direct order procedures. Remember, too, to check out the Performing Arts or similarly named sections of video rental outlets for a sense of new and/or discontinued titles.

Dance Book Club, Princeton Book Company, Publishers, 12 W. Delaware Avenue, Pennington, NJ 08534; phone: (800) 220-7149, fax: (609) 737-1869.

Home Vision Cinema, 5547 N. Ravenswood Avenue, Chicago, IL 60640-1199; phone: (800) 826-3456.

Kultur, 195 Highway 36, West Long Branch, NJ 07764; phone: (908) 229-2343, fax: (908) 229-0066, phone orders: (800) 4-KULTUR.

Video Artists International, Inc. (VAI), 158 Linwood Plaza, Suite 301, Fort Lee, NJ 07024-3790; phone: (201) 944-0099, fax: (201) 947-8850.

V.I.E.W., Inc., 34 East 23 Street, New York, NY 10010; phone: (800) 843-9843.

Direct Cinema has a limited number of dance titles, some of which are not available for sale or rental at local stores. Ordering number: (800) 525-0000.

"The Balanchine Library," (Nonesuch Dance Collection) has a phone order number: (800) 381-6464.

A frequently updated catalogue that includes dance videos is put out by Melvin Jahn for Tower Classics (Audio and Video). The price is $10.95 plus $2 postage; the address for purchasing the "Tower Records Guide to Classical Music on Video" is Bayside Distribution, Classical Division, 2516-A Durant Avenue, Berkeley, CA 94704, Attn: Melvin Jahn. You can receive updated information if you include your e-mail address with your order.

SELECTED BIBLIOGRAPHY

This selection of supplementary readings is far from complete. Because of the large number of biographies focused on individual dancers and choreographers, these have not been included here. Since the dancer's or choreographer's name usually appears in biography titles, you should not have difficulty locating such works. Dance dictionaries or encyclopedia entries often give choice bibliographies at the end of listings for individuals.

Dictionaries

Atkinson, Margaret F., and May Hillman. *Dancers of the Ballet: Biographies.* New York: Knopf, 1955.

Bremser, Martha, ed. *International Dictionary of Ballet.* 2 vols. Detroit, London, Washington, D.C.: St. James Press, 1993.

Chujoy, Anatole, ed. *The Dance Encyclopedia.* New York: A. S. Barnes, 1949.

———, and P. W. Manchester, eds. *The Dance Encyclopedia.* rev. and enl. ed. New York: Simon & Schuster, 1967.

Clarke, Mary, and David Vaughan, eds. *The Encyclopedia of Dance & Ballet.* London: Pitman Publishing, 1977.

Cohen, Selma Jeanne, founding ed. *International Encyclopedia of Dance.* 6 vols. New York: Oxford University Press, 1998.

Cohen-Stratyner, Barbara Naomi. *Biographical Dictionary of Dance.* New York: Schirmer Books, 1982.

Crosland, Margaret. *Ballet Lovers' Dictionary.* London: Arco Publications, 1962.

Gadan, Francis, and Robert Maillard, eds.; Selma Jeanne Cohen, American ed. *Dictionary of Modern Ballet.* Translated from the French by John Montague and Peggie Cochrane. New York: Tudor Publishing, 1959.

Koegler, Horst. *The Concise Oxford Dictionary of Ballet.* 2d ed. London and New York: Oxford University Press, 1987.

Wilson, G. B. L. A *Dictionary of Ballet*. 3d ed., rev. and enl. New York: Theatre Arts Books, 1974.

Dance Collection of the New York Public Library (NYPL): References

Bibliographic Guide to Dance. 1975–present. Boston: G. K. Hall. This guide serves as an annual supplement to the *Dictionary Catalog of the Dance Collection*, published by the Performing Arts Research Center of the NYPL. Includes dance works in many languages and various forms (e.g., motion pictures, videotapes, photographs).

Dance on Disc. Boston: G. K. Hall, 1975–present. The complete catalog of the Dance Collection of the NYPL on CD ROM. Includes the ten-volume *Dictionary Catalog of the Dance Collection* (See below) with the seventeen supplements that have been published as the annual *Bibliographic Guide to Dance* (See above), of approximately 189,000 records covering all aspects of dance, in various languages and in all media. Also includes the Dance Collection authority file of 153,000 names, dance titles, and subjects, with cross-references and first performance history notes.

Dictionary Catalog of the Dance Collection. Boston: G. K. Hall, 1974. "This catalogue . . . consists of bibliographic data for materials catalogued prior to October 1, 1973. It contains approximately 300,000 entries representing 96,000 catalogued items." Introd. 1975.

Index to Dance Periodicals. Boston: G. K. Hall, 1992–present.

Chronologies of Ballets and Lists of Works

Choreography by George Balanchine: A Catalogue of Works. Project directors: Leslie George Katz, Nancy Lassalle, and Harvey Simmonds. New York: Viking, 1984.

Cohen, Selma Jeanne, and A. J. Pischl. "The American Ballet Theatre: 1940–1960." *Dance Perspectives* 6 (1960).

George Balanchine: A Reference Guide, 1987. New York: Ballet Society, July 1987. This supplements *Choreography by George Balanchine: A Catalogue of Works* by updating the bibliography and the listings of stagings and telecasts. Information on photographers and addresses of sources is also included.

Henry, Tricia. "The Joy of Modem: Computer Access to Resources in Dance." *DRJ* 26, no. 1 (Spring 1994): 56–58.

Reynolds, Nancy. *Repertory in Review: 40 Years of the New York City Ballet*. Introduction by Lincoln Kirstein. New York: Dial Press, 1977.

Guides to Individual Ballets

Balanchine, George. *Balanchine's Complete Stories of the Great Ballets.* Edited by Francis Mason. Garden City, N.Y.: Doubleday, 1954.

———. *Balanchine's New Complete Stories of the Great Ballets.* Edited by Francis Mason. Garden City, N.Y.: Doubleday, 1968.

———, and Francis Mason. *Balanchine's Complete Stories of the Great Ballets.* Rev. and enl. ed. Garden City, N.Y.: Doubleday, 1977.

———. *101 Stories of the Great Ballets.* Garden City, N.Y.: Doubleday, 1975.

Beaumont, Cyril. *Ballets Past & Present: Being a Third Supplement to the Complete Book of Ballets.* London: Putnam, 1955.

———. *Ballets of Today: Being a Second Supplement to the Complete Book of Ballets.* London: Putnam, 1954.

———. *Complete Book of Ballets: A Guide to the Principal Ballets of the Nineteenth and Twentieth Centuries.* New York: Grosset & Dunlap, 1938.

———. *The Sadler's Wells Ballet: A Detailed Account of the Works in the Permanent Repertory with Critical Notes.* Rev. ed. London: C. W. Beaumont, 1947.

———. *Supplement to Complete Book of Ballets.* London: Putnam, 1952.

Brinson, Peter, and Clement Crisp. *Ballet and Dance: A Guide to the Repertory.* Rev. and enl. ed. Newton Abbot, Devon, and London: David & Charles, 1980. First published as *Ballet for All: A Guide to One Hundred Ballets* by Pan Books, London, 1970.

———. *The International Book of Ballet.* With contributions by Don McDonagh and John Percival. New York: Stein and Day Publishers, 1971. First published in England as *Ballet For All: A Guide to One Hundred Ballets.* London: Pan Books, 1970.

Crosland, Margaret. *Ballet Carnival: A Companion to Ballet.* London: Arco Publishers, 1955.

Davidson, Gladys. *More Ballet Stories for Young People.* London: Cassell, 1961.

———. *Stories of the Ballets.* London: T. Werner Laurie, 1949.

Drew, David. *The Decca Book of Ballet.* Introduction by Ernest Ansermet and a short history of ballet by Arnold L. Haskell. London: Frederick Muller, 1958.

Goode, Gerald, ed. *The Book of Ballets: Classic and Modern.* Introduction by Leonide Massine. New York: Crown Publishers, 1939.

Gruen, John. *The World's Great Ballets: "La Fille Mal Gardée" to "Davidsbündlertänze."* New York: Abrams, 1981.

Heath, Charles. *Beauties of the Opera and Ballet.* New York: Da Capo Press, 1977. Reprint. Originally published under the same title by David Bogue, London, c. 1845, an English edition of *Les Beautés de l'Opéra* by Gautier, Janin, and Chasles. Paris: Soulié, 1845.

Kirstein, Lincoln. *Four Centuries of Ballet: Fifty Masterworks*. New York: Dover Publications, 1984. Unabridged, corrected version of *Movement & Metaphor: Four Centuries of Ballet*, New York: Praeger Publishers, 1970.

Krokover, Rosalyn. *The New Borzoi Book of Ballets*. New York: Knopf, 1956.

Lawrence, Robert. *The Victor Book of Ballets and Ballet Music*. New York: Simon & Schuster, 1950.

Reynolds, Nancy. *Repertory in Review: 40 Years of the New York City Ballet*. Introduction by Lincoln Kirstein. New York: Dial Press, 1977.

———, and Susan Reimer-Torn. *Dance Classics: A Viewer's Guide to the Best-Loved Ballets and Modern Dances*. Pennington, N.J.: A Cappella Books, 1991. Originally published as *In Performance: A Companion to the Classics of Dance*. New York: Harmony Books, 1980.

Robert, Grace. *The Borzoi Book of Ballets*. New York: Knopf, 1947. Stokes, Adrian. *Russian Ballets*. London: Faber & Faber, 1935; reprint, New York: Da Capo Press, 1982.

Terry, Walter. *Ballet Guide*. New York: Dodd, Mead, 1976. Background, listings, credits, and descriptions of more than five hundred of the world's major ballets.

———. *Ballet: A New Guide to the Liveliest Art*. New York: Dell Publishing, 1959.

Verwer, Hans. *Guide to the Ballet*. Translated from the Dutch by Henry Mins. New York: Barnes & Noble, 1963.

Critical Essays

Anderson, Jack. *Choreography Observed*. Iowa City: University of Iowa Press, 1987.

Beaumont, Cyril W. *Dancers Under My Lens: Essays in Ballet Criticism*. London: C. W. Beaumont, 1949.

Bland, Alexander. *Observer of the Dance 1958–1982*. London: Dance Books, 1985.

Buckle, Richard. *Buckle at the Ballet*. New York: Atheneum, 1980.

Coton, A. V. *Writings on Dance 1938–68*. Selected and edited by Kathrine Sorley Walker and Lilian Haddakin. London: Dance Books, 1975.

Croce, Arlene. *Afterimages*. New York: Knopf, 1977.

———. *Going to the Dance*. New York: Knopf, 1982.

———. *Sight Lines*. New York: Knopf, 1987.

Denby, Edwin. *Dancers, Buildings and People in the Streets*. Introduction by Frank O'Hara. New York: Horizon Press, 1965.

———. *Dance Writings*. Edited by Robert Cornfield and William MacKay.

New York: Knopf, 1986. Includes a biographical essay, "Edwin Denby, 1903–1983," by William MacKay.

———. *Looking at the Dance*. New York: Pellegrini & Cudahy, 1949; reprint, with introduction by B. H. Haggin. New York: Horizon Press, 1968.

Gautier, Théophile. *Gautier on Dance*. Selected, translated, and annotated by Ivor Guest. London: Dance Books, 1986.

———. *The Romantic Ballet as Seen by Théophile Gautier*. "Being his Notices of all the Principal Performances of Ballet Given at Paris During the Years 1837–1848." Translated from the French by Cyril W. Beaumont. London: C. W. Beaumont, 1932; rev. ed. 1947; reprint of 1947 ed., Brooklyn, N.Y.: Dance Horizons, 1973.

Haggin, B. H. *Ballet Chronicle*. New York: Horizon Press, 1970.

Jackson, Graham. *Dance as Dance: Selected Reviews and Essays*. Scarborough, Ontario: Catalyst, 1978.

Jowitt, Deborah. *Dance Beat: Selected Views and Reviews 1967–1976*. New York and Basel, Switzerland: Marcel Dekker, 1977.

———. *The Dance in Mind: Profiles and Reviews 1976–1983*. Boston: David R. Godine, 1985.

Kirstein, Lincoln. *Ballet: Bias and Belief*. New York: Dance Horizons, 1983.

Levinson, André. *André Levinson on Dance: Writings from Paris in the Twenties*. Edited and with an introduction by Joan Acocella and Lynn Garafola. Hanover, N.H., and London: University Press of New England/Wesleyan University Press, 1991.

———. *Ballet Old and New*. Translated from the Russian by Susan Cook Summer. New York: Dance Horizons, 1982. Gradually accumulated theatrical impressions recorded as descriptive essays.

Macaulay, Alastair. *Some Views and Reviews of Ashton's Choreography*. Collected Writings, No. 1. Guildford, Surrey: National Resource Centre for Dance, 1987.

Macdonald, Nesta. *Diaghilev Observed: By Critics in England and the United States, 1911–1929*. New York: Dance Horizons; London: Dance Books, 1975.

Parker, H. T. *Motion Arrested: Dance Reviews of H. T. Parker*. Edited by Olive Holmes. Middletown, Conn.: Wesleyan University Press, 1982.

Siegel, Marcia B. At *the Vanishing Point: A Critic Looks at Dance*. New York: Saturday Review Press, 1972.

———. *The Shapes of Change: Images of American Dance*. Boston: Houghton Mifflin, 1979; reprint Berkeley, Los Angeles, London: University of California Press, 1985.

———. *The Tail of the Dragon: New Dance, 1976–1982*. Durham, N.C., and London: Duke University Press, 1991.

———. *Watching the Dance* Go *By*. Boston: Houghton Mifflin, 1977.

Swinson, Cyril, ed. *Dancers and Critics*. London: Adam & Charles Black, 1950. Contributions by Cyril Beaumont, Caryl Brahms, Anatole Chujoy, A. V. Coton, A. H. Franks, Arnold L. Haskell, Joan Lawson, Irène Lidova, P. W. Manchester, Pierre Michaut, Walter Terry, Léandre Vaillat, and Audrey Williamson.

Terry, Walter. *I Was There: Selected Dance Reviews and Articles, 1936–1976*. Edited by Andrew Mark Wentink. Foreword by Anna Kisselgoff. New York and Basel, Switzerland: Marcel Dekker, 1978.

Readings in Dance History, Theory, and Criticism

Cohen, Selma Jeanne, ed. *Dance as a Theatre Art: Source Readings in Dance History from 1518 to the Present*. Princeton, N.J.: Princeton Book Company, 1992.

Copeland, Roger, and Marshall Cohen, eds. *What Is Dance? Readings in Theory and Criticism*. New York: Oxford University Press, 1983.

Steinberg, Cobbett, ed. *The Dance Anthology*. New York and London: New American Library, c. 1980.

General Ballet Histories

Anderson, Jack. *Ballet & Modern Dance: A Concise History*. 2d ed., rev. and enl. Princeton, N.J.: Princeton Book Company, 1992.

———. *Dance*. New York: Newsweek Books, c. 1974.

Au, Susan. *Ballet & Modern Dance*. Introduction by Selma Jeanne Cohen. World of Art. London and New York: Thames and Hudson, 1988.

Beaumont, Cyril W. *A Short History of Ballet*. Essays on Dancing and Dancers, No. 4. London: C. W. Beaumont, 1944.

Clarke, Mary, and Clement Crisp. *Ballet: An Illustrated History*. 2d ed., rev. and enl. London: Hamish Hamilton, 1992.

Conyn, Cornelius. *Three Centuries of Ballet*. Houston and New York: Elsevier Press, 1953.

De Mille, Agnes. *The Book of the Dance*. New York: Golden Press; London: Paul Hamlyn, 1963.

Fonteyn, Margot. *The Magic of Dance*. New York: Knopf, 1979.

Guest, Ivor. *A Dancer's Heritage: A Short History of Ballet*. Foreword by Dame Margot Fonteyn. 6th ed., updated by Kathrine Sorley Walker. London: Dancing Times, 1988.

Haskell, Arnold L. *Ballet Panorama: An Illustrated Chronicle of Three Centuries*. 3d rev. ed. London and New York: B. T. Batsford, 1948.

———. *A Picture History of Ballet*. Rev. ed. London: Hulton Press, 1957.

Kirstein, Lincoln. *The Book of the Dance*. New York: Garden City Publishing, 1942. Reissue with additional chapter of *Dance: A Short History of Classic Theatrical Dancing*.

———. *Dance: A Short History of Classic Theatrical Dancing*. New York: G. P. Putnam's Sons, 1935; reprint, Princeton, N.J.: Princeton Book Company, 1986.

Lawson, Joan. *A History of Ballet and Its Makers*. New York and London: Pitman Publishing, 1964.

Lynham, Deryck. *Ballet Then and Now: A History of the Ballet in Europe*. London: Sylvan Press, 1947.

Magriel, Paul. *Ballet: An Illustrated Outline*. New York: Kamin Publishers, c. 1938.

Reyna, Ferdinando. *A Concise History of Ballet*. Translated from the French by Pat Wardroper. London: Thames and Hudson, c. 1965.

Ryan, June. *Ballet History*. New York: Roy Publishers, 1960.

Terry, Walter. *Ballet: A Pictorial History*. New York: Van Nostrand Reinhold, 1970.

Period Histories

Arbeau, Thoinot (pseudonym of Jehan Tabouret). *Orchesography* (1588). Translated by Mary Steware Evans. New York: Kamin Dance Publications, 1948; reprint with new introduction and notes by Julie Sutton. New York: Dover Publications, 1967.

Caroso, Fabritio. *Noblità de Dame* (1600). Translated and edited by Julia Sutton; music edited by F. Marian Walker. New York: Oxford University Press, 1986.

Chaffee, George. "The Romantic Ballet in London: 1821–1858, Some Hitherto Unremarked Aspects." *Dance Index* 2, nos. 9–12 (September–December 1943).

Chazin-Bennahum, Judith. *Dance in the Shadow of the Guillotine*. Carbondale, Ill.: Southern Illinois University Press, 1988.

Demidov, Alexander. *The Russian Ballet: Past and Present*. Translated by Guy Daniels. Garden City, N.Y.: Doubleday, 1977.

Foster, Susan Leigh. *Choreography and Narrative: Ballet's Staging of Story and Desire*. Bloomington and Indianapolis: Indiana University Press, 1996.

Guest, Ivor. "The Alhambra Ballet." *Dance Perspectives* 4 (Autumn 1959).

———. *Ballet in Leicester Square: The Alhambra and the Empire 1860–1915*. London: Dance Books, 1992.

———. *The Ballet of the Enlightenment*. London: Dance Books, 1996.

———. *The Ballet of the Second Empire*. Middletown, Conn.: Wesleyan University Press, 1974. First published as two volumes, London: Pitman Publishing, 1953 and 1955.

———. *The Ballet of the Second Empire 1847–1858*. London: Adam and Charles Black, 1955.

———. *The Ballet of the Second Empire 1858–1870*. Preface by Serge Lifar. London: Adam and Charles Black, 1953.

———. *The Empire Ballet*. London: Society for Theatre Research, 1962.

———. *The Romantic Ballet in England: Its Development, Fulfilment and Decline*. London: Phoenix House, 1954; reprint Middletown, Conn.: Wesleyan University Press, 1972.

———. *The Romantic Ballet in Paris*. Foreword by Dame Ninette de Valois. London: Sir Isaac Pitman and Sons, 1966; 2d rev. ed., with foreword by Lillian Moore, London: Dance Books, 1980.

Haskell, Arnold. *Balletomania: Then and Now*. New York: Knopf, 1977.

Hilton, Wendy. *Dance and Music of Court and Theater: Selected Writings of Wendy Hilton*. Dance & Music Series, No. 10. Stuyvesant, N.Y.: Pendragon Press, 1997. This collection of Hilton's selected writings includes a complete facsimile of her 1981 *Dance of Court and Theater* as well as more recent writings.

Noble, Peter, ed. *British Ballet*. London: Skelton Robinson, 1949.

Ralph, Richard. *The Life and Works of John Weaver*. New York: Dance Horizons, 1985.

Roslavleva, Natalia. *Era of the Russian Ballet*. New York: Dutton, 1966; reprint New York: Da Capo Press, 1979.

Scholl, Tim. *From Petipa to Balanchine: Classical Revival and the Modernization of Ballet*. London and New York: Routledge, 1994.

Skeaping, Mary. "Ballet Under the Three Crowns." *Dance Perspectives* 32 (Winter 1967). A study of ballet in Sweden, 1648–1792.

Slonimsky, Juri. *The Soviet Ballet*. New York Philosophical Library, 1947.

Souritz, Elizabeth. *Soviet Choreographers in the 1920s*. Translated from the Russian by Lynn Visson. Edited, with additional translation, by Sally Banes. Durham, N.C., and London: Duke University Press, 1990.

Wiley, Roland John. *A Century of Russian Ballet: Documents and Accounts, 1810–1910*. Oxford, U.K.: Clarendon Press, 1990.

Winter, Marian Hannah. *The Pre-Romantic Ballet*. London: Sir Isaac Pitman and Sons, 1974; Brooklyn, N.Y.: Dance Horizons, 1975.

Ballet Histories by Country

Amberg, George. *Ballet in America: The Emergence of an American Art*. New York: Duell, Sloan and Pearce, 1949. This is a joint publication with New

American Library whose paperback edition is entitled *Ballet: The Emergence of an American Art.*

"Ballet in Canada Today." *Dance Magazine* 45, no. 4 (April 1971). A special issue surveying the Canadian dance scene. Olga Maynard, "Idea, Image, and Purpose: Ballet in Canada Today," 32–74; "Idea: Arnold Spohr and the Royal Winnipeg Ballet," 38–44; "Image: Celia Franca and the National Ballet of Canada," 46–54; "Purpose: Ludmilla Chiriaeff and Les Grands Ballets Canadiens," 56–64. Greg Thomson, "Dance with a Liberal Education," 66–67, (dance studies at York University): "Canadian Carousel: A Pictorial Statement About Dance's Moods Today," 68–69. Barbara Gail Rowes, "Toronto Dance Theatre," 70–72. Doris Hering, "Neither Floods Nor . . . ," 74–75, look at the accomplishments of Gweneth Lloyd, Diana Jablokova-Vorps, and Nesta Toumine, three pioneers in the Canadian regional ballet movement.

Barnes, Clive. *Ballet in Britain Since the War.* Thrift Book, No. 21. London: C. A. Watts & Co., 1953.

Beaumont, Cyril W. *A History of Ballet in Russia (1613–1881).* Preface by André Levinson. London: C. W. Beaumont, 1930.

De Mille, Agnes. *American Dances.* New York: Macmillan; London: Collier Macmillan, 1980.

Grut, Marina. *The History of Ballet in South Africa.* Capetown, Pretoria, Johannesburg: Human & Rousseau, 1981.

Haskell, Arnold. "Ballet in Britain 1934–1944." *Dance Index* 4, no. 10 (October 1945).

———. *Ballet Since 1939.* The Arts in Britain, No. 2. London, New York, Toronto: Longmans, Green, 1946.

Lawson, Joan. "The Soviet Ballet, 1917–1943." *Dance Index* 2, nos. 6–7 (June–July 1943).

Lifar, Serge. *A History of Russian Ballet from its Origins to the Present Day.* Translated by Arnold Haskell. London: Hutchinson, 1954.

Moore, Lillian. *Echoes of American Ballet.* New York: Dance Horizons, 1976.

Pask, Edward H. *Ballet in Australia: The Second Act, 1940–1980.* Melbourne and New York: Oxford University Press, 1982.

Roslavleva, Natalia. *Era of the Russian Ballet.* Foreword by Dame Ninette de Valois. London: Victor Gollancz, 1966; reprint New York: Da Capo Press, 1979.

Swift, Mary Grace. *The Art of the Dance in the U.S.S.R.* Notre Dame, Ind.: University of Notre Dame Press, 1968.

Van Praagh, Peggy. *Ballet in Australia.* The Arts in Australia. Victoria, Australia: Longmans, 1965.

Wyman, Max. *Dance Canada: An Illustrated History.* Vancouver and Toronto: Douglas & McIntyre, 1989.

Ballet Company Histories

Anderson, Jack. *The One and Only: The Ballet Russe de Monte Carlo*. New York: Dance Horizons, 1981.

———. "An Introduction to the Ballets Suédois." *Ballet Review* 7, nos. 2–3 (1978–1979):28–59.

Beaumont, Cyril. *Bookseller at the Ballet: Memoirs 1891 to 1929*. London: C. W. Beaumont, 1975. A record of bookselling, balletgoing, publishing, and writing. Incorporates *The Diaghilev Ballet in London*. 3d rev. ed. London: Adam and Charles Black, 1951.

———. *The Diaghilev Ballet in London*. 3d rev. ed. London: Adam and Charles Black, 1951. Incorporated in Beaumont's *Bookseller at the Ballet: Memoirs 1891 to 1929*.

———. *The Monte Carlo Russian Ballet* (*Les Ballets Russes du Col. W. de Basil*). Essays on Dancing and Dancers, No. 5. London: C. W. Beaumont, 1934.

———. *The Vic-Wells Ballet*. Essays on Dancing and Dancers, No. 7. London: C. W. Beaumont, 1935.

Bell, Ken, photography. *The National Ballet of Canada: A Celebration*. Includes memoir by Celia Franca. Toronto and London: University of Toronto Press, c. 1978.

Bland, Alexander. *The Royal Ballet: The First Fifty Years*. Foreword by Dame Ninette de Valois. Garden City, N.Y.: Doubleday, 1981.

Bradley, Lionel. *Sixteen Years of Ballet Rambert*. London: Hinrichsen Edition, 1946.

Brown, Ian F., ed. *The Australian Ballet 1962–1965: A Record of the Company, Its Dancers, and Its Ballets*. Victoria, Australia: Longmans, c. 1967.

Chujoy, Anatole. *The New York City Ballet*. New York: Knopf, 1953; reprint, with a new preface by Edward Villella, New York: Da Capo Press, 1981.

Clarke, Mary. *Dancers of Mercury: The Story of Ballet Rambert*. London: Adam and Charles Black, 1962.

———. *The Sadler's Wells Ballet: A History and an Appreciation*. London: Adam and Charles Black, 1955; reprint, with a new foreword by the author, New York: Da Capo Press, 1977.

Cohen, Selma Jeanne, and A. J. Pischl. "The American Ballet Theatre: 1940–1960." *Dance Perspectives* 6 (1960).

Crisp, Clement, Anya Sainsbury, and Peter Williams. *Ballet Rambert: 50 Years and On*. Rev. and enl. ed., n.p., 1981.

Dafoe, Christopher. *Dancing Through Time: The First Fifty Years of Canada's Royal Winnipeg Ballet*. Winnipeg: Portage & Main Press, 1990.

Fisher, Hugh. *The Sadler's Wells Theatre Ballet*. London: Adam and Charles Black, 1956.

———. *The Story of the Sadler's Wells Ballet*. London: Adam and Charles Black, 1954.

Garafola, Lynn. *Diaghilev's Ballets Russes*. New York and Oxford: Oxford University Press, 1989.

García-Márquez, Vicente. *The Ballets Russes: Colonel de Basil's Ballets Russes de Monte Carlo 1932–1952*. New York: Knopf, 1990.

Goodwin, Noël. *A Ballet for Scotland: The First Ten Years of the Scottish Ballet*. Edinburgh: Canongate Publishing, 1979.

Grigoriev, S. L. *The Diaghilev Ballet 1909–1929*. Translated and edited by Vera Bowen. London: Constable, 1953.

Häger, Bengt. *Ballets Suédois (The Swedish Ballet)*. New York: Abrams, 1990.

Haskell, Arnold L. *The National Ballet: A History and a Manifesto*. Overture by Ninette de Valois. London: Adam and Charles Black, 1943.

Kirstein, Lincoln, text, with photography by Martha Swope and George Platt Lynes. *New York City Ballet*. New York: Knopf, 1973.

———. *Thirty Years: Lincoln Kirstein's "The New York City Ballet."* New York: Knopf, 1978. Expanded to include 1973–1978 in celebration of the company's thirtieth anniversary.

Kochno, Boris. *Diaghilev and the Ballets Russes*. Translated from the French by Adrienne Foulke. New York and Evanston, Ill.: Harper & Row, 1970.

Kragh-Jacobsen, Svend. *The Royal Danish Ballet: An Old Tradition and a Living Present*. Copenhagen: Det Danske Selskab; London: Adam and Charles Black, 1955.

Lieven, Prince Peter. *The Birth of Ballets-Russes*. Translated from the Russian by L. Zarine. London: George Allen & Unwin, 1973.

Manchester, P. W. *Vic-Wells: A Ballet Progress*. London: Victor Gollancz, 1942.

Maynard, Olga. *The American Ballet*. Philadelphia: Macrae Smith, 1959.

Neufeld, James. *Power to Rise: The Story of the National Ballet of Canada*. Toronto, Buffalo, London: University of Toronto Press, 1996.

Payne, Charles. *American Ballet Theatre*. With essays by Alicia Alonso, Erik Bruhn, Lucia Chase, and Nora Kaye. New York: Knopf, 1978.

Propert, W. A. *The Russian Ballet in Western Europe, 1909–1920*. With a chapter on the music by Eugène Goossens. London: John Lane The Bodley Head, 1921; reprint New York: Benjamin Blom, 1972.

———. *The Russian Ballet 1921–1929*. Preface by Jacques Emile Blanche. London: John Lane The Bodley Head, 1931.

Sexton, Jean Deitz. *San Jose/Cleveland Ballet: A Legacy for the Future*. San Francisco: Henry Holt & Company, 1993.

Shead, Richard. *Ballets Russes*. Secaucus, N.J.: Wellfleet Press, 1989.

Sorley Walker, Kathrine. *De Basil's Ballets Russes*. London: Hutchinson, 1982.

———, and Sarah C. Woodcock. *The Royal Ballet: A Picture History*. London: Threshold Books, 1981.

Steinberg, Cobbett. *San Francisco Ballet: The First Fifty Years*. Edited by Laura Leivick. Researched by Russell Hartley. Introduction by Lew Christensen and Michael Smuin. Forewords by Lincoln Kirstein, Oliver Smith, and Lucia Chase. San Francisco: San Francisco Ballet Association and Chronicle Books, c. 1983.

Whittaker, Herbert. *Canada's National Ballet*. Toronto and Montreal: McClelland and Stewart, 1967.

Woodcock, Sarah C. *The Sadler's Wells Royal Ballet: Now the Birmingham Royal Ballet*. London: Sinclair-Stevenson, c. 1991.

Wyman, Max. *The Royal Winnipeg Ballet: The First Forty Years*. Garden City, N.Y.: Doubleday, 1978.

Histories of Individual Ballet

Anderson, Jack. *The Nutcracker Ballet*. New York: Mayflower Books, 1979.

Beaumont, Cyril W. *The Ballet Called Giselle*. London: Cyril W. Beaumont, 1944; reprint, New York: Dance Horizons, 1969.

———. *The Ballet Called Swan Lake*. London: Cyril W. Beaumont, 1952.

———. *Michel Fokine and His Ballets*. London: Cyril W. Beaumont, 1935; reprint 1945.

Berg, Shelly C. *Le Sacre du Printemps: Seven Productions from Nijinsky to Martha Graham*. Ann Arbor, Mich.: UMI Research Press, 1988.

Buckle, Richard. *L'Après-midi d'un Faune*. New York: Dance Horizons, 1983.

Hodson, Millicent. *Nijinsky's Crime Against Grace: Reconstruction Score of the Original Choreography for "Le Sacre du Printemps."* Dance & Music Series, No. 8. Stuyvesant, N.Y.: Pendragon Press, 1996.

Vaughan, David. *Frederick Ashton and His Ballets*. New York: Knopf, 1977.

Wiley, Roland John. *The Life and Ballets of Lev Ivanov: Choreographer of "The Nutcracker" and "Swan Lake."* Oxford, U.K.: Clarendon Press, 1997.

Tchaikovsky's Ballets: Swan Lake, Sleeping Beauty, Nutcracker. Oxford, U.K.: Clarendon Press, 1985.

The Art of Choreography

Noverre, Jean Georges. *Letters on Dancing and Ballets* [1760]. Translated by Cyril W. Beaumont from the rev. and enl. ed. published at St. Petersburg, 1803. London: C. W. Beaumont, 1951.

Sorely Walker, Kathrine. *Dance and Its Creators: Choreographers at Work*. New York: John Day Company, 1972.

Van Praagh, Peggy, and Peter Brinson. *The Choreographic Art: An Outline of Its Principles and Craft*. London: Adam & Charles Black, 1963.

The Art of the Dancer

Ashley, Merrill. *Dancing for Balanchine*. New York: E. P. Dutton, 1984.

Austin, Richard. *The Art of the Dancer*. London: Barrie & Jenkins, 1982.

———, *The Ballerina*. London: Vision, 1974.

Balsis, Carlo. *The Code of Terpsichore* [1828]. Translated by R. Barton. New York: Dance Horizons, 1976.

Bland, Alexander, and John Percival. *Men Dancing: Performers and Performances*. New York: Macmillan, 1984.

Bournonville, August. *My Theatre Life*. Translated by Patricia W. McAndrew. Middletown, Conn.: Wesleyan University Press, 1979.

Bruhn, Erik, and Lillian Moore. *Bournonville and Ballet Technique*. London: Adam and Charles Black, 1961; reprint, New York: Dance Horizons, n.d.

Clarke, Mary, and Clement Crisp. *Ballerina: The Art of Women in Classical Ballet*. London: BBC Books, 1987; reprint, Princeton, N.J.: Princeton Book Company, 1988.

———. *Dancer: Men in Dance*. London: British Broadcasting Corp., 1984.

Cohen, Selma Jeanne, ed. "The Male Image." *Dance Perspectives* 40 (Winter 1969).

Gale, Joseph. *Behind Barres: The Mystique of Masterly Teaching*. New York: Dance Horizons, 1980.

Gruen, John. *The Private World of Ballet*. New York: Viking, 1975.

Jürgenson, Knud Arne. *The Bournonville Ballets: A Photographic Record, 1844–1933*. London: Dance Books Ltd., 1987.

Kirstein, Lincoln. *Nijinsky Dancing*. New York: Knopf, 1975.

Lazzarini, John and Roberta. *Pavlova: Repertoire of a Legend*. New York: Schirmer Books, 1980.

Magriel, Paul, ed. *Nijinsky, Pavlova, Duncan: Three Lives in Dance*. New York: Da Capo Press, 1977.

Money, Keith. *Anna Pavlova: Her Life and Art*. New York: Knopf, 1980.

Mason, Francis. *I Remember Balanchine: Recollections of the Ballet Master by Those Who Knew Him*. New York: Doubleday, 1991.

McConnell, Jane T. *Famous Ballet Dancers*. New York: Thomas Y. Crowell Company, 1955.

Migel, Parmenia. *The Ballerinas: From the Court of Louis XIV to Pavlova.* New York: Macmillan, 1972.

Montague, Sarah. *The Ballerina: Famous Dancers and Rising Stars of Our Time.* New York: Universe Books, 1980.

———. *Pas de Deux: Great Partnerships in Dance.* New York: Universe Books, 1981.

Petipa, Marius. *Russian Ballet Master: The Memoirs of Marius Petipa.* Translated by Helen Wittaker. London: Adam & Charles Black, 1958; reprint, New York: Dance Horizons, n.d.

Philip, Richard, and Mary Whitney. *Danseur: The Male in Ballet.* New York: McGraw-Hill, 1977.

Smakov, Gennady. *The Great Russian Dancers.* New York: Knopf, 1984.

Swift, Mary Grace. *Bells & Beaux on Their Toes: Dancing Stars in Young America.* Washington, D.C.: University Press of America, 1980.

Swinson, Cyril. *Great Male Dancers.* Dancers of To-Day, No. 16. London: Adam & Charles Black, 1964. Completed by Ivor Guest after the author's death.

Switzer, Ellen. *Dancers! Horizons in American Dance.* New York: Atheneum, 1982.

Terry, Walter. *Great Male Dancers of the Ballet.* New York: Anchor Books, 1978.

———. *On Pointe: The Story of Dancing and Dancers on Toe.* New York: Dodd, Mead, 1962.

Tracy, Robert, with Sharon DeLano. *Balanchine's Ballerinas: Conversations with the Muses.* New York: Simon & Schuster, 1983.

Technical Term Books

Grant, Gail. *Technical Manual and Dictionary of Classical Ballet.* New York: Dover, 1982.

Hammond, Sandra Noll. *Ballet: Beyond the Basics.* Palo Alto, Calif.: Mayfield, 1982.

Kersley, Leo and Janet Sinclair. *A Dictionary of Ballet Terms.* London: A & C Black. 1977. Reprint New York: Da Capo Press, 1979.

Kirstein, Lincoln, historical development, Muriel Stuart, descriptive text, Carlus Dyer, illustrations. *The Classic Ballet: Basic Technique and Terminology.* Preface by George Balanchine. New York: Knopf, c. 1952.

Lawson, Joan. *The Principles of Classical Dance.* New York: Knopf, 1980.

Messerer, Asaf. *Classes in Classical Dance.* Garden City, N.Y.: Doubleday, 1975.

Shook, Karel. *Elements of Classical Ballet Technique.* New York: Dance Horizons, 1977.

Tarasov, Nikolai Ivanovich. *Ballet Technique for the Male Dancer.* Garden City, N.Y.: Doubleday, 1985.

Vaganova, Agrippina. *Basic Principles of Classical Ballet.* New York: Dover, 1969.

Warren, Gretchen Ward. *Classical Ballet Technique.* Gainesville, Fla.: University of South Florida Press, 1989.

Dance Periodicals

Ballet is covered in most monthly and quarterly periodicals devoted to dance. The most prominent of these in the United States is *Dance Magazine*; in Britain, it is *The Dancing Times*. Both are monthlies with regular coverage of ballet dancing and dancers. *Dance & The Arts* is a bimonthly. U.S. quarterlies include *Ballet Review*, *Dance Chronicle*, and *DanceView*. *Dance Research Journal* is a publication of the Congress on Research in Dance, and comes out biannually. Foreign English-language publications include *Dance Australia* (bimonthly); *Choreography and Dance* (irregular quarterly, British); *Dance Europe* (bimonthly); *Dance Gazette* (three times a year, British), *Dance Now* (quarterly, British), *Dance Research* (biannual, British); and *Dance Theatre Journal* (three issues per year, British). All these publications and more are listed with synopses regarding contents, plus new publications news in the monthly newsletter *Attitudes & Arabesques* is edited by Leslie Getz and available only by subscription, 150 Claremont Avenue, Suite # 2-C, New York, NY 10027-4672. A bimonthly newsletter, available only by subscription, specifically dedicated to ballet news and issues is published as an offshoot of *DanceView*, called *Ballet Alert*; either or both can be subscribed to by contacting: *Ballet Alert* or *DanceView*, P.O. Box 34435, Martin Luther King Station, Washington, D.C. 20043.

Acknowledgments

My first book has me recall my beginnings, and I am most indebted to Arlene Croce who first asked me to write about ballet, and to Charles France, Edward Gorey, and Robert Cornfield, now my agent and the source of this project, for encouraging me to keep on going. The late Edwin Denby, Richard Hayes, and Anita Finkel variously insisted there was something to read in what I was writing. Jennifer Dunning, Joan Acocella, Mindy Aloff, and Lewis Segal have all been continuing sources of encouragement. During the particular time of this book, Alexander Meinertz, Alexandra Tomalonis, and Dawn Lille Horwitz each calmly spurred me on. Ever since my blissfully ignorant ventures into adult-beginner ballet classes with a patient and knowledgeable Celene Keller, I have been continually grateful to all the dancers and choreographers for keeping my ballet-going ever green, and to numerous writers past and present who have enlightened those experiences. Several individuals were of invaluable assistance with the nuts and bolts of this text, namely Ed Willinger for his encyclopedic memory, Amy Greenhouse for her music notes, Melvin Jahn for his video listings, and Leslie Getz for her bibliographic information. Deep gratitude goes to Mikhail Baryshnikov for finding time to look over my take on his art and to comment on it from the public's side of the footlights. Finally, I am especially grateful to my soft spoken and unobtrusive editor, David Cashion, and to Curtis Robertson, who's plain advice and gentle prodding—"just sally forth and do your best"—sustained me at more than one impasse.

INDEX

From the Sahara to Samarkand

From the Sahara to Samarkand

Selected Travel Writings of Rosita Forbes, 1919–1937

Edited with an Introduction by
Margaret Bald